CHRISTIAN INITIATION

THE CATHOLIC UNIVERSITY OF AMERICA STUDIES IN CHRISTIAN ANTIQUITY

EDITED BY

JOHANNES QUASTEN

Professor of Ancient Church History and Christian Archaeology
The Catholic University of America

No. 17

THE CATHOLIC UNIVERSITY OF AMERICA PRESS
CONSORTIUM PRESS
WASHINGTON, D.C.
1974

CHRISTIAN INITIATION

A Comparative Study
of the Interpretation of the
Baptismal Liturgy
in the Mystagogical Writings of
Cyril of Jerusalem
John Chrysostom
Theodore of Mopsuestia
and Ambrose of Milan

BY

HUGH M. RILEY

THE CATHOLIC UNIVERSITY OF AMERICA PRESS
CONSORTIUM PRESS
WASHINGTON, D.C.
1974

Manufactured in the United States
of America

ACKNOWLEDGEMENTS

Thanks are due to Rev. Dr. Balthasar Fischer, Professor of Liturgical Science at the Theology Faculty of Trier, W. Germany. At his suggestion as chairman of the Roman Committee entrusted with the reform of the Baptismal rites commissioned by the Second Vatican Council this work was undertaken and continued with his constructive criticism and encouragement. My most grateful acknowledgement is due to Rev. Dr. Bruno Kleinheyer, Professor of Liturgical Science at the University of Regensburg, W. Germany, for his gracious and competent criticism which accompanied the preparation of my manuscript. I am also grateful to Dr. Norbert Brox, Professor of Church History at the University of Regensburg, for his reading and criticism of the manuscript. Rev. Dr. Michael A. Fahey, S.J., Professor of Theology at the Weston College School of Theology, Cambridge, Massachusetts, U.S.A., provided invaluable assistance in the proofreading of the text and in the preparation of the indexes. My thanks are also due to Very Rev. William G. Guindon, S.J., Provincial Superior of the Society of Jesus of New England, for his understanding and support of this project.

For My Mother

TABLE OF CONTENTS

PAGE

PAGE

PAGE

CHAPTER THREE PAGE

PAGE

PAGE

PAGE

LIST OF SYNOPTIC CHARTS

LIST OF ESSAYS

ABBREVIATIONS

Titles of collections have been abbreviated as follows; titles of periodical literature, however, have been given in full.

AAS	*Acta apostolicae sedis* (Vatican City, 1909 ff.)
AC	*Antike und Christentum,* ed., F. Dölger (Münster, 1929 ff.)
ACW	*Ancient Christian Writers,* eds., J. Quasten, W. Burghardt (Westminster, Maryland and London, 1946 ff.)
CCL	*Corpus christianorum.* Series Latina (Turnhout and Paris, 1953 ff.)
CSEL	*Corpus scriptorum ecclesiasticorum latinorum* (Vienna, 1866 ff.)
DACL	*Dictionnaire d'archéologie chrétienne et de liturgie,* eds., F. Cabrol, H. Leclercq (Paris, 1907-1953).
FC	*The Fathers of the Church,* ed., R. Deferrari (New York, 1947 ff.)
FP	*Florilegium patristicum,* eds., B. Geyer, J. Zellinger (Bonn, 1904 ff.)
GCP	*Graecitas christianorum primaeva,* eds., C. Mohrmann, J. Ross (Nijmegen, 1962 ff.)
ICEL	*The International Commission for English in the Liturgy.*
LQF	*Liturgiewissenschaftliche Quellen und Forschungen,* eds., K. Mohlberg, J. Quasten, H. Frank, O. Heiming (Münster, 1939 ff.)

LS	*Liturgical Studies,* ed., M. Mathis (Notre Dame, Indiana, 1954 ff.)
MG	J. Migne, *Patrologia graeca* (Paris, 1886 ff.)
ML	J. Migne, *Patrologia latina* (Paris, 1844 ff.)
RAC	*Reallexikon für Antike und Christentum,* ed., Th. Klauser (Stuttgart, 1941 ff.)
SC	*Sources chrétiennes,* eds., H. de Lubac, J. Daniélou (Paris, 1941 ff.)
SeT	*Studi e Testi* (Vatican City, 1900 ff.)
SP	*Studia patristica.* Papers presented to the International Conference on Patristic Studies (Berlin, 1957 ff.)
SPCK	*The Society for Promoting Christian Knowledge* (London).
TU	*Texte und Untersuchungen zur Geschichte der altchristlichen Literatur* (Leipzig and Berlin, 1882 ff.)
TWB	*Theologisches Wörterbuch zum Neuen Testament,* ed., G. Kittel (Stuttgart, 1933 ff.)
VGS	*Varia graeca sacra:* Sbornik greceskikh neidannikh bogoslovskikh tekstov IV-XV vekov, ed. A. Papadopoulos-Kerameus (St. Petersburg, 1909).
WS	*Woodbrooke Studies* (Cambridge).

ABBREVIATIONS OF SOURCES

Principal Authors

Ambrose:

Myst.	*De Mysteriis*
Sacr.	*De Sacramentis*

Chrysostom:

P.K.	*Baptismal Instructions. Catecheses,* series Papadopoulos-Kerameus.
Stav.	*Baptismal Instructions. Catecheses,* series Stavronikita.
Montf.	*Baptismal Instructions. Catecheses ad Illuminandos prima et altera* (Montfaucon).
De res. dom.	*De resurrectione domini nostri Jesu Christi homilia.*
In act. apost.	*In acta apostolorum homiliae 1-55.*
In Col.	*In epistolam ad Colossenses homiliae 1-12.*
In 1 Co.	*In epistolam 1 ad Corinthios homiliae 1-44.*
In Gal.	*In epistolam ad Galatas commentarius.*
In Jn.	*In sancti Johannis evangelium homiliae 1-88.*
In Mt.	*In sancti Matthei evangelium homiliae 1-91.*
In Rm.	*In epistolam ad Romanos homiliae 1-32.*

Cyril:

Procat.	*Procatechesis*
Bapt. Cat.	*Baptismal Catecheses*
Myst. Cat.	*Mystagogical Catecheses*

Theodore:

Bapt. Hom.	*Baptismal Homilies*

Other

Hippolytus

Trad. apost.	*Traditio apostolica*

Jerome

Epist.	*Epistola ad Fabiolam*

Proclus

Cat. de bapt. myst.	*Catechesis de baptismo mystagogica*

Tertullian

De bapt.	*De baptismo*
De carn. res.	*De resurrectione mortuorum (De carnis resurrectione)*
De pudic.	*De pudicitia*
De spect.	*De spectaculis*

Test. D.N.J.C.	*Testamentum Domini nostri Jesu Christi*

Theodorus Lector:

Hist. eccl.	*Historia ecclesiastica*

OTHER ABBREVIATIONS

art. cit.	in the article cited
cf.	compare
ch.	chapter
col., cols.	column(s)
diss.	dissertation
ed., eds.	editor(s), edition(s)
esp.	especially
f., ff.	and the following
fol., foll.	folio(s)
hom.	homily
ibid.	in the same place
idem	the same
n., nn.	note(s)
no., nos.	number(s)
op. cit.	in the work cited
p., pp.	page(s)
passim	throughout the work, here and there
text	the resumé of the ritual (Theodore)
tr.	translator, translation
vol., vols.	volume(s)
vs.	verse

BIBLIOGRAPHY

Sources

Principal Authors

Ambrose:

De Mysteriis. B. Botte, ed., *Ambroise de Milan: Des Sacraments, Des Mystères,* SC 25bis (Paris, 1961), pp. 156-192.
De Sacramentis. Ibid., pp. 60-154.

Chrysostom:

Catecheses (Series Papadopoulos-Kerameus) 2-4. A. Papadopoulos-Kerameus, ed., *Varia graeca sacra* (St. Petersburg, 1909), pp. 154-183.
Catecheses (Series Stavronikita) 1-8. A. Wenger, ed., *Jean Chrysostome: Huit catéchèses baptismales inédites,* SC 50, SC 50bis (Paris, 1957, 1970).
Catechesis ad illuminandos prima et altera. (Series Montfaucon) B. Monfaucon, ed., MG 49.223-240 (Paris, 1862).
De bap. Christi. MG 49.365-372 (Paris, 1862).
De res. dom. MG 50.433-442 (Paris, 1862).
Exp. in Ps. 44. MG 55.182-203 (Paris, 1862).
In act. apost. 1-55. MG 60.1-384 (Paris, 1862).
In Col. 1-12. MG 62.299-392 (Paris, 1862).
In 1 Co. 1-44. MG 61.11-382 (Paris, 1862).
In Gal. MG 61.611-682 (Paris, 1862).
In Jn. 1-88. MG 59.24-482 (Paris, 1862).
In Mt. 1-91. MG 57.58.794 (Paris, 1862).
In prin. ac. 1-4. MG 51.65-112 (Paris, 1862).
In Rm. 1-32. MG 60.391-682 (Paris, 1862).
Sermo ad neophytos. A. Wenger, ed., SC 50, SC 50bis (Paris, 1957, 1970), pp. 168 -181.

Cyril:

Procatechesis. F. Cross, ed., *St. Cyril of Jerusalem's Lectures on the Christian Sacraments: the Procatechesis and the Five Mystagogical Catecheses,* SPCK, Texts for Students 51 (London, 1966), pp. 1-11.
Baptismal Catecheses I-XVIII. MG 33.367-1060 (Paris, 1903).
Mystagogical Catecheses I (XIX) – V (XXIV). A. Piédagnel, ed., *Cyrille de Jérusalem: Catéchèses Mystagogiques,* SC 126 (Paris, 1966), pp. 82-174.

Theodore:

Baptismal Homilies I-III. R. Tonneau, R. Devreesse, eds., *Les Homélies Catéchétiques de Théodore de Mopsueste,* Reproduction phototypique du MS. Mingana Syr. 561, SeT 145 (Vatican City, 1949), pp. 320-460. Tr., A. Mingana, *Commentary of Theodore of Mopsuestia on the Lord's Prayer and on the Sacraments of Baptism and the Eucharist,* WS VI (Cambridge, 1933), pp. 16-70.

Commentary on the Lord's Prayer. Tonneau-Devreesse, SeT 145, pp. 280-330. Tr., Mingana, WS VI, pp. 1-16.

Homilies on the Eucharist and the Liturgy I-II. Tonneau-Devreesse, SeT 145, pp. 460-604. Tr. Mingana, WS VI, pp. 70-123.

Other

Augustine, *Sermo 172.* ML 39.2075-2076 (Paris, 1841).

Constitutiones apostolorum 7, 39-45. J. Quasten, ed., FP 7 (Bonn, 1936), pp. 186-196.

Cyprian, *Epistula 73.* W. Hartel, ed., CSEL 3/2.778-799 (Vienna, 1868-1871).

Didascalia et Constitutiones Apostolorum. F. Funk, ed. (Paderborn, 1905).

Durandus, G., *Rationale divinorum officiorum* (Lyons, 1592).

Etheria, *Peregrinatio Aetheriae.* H. Pétré, ed., SC 21 (Paris, 1948).

Hippolytus, *Traditio apostolica.* B. Botte, ed., LQF 39 (Münster, 1963).

Jerome, *Epistula 64, ad Fabiolam.* I. Hilberg, ed., CSEL 54.586-615 (Vienna, Leipzig, 1910).

Narsai, *Liturgical Homilies.* R. Connolly, ed., Texts and Studies VIII.1 (Cambridge, 1909).

Ordo of Constantinople. F. Conybeare, J. MacLean, eds., *Rituale Armenorum* (Oxford, 1905), pp. 438-442.

Palladius, *Dialogus de Vita Sancti Johannis Chrysostomi.* MG 47.5-82 (Paris, 1863).

Proclus of Constantinople, *Catechesis de baptismo mystagogica,* Codex sinaïticus graecus 491, foll. 129v.-141v.

Tertullian, *De baptismo.* J. Borleffs, ed., CCL 1.275-295 (Turnhout, 1954)

Tertullian, *De pudicitia.* E. Dekkers, ed., CCL 2.1279-1330 (Turnhout, 1954).

Tertullian, *De resurrectione mortuorum.* J. Borleffs, ed., CCL 2.919-1012 (Turnhout, 1954).

Tertullian, *De spectaculis.* E. Dekkers, ed., CCL 1.225-253 (Turnhout, 1954).

Testamentum Domini nostri Jesu Christi 1-2. J. Quasten, ed., FP 7 (Bonn, 1936), pp. 235-273.

Theodorus Lector, *Historia ecclesiastica* 2. MG 86. 184-216 (Paris, 1865).

Vatican II, *Constitutio de sacra liturgia.* AAS 56 (1964), pp. 97-135.

GENERAL BIBLIOGRAPHY

Abbott, W., ed., *The Documents of Vatican II* (New York, 1966).

Abramowski, L., "Zur Theologie Theodors von Mopsuestia," *Zeitschrift für Kirchengeschichte* 72 (1961), 263-293.

Altaner, B., and Stuiber, A., *Patrologie: Leben, Schriften und Lehre der Kirchenväter,* 7th ed. (Freiburg i. Br., 1966).

Anrich, G., *Das antike Mysterienwesen in seinem Einfluss auf das Christentum* (Göttingen, 1894).

Assemani, J., *Codex Liturgicus Ecclesiae Universae.* I. De Catechumenis; II. De Baptismo (Rome, 1749); III. De Confirmatione (Rome, 1750). (Reprint, Paris and Leipzig, 1902).

Baumstark, A., *Comparative Liturgy,* revision B. Botte, tr. F. Cross (Westminster, Maryland, 1957).

Baumstark, *Festbrevier und Kirchenjahr der syrischen Jakobiten* (Paderborn, 1910).

Baur, C., *John Chrysostom and His Time,* tr. M. Gonzaga, 2nd ed., 2 vols., Vol. 1: Antioch, Vol. 2: Constantinople (Westminster, Maryland, 1959, 1960).

Bedard, W., *The Symbolism of the Baptismal Font in Early Christian Thought,* The Catholic University of America Studies in Sacred Theology II.45 (Washington, 1951).

Bohen, M., *The Mystery of Confirmation* (New York, 1963).

Boismard, M., "Je renonce à Satan . . . ," *Lumière et Vie* 26 (1956), 105-110 (249-254).

Boismard, "I renounce Satan, his Pomps and his Works," in *Baptism in the New Testament: A Symposium,* tr. D. Askew (Baltimore, 1964), pp. 107-114.

Borella, P., "Gli esorcismi nel battesimo e la estrema-unzione," *Ambrosius* 20 1944), 40-45.

Botte, B., *Ambroise de Milan: Des Sacraments, Des Mystères.* SC 25bis (Paris, 1961).

Botte, *La Tradition Apostolique de saint Hippolyte,* 2nd ed., LQF 39 (Münster, 1963).

Botte, "La sputation, antique rite baptismale? " in *Mélanges offerts à Mademoiselle Christine Mohrmann* (Utrecht, 1963), 196-201.

Botte, "Le Baptême dans l'Église Syrienne," *Orient Syrien* 1 (1956), 137-155.

Bouvet, J., *Saint Cyrille de Jérusalem, Catéchèses baptismales et mystagogiques* (Namur, 1961).

Bouyer, L., *Rite and Man: Natural Sacredness and Christian Liturgy,* tr., M. Costelloe, LS (Notre Dame, Indiana, 1963).

Burghardt, W., "Catechetics in the Early Church: Program and Psychology," *The Living Light* 1 (1964), 100-118.

Camelot, P.-Th., *Spiritualité du Baptéme,* Lex Orandi 30 (Paris, 1960).

Casel, O., *Das christliche Kultmysterium,* 3rd ed. (Regensburg, 1948).

Casel, *The Mystery of Christian Worship,* tr., B. Neunheuser (Westminster, Maryland, 1962).

Casel, "Die Taufe als Brautbad der Kirche," *Jahrbuch für Liturgiewissenschaft* 5 (1925), 144-147.

Casel, "Neue Zeugnisse für das Kultmysterium," *Jahrbuch für Liturgiewissenschaft* 13 (1933), 99-171.

Chadwick, H., ed., *St. Ambrose: On the Sacraments,* Studies in Eucharistic Faith and Practice 5 (London, 1960).

Connolly, R., *The Liturgical Homilies of Narsai,* Texts and Studies VIII,1 (Cambridge, 1909).

Connolly, ed., *Didascalia Apostolorum* (Oxford, 1929).

Conybeare, F. and MacLean, J., eds., *Rituale Armenorum* (Oxford, 1905).

Crehan, J., *Early Christian Baptism and the Creed.* The Bellarmine Series 13 (London, 1950).

Crehan, "Ten Years' Work on Baptism and Confirmation, 1945-1955," *Theological Studies* 17 (1956), 494-515.

Cross, F., ed., *St. Cyril of Jerusalem's Lectures on the Christian Sacraments: the Procatechesis and the Five Mystagogical Catecheses,* SPCK, Texts for Students 51 (London, 1966).

Daniélou, J., *From Shadows to Reality: Studies in the Biblical Typology of the Fathers,* tr., W. Hibberd (London, 1960).

Daniélou, *Les symboles chrétiens primitifs* (Paris, 1961).

Daniélou, *The Bible and the Liturgy,* LS 3 (Notre Dame, Indiana, 1956).

Daniélou, "Le symbolisme des rites baptismaux," *Dieu vivant* 1 (1945), 17-43.

Daniélou, "Die Symbolik des Taufritus," *Liturgie und Mönchtum* 3 (1949), 45-68.

Daniélou, "The Problem of Symbolism," *Thought* (1950), 423-440.

Daniélou, "Traversée de la Mer Rouge et le baptême aux premiers siècles," *Recherches de science religieuse* 33 (1946), 402-430.

Davies, J., *The Architectural Setting of Baptism* (London, 1962).

Deferrari, R., tr., *Saint Ambrose: Theological and Dogmatic Works,* FC 44 (Washington, 1963).

Denzinger, H. *Ritus Orientalium, Coptorum, Syrorum et Armenorum in administrandis Sacramentis,* 2 vols. (Würzburg, 1863-1864). (Reprint, Graz, 1961).

DePuniet, P., "Baptême," DACL 2.1 (1910), 251-346.

DePuniet, "Confirmation," DACL 3.2 (1913), 2515-2544.

Dinkler, E., "Die Taufterminologie in 2 Kor. I.21f," *Novum Testamentum,* Supplementum 6, Festschrift O. Cullmann (Leiden, 1962), 173-191.

Dölger, F., *Das Fischsymbol* (Münster, 1928).

Dölger, *Der Exorzismus im altchristlichen Taufritual: Eine religionsgeschichtliche Studie,* Studien zur Geschichte und Kultur des Altertums 3, 1/2 (Padernborn 1909).

Dölger, *Die christliche Taufe und das antike Mysterienwesen* (Cologne, 1912).

Dölger, *Die Sonne der Gerechtigkeit und der Schwarze, Eine religionsgeschichtliche Studie zum Taufgelöbnis,* 2nd ed., LQF 14 (Münster, 1918).

Dölger, *Sol Salutis: Gebet und Gesang im christlichen Altertum mit besonderer Rücksicht auf die Ostung in Gebet und Liturgie,* 2nd ed., LQF 16/17 (Münster, 1925).

Dölger, *Sphragis: Eine altchristliche Taufbezeichnung in ihren Beziehungen zur profanen und religiösen Kultur des Altertums,* Studien zur Geschichte und Kultur des Altertums 5, 3/4 (Paderborn, 1911).

Dölger, "Der Durchzug durch das rote Meer als Sinnbild der christlichen Taufe," AC 2 (1930), 63-69.

Dölger, "Der Durchzug durch den Jordan als Sinnbild der christlichen Taufe, AC 2 (1930), 70-79.

Dölger, "Der Kampf mit dem Ägypter in der Perpetua-Vision. Das Martyrium als Kampf mit dem Teufel," AC 3 (1932), 177-188.

Dölger, "Sacramentum militiae," AC 2 (1930), 268-280.

Dölger, "Zur Symbolik des altkirchlichen Taufhauses I," AC 4 (1934), 153-187.

Duchesne, L., *Christian Worship: Its Origin and Development,* tr. M. McClure (London, 1949).

Durandus, G., *Rationale divinorum officiorum* (Lyons, 1592).

Ehrhard, A., Review of *Varia graeca sacra, Byzantinische Zeitschrift* 20 (1911), 257-261.

Elfers, H. *Die Kirchenordnung Hippolyts von Rom* (Paderborn, 1938).

Elfers, "Gehört die Salbung mit Chrisma im ältesten Initiationsritus zur Taufe oder zur Firmung?" *Theologie und Glaube* 34 (1942), 334-341.

Eliade, M., *Das Mysterium der Wiedergeburt. Initiationsriten, ihre kulturelle und religiose Bedeutung* (Zürich, Stuttgart, 1961).

Eliade, *Ewige Bilder und Sinnbilder. Vom unvergänglichen menschlichen Seelenraum* (Freiburg i. Br., 1958).

Faller, O., ed., *Sancti Ambrosii Opera VII,* CSEL 73 (Vienna, 1955).

Faller, "Das Teufelanspeien im Mailänder Taufritual?" *Jahrbuch für Liturgiewissenschaft* 9 (1929), 128-132.

Feron, E., and Battaglini, F., *Codices manuscripti graeci Ottoboniani Bibliothecae Vaticanae,* MS Ottoboni graecus 175 (Rome, 1893), foll. 47-70.

Finn, T., *The Liturgy of Baptism in the Baptismal Instructions of St. John Chrysostom,* The Catholic University of America Studies in Christian Antiquity 15, ed., J. Quasten (Washington, 1967).

Finn, "Baptismal Death and Resurrection: a Study in Fourth Century Eastern Baptismal Terminology," *Worship* 43 (1969), 175-189.

Forstner, D., *Die Welt der Symbole* (Innsbruck, 1960).

Freburger, W., ed., *Baptism; The Sacramental Rite for Children,* tr. ICEL (New York, 1970).

Funk, F., ed., *Didascalia et Constitutiones Apostolorum,* 2 vols. (Paderborn, 1905).

Galtier, P., "La consignation dans les églises d'Occident," *Revue d'Histoire ecclésiastique* 13 (1912), 257-301.

Gamber, K., "Ist Niceta von Remesiana der Verfasser von De Sacramentis?" *Ostkirchliche Studien* 7 (1958), 153-172.

Gamber, "Zur ältesten Liturgie von Mailand," *Ephemerides liturgicae* 77 (1963), 391-395.

Green, H., "The Significance of the Pre-Baptismal Seal in St. John Chrysostom," *SP,* Vol. VI, Part IV, TU 81 (Berlin, 1962), 84-90.

Greer, R., *Theodore of Mopsuestia: Exegete and Theologian* (London, 1961).

Haidacher, S., "Eine unbeachtete Rede des hl. Chrysostomus an Neugetaufte," *Zeitschrift für Katholische Theologie* 28 (1904), 168-186.

Hamann, A., *Le Baptême d'après les Péres de L'Eglise: Textes choisis et présentés.* Lettres Chrétiennes 5 (Paris, 1962).

Harkins, P., tr., *St. John Chrysostom: Baptismal Instructions,* ACW 31 (Westminster, Maryland, London 1963).

Harkins, "Pre-Baptismal Rites in Chrysostom's Baptismal Catecheses," *SP,* Vol. VIII, Part II, TU 93 (Berlin, 1966), 219-238.

Hermann, A., "Cilicium," RAC 3 (1957), cols. 127-136.

Hoffmann, K., "Taufgeschehen und Taufverwirklichung nach den Taufkatechesen des hl. Johannes Chrysostomus," diss. (Trier, 1963).

Hofmeister, Ph., *Die Heligen Öle in der morgen- und abendländischen Kirche.*

Eine Kirchenrechtliche-liturgische Abhandlung. Das östliche Christentum, Neue Folge, Heft 6/7 (Würzburg, 1948).

Illert, D., "Die Taufe bei Ambrosius von Mailand," diss. (Kiel, 1962).

Jungmann, J., *Symbolik der katholischen Kirche,* Symbolik der Religionen 6 (Stuttgart, 1960).

Jungmann, *The Early Liturgy to the Time of Gregory the Great,* tr. F. Brunner (Notre Dame, Indiana, 1959).

Kavanagh, A., "Liturgical Needs for Today and Tomorrow," *Worship* 43 (1969), 488-495.

Kelly, J., *Early Christian Creeds* (London, 1950).

Kirchgässner, A., *Die mächtigen Zeichen, Ursprünge, Formen und Gesetze des Kultes* (Basel, Freiburg i. Br., Vienna, 1959).

Kirsten, H. *Die Taufabsage. Eine Untersuchung zu Gestalt und Geschichte der Taufe nach den altkirchlichen Taufliturgien* (Berlin, 1960).

Klauser, Th., "Taufet in lebendigem Wasser," in *Pisciculi, Studien zur Religion und Kultur des Altertums* (Münster, 1939), 157-164.

Kretschmar, G., *Die Geschichte des Taufgottesdienstes in der alten Kirche,* in Leiturgia, Handbuch des evangelischen Gottesdienstes, eds., K. Müller, W. Blankenburg, Vol. V, *Der Taufgottesdienst* (Kassel, 1970), 1-349.

Kretschmar, "Die frühe Geschichte der Jerusalemer Liturgie," *Jahrbuch für Liturgik und Hymnologie* 2 (1956), 22-46.

Kretschmar, "Die Zwei Imperien und die zwei Reiche," *Ecclesia und Res publica,* für K.D. Schmidt (Göttingen, 1961), 89-112.

Lampe, G., *The Seal of the Spirit,* 2nd ed. (London, 1967).

Lebreton, J., "Les origines du symbole baptismal," *Recherches de Science Religieuse* 20 (1930), 97-124.

Lécuyer, J., "San Juan Crisostomo y la confirmación," *Orbis Catholicus* (Barcelona, 1958), 385-387.

Lietzmann, H., *Die Liturgie des Theodor von Mopsuestia,* Sonderausgabe aus den Sitzungsberichten der Preussischen Akademie der Wissenschaft, Phil. Hist. Klasse 23 (Berlin, 1933). Reprinted in *Kleine Schriften* 3: Studia zur Liturgie und Symbolgeschichte, TU 74 (Berlin, 1962), 71-97.

Ligier, L., "Le symbolisme biblique du baptême selon les Pères et la liturgie," *Concilium* 22 (1967), 21-32.

Lubienska de Lenval, H., *Die Liturgie der Gebärde* (Klosterneuburg, 1959).

Lundberg, P., *La Typologie baptismale dans l'ancienne église* (Uppsala, Leipzig, 1942).

Maertens, Th., *Histoire et pastorale du rituel du catéchuménat et du baptême.* Paroisse et Liturgie, Collection de Pastorale Liturgique 56 (Bruges, 1962).

Marsh, T., "Confirmation and its Relation to Baptism," *Irish Theological Quarterly* 27 (1960), 259-293.

Marsh, "The History and Significance of the Post-Baptismal Rites," *Irish Theological Quarterly* 29 (1962), 175-206.

Martimort, A.-G., ed., *Handbuch der Liturgiewissenschaft* 2 vols. (Freiburg, Basel, Vienna, 1963, 1965).

McKenzie, J., "A new Study of Theodore of Mopsuestia," *Theological Studies* 10 (1949), 394-408.

Michiels, D., "L'initiation chrétienne selon saint Ambroise" *Les Questions Liturgiques et Paroissiales* 34 (1953), 109-114, 164-169.

Mingana, A., ed., *Commentary of Theodore of Mopsuestia on the Lord's Prayer and on the Sacraments of Baptism and the Eucharist,* WS VI (Cambridge, 1933).

Mingana, ed., *Commentary of Theodore of Mopsuestia on the Nicene Creed,* WS V (Cambridge, 1932).
Mitchell, L., *Baptismal Anointing,* SPCK, Alcuin Club Collections 48 (London 1966).
Mitchell, "Ambrosian Baptismal Rites," *Studia Liturgica* (1962), 241-253.
Mitchell, "The Baptismal Rite in Chrysostom," *Anglican Theological Review* 43 (1961), 397-403.
Morin, G., "La Sputation, rite baptismal de l'église de Milan au IVe siècle, d'après un passage corrigé du *De mysteriis* de S. Ambroise," *Revue Bénédictine* 16 (1899), 414-418.
Neunheuser, B., "De benedictione aquae baptismalis," *Ephemerides Liturgicae* 44 (1930), 194-207, 258-281, 369-412, 455-492.
Oepke, A., "bapto, baptizo," *TWB* I.527-544.
Ohm, T., *Die Gebetsgebärden der Völker und das Christentum* (Leiden, 1944).
Oppenheim, Ph., *Symbolik und religiöse Wertung des Mönchskleides im christlichen Altertum* (Münster, 1932).
Papadopoulos-Kerameus, A., ed., *Varia graeca sacra: Sbornik greceskikh neidannikh bogoslovskikh tekstov IV-XV vekov,* Collection Zapiski, istor.- fil. fakulteta S. Peterburgskago Universiteta 93-95 (St. Petersburg, 1909).
Pascher, J., *Form und Formenwandel sakramentaler Feier. Ein Beitrag zur Gestaltenlehre heiliger Zeichen* (Münster, 1949).
Paulin, A., *Saint Cyrille of Jérusalem, Catéchète,* Lex Orandi 29 (Paris, 1959).
Peterson, E., *Pour une théologie du vêtement* (Lyons, 1943).
Peterson, "Die geschichtliche Bedeutung der jüdischen Gebetsrichtung," *Theologische Zeitschrift* 3 (1947), 1-15.
Peterson, *Frühkirche, Judentum und Gnosis* (Freiburg i. Br., 1959).
Pétré, H., ed., *Ethérie: Journal de voyage,* SC 21 (Paris, 1948).
Piédagnel, A., ed., *Cyrille de Jérusalem: Catéchèses Mystagogiques,* SC 126 (Paris, 1966).
Pöll, W., *Religionspsychologie: Formen der religiösen Kenntnisnahme* (Munich, 1965).
Prümm, K., *Religionsgeschichtliches Handbuch für den Raum der altchristlichen Umwelt. Heidnische-römische Geistesströmungen und Kulte mit Beachtung des Eigenlebens der Provinzen* (Freiburg i. Br., 1943).
Quasten, J., *Patrology,* 3 vols. (Westminster, Maryland, Utrecht, Antwerp, 1950, 1958, 1960).
Quasten, ed., *Monumenta eucharistica et liturgica vestustissima,* FP 7, 7 Parts (Bonn, 1935-1937).
Quasten, "A Pythagorean Idea in Jerome," *American Journal of Philology* 63 (1942), 207-215.
Quasten, "Baptismal Creed and Baptismal Act in St. Ambrose's *De Mysteriis* and *De Sacramentis,*" in *Mélanges Jos. de Ghellinck,* Tome I, *Antiquité,* Museum Lessianum, Section Historique, No. 13 (Gembloux, 1951), 223-234.
Quasten, "Die Ostervigil im Testamentum Domini," in *Paschatis Sollemnia,* eds., B. Fischer, J. Wagner (Freiburg i. Br., 1959), 87-95.
Quasten, "The Blessing of the Baptismal Font in the Syrian Rite of the Fourth Century," *Theological Studies* 7 (1946) 309-313.
Quasten, "The Garment of Immortality: A Study of 'Accipe Vestem Candidam'," *Miscellanea Liturgica in onore il Card. G. Lercaro,* Vol. I (Rome, 1966), 391-401.
Quasten, "The Liturgical Mysticism of Theodore of Mopsuestia," *Theological Studies* 15 (1954), 431-439.

Quasten, "Theodore of Mopsuestia on the Exorcism of the Cilicium," *Harvard Theological Review* 35 (1942), 209-219.

Rahmani, I., *Testamentum Domini nostri Jesu Christi* (Mainz, 1899).

Rahner, H., *Griechische Mythen in christlicher Deutung,* 3rd ed. (Zürich, 1966).

Rahner, *Greek Myths and Christian Mystery,* tr. B. Battershaw (New York, 1963).

Rahner, "Pompa Diaboli," *Zeitschrift für Katholische Theologie* 55 (1931), 239-273.

Reicke, Bo, *The Disobedient Spirits and Christian Baptism* (Copenhagen, 1946).

Reischl, G. and Rupp, J., eds., *S. Patris Nostri Cyrilli Hierosolymorum Archiepiscopi Opera Quae Supersunt Omnia,* 2 vols. (Munich, 1848, 1860).

Riley, H., "The Salt Ceremony in Christian Initiation," diss. (Trier, 1968).

Roques, R., *Anselme de Cantorbéry, Pourquoi Dieu s'est fait homme,* SC 91 (Paris, 1963).

Rothenhauser, M. "Apotaxis," RAC 1 (1950), 558-564.

Sawhill, J., *The Use of Athletic Metaphors in the Biblical Homilies of John Chrysostom* (Princeton, 1928).

Scheidt, H., *Die Taufwasserweihegebete im Sinne vergleichender Liturgieforschung untersucht,* LQF 29 (Münster, 1945).

Schelkle, K.-H., *Paulus, Lehrer der Väter* (Düsseldorf, 1957).

Schnackenburg, R., *Das Heilsgeschehen bei der Taufe nach dem Apostel Paulus* (Munich, 1950).

Schnackenburg, *Baptism in the Thought of St. Paul,* tr. G. Beasley-Murray (New York, 1964).

Srawley, J., ed., Thompson, T., tr., *On the Sacraments and on the Mysteries,* SPCK (London, 1950).

Stenzel, A., *Die Taufe: eine genetische Erklärung der Taufliturgie,* Forschungen zur Geschichte der Theologie und des innerkirchlichen Lebens VII/VIII, eds., H. Rahner und J. Jungmann (Innsbruck, 1958).

Stommel, E., *Studien zur Epiclese der römischen Taufwasserweihe* (Bonn, 1950).

Stommel, " 'Begraben mit Christus' (Röm 6,4) und der Taufritus," *Römische Quartalschrift für christliche Altertumskunde und für Kirchengeschichte* 49 (1954), 1-20.

Stommel, "Christliche Taufriten und antike Badesitten," *Jahrbuch für Antike und Christentum* 2 (1959), 5-14.

Stommel, "Das 'Abbild seines Todes' (Röm 6,5) und der Taufritus," *Römische Quartalschrift für christliche Altertumskunde und für Kirchengeschichte* 50 (1955), 1-21.

Swaans, W., "A propos des Catéchèses mystagogiques attribuées à Saint Cyrille de Jerusalem," *Muséon* 55 (1942), 1-43.

Symposium, *Baptism in the New Testament: A Symposium,* tr., D. Askew (Baltimore, 1964).

Tonneau, R., and Devreesse, T. eds., *Les Homélies Catéchètiques de Théodore de Mopsueste,* SeT 145 (Vatican City, 1949).

Van Unnik, W., "Les cheveux défaits des femmes baptisées: un rite de baptême dans l'ordre ecclésiastique d'Hippolyte," *Vigiliae Christianae* 1 (1947), 77-100.

Van Unnik, "Parrhesia in the 'Catechetical Homilies' of Theodore of Mopsuestia," in *Melanges offerts à Mademoiselle Christine Mohrmann* (Utrecht, 1963), 12-22

Vogel, C., "Versus ad Orientem: l'orientation dans les *Ordines Romani* du haut moyen âge," *La Maison Dieu* 70 (1962), 67-99.

Waszink, J., "Pompa Diaboli," *Vigiliae Christianae* (1947), 13-41.

Weaver, J., "Catechetical Themes in the Post-Baptismal Teaching of St. John Chrysostom," diss. (Catholic University of America, Washington, 1964).

Welte, B., *Die postbaptismale Salbung,* Freiburger Theologische Studien 51 (Freiburg i. Br., 1939).

Wenger, A., *Jean Chrysostome: Huit catéchèses baptismales inédites,* SC 50, SC 50bis (Paris, 1957, 1970).

Wenger, "La tradition des oeuvres de saint Jean Chrysostome I. Catéchèses inconnues et homélies peu connues," *Revue des Études Byzantines* 14 (1956), 5-48.

Whitaker, E., *Documents of the baptismal Liturgy* (London 1960).

Ysebaert, J., *Greek Baptismal Terminology: Its Origins and Early Development,* GCP I (Nijmegen, 1962).

Ziegenhaus, A., "Das Menschenbild des Theodore von Mopsuestia," diss. (Munich, 1963).

INTRODUCTION

THE LITURGY OF CHRISTIAN INITIATION: A SYMBOLIC RITE OF PASSAGE

The liturgy of Christian Initiation provides for its participants, the catechumens, a unique event. It introduces them into a new world which reveals itself to them through the words and gestures of the liturgical rites and it elicits their personal engagement in this world. At the same time, this symbolic rite of passage into a new world does not remove them from the world in which they live. The words and gestures which form the symbolism of the initiation rites themselves depend on and are drawn from the world of the catechumen. Rather than rupturing his relationship to the world, this liturgy initiates the catechumen into a deeper understanding of his own world, and a way of viewing it at a level heretofore inaccessible to him. Having heard the divine call through the preaching of the Good News, and attempting to respond to this call in the act of faith, the candidate will be initiated through the medium of symbolic word and action into the depth and scope of the hitherto invisible mystery of God's salvific plan for the world and his position in this plan, his response to this revelation. This symbolic initiation will give him a new orientation and provide a new meaning to his own life, in his relationship to himself and to others, to his whole environment, to history and to God.

Engaged by the medium of visible symbol which comprises the liturgical initiation the candidate, in what he says and does and in what is said and done to him, is enlightened to discover the meaning of salvation history. Not through abstract instruction, but through concrete engagement in physical symbolic action the candidate performs his rite of passage from the visible world into the invisible world. In this rite of passage his known world of experience is not destroyed, but illumined in its ultimate depth, in its heretofore hidden and unrevealed intersection with the plan of God. Passing symbolically in word and gesture through the crisis points of human existence, birth, commitment to the realization of one's life and death, the candidate is initiated into the meaning of his own life in the light of God's plan. Having undergone the symbolic rite of passage, he returns to this very same life, now to live it at a level of more profound understanding, engaged in a new partnership with the invisible God, a partnership mediated to him by the symbolic rites of the liturgy of Christian Initiation.

Mystagogy

Those undertaking a journey need a guide. Those who conduct the candidates through the symbolic rite of passage which is the liturgy of Christian Initiation are the guides, those who conduct one through the mysteries, or the "mystagogues." The instruction which is imparted to help the candidates understand the meaning of what is said and what is done in the liturgy of his initiation into the Christian life is called "mystagogy", instruction in the meaning of the mysteries.

In discharging his function of mystagogy the mystagogue must bear in mind three things: *first*, the liturgical rite itself, what is said and what is done; *second*, the actual condition of a real group of candidates, their relationship to their environment; *third,* the material which can most adequately explain, given *this* liturgical complex of ceremonies and *this* group of candidates, what these symbolic words and gestures of the initiation rite mean.

Mystagogy, then, is a pastoral function. It is a task which is never completed, but must be creatively renewed, since the actual liturgy itself of Christian Initiation undergoes changes in its developing history, the world and the consciousness of those who hear the divine call to faith is constantly varied, and the creative and historically educated insight into the rich meaning of the symbols of which the liturgy is composed is constantly capable of development.

Reason for the Present Investigation

In view of such an ongoing pastoral task it will be not without value to provide those entrusted with the office of initiating candidates into the Christian life with a scientific study of mystagogical instruction as it took place historically in a form that is recognized as classic coming from the hands of recognized masters in this area of creative pastoral endeavor. From a detailed scientific investigation of how highly gifted pastors provided their catechumens with a mystagogy of the liturgy of Christian Initiation, taking into account the liturgy itself from beginning to end, that is, its individual ceremonies as well as its coherence as a totality, the world of consciousness of the candidates, and the materials chosen by these mystagogues to provide a sensitive and intelligible exposition of the words and actions of this liturgy, principles can emerge which will be of invaluable assistance to those whose responsibility it is to provide a mystagogy of the present initiation liturgy, which has undergone a historical development, the candidates for which have a different world of consciousness, and the material for explaining which has reached a new stage of understanding.

Three developments of the present day render a scientific investigation of a classical initiation mystagogy particularly valuable and even imperative. *First*, there is the historically momentous reform of the liturgy of Christian Initiation itself commissioned by the *Constitution on the Sacred Liturgy* of the Second Vatican Council.[1] The execution of this commis-

[1]*Constitutio de sacra liturgia, AAS* LVI (1964), 97-138, esp. nos. 1, 4, pp. 97, 98; tr. *The Documents of Vatican II*, ed. W. Abbott (New York, 1966), pp. 137-178, esp. pp. 137, 138.

The Constitution enunciates the following principles: "Sacrosanctum Concilium, cum sibi proponat vitam christianam inter fideles in diem augere; eas institutiones quae mutationibus obnoxiae sunt, ad nostrae aetatis necessitates melius accomodare. (It is the goal of this most sacred Council to intensify the daily growth of Catholics in Christian living; to make more responsive to the requitements of our time those Church observances which are open to adaptation)." (No. 1).

"Sacrosanctum Concilium . . . optat ut, ubi opus sit, caute ex integro ad mentem sanae traditionis recognoscantur et novo vigore, pro hodiernis adjunctis et necession as it pertains to the liturgy of Christian Initiation is currently effecting changes in this liturgy which are unprecedented in its entire history for their scope and rapidity within such a brief span of time and effecting so many people. One need only draw attention to the fact that the newly published rite of infant baptism[2] is a complete *novum* in the history of the liturgy of Christian Initiation in the sense that the rite is specifically and exclusively intended for the real circumstances of the baptism of infants,[3] whereas previously this rite was only in form an independent liturgy, but in reality only an abbreviation and adaptation, often quite inadequate, of the rite of adult initiation,[4] a rite, indeed, which, at the time of its adaptation, was by no means itself a living liturgy suited to the actual conditions of the candidates whom it was supposed to serve.

Such current momentous changes in the previous initiation liturgy around which the mystagogical interpretation had been built for better or for worse for centuries now require an entirely new approach if the mystagogy is to be suitable to this renewed liturgy. An investigation of a given classic and living liturgy and how it was exposed mystagogically can provide perspective and insight for the present day work.

In the wake of the authorized reform of the liturgy have come as well from various Christian communities unofficial

---

sitatibus, donentur. (The most sacred Council . . . desires that, where necessary, the rites be carefully and thoroughly revised in the light of sound tradition, and that they be given new vigor to meet the circumstances and needs of modern times)." (No. 4).

[2] *Baptism: The Sacramental Rite for Children,* tr. *ICEL.*, ed. W. Freburger (New York, 1970), pp. 14-26. For the previous rite see the *Rituale Romanum*, first issued by Paul V in 1614, revised by Pius XII in 1952, "Ordo Baptismi Parvulorum," Titulus II, Caput 2.

[3] This reform of the infant baptismal rite corresponds to the commission of Vatican II in the *Constitutio de sacra liturgia*: "Ritus baptizandi parvulos recognoscatur et verae infantium condicioni accomodetur. (The rite for the baptism of infants is to be revised and should be adapted to the circumstances that those to be baptized are, in fact, infants)." (No. 67). *AAS* LVI (1964), p. 118; tr. Abbott, p. 160.

[4] This rite of adult initiation appears in the *Rituale Romanum* of Paul V, issued in 1614 and revised by Pius XII in 1952, "Ordo Baptismi Adultorum," Titulus II, Caput 4.

attempts to provide liturgies of Christian Initiation which display results of promising, but also, despite the zeal of their composers, questionable value. If responsible pastors are to be helped in fulfilling their task as mystagogues both in respect to understanding changes in the authorized liturgy as well as in the task of evaluating and sifting the unauthorized forms, a historical study which throws into relief the classic principles to which a mystagogue may refer in dealing with these symbolic rites will be helpful. The principles which will emerge in learning how a mystagogy was provided for a classic liturgy at a certain period of historical development will yield valuable criteria for approaching the present task, criteria which will reveal the difficulty of the task, the sensitivity required to avoid missing the mark and so guard against an unschooled arbitrariness which does no service to the historical tradition of Christian Initiation.

The official impetus which Vatican II provided for the liturgical movement and its current results in the reform of the liturgy are a reflection of the *second* circumstance which warrants a scientific investigation of a classic mystagogy of the initiation rites. That circumstance is the rapid growth of human consciousness on a global level expedited particularly by the communications media leading to a new unified awareness and self-consciousness of such universally valid anthropological symbols as human birth, commitment and growth. If changes in the given liturgy itself demand a revised mystagogy to provide a coherent and plausible explanation of the ceremonies, so, too, developments, especially when they are rapid, pervasive and widespread, in the consciousness of the candidates who are performing this liturgy, will be neglected by the mystagogue only at the risk of compelling the candidates to serve the given liturgy in a personally unauthentic manner instead of allowing the given liturgy to serve the candidates in mediating their initiation into the Christian life. It will not do for the mystagogue merely to understand the history and principles of coherence of the given liturgy. In making its symbolism intelligible to his hearers he must also take into account the rapidly changing world of consciousness, the imaginative and emotive orientation of his hearers on the basic of which they must find a rapport with the given symbolic rites. The liturgical symbolism must, of course, speak for itself. This is one of the *desiderata* of the liturgical reform.[5] But the liturgy of itself cannot do this entirely, a fact which lies in the very inexhaustibility of genuine symbolism. The guide, the mystagogue, is still indispensable, as in any journey of initiation, to provide emphasis, to suggest connections and nuances, to reveal the salvation history, the mystery of faith, inherent in the initiation symbolism and to relate it to the real life of the candidates.[6] It is this world of consciousness, after all, which forms the matrix which the candidate brings with him to his initiation. Great creative skill is required of the mystagogue to resonate with this consciousness which forms the candidate's understanding of himself and his world so that he can be escorted through the symbolic action of the initiation rites in a way that will make them meaningful *to him*, and not merely meaningful in themselves from a detached and "objective" standpoint. Success or failure in this creative interpretation of the given ceremonies will depend on the mystagogue's capacity to provide pedagogically the rapport between the candidate's world of consciousness and the wide flow of meaning which the liturgical symbolism is capable of yielding, thus en-

[5] "Ritus . . . sint fidelium captui accomodati, neque generatim multis indigeant explanationibus. (The rites . . . should be within the people's powers of comprehension and normally should not require much explanation)." *Constitutio de sacra liturgia*, no. 34, *AAS* LVI (1964), p. 109; tr. Abbott, p. 149.

[6] Theodore of Mopsuestia states the need as follows: "Every sacrament consists in the representation of unseen and unspeakable things through signs and emblems. Such things require explanation and interpretation, for the sake of the person who draws nigh to the sacrament, so that he might know its power. If it only consisted in the visible elements themselves, words would have been useless, as sight itself would have been able to show us one by one all the happenings that take place, but since a sacrament contains the signs of things that take place or have already taken place, words are needed to explain the power of signs and mysteries," *Bapt. Hom.* I.2 (Tonneau-Devreesse, *SeT* 145, 324; tr. Mingana, *WS* VI, 17).

St. Cyril of Jerusalem offers as his justification for this mystagogical explanation of the ceremonies: "that you may know the deep meaning to you of what was done on that evening of your baptism (*ἵνα εἰδῆτε τὴν ἔμφασιν τὴν πρὸς ὑμᾶς κατ' ἐκείνην γεγενημένην τοῦ βαπτίσματος τὴν ἑσπέραν*)." *Myst. Cat.* I. 1 (Piédagnel, *SC* 126, 84; tr. Cross, *SPCK*, 53).

abling him to enter the world of salvation history successfully and so achieve the purpose of engaging in the rites of initiation — an enlightenment and transformation of his own world as a result of answering the divine call in his act of faith, concretely embodied in the performance of the liturgical rites.

Here, too, a study of classic mystagogy yields insight into just how the mystagogue, in view of the world of consciousness of his hearers, went about emphasizing now this, now that aspect of the liturgical rites in such a way as to reveal their relationship to the life experience of the candidates. Indeed, the liturgy has changed and is changing; the candidates' world has changed and is changing. These principles can be learned from the masters who, although they dealt with another world and a somewhat different liturgy, were able to succeed in the task of relating their candidates to the variegated possibilities of the liturgical symbolism, neither doing violence to the liturgy itself nor to the candidates' capacity for understanding and participating in it.

A *third* current development which makes a scientific investigation of classic mystagogy useful is the rapid expansion of the modern psychological sciences which are revealing the importance of symbol in the conscious and unconscious world of man, distinguishing the universally valid archetypal symbols from those culturally conditioned, and revealing the varied processes of human apprehension. A study of how classic mystagogy approached the interpretation of the symbolic rites of initiation, examining the materials on which the mystagogues drew in the natural, cultural and religious level known to them to explain to the candidates the meaning of the rites can also provide criteria for the application of our growing wealth of psychological knowledge in the development of a suitable mystagogy of Christian Initiation.

The Investigation

This work investigates the mystagogical interpretation of the liturgy of baptism in the later part of the fourth century as this mystagogy is found in the *Mystagogical Catecheses* attributed to St. Cyril of Jerusalem, in the *De Sacramentis* and *De Mysteriis* of St. Ambrose of Milan, in the *Baptismal Instructions* of St. John Chrysostom, and in the *Baptismal Homilies* of Theodore of Mopsuestia. These writings reflect a period which is considered a classical age of the catechumenate and the liturgy of baptism.

While numerous works have appeared on all of these four fathers and their works as a whole, the number of works which treat formally of their mystagogical writings on the liturgy of baptism in detail is practically non-existent, being limited for the most part either to brief articles on some aspect or passage in the mystagogical writings, or to general introductions contained in various editions of the mystagogical writings themselves. A small number of articles in the field of liturgiology treat aspects of certain ceremonies mentioned in the mystagogical writings, but they, too, make no formal study of the total mystagogy of baptism of any one father as such. Works on the history of the liturgy of baptism, because of their wide scope, cannot pause for a formal, unified treatment of the baptismal mystagogy of any one father. And monographs which, for example, treat of a complex of baptismal ceremonies such as the renunciation of Satan and commitment to Christ, or the recitation of the creed, or the anointings, cannot afford, by their nature, to focus on the mystagogy of baptism in a single father in its wholeness. Their interest, moreover, veers more to dogmatic or sacramental theology, rather than to that pastoral theology which includes mystagogy.

As a matter of fact, the astounding lack of *any significant monograph* treating professedly the mystagogy of baptism in any one of these four fathers must be attributed more to the lack of comprehension of the unique and peculiar genius and presuppositions of mystagogical writings than to any dearth in the writings themselves, which provide ample matter for study.[7] Furthermore, the hopeless state of fossilization of the

[7] In 1951 the work of J. Daniélou exemplified particularly in *Bible et Liturgie* was a pioneering beginning in awakening the long dormant appreciation of mystagogy. However, Daniélou's work does not treat classical mystagogical works in their individual teleology. He rather draws on mystagogical interpretation of various

initiation liturgy until recently helps also to explain this lack of interest in treating the mystagogical explanation of baptism, because the very unsuitability of the baptismal rites themselves provided little interest for attempting to explain them, an explanation which would only further reveal their embarrassing inadequacy. Further, the concentration on dogmatic theology sometimes served to degrade the mystagogical writings merely to the function of an arsenal from which ammunition might be drawn to corroborate later theories of sacramental theology without due reference to the true nature of mystagogical writings and their reference to a given historical liturgy, or to concrete candidates existing in a given cultural milieu.

In addressing itself to this scientific *lacuna* this present work sets before it a twofold purpose: to provide a detailed analysis of the *interpretation* of the liturgy of baptism in the above-mentioned works of Cyril, Chrysostom, Theodore and Ambrose. How did these four fathers go about explaining to their candidates the meaning of what was said and what was done in the dramatic liturgy of initiation which characterized the baptismal rites of the time? What interpretative materials did they use? How did they present their interpretative

---

and widely differing baptismal rites covering a long period of history and from a great number of fathers to present a very general, and somewhat diffuse picture, of the possibilities of this kind of understanding of Christian Initiation. Moreover, only in 1957, with the publication of the fiftieth volume of the *Sources chrétiennes* series by A. Wenger were seven important and previously unknown instructions of Chrysostom made available, works which were unavailable to Daniélou when he prepared his work. Moreover, Daniélou does not take cognizance of the Montfaucon series of instructions of Chrysostom, or the series of Papadopoulos-Kerameus. (See below, pp. 12-13 and n. 24). This is not surprising however, since Daniélou is presenting a rather general survey of mystagogical directions, rather than an analysis of any father's mystagogy, much less a particularized comparative study in mystagogy.

A monograph such as that appearing in 1967 by T. Finn, *The Liturgy of Baptism in the Baptismal Instructions of St. John Chrysostom*, The Catholic University of America Studies in Christian Antiquity, No. 15, ed. J. Quasten (Washington, D.C.), does take into account these newly available works of Chrysostom. His work, however, is not formally a work on Chrysostom as mystagogue, but on Chrysostom's liturgy principally, while at the same time he does make constant and valuable reference to Chrysostom's interpretation of the rites. The scope of the work, however, limited as it is to Chrysostom, cannot provide a formal analysis and comparison of the mystagogies of Cyril, Ambrose and Theodore.

materials to their candidates in view of the actual liturgies they were called upon to explain? Then, having examined the teleology of each father's work, his particular style and mystagogical genius, a comparison and contrast is made among these four mystagogies of the rite of baptism. From this comparative study of these four classic mystagogies of the baptismal rites, it is hoped that principles will emerge which will be of some service for the aforementioned task in developing a mystagogy for present-day pastors in helping their candidates to profit from their participation in the reformed rites of Christian Initiation.

The fact that our investigation can provide not only an analysis of the mystagogical interpretation which each of these four fathers gives to the baptismal rites, but also a comparison among the four, is made possible methodologically by the fact that the respective baptismal liturgies which they interpret, while differing in some aspects, present on the whole remarkable similarity in the ceremonies which form the total complex of these liturgies. While showing what these individual variations mean for the mystagogical approach, emphasis and choice of material on the part of each father for interpreting his particular liturgy, it is also possible on the basis of the essential unity of the four liturgies in question to make an effective and instructive comparison of the four mystagogies.

The Sources: Origin, Dates, Authenticity.

The mystagogies of the baptismal rites which are subject to analysis and comparison in this work are contained principally in the following writings.

St. Cyril of Jerusalem (d. 387)

In the tradition of the works attributed to St. Cyril, bishop of Jerusalem, tradition accords the first place to the *Catecheses.* These *Catecheses* consist of a *Procatechesis*, eighteen *Baptismal Catecheses* and five *Mystagogical Catecheses.* These five *Mystagogical Catecheses* bear in the manuscripts the epithet "*μυσταγωγικαί*," that is, "concerning the initiation into the mysteries," and are addressed to the "νεοφωτίστους," that is, "those who had been newly illumined," by baptism. They were delivered in the *Anastasis*, the "Rotunda of the Resurrection," the small chapel which contained the Holy Sepulcher,[8] to those who had reconvened during the Paschal Octave, the "week of the white robes" to hear these instructions on the meaning of the mysteries of baptism and the Eucharist into which they had been initiated during the Easter Vigil. The fourth and fifth *Mystagogical Catecheses* concern the Eucharist. The first three are on the mystery of baptism and in content are divided into 1) the renunciation of Satan and the act of commitment to Christ, 2) the mystery of baptism, and 3) the chrismation. It is these three *Catecheses* which contain the principal mystagogy of Cyril on the ceremonies of the baptismal liturgy.

The date of the *Catecheses* is placed between 347 and 350, the latter year being the probable beginning of Cyril's episcopate.[9]

Uncertainty still remains in the long investigation concerning Cyril's authorship of the *Catecheses,* the possibility being open that his successor as bishop of Jerusalem, John II (387-417), had to do with the final redaction of the *Catecheses* as we know them today.[10]

In considering the text of the *Mystagogical Catecheses* of St. Cyril of Jerusalem we have used throughout the work the critical edition of A. Piédagnel, published in 1966 as volume 126 of the *Sources chrétiennes* series. The work of Piédagnel contains lengthy introductory material covering amply the discussion of the authorship and the manuscript tradition, extremely valuable footnotes which look particularly to the actual unfolding of the liturgical ceremonies and takes into consideration parallels in other baptismal liturgies of the sec-

[8]See *Bapt. Cat.* XVIII. 33 (*MG* 33.1056).

[9]See *Cyrille de Jérusalem, Catéchèses Mystagogiques,* ed. A. Piédagnel, *SC* 126 (Paris, 1966), p. 14.

[10]On this subject see Piédagnel, *SC* 126, 18-40, 75-78. Given this uncertainty we follow Piédagnel in using the traditional designation of the *Catecheses of St. Cyril of Jerusalem.*

ond half of the fourth century. These have been of some help in the work we have had to perform in reconstructing the baptismal liturgy in Jerusalem as an indispensable preliminary step to considering Cyril's mystagogical explanation of this liturgy.

English translation of the texts cited from the *Mystagogical Catecheses* is that of R. Church first published in 1838 and most readily available as reproduced, somewhat amended, in the edition of the *Procatechesis* and *Mystagogical Catecheses* first published under the editorship of F. Cross in 1951, and since reprinted in 1960 and 1966.[11] We have altered this English translation where necessary to correspond to the critical text by Piédagnel.

St. John Chrysostom (d. 407)

Chrysostom's mystagogy of baptism is contained principally in three series of catechetical homilies delivered in Antioch between the years 386 and 398.[12]

The Series of Montfaucon[13]

This series consists of two instructions published in the eighteenth century by the Benedictine scholar B. Montfaucon and entitled *Ad illuminandos catechesis prima et altera.* They are not the first and second of the same series, however. The second Montfaucon instruction is the second of a series now lost, and was delivered twenty days after Lent began in 390 (?). The first Montfaucon instruction is identical with the first of the Papadopoulos-Kerameus series, and was delivered ten days after Lent began in 388.

[11] *St. Cyril of Jerusalem's Lectures on the Christian Sacraments. The Procatechesis and the Five Mystagogical Catecheses,* ed. F. Cross, *SPCK* (London, 1966).

[12] See *Jean Chrysostom, Huit catéchèses baptismales inédites,* ed. A. Wenger, 2nd ed., *SC* 50bis (Paris, 1970), p. 22. This "second edition" is, according to the note on p. 4, nothing more than a reprinting of the first edition which appeared in 1957 as *SC* 50, containing only some slight technical alterations such as punctuation. An afterword and three small notes have been added in two additional pages at the end of the volume. Otherwise *SC* 50 and *SC* 50bis remain identical.

For the following summary on Chrysostom's *Baptismal Instructions* see pp. 22-65 of Wenger's work, and also the briefer treatment, following Wenger, by T. Finn, *op. cit.*, pp. 5-13. See also *St. John Chrysostom: Baptismal Instructions,* tr. P. Harkins, *ACW* 31 (Westminster, Maryland, 1963), pp. 8-19.

[13] See Wenger, *SC* 50, 24-26; Harkins, *ACW* 31, 9-10.

The Papadopoulos-Kerameus Series[14]

In 1909 the Byzantine scholar A. Papadopoulos-Kerameus discovered the first complete set of Chrysostom's *Baptismal Instructions,* four in number, in MS *Codex graecus* 215 of the Synodal Library of Moscow.[15] The first of these is identical with the first of the Montfaucon series. The other three were relatively unknown until recently because they were published in 1909 as part of a little known Russian series from the then University of St. Petersburg.[16] The second instruction of this series was preached twenty days after Lent began in 388; the third on Holy Thursday of 388. The fourth of this series was delivered immediately after baptism sometime between 388 and 390. This fourth instruction, known already to St. Augustine[17] had been known in Latin translation, the *Sermo ad neophytos,* prior to Papadopoulos-Kerameus' discovery of the Greek MS.

As it has now turned out this fourth Papadopoulos-Kerameus instruction is basically the same as the third instruction now recently come to light in the Stavronikita series.

Therefore, since the first instruction of the Papadopoulos-Kerameus series is identical with the first Montfaucon and the fourth was already known in Latin translation, the discovery of Papadopoulos-Kerameus brought to light two previously unknown instructions, the second and third of the series, as well as the Greek text of the *Sermo ad neophytos.*

[14] See Wenger, *SC* 50, 26-27; Harkins, *ACW* 31, 10-11.

[15] The MS is now in the Moscow Historical Museum.

[16] A. Papadopoulos-Kerameus, *Varia graeca sacra. Sbornik greceskikh neidannikh bogoslovskikh tekstov IV-XV vekov,* in the collection Zapiski, istor.-fil. fakulteta S. Peterburgskago Universiteta 93-95 (St. Petersburg, 1909), pp. 154-183. (The Russian sub-title means: A collection of unedited Greek theological texts from the first to the fifteenth centuries).

This work is reviewed by A. Ehrhard, *Byzantinische Zeitschrift* 20 (1911) 257-261.

[17] For the tradition of the text and St. Augustine's use of it see Wenger, *SC* 50, 30-34.

The Stavronikita Series[18]

In 1955 A. Wenger found a complete set of eight baptismal instructions of Chrysostom at the monastery of Stavronikita on Mount Athos. There he noticed in the first fifty-one folios of Stavronikita MS 6, an eleventh century parchment codex containing forty-seven homilies of Chrysostom in four hundred and fifty-three folios, these eight instructions.

The first two instructions were given before baptism. The third is identical with the fourth Papadopoulos-Kerameus instruction, both of which are substantially the same as the *Sermo ad neophytos.* The last five were delivered during Easter week. This important find, then, added seven new instructions of Chrysostom not known prior to Wenger's publication in 1957 of these eight instructions accompanied by a French translation, lengthy introduction and notes, in the fiftieth volume of the *Sources chrétiennes.*

In summary, the available instructions which form the object of our investigation of Chrysostom's mystagogy of baptism are as follows.[19]

Stav. 1		10 days after Lent began	390
Stav. 2		Shortly after Easter	390
Stav. 3	(*P.K.* 4; *Sermo ad neophytos*)	Immediately after baptism	388 390
Stav. 4		Easter Sun. or Mon.	390
Stav. 5		Easter Tues.	390
Stav. 6		Easter Wed.	390
Stav. 7		Easter Thurs.	390
Stav. 8		Easter Fri.	390
P.K. 1	(*Montf.* 1)	10 days after Lent began	388
P.K. 2		20 days after Lent began	388
P.K. 3		Holy Thurs.	388
Montf. 2		20 days after Lent began	390 (?)

[18]See Wenger, *SC* 50, 7-21; 36-59; Harkins, *ACW* 31, 12-14.

[19]The discussion of the origin, date and authenticity of the instructions is contained in Wenger, *SC* 50, 48-65; Finn, *op. cit.*, pp. 8-10.

Unlike the more ordered instructions of Cyril or Theodore, these homilies bear particularly the *ad hoc* pastoral mark, and the mystagogy as such must be gleaned from them in various places.

In presenting the texts of these instructions we have used for the Stavronikita series the edition of A. Wenger;[20] for the second and third of the Papadopoulos-Kerameus series the publication of the texts by that scholar.[21] The instructions of the Montfaucon series are found in volume forty-nine of J. Migne's *Patrologia Graeca*, columns 221–240.[22]

The English translations are those of P. Harkins, published in 1963 as volume thirty-one of the *Ancient Christian Writers* series.[23] This volume contains valuable notes and cross-references to pertinent baptismal thought of Chrysostom in his other works.[24]

Theodore of Mopsuestia (d. 428)

A Syriac version of sixteen catechetical homilies of the fellow student and lifelong friend of St. John Chrysostom, Theodore of Mopsuestia, is preserved in the Selly Oaks Colleges' Library, Birmingham, and dates from about 1340.[25] This MS

[20] See above, n. 12.

[21] See above, n. 16. Throughout our work we shall refer to Papadopoulos-Kerameus, *Varia graeca sacra* as *VGS*. In presenting the Greek texts for these two instructions we follow the section numbering of the *VGS*, adding as well the more convenient paragraph numbering of Harkins' translation, *ACW* 31, 147-172. In the synoptic charts, however, only the Harkins' numbering is given. Since the *VGS* is not easily attainable, and the space in the charts is limited, this seems to be the most realistic policy. The corresponding *VGS* numbering (and page) can always be found in our index of ancient authors as well as in the body of this work.

[22] In presenting the Greek texts of these two Montfaucon instructions we shall use the paragraph numbering found in Harkins translation, *ACW* 31, 131-146; 173-192, as well as giving the column in Migne.

[23] See above, n. 12.

[24] Harkins' translation of the Papadopoulos-Kerameus series also performs the service of making these virtually unknown instructions available to the Western world for the first time. He notes that even a specialist like C. Baur makes no mention of them in his exhaustive bibliography. (*ACW* 31, 201, n. 16). See C. Baur, *John Chrysostom and His Time*, tr. M. Gonzaga, 2nd. ed. (Westminster, Maryland, 1959-1960).

[25] See *Les Homélies Catéchétiques de Théodore de Mopsuestia*, eds. R. Tonneau, R. Devreesse, *SeT* 145 (Vatican City, 1949), p. X.

is reproduced in volume 145 of *Studi e Testi* in phototype, edited by R. Tonneau and R. Devreesse. Of these sixteen homilies, number 12, 13, and 14 concern the baptismal liturgy and will be referred to hereafter as *Baptismal Homily* I, II, III.

Though their Syrian origin and authenticity is not questioned there is still some question about the date and place of delivery of these homilies.[26] The fact that A. Wenger has established Antioch as the place where Chrysostom's instructions were held gives added weight to H. Lietzmann's position that Theodore's instructions were delivered in Mopsuestia during his episcopacy from 392 to 428,[27] since it is unlikely that both Chrysostom's and Theodore's instructions could have been delivered in the same city at the same time. Mopsuestia was a country see jurisdictionally and liturgically under the influence of Antioch, the center of fourth-century Syrian Christianity. While the liturgies reflected in the mystagogy of Chrysostom and Theodore are substantially the same, as we shall see in our reconstruction, Theodore's represents a development showing a date later than Chrysostom.

In these three *Baptismal Homilies* Theodore treats of the process of initiation from the enrollment in the ecclesiastical books under the patronage of a godparent through the exorcisms to the profession of faith (I); the renunciation of Satan and act of commitment to Christ with its concluding anointing and reception of the *orarium* (II); the baptismal act itself with the final anointing (III). Each of these three *Baptismal Homilies* is preceded by a resumé of the text of the liturgical ritual which is to be explained.

Due principally to technical and financial considerations it has not been possible to reproduce in this work the Syriac text of the fourteenth century MS Mingana Syr. 561 which contains the version of the *Baptismal Homilies* which has come

[26] R. Tonneau assigns Antioch, before 392, as place and date of origin. (*Ibid.*, p. XVI).

[27] H. Lietzmann, *Die Liturgie des Theodor von Mopsuestia*, Sonderausgabe aus den Sitzungsberichten der preussischen Akademie der Wissenschaft, Phil.- Hist. Klasse 23 (Berlin, 1933), p.3.

In quoting Theodore we use the paragraph numbering of the French translation provided by Tonneau-Devreesse, *SeT* 145, since the Mingana translation provided none.

down to us (folios 81r. to 116r). This text, however, is readily available in the phototype published in volume 145 of the *Studi e Testi* series published in 1949, pp. 320-460.

For the English translation we have used that of A. Mingana published in 1933 as volume VI of the *Woodbrooke Studies*,[28] compared and altered where it seemed necessary with the help of the French translation provided by R. Tonneau and R. Devreesse which accompanies the Syriac text given in *Studie Testi*, volume 145.

St. Ambrose (d. 397)

St. Ambrose's treatise *The Mysteries* is a mystagogical explanation of the initiation rites of baptism, confirmation and the Eucharist. In the manuscripts the title of the treatise varies, some having *De mysteriis sive initiandis*, the most ancient, however, having *De divinis mysteriis* or simply *De mysteriis*.

The Sacraments is a series of sermons, presenting a longer, more detailed mystagogy of the initiation rites, consisting of six addresses delivered to the newly baptized on six successive days from Easter Tuesday through the following Sunday.

In his critical edition of the two works appearing in 1961 as volume 25 bis of the *Sources chrétiennes* B. Botte places the date of the *De Sacramentis* between 380 and 390, that of *De Mysteriis* between 387 and 391, considering *De Sacramentis* as a representation of Ambrose's actual preaching to have preceded *De Mysteriis* but finding a more exact fixation of the dates impossible.[29]

In his introduction Botte devotes considerable discussion to the long and ever-recurring debate on the authenticity of the *De Sacramentis* as attributed to St. Ambrose.[30] While the *De Sacramentis* is actually a series of sermons, the treatise *De Mysteriis* adopts this form of addressing a group of hearers as a literary device, a form also used in other works of St. Ambrose. In reality, however, the treatise goes beyond the pro-

[28] A. Mingana, ed., *Commentary of Theodore of Mopsuestia on the Lord's Prayer and on the Sacraments of Baptism and the Eucharist*, WS VI (Cambridge, 1933).
[29] *SC* 25bis, 25.
[30] *Ibid.*, pp. 7-21.

portion of a sermon and is actually addressed to readers and not to hearers. The stylistic differences between *De Sacramentis* and *De Mysteriis*, while perhaps exaggerated by critics of the authenticity of *De Sacramentis* are nonetheless real, the *De Sacramentis* being decidedly inferior to the *De Mysteriis* and other certainly authentic works of St. Ambrose.[31]

Botte concludes that the indications emerging from his reconstruction of the *De Sacramentis* over against the weakness of the various negative hypotheses favor the argument of authenticity of the *De Sacramentis* as a work of St. Ambrose.[32]

In presenting the texts of the *De Sacramentis* and the *De Mysteriis* we use this edition of Botte. For the English translation of the passages we have used that published in 1963 by R. Deferrari, volume 44 of the *Fathers of the Church* series. However, it has been necessary to alter this translation in certain places where it has been deemed less than clear.

The Method

In presenting this comparative study of the baptismal mystagogy of Cyril, Chrysostom, Theodore and Ambrose the work has been divided into three chapters: the rite of renunciation and profession (chapter one), baptism (chapter two), and the post-baptismal ceremonies (chapter three). This divi-

[31] *Ibid.*, p. 8.

[32] *Ibid.*, 20-21. K. Gamber argues with especial vehemence against the genuineness of St. Ambrose's authorship of *De Sacramentis.* See K. Gamber, "Ist Niceta von Remesiana der Verfasser von De Sacramentis?" *Ostkirchliche Studien* 7 (1958), 153-172; K. Gamber, "Zur ältesten Liturgie von Mailand," *Ephemerides liturgicae* 77 (1963), 391-395. His argument pertains particularly to the commentary of *De Sacramentis* on the Eucharist, namely that *De Sacramentis* comments on the Roman canon or one very akin to it, and not the northern Italian-Gallican tradition which is assumed for Milan in the fourth century. Be that as it may, as far as the baptismal liturgy is concerned, *De Sacramentis* shows no essential difference from *De Mysteriis.* G. Kretschmar remains similarly unconvinced by Gamber's argumentation, noting that the similarities between *De Mysteriis* and *De Sacramentis* and other works of Ambrose in respect to the baptismal liturgy which they presume is too great to assume different authors. See G. Kretschmar, *Die Geschichte des Taufgottesdienstes in der alten Kirche,* in *Leiturgia,* Handbuch des evangelischen Gottedienstes, eds., K. Müller, W. Blankenburg, Vol. V, *Der Taufgottesdienst* (Kassel, 1970) pp. 222, 229, 236-237.

sion follows in general the division which the fathers themselves make in treating the initiation liturgy. Given the homiletic nature of the mystagogical writings, of course, which for the most part are aimed at particular groups of hearers, one does not immediately discover such a clear schematic presentation of the mystagogy. However, given the basic unity of chronological development and action in the separate initiation liturgies, such a presentation can be presented without danger of distorting the mystagogy by presenting it here in such schematic form. Moreover, this schematization is indispensable if a comparative study is to be at all possible. The necessary detailed analysis of the mystagogy of each father, the particular ceremonies which each liturgy presents, the different materials each father draws on as well as his own peculiar style, require constant reference to a general frame work if the work of comparison is to succeed in an intelligible fashion.

Each of these three chapters commences with a synopsis of the ceremonies in each of the four baptismal liturgies. These synopses are a critical reconstruction of the liturgy itself which is based principally on the indications provided by implication in the mystagogical writings themselves and collateral sources, an undertaking necessitated by the fact that no ritual orders of divine service are available for the four specific liturgies.

The liturgies being established, the chapters then treat of the mystagogical interpretation which the four fathers give to them. Here, too, schematic groupings of the different aspects of the ceremonies have been necessary in the analytic presentation of the respective mystagogies and for the work of comparison. The different principles employed in determining the schematic presentation of the different aspects of the ceremonies and their mystagogical interpretation in any given part of a chapter depend on the importance and emphasis attached to these aspects of the ceremonies by the fathers and on facilitating the comparison of the four mystagogies. The individual mystagogies are first presented in detail for each father. Individual "summaries" of separate mystagogical points are made where the wealth of material could lead the reader to lose sight of the general picture. Once this individual mystagogy is presented on the ceremonies grouped under these schematic principles, the work of comparison among the four fathers is presented, the "comparative summaries".

The temptation to provide a single aprioristic and exclusive method of schematic consistency in undertaking this work of comparison has been rejected since it would risk distorting the varied and amorphous ceremonies and their peculiar and unique methods of mystagogical interpretation for the sake of schematic clarity. Rather, it has been the different types of ceremonies in the various sections of the baptismal liturgies and the fathers' unique mystagogical approaches to these ceremonies which ultimately have been permitted to determine the manner of presenting the comparisons at different points in the work. To provide the necessary clarity, however, numerous synoptic charts have been included which show both the ceremonies themselves and the mystagogical interpretation of these ceremonies. These synoptic charts indicate both the *loci* in the mystagogical writings and the principal material of mystagogical interpretation.

Particular problems and important tangential results emerging from the investigation are treated in their place in a series of essays.

Direct quotation from the mystagogical works of the four fathers has been deemed generally preferable to mere paraphrasing, since the purpose of the work is to provide a feeling for mystagogical interpretation as a living pastoral function. The four fathers reveal such individual genius and style in their homiletic approach that exclusive circumlocution rather than direct quotation would risk reducing this study of mystagogy to a pale abstraction of principles alone which would not provide the real coloration which is the very nature of that pastoral *genus* which is mystagogy. Since such direct quotation must obviously be limited by technical considerations, its extent has been subject throughout the work to a principle of discrimination which attempts in any given section for an individual father to present sufficiently the high points of his mystagogical approach. Since this work purports to fill to some extent the egregious *lacuna* of scientific theological investigation *vis-à-vis* mystagogy and its obtuse neglect of this pastoral theological area due to an exclusive concentration on the dogmatic aspects of sacramental theology and its reduction of mystagogy to a source supply, a neglect of which liturgiology itself has also been not without guilt in failing to sufficiently unfold the implications of the *praedicatio verbi* in the liturgy, it is hoped that by allowing the fathers to speak for themselves within the scientific framework provided, the imaginative, psychological and pastoral genius of mystagogy might regain some of its rightful inheritance in the field of theology.

SYNOPTIC CHART

The Ceremonies of the Baptismal Initiation

Cyril	*Chrysostom*	*Theodore*	*Ambrose*
			Anointing
Renunciation- Commitment	Renunciation- Commitment Anointing	Renunciation- Commitment Anointing	Renunciation
Stripping	Stripping	Stripping	
Anointing	Anointing	Anointing	
BAPTISM	BAPTISM	BAPTISM	BAPTISM
Anointing		White Garment	Anointing
	(Kiss)		(Foot-Washing)
White Garment	White Garment	Anointing	White Garment
	(Lamp?)		Consignation

CHAPTER ONE

THE RITE OF RENUNCIATION AND PROFESSION

This chapter will deal with the first of the solemn liturgical rites of Christian Initiation, the renunciation of Satan and the profession of allegiance to Christ. The interior dynamic which takes place in the process of believing in the Good News[1] is that of a passage from non-belief to belief. Essentially a transition between two poles, this interior dynamic will seek an expression of its presence in some exterior sign. In its simplest *NT* form, this visible expression of the presence of belief, that is, the expression of the more important or positive pole, is the confession of belief in Jesus Christ, Who Himself is the content of the Good News.[2] In addition to this positive expression of the belief which has come to an individual as the answer of the open heart to the kerygma, there is also implied a rejection of the previous position from which one has departed, the posture of non-belief, a posture which one becomes acutely aware of when confronted with the Good News and its appeal for acceptance. The acceptance of the Good News, belief, and its visible expression, the confession of belief in Jesus Christ, will also naturally strive to give a concrete expression to the rejection of the former position, the unbelief, which has now become no longer tenable. The presence of the individual's radical shift of posture, changing one's way of thinking radically from non-belief to belief, *metanoia*, or penance, is indispensable, as the *NT* frequently indicates in its call to repent as the negative pole to the positive acceptance of the Good News.[3] The external expression of this internal disposition of penance, this negative pole of the process, can take various forms covering a wide range of possibilities; it can be spelled our in var-

[1] *Cf. Ep.* 1:13.
[2] *Cf. Ac.* 8:12; 16:31; 18:8; *Rm.* 10:9-10.
[3] *Cf. Mk.* 1:4; *Lk.* 3:3; *Ac.* 2:38.

ious ways. Just as the interior presence of faith must be externalized by the confession of faith in Jesus Christ before one can be baptized, so too, unbelief, its recognition and rejection, this necessary interior disposition, will find some externally verifiable expression. While considering this attitude of *metanoia*, of penance, indispensable, the *NT* however demands no single concrete form by which this must be expressed. Various expressions of this attitude are recorded in the *NT*, ranging, for example, from the astounding demands of John the Baptist[4] through Zacchaeus' assurance of what he has done to manifest his sincere interior change of heart,[5] to the case of the baptism of the three thousand, where due to the circumstances described one cannot conceive of much more external expression of penance than some general indication of good will.[6] The *NT* sets up no binding expression in word (as, for example, a particular formula for confessing one's guilt) or in act (as, for example, certain practices like fasting or almsgiving) for indicating externally one's rejection of his position of unbelief. When the positive pole, belief in the Good News of the Kingdom of God present in Jesus Christ is expressed with sincere heart, the confession of faith, no more is required for admission to baptism from the standpoint of a binding, concretely verifiable expression of the proper interior dispositions.[7]

Nevertheless, the concrete expression of this negative pole, the rejection of non-belief, quickly took on various forms which coalesced into various ritual expressions, just as its positive, more important counterpart, the confession of faith, quickly gained ritual form. By the fourth century, the presence of belief and the rejection of its opposite pole, nonbelief, had found visible expression in a specific liturgical form which dealt with the handling of the catechumens in their process of Christian Initiation. This complex of liturgical word

[4] *Cf. Lk.* 3:10-14.
[5] *Cf. Lk.* 19:8.
[6] *Cf. Ac.* 2:41.
[7] *Cf.Ac.* 8:35-39; 16:30-34; 18:8.

and act had, by this time, become the rite of the renunciation of Satan and the profession of adherence to Christ. The interior dynamic of the transition from non-faith to faith is expressed in visible ritual form as a turning *away* from Satan, the "*apotaxis*," or "*abrenuntio*," the name derived from the first word in the liturgical formula of the rite, "*ἀποτάσσομαι*,"[8] ("renounce, give up, part company with, leave the ranks of"), and a turning *towards* Christ, the *syntaxis*," or "*professio,*" derived from the second verb in the formula, "*συντάσσομαι*,"[9] ("enter the service of, join the ranks of, adhere to") thus, *ἀπο* and *τάξις*, to turn away from the ranks of Satan, and to join the ranks of Christ, *σὺν* and *τάξις*. The interior dispositions are made visible through the enactment of the ritual drama.

Before proceeding to our comparative analysis of how Cyril, Ambrose, Chrysostom and Theodore interpret this ritual drama for the benefit of those involved in it, the neophytes that is, or the candidates for baptism in the case of some of the mystagogical writings, it will be necessary, first of all, for purposes of comparison and reference, to present the ritual itself, what was said and what was done, this first group of ceremonies which comprise the ritual of Christian Initiation in the liturgies which were employed for this purpose and which are reflected in the mystagogical writings of these four fathers.

Synopsis of the Ceremonies

Cyril

The candidates for baptism enter "the vestibule of the baptistery (*τὸν προαύλιον τοῦ βαπτίσματος οἶκον*)."[10] There they

[8] See formulas below, pp. 25, 27-28, 30, 32.

[9] See formula below, p. 31.

[10] *Myst. Cat.* I.2 (Piédagnel, *SC* 126, 84; tr. Cross, *SPCK*, 53). A further description of the place where the ceremonies are performed occurs in the conclusion of this first *Mystagogical Catechesis:* "in the outer chamber (*ἐν τῷ ἐξωτέρῳ . . . οἴκῳ*)." (See *Myst. Cat.* I. 11 (Piédagnel, *SC* 126, 102; tr. Cross, *SPCK*, 58). A baptismal complex in Nisibis, the present day Mâr Ya' qûb, which dates from the year

stand, facing towards the West, and listen.[11] At a given command they stretch forth their hand,[12] and then they are told to address the following words to Satan as though he were actually present there: "I renounce you, Satan (Ἀποτάσσομαι σοι, Σατανᾶ)."[13] This sentence of renunciation is then prolonged by a triple formula which the candidates are instructed to add: "and all your works (καὶ πᾶσι τοῖς ἔργοις σου),[14] and all his pomp (καὶ πάσῃ τῇ πομπῇ αὐτοῦ),[15] and your cult (καὶ τῇ λατρείᾳ σου)."[16]

The candidates then turn to the East, and are told to say, "I believe in the Father, and in the Son, and in the Holy Spirit, and in one baptism of repentance (Πιστεύω εἰς τὸν Πατέρα καὶ εἰς τὸν Υἱὸν καὶ εἰς τὸ ἅγιον Πνεῦμα καὶ εἰς ἓν βάπτισμα μετανοίας)."[17]

359, corresponds closely to the data given in these Jerusalem *Catecheses* for the ceremonies of Initiation. For a diagram and explanation of the reconstruction of this building according to E. Herzfeld, see G. Kretschmar, *Die Geschichte des Taufgottesdienstes in der alten Kirche,* in *Leiturgia,* Handbuch des evangelischen Gottesdienstes, eds. K. Müller and W. Blankenburg, Vol. V, *Der Taufgottesdienst,* No. 33 (Kassel, 1966), pp. 204-206.

[11] *Myst. Cat.* I.2 (Piédagnel, *SC* 126, 84; tr. Cross, *SPCK,* 53).

[12] *Idem.*

[13] *Myst. Cat.* I.4 (Piédagnel, *SC* 126, 88; tr. Cross, *SPCK,* 54).

[14] *Ibid.,* I.5 (*Ibid.,* 88; tr. *ibid.,* 55).

[15] *Ibid.,* I.6 (*Ibid.,* 92; tr. *ibid.,* 55). Piédagnel notes that almost all the manuscripts attest the change from the expected σου to the third person, αὐτοῦ. In view of the free style of the *Catecheses* in describing the liturgy, this does not lead to the conclusion that the actual liturgical formula was in the third person, but rather, like the other two members, remained in the second person. See Piédagnel, *SC* 126, 92, n. 1.

[16] *Myst. Cat.* I.8 (Piédagnel, *SC* 126, 94; tr. Cross, *SPCK,* 56).

[17] *Ibid.,* I.9 (*Ibid.,* 98; tr. *ibid.,* 58). Piédagnel (*SC* 126, 99, n. 4) draws attention to the absence of the phrase "and in one baptism of repentance" in any other documents of the rite of baptism, and he asks whether this sentence is the actual liturgical formula or a simple resumé of it. In approaching the complex problem of the time, the place and the nature of the various expressions of faith which occurred in the Initiation ceremonies, one must bear in mind three things: the distinction between the recitation of the creed (*redditio symboli*) at some time during the catechumenate or just before baptism (see J. Kelly, *Early Christian Creeds* (London, 1950), the confession of faith attached to the baptismal act itself (see J. Quasten, "Baptismal Creed and Baptismal Act in St. Ambrose's *De Mysteriis* and *De Sacramentis,* " in *Mélanges Jos. de Ghellinck,* Tome I, *Antiquité,* Museum Lessianum, Section Historique, No. 13 (Gembloux, 1951), pp. 223-234; T. Finn, *The Liturgy of Baptism in the Baptismal Instructions of St. John Chrysos-*

tom, The Catholic University of America Studies in Christian Antiquity, ed. J. Quasten, No. 15 (Washington, D.C., 1967), pp. 110-112; P. Harkins, "Pre-Baptismal Rites in Chrysostom's Baptismal Catecheses," *SP,* ed. F. Cross, Vol. VIII, Part II, Texte und Untersuchungen zur Geschichte der altchristlichen Literatur, Band 93 (Berlin, 1966), pp. 233-234, and finally the act of commitment to Christ which seems to have developed as a counterpart to the act of renunciation of Satan at a time when this rite, due, e.g. to the large number of candidates, had severed itself from the baptismal act. In the quasi-independent rite of renouncing Satan, the profession of faith attached to the baptismal act itself could no longer serve as the act of profession corresponding to the act of renunciation, due to its ever-increasing distance in time away from the rite of renunciation. This would naturally lead to the development of a second act of commitment, independent of the profession of faith in the baptismal act itself, in order to provide a liturgical balance for the act of renunciation. On inspecting the synopsis of the ceremonies in the four fathers, such a development does not seem unfeasible, and this would explain the wide variation in the formula for the act of commitment in the rite of renunciation and profession. The oldest tradition would, then, be reflected by Ambrose, who gives no formula of commitment to correspond to the formula of renunciation. In this case, the act of renunciation is so close in time to the baptismal act that the profession of faith contained in the baptismal immersions and emersions renders the development of any counterpiece to the act of renunciation quite superfluous. The order of ceremonies given by Ambrose corroborates this supposition. (See below, pp. 27-28 and ch. 2, pp. 149-150). Stylistically, the profession of faith in question and answer from during the immersion corresponds to the act of renunciation in question and answer form. Further, the anointing has been performed *before* the act of renunciation and not between it and the baptism. And from Ambrose's description, the candidate immediately after the act of renunciation turns and proceeds to the font.

On the other extreme of development one sees reflected in the liturgies of Chrysostom and Theodore a rite of renunciation and commitment far more independent of the baptismal act than is the case in Ambrose's liturgy. (See below, pp. 28-33 and ch. 2, pp. 146-148). Cyril, as well, shows this more complex development. (See p. 24 and ch. 2, pp. 144-146). In Chrysostom, the rite of renunciation and commitment has moved from Holy Saturday evening to Good Friday afternoon. Both Chrysostom and Theodore have an anointing which they interpret in terms of a conclusion on the rite (see below, pp. 111-138), and this anointing is independent of a second ritual stripping of clothing and anointing prior to the baptismal act. Theodore further has the ceremony of the *orarium* intervening between the act of renunciation and commitment and the baptism itself. In Cyril, the emphasis on the symbolism of the act of renunciation and commitment taking place in one part of the baptistery complex, and then the movement to the inner chamber, with the ritual stripping and anointing, also point to a sufficiently long time lapse between the act of renunciation and the baptismal act.

All of this indicates a development of the act of renunciation separate from the baptismal act itself, a development which would require for balance sake a second profession of faith, other than the profession occurring in the baptismal act. In the simpler arrangements of Ambrose, anointing, act of renunciation, immersion with act of commitment, all done within the briefest time and space, such a second act of commitment is unneccessary, which explains its absence. The more complex development of the liturgy reflected by Cyril, Chrysostom and Theodore show how the development of a second act of commitment might take place, and help to explain the marked differences in the formulas of this act of commitment.

Ambrose

On the evening of Holy Saturday,[18] upon completion of the "Effetha" ceremony[19] the candidates enter the baptistery [20] which is called by Ambrose the "holy of holies (sancta sanctorum)," and the "sanctuary of rebirth (sanctuarium regenerationis)."[21] The candidates remain, however, a little distance removed from the baptismal font itself.[22]

Then each candidate is anointed by a deacon and a priest ("occurrit tibi levita, occurrit presbyter").[23] Because it is not the bishop ("sacerdos") who performs this anointing, and because it requires the joint cooperation of a priest and a deacon, and because the image is that of an athlete being rubbed down with oil in preparation for combat with his adversary—"you are anointed as an athlete of Christ (unctus es quasi athleta Christi),"[24] one may safely conclude that this is an anointing of the body and not merely of the forehead or head.

While the candidate is facing the West[25] the following questions are put to him, which he answers: "Do you renounce the devil and his works (abrenuntias diabolo et operibus ejus)?" "I do renounce (abrenuntio)." "Do you renounce the

[18]See *Sacr.* I.2 (Botte, *SC* 25bis, 60; tr. Deferrari, *FC* 44, 269).

[19]*Idem.* On the ceremony of the *apertio* see Botte, *SC* 25bis, 25-26.

[20]*Sacr.* I.4; *Myst.* 5 (Botte, *SC* 25bis, 62, 158; tr. Deferrari, *FC* 44, 6, 270). Present excavations before the present cathedral in Milan have revealed the ground-plan of Ambrose's cathedral and baptistery. The baptistery is octagonal in shape and has a central bath. No adjacent rooms have been discovered and all the ceremonies described in *Sacr.* and *Myst.,* except the *apertio,* seem to have taken place in this single baptismal room. For a diagram of this baptistery and its relationship to the cathedral see G. Kretschmar, *op. cit.,* p. 230. The complex of the baptismal building, then, differs from Cyril's more complex structure. We shall see how, in both of these fathers, the physical construction of the baptistery is utilized in providing mystagogical interpretation of the ceremonies. (See below, pp. 45-50; ch. 2, pp. 228-230, 247-248).

[21]*Myst.* 5 (Botte, *SC* 25bis, 158; tr. Deferrari, *FC* 44, 6).

[22]See *Sacr.* I.9 (*Ibid.*, 64; tr. *ibid.*, 272).

[23]*Ibid.,* I.4 (*Ibid.*, 62; tr. *ibid.,* 270).

[24]*Idem.*

[25]While it is not explicitly stated that the candidate faces the West for the renunciation, and no mystagogy is provided for this position, the fact that the turning to the East with an attendant mystagogy is explicitly mentioned makes it clear, See *Myst.* 7 (Botte, *SC* 25bis, 158; tr. Deferrari, *FC* 44, 7).

world and its pleasures (abrenuntias saeculo et voluptatibus ejus)?" "I do renounce (abrenuntio)."[26]

Having rejected Satan to his face as though personally present,[27] the candidate then turns and faces the East.[28]

Chrysostom

On Good Friday afternoon at three o'clock[29] the priests[30]

[26] *Sacr.* I.5 (Botte, SC 25bis, 62; tr. Deferrari, *FC* 44, 271).

[27] *Myst.* 7 (*Ibid.,* 158; tr. *ibid.*, 7). The sentence of *Myst.* 7. "You entered, then, that you might recognize your adversary, whom you thought it necessary to renounce to his face (ingressus igitur ut adversarium tuum cerneres cui renuntiandum in os putaris)," was the subject of a thesis that here was a ritual of symbolically spitting at the devil. This thesis was based on the variant reading *sputaris* instead of *putaris* of one manuscript. See G. Morin, "La sputation, rite baptismale de l'Eglise de Milan de VIe siècle," *Revue bénédictine* 16 (1899), 414-418. O. Faller has shown through the rules of criticism that this was an orthographical error due to the reduplication of the final *s* of *os.* See "Das Teufelanspeien im Mailänder Ritual?" *Jahrbuch für Liturgiewissenschaft* 9 (1929), 128-132. Furthermore, acceptance of the variant *sputaris* would require a change of *renuntiandum* to *renuntiando,* otherwise unattested in the manuscript tradition. Such a rite of spitting is unknown in the West, and in addition Ambrose provides no mystagogy for such a rite. For spitting in the East, see F. Dölger, *Die Sonne der Gerechtigkeit und der Schwarze, LQF* 2 (Münster, 1918), pp. 13-19; B. Botte, "La sputation, antique rite baptismale?" in *Mélanges offertes à Chr. Mohrmann* (Utrecht, 1963), pp. 196-201.

[28] *Myst.* 7 (Botte, *SC* 25bis, 158; tr. Deferrari, *FC* 44,7).

[29] See *P.K.* 3.4 (*VGS,* 171; tr. Harkins, *ACW* 31, 166, nos. 19-20). Along with *P.K.* 3, *Stav.* 2 also describes the rite of renunciation and profession. While the latter *Instruction* does not specify the time of the rite, its manner of commenting on the order of ceremonies indicates no lapse of time between the rite of renunciation, with its concluding anointing of the forehead and the rite of baptism proper, with its preceding stripping off of garments and anointing of the entire body. However, Chrysostom says that this latter, the baptismal rite proper, took place in the full darkness of night. See *Stav.* 2.24 (Wenger, *SC* 50, 147; tr. Harkins, *ACW* 31, 52). How resolve, then, this apparent contradiction whereby the rite of renunciation clearly occurs on Good Friday at three in the afternoon according to *P.K.* 3, and according to *Stav.* 2 seems to occur just before baptism on Holy Saturday night? Wenger (*SC* 50, 80) offers the following solution. When Chrysostom himself was baptized in 372, the renunciation and profession occurred at the customary time, on Holy Saturday night shortly before baptism. See J. Quasten, "Die Ostervigil im *Testamentum Domini,*" in *Paschatis Sollemnia,* eds., B. Fischer and J. Wagner (Freiburg i. Breisgau, 1959). pp. 87-95. However, the increasing number of candidates following the accession of Theodosius in 379 required moving the renunciation rite to Good Friday afternoon for convenience sake as well as to heighten its importance through such a symbolic hour. While both of the *Instructions* in question were delivered well after this alteration of

lead the candidates into the church.[31] All together the candidates are told by the priests to kneel down and stretch out

---

time, *P.K.* 3 at Antioch on Holy Thursday of the year 388, and *Stav.* 2 at Antioch shortly before Easter of the year 390 (see T. Finn, *op. cit.*, pp. 8-10), Chrysostom, in delivering *Stav.* 2, is speaking of the ceremonies not as they were in 390, but as they occurred during the night vigil of his own baptism back in 372. Reason for Chrysostom's flashback to the Saturday night vigil order instead of mentioning the by that time current Good Friday order is Chrysostom's sudden emotion when he comes to the words "I renounce you, Satan." The very mention of the liturgical formula has such an emotional effect on Chrysostom that he breaks down in tears in the middle of his discourse: "Now tears and bitter groans assail me. For I thought of the day on which I too was judged worthy to speak these words (*Δαπρῦσαί μοι νῦν ἔπεισι καὶ ἀνοιμῶξαι μέγα·. ἐνενόησα γὰρ τὴν ἡμέραν ἐκείνην καθ' ἥν καὶ αυτος κατηξιώθην ταύτην ἀφεῖναι τὴν φωνήν*)." *Stav.* 2. 19 (Wenger, *SC* 50, 144; tr. Harkins, *ACW* 31, 50). Carried away emotionally, Chrysostom starts thinking not of the current order, but of the earlier order, the imaginative framework of the night when his own baptism took place.

Wenger's solution to this problem is not implausible. Although the rite of renunciation took place traditionally before baptism on Holy Saturday evening, it is indisputably clear from *P.K.* 3 that it had moved to Good Friday afternoon. In addition, the *Ordo of Constantinople* (F. Conybeare, J. Mac Lean eds., *Rituale Armenorum* (Oxford, 1905), p. 438) and Theodore the Lector (*Historia ecclesiastica* 2, frag. 32, *MG* 86.201) verify Good Friday as the time of the renunciation where the liturgical influence of Constantinople prevailed in the fifth century. The fifth-sixth century *Ordo of Constantinople* is considered by Wenger to be one of the liturgical practices Chrysostom brought from Antioch to Constantinople (*SC* 50, 84), and the *Ordo* is perhaps even attributable to Chrysostom himself, if not to Proclus or another 5th-6th century patriarch (*SC* 50, 85).

The rite is valuable for comparison with the liturgy recorded by Chrysostom's *Baptismal Instructions.* It may be found in F. Conybeare, J. Mac Lean, eds., *Rituale Armenorum,* pp. 438-442 according to the eighth century MS of the Barberini collection in the Vatican library. Wenger *(SC* 50, 85-90) publishes a French translation of this following the published Greek text of the Barberini MS, but correcting this with the unpublished eleventh century MS, Ottoboni graecus 175 (E. Feron, F. Battaglini, *Codices manuscripti graeci Ottoboniani Bibliothecae Vaticanae* (Rome, 1893), foll. 47-70). An English translation following Wenger's work is provided by T. Finn, *op. cit.,* pp. 114-118. A study of the *apotaxis-syntaxis* with reference to the *Ordo of Constantinople* is made by P. Harkins, "Pre-Baptismal Rites in Chrysostom's Baptismal Catecheses," *SP,* ed. F. Cross, Vol. VIII, Part II, TU, 93 (Berlin, 1966), pp. 228-238.

30 See *Stav.* 2.18 (Wenger, *SC* 50, 143; tr. Harkins, *ACW* 31, 50).

31 See *P.K.* 3.4 *(VGS,* 171; tr. Harkins, *ACW* 31, 166, no. 20); *Stav.* 2.18 (Wenger, *SC* 50, 143; tr. Harkins, *ACW* 31, 50). Both of these *Instructions* say merely that the candidates are "led in," without specifying whether it is to the church or the baptistery, and this may have depended on the number of candidates. On the "Great Church" at Antioch built by the Emperor Constantine, see C. Baur, *John Chrysostom and His Time,* tr. M. Gonzaga, 2nd ed. (Westminster,

their hands toward heaven.[32] It is most probably the bishop himself[33] who approaches each kneeling candidate, one by one,[34] preparing him to recite his act of renunciation of Satan which Chrysostom calls, "*ἡ ἀποταγή*," and his profession of adherence to Christ, which Chrysostom calls "*ἡ συνταγή*."[35] Apparently in a question and answer dialogue[36] with the bishop, the candidate says, "I renounce you, Satan, your pomps, your service and your works (*Ἀποτάσσομαί σοι, Σατανᾶ, καὶ τῇ πομπῇ σου καὶ τῇ λατρείᾳ σου καὶ τοῖς ἔργοις σου*)."[37] After this act of renunciation, again, apparently in answer to a question from the bishop, the candidate makes his profession of adherence to Christ with the words,

---

Maryland, 1959), Vol. I, pp. 30-31. Unlike Cyril and Ambrose, Chrysostom makes no mystagogical point about the structure of the building where the rite of renunciation and commitment is held. The *Ordo of Constantinople* (Conybeare-Mac Lean, *Rituale Armenorum*, p. 438) states that the ritual took place in the church, probably meaning the body of the church since it is a question of a renunciation *en masse*. Archaeological remains of the church of Antioch at the time described in Chrysostom's Baptismal Instructions are not present. A baptistery built by Bishop Theodot (424-428?) onto a *martyrium* at the gates of the city has been excavated and is the only archaeological remnant corresponding to literary sources on baptism in Antioch before 450. For a diagram and exposition, see G. Kretschmar, *op. cit.*, pp. 183-184.

[32]See *P.K.* 3.4 (*VGS*, 171; tr. Harkins, *ACW* 31, 167, no. 21); *Stav.* 2.18 (Wenger, *SC* 50, 143-144; tr. Harkins, *ACW* 1,50).

[33]In *Stav.* 2.18 it is the "priests (ἱερεῖς)" who lead the candidates in, telling them to kneel and stretch out their arms to heaven, but the "priest (ἱερεύς)" who then comes to the candidates one by one to receive the act of renunciation and profession. *Cf.* also *Stav.* 2.20 (Wenger, *SC* 50, 145; tr. Harkins, *ACW* 31 51), where it is the "ἱερεύς" who has the candidate speak the formula in *P. K.* 3. 4 (*VGS*, 171; tr. Harkins, *ACW* 31, 167, no. 22) Chrysostom uses only the general term, speaking of "those who initiate (μυσταγογοῦντες)" the candidates into the rite. From the way Chrysostom uses the term "priest" (see T. Finn, *op. cit.*, pp. 18-21) it seems clear that the bishop is the one who receives the act of renunciation and commitment, assisted by the priests.

[34]See *Stav.* 2.18 (Wenger, *SC* 50,.144; tr. Harkins, *ACW* 31,50). In fifth century Constantinople there was a group renunciation and profession. See *Ordo of Constantinople* (Conybeare-MacLean, *Rituale Armenorum*, p. 440).

[35]See *P.K.* 3.7 (*VGS*, 173; tr. Harkins, *ACW* 31, 169, no. 27).

[36]In *P.K.* 3.4 (*VGS*, 171; tr. Harkins, *ACW* 31, 166, no. 19) Chrysostom tells the candidates that certain questions must be asked of them.

[37]*Stav.* 2.20 (Wenger, *SC* 50, 145; *tr. Harkins*, *ACW* 31, 51). This is the most complete Antiochene formula. For partial formulas see *P.K.* 3.4,6 (*VGS*, 172; tr. Harkins, *ACW* 31, 167-168; nos. 22,24); *Montf. 2 (MG* 49; 239, 240; tr. Harkins, *ACW* 31, 188, 191, nos. 48, 60).

"And I enter into your service, O Christ (*καὶ συντάσσομαί σοι, Χριστέ*)."[38]

Again, it is most probably the bishop[39] who at this point, after the candidate has spoken his formula of renunciation of Satan, and his profession of adherence to Christ, anoints him on the forehead "with the spiritual unguent (*τῷ μύρῳ τῷ πνευματικῷ*)."[40] "This chrism is a mixture of olive oil and unguent (*τὸ δε χρῖσμα τοῦτο ἔλαιον ὁμοῦ καὶ μύρον ἐστί*)."[41] The anointing is done with the sign of the cross,[42] with the words: "So-and-so is anointed in the name of the Father and of the Son and of the Holy Spirit (*χρίεται ὁ δεῖνα εἰς τὸ ὄνομα τοῦ Πατρὸς καὶ τοῦ Υἱοῦ καὶ τοῦ ἁγίου Πνεύματος*)."[43]

Theodore

The candidates for baptism stand barefoot on the "*cilicium,*" a sack-cloth made of goats' hair, and their outer garment is removed. They stretch forth their hands towards God implor-

[38] *Stav.* 2.21 (Wenger, *SC* 50, 145; tr. Harkins, *ACW* 31, 51); *P.K.* 3.6 (*VGS,* 172; tr. Harkins, *ACW* 31, 168, no. 24). See also *Montf.* 2 *MG* 49.240 (tr. Harkins, *ACW* 31, 191, no. 60). Chrysostom attests that this same formula was used in Constantinople. See *In Col.* 6 (*MG* 62.342). It is also contained in the unpublished instruction of Proclus of Constantinople. See *Catechesis de baptismo mystagogica,* Codex Sinaiticus graecus 491, folio 131, cited in Wenger, *SC* 50, 82).

[39] See *Stav.* 2.22 (Wenger, *SC* 50, 145; tr. Harkins, *ACW* 31, 51). The text says, "He anoints on the forehead (*ἀλείφει ἐπὶ τοῦ μετώπου*)" employing a transitive verb without giving the subject of the verb. The subject, however, is from the context the *ἱερεύς* whom we have already seen to be the bishop who comes to the candidates one by one and has them make their act of renunciation and commitment. *Cf.* above, n. 33.

[40] *Stav.* 2.22 (Wenger, *SC* 50, 145; tr. Harkins, *ACW* 31,51).

[41] *P.K.* 3.7 (*VGS,* 173; tr. Harkins, *ACW* 31, 169, no. 27).

[42] "[The priest] anoints [you] on the forehead with the spiritual unguent, imposing the seal (*ἀλείφει ἐπὶ τοῦ μετώπου τῷ μύρῳ τῷ πνευματικῷ, τὴν σφραγῖδα ἐπιτιθείς*)." *Stav.* 2.22 (Wenger, *SC* 50, 145-146; tr. Harkins, *ACW* 31, 51). "For through the chrism the cross is stamped [on you] (*ἐντυποῦται δὲ ὁ σταυρὸς διὰ τοῦ χρίσματος*)." *P.K.* 3.7 (*VGS,* 173, tr. Harkins, *ACW* 31, 169, no. 27).

[43] *Stav.* 2.22 (Wenger, *SC* 50, 146; tr. Harkins, *ACW* 31, 51).

ingly.[44] They then kneel down on the sackcloth, body erect, arms still outstretched imploringly to God, with their gaze fixed toward heaven.[45]

Then ministers appointed for the service approach them and speak to them a message which is an elaboration of the message of the angel to Cornelius, "Your prayers have been heard and your supplications answered."[46] The text spoken to the kneeling candidates is this:

> God has looked upon your tribulations which you were previously undergoing and had mercy upon you because you were for a long time captives of the tyrant and served a cruel servitude to him. He saw the number and nature of the calamities which you have endured, and this moved Him to deliver you from that servitude and from the great number of your ancient tribulations, and to bring you to freedom and to grant you to participate in the ineffable heavenly benefits, which immediately after you have received, you become undoubtedly free from all calamities. It is now time for you to learn the things through which you will surely receive deliverance from your ancient tribulations and enjoy the good things that have been shown to you.[47]

Deacons then approach the candidate, who have remained in the same position, and prepare them for the recitation of the solemn formula of renunciation and profession of commitment. The candidates say: "I renounce Satan, all his angels, all his works, all his service, all his vanity, and all his wordly glamor; and I engage myself by vow, I believe, and am bap-

[44] See *Bapt. Hom.* II. text and 2 (Tonneau-Devreesse, *SeT* 145, 366, 368; tr. Mingana, *WS* VI, 34, 36). The candidates also stand on this *cilicium* during the exorcism ceremonies. See *Bapt. Hom.* I.25 (Tonneau-Devreesse, *SeT* 145, 360; tr. Mingana, *WS* VI, 32). On Theodore as the earliest witness of this so-called "Rite of the *Cilicium*" see J. Quasten, "Theodore of Mopsuestia on the Exorcism of the Cilicium," *Harvard Theological Review* 35 (1942) 209-219. See also A. Hermann, "Cilicium," *RAC* 3 (1957), cols. 127-136, esp. col. 130 f.

[45] See *Bapt. Hom.* II.3-4 (Tonneau-Devreesse, *SeT* 145, 370, 372; tr. Mingana, *WS* VI, 36).

[46] *Cf. Ac.* 10:4.

[47] *Bapt. Hom.* II. 4 (Tonneau-Devreesse, *SeT* 145, 372; tr. Mingana, *WS* VI, 37).

tized in the name of the Father and of the Son and of the Holy Spirit."[48]

The pontiff, who has changed his previous garments, and is now clad in a supple and radiant linen robe, approaches the candidates and signs them on the forehead with the oil of anointing and says: "So-and-so is signed in the name of the Father and of the Son and of the Holy Spirit."[49]

Immediately after this each candidate's godfather standing behind him spreads an "orarium" of linen on his head, raises him and makes him stand erect.[50]

SYNOPTIC CHART

The Rite of Renunciation and Profession

Cyril	*Ambrose*	*Chrysostom*	*Theodore*
Holy Saturday Evening	Holy Saturday Evening	Good Friday, 3 p.m.	
Vestibule of baptistery	In baptistery, a little removed from font	Priests lead candidates into church	
	Anointing of body by deacon and priest		
			Candidates stand barefoot on *cilicium*, are divested of outer garment, stretch hands out to God

[48]*Ibid.,* II. text and 5 (*Ibid.,* 366, 372, 374; tr. *ibid.,* 35, 37). The phrase of the renunciation formula "all his works," which is present in the resumé text at the beginning of the *Homily* is missing in paragraph 5, presumably because Theodore does not choose to comment upon it in the *Homily* itself.

[49]*Bapt. Hom.* II. text and 17 (Tonneau-Devreesse, *SeT* 145, 368, 394, 396; tr. Mingana, *WS* VI, 35, 45-46).

[50]*Ibid.,* II. text and 19 (*ibid.,* 368, 398; tr. *ibid.,* 35, 47).

The Rite of Renunciation and Profession—continued

Cyril	*Ambrose*	*Chrysostom*	*Theodore*
Candidates stand, facing West, listen	Candidates face West	Candidates kneel together at command of priests	Candidates kneel on *cilicium*, body erect, gaze toward heaven
At command, stretch forth hand in rejection		Stretch hands out to heaven	Arms outstretched to God
			Ministers recite formula from *Ac.* 10:4
			Deacons approach
Candidates told to say:	Questions put to candidates:	Candidates dialog with bishop:	Candidates say:
I renounce you, Satan, and all your works, and all your pomps, and all your cult.	Do you renounce the devil and his works? I do renounce. Do you renounce the world and its pleasures? I do renounce.	I renounce you, Satan, your pomps, your service and your works.	I renounce Satan, all his angels, all his works, all his service, all his vanity, and all his worldly glamor.
Turn to East	Turn to East		
I believe in the Father, and in the Son, and in the Holy Spirit, and in one baptism of repentance.		And I enter into your service, O Christ.	I engage myself by vow, I believe and am baptized in the name of the Father, of the Son, and of the Holy Spirit.

The Rite of Renunciation and Profession—continued

Cyril	*Ambrose*	*Chrysostom*	*Theodore*
		Bishop anoints candidates with "spiritual unguent" on forehead in form of cross, saying: "So-and-so is anointed in the name of the Father and of the Son and of the Holy Spirit."	Bishop, clad in linen robe, anoints candidates with "oil of anointing" on forehead in form of cross, saying: "So-and-so is signed in the name of the Father and of the Son and of the Holy Spirit."
			Godfather, standing behind candidate, spreads *orarium* on head.
			Raises him from knees to erect position.

The Mystagogical Interpretation of the Ceremonies

It has been necessary to present the rite of the renunciation of Satan and commitment to Christ in a synoptic view for purposes of comparison and reference. The rite as found in the mystagogical writings of the four fathers has been sufficiently reconstructed from the indications that are found there so as to provide a working model around which their mystagogical interpretation of the ceremonies may be grouped. Given this received liturgy, the time and the place of the rite, the words and the actions which we have just seen in synoptic view, the question to which we now address ourselves is this: how do the four fathers, Cyril, Ambrose, Chrysostom and Theodore, in their mystagogical writings concerning this rite, interpret the meaning of these liturgical ceremonies? What materials do they bring to bear on the rite of renunciation and commitment which will serve to explain them to their hearers, as Cyril puts it: "that you may know the deep meaning of what was done on that evening of your baptism?"[51] The obvious similarity in the structure of the rite evidenced in the four fathers makes such a comparison possible, even though there are some differences among them. For presentation we have grouped the interpretation into three categories, the bodily movements, the recitation of the formula and the concluding anointing, and prefaced these with a consideration of the dramatic framework of the ceremonies, which is itself interpretative of the rite as a whole. Synoptic charts accompanying each of these divisions show the principal *loci* in the mystagogical writings where interpretation is given, and the principal interpretative material used.

Presuppositions: The Dramatic Framework of the Ceremonies

The Drama of Salvation History

The rite itself of renunciation of Satan and commitment to Christ seems, on inspection in the synopsis of the ceremonies, remarkably simple, not overladen with symbolism, and containing an obvious dramatic structure, with its clearly delineated time, place, *dramatis personae,* text and action: the ritual drama. The careful reading of the texts which have been cited in reconstructing the rite will reveal the obvious sense of drama which the mystagogues see in this rite. The very context and way in which the fathers present the ceremonies

[51] *Myst. Cat.* I.1 (Piédagnel, *SC* 126, 84; tr. Cross, *SPCK,* 53): *ἵνα εἰδῆτε τὴν ἔμφασιν τὴν πρὸς ὑμῶν κατ' ἐκείνην γενομένην τοῦ βαπτίσματος τὴν ἑσπέραν.*

for reflection on the part of their hearers is in itself a form of interpretation in the mystagogical writings.

It is object of the mystagogical writings to aid the hearers who are to be or have been initiated into the Christian Church in becoming aware of the world into which they have come by their passage through the words and the actions which constitute the ceremonies of Christian Initiation. Behind the liturgy as found by the fathers at this time and explained by them, there shines forth always the central core of the Christian experience as recorded in the *NT*, one believes and is baptized. This "believing" implies an event, a dynamic passage from one state to another, a turning, a *metanoia* an introduction into a new world of consciousness, insertion into a history which absorbs past, present and future, and recapitulates it interiorly and transcendentally in the mystery of Christian Initiation. This drama of Christian Initiation is described in various ways, from its simplest form, as, for example, in the story of the meeting on the Jerusalem-Gaza road of the deacon Philip with the Ethiopian eunuch on pilgrimage to Jerusalem,[52] or in the conversion of Saul on the road to Damascus[53] to its more elaborately developed rituals. The ritual manifestation of this event, as the fathers found it in the fourth century liturgy, as will easily be surmised, had passed from simpler forms to ritual forms suited to the changed conditions in which the Good News was preached and the act of belief, and its negative counterpart, the act of renunciation of unbelief, took place. The dramatic elements, the time of day, the pilgrimage, the road, the encounter, obvious in the portrayal of the conversion of the Ethiopian eunuch or Saul, remain present, however, even in the more highly developed ritual, because of the very nature of the mystery of Christian Initiation as a passage into a new world of consciousness, the world of salvation history. Place, time, characters, dialogue, event: all continue to play their role in describing the process of this mystery of initiation.

[52] *Ac.* 8:26-40.
[53] *Ac.* 9:1-19.

Whatever cultural refractions the explanation of the mystery might pass through, central to the interpretation of the four fathers is the biblical symbolism which emerges in their mystagogy as the common tradition linking them with the apostolic writings. In order to explain to the hearers what it means to be drawn into the mystery of Christ by believing and being baptized, and in order to expose the full scope of that mystery, it is through their use of biblical symbolism that the fathers provide their principal interpretation of the ritual.[54]

A presupposition for the mystagogical interpretation of the rite of renunciation and commitment is that it is a re-enactment of the drama of salvation history. The biblical symbolism of which the fathers make use in order to explain the meaning of the rite is designated by the name of *typology*.[55] The *OT* saw that in the future God would perform deeds for the chosen people even greater than what past history recorded. In time of constraint, as in the Captivity, a promised liberation was sought, a new Exodus, in which God would destroy the tyranny that held man in bondage, just as He had once destroyed Pharaoh and the Egyptians. The suffering

[54] "The biblical symbolism, therefore, constitutes the primitive foundation which gives us the true significance of the sacraments in their original institution. Later on, in the midst of a Hellenistic culture, other kinds of symbolism were grafted on to this primitive stock—symbols borrowed from the customs of the Greek world. In this way, for example, the *sphragis* was first interpreted in relation to the Jewish rite of circumcision, but later on was compared to the brand or sign with which sheep, soldiers or priests were marked. Or again the dove originally referring to the Spirit of God hovering over the waters, was later considered to be a symbol of peace. But these later interpretations have never entirely covered over the original biblical foundation which the Fathers have preserved for us. And so their sacramental theology must be considered as essentially biblical." J. Daniélou, *The Bible and the Liturgy,* LS 3 (Notre Dame, Indiana, 1956), p. 7. For detailed examples from various fathers of biblical and cultural symbolism used in connection with the baptismal rites see, in addition to *The Bible and the Liturgy,* also J. Daniélou, "Le symbolisme des rites baptismaux," *Dieu vivant* 1 (1945) 17-43. This article re-appears in German translation, "Die Symbolik des Taufritus," *Liturgie und Mönchtum* 3 (1949) 45-68.

[55] For a discussion of typology within the wider framework of symbolism, and its problematic, see J. Daniélou, "The Problem of Symbolism," *Thought* (1950) 423-440. See also J. Daniélou, *From Shadows to Reality: Studies in the Biblical Typology of the Fathers,* tr. W. Hibberd (London, 1960).

attendant on man's loss of God's friendship would be wiped away like tears by man's introduction into a new Paradise, restoring what was once lost in the Garden of Eden. Such eschatological hope was the message of the prophets. In the *NT*, this future hope is seen as being realized. Baptism, for example, becomes the "*antitype*" of the Deluge which destroyed sinful man,[56] a symbolism which has its foundation in the unity of the plan of God, the history of salvation, the correspondence between different moments of sacred history. This typological awareness is manifest in the mystagogical writings. Similarly manifest in them is the awareness of the *NT* teaching and tradition that the eschatological hope present in the *OT* finds its realization in the person of Jesus of Nazareth. Jesus enters Paradise as the new Adam, the old Adam having been a figure, a "*type*" of Christ, as St. Paul calls him.[57] Antitype of the Exodus is the accomplishment of Jesus Who in His Exodus delivers mankind from tyranny and slavery to sin. What was eschatological hope in the *OT* is accomplished in Jesus, His life, death and resurrection. This mode of interpretation forms an essential part of the interpretation of the ceremonies of Initiation in the mystagogical writings.

However, the biblical interpretation of the ceremonies of Initiation goes even a step further, and it is this step which characterizes their unique liturgical creativity. It is precisely the creative genius of the mystagogical writings to penetrate *in the liturgical action* the different dimensions of the mystery of the saving activity of Christ, hoped for in the *OT*, accomplished once and for all in His sacrifice, and awaiting final revelation in the *Parousia.* Bringing to bear on the ceremonies biblical typology as vehicle of interpretation, they reveal the here-and-now situation of the mystery that is taking place. In the life, death and resurrection of Christ the *NT* sees the advent of eschatological realities hoped for in the *OT.* The fathers see this life, death and resurrection of Christ *contained in the sacraments of the Church* which fill the interval which

[56] 1 *P.* 3:19.
[57] *Rm.* 5:16.

exists between the Ascension and the Parousia. Their mystagogy of the ceremonies tends to show how this mystery of Christ is contained in the liturgical action.

It will not be surprising, then, to discover that the core of the mystagogy, be it biblical, natural or cultural symbolism, or whether it analyzes the interior, pneumatic action transpiring in the candidate, or reaches into the transcendental or eschatological repercussions of the baptismal rite, the core of the interpretation is Christological, the action of Christ encountering in the mystery of His life, death, and resurrection, the candidate here and now, in the full scope of salvation history as the bible understands it. Since the catecheses are not theological treatises as such, but rather *ad hoc* explanations of a given liturgical process to specific hearers on a specific occasion, it does not become immediately evident upon initial perusal that this Christological element is the central core upon which the interpretation of the ceremonies is constructed. Given the very nature of catechetical homilies, they cannot be presented in the closed, ordered form of the theological treatise. Subject to analysis, however, this inner structure of interpretation from the standpoint of salvation history is revealed as the presupposition of the interpretation of the ceremonies in the mystagogical writings. The program of the catecheses is pastoral, their use of biblical symbolism summed up by St. Paul: "And indeed, everything that was written long ago in the scriptures was meant to teach us something about hope from the examples scripture gives us of how people who did not give up were helped by God. And may He Who helps us when we refuse to give up, help you all to be tolerant with each other, so that united in mind and voice, you may give glory to God and the Father of Our Lord Jesus Christ."[58]

Not merely on the occasion of, but in and through the ceremonies is the candidate brought face to face with the drama of the whole Christ, active in himself and in history, the Christ of the *OT,* the Messiah, Jesus of Nazareth in His life, death, and resurrection, the glorified Lord, Christ united here and

[58] *Rm.* 15:4-6.

now with the candidate in his own conversion, his *metanoia,* his transformation from not seeing to seeing, from unbelief to belief.

This recapitulation of the life of Christ, His passion, death, and resurrection, as well as its foreshadowing in the *OT* and its consummation in the eschaton of glory, is interpreted and explained in different ways, under different modalities, as it were, depending on the nature of the ceremonies in question, and the possibilities they provide for such plausible symbolic interpretation.

The particular modality by which recapitulation of the mystery of Christ, and the candidate's encounter with Him, is presented in the first of the solemn rites of Initiation, the rite of renunciation of Satan and profession to Christ, is the modality of the central act of faith required for admission to the baptismal bath, and its concomitant negative pole, the rejection of the previous posture of non-faith. The fathers see in the rite of renunciation and commitment the visible representation of this *metanoia,* this conversion or turning, and their interpretation of the ceremonies shows this as the underlying premise. Their interpretations of the words and actions of the ceremonies reflect this act of faith and its implications, which are spelled out in greater or lesser degree according to the cultural context, as, for example, in the elaborations of the formula of renunciation of Satan.

This act of renunciation and commitment, then, is seen as a drama, in which the correspondence between the different moments of sacred history is re-presented.

SYNOPTIC CHART

The Dramatic Framework of the Ceremonies

Cyril	*Ambrose*	*Chrysostom*	*Theodore*
Reading: 1 *P.* 5:8-11		Devil as lion	
Myst.Cat. I.10		*Stav.* 2.23 1 *P.* 5:8	

The Dramatic Framework of the Ceremonies—continued

Cyril	*Ambrose*	*Chrysostom*	*Theodore*
Time: Night Vigil Darkness		*Time:* Good Fri., 3 p.m. Light-Darkness	
Myst.Cat. I.1		*P.K.* 3.19 *Lk.* 23:44	
Place: Vestibule of baptistery	*Place:* In baptistery vs. "Effetha" outside		
Myst.Cat. I.2, 11	*Myst.* 5 *Sacr.* I.4		
-Entrance to "king's house" *Procat.* 1	-Holy of Holies -Sanctuary of rebirth -No longer tomb		
	Myst. 5 Removed from font		
	Sacr. I.9		
Circumstances: Silence; Facing West and East	*Circumstances:* Facing West and East		
Myst.Cat. I.2	*Myst.* 7		
God's Book	Book of living	Heavenly Books	
Myst.Cat. I.5	*Myst.* 5	*Stav.* 2.20	
Personae: Presence of Satan	*Personae:* Face to face with Satan	*Personae:* Candidates in fear of Satan	*Personae:* Candidates in fear of Satan
Myst.Cat. I.2 (*Procat.* 16)	*Myst.* 7	*Stav.* 2.18 *P. K.* 3.24	*Bapt.Hom.* I. 23-25
Power of death *Myst.Cat.* I.10			
	Angels	Angels	

The Dramatic Framework of the Ceremonies—continued

Cyril	*Ambrose*	*Chrysostom*	*Theodore*
	Sacr. I.6	*Stav.* 2.20	
	Myst. 6		
Action: Satan pursues candidates to font	*Action:*	*Action:* Rage of Satan	*Action:*
		Stav. 2.22-23 *P.K.* 3.27	
Myst.Cat. I.3 (*Procat.* 16)			
	Combat with Satan	Combat with Satan	
	Myst. 7	*Stav.* 2.23	
	Sacr. I.4		
			Courtroom Scene
			Bapt.Hom. I. 22-25
Typology OT-NT:	*Typology OT-NT:*	*Typology OT-NT:*	
Myst.Cat. I.2-3	*Myst.* 12	*Stav.* 3 - *P.K.* 4. 13-15, 23-24	
Pharaoh-Satan (sin/death); Israelites-God's new people; Moses-Christ	Egyptian drown; Hebrews pass. Sin, error drown; piety innocence pass		
Red Sea-Font	Red Sea-Font	Red Sea-Font	
Ex. 12:7; 13: 22-23; 14:22-30			

The Dramatic Framework of the Ceremonies—continued

Cyril	*Ambrose*	*Chrysostom*	*Theodore*
Blood of Lamb-Christ		Blood of Lamb-Christ-Eucharist	
1 *P.* 1:19		Door-posts of Israelites - mouths of faithful	
		Stav. 3-*P.K.* 4.15 *Ex.* 12:21-25	
		Statues of Theodosius as asylum	
		Stav. 3-*P.K.* 4-14	

1. Cyril

In a unique overture to the interpretation of the rite of renunciation and commitment Cyril establishes the dramatic framework of salvation history as a presupposition for his mystagogical interpretation of the rite. His first *Mystagogical Catechesis* is in form actually a commentary on a brief section of the *NT,* which is first read out to the newly baptized, who have gathered for the instruction. This pattern is also followed in the subsequent four *Catecheses.* Cyril alludes to the fact of this public reading at the conclusion of the *Catechesis,*[59] where he also quotes part of it again. The manuscripts preserve the indications of the readings which were held. In this case the reading is 1 *P.* 5:8-11:[60] "Be calm but vigilant, because your enemy the devil is prowling round like a roaring lion, looking for someone to eat. Stand up to him strong in faith and in the knowledge that your brothers all over the world are suffering the same things. You will have to suffer only for a little while;

[59] See *Myst. Cat.* I.10 (Piédagnel, *SC* 126, 100; tr. Cross, *SPCK,* 58).
[60] See Piédagnel, *SC* 126, 82.

the God of all grace Who called you to eternal glory in Christ will see that all is well again; He will confirm, strengthen and support you. His power lasts forever and ever. Amen."

This reading, which, of course, pertains itself to the biblical interpretation of the rite, constituting as it does a part of the *Catechesis,* provides the themes of the rite of renunciation and commitment as we shall see them emerge in all four of the fathers: the dramatic pursuit of Satan to enslave men, fear giving way to strength based on faith and the support of the brotherhood, which enables one to stand up to Satan to his face and break his power and enslavement, God's power strengthening one in this endeavor.

The candidates begin their pilgrimage to vision and awareness under the age-old biblical admonition to vigilance. In the darkness of night,[61] standing in the vestibule of the baptistery and facing the West, region of darkness itself, listening in hushed silence, the candidates begin their Easter Vigil. "First you entered the vestibule of the baptistery; standing, facing the West, you listened, and you heard the order to stretch out your hand, and, as though he were actually present there, you renounced Satan."[62] In simple, yet obviously dramatic terms, Cyril recreated that night when the candidates were plunged into the struggle and glory of salvation history, into what will be no less than a new birth, a new life.

In the hushed darkness the drama begins. A command is heard. The candidates are told to stretch out their hand in sign of rejection – for in this darkness the ancient adversary himself becomes present. He is in fearsome pursuit of the candidates right up to the very font of baptism itself! [63]

[61]See *Myst. Cat.* I.1 (Piédagnel, *SC* 126, 84; tr. Cross, *SPCK,* 53), where the evening is specifically mentioned.

[62]*Ibid.,* I.2 (*Ibid.,* 84; tr. *ibid.,* 53): *Εἰσῄειτε πρῶτον εἰς τὸν προαύλιον τοῦ βαπτίσματος οἶκον καὶ πρὸς τὰς δυσμὰς ἑστῶτες ἠκούετε καὶ προσετάττεσθε ἐκτείνειν τὴν χεῖρα, καὶ ὡς παρόντι ἀπετάττεσθε τῷ Σατανᾷ.*

[63]See *ibid.,* I.3 (*Ibid.,* 86; tr. *ibid.,* 54) A similar, but differently nuanced image of Satan pursuing the candidates up to the very font of baptism occurs in *Procat.* 16 (Cross, *SPCK,* 11; tr. *ibid.,* 51). Here the catechumens are advised to treat the eventual encounter with their townsmen who see them on the way to be baptized and ask with sarcastic humor if the town does not provide sufficient public bathing facilities without their having to go to a baptismal pool, as a plot of Satan along the way to prevent their arrival at the pool.

This scriptural reading, and Cyril's dramatic application of it in his re-creation of the ceremony, interprets the scene on the night of baptism: the solemnity of the moment, calm, yet earnest, because one is moving into a new, invisible world of struggle, beginning here in the vestibule of baptistery. Satan has sought the candidates up until now to do them harm.[64] Their calmness is not shattered, however, even in this final, crucial confrontation in the darkness. They are able to stand, to stretch forth their hand in rejection, because "strong in faith", derived from the consciousness that they are not alone in the struggle, but that in the history of the chosen people in Egypt and now, on this evening, the struggle will end in victory, for God will give them the strength to do what must be done, even to the point of overcoming Satan, whose devouring power becomes the power of death itself.[65] And this victory will be gained in Christ.

This *NT* selection, then, and Cyril's application of it, provides the first general mystagogy of the rite of renunciation and commitment, and Cyril makes of the opening scene thereby a dramatic scene of salvation history. The themes are set forth here, the presence of Satan, his pursuit of the faithful, fear of him giving way to strength based on faith supported by the brotherhood, the power of death, suffering with Christ in the face of death, and they run through the interpretations of the other fathers as well.

Cyril uses an *OT* type to interpret the rite, working it out more elaborately than either Chrysostom or Ambrose, who also use it. It serves to interpret the first actions of the candidates, the symbolic meaning of their movement into the vestibule of the baptistery, moving eventually to the baptismal font

[64] See *Myst. Cat.* I. 3 (Piédagnel, *SC* 126, 86; Cross, *SPCK,* 54). *Procat.* 16 (Cross, *SPCK,* 10-11; tr. *ibid.,* 50-51) pictures Satan as lying by the wayside waiting to bite the catechumens with "unbelief (ἀπιστία)," to devour them before they receive salvation. The struggle dramatized in the rite is between the power of unbelief in the candidate and his whole environment and belief. On the subject of the exorcisms as a struggle against Satan see F. Dölger, "Der Kampf mit dem Ägypter in der Perpetua-Vision. Das Martyrium als Kampf mit dem Teufel," *AC* 3 (1932), 177-188.

[65] See *Myst. Cat.* I.10 (Piédagnel, *SC* 126, 100; tr. Cross, *SPCK,* 58).

later, on Holy Saturday night, the Passover, facing West, and stretching out their hand to renounce Satan. The candidates standing there at this moment are the Hebrew people pursued by Pharaoh. "Now you must understand that this figure (τύπος) is found in ancient history."[66] Cyril sketches the events of *Exodus.*[67] Then he invites the candidates to turn "from the ancient to the recent, from the type (τύπου) to the reality (ἀλήθειαν)."[68]

Pharaoh, a tyrant, has enslaved and oppressed the Hebrews—mankind has been oppressed by sins. Moses is sent by God to lead the Hebrews out of Egypt to freedom—Christ is sent by His Father to rescue mankind. The blood of the lamb is the spell against the destroyer—now the blood of the Immaculate Lamb Jesus Christ[69] is refuge from the evil spirits. Yet, Pharaoh continues his pursuit of the Hebrews right up to the Red Sea—so the shameless demon has continued his pursuit of the candidates "right up to the saving streams themselves."[70] Pharaoh followed Moses and the Hebrews right into the Red Sea and was engulfed by the sea—the present tyrant pursuing the faithful right up to the baptistry will be also drowned "in the saving water."[71]

With this type from the *OT*, then, with its notion of bondage and liberation, death and suffering, pursuit to the very edge of liberation, and the power of God, Cyril interprets the

[66] *Ibid.*, I.2 (*Ibid.*, 84; tr. *ibid.*, 53): Χρὴ δὲ τοῦτο ὑμᾶς εἰδέναι, ὅτι ἐν παλαιᾷ ἱστορίᾳ οὗτος κεῖται ὁ τύπος·

[67] *Cf. Ex.* 12:7; 13:22-23; 14:22-30. On the Exodus as type of baptism see J. Daniélou, "Traversée de la mer Rouge et baptême aux premiers siècles," *Recherches de science religieuse* 33 (1946) 402-430; F. Dölger, "Der Durchzug durch das rote Meer als Sinnbild der christlichen Taufe," *AC* 2 (1930)63-69.

[68] *Myst. Cat.* I.3 (Piédagnel, *SC* 126, 86; tr. Cross, *SPCK,* 54): ἀπὸ τῶν παλαιῶν ἐπὶ τὰ νέα, ἀπὸ τοῦ τύπου ἐπὶ τὴν ἀλήθειαν. *Cf.* the same expression of type ("figura") and reality ("veritas") by Ambrose, *Sacr.* II.2 (Botte, *SC* 25bis, 74; tr. Deferrari, *FC* 44, 280) and by Chrysostom, below, p. 52 and n. 100.

[69] *Cf.* 1 *P.* 1:19.

[70] *Myst. Cat.* I.3 (Piédagnel, *SC* 126, 86; tr. Cross, *SPCK,* 54): ἕως αὐτῶν . . . τῶν σωτηρίων ναμάτων.

[71] *Idem*: ἐν τῷ σωτηρίῳ ὕδατι.

time: the night journey of the Hebrews with Pharaoh in pursuit—the baptismal vigil with Satan in pursuit of the candidates; the *place*: the journey to the waters of the Red Sea—the arrival in the vestibule of the baptistery, with the font-Red Sea within; the *action*: facing the West and stretching forth the hand in rejection of slavery before passing into the inner chamber, into final freedom through entering the waters of the font-Red Sea, the saving waters of baptism.

2. *Ambrose*

Like Cyril, Ambrose also sees the rite of renunciation as a drama, and in his catecheses he indicates his awareness of this frame of reference in providing a mystagogical interpretation. By his remarks on the ceremony he sets a stage. He calls the baptistery interpretatively the "holy of holies (sancta sanctorum),"[72] distinguishing the locale for the rite of renunciation interpretatively from the place where the "Effetha" ceremony had taken place, namely before the door of the baptistery.[73] Ambrose indicates thereby a graduated dramatic introduction into the mystery based on the physical appointments of the baptistery, a mystagogy which occurs again, and more importantly, in explaining the baptismal act itself, where the resemblance of the baptistery to a tomb is indicated.[74] Cyril had also used this dramatic interpretation of the physical locale, when, by noting that the renunciation took place in the vestibule of the baptistery[75] he indicated his awareness of the physical locale and progression of the ceremony as a frame of interpretation by dramatic progression up to the baptismal act itself. In the *Procatechesis* Cyril had called this vestibule "the entrance hall to the King's house,"[76] expressing the wish that King Himself would lead the candidates

[72] See above, p. 27.
[73] *Idem.*
[74] See below, ch. 2, p. 247
[75] See above, p. 45.
[76] *Procat.* 1 (Cross, *SPCK,* 1; tr. *ibid.,* 40): τὸ προαύλιον τῶν βασιλείων.

into His house. Even though the Milanese baptistery did not have this vestibule of its Jerusalem counterpart, and Ambrose's candidates were already in the baptistery proper for the rite of renunciation, Ambrose shows this same concern with this dramatic interpretation in the following. Apart from the obvious considerations of liturgical practicality in dealing with a number of candidates in a ritual of complex parts as renunciation, anointings, removal and putting on of clothing, immersion etc., Ambrose's interpretation sees in the fact that the candidates have not yet been allowed to come close to the font itself, and do not yet see it, a dramatic meaning.[77] That the candidates stand somewhat removed from the font and facing away from it is interpreted as the establishment of a kind of combat arena where the struggle with Satan will be acted out. "You entered, then, in order to confront your adversary, whom you had to renounce to his face (ingressus igitur ut adversarium tuum cerneres cui renuntiandum in os putaris)."[78] Thus, like Cyril, Ambrose sees a quasi-physical presence of Satan as antagonist in a drama taking place between the door of the baptistery and arrival at the edge of the font itself.

The interpretation of the anointing which takes place before the act of renunciation confirms this interpretation. The candidate receives an anointing of the entire body.[79] Ambrose interprets this anointing by the image of an athlete being rubbed down with oil in preparation for combat with his adversary. "You are anointed as an athlete of Christ (unctus es quasi athleta Christi)."[80]

Further elements of the dramatic framework of interpretation are presented when Ambrose considers the words of the re-

[77]See above, p.27 and n. 22. Ambrose indicates that the candidates could not yet even see the font. Given the Milanese baptistery this seems physically impossible until one remembers that the candidates faced West, and then, after the act of renunciation turned East and then saw the font, at least "ritually" for the first time, as Ambrose says.

[78]*Myst.* 7 (Botte, *SC* 25bis, 158; tr. Deferrari, *FC* 44,7).

[79]See above, p. 27.

[80]See above, p. 27 and n. 24.

nunciation formula as being uttered in the baptistery,[81] but actually recorded in the heavenly book. "Your word is not kept in the tomb of the dead, but in the book of the living (tenetur vox tua non in tumulo mortuorum, sed in libro viventium)."[82] The figures of the deacons, the priests and the bishop and their ministry is likened to the work of the angels.[83]

Ambrose also employs the *Exodus* type, as did Cyril to describe the drama of the rite as one of salvation history. Like Cyril he calls it a "figure of holy baptism (figura sancti baptismatis)."[84] As the Egyptian perished and the Hebrew was saved, so sin is drowned and error abolished, piety and innocence pass through unscathed. However, he does not go into the comparative detail of Cyril and Chrysostom in connection with the rite of renunciation, but applies the figure more to the baptismal bath itself.[85]

The action of turning from West to East receives also its dramatic cast with Satan present on the one side and Christ appearing on the other.[86]

Thus, Ambrose, like Cyril, establishes a mystagogical framework in which place, action and dialogue as provided in the relatively simple liturgical ceremony of renunciation are elevated into salvation history. Elements of the past history of God's power and its presence in Christ and the mystery of the action of Christ in the sacrament of Initiation are shown in this first of the solemn rites of Initiation.

3. *Chrysostom*

While the time, the place and the ceremonies differ in some details from the liturgy recorded by Cyril, as we have seen in

[81] Ambrose proleptically interprets the baptistery as resembling a tomb, a view which will play a role in the interpretation of the baptismal act. See below, ch. 2. p. 247.

[82] *Myst.* 5 (Botte, *SC* 25bis, 158; tr. Deferrari, *FC*44,6). *Cf. Myst. Cat.* I. 5 (Piédagnel, *SC* 126,90; tr. Cross, *SPCK,* 55); *Ex.* 33:32; *Ps.* 69:28; *Rm.* 3:5.

[83] See *Sacr.* I.6; *Myst.* 6 (Botte, *SC* 25bis, 62, 64, 158; tr. Deferrari, *FC* 44, 271, 6-7).

[84] *Myst.* 12 (Botte, *SC* 25bis, 162; tr. Deferrari, *FC* 44,9). *Cf.* p. 47 and n. 68; *Sacr.* II.2 (*Ibid.,* 74; tr. *ibid.,* 279-280).

[85] See *Sacr.* I.2 (*Ibid.,* 66; tr. *ibid.,* 273).

[86] See *Myst.* 7 (*Ibid.,* 158; tr. *ibid.,* 7).

the synopsis of the ceremonies,[87] it is obvious that Chrysostom, like Cyril, sees the liturgy as a drama to be interpreted from the standpoint of salvation history. His description of the kneeling candidates with their hands outstretched to heaven at the solemn moment of renunciation, an act which Chrysostom calls awesome and frightening,[88] the presence of angels at the scene who bring the words from the candidates' tongues to be inscribed in the heavenly books,[89] the candidates whom Chrysostom describes as quivering with fear at the thought of renouncing Satan,[90] the implied presence of Satan himself seen in the vivid description of his rage, frenzy, and desire to assault the candidates when he sees them marked on the forehead with the sign of the cross,[91] the imaginative picture of the candidates being led into the arena by the priests as athletes of Christ to engage in the combat,[92] even the allusion to Satan going about as a roaring lion, reminiscent of the scripture reading which is Cyril's point of departure,[93] the dramatic moment of three o'clock on Good Friday afternoon,[94]—all of these dramatic touches which we are about to analyze in greater detail show that the framework of the interpretation for the rite is that of a drama. The candidates, the angels, Christ, Satan, are the *dramatis personae*, the script is the dramatic dialogue of the renunciation, the stage directions are kneeling and trembling and raising the arms to heaven, the "lighting" is the allusion to the light and darkness of Good Friday afternoon. Partly from the liturgy itself, partly from imaginative metaphor Chrysostom establishes the dramatic framework as the pattern of his mystagogical interpretation of this rite.

As in Cyril, so here, too, this drama is the drama of salvation history. The chief vehicle for conveying this is the same

[87]See above, pp. 24-26, 28-31.
[88]See *Stav.* 2.18 (Wenger, *SC* 50, 144; tr. Harkins, *ACW* 31, 50).
[89]See *Ibid.,* 2.20 (*Ibid.*, 145; tr. *ibid.*, 51). *Cf.* above p. 49 and nn. 82, 83.
[90]See *P.K.* 3.6 (*VGS,* 172; tr. Harkins, *ACW* 31, 168, no. 24).
[91]See *Stav.* 2.22-23; *P.K.* 3.7 (Wenger, *SC* 50, 145-147; *VGS,* 173; tr. Harkins, *ACW* 31, 51-52, 169, no. 27).
[92]See *Stav.* 2.23 (Wenger, *SC* 50, 146-147; tr. Harkins, *ACW* 31, 52).
[93]*Idem.* See above, pp. 44-46.
[94]*P.K.* 3.4 (*VGS.* 171; tr. Harkins, *ACW* 31, 166, no. 19).

as in Cyril, the Exodus as type.[95] The miracles that the Jews saw are repeated on a greater scale when the candidates pass through the sea of death (the baptismal immersion) and so are freed from the demon, as the Jews pass through the Red Sea to freedom. The candidates did not see Pharaoh and his armies drown in the sea, but they did witness the drowning of the devil and his armies in the font. The Jews were delivered from the Egyptians and servitude; the candidates will be freed from the demon and servitude to sin.

Also like Cyril in this *Exodus* parallel Chrysostom draws the comparison between the blood of the Paschal lamb smeared on the door posts of the Israelite Houses, and the power of the Blood of Christ which delivers the new people of God.[96] Here Chrysostom goes beyond Cyril in that he pictures the Blood as the Blood of the Eucharist "smeared on the mouths of the faithful, since these mouths have become doors of a temple which holds Christ."[97] He also adds a comparison from his own political circumstances in this connection of the protection of the Israelites due to the blood of the lamb, and the protection of the faithful due to power of the Blood of Christ. A law of Theodosius in 386 had extended the right of sanctuary to the statues of the emperor.[98] These statues provided refuge not because they are of bronze, but because they are images of the emperor. So, too, the blood of the Paschal lamb saved the Jews, not because it was blood, but because it was a type of the Blood of Christ.[99] Through this comparison Chrysostom tries to make clear the typology of the Blood of Christ, and how Its strength protects those who have to make the frightening renunciation of Satan. In terms identical with Cyril's typological explanation he instructs the candidates: "Learn the power of the type (τύπου) that you may

[95]See *Stav.* 3-*P.K.* 4.23-24 (Wenger, *SC* 50, 164-165; tr. Harkins, *ACW* 31, 64). For parallel references to this baptismal type in Chrysostom's works, see Harkins, *ACW* 31, 240, nn. 52, 53.

[96]See *Stav.* 3-*P.K.* 4.13-15 (Wenger, *SC* 50, 158-160; tr. Harkins, *ACW* 31, 60-61).

[97]*Stav.* 3-*P.K.* 4.15 (*Ibid.*, 159; tr. *ibid.*, 61).

[98]See Harkins, *ACW* 31, p. 235, n. 30.

[99]See *Stav.* 3-*P.K.* 4.14 (Wenger, *SC* 50, 159; tr. Harkins, *ACW* 31, 61).

learn the strength of the truth (ἀλήθειας)."[100] And he concludes: "If the angel stood in awe when he saw the type, much more likely is it that the devil will flee when he sees the truth."[101]

4. *Theodore*

Theodore's presentation of the rite of renunciation and commitment is less characterized by an attempt to provide a dramatic framework than is that of Cyril, Ambrose and Chrysostom. Aside from the dramatic structure inherent in the ceremonies themselves, which Theodore notes in detail for the benefits of his hearers,[102] the coloration which the other three fathers give to the ceremonies in order to enhance, for purposes of interpretation, their already dramatic liturgical structure, is not as obvious when Theodore describes the ceremonies and their meaning. He limits himself for the most part to recollecting what was said and done, and immediately presents his material to interpret this without those many touches with which have seen Cyril, Ambrose and Chrysostom set, as it were, a stage.

In describing the ceremony for exorcism as a kind of courtroom scene,[103] Theodore had to some extent already provided a dramatic framework of interpretation for a ceremony which is an extension of the renunciation of Satan. Here he describes, for example, the candidates as standing in fear and dread of the tyrant, Satan.[104] But in general, Theodore's principal concern in his *Baptismal Homily* on the act of renuncia-

[100] *Cf.* the same expression of "type" and "reality" in Cyril, above, p. 47 and Ambrose, above, n. 68. *Stav. 3-P.K.* 4.13 (Wenger, *SC* 50, 159; tr. Harkins, *ACW* 31, 60): Μάθε τοῦ τύπου τὴν δύναμιν ἵνα μάθῃς καὶ τῆς ἀληθειάς τὴν ἰσχύν.

[101] *Stav. 3-P.K.* 4.15 (Wenger, *SC* 50, 160; tr. Harkins, *ACW* 31, 61): Εἰ γὰρ ἄγγελος ἰδὼν τὸν τύπον ᾐδέσθη, πολλῷ μᾶλλον ὁ διάβολος ἰδὼν τὴν ἀλήθειαν φεύξεται.

[102] See *Bapt. Hom.* II. *passim* (Tonneau-Devreesse, *SeT* 145, 367-401; tr. Mingana, *WS* VI, 34-48).

[103] See *Bapt. Hom.* I. 22-25 (*Ibid.*, 356-362; tr. *ibid.*, 30-33).

[104] See *ibid.*, I. 23 (*Ibid.*, 360; tr. *ibid.*, 31).

tion and commitment is to explain in great detail the terms of the formula of renunciation itself[105] and all manner of applications of it from such groups as poets, philosophers and heretical theologians, whom Theodore calls "angels of Satan", through bird omens and dancing. Thus, his presentation, and his own talent, lean more on the analytical and theological presentation of the meaning of the ceremonies, than to the imaginative and dramatic frame of mystagogical reference. We have sketched the mystagogy of the ceremonies of the rite of renunciation and commitment in Cyril, Ambrose, Chrysostom and Theodore in a general and summary way in order to show by this rapid condensation important presuppositions which must not be overlooked when analyzing the mystagogical interpretation of these ceremonies in detail, namely the dramatic framework which the fathers establish as a frame for their mystagogical explanations, and the importance of biblical typology as the principal method which makes of this drama a drama of salvation history.

Our next step will be to analyze in detail the different materials which the four fathers use in explaining different points of the ceremony, and to summarize their respective approaches and techniques in handling the mystagogy and to compare these with one another. Though the fathers themselves follow no logical scheme in the presentation of their mystagogy—they simply follow the course of the liturgy itself and comment on it—still it is necessary for purposes of presentation and comparison to provide such a scheme. The interpretation of the rite may be grouped under I, bodily movements; II, the recitation of the formula; III, the concluding anointing.

I

THE BODILY MOVEMENTS

The interpretation which the four fathers give to the physical movements involved in the act of renunciation and commitment affords an excellent opportunity to study the pro-

[105] See *Bapt. Hom.* II. 5-12 (*Ibid.,* 372-388; *ibid.*, 37-43).

cess of how a mystagogy is developed in respect to a given liturgy. The rite itself, of course, obviously expresses *metanoia*, or that conversion which the act of faith presupposes. In elementary form this turning *away* from something or someone, and turning *to* something or someone. It is insufficient mystagogically, however, to bring material to bear on this elementary notion without reference to the given liturgical ceremony which concretely expresses this notion, or, at least, can plausibly be so interpreted. In the liturgy described by Cyril and Ambrose, the candidates are standing, and turn, first facing West then East, in making the act of renunciation and commitment. In that liturgy described by Chrysostom and Theodore, the candidates do not stand and turn, but they perform the renunciation and commitment kneeling, their eyes facing heaven. The gestures of the hands also differ. Cyril describes a stretching forth of the hand toward the West in a gesture of rejection for the renunciation. The liturgical prescriptions for the hands of the candidates in the liturgy of Chrysostom and Theodore are different. Not a gesture of rejection toward the West, but outstretched arms with an imploring gesture of the hands towards heaven. The position of the eyes also differs. While the candidates of Cyril and Ambrose face West, then East, those of Chrysostom and Theodore gaze heavenward. Thus, the act of renunciation and commitment is made in the liturgies of the different fathers with different bodily comportment.[106]

Given the essential abstract unity of the meaning of conversion, it is instructive to study how the different fathers proceed to apply the material of their mystagogical interpretation in order to provide a plausible explanation of the essential meaning of conversion which is connected to the difference of the somewhat dissimilar liturgical expressions with which this "given" liturgy requires them to work. How can the liturgical requirements for these bodily gestures different as they are in the several liturgies, be interpreted in order to show the meaning of *metanoia,* of conversion, to

[106]See above, pp. 24-33.

which this rite is meant to give visible expression? On what materials will the fathers draw to reveal the meaning of these gestures to the hearers? This will depend, of course, on the liturgically prescribed gestures themselves, which naturally present certain limitations, as well as on the individual mystagogical genius of each father in his attempt to present the interpretative material he chooses in order to provide a coherent explanation to his particular group of hearers.

SYNOPTIC CHART

The Bodily Movements

Cyril	*Ambrose*	*Chrysostom*	*Theodore*
TURNING:		*KNEELING:*	*KNEELING:*
From evil works			
Myst.Cat. I.4-9			
From slavery to freedom		Slavery, Captivity	Slavery; Fall of Man
Myst.Cat. I.8		*Stav.* 2.14,18	*Bapt.Hom.* II.3-4 *Ac.* 26:14
		Acknowledging Christ as Lord	Acknowledging Christ as Lord
		P.K. 3.22 *Ph.* 2:10	*Bapt.Hom.* II.3 *Ph.* 2:10-11
		Equality of all candidates in Christ	
		P.K. 3.21 *Stav.* 2.13 *Ga.* 3:28	
			Paul on road to Damascus
			Bapt.Hom. II.3 *Ac.* 26:14,16, 17-20

The Bodily Movements—continued

Cyril	*Ambrose*	*Chrysostom*	*Theodore*
			Prayer of Cornelius *Bapt.Hom.* II.4 *Ac.* 10:4
OT Types: Lot's wife *Myst.Cat.* I.8,6 *Gn.* 19:15-26 *Ps.* 119:37 -Moral *Dt.* 4:23 -Irrevocable *Lk.* 9:62 -Eschatological *Dn.* 2:34-35, 45			
			RISING: *Bapt.Hom.* II.19 - Freedom - Overcoming fall of man - Confession of Christ's Lordship accepted - Prayer accepted
HAND:		*ARMS OUTSTRETCHED TO HEAVEN*	*HANDS OUTSTRETCHED; GAZE TO HEAVEN*
Rejection of world of Satan *Myst.Cat.* I.2			

The Bodily Movements—continued

Cyril	*Ambrose*	*Chrysostom*	*Theodore*
		Deliverance from evil; dedication to good deeds	Prayer for deliverance from Satan
		Stav. 2.18	*Bapt.Hom.* II.3,16
		Thanks for faith	
		P.K. 3.21	
			Reminder of fall and slavery
			Bapt.Hom. II.2,4
			Adoration of God
			Bapt.Hom. II.16

FACING WEST AND EAST	*TURNING FROM WEST TO EAST*	*LIGHT-DARKNESS:*	*LIGHT-DARKNESS:*
		P.K. 3.19-20	*Bapt.Hom.* II.3-4
		Good Friday, 3 p.m. (9th hour)	Cornelius: vision (9th hour)
		Lk. 23:44	*Ac.* 10:3
	Darkness-Devil; Light-Messiah from East	Messiah, Sun of Justice, shines from cross	Paul: light brighter than sun
	Myst. 7 *Sacr.* I.6-8 *Mt.* 24:27-28		*Ac.* 26:13-14

The Bodily Movements—continued

Cyril	*Ambrose*	*Chrysostom*	*Theodore*
Darkness-Hell; Light-Paradise in East		Good Thief and Candidate enter Paradise at Lord's Word	Paul: blind, sight restored
			Ac. 9:17
Myst.Cat. I.9,4 *Procat.* 15 *Gn.* 2:8;3:23 *Ps.* 139:12		*Lk.* 23:46	

A. CYRIL

1. *Turning; the Hand*

The liturgical gesture of the *turning* itself, "τὸ στραφῆναι,"[107] receives its mystagogical interpretation from Cyril in the context of his explanation of the triple term of the renunciation formula itself, the renunciation of the "work", the "pomp", and the "cult" of Satan.[108] That the candidates turn from one direction to another symbolizes on the obvious natural level that they are turning away in their lives from those things which Cyril spells out in his own cultural context, *apropos* of the triple formula, pomp, cult, as disconsonant with the confession of faith in Christ, and also that they are turning away from the person who represents these evils, Satan. On the opposite pole, they are turning toward Christ and the things which He represents.

This natural symbol of turning is then deepened by Cyril's mystagogy in several ways. This turning is irrevocable, and any attempt to reverse it and to turn back to the works one has renounced will not return the candidate to his original position, but to a position far worse than before. Cyril shows this by employing the concrete image of slavery, being possessed by a cruel master *versus* the freedom experienced in belonging to Christ: "For if after renouncing Satan and at-

[107] *Myst. Cat.* I.9 (Piédagnel, *SC* 126, 98; tr. Cross, *SPCK,* 58).
[108] *Ibid.,* I. 4-8 (*Ibid.,* 88-98; tr. *ibid.,* 54-57).

taching yourself to the service of Christ you fall under the influence of these things, you will find the tyrant more cruel, who once treated you as his own, and has released you from his cruel slavery, but who now has been terribly exasperated by you, and then you will be deprived of Christ."[109] This image of turning from slavery, "*δουλεῖα*" to freedom "*ἐλευθερία*" is well known in the cultural context of antiquity and is a familiar image to the fathers of the Church.[110] We shall encounter it again in the mystagogy of Chrysostom and Theodore.[111]

In addition to the natural and cultural symbol to explain the turning, Cyril chooses an *OT* type: the story of Lot and his family.[112] Lot and his daughters escaped from the evil city and were saved because they kept on going to the mountain without turning around to look back. Lot's wife, however, though she too had turned from the city and set out for the safety of the mountain, turned around again to look back, and so was transformed into a pillar of salt, "a perpetual frozen memorial of her depraved will and her turning to look behind."[113] Cyril had already intimated this symbolic interpretation of the turning when explaining the meaning of the pomp of Satan in the triple formula as the entire gamut of corrupt spectacles and entertainment which the pagan city provides, remarking that the psalmist meant this when he prayed: "Turn away my eyes from the beholding vanity."[114]

[109] *Ibid.*, I.8 (*Ibid.*, 96; tr. *ibid.*, 57): *εἰ γὰρ τούτοις ὑποπξσοις μετὰ τὴν ἀπόταξιν τοῦ Σατανᾶ καὶ τὴν πρὸς τὸν Χριστὸν σύνταξιν, πικροτέρου πειραθήσῃ τοῦ τυρράνου, ἴσως ὡς οἰκείου περιέποντος πάλαι, καὶ τὴν πικρᾶς ἀνιέντος σε δουλείας, νῦν δὲ σφόδρα παρὰ σοῦ καταπικρανθέντος, καὶ τοῦ Χριστοῦ στερηθήσῃ.*

[110] See *e.g.* Chrysostom, *Stav.* 2.14,27; *Stav. 3-P.K.* 4.24 (Wenger, *SC* 50, 141, 148, 165; tr. Harkins, *ACW* 31, 48, 53, 64); Theodore, *Bapt. Hom.* I.19,23 (Tonneau-Decreesse, *SeT* 145, 358-360).

[111] See below, pp. 64, 70.

[112] *Cf. Gn.* 19:15-26.

[113] *Myst. Cat.* I.8 (Piédagnel, *SC* 126, 96, 98; tr. Cross, *SPCK,* 57): *ἐστηλιτευμένη διαἰῶνος, ἔχουσα τῆς πονηρᾶς προαιρέσεως και ὑποστροφῆς την μνήμην.*

[114] *Ps.* 119:37. See *Myst. Cat.* I.6 (*Ibid.*, 92; tr. *ibid.*, 56).

The commitment to the service of Christ, seen in this biblical interpretation of the liturgical gesture of turning has set the candidates in the direction of the mountain, where they will be next to Jesus Christ, freed from the destruction of the evil city, abode of Satan, plagued with the godlessness which Cyril has described in his exposition of the triple formula of renunciation. To turn around and to look back would imply a longing to return "to the brackish activity of this life,"[115] and to risk the sterile paralysis exemplified in the forlorn and lifeless column of salt on the landscape of the plain, perpetual memorial to Lot's wife, and warning to any who turn back.[116] Here Cyril adds the admonition of *Lk.* 9:62 against whoever puts his hand to the plow and looks back.

Thus, through natural, cultural and biblical symbol Cyril provides a mystagogy of the turning not merely on the moral level, "Look to yourself, therefore, and do not turn back,"[117] but precisely on the moral level because this turning is invested with the eschatological significance which both *OT* and *NT* provides: "Flee to the mountain[118] next to Jesus Christ, the stone hewn without hands which has filled the whole world."[119] In this closing sentence of his mystagogy of the act of turning Cyril sounds the call of the final judgement and the fulfilment of the universe in Christ, showing that the turning symbolizes a profound, irrevocable conversion, a *metanoia*, involving the whole relationship of the candidate with the world.

[115] *Myst. Cat.* I.8 (*Ibid.*, 98; tr. *ibid.*, 57): *εἰς τὴν ἁλμυρὰν τοῦ βίου τούτου πρᾶξιν.*

[116] Salt as symbol of sterility in baptismal mystagogy comes in interesting contrast here to the mystagogy of the salt ceremony in the Latin Initiation tradition. See the unpublished diss. of H. Riley, "The Salt Ceremony in Christian Initiation," (Trier, Liturgisches Institut, 1968).

[117] *Cf. Dt.* 4:23; *Tb.* 4:13.

[118] *Cf. Gn.* 19:17, and also *Mt.* 24:15, where this command comes in context of the description of the end of the world.

[119] *Cf. Dn.* 2:34-35,45. *Myst. Cat.* I.8 (Piédagnel, *SC* 126, 98; tr. Cross, *SPCK*, 57). *φεῦγε εἰς τό ὄρος πρὸς Ἰησοῦν Χριστόν τὸν τμηθέντα λίθον ἄνευ χειρῶν, καὶ τὴν οἰκουμένην πληρώσαντα.*

In this connection the gesture of the hand in sign of rejection toward the West[120] symbolizes this rejection of the world dominated by Satan.

2. *Facing West and East*

Further significance is attached to the gesture of turning by a consideration of the direction from which the candidate turns, the West, to the direction he eventually faces, the East. Clearest on this point, both in fact of the gesture and the use of natural and biblical material to interpret it is Cyril: "When, therefore, you renounce Satan, utterly breaking all covenant with him, that ancient pact with hell, there is opened to you the Paradise of God, which He planted towards the East and from which our first father was exiled for his sin.[121] The symbol of this was your turning from the West to the East, the place of light."[122] Cyril had already indicated to the neophytes why they had been facing West to make their act of renunciation: "I wish to say why you stand facing the West, for it is necessary. Since the West is the region of sensible darkness, and he being darkness has his dominion also in darkness, you therefore, looking with a symbolical meaning towards the West, renounce that dark and gloomy potentate."[123]

This same imagery of light and darkness, breaking the pact with hell and entering Paradise, had already been summed up by Cyril in his introduction to the ceremonies in the *Procatechesis*. After discussing the effect of the exorcisms in

[120] See above, p. 25.

[121] *Cf. Gn.* 2:8; 3:23.

[122] *Myst. Cat.* I.9 (Piédagnel, *SC* 126, 98; tr. Cross, *SPCK*, 57-58): Ὅτε οὖν τῷ Σατανᾷ αποτάττῃ, πᾶσαν τὴν πρὸς αὐτὸν πατῶν διαθήκην, λύεις τὰς παλαιὰς πρὸς τὸν ᾅδην συνθήκας, ἀνοίγεταί σοι ὁ παράδεισος τοῦ Θεοῦ, ὃν ἐφύτευσε κατὰ ἀνατολας, ὅθεν διὰ τὴν παράβασιν ἐξόριστος γέγονεν ὁ ἡμέτερος προπάτωρ.

[123] *Ibid.*, I.4 (*Ibid.*, 88; tr. *ibid.*, 54-55): Βούλομαι καὶ τίνος ἕνεκεν ἵστασθε πρὸς δυσμὰς εἰπεῖν· ἀναγκαῖον γάρ. Ἐπειδὴ τοῦ φαινομένου σκότους τόπος αἱ δυσμαί, ἐκεῖνος δὲ σκότος τυγχάνων ἐν σκότῳ ἔχει καὶ τὸ κράτος· τούτου χάριν συμβολικῶς πρὸς δυσμὰς ἀποβλέποντες, ἀποτάσσεσθε τῷ σκοτεινῷ ἐκείνῳ καὶ ζοφερῷ ἄρχοντι.

symbolic terms he says: "May God at length show you that night, that darkness which shows like the day, concerning which it is said, 'The darkness shall not be dark to you, and night shall be light as the day.'[124] At the time to each man and woman among you may the gate of Paradise be opened."[125]

The natural significance of the darkness in the region of the sunset and sunrise in the East is combined with the biblical symbol of the Garden of Paradise planted in the East,[126] from which Adam was exiled for his transgression.[127] Turning to the East "you were told to say: I believe in the Father and the Son and the Holy Spirit and in one baptism of repentance (μετανοίας)."[128]

The repentance, or *metanoia*, meant, then, a turning which brings one back to the East, the symbolic location of the Garden of Paradise, from which man was exiled.

B. Ambrose

Turning from West to East

The mystagogical interpretation which Ambrose gives to the gesture of turning from the West to the East occurs in this statement: "Having entered, then, in order to confront your adversary whom you had to renounce to his face, you turned to the East, for he who renounces the devil turns to Christ; he looks at Him face to face."[129]

This somewhat mysterious statement is, in fact, an interpretation based on the primitive meaning of orientation in

[124] *Ps.* 139:12.

[125] *Procat.* 15 (Cross, *SPCK,* 9; tr. *ibid.,* 49): Ποτὲ ὑμίν δείξῃ ὁ θεος ἐκείνην τὴν νύκτα, τὸ σκότος τὸ ἡμεροφανές, περὶ οὗ εἴρηται· "Σκότος οὐ σκοτισθήσεται ἀπο σοῦ, καὶ νὺξ ὡς ἡ ἡμέρα φωτισθήσεται·" τότε ὑμῶν ἑκάστῳ καὶ ἑκάστῃ πραρδείσου θύρα ἀνοιχθῇ.

[126] *Cf. Gn.* 2:8.

[127] *Cf. Gn.* 3:33.

[128] *Myst. Cat.* I.9 (Piédagnel, *SC* 126, 98; tr. Cross *SPCK,* 58): σοι ἐλέγετο εἰπεῖν· "Πιστεύω εἰς τὸν Πατέρα καὶ εἰς τὸν Υἱὸν καὶ εἰς τὸ ἅγιον Πνεῦμα καὶ εἰς ἓν βάπτισμα μετανοίας."

[129] *Myst.* 7 (Botte, *SC* 25bis, 158; tr. Deferrari, *FC* 44, 7). "Ingressus igitur ut adversarium tuum cerneres cui renuntiandum in os putaris, ad orientem converteris: qui enim renuntiat diabolo ad Christum convertitur, illum directo cernit obtutu."

Christian prayer. The eschatological emphasis on waiting for Christ's appearance at the end of time was soon attenuated, and the East became synonymous with Christ Himself, a symbolism connected with *Zc.* 6:12, "The Orient is His name." In explaining the rite of renunciation and commitment, particularly in his emphasis on the meaning of the contract,[130] Ambrose uses eschatological imagery: "Your surety is held not on earth but in heaven. Consider where you receive the heavenly sacraments. If the body of Christ is here, here too are the angels established. 'Wherever the body shall be there also shall the eagles be,'[131] as you have read in the Gospel."[132] The previous verse of the Gospel text which Ambrose quotes here is: "As the lightning appears from the East, so shall the Son of Man appear," one of the origins of the East-light-Messiah notions.

C. Chrysostom

1. *Kneeling; the Hands*

Since the candidates kneel for the act of renunciation and commitment with hands outstretched to heaven in the liturgy described by Chrysostom rather than standing and turning as in Cyril and Ambrose, it is this bodily comportment which must determine his mystagogy of the rite of conversion.

Chrysostom sees in the gesture of kneeling the external attitude of captivity, the sign of bondage to Satan,[133] the same common cultural symbol which Cyril had used to interpret the turning as a turning away from slavery and toward freedom.[134] Chrysostom had indicated this already in his inter-

[130] See below, p. 96.
[131] *Mt.* 24:28.
[132] *Sacr.* I.6 (Botte, *SC* 25bis, 62, 64; tr. Deferrari, *FC* 44, 271): "Chirographum tuum tenetur non in terra sed in caelo. Considera ubi capias sacramenta caelestia. Si hic corpus est Christi, hic et angeli constituti sunt: 'ubi corpus ibi et aquilae,' legisti in evangelio."
[133] See *Stav.* 2.18, *P.K.* 3.4 (Wenger, *SC* 50, 143-144; *VGS* 170-171; tr. Harkins *ACW* 31, 50, 167, no. 22).
[134] *Cf.* above, pp. 59-60.

pretation of the kneeling posture for the exorcisms: "Those who endure captivity of the body show by their posture their dejection at the disaster which has overcome them. So, too, when the devil's captives are about to be set free from his damnation and to come under the yoke of goodness, they first remind themselves of their prior condition by their external attitude. They do this that they may be able to know from what evil they are being delivered and to what good they are hurrying."[135]

At the same time this kneeling is not only a sign of slavery to Satan, but Chrysostom sees in it also a sign of confessing the absolute rule of Christ as well, using a passage from St. Paul to establish this: "Sacred custom bids you to remain on your knees, so as to acknowledge His absolute rule (*ὁμολογῆσαι τὴν δεσποτεῖαν*) even by your posture, for to bend the knee is a mark of those who acknowledge their servitude. Hear what St. Paul says: 'To Him every knee shall bend of those in heaven, on earth and under the earth.' "[136]

Thus, the kneeling position for the act of renunciation and commitment means for Chrysostom two things, and it corresponds in its own way to Cyril's interpretation of turning from servitude to the freedom which comes from the confession of faith in Christ as Messiah. It represents both man's fall and consequent enslavement, but it expresses at the same time what happens in the act of commitment to Christ. Kneeling expresses that one "confesses the absolute rule (*ὁμολογῆσαι τὴν δεσποτεῖαν*)" of Christ, that is to say, this

[135] *Stav.* 2.14 (Wenger, *SC* 50, 141; tr. Harkins, *ACW* 31, 48): *Οἱ τὴν αἰχμαλωσίαν ταύτην τὴν σωματικὴν ὑπομένοντες καὶ διὰ τοῦ σχήματος τὴν κατήφειαν δεικνύουσι τῆς καταλαβούσης αὐτοὺς συμφορᾶς, οὕτω καὶ οὗτοι αἰχμάλωτοι γενόμενοι ὑπὸ τοῦ διαβόλου, ἐπειδὴ μέλλουσιν ἐλευθεροῦσθαι τῆς ἐκείνου τυραννίδος καὶ ὑπὸ τὸν ζυγὸν ἔρχεσθαι τὸν χρηστόν, πρότερον διὰ τοῦ σχήματος ὑπομιμνήσκουσιν ἑαυτοὺς τῆς προτέρας καταστάσεως ἵν' εἰδέναι ἔχωσι τίνος μὲν ἀπαλλάττονται, τίνι δὲ προστρέχουσι.*

[136] *Ph.* 2:10. *P.K.* 3.4 (*VGS.* 171-172; tr. Harkins, *ACW* 31, 167, no. 22): *ἐπὶ γόνυ δὲ οἱ ἱεροὶ κελεύουσι κεῖσθαι νόμοι, ὥστε καὶ διὰ τοῦ σχήματος ὁμολογῆσαι τὴν δεσποτείαν. ὅτι γὰρ τὸ γόνυ κάμψαι (τῶν) τὴν δουλείαν ὁμολογούντων ἐστίν, ἄκουσον τί φησιν ὁ Παῦλος· ὅτι "αὐτῷ κάμψαι πᾶν γόνυ ἐπουρανίων καὶ ἐπιγείων καὶ καταχθονίων."*

gesture dramatizes the confession of commitment which the candidate makes with his lips, the confession that Jesus is the *Kyrios*. The text of *Ph.* 2 which Chrysostom quotes to interpret this gesture contains as a matter of fact immediately after the verse quoted the confession of faith or commitment to Christ "and that every tongue should acclaim Jesus Christ as Lord to the glory of God the Father."[137] Chrysostom has simply taken over the Pauline image of kneeling as sign of acknowledging the universal Lordship of Christ, the bodily sign which symbolizes the confession of this faith, which is what the candidates confess when they say: "And I enter into your service, O Christ."[138]

In interpreting the turning to the East Cyril had put the act of faith in conjunction with the eschatological picture of Christ on the mountain, "the stone hewn without hands which has filled in the whole world."[139] In interpreting the kneeling in connection with the sign of the servitude of man's dominion to Satan, and then St. Paul's image of kneeling to confess the universal sovereignty of Christ, Chrysostom also presents a consistent mystagogy. While the gestures differ, standing and turning, and kneeling, they both represent the same thing, the dramatiation through bodily gesture of the conversion from Satan to Christ which the act of renunciation and commitment bespeaks.

Unique to Chrysostom is his interpretation of the kneeling posture by means of reference to *Ga.* 3:28, where St. Paul says that in those who are baptized "there are no more distinctions of Jew and Greek, slave and free, male and female," but all are one in Christ Jesus. Chrysostom in his mystagogy makes much of the fact that on entering the church all the candidates must kneel down together, and he insists that no one stand erect because the gifts are given to all in common.[140] The liturgical requirement that all kneel down

[137] *Ph.* 2:11.
[138] See above, p. 31.
[139] See above, p. 61.
[140] See *P.K.* 3.4 (*VGS.* 171; tr. Harkins, *ACW* 31, 167, no. 21).

shows that the rich man may not look down on the poor man, nor the poor man consider he has any less than the rich man. Equality before God is a favorite theme of Chrysostom. He had already touched on this mystagogy in his commentary on the ceremonies of exorcism,[141] where he notes that regardless of a man's lineage, wealth, or worldly honor, he stands side by side with the beggar and often with the blind and the lame. Difference and distinction of rank, says Chrysostom, have no place in the world of the spirit where one looks only for a soul that is well-disposed. Here, however, in *P.K.* 3,[142] with its reference to *Ga.* 3:28, Chrysostom's interpretation of the liturgical directive that all kneel down together for the act of renunciation and commitment takes us into the more profound idea of oneness with Christ. This is Paul's commentary on baptism and the act of faith and its social repercussions. By applying it to this gesture as a mystagogical interpretation Chrysostom shows graphically how the bodily gesture expresses the meaning of this act using a symbol which culturally and sociologically would not escape his hearers. He lets the gesture spell out in sociological terms what the renunciation of Satan and conversion to Christ must mean. His emphasis on fraternity and equality here, something that could hardly be missed by his hearers, given the social structure of the times,[143] is not based on a merely humanitarian notion but on a profound meditation on the doctrine of the Mystical Body of Christ, and the reality which the act of faith brings to a human being's relationship to society. Indeed, Chysostom spells out the meaning of *metanoia* in sociological terms with this mystagogy, but these terms are based on eschatological awareness, based on the Pauline exegesis of the act of faith, confessing Jesus as universal Lord.

Actually, the way Cyril puts it, turning, following Christ to the mountain and avoiding the salt-savor of this world's evil

[141] See *Stav.* 2.13 (Wenger, *SC* 50, 140; tr. Harkins, *ACW* 31, 48).

[142] See above, n. 140.

[143] Two beautiful parallel passages of Chrysostom on this subject of the lack of distinction of persons in the Christian fraternity are found in *In 1 Co.* 10.1 (*MG* 51.247) and in an Easter sermon, *De res. dom.* (*MG* 50.437). Harkins, *ACW* 31, 219, n. 30, provides an English translation of the former.

doings, and the concrete way Chrysostom puts it, kneeling down together, "that the rich man may not look down on the poor man," are similar, but nuanced expressions of the renunciation of the way of Satan and commitment to the way of Christ. Thus, it would hardly do justice to such a mystagogy of kneeling as Chrysostom gives here to view it as the preacher's occasion to draw from his notebook of *loci communes* to score a point on a favorite local problem. It is, rather, Chrysostom's peculiar way of analyzing the conversion experience, and showing how this gesture expresses its meaning.

Unlike the gesture of rejection to the West described by Cyril as a requirement of the candidates, Chrysostom's candidates have their arms outstretched to heaven. Again, the gesture is connected to the conversion dynamic. First, Chrysostom sees it as a natural expression, connected with the kneeling, to remind the candidates from what evil they have been delivered and to what good they will dedicate themselves.[144] He further interprets this gesture as a sign of thankfulness to God for the gift of faith.[145]

2. *Light and Darkness*

Although Chrysostom does not mention specifically whether his candidates faced West for the renunciation and then turned to the East for the act of commitment, still his *Instruction* on the ceremonies at this point reveal the same symbolic awareness found in Cyril and Ambrose who comment on the matter, namely the symbolism of light and darkness, and that of the return to Paradise as a result of destroying the pact with hell:

> Tomorrow, on Friday at the ninth hour, you must have certain questions asked of you and you must present your contracts to the Master. Nor do I make mention to you of that day and that hour without some purpose. A mystical lesson can be learned from them. For on Friday at the

[144] See *Stav.* 2.18 (Wenger, *SC 50,* 143-144; tr. Harkins, *ACW* 31, 50).
[145] See *P.K.* 3.4 (*VGS,* 171; tr. Harkins, *ACW* 31, 167, no. 21).

> ninth hour the thief entered Paradise; the darkness, which lasted from the sixth to the ninth hour was dissolved;[146] and the Light, perceived by both body and mind, was taken up as a sacrifice for the whole world. For at that hour Christ said: 'Father, into thy hands I commend my spirit.'[147] Then the sun we see looked on the Sun of Justice shining from the cross and turned back its own rays. Therefore, when you are about to be led [into the church] at the ninth hour, do you also recall to mind the great number of your virtuous deeds and count those gifts which await you; you will no longer be on earth, but your soul will raise itself up and lay hold of heaven itself.[148]

Here, the symbolism of both the Messiahship of Christ as Sun of Justice and the re-entry into Paradise appear in the framework of the symbolism of light, albeit in a different way from that presented by Cyril and Ambrose in their interpretation of the facing West, region of darkness, and East, region of light and symbolic location of Paradise. Chrysostom's mystagogy is more directly Christological, due to the different circumstances of his liturgy, the gestures and the time. He utilizes the advantage of the Good Friday hour to provide the mystagogy which in import is essentially the same as that of Cyril and Ambrose, light-darkness, the Messiahship of Christ, the return to Paradise.

[146] *Cf. Lk.* 23:44.

[147] *Lk.* 23:46.

[148] *P.K.* 3.4 (*VGS,* 171; tr. Harkins, *ACW* 31, 167, nos. 19-20): Μετὰ τὴν αὔριον τῇ Παρασκευῇ, ὥρᾳ ἐνάτῃ, ἀνάγκη τινὰ ὑμᾶς ἀπαιτηθῆναι ῥήματα καὶ συνθήκας θέσθαι πρὸς τὸν δεσπότην. οὐχ ἁπλῶς δὲ ὑμᾶς οὐδε τὴν ἡμέραν οὐδε τὴν ὥραν ἀνέμνησα ταύτην· ἀλλὰ ἔστι καὶ ἀπο τούτων μαθεῖν τὶ μυστικόν. καὶ γὰρ τῇ Παρασκευῇ, ἐνάτῃ ὥρᾳ, ὁ ληστὴς εἰς τὸν παράδεισον εἰσηλθε καὶ τὸ σκότος κατελύθη τὸ ἀπο τῆς ἕκτης ὥρας ἕως τῆς ἐνάτης, καὶ τὸ αἰσθητον καὶ τὸ νοητὸν φῶς τότε ὑπερ τῆς οἰκουμένης ἀνηνέχθη θυσία· τότε γὰρ φησιν ὁ Χριστος·" πάτερ, εἰς χεῖρας σου παραθήσομαι τὸ πνεῦμα μου". τότε τὸν ἥλιον τῆς δικαιοσύνης ιδων ἀπο του σταυροῦ λάμποντα ὁ αἰσθητος οὑτος ἥλιος τὰς ἀκτῖνας ἀπέστρεψεν. ὅταν οὖν μέλλῃς εἰσάγεσθαι καὶ συ κατὰ τὴν ἐνάτην ὥραν, ἀναμιμνήσκου καὶ συ τοῦ μεγέθους τῶν κατορθω μάτων καὶ τὰς δωρεὰς ἀρίθμει ταύτας παρὰ σαυτῷ, καὶ οὐκ ἔσῃ λοιπὸν ἐπὶ τῆς γῆς, ἀλλὰ διαναστήσῃ καὶ τῶν οὐρανῶν αὐτων ἐπιλήψῃ τῇ ψυχῇ.

D. Theodore

1. *Kneeling and Rising*

More similar generally to the liturgy of Chrysostom than to that of Cyril or Ambrose, Theodore's liturgy also has the candidates kneel gazing toward heaven with outstretched arms for the act of renunciation and commitment. A careful study of Theodore's introductory mystagogy of the rite reveals the astonishing skill with which *OT* and *NT* images, particularly Pauline notions, are applied to show the candidates the meaning of what they are doing:

> First you genuflect, while the rest of your body is erect, and in the posture of one who prays you stretch out your arms towards God. As we have all of us fallen into sin and been driven to the dust by the sentence of death, it behooves us to "bow our knees in the name of Jesus Christ," as the blessed Paul said, "and to confess that Jesus Christ is the Lord to the glory of God His Father."[149] In this confession we show the things that accrue to us from the divine nature through the Economy of Christ our Lord, whom [God] raised up to heaven and showed as Lord of all and head of our salvation. Because all these things have to be performed by us all who "are fallen to the earth" according to the words of blessed Paul[150] it is with justice that you who through the Sacrament become partakers of the ineffable benefits to which you have been called by your faith in Christ, bow your knees and make manifest your ancient fall, and worship God the cause of all those benefits.[151]

Here we see, first, that Theodore's interpretation of the gesture of kneeling parallels that of Chrysostom in that it is a symbol of man's servitude as a result of his original fall. The kneeling symbolizes man's return to the dust of the earth through God's sentence of death and consequent servitude to

[149] *Ph.* 2:10-11.
[150] *Ac.* 26:14.
[151] *Bapt. Hom.* II.3 (Tonneau-Devreesse, *SeT* 145, 370; tr. Mingana, *WS* VI, 36).

Satan.[152] This familiar theme of slavery to Satan and deliverance to freedom is expressed particularly by the formula developed from the message of the angel to Cornelius[153] which those appointed for the service speak to the kneeling candidates. The long prayers of the catechumenate, the time of exorcism, the awareness of servitude are the content of this message.

Also like Chrysostom, Theodore quotes *Ph.* 2 to interpret the kneeling as a gesture which expresses that total adoration of Jesus as Lord which the confession of faith bespeaks.

The same mystagogy of the conversion dynamic is present here, then, in this interpretation of the kneeling as was present in Chrysostom, man's fall and consequent enslavement, and at the same time his confession of Jesus' Lordship over the whole of creation, on bended knee, a gesture symbolically suited to the act of faith from *Ph.* 2.

[152]Theodore develops this theme of servitude to Satan particularly in his mystagogy of the ceremonies of exorcism: "In this same way when the words called the words of exorcism are pronounced you stand perfectly quiet, as if you had no voice and as if you were still in fear and dread of the Tyrant, not being in a position even to look at him on account of the great injustice which he did to you and to your fathers, in the fact that he led you into captivity, brought you into a dire and cruel servitude, and inflicted upon you wounds that leave indelible scars, through the punishment of death which he placed in your midst; and in the fact that he has been for a long time the master of the servitude which you, with your own hands, brought upon yourselves. You stand, therefore, with outstretched arms in the posture of one who prays, and look downwards and remain in that state in order to move the judge to mercy. And you take off your outer garment and stand barefooted in order to show in yourself the state of the cruel servitude in which you served the Devil for a long time, according to the rules of captivity, and in which you did all his work for him according to his requirements. Your aim in this posture is also to move the judge to mercy, and it is this picture of captivity that is implied in the words of God who spoke thus through the prophet Isaiah: 'Like as my servant Isaiah hath walked naked and barefoot for three years in order that he might become a sign for the Egyptians and the Ethiopians captives, young and old, naked and barefoot.' "*Is.* 20:3-4. *Bapt. Hom.* I.23-24, (Tonneau-Devreesse, *SeT* 145, 358, 360; tr. Mingana, *WS* VI, 31-32).

Here it is not the kneeling, but the nakedness and the bare feet of the candidates, their looking downwards in silence, fearful even to look at the tyrant, and the arms outstretched imploring mercy, which suggests slavery.

[153]See above, p. 32.

Most remarkable, however, in Theodore's mystagogy of the kneeling (and subsequent rising)[154] is the use of St. Paul's conversion on the road to Damascus, where, as Theodore notes, he and his companions, like the candidates, all fell to the ground.[155] Theodore proceeds to show the *metanoia* that takes place, demonstrating how the candidates, like St. Paul, will eventually be extricated from this *impasse*. It is through faith in Christ that the turning point comes. The message is the same, but the interpretation although biblical, quite different from that of Cyril. Cyril had interpreted the "turning (το στραφῆναι)," using the picture of Lot's wife on the one hand and Jesus on the mountain, with the eschatological overtones on the other hand to describe the implications of the process of conversion.[156] Here, Theodore emphasizes not the *turning*, but the *falling* and *rising*. Paul and his companions all fell to the ground, like Adam, like the kneeling candidates. That they are able to get up again is due to the power of Jesus, who tells Paul: "Get up, and stand on your feet,"[157] just as the candidates, after their renunciation and confession of the Lordship of Jesus, as Theodore indicates in his quotation from *Ph.* 2:10-11, will be helped to their feet by their godparents.[158] Paul proceeded to baptism after his "fall" and "rising," his rite of renunciation and commitment, and so, too, the candidates, who liturgically express their *metanoia* in this way, and proceed after this to baptism. That Theodore intends the parallel between the conversion of St. Paul and the rite of renunciation and commitment that he is describing becomes clear from the obvious baptismal allusions present when one reads further in this text from *Ac.*: "I shall deliver you from the people and from the pagans, to whom I am sending you to open their eyes, so that they may turn from darkness to light, from the

[154] See above, p. 33.
[155] *Ac.* 26:14. See *Bapt. Hom.* II.3, above, p. 70.
[156] See above, pp. 59-62.
[157] *Ac.* 26:16.
[158] See above, p. 33.

dominion of Satan to God, and receive, through faith in me, forgiveness of their sins and a share in the inheritance of the sanctified."[159]

And Paul goes on to add that he became preacher of this *metanoia* which he himself had undergone beginning with his falling to the ground and rising on the Damascus road: "I started preaching, first to the people of Damascus, then to those of Jerusalem and all the country-side of Judea, and also to the pagans, urging them to repent (μετανοεῖν) and to turn (ἐπιστρεφεῖν) to God, proving their change of heart (μετανοίας) by their deeds."[160]

Thus, Theodore interprets the posture of kneeling for the act of renunciation and commitment as sign of man's fall and servitude, and adds the image of conversion in the story of Cornelius the centurion from *Ac.* whose prayers for deliverance were finally heard. Through the use of the Pauline image of kneeling from *Ph.* 2 he sees the kneeling of the candidates also as a gesture which dramatizes the confession of Jesus universal Lordship in the act of commitment. The conversion of St. Paul described in *Ac.*, with its falling to the ground and rising again provides Theodore with further mystagogical material for a parallel with the ceremony of kneeling and rising.

At the end of the service the godfather of the candidate makes him stand up. Theodore interprets this gesture of standing as a sign that the ancient fall and captivity expressed by the kneeling has been overcome and that the confession of the Lordship of Christ expressed by the same gesture of kneeling has been accepted:

> By your rising from your genuflexion you show that you have cast away your ancient fall, that you have no more communion with earth and earthly things, that your adoration and prayer to God has been accepted, that you have received the stamp which is the sign of your election to the ineffable military service, that you have been called

[159] *Ac.* 26:17-18.
[160] *Ac.* 26:20.

> to heaven, and that you ought henceforth to direct your course to its life and citizenship while spurning all earthly things.[161]

2. *The Hands and the Gaze*

The gaze of the candidates has been directed to heaven and their hands have been outstretched toward heaven during the act of renunciation and commitment. Theodore describes this gesture as "the posture of one who prays."[162]

The gesture is for Theodore's mystagogy as for Chrysostom's, a reminder of the ancient fall and slavery, since it is a gesture of prayer that one be delivered from this slavery. By the fact that it is a sign of imploring, it reveals the need of the candidates of God's help toward freedom, to rise from the ancient fall, summing up the import of the exorcistic ceremonies of the catechumenate which were meant to help to this purpose of liberating the candidate fallen under the power of evil. The story of Cornelius the centurion which is suggested to the candidates by the formula which the assistants speak to them while they are in this position encourages them that their long prayers of the past weeks of preparation will now be heard by God, as were those of Cornelius who was also led to baptism. While they are kneeling there with outstretched arms and gaze toward heaven, Theodore reminds the candidates of what their interior dispositions should be: "In this posture you offer prayer to God, and implore Him to grant you deliverance from the ancient fall and participation in the heavenly benefits."[163]

This gesture expresses not only the request for deliverance from servitude and the ancient fall, but it also corresponds to the kneeling as Theodore interprets it as a sign of confession of Christ as the Lord, the very confession which will bring about the deliverance from the servitude of belonging to Satan

[161] *Bapt. Hom.* II.19 (Tonneau-Devreesse, *SeT* 145, 398, 400; tr. Mingana, *WS* VI, 47).

[162] *Bapt. Hom.* II. text and 3,16 (*Ibid.*, 366-370, 394; tr. *ibid.*, 35, 36, 45).

[163] *Ibid.*, II.4 (*Ibid.*, 372; tr. *ibid.*, 36-37).

to the freedom of belonging to Christ as the new Master. Theodore sums us his mystagogy as follows:

> These engagements and promises you make in the posture which we have described above, while your knee is bowed to the ground both as a sign of adoration from you to God, and as a manifestation of your ancient fall to the ground; the rest of the body is erect and looks upward toward heaven, and your hands are outstretched in the guise of one who prays so that you may be seen to worship the God Who is in heaven, from Whom you expect to rise from your ancient fall. This is the reason why you have, through the promises and engagements which we have already described, directed your course towards Him and have promised to Him that you will make yourself worthy of the expected gift. After you have looked towards Him with outstretched hands, asked grace from Him, risen from your fall and rejoiced in (future) benefits, you will necessarily receive the first-fruits of the sacrament which we believe to be the earnest of the good and ineffable things found in heaven.[164]

3. *Light and Darkness*

While the obvious East-West aspect of the ritual expression of *metanoia* is not present in Theodore's liturgy, he, though less explicitly than Chrysostom in his reference to the Good Friday hour of three in the afternoon and the Sun of Justice shining from the cross, also indicates a mystagogy based on this natural symbol of light and darkness. While not able to be as explicit as Cyril and Ambrose who presume on the tradition of orientation in Christian and Jewish prayer as the direction from which one expects the Messiah, or the East as the symbolic location of Paradise which is "reopened" by the confession that Jesus is Lord of the universe, and without the image of Jesus on the cross which Chrysostom presents in this connection, where Christ as Messiah shines from the cross as Sun of Justice and the natural sun turns back its rays, and where the candidates, kneeling, as it were, at the foot of the

[164] *Ibid.,* II.16 (*Ibid.,* 394; tr. *ibid.,* 45).

cross, by their act of faith recognize His Lordship and hear Him say to the good thief and to them, "Amen, I say to thee, this day thou shalt be with me in Paradise," still Theodore in his way also suggests such a mystagogy.

It is not far-fetched, in view of our analysis of how the fathers construct a mystagogy to suit their liturgical circumstances, to suggest that Theodore must be consciously aware that in the two biblical examples he uses from *Ac.*, the conversion of Cornelius the centurion[165] and the conversion of St. Paul[166] there are these symbolic features of the light and darkness in connection with the description of the conversion experience, which are fundamentally in the same line as the orientation symbol as underlining the expression of faith in Christ's Lordship. Cyril and Ambrose's candidates look to the East, from where the Messiah will come, and the symbolic location of Paradise; Chrysostom's candidates look up at the symbolic ninth hour and see the Messiah shining from the cross, "brighter than the sun," and opening Paradise, Christ "become" Messiah through His sacrificial offering.

The story of the conversion of Cornelius the centurion, which is used in paraphrase in Theodore's liturgy[167] begins explicity, "One day at the ninth hour Cornelius had a vision,"[168] and continues with symbolic-ritualistic overtones to describe his process of conversion and baptism. Peter reaches Cornelius' house and the latter, "went out to meet him, knelt at his feet, and prostrated himself. But Peter helped him up. 'Stand up,' he said."[169]

Again, Paul's description of his conversion begins: ". . . and at midday as I was on my way, your Majesty, I saw a light brighter than the sun come down from heaven. It shone brilliantly around me and my fellow travellers. We all fell to the ground."[170] When Paul recognizes it is Jesus speaking, we read:

[165] *Cf. Ac.* 10.
[166] *Cf. Ac.* 9; 26:13-23.
[167] See above p. 32.
[168] *Ac.* 10:3.
[169] *Ac.* 10:25-26.
[170] *Ac.* 26:13-14.

"But get up, and stand on your feet,"[171] and the words of Jesus are couched in the *OT* terms used about the two great prophetic figures, Jeremiah and the Servant of Yahweh: "I shall deliver you from the people and from the pagans to whom I am sending you, to open their eyes, so that they may turn (*ἐπιστρέψαι*) from darkness to light, from the dominion of Satan to God, and receive, through faith in me, forgiveness of their sins and a share in the inheritance of the sanctified."[172] In *Ac.* 9:17-18, Paul, his sight restored, passes from darkness to light; in *Ac.* 22:16[173] Paul is ordered to wash away his sins by baptism.

The hour of the day when Jesus as Lord appears in these conversion accounts is the hour of the temple sacrifice and the sacrificial death of Jesus on the cross as Chrysostom has already made use of it in his mystagogy, the appearance of Jesus as Messiah and Lord in the symbolism of the brilliant light, "brighter than the sun," which Chrysostom also uses in describing the Messiah on the cross appearing to the candidates, the falling to the ground and rising, the turning "from darkness to light, from the dominion of Satan to God" through the act of confession of faith in Jesus, the forgiveness of sins in baptism: in these two descriptions from *Ac.* these various features of the rite of Initiation are suggested.

Thus, in his own way, and given his own liturgy, Theodore is able to suggest the same things that Cyril and Ambrose bring with their mystagogy of orientation or which Chrysostom brings with the image of the crucifixion. The light-darkness imagery, already present as symbol in the scriptural description of conversion, is present here for the candidates who face not East, region of light and the coming Messiah and Paradise, not up to Jesus, shining as Messiah from the cross and re-opening Paradise, but heavenwards, to Christ, "Whom (God) raised up to heaven and showed as Lord of all, and head of our salvation."[174]

[171] *Ac.* 24:16.
[172] *Ac.* 26:17-18.
[173] *Cf. Ac.* 9:18.
[174] *Bapt. Hom.* II.3. See above, p. 70.

Comparative Summary

Remarkable is the versatility which the fathers manifest in selecting material tailored to the requirements of their diverse liturgies and the synthetic genius they reveal in putting this material into a plausible and coherent mystagogy of the given liturgy.

These gestures underline the interior process of believing in Christ and consequently levaing the anterior position of adherence to Satan. This basic unity in the mystagogical interpretation is maintained throughout the four mystagogies of the bodily movements. Yet, despite marked differences in the prescriptions of liturgical gesture in what concerns these movements, the fathers are able to find ample material which provides an interpretation by no means forced or implausible of these gestures and also one that is readily understandable on a basic anthropological plane. Here, perhaps, is a very real case of *ars celat artem*. The very fact that after sixteen hundred years such a mystagogy can be quite intelligible to a modern hearer is by no means an obviosity. It is the very skillful avoidance of the exotic and the *recherché* coupled with the true catholicity which comes from an understanding of biblical anthropology which makes the mystagogy classic.

Presented with the gesture of *turning* Cyril is able to explain *metanoia* by bringing to the obvious natural symbolism of turning from one position to another opposite position the cultural symbolism of turning from slavery to freedom, of escape from bondage, a symbol so well understood in the social context of antiquity (and hardly limited to antiquity although some of the concrete manifestations may have changed!)[175]

[175] On the opposition of slavery and freedom in the sociological context of antiquity see R. Roques, *Anselme de Cantorbéry, Pourquoi Dieu s'est fait homme, SC* 91, Introd., p. 119 and n. 1.

Presented in their liturgies not with the natural gesture of *turning* but that of *kneeling*, Chrysostom and Theodore are equally able to point to the same meaning in a different way. Man brought to his knees, also a sign helpless degradation and captivity clearly understood on a natural plane, is applied to the concrete social context of the various forms of enslavement which the candidates could well conjure up from personal experience. This personal experience recapitulated by the experience of kneeling is then given the religious dimension by drawing it into the fall of Adam, his degradation to the dust of the earth, the refusal to adore God and the consequent enslavement of man which this very act of disobedience brought with it in the history of man's various forms of enslavement. While beginning with the natural and cultural symbolism of the gesture of slavery, the specifically Christian dimension is added always in the mystagogy by recourse to the material of biblical revelation which does not deny the natural and cultural symbolism but illuminates its hidden roots through the symbolic language which revelation employs.[176]

Both Chrysostom and Theodore, using *Ph.* 2:10 are able to show how kneeling expresses not only the sad perversion of the captivity which the refusal of adoration as man's ultimate calling and fulfilment in life has wrought, but also out of the very same gesture to show how this expresses the positive return to this adoration, the acknowledgement of Christ as Lord of the universe, a return, however, not to the kneeling before a despotic master in degrading adoration, but a

[176] It should not be overlooked that the falling and rising symbolism that Theodore makes so much of, "We all fell to the ground," (*Ac.* 26:14), and, "But get up and stand on your feet," (*Ac.* 26:16), is also present in the Petrine writings just preceding the text used by Cyril in his first *Mystagogical Catechesis:* "Bow down, therefore, before the power of God now, and He will raise you up on the appointed day," (1 *P.* 5:6), although Cyril does not use the falling and rising symbolism presumably because the candidates in Jerusalem stand and turn, while Theodore's candidates fall to their knees and are later raised up. Central to both the Petrine text and the description of *Ac.* — and Theodore quotes from it specifically (*Bapt. Hom.* II.3, see above, p. 70)—is. *Ph.* 2:5-11, the ancient Christian hymn of the *kenosis* of Christ, the "falling" and the "rising" of Christ.

free kneeling in reverent answer to the possibility of restoring man's lost fulfilment by choosing to accept the Gospel call of the Son of God in a partnership of free adoration which liberates rather than enslaves.

Chrysostom's unique further step in this mystagogy of the kneeling, its expression of the equality of all men before God, again combines the problem of social injustice symbolized by the arrogant refusal of the washed to have part in kneeling with the unwashed with the call to recognize both the unity of sinfulness in all expressed in the kneeling and the new unity of the level of common faith in confessing Christ's Headship.

Cyril then follows the line of *OT* typology which best interprets the religious dimension of turning by the story of Lot's wife and the interweaving of other biblical material which reveals the moral and eschatological dimension of the act. Theodore, having received the gesture of kneeling, repairs to the *NT* conversion descriptions of the conversion of Paul and Cornelius the centurion where kneeling plays a role in the act preparatory to baptism. He alone spells out the symbolic meaning of the eventual rising from the knees as the reversal of slavery and its roots in the fall of man, the sign that the adoration of Christ is accepted and the prayers for deliverance answered.

These same dissimilarities of liturgical tradition pose no problem in interpreting the different *hand* gestures prescribed. A natural sign of rejection of Satan is Cyril's mystagogy. The somewhat different gestures of the outstretched arms not toward the West or Satan but in the direction of heaven is sign of deliverance from evil and willingness to strive for good deeds as well as gratitude for the gift of faith in Chrysostom's mystagogy. Theodore sees this same gesture as a reminder of the helplessness and the need that the fall into slavery brought as well as a prayer for deliverance from this and also a sign of adoration of God.

All four fathers utilize the various levels of the *West-East, light-darkness* symbolism again on manifold levels and with material nuanced to fit their different liturgical situations.[177]

The candidates of Cyril and Ambrose turned from West to East. In their mystagogy there is the factor of the natural darkness of the night vigil. Chrysostom and Theodore's candidates do not make this gesture of turning from West to East.[178]

[177]On the subject of orientation in the baptismal liturgy, see J. Daniélou, "Die Symbolik des Taufritus," *Liturgie und Mönchtum* 3 (1949) 47-55; J. Daniélou, *The Bible and the Liturgy, LS* 3 (Notre Dame, Indiana, 1966), pp. 30-33; F. Dölger, *Die Sonne der Gerechtigkeit und der Schwarze, LQF* 2 (Münster, 1918), pp. 1-18; F. Dölger, *Sol Salutis, Gebet und Gesang im christlichen Altertum mit besonderer Rücksicht auf die Ostung in Gebet und Liturgie, LQF* 4-5 (Münster, 1920). For a discussion of the various levels of this symbolism, the natural symbolism of sunrise and light the symbolism of praying facing the East as the direction from which the Messiah was expected and the symbolism of the return to Paradise, planted towards the East (*Cf. Gn.* 2:8), see C. Vogel, "Versus Orientem," *La Maison Dieu* 70 (2, 1962) 67-99, esp. 67-70, which contains references to sources and studies.

[178]It is apparently the antiquity of the custom of orientation for the act of commitment, its explicit mention by Cyril and Ambrose as well as by such liturgies as recorded in the *Testamentum Domini nostri Jesu Christi* 2,8 (Quasten, *FP* 7, 269) and the *Ordo of Constantinople* (Conybeare-MacLean, eds., *Rituale Armenorum,* 439-440), which leads Harkins (*ACW* 31, p. 224, n.47) to say: "Although neither Theodore nor Chrysostom mentions anything about the orientation of the candidate, it seems not unlikely that he turned to the West to renounce Satan and to the East to make his pledge to Christ." Finn, *op. cit,* p. 107, thinks that Chrysostom's presentation of the baptismal action as if it were situated in the garden of Paradise (see below, pp. 262-263), as well as his mystagogy of the Good Friday hour, "For on Friday at the ninth hour the thief entered Paradise," (see above, p. 69), adds to the likelihood of orientation for the profession of allegiance in the baptismal liturgy of Antioch. However, several things make this likelihood improbable. Both Chrysostom and Theodore are silent on the fact of orientation, as also are the *Constitutiones apostolorum* 7, 40-41 (Quasten, *FP* 7, 190), a fact, which, as Finn admits (*op. cit.,* p. 106), suggests that orientation may not have been the custom in West Syria. Furthermore, in the liturgies described by Chrysostom and Theodore the candidates kneel for the act of renunciation and commitment. Were there a turning from West to East one must imagine a rather cumbersome ceremonial action, given the brief formula of renunciation and commitment and the apparently large number of candidates. The candidates would first kneel, facing the West, make the renunciation, then all stand, turn to the East, kneel down again, and then make the act of commitment. Aside from such a complex movement, given the brevity of the formula, both Theodore and Chrysostom say that the candidates, for the act of renunciation and commitment, have their arms outstretched to heaven, with Theodore adding explicitly, what is obvious anyway, that the gaze of the candidates is toward heaven, and not toward the West or East, with an attendant mystagogy not of orientation but of prayer for deliverance, dedication to good deeds, gratitude for faith, reminder of the fall and slavery and of adoration.

Given these considerations, Finn's argument from Chrysostom's Good Friday

Chrysostom's rite clearly takes place in the afternoon of Good Friday. When Theodore's takes place is not possible to say with certainty and from his mystagogy little is said which could lead to a supposition of the time of the rite.

Most instructive is how the separate mystagogies are developed, given these differences. The natural darkness of the hour and the West as symbol of darkness *versus* the East, place of the sunrise and light are used by Cyril and Ambrose as sign of the darkness of Satanic works and hell. Cyril adds the scriptural reference that conversion, turning to the East, means not only turning to the light but also towards Paradise planted in the East according to the biblical account.[179] Ambrose's emphasis is not on Paradise here, but on the traditional orientation in prayer which expected the Messiah from the East.[180] Chrysostom "creates" the absent natural dark-

---

mystagogy of the good thief entering Paradise and the mystagogy of the baptismal scene as situated in the garden of Paradise adds nothing to the likelihood of orientation. As a matter of fact, it seems that the mystagogy of Chrysostom and Theodore as well is developed as a conscious effort to work into a liturgy which requires kneeling and looking upward to heaven, rather than standing and turning, a mystagogical explanation which takes into account the traditional imagery of light-darkness, Paradise and the Messiah, even though the liturgical requirements themselves do not provide the ceremony of turning from West to East. Why else the total lack of any mention of the orientation by Chrysostom and Theodore, which would seem obviously called for if it were really present liturgically? Thus, in Chrysostom, the reference to the hour of three in the afternoon of Good Friday from the Lukan account of the crucifixion, with its light-darkness, Messiah and Paradise imagery, shows mystagogically to the candidates kneeling and gazing to heaven what Cyril and Ambrose can do by reference to the facing West and East. And in Theodore, the use of the symbolism from *Ac.* serves the same function *in lieu* of an actual liturgical orientation.

[179]See "Die Gebetsostung als Ausdruck der Sehnsucht nach Paradise," in F. Dölger, *Sol Salutis,* pp. 220-258.

[180]E. Peterson goes beyond the natural symbolism of the pagan custom of praying toward the rising sun shown by Dölger (*Sol Salutis,* pp. 220-258), and establishes the connection of the usage with the controversies between Jews and Christians as to the place where the Messiah would appear at the end of time. Prayer to the East designates Christianity as opposed to prayer toward Jerusalem for the Jews, and later toward Mecca for the Moslems. See E. Peterson, "Die geschichtliche Bedeutung der jüdischen Gebetsrichtung," *Theologische Zeitschrift* 3 (1947) 1-15; E. Peterson, *Frühkirche, Judentum und Gnosis* (Freiburg i. Breisgau, 1959), pp. 1-35.

ness of the vigil by recourse to the darkness spoken of in the Lukan account of the crucifixion. By recourse to this crucifixion scene, in which the kneeling candidate mystically finds himself, he is able to bring in both symbols, the looking towards the Messiah and Paradise. Not in the East, region of light, but shining from the cross the glorious Messiah appears to the candidate in mystical symbolism, the Son of Justice, brighter than the natural sun which rises in the East. Paradise in its turn comes closer than its *OT* description of being planted in the East because the word of Christ accepts the candidate's adoration and commitment as He accepted that of the good thief on the cross and admits him to Paradise.

Theodore in his turn avails himself of the light-darkness symbolism completely through the symbolic medium already present in the conversion accounts of *Ac.* without going into any concrete association of these with the actual time of the liturgy, and without any reference to the turning, since, of course, his candidates kneel, like those of Chrysostom. Cornelius' vision is at the ninth hour, or three in the afternoon, time of the crucifixion and of the temple sacrifice. Paul sees a light brighter than the sun when he falls to his knees. His sight is restored, a Messianic work and symbol of his conversion.

Thus, the four fathers by drawing on different material and cultural symbols and with apt interpretative employment of Scripture are able to develop a mystagogy for the bodily engagement which underscores in some breadth and depth the act of renunciation and commitment. Their selection of materials remains linked in an unforced way to the exigencies of their respective liturgies. At the same time the reach of their symbols into the real lives of the candidates in question ensures that the renunciation of Satan and commitment to Christ will be grasped in the fullest possible way as a radical change in one's entire life, touching the central areas where a human being most deeply lives.

The body language of this first step in Christian Initiation rites contains a remarkable scope. Turning, kneeling and rising, stretching out the hand or arms, the gaze towards heaven, or facing West and East, the apprehension of light or darkness;

from an interpretation of these gestures the four fathers show the candidates what this act means. It is a turning from evil works to good works, from slavery to freedom. It is rising from slavery and all forms of human degradation and captivity. It is joining the entire universe in acknowledging Christ's Lordship. It is a prayer for help and grace and an admission of universal sinfulness and redemption excluding and favoring no one. It is a serious moral choice, irrevocable because of its eschatological overtones. It is linked historically with God's specific action in the conversion of such individuals as Cornelius and St. Paul. It is a rejection of all in the world which pertains to slavery and exploitation through fear, and it presents a new freedom and partnership with a new kind of Master in the struggle for good. It reaches into the roots of human history presaging a return to the lost Paradise of man by reinstating the candidate into a human pilgrimage toward the coming Messiah of glory. And on the way to this final fulfilment it presents in mystical light Jesus the God-man, meeting the candidate on the road, restoring his sight, giving him strength to rise from his fall, and assuring him from the glory which shines through His suffering on the cross that his act of commitment to Christ will not be in vain but accepted by Christ, Who is Himself the way.

II

RECITING THE FORMULA

Until now we have examined the mystagogy of the bodily movements which are involved in the rite of renunciation and profession: turning, kneeling and rising, the gesture of the hands, gazing heavenwards or facing West and East. These gestures, in fact, only serve to dramatize the core of the rite, the personal act of renouncing Satan and committing oneself to Christ which the candidate must make verbally according to the several ritual formulas of the respective liturgies under consideration.

The fathers emphasize the solemnity of the moment when this verbal act is made. How do they explain mystagogically to their hearers what it means to perform this act?[181]

One of the *leitmotivs* in the interpretation of the solemn verbal act of renouncing Satan and committing oneself to Christ is the presupposition that the man who wishes to turn to Christ and commit Himself to Him and His service is impeded in so doing by an ancient contract that holds man in servitude to another master, Satan. Man himself was not responsible for this contract, but he has inherited it. Nor can he void the contract by his own power alone—the master is too strong. Thus the uttering the words of renunciation and commitment become a solemn, dramatic moment of crisis for the candidate. He must indeed speak for himself, but encircling him is a battle of invisible powers and there is a struggle to possess him.[182] In uttering the words of renunciation and commitment, the candidate passes from slavery to freedom. It is not enough that one commit oneself to Christ, at least liturgically. The implication of this commitment to Christ has its counterpart in the awareness that to enter a life of service to Christ, a new awareness of "His world" one has in the process of preparation for this step become painfully aware of the impediments both exterior and interior that prevent the self-determination that such a step requires. Both in oneself and in one's environment lie so many snares of unfreedom. This unfreedom, particularly in the environment of the candidates, is spelled out at length and concretely by the fathers in their

[181] It is not our purpose to investigate the history of the liturgical formulas of renouncing Satan, but to compare the mystagogical interpretation among the four fathers of the act of reciting this formula. For the history of the formula see H. Kirsten, *Die Taufabsage. Eine Untersuchung zu Gestalt und Geschichte der Taufe nach den altkirchlichen Taufliturgien* (Berlin, 1960); M. Boismard, "Je renonce à Satan . . ." *Lumière et Vie* 26 (1956) 105-110 (249-254). Boismard's work also appears in English: "I renounce Satan, his Pomps and his Works," in the symposium, *Baptism in the New Testament*, tr. D. Askew (Baltimore, 1964), pp. 107-112.

[182] On this subject of the power of Satan and of death see Bo Reicke, *The Disobedient Spirits and Christian Baptism* (Lund, 1948).

interpretation of the formula of renunciation, where they spell out what the pomps, works and service of Satan are in the concrete cultural context of the candidates.[183] The essential freedom expressed by the candidates in the renunciation of Satan will symbolically confront these internal and external hindrances in its attempt to win effectiveness.

It is against this general background that the candidates say: "I renounce you, Satan, and I enter your service, O Christ."[184] The material which the mystagogical discourses make use of to explain to the candidates what their verbal act means, reveals this background. They spell out the symbolic confrontation of servitude and freedom that takes place when the candidate utters the formula, and they illuminate the significance of the verbal act in its various depths.

[183]See H. Rahner, "Pompa Diaboli," *Zeitschrift für katholische Theologie* 55 (1931) 239-273; J. Waszink, "Pompa Diaboli," *Vigiliae Christianae* I (1947) 13-41.
[184]See above p. 30.

SYNOPTIC CHART

Reciting the Formula

Cyril	*Ambrose*	*Chrysostom*	*Theodore*
A. *The Encounter with Satan:*			
Virtual Presence	Virtual Presence ("to his face")	Virtual Presence (Fear in candidates)	Virtual Presence (Fear in candidates)
Myst.Cat. I.4	*Myst.* 7	*P.K.* 3.24	*Bapt.Hom.* I. 23-25; II.5-6
Personal Formula		Personal Formula	
Myst.Cat. I.4		*Stav.* 2.20	

Reciting the Formula—continued

Cyril	*Ambrose*	*Chrysostom*	*Theodore*
B. *The Contract with Satan:*			
		Contract *Stav.* 2.17-22	
Tyrant, Slavery Death *Myst.Cat.* I.4 *Heb.* 2:14-15			
Pact with Hell *Myst.Cat.* I.9 *Is.* 28:15		Old Contract *Stav.* 3-*P.K.* 4 20-21	Pact with Hell *Bapt.Hom.* II.5
C. *Union with Christ and Contract with Him:*			
Bond with Christ's human- ity, *kenosis* *Myst.Cat.* I.4 *Hb.* 2:14-15		Bond with Christ's human- ity, *kenosis:* -Equality in Christ *P.K.* 3:21 *Ga.* 3:28 -Crucifixion *P.K.* 3.19-20 -Christ as refuge *P.K.* 3.24 -Christ as Olympic Judge: -On side of candidate *Stav.* 3-*P.K.*4.9	Divine decree: grace of Christ *Bapt.Hom.* II.5-6

Reciting the Formula—continued

Cyril	*Ambrose*	*Chrysostom*	*Theodore*
		-Gave life to assure victory of candidate	
		*Stav.*3-*P.K.*4.8	
		-Gives armor	
		*Stav.*3-*P.K.*4.11	
Contract	Contract	Contract	Contract
*Myst.Cat.*I.5	*Sacr.* I.5	*Stav.* 2.17-22	*Bapt.Hom.*II.16
		-Christ ransoms Satan's slaves with blood	
		Montf. 2.50 1 *Co.* 7:23	
		-Erases contract with Satan on cross	
		Stav. 3-*P.K.*4.21-22 *Col.* 2:14	
		-Free, not forced contract *vs.* worldly contract	
		-Christ pays price before we agree	
		Montf. 2.50 1 *Co.* 7:23	
		-*Syntaxis* as dowry to Bridegroom	

Reciting the Formula—continued

Cyril	*Ambrose*	*Chrysostom*	*Theodore*
		P.K. 3.26 *Stav.* 1.16-18 *Rm.* 10:12	
		-Confession of faith as candidate's part of contract	
		Stav. 1.19 *Stav.* 4.31 *Rm.* 10:10	
Recorded in God's Book	Recorded in Book of Living	Recorded in Heavenly Books	
Myst.Cat. I.5	*Myst.* 5	*Stav.* 2.20	

A. The Encounter with Satan

Cyril and Ambrose emphasize particularly an almost physical presence of Satan. Cyril notes that the candidates were told to speak their formula of renunciation of Satan "as though he were actually present (ὡς πρὸς πάροντα)."[185] We have already seen how such a dramatic liturgical emphasis fits in with Cyril's entire mystagogy of the *OT* type of the flight from Egypt with Pharaoh in pursuit.[186]

Ambrose also indicates an awareness of the personal presence of Satan, the adversary "whom you think you should renounce to his face (cui renuntiandum in os putaris)."[187]

[185] *Myst. Cat.* I.4 (Piédagnel, *SC* 126, 88; tr. Cross, *SPCK*, 54). *Myst. Cat.* I.2 (*Ibid.*, 84; tr. *ibid.*, 53) contains the same idea: "You renounced Satan as though he were present (ὡς παρόντι ἀπετάττεσθε τῷ Σατανᾶ)."

[186] See above, pp. 46-47.

[187] *Myst.* 7 (Botte, *SC* 25bis, 158; tr. Deferrari, *FC* 44, 7).

Both Cyril and Chrysostom have formulas of renunciation using the second personal pronoun, "I renounce you, Satan.[188] While Theodore uses the third person, "I renounce you, Satan,"[189] and not the personal pronoun, his moving description of the candidate's frame of mind as he kneels there, perhaps even more than the other fathers, indicates an interpretation of the act which implies an almost face to face encounter with the tyrant:

> It is in place here to explain to you the power of these words, in order that you may know the force of the engagements, promises and words of asserveration through which you receive the happiness of this great gift. Because the devil, to whom you had listened, was for you the cause of numerous and great calamities—as he has begun his work from the time of the fathers of your race—you promise to abjure him, since facts themselves and your own experience had made you feel his injuries. This is the reason why you say, "I abjure you, Satan." Formerly, even if you wished it, you did not dare make use of these words, because you were afraid of his servitude, but as you have, by a divine decree received deliverance from him, you proclaim and abjure him with confidence and by your own words, and this is the reason why you say, "I abjure Satan." In this you imply both your present separation from him, and the former association that you had with him.
>
> You rightly say, "I abjure Satan," but you can hardly realize, that after formerly having felt the injury which he inflicted upon you in his relation to you, you could be in a postion to be delivered from him.[190]

[188]See above, pp. 25-30.

[189]See above, p. 32.

[190]*Bapt. Hom.* II.5-6 (Tonneau-Devreesse, *SeT* 145, 374; tr. Mingana, *WS* VI, 37-38). *Cf. Bapt. Hom.* I.23 (*Ibid.*, 358, 360; tr. *ibid.*, 31) where the dramatic courtroom scene in the exorcism rite is envisaged. Here the candidate stands in silent fear of his present adversary.

In the same way Chrysostom emphasizes the drama of personal confrontation, reminding the candidates that they were quivering with fear as they pronounced the words of rebellion against their cruel master.[191]

It is this emphasis on the virtual presence of Satan, and the necessity of personal repudiation on the part of the candidate which indicates the common biblical theme which the fathers use to interpret the verbal act involved in the apotaxis. The theme is the power or sway which Satan has over man. Biblical material indicative of this power is interspersed throughout the explanation of the meaning of the act.

B. The Contract with Satan

1. *Cyril*

According to Cyril Satan is a "wicked and cruel tyrant."[192] His domain is described by words from *Heb.* 2:14-15 as being a power which holds men in bondage because they are slaves, living in fear of death, over which they have no control. He is the clever and ruthless serpent who, under guise of friendship, brought our first parents to their "apostasy."[193] The words of

[191] See *P.K.* 3.6 (*VGS,* 172, tr. Harkins, *ACW* 31, 168, no. 24).

[192] *Myst. Cat.* I.4 (Piédagnel, *SC* 126, 88; Cross, *SPCK* 55): πονηρῷ καὶ ὠμοτάτῳ τυράννῳ.

[193] *Idem:* ἀποστασίαν.

renunciation are designed to break the ancient pact, or covenant with hell, as indicated in *Is.* 28:15, the covenant with Mot and the pact with Sheol. "When you renounce Satan, trampling under foot all covenant (διαθήκην) with him, you break the ancient treaties (συνθήκας) with hell."[194]

2. *Theodore*

This same idea of a pact with hell, resulting in mankind's slavery, is found in Theodore:

> The use of this expression [I abjure Satan] is especially incumbent upon you, as you had relation with him from the time of your forefathers, together with that cruel and ancient pact, which resulted in the calamitous servitude to him, under which you lived.[195]

3. *Chrysostom*

Indeed, in Chrysostom, the notion of a contract is the central vehicle whereby he interprets the act of renunciation and profession.[196] In his mystagogy, however, Chrysostom goes further than either Cyril or Theodore in elaborating the notion of the contract, weaving into it both biblical material and secular understanding of the contract.

The term "the contact (ἡ συνθήκη)," which occurs more than twenty times in the *Baptismal Instructions* of Chrysostom,[197] is used to interpret several aspects of the rite of renunciation and profession. The verbal act by which the candidate expresses his turning away from Satan and turning toward Christ is called by Chrysostom his "contract (ἡ συνθήκη)."[198]

[194] *Ibid.*, I.9 (*Ibid.*, 98; tr. *ibid.*, 57) See above, n. 122.
[195] *Bapt. Hom.* II.5 (Tonneau-Devreesse, *SeT* 145, 374; tr. Mingana, *WS* VI, 38).
[196] See Finn, *op. cit.*, pp. 93-95; 102-104; 108-110.
[197] *Ibid.*, p. 93.
[198] *Stav.* 2.17 (Wenger, *SC* 50, 143; tr. Harkins, *ACW* 31, 50).

The terms of the contract are the two liturgical formulas, "I renounce you, Satan, your pomps, your service and your works," and "I enter into your service, O Christ."[199] The first term of the contract is the "renunciation (ἀποταγή),"[200] and the second term is called the "profession (ὁμολογία)"[201] of "attachment (συνταγή)."[202] This agreement (συνθήκη)"[203] between the contracting parties is not some paper and ink document, however, but it is rather written by the Spirit. This contract is also called "faith (πίστις),"[204] since its content is invisible, seen only by the eyes of the spirit. This verbal act, whereby the contract is constituted, is called by Chrysostom a "conversion (ἐπιστροφῆ)."[205]

If the verbal act of renunciation and commitment is a "contract," in Chrysostom's mystagogy, then, like Cyril and Theodore he sees the presence of a previous contract, the one which man had with Satan, which is now made void by the new contract, which is seen as coming into existence by the liturgical act of the renunciation and commitment: "We confessed [Christ's] sovereignty; we rejected the domination of the devil. This was the signature, this the agreement, this the contract. See to it that we do not again become debtors to the old contract. . . . Adam contracted the debt; by our subsequent sins we increased the amount owed. In this contract are written a curse, and sin, and death, and the condemnation of the law."[206]

[199] *Ibid.*, 2.20, 21. See above, p. 31.

[200] *Ibid.*, 2.22 (Wenger, *SC* 50, 145; tr. Harkins, *ACW* 31, 51). *Cf.* also above, p. 24.

[201] *Ibid.*, 2.18 (*Ibid.*, 144; tr. *ibid.*, 50.).

[202] *Ibid.*, 2.22 (*Ibid.*, 145; tr. *ibid.*, 51).

[203] *Ibid.*, 2.17 (*Ibid.*, 143; tr. *ibid.*, 50).

[204] *Idem.*

[205] *Ibid.*, 2.20 (*Ibid.*, 145; tr. *ibid.*, 51).

[206] *Stav.* 3-P.K. 4.20-21 (Wenger, *SC* 50, 163, tr. Harkins, *ACW* 31, 63): 'Ὡμολογήσαμεν αὐτοῦ τὴν δεσποτείαν, ἠρνησάμεθα τὴν τυρρανίδα τὴν διαβολικήν, τοῦτο μειρόγραφον ἐγένετο, τοῦτο συνθήκη, τοῦτο γραμματεῖον. Ὁρᾶτε μὴ πάλιν ὑποχείριοι γενώμεθα τῷ γραμματείῳ τούτῳ....' Ἐκεῖνος τὴν ἀρχὴν εἰσήνεγκε τοῦ χρέους, ἡμεῖς τὸ δάνειον ηὐξήσαμεν ταῖς μετὰ ταῦτα ἁμαρτίαις. Κατάρα ἦν ἐκεῖ καὶ ἁμαρτία καὶ θάνατος καὶ νόμου κατάκρισις.

Here, like Cyril and Ambrose, Chrysostom also emphasizes the solemn nature of the contract by reminding the hearers that the words of this contract are recorded in heaven: "The words are few but their power is great. The angels who are standing by and the invisible powers rejoice at your conversion, receive the words from your tongues, and carry them up to the common Master of all things. There they are inscribed in the books of heaven."[207]

C. Union with Christ and the Contract with Him

The dramatic picture which the fathers draw of the verbal act of renunciation and commitment where the candidate encounters Satan in fear and trembling because he knows he is in servitude to an ancient contract, is balanced on the other side by a mystagogy which sees the power of Christ supporting the candidate at this decisive moment, helping him to break the ancient contract and its power and to enter into a new contract of free service to a far different Master. A key biblical notion is used by the fathers to interpret the act. It is the teaching that the candidate is not alone in his act of repudiating the contract with Satan, but that in so doing he derives power from union with the humanity of Christ, Whose suffering on the cross has made this act possible. The humiliation and the slavery of the candidates is not hopeless, because there is One, Who, by taking on the form of a slave, has already overthrown once and for all the power of Satan, and it is in the power of this victory already achieved that the candidates are themselves able to participate in this liberation from the old contract.

[207] *Stav.* 2.20 (*Ibid.*, 145; tr. *ibid.*, 51): Ὀλίγα τὰ ῥήματα ἀλλὰ μεγάλη τούτων ἡ δύναμις. Καὶ γὰρ ἄγγελοι παραστηκότες καὶ αἱ ἀόρατοι δυνάμεις ἡδόμενει ἐπὶ τῇ ὑμετέρᾳ ἐπιστροφῇ δέχονται παρὰ τῆς ὑμετέρας γλώττης τὰς φωνὰς καὶ ἀναφέρουσι τῷ κοινῷ πάντων δεσπότῃ καὶ ἐν ταῖς βίβλοις ταῖς οὐρανίοις αὗται ἐγγράφονται.

1. *Cyril*

Cyril interprets the apotaxis in this way: "What did each of you standing up say? 'I renounce you, Satan, you wicked and most cruel tyrant!' meaning, 'I fear your might no longer, for Christ has overthrown it, having partaken with me of flesh and blood, that through these He might by death destroy death, that I might not forever be subject to bondage.' "[208]

Thus, even though it is the candidate himself who in personal responsibility performs the act of renunciation and commitment, he is enabled to do so by virtue of the "common bond of flesh and blood which he has with Christ."[209] In other words, the power of the salvific act of Christ, united in the bond of common humanity with the candidate, lends him the power to break the ancient covenant with hell and death.

This union of the candidate with the power of Christ at the moment of his act of renunciation and commitment lends to his action a solemn, contractual nature which Cyril explains in the following way: "Only know this: that all that you say, especially at this most thrilling hour, is written in God's books; when, therefore, you do anything contrary to these, you shall be judged as a 'transgressor.' "[210]

2. *Theodore*

This same association of the *kenosis* of Christ with the power to repudiate Satan is indicated also by Theodore. It is by

[208] *Cf. Heb.* 2:14-15. *Myst. Cat.* I.4 (Piédagnel, *SC* 126, 88; tr. Cross, *SPCK*, 55): Τὶ οὖν ὑμῶν ἕκαστος ἑστὼς ἔλεγεν; Ἀποτάσσομαί σοι, Σατανᾶ, σοι τῷ πονηρῷ καὶ ὠμοτατῳ τυρράνῳ· οὐκέτι σου δέδοικα, λέγων, τὴν ἰσχύν. Κατέλυσε γὰρ ταύτην ὁ Χριστός, αἵματός μοι καὶ σαρκὸς κοινωνήσας, ἵνα διὰ τούτων τῶν παθημάτων καταργήσῃ θανάτῳ, τὸν θάνατον, ὅπως μὴ διὰ παντὸς ἔνοχος γένωμαι δουλείας.

[209] *Ibid.*: αἵματος μοι καὶ σαρκὸς κοινωνήσας.

[210] *Cf. Ga.* 2:18. *Myst. Cat.* I. 5 (*Ibid.*, 90; tr. *ibid.*, 55): Πλὴν τοῦτο ἴσθι ὅτι ὅσα λέγεις, μάλιστα κατ' ἐκείνην τὴν φρικωδεστάτην ὥραν, ἔγγραφά ἐστὶν ἐν τοῖς ἀοράτοις τοῦ Θεοῦ γραφόμενα βιβλίοις· Ἐπειδὰν τοίνυν ἐναντίως τὶ διαπραττόμενος τούτοις ἁλῷς, ὡς παραβάτης κριθήσῃ.

"divine decree" that the candidate, having received deliverance from Satan, is able to say the words, "I abjure Satan."[211] This is the "great and wonderful grace, which was manifest through Christ, and which freed us from the Tyrant and delivered us from his servitude and granted us this wonderful participation in His benefits."[212]

What has resulted from this act is also described in contractual terms as "engagements and promises."[213]

3. *Ambrose*

The act of renunciation and commitment is also provided by Ambrose with a mystagogy which elevates the act into a contract with heaven, and here Ambrose uses terms remarkably similar to Cyril. Speaking of the solemn formula of renunciation which the candidate has made, Ambrose says: "Your utterance is kept not in the tomb of the dead, but in the book of the living."[214] And even more specifically he explains the contractual nature of the act in legal terms: "Remember these words of yours and never lose sight of the consequences of the promise (cautionis) which you have given. If you give a man bond (chirographum), you are held responsible, so that you may receive his money; you are held bound, and the lender compels you if you resist. If you refuse, you go to the judge, and there you will be convicted by your own promise (cautione)."[215]

4. *Chrysostom*

It is the piety of Chrysostom, however, which brings to bear most vividly the mystical relationship between the candidate

[211] See *Bapt. Hom.* II.5 (Tonneau-Devreesse, *SeT* 145, 374; tr. Mingana, *WS* VI, 38).

[212] *Ibid.*, II.6 (*Ibid.*, 377; tr. *ibid.*, 38).

[213] *Ibid.*, II. 16 (*Ibid.*, 394; tr. *ibid.*, 45).

[214] *Myst.* 5. *Cf.* above, p. 50 and n. 82.

[215] *Sacr.* I.5 (Botte, *SC* 25bis, 62; tr. Deferrari, *FC* 44, 271): "Memor esto sermonis tui et numquam tibi excidat tuae series cautionis. Si chirographum homini dederis, teneris obnoxius, ut pecunia ejus accipias, teneris adstrictus et reluctantem te foenerator adstringit. Si recusas vadis ad judicem atque illic tua cautione convinceris."

and Christ in the act of renouncing Satan. Christ is the central figure playing a dominant role in the action. At the very outset of his interpretation of the rite, Chrysostom places the candidates at the foot of the cross, reminding them that the ceremony of renunciation and commitment took place on Good Friday at the ninth hour.[216] Through the power of Christ's death on the cross they are enabled to break the power of Satan which held them banned from Paradise. Chrysostom continues the association of the candidate with Christ in a passage which we have already seen, where the kneeling candidates are seen as equal to one another in their common humanity, because they are one in Christ through faith, and here *Ga.* 3:28 is quoted.[217] Christ is the strong place of refuge, an ally, Who has made the candidate superior to the demon, although previously he was trembling and afraid.[218] Finally in the image of the Olympic games, Christ is compared to the Olympic judge. In the Olympic games, the judge stands in the middle, because his judgement must be impartial in respect to the candidates striving for the prize. But in the combat with the devil, Christ does not stand aloof, but is, rather, entirely on the side of the combatant.[219] Christ, the judge of the contest, is the one who has laid down His life for us, a fact which is both an honor for the candidate and an assurance of the victory in the contest.[220] It is Christ Who has given the candidate the armor for the battle, a new kind of armor for a new kind of combat.[221] Moreover, the concrete image of Christ paying the price for us by paying over His own blood as a way of ransoming slaves from Satan is also used by Chrysostom following St. Paul[222] to bring out the relationship of the act of renunciation and commitment to the historical act of Jesus on the cross, and the present power of this act of Jesus at work

[216]See above, pp. 68-69.

[217]See above, p. 67.

[218]See *P.K.* 3.6 (*VGS,* 172; tr. Harkins, *ACW* 31, 64, no. 24).

[219]See *Stav.* 3-*P.K.* 4.9 (Wenger, *SC* 50, 155-156; tr. Harkins, *ACW* 31, 58).

[220]See *Stav.* 3-*P.K.* 4.8 (*Ibid.,* 155; tr. *ibid.,* 58).

[221]See *Stav.* 3-*P.K.* 4.11 (*Ibid.,* 157; tr. *ibid.,* 59).

[222]1 *Co.* 7:23.

empowering the candidates to make effective by their verbal act the salvation already won for them by Christ.[223]

In an unusually vivid passage suggested by *Col.* 2:14 Chrysostom combines in vivid rhetoric the various biblical materials which we have seen in the different fathers to interpret the verbal act of renunciation and commitment: the notion of the power of Satan, his sway over man through the pact with our first parents which caused our servitude, the power invested in the act itself due to the *kenosis,* the sacrificial offering of the blood of Christ on the cross:

> Christ came once; He found the certificate of our ancestral indebtedness which Adam wrote and signed. Adam contracted the debt; by our subsequent sins we increased the amount we owed. In this contract are written a curse, and sin, and death, and the condemnation of the law. Christ took all these away and pardoned them. St. Paul cries out and says: "The decree of our sins which was against us, He has taken completely away, nailing it to the cross."[224] He did no say "erasing the decree," nor did he say "blotting it out," but "nailing it to the cross", so that no trace of it might remain. This is why he did not erase it, but tore it to pieces. The nails of the cross tore up the decree and destroyed it utterly, so that it would not hold good for the future, nor did he destroy the note of our debt in some secret corner but in full view of the world, from a lofty stage. Let the angels see it, He says, let the archangels and powers above behold; let the wicked demons and the devil himself see! It was these wicked ones who made us liable to our creditors for our debts, but now the contract is destroyed, so that they may not hereafter assail us.[225]

[223] *Montf.* 2 (*MG* 49.239; tr. Harkins, *ACW* 31, 188, no. 50).

[224] *Col.* 2:14.

[225] *Stav.* 3-*P.K.* 4.21-22 (Wenger, *SC* 50, 163-164; tr. Harkins *ACW* 31, 63): *Ἦλθεν ἅπαξ ὁ Χριστός, εὗρεν ἡμῶν χειρόγραφον πατρῷον ὅπερ ἔγραψεν ὁ Ἀδάμ. Ἐκεῖνος τὴν ἀρχὴν εἰσήνεγκε τοῦ χρέους, ἡμεῖς τὸ δάνειον ηὐξήσαμεν ταῖς μετὰ ταῦτα ἁμαρτίαις. Κατάρα ἦν ἐκεῖ καὶ ἁμαρτία καὶ θάνατος καὶ νόμου κατάκρισις πάντα ταῦτα ἀνεῖλεν ὁ Χριστὸς καὶ συνεχώρησε. Καὶ βοᾷ ὁ Παῦλος λέγων. "Τὸ χειρόγραφον τῶν ἁμαρτιῶν ἡμῶν ὅ ἦν ὑπεναντίον ἡμῖν, καὶ αὐτο ἦρκεν ἀπὸ τοῦ μέσου, προσηλώσας, αὐτο τῷ σταυρῷ." Οὐκ εἶπεν ἀπαλείψας*

In further elaboration of his image of the contract, Chrysostom brings also two other aspects of biblical interpretation to bear on the ceremony. Although the old contract is destroyed by the ransom paid by Christ in his once-for-all salvific act, still the candidate is not forced to avail himself of this salvation. His "renunciation" and "profession of attachment" to Christ, that is his "contract" is not a forced mastership imposed by Christ. Christ, indeed asks us if we are willing to serve Him, and we answer by our contract. However, unlike an earthly master, Christ has paid the ransom price for us slaves even before we have answered Him, and regardless of the answer we might give, while a wordly master would first await an affirmative guarantee of service on our part before paying out the price for our ransom. Despite the fact that He has already paid the ransom price of his blood for us even before asking us whether we want to serve Him or not, He does not demand of us an affirmative answer: "He paid the price for all of us, His precious blood. 'You have been bought with a price,' says St. Paul.[226] And even so He does not force those to serve Him who are unwilling to do so. Unless you are grateful, He says, and are willing of yourself and of your own accord to be enrolled under Me as your Master, I do not force or compel you."[227]

αὐτο, οὐκ εἶπεν χ α ρ ἀ ξ α ς ἀλλα π ρ ο σ η λ ώ σ α ς αὐτὸ τῷ σταυρῷ ἵνα μηδὲ ἴχνος αὐτοῦ μείνῃ. Διὰ τοῦτο οὐκ ἀπήλειψεν ἀλλὰ διέρρηξεν. οἱ γάρ ἧλοι τοῦ σταυροῦ διέρρηξαν αὐτὸ καὶ διὲφθειραν ἵνα ἄχρηστον γένηται τοῦ λοιτοῦ.

Καὶ οὐκ ἐν γωνίᾳ καὶ λάθρᾳ ἀλλ' ἐν μέσῳ τῆς οἰκουμένης ἐφ' ὑψηλοῦ τοῦ ἰκρίου τὴν διάλυσιν ἐποιήσατο. Βλεπέτωσαν ἄγγελοι, φησίν, βλεπέτωσαν ἀρχάγγελοι, βλεπέτωσαν αἱ ἄνω δυνάμεις, βλεπέτωσαν καὶ οἱ πονηροὶ δαίμονες καὶ αὐτος ὁ διάβολος, οἱ ποιήσαντες ὑπευθύνους ἡμᾶς τῶν ὀφλημάτων ἐπι τῶν δανειστῶν· διαρρήγνυται τὸ χειρόγραφον ἵνα μὴ μετα ταυτὰ ἡμῖν ἐπιπηδήσωσιν.

226 1 *Co.* 7:23.

227 *Montf.* 2 (*MG* 49.239; tr. Harkins, *ACW* 31, 188, no. 50: *Τὴν τιμὴν κατέβαλεν ὑπερ ἁπάντων ἡμῶν, τὸ τὶμιον αὐτοῦ αἱμα. "Τιμῆς γὰρ," φησὶν, "ἠγοράσθητε·" καὶ ὅμως οὐδὲ οὕτως ἀναγκάζει μὴ βουλεμένους αὐτῷ δουλεῦσαι, ἀλλ' εἰ μὴ χάριν ἔχεις, φησὶ, καὶ παρὰ σαυτοῦ καὶ ἑκὼν θέλεις ἐπιγράψασθαι τὴν δεσποτείαν, οὐκ ἀναγκάζω οὐδὲ βιάζομαι.*

Along with this scriptural refinement of the freedom[228] of the candidate *vis-à-vis* the fact of the universal salvation purchased by the blood of Christ in entering into the ratification of a contract of service, which is the act of renunciation and commitment, Chrysostom adds two more biblical analyses devoted especially to the second part of the contract, the syntaxis, or profession of attachment, when the candidate declares: "And I enter into Your service, O Christ."[229]

These words are not only interpreted under the image of the contract in Chrysostom's mystagogy; they are also seen as an engagement with the Bridegroom. The formula of commitment is the dowry which the candidate freely contributes. The Bridegroom has contributed His gift of salvation, a Bridegroom Who, as Chrysostom says, quoting St. Paul, is "rich towards all and for all who call upon Him."[230]

The other interpretation of the act of commitment to Christ which Chrysostom gives is contained in his analysis of it in Pauline terms as a confession of faith.[231] Following the Pauline commentary on the biblical anthropology of the act of faith from *Rm.* 10:10, Chrysostom instructs the candidates to contribute their "fair share,"[232] that is, to make a confession of faith in Christ, not only with the lips, but also with the understanding. "For with the heart a man believes unto justice; and with the mouth profession of faith is made unto salvation."[233] "For the understanding must be strongly fixed in pious faith, and the tongue must herald forth by its confession the solid resolution of the mind."[234] The distinction between "faith (πίστις)" and "confession (ὁμολογία)," where faith is

[228]Harkins, *ACW* 31, p. 337, n. 73, draws attention to a similar passage from *In Mt.* 56 (*MG* 58.541) which shows how Christ invites the candidate, but does not compel him.

[229]See above, p. 31.

[230]*Rm.* 10:12. See *P.K.* 3.6 (*VGS,* 173; tr. Harkins, *ACW* 31, 168-169, no. 26).

[231]See *Stav.* 1.19 (Wenger, *SC* 50, 118; tr. Harkins, *ACW* 31, 30).

[232]*τὰ παρ' ἑαυτῶν εἰσενέγκατε.*

[233]*Rm.* 10:10.

[234]*Δεῖ γαρ καὶ τὴν διάνοιαν ἐστηρίχθαι βεβαίως ἐν τῇ εὐσεβεῖ πίστει καὶ τὴν γλῶτταν διὰ τῆς ὁμολογίας κηρύττειν τὸ πεπηγὸς τῆς διανοίας.*

primarily the candidate's interior disposition and confession the verbal manifestation of his interior disposition, is seen in *Stav.* 4.31.[235]

Thus, Chrysostom in his mystagogy, in an even more elaborate way than Theodore, Cyril or Ambrose, reveals the candidate's union with the power of Christ and the contractual nature of the act of renunciation and commitment.

Comparative Summary

Important though the body language be in revealing the breadth and depth of the act of renunciation and commitment, the place of signal importance in the rite remains reserved for the utterance of the word itself, the verbal act of renouncing Satan and confessing one's allegiance to Christ. The symbolic language of the bodily movement actually plays an assisting role of underscoring more completely the verbal act.

In providing a mystagogy for this verbal act the fathers rest solidly on the natural symbol: the indispensable importance of the spoken word of a human being in revealing his state of mind and heart. The interior act of conversion must be brought onto the actual stage of life and made visible and interpersonal. When the stakes are as dramatically high as in the act of renunciation and commitment, and mean so much as far as a person's relationship to others and to the world is concerned, it is doubly important that the word be solemnized.

In their mystagogical interpretation of this verbal act, then, the fathers rely on this natural symbol of the spoken word in placing the individual in a dramatic inter-personal relationship. It is this symbolism which is at the root of the consistent mystagogy of all four fathers that in uttering the formula the candidate, by his own word, dramatically confronts Satan, who

[235] Wenger, *SC* 50, 198; tr. Harkins, *ACW* 31, 78. "Keep strong your contract with the Master, which you wrote not with ink nor on paper, but with faith and in confession (Τὰς *συνθήκας τοίνυν ἅς πρὸς τὸν δεσπότην ἔθεσθε, οὐ μέλανι οὐδὲ χάρτῃ ταύτας ἐγγράψαντες ἀλλὰ τῇ πίστει καὶ τῃ ὁμολογίᾳ, βεβαίους καὶ ἀκινήος φυλάξαντες*).

becomes virtually present to him. If the candidate in his preparation for baptism has in his journey toward faith become aware of the enslaving impediments which hinder his free confession of faith in Christ, then just prior to that confession of faith he sums up the totality of what he rejects by means of this personal word of rejection uttered in the face of the one who biblically symbolizes the works of evil and unfreedom, Satan.

Thus, all four fathers develop a mystagogy for reciting the formula which emphasizes that the candidates are involved not in a dead formula, but in a verbal, personal confrontation of Satan. Cyril sees Satan as present to hear his own rejection. Ambrose dramatizes the confrontation by emphasizing that the rejection is hurled in Satan's face. Chrysostom and Theodore raise the act to a personal plane by making the candidates conscious of the network of enslavement to evil which had become so strong and almost hopeless that the utterance of the word of rejection against such a despotic adversary terrifies them.

The mystagogical interpretation of this verbal act then moves a step further in availing itself of the cultural symbol, the word as sign of a human contract in legal terms. Both natural and cultural symbol are already present in Scripture. Cyril, Chrysostom and Theodore all contrast the verbal act of renunciation with a previous contract which Scripture describes as man having made with Satan as enslaving tyrant, with death, with hell. Man's ratification of this contract through the word of Adam had enslaving consequences as the contract was carried out in history. The word of rejection is now about to dissolve this age-old contract and establish a new contract. The union with Satan as a result of the old contract is at the moment of reciting the formula to be replaced by the contract with Christ and union with Him. This mystagogy of the contract, relying on Scripture, is most highly developed by Chrysostom.

Just as there was a previous contract with Satan, so, too, the verbal act established a new, solemn contract with Christ. Indeed, the candidate utters the formula, but once uttered it has binding, transcendental consequences. This aspect of the verbal act is emphasized in all four fathers by their recourse to specific legal terminology in describing the act as a binding contract. Cyril, Ambrose, and Chrysostom further reinforce its solemn nature by carrying this mystagogy based on legal terminology over to the image that God Himself records the contract in a heavenly book, just as an earthly probate court would make an agreement valid and binding by recording it officially.

Again, it is Chrysostom who goes into some detail with the contract image, basing his mystagogical development on Pauline utterances. The price of invalidating the old contract is paid by Christ with His blood on the cross. Even though the candidate finds the price paid already, still he is not compelled to agree to the contract. He accepts it freely. It differs from a secular contract here in that Christ paid the price even before He has the assurance that the candidate will accept the contract. The contract remains a non-compulsory gift, whereby its unusual freedom from coercion is emphasized. Chrysostom moves from here out of the merely legal mystagogy to the bridal metaphor, which emphasizes the personal relationship of love involved in the verbal "Yes" to the contract. The verbal act is more than a mere contract; it is the highly personal answer of intimate love of the bride to the gift of Himself which the Bridegroom is making. The act of commitment to Christ becomes then the dowry which the bride happily brings to the Bridegroom.

In this development of Chrysostom the mystagogy of the verbal act, and what it really means, an intimate answer yet at the same time a public contractual confession of commitment to Christ as in a marriage bond, reaches, as it were, its high point of development. It rests on verbal, cultural and scriptural symbol and is infused with a personalism which comes from the author's own mystical experience.

The helplessness of the candidate and his fear in confronting Satan are overcome by the mystagogical emphasis on the fact that, while the candidate himself must say the word, he is united with the struggle and victory of Christ in liberating him from Satan. Cyril and Theodore both emphasize the candidate's bond with Christ's humanity at this decisive moment. Chrysostom colors this mystagogy even further by referring the candidate's struggle at this moment to the struggle of Christ on the cross, and emphasizes the consolation of victory by the metaphor of the struggle in the Olympic games, where Christ as Olympic Judge decides for the candidate.

Essay: The Anointings

As has been indicated by the synoptic presentation of the ceremonies of renunciation and profession, both Chrysostom and Theodore show that the rite is brought to a conclusion or "sealed" by an anointing.[236] Before presenting in greater detail the mystagogical commentaries of Chrysostom and Theodore which serve to interpret the meaning of this ritual action of anointing, it will be advisable, for the sake of clarity, to group together here all the anointings mentioned in the mystagogical writings, and at least provisionally to distribute them into several categories or groups, the justification for which will emerge as they are treated in detail in the context of the unfolding ceremonies. It would be possible to draw together the interpretations of all the anointings and compare them in a separate chapter. This would serve the purpose of a convenient survey by having them all together in one place. However, it would have the disadvantage of removing them from their context in the unfolding ceremonies, and it is precisely this context which is important in order to understand how the fathers used such ceremonies, which they found as a "given" in the liturgies upon which they were called to comment, to illustrate the meaning of the main sections of the rite of initiation. Common material was already at hand for the fathers to use in interpreting the anointings, since they had already undergone certain historical development. The fathers used this material applying their own emphasis in a creative way in order to interpret mystagogically the main actions of the bap-

[236] See above, pp. 31, 33.

tismal rite. It must not be expected that this was done in a very systematic way, however, because at the time the fathers wrote, the liturgy of the anointings had already been subject to different emphases, as, for example, cultural and theological, and was itself changing. Studies in comparative liturgy of the times point up such problems of reduplications in the anointing, separation in time due, for example, to the number of candidates, or the absence of the bishop in outlying churches and the like. Therefore the fathers' comments on the anointings must be seen in the context of the ceremonies themselves in order to understand their particular emphasis. The mystagogical writings are not a history of liturgy or a liturgical analysis, but a pastoral tool to help the newly baptized understand the meaning of the ceremonies as they were actually performed. Since this is their purpose, it will not be surprising to see that one of the fathers will use material to interpret a pre-baptismal anointing, and that another father will use the same material to interpret an anointing which comes subsequent to the baptismal act.[237]

A compromise solution of methodology, therefore, has been essayed here in which a general listing and hypothetical interpretative grouping of all the anointings is presented, which may serve as a scheme of reference. Then the anointings will be treated separately in their actual individual place in the context of the unfolding ceremonies. This treatment in context will, it is hoped, serve to justify the hypothetical interpretative groupings here given.

In the mystagogical writings under consideration, Cyril, Chrysostom, Theodore and Ambrose provide explanations for a total of nine ceremonies which involve some kind of an anointing with oil. Cyril records two, Chrysostom records two, Theodore records three and Ambrose indicates two. (There is also the possibility that the final ceremony of "sealing" recorded by Ambrose also involves the use of oil).

[237]See, *e.g.*, Theodore's mystagogy of the anointing concluding the rite of renunciation and commitment (below, pp. 126-131), where material used there is used by Cyril in his mystagogy of the post-baptismal anointing (below, ch. 3, pp. 370-373).

Taking the general structure of the initiation rite as the fathers themselves treat it in their mystagogical writings, a framework we have followed in our three chapter divisions as *first*, the rite of renunciation and profession, *second*, the baptismal act, and *third*, the post-baptismal ceremonies, these anointings are located as follows.

First: Ambrose records an anointing before the act of renunciation and profession.[238] Chrysostom and Theodore record an anointing after the act of renunciation and profession.[239]

Second: Cyril, Chrysostom and Theodore record an anointing just prior to the baptismal bath.[240]

Third: Cyril, Theodore and Ambrose record an anointing just after the baptismal bath.[241]

(Ambrose does not disclose whether a later ceremony, the "sealing" which takes place after the washing of the feet, is performed with oil or not).[242]

If we seek a least common denominator in the *kind* of anointing (*e.g.* forehead or whole body), in its *place* in relationship to the total initiation rite, and in the chief *emphasis of mystagogical interpretation* accorded to it in the commentaries of the four fathers on these nine anointings, we can provisionally divide the anointings into three groups.

Group one is the anointing of the forehead with the sign of the cross, taking place after the act of renunciation and profession, which is viewed as a conclusion ritually to this ceremonial act. The mystagogy emphasizes the sign of the cross as the "sphragis" or "seal" of belonging to Christ and ownership by Him.

To this group belong the anointing recorded by Chrysostom and that recorded by Theodore after the act of renunciation and profession.

Group two is an anointing of the body prior to the baptismal bath. This anointing is viewed as a preparation for this

[238] See above, p. 27.
[239] See above, pp. 31, 33.
[240] See below, ch. 2, pp. 144-148.
[241] See below, ch. 3, pp. 349, 351-353.
[242] See below, p. 353, and the discussion, ch. 3, n. 30, p. 354.

bath. Exorcistic considerations and their ramifications in connection with the meaning of the baptismal bath are the point of departure for the mystagogy of this anointing.

To this group belong the anointings before the baptismal bath recorded by Cyril, Chrysostom and Theodore, and also the anointing recorded by Ambrose before the act of renunciation and profession.

Group three is somewhat amorphous. There is an anointing of the bodily senses directly after the bath recorded by Cyril, mystagogically emphasizing the coming of the Holy Spirit. There is an anointing of the forehead directly after the baptismal bath recorded by Theodore also emphasizing in its mystagogical interpretation the coming of the Holy Spirit. (Further, the "sealing" ceremony recorded by Ambrose after the foot-washing, where there is a possible use of oil, emphasizes in a similar way the coming of the Holy Spirit).

Belonging to none of these three groups is the anointing of the head directly after the baptismal bath recorded by Ambrose where the mystagogical emphasis has nothing to do with the coming of the Holy Spirit, but rather unfolds symbolically the meaning of the baptismal bath in association with resurrection and immortality.

The following synoptic chart, composed according to these groupings suggested, will serve as an orientation in the rite of initiation as recorded in the mystagogical writings under consideration.

SYNOPTIC CHART

The Anointings

Type	*Place*	*Father*	*Mystagogy*
Group One:			
Forehead	After Renunciation	Chrysostom	Sphragis (Cross)
Forehead	After Renunciation	Theodore	Sphragis (Cross)
Group Two:			
Body	Before Renunciation	Ambrose	Exorcistic
Body	Before Bath	Cyril	Exorcistic
Body	Before Bath	Theodore	Exorcistic-Immortality
Body	Before Bath	Chrysostom	Exorcistic
Group Three:			
Body Senses	After Bath	Cyril	Sphragis (Spirit)
Forehead	After Bath	Theodore	Sphragis (Spirit)
?	After Foot-Washing	Ambrose	Sphragis (Spirit)
Head	After Bath	Ambrose	Immortality-Resurrection

Materials which the fathers use to interpret these anointings which they found in the initiation liturgy upon which they were called to comment in their mystagogical writings are dispersed in a way that there is some over-lapping in the use of these materials, and the mystagogy of one anointing is not always clearly and completely separate from that of another in the application of the mystagogical materials. This will come as no surprise when one realizes that numerous traditions come together in these anointing rites. For example, it will be observed from an examination of the groupings we have presented that the anointing as *sphragis* or seal is viewed by Chrysostom and Theodore in group one from the standpoint of the theology of the cross, the marking with the sign of the cross, which seals the covenant or contract which they consider the act of renunciation and profession to establish between the candidate and Christ, and it forms a conclusion to that rite. That rite, due to the number of candidates, had gradually grown and severed itself from the Holy Saturdy vigil, thus requiring liturgically some kind of ritual conclusion, since the baptismal profession of faith would not take place immediately thereafter, as it does, for example, in the liturgy of Ambrose, where the *syntaxis* itself seems to be the triple profession involved in the triple immersion of the baptismal bath itself, instead of a separate declaration as in Theodore and Chrysostom. This same notion of the Christian commitment, a "sealing," reappears in Cyril and in Ambrose *after* the baptismal bath itself. Here the material used to interpret such a sealing is not so much the theology of the sign of the cross, but rather the theology of the Holy Spirit, Who is given as gift to the candidate, a testimony of God's ratification of the covenant of faith which the total initiation represents, much as Jesus in the Jordan was approved by the Spirit.

Ambrose himself seems to be aware of the mystagogical and to some extent theological "embarrassment" involved in the inability to present a totally clear distinction in the meaning of the different liturgical ceremonies when he says:

> The Father, the Son and the Spirit are everywhere, with one working, one sanctification. But certain things are seen in praticular to each Person. How may this be? God has anointed you, the Lord has marked you with His seal, and He has put the Holy Spirit into your heart.[243] You have, then, received the Holy Spirit in your heart. Receive something else as well: for, as the Holy Spirit is in your heart, so Christ is in your heart. How? You possess that Christ Who said to the Church in the Canticle: "Put me as a seal on your heart, as a seal on your arms."[244] Therefore God has anointed you, Christ has marked you with His seal. How? You were marked with the sign of His cross, with the sign of His passion. You have received the sign in order to be like Him . . .[245]

Here, then, is an example of how the theme of the *sphragis* is on the one hand related to Christ crucified because it is the impression of the sign of the cross,[246] yet on the other hand it is related to the Holy Spirit. Depending on the emphasis which a mystagogical writer wishes to give to the ceremony, he has a variety of traditions to choose from. This serves to explain the various "unschematic" overlapping of materials, and warns away from an approach which would try to fit the interpretations into neat categories. This is added reason to use a methodology in studying the anointings which treats them in their context, rather than attempting to compare them in a "schematic" way which would lead to the

[243] *Cf. 2 Co.* 1:21-22.

[244] *Sg.* 8:6

[245] *Sacr.* VI.5-7 (Botte, *SC* 25 bis, 140; tr. Deferrari, *FC* 44, 320-321: "Ubique pater, filius et spiritus sanctus, una operatio, una sanctificatio, etsi quaedam veluti specialia esse videantur. Quomodo? Deus, qui te unxit et signavit te dominus, et posuit spiritum sanctum in corde tuo. Accepisti ergo spiritum sanctum in corde tuo. Accipe aliud, quia quemadmodum sanctus spiritus in corde, ita etiam Christus in corde. Quomodo? Habes hoc in Canticis canticorum, Christum dicentem ad ecclesiam: 'Pone me sicut signaculum in corde tuo, sicut signaculum in bracchiis tuis.' Ergo unxit te deus, signavit te Christus. Quomodo? Quia ad crucis ipsius signatus es formam ad illius passionem. Accepisti signaculum ad illius similitudinem......"

[246] *Cf. Myst.* 20 (Botte, *SC* 25bis, 166; tr. Deferrari, *FC* 44, 12).

temptation to develop a "thesis" on the subject, or to attempt to fit them into later theological categories. The groupings we have given are not presented to assert a "thesis" but merely as a general aid to assist the reader in maintaining some clarity, since the anointings are so numerous throughout the initiation rite. It is not our purpose to develop a "thesis" in sacramental theology on this subject, but rather to show in a comparative study of mystagogical interpretation how these four fathers used their biblical and other materials to interpret a given liturgy. Individual genius and style as well as common trends will emerge through analysis and comparison of this mystagogy which may well serve an eventual "thesis" on the subject. Our study, however, is primarily a study in mystagogy.

III

THE CONCLUDING ANOINTING

The mystagogical writings of both Chrysostom and Theodore reveal that the rite of renunciation and commitment comes to its conclusion with an anointing of the candidate. Details of the action and the accompanying formulas have already been presented in the synopsis of the ceremonies.[247] In both the *Baptismal Instructions* of Chrysostom and the *Baptismal Homilies* of Theodore, it is clear that whatever the liturgical origin and history of this anointing was, it is treated in the mystagogical interpretation of these two fathers as a conclusion or a kind of rounding off of the rite of renunciation and profession. After it there is a definite *caesura* before the next phase of the initiation begins, the baptism proper with its attendant preparatory and concluding ceremonies. The mystagogical interpretation of this anointing is, then influenced by its deliberate association with the act of renunciation and profession in the presentation of these two mystagogues.

[247]See above, pp. 31, 33.

How does Theodore interpret this action in which the pontiff, having exchanged his garments for a supple and radiant linen robe, approaches the kneeling candidate, and with the oil of anointing traces on the forehead of each one of them the sign of the cross saying, "So-and-so is signed in the name of the Father and of the Son of the Holy Spirit."[248] What meaning does Chrysostom attach to a very similar ceremony, likewise occuring after the candidate has spoken his formula of renunciation of Satan and attachment to Christ, where the bishop anoints him of the forehead with the "spiritual unguent (μύρῳ πνευματικῷ)" in the form of the cross saying, "So-and-so is anointed in the name of the Father and of the Son and of the Holy Spirit?"[249]

Both Chrysostom and Theodore use as their point of departure in interpreting this ceremony the traditional Christian notion of the "sphragis," the "seal" as denoting the mark of ownership and the implication of protection on the part of the owner for those who bore this seal.[250] By the time of Chrysostom and Theodore, the use of the term "sphragis" and its derivatives refers to the rites of imposition of hands and anointing in the form of a cross, particularly in the baptismal liturgy.[251] Chrysostom says explicitly: "through the chrism the cross is stamped on you."[252] A comparison of the principal texts in which this anointing ceremony is interpreted show this common point of departure in interpreting

[248]See above, p. 33.

[249]See above, p. 31. For recent contributions on this, see H. Green, "The Significance of the Pre-Baptismal Seal in St. John Chrysostom," *SP*, ed. F. Cross, Vol. VI, Part IV, TU 81 (Berlin, 1962), pp. 84-90; P. Harkins, "Pre-Baptismal Rites in Chrysostom's Baptismal Catecheses," *SP*, ed. F. Cross, Vol. VIII, Part II, TU 93 (Berlin, 1966), pp. 219-238; L. Mitchell, "The Baptismal Rite in Chrysostom," *Anglican Theological Review* 43 (1961) 400-401.

[250]The evolution of the term "Sphragis" is traced in J. Ysebaert, *Greek Baptismal Terminology: Its Origins and Early Development, GCP* 1, eds. C. Mohrmann, J. Ross (Nijmegen, 1962), pp. 204-226. Ysebaert's intention is to collect and rearrange the material of Dölger, particularly in *Sphragis: Eine altchristliche Taufbezeichnung in ihren Beziehungen zur profanen und religiösen Kultur des Altertums* (Paderborn, 1911).

[251]*Cf.* Ysebaert, *op. cit.*, p. 420.

[252]*P.K.* 3.7 (VGS, 173, tr. Harkins, *ACW* 31, 169, no. 27): ἐντυποῦται δὲ ὁ σταυρὸς διὰ τοῦ χρίσματος.

the signing with the cross as sealing the candidate with a mark of ownership.[253]

The notion of ownership, or "belonging" in the commonly used examples of the sacred and profane literature of antiquity (*e.g.* the soldier's tatoo marking him for the imperial military service, the brand on an animal showing whose property he is) is accepted as fundamental interpretation of this anointing with the sign of the cross on the forehead of the candidate both by Theodore and by Chrysostom. In connection with this traditional "sphragis" interpretation of the anointing, however, it is essential to note that it is not the ceremony of the anointing with the sign of the cross which *brings about* the ownership of the candidate by Christ, or his separation from Satan and the world for the task of the Christian life through combat to glory under the special protection of the cross of Christ. This particular status of belonging, task-orientation, and confidence in protection to final victory has come to be in the candidate not through the anointing, but through the words of renunciation and commitment which he has just uttered, the contract of faith. Chrysostom is especially explicit on this point, always referring the anointing to the act of renunciation and commitment which has just taken place: "After these words, after the renunciation of the devil and the covenant with Christ, in as much as you have henceforth become His very own, and have nothing in common with that Evil One, He straightway bids you to be marked and places on your forehead the sign of the cross."[254] Thus, one has become Christ's "very own" not through the anointing with the sign of the cross, but through his act of renunciation and

[253] See *P.K.* 3.7 (*VGS,* 173; tr. Harkins, *ACW* 31, 169, no. 27); *Stav.* 2.22-23 (Wenger, *SC* 50, 145-146; tr. Harkins, *ACW* 31, 51-52); *Bapt. Hom.* II.17-19; III.1 (Tonneau-Devreesse, *SeT* 145, 394-400, 402, 404; tr. Mingana, *WS* VI, 46-47, 49).

[254] *P.K.* 3.7 (*VGS*, 173; tr. Harkins, *ACW* 31, 169, no. 27): Μετὰ δὲ τά ῥήματα ταῦτα, μετὰ τὴν ἀποταγὴν τοῦ διαβόλου, μετὰ τὴν συνταγὴν τὴν πρὸς τὸν Χριστόν, ἅτε οἰκείους γεγενημένους λοιπὸν καὶ οὐδὲν κοινὸν ἔχοντας πρὸς ἐκεῖνον, εὐθέως σφραγίζεσθαι κελεύει καὶ ἐπὶ τοῦ μετώπου δίδωσι σοι τὸν σταυρόν.

commitment. Then Christ seals the candidate, after he has made his contract of faith with Him. This same association of the anointing with the apotaxis-syntaxis occurs again in Chrysostom: "After that contract of renunciation and attachment, after you have confessed His sovereignty and by the words you spoke have attached yourself to Christ, in the next place, as if you were a combatant chosen for the spiritual arena, the priest anoints you on the forehead with the spiritual unguent and signs you saying: 'So-and-so is anointed in the name of the Father and of the Son and of the Holy Spirit.' "[255]

Thus, the existential fact of belonging to Christ and being separated from Satan, attachment and renunciation, is achieved not through the anointing but through the candidate's previously made contract. The anointing with the sign of the cross, then, is interpreted as a sort of elucidation, ceremonial confirmation, and elaboration of the implications of the event that has just taken place through the candidate's act of renunciation and commitment. It is not causative, but illustrative of the existential situation which has been brought about by the act of renunciation and commitment.

Theodore likewise links the anointing ceremony with the preceding act of renunciation and commitment. Before describing the anointing, he reminds the candidates of their posture in which they had made their "engagement" and "promises," kneeling as the sign of adoration of God and of the ancient fall, yet the rest of the body erect and hands outstretched to the God from Whom one expects to rise from that ancient fall. It is through the "promises and engagements"

[255] *Stav.* 2.22 (Wenger, *SC* 50, 145-146; tr. Harkins, *ACW* 31, 51): Εἶτα μετὰ τὴν συνθήκην ταύτην, καὶ τὴν ἀποταγὴν καὶ τὴν συνιαγήν, ἐπειδὴ ὡμολόγησας τὴν δεσποτείαν καὶ διὰ τῶν τῆς γλώττης ῥημάτων συνετάξω τῷ Χριστῷ, λοιπὸν ὡς στρατιώτην καὶ εἰς τὸ στάδιον καταλεγέντα τὸ πνευματικόν, ἀλείφει ἐπὶ τοῦ μετώπου τῷ μύρῳ τῷ πνευματικῷ, τὴν σφραγῖδα ἐπιτιθεὶς καὶ λέγων. "Χρίεται ὁ δεῖνα εἰς τὸ ὄνομα τοῦ Πατρος καὶ τοῦ Υἱοῦ καὶ τοῦ ἁγίου Πνεύματος."

that the candidate has come to belong to Christ. The anointing is an elucidation of the benefits which come as a result of this commitment. The anointing is the "first-fruits" of the sacrament. Orientation and access to these first-fruits has come about through the fundamental choice which occured in the act of renunciation and commitment: "This is the reason why you have, through the promises and engagements which we have already described, directed your course towards Him and have promised to Him that you will make yourself worthy of the expected gift."[256]

Understanding, then, how Theodore and Chrysostom relate the anointing ceremony to the act of renunciation and commitment, not as another parallel step in the process of initiation but rather as an elucidation through symbolism of the way of life and some of its implications to which one has committed himself through the act of renunciation of Satan and commitment to Christ, one can proceed to compare and contrast their different emphases in their instructions on its meaning.

Theodore and Chrysostom interpret this anointing of the candidate with oil under three aspects, although with somewhat different emphases. They interpret the ceremony as a sign, *first,* of the status of belonging (on the part of the sealed candidate) and ownership (on the part of Christ), *second,* appointment to a life task together with a claim to effective protection in pursuing this life task, and *third,* a sign of the first-fruits of final victory.

[256] *Bapt. Hom.* II. 16 (Tonneau-Devreesse, *SeT* 145, 394; tr. Mingana, *WS* VI, 45).

SYNOPTIC CHART

The Concluding Anointing

Chrysostom	*Theodore*
A. Belonging and Ownership:	
Christ Himself marks candidate as His own with sign of cross *P.K.* 3.27 2 *Co.* 1:21	
	Animal brand, Military tatoo, Household name-plate *Bapt.Hom* II. 17-19 *Ep.* 2:19 *Ph.* 3:20
B. Appointment for Life-Task and Protection:	
Athlete in spiritual arena on Christ's team *Stav.* 2.22 Strife-Counterstrife *Stav.* 2.23 Olive oil for athlete *P.K.* 3.27 Anointing with cross by God for protection in combat	
-Satan blinded by chrism *P.K.* 3.27 *Stav.* 2.23	Seal frightens demons *Bapt.Hom.* II.18
-Protection in daily life *Montf.* 2.60	
	Life-long union with cross of Christ *Bapt.Hom.* III.1 2 *Tm.* 2:11-13

The Concluding Anointing—continued

	Theodore
C. The First-fruits of Final Victory:	
	Communion with Christ the heavenly King *Bapt.Hom.* II.16; III.1 *Jn.* 17:24 *Ga.* 4:26 Circumstances surrounding anointing -Bishop's linen rob: Sign of Heaven: joy, radiance, suppleness *Bapt.Hom.* II.17 -*Orarium* of free citizen *Bapt.Hom.* II.19 *Ga.* 4.26 -Rising from knees as sign of freedom *Bapt.Hom.* II.19 Sign of possession of confidence (*parrhesia*) *Bapt.Hom.* I.29; II.17-18 *Commentary on Lord's Prayer,* 7 (Mingana, pp.6-7, Tonneau-Devreesse, p.297) *Ga.* 4:5,26 *Rm.* 8:15 *Ph.* 3:20 -Looking at God with unveiled face 1 *Co.* 12:12; 2 *Co.* 3:18 *Homily on Eucharist,* II.6 (Mingana, p.100; Tonneau-Devreesse, p. 543) *Is.* 6:3 -Bishop's garments inspire with awe, fear, love *Bapt.Hom.* II.17 -Right of heavenly citizenship *Bapt.Hom.* II.19 -Participation in Christ's *parrhesia,* free intercourse with God *Bapt.Hom.* I. 7,9,10 *Rm.* 6:3-4

A. Belonging and Ownership

1. *Chrysostom*

As might be expected from what we have already seen of Chrysostom's approach to the idea of the candidate's union with Christ in the unfolding of the liturgy of initiation, his approach to the mystagogy of the sealing as a sign of belonging, which was accomplished by the candidate's avowal of service to Christ and attachment to Him, is quite direct. It is Christ Himself Who bids the candidate to be marked with the sign of His cross, Christ Himself Who places this sign on the candidates forehead.[257] This is because the candidate, through his syntaxis, has become "His very own,"[258] a result of his contract with the Master. The candidate now has "nothing in common with Satan."[259] his former master. "It is not a man, but God Himself Who anoints you through the hand of the priest."[260]

Chrysostom also chooses a text from St Paul. With Chrysostom, it is consistent with the direct christological mystagogy emphasizing Christ's taking possessing of the candidate, signified in this anointing with the cross: "It is God Who is warrant for us, and for you in Christ, Who has anointed us."[261]

2. *Theodore*

Theodore compares the sign of the cross with which the candidate has been anointed on the forehead with the brand

[257] *P.K.* 3.7. See above, p. 113 and n. 254.

[258] *Idem.*

[259] *Idem.*

[260] *Ibid.* (*Ibid.*, 173; tr. *ibid.*, 160): *οὐκ ἄνθρωπος, ἀλλ' αὐτὸς σε χρίει ὁ Θεὸς διὰ τῆς τοῦ ἱερέως χειρός.*

[261] *Cf.* 2 *Co.* 1:21. *P.K.* 3.7 (*VGS*, 173; tr. Harkins, *ACW* 31, 169, no. 27): *ὁ δὲ βεβαιῶν ἡμᾶς σὺν ὑμῖν εἰς Χριστὸν καὶ χρίσας ἡμᾶς, Θεός.*

which an owner places immediately on a lamb so that it will belong to his flock and graze in his pastures with his other lambs. He also compares this seal with the tatoo a soldier receives on his hand as a sign that his enlistment has found acceptance, and that he will henceforth offer his service to a certain king. Like Chrysostom, Theodore also reaches to St. Paul, using *Ep.* 2:19, where Paul calls Christians no longer "aliens or foreign visitors," but "citizens and part of God's household." Theodore also compares this stamp with a mark of ownership which one is able to display (perhaps a nameplate around the neck), to show he is a member of a certain household. In this case it is God's household to which one belongs and citizenship in heaven which one possesses.[262] Thus, through the seal interpreted in traditional images of belonging and ownership, and explained by recourse to Pauline writings, Theodore sees the candidate as consecrated to the participation in the life of a new, heavenly world: "When the priest performs these things for you and signs you with a sign on your forehead, he separates you from the rest as a consequence of the aforesaid words, and decides that you are a soldier of the true king and a citizen of heaven. The sign (with which you have been signed) demonstrates that you have communion with and participation in these things."[263]

B. Appointment for Life Task and Protection

While one sees a common traditional attention to the seal as sign of ownership and belonging, expressed in these different ways, one notes a divergent emphasis in interpreting the function of the seal. Chrysostom sees the seal as a sign of and equipment for the struggle against Satan in this world. Theodore interprets it more as a sign of the interior victory already achieved through conversion to Christ, and so participation in

[262] See *Bapt. Hom.* II.17 (Tonneau-Devreesse, *SeT* 145, 396; tr. Mingana, *WS* VI, 46).

[263] *Ibid.*, II.19 (*Ibid.*, 398; tr. *ibid.*, 47).

His union with the Godhead. To be sure, elements of both aspects are present in both fathers, but the preponderant emphasis in Chrysostom is on the struggle now, while Theodore points out more the aspects of an achieved victory seen as a participation now in a heavenly life already begun, evidenced by this sign which is impressed with oil on the forehead.

1. *Chrysostom*

Using the athletic metaphor of which he is so fond,[264] Chrysostom sees the anointing with the cross as a sign that the candidate has been chosen as a combatant in the spiritual arena, playing in the game on the side of Christ.[265] Because this mark indicates that he has gone over from the side of Satan to the side of Christ, belonging now go Christ's team, a struggle situation is thus announced in which the candidate must be involved: "Hence, from that day there is strife and counterstrife with [Satan,] and on this account the priest leads you into the spiritual arena as athletes of Christ by virtue of this anointing."[266]

In describing the composition of the "spiritual unguent," Chrysostom notes that the olive oil component is for the athlete. "This chrism is a mixture of olive oil and unguent; the unguent is for the bride, the olive oil for the athlete."[267] The allusion in this mystagogy is to the obvious use of olive oil to rub down athletes before their participation in a contest, and to the perfume for the bride.

Through his rejection of Satan the candidate has infuriated him, and he has become his raging enemy. For protection

[264] See J. Sawhill, "The Use of Athletic Metaphors in the Biblical Homilies of St. John Chrysostom," diss. (Princeton, New Jersey, 1928); P. Harkins, *art. cit.*

[265] See *Stav.* 2.22 (Wenger, *SC* 50, 145; tr. Harkins, *ACW* 31, 51).

[266] *Ibid.*, 2,23 (*Ibid.*, 147; tr. *ibid.*, 52): *Λοιπὸν γὰρ μάχη καὶ ἀντίστασις ἐξ ἐκείνου πρὸς αὐτὸν γίνεται καὶ διὰ τοῦτο καθάπερ ἀθλητάς τινὰς Χριστοῦ οὕτω διὰ τῆς ἀλοιφῆς εἰς τὸ στάδιον τὸ πνευματικὸν εἰσάγει.*

[267] *P.K.* 3.7 (*VGS*, 173; tr. Harkins, *ACW* 31, 169, no. 27): *τὸ δὲ χρῖσμα τοῦτο ἔλαιον ὁμοῦ καὶ μύρον ἐστί, μύρον μεν ὡς νύμφην, ἔλαιον δὲ ὡς ἀθλητήν.*

against assault, "[God] anoints your countenance and stamps thereon the sign of the cross."[268] The seal thus becomes the protective device to turn back Satan, who will not dare to look upon the sign of the cross: "Just as if he beheld the rays of the sun, and had leaped away, so will his eyes be blinded by the sign of your face and he will depart; for through the chrism the cross is stamped on you."[269]

Reflection on Chrysostom's interpretation of the anointing indicates that he goes far beyond the notion of a merely extrinsic, exorcistic "talisman" to protect one. In order to grasp the fact that this mystagogy is based on a profound mystical meditation, it will be recalled how Chrysostom used the light and darkness imagery of Good Friday to lead the candidates to Christ, the "Sun of Justice" shining forth from the cross so brightly that the sun turned back its own rays.[270] From this same source, Chrysostom again relates the ceremonies of Christian Initiation to the power of the cross of Christ. Christ, Who has taken possession of the candidate as His own, has become one with him, and it is His own power which shines from the cross stamped on the candidate's forehead, because "through this chrism the cross was stamped on you."[271] Through his contract with Christ, sign for which is this sealing, the candidate joins Christ in the struggle which His cross represents, and through the power of that cross he is protected in reliving that struggle in his own life. Thus, the seal of the cross on the candidate's forehead radiates a power for the combat which confounds the adversaries: "Therefore [the priest] anoints you on the forehead and puts on you the sign in order that the enemy may turn away his eyes. For he does not dare to look you in the face when he sees the lightning

[268] *Idem:* διὰ τοῦ χρίσματος ἐντυπῶν σου τῷ προσώπῳ τὸν σταυρόν.

[269] *Ibid.;* ὥσπερ ἀκτῖνας ὁρῶν ἐκπηδώσας ἐκεῖθεν, οὕτως ἀποτυφλωθεὶς τοὺς ὀφθαλμους ἄπεισιν. ἐντυποῦται δὲ ὁ σταυρὸς διὰ τοῦ χρίσματος. See also F. Dölger, *Sphragis,* p. 120; H. Green, *art. cit.,* pp. 88 ff.

[270] See above, p. 69.

[271] See above, n. 269.

flash which leaps forth from it and blinds his eyes."[272] This is the spiritual weapon, sign of the candidate's renunciation and commitment, which will accompany him in the Christian struggle, the struggle upon which he embarks when he renounces Satan and joins Christ. Chrysostom sums up this mystagogy of the anointing as sign of appointment to this life task and the protection it implies in pursuing this task as follows:

> When you are going to cross the threshold of a doorway, first speak these words: "I renounce you, Satan, your pomps and your service, and I enter into your service, O Christ." And never go forth without saying these words. This will be your staff, this will be your armor, this will be your impregnable tower. And after you speak these words, make the sign of the cross on your forehead. In this way no man will be able to hurt you, nor will the devil himself be able to do so, when he sees you appear with these weapons to protect you on every side.[273]

Thus, the anointing is interpreted as a sign of the Christian athletic combat in mystical union with the struggle of Christ under the victorious and so protective power of His cross.

2. *Theodore*

Theodore also sees the sealing with the cross on the forehead as a sign of appointment for the task of a Christian life on earth. He does not elaborate, however, with the combat

[272] *Stav.* 2.23 (Wenger, *SC* 50, 146-147; tr. Harkins, *ACW* 31, 52): *διὰ τοῦτο ἀλείφει ἐπὶ τοῦ μετώπου καὶ τὴν σφραγῖδα ἐπιτίθησιν ἵνα ἀποστρέψῃ τὰς ὄψεις ἐκεῖνος. Οὐδε γὰρ ἀντιβλέψαι τολμᾷ ὁρῶν τὴν ἐκεῖθεν ἀστραπὴν ἐκπηδῶσαν καὶ ἀποτυφλοῦσαν αὐτοῦ τὰς ὄψεις.*

[273] *Montf.* 2 (*MG* 49.240; tr. Harkins, *ACW* 31, 191, no. 60): *Ὅταν μέλλῃς ὑπερβαίνειν τὰ πρόθυρα τοῦ πυλῶνος, τοῦτο φθέγξαι τὸ ῥῆμα πρότερον· " Ἀποτάσσομαί σοι, Σατανᾶ, καὶ τῇ πομπῇ σου, καὶ τῇ λατρείᾳ σου, καὶ συντάσσομαι σοι, Χριστέ." καὶ μηδέποτε χωρὶς τῆς φωνῆς ταύτης ἐξέλθῃς· τουτό σοι βακτήρια ἔσται, τοῦτο ὅπλον, τοῦτο πύργος ἄμαχος. Καὶ μετὰ τοῦ ῥήματος τούτου, καὶ τὸν σταυρὸν ἐπι τοῦ μετώπου διατύπωσον. οὔτω γὰρ οὐ μόνον, ἄνθρωπος ἀπαντῶν, ἀλλ' οὐδὲ αὐτὸς ὁ διάβολος βλάψαι τὶ δυνήσεται, μετὰ τούτων σε ὁρῶν τῶν ὅπλων πανταχοῦ φαινόμενον.*

and athletic metaphors of Chrysostom and the emphasis on the battle itself, nor does he display Chrysostom's characteristic meditation on the cross of Christ. He sums up this aspect of union with the cross of Christ in the struggle by reference to the hymn in 2 *Tm.* 2:11-13: "If we have died with Him, then we shall live with Him. If we hold firm, then we shall reign with Him. If we disown Him, then He will disown us. We may be unfaithful, but He is always faithful, for He cannot disown His own self."

The belonging to Christ, which the seal implies, is an appointment for a life task on earth: "We expect to reign with Him, if, as the blessed Paul said, through our suffering we show our love for Him; and we shall be with Him in heaven and partakers of that great glory. It is for this task that you have been signed and it is through this signing that you are known to have been chosen for the service of heaven."[274]

C. The First-Fruits of Final Victory

Theodore

The chief emphasis which Theodore gives to the function of the seal comes more, however, in the context of its significance as indication of the achieved victory of the heavenly life, whose "first-fruits" are already present through this sealing.[275] It is a sign that the candidate has been called to the service of heaven, where Christ has established His Kingdom. It is a sign of "communion with heaven, where all of us will move and where our King is, as He Himself said, 'I will that they be with me, where I am.'"[276]

To establish this mystagogical emphasis Theodore draws attention to several features which surround the ceremony of

[274] *Bapt. Hom.* III.1 (Tonneau-Devreesse, *SeT* 145, 404; tr. Mingana, *WS* VI, 49).

[275] See *ibid.*, II. 16 (*Ibid.*, 394; tr. *ibid.*, 45).

[276] *Jn.* 17:24. *Bapt. Hom.* III.1 (*Ibid.*, 404; tr. *ibid.*, 49).

the sealing, and which put it into the context of the life to come. He remarks that the bishop has exchanged his ordinary garments for a linen robe. In its joyful appearance it symbolizes the joy of the world to come; in its shining whiteness the radiance of the life to come; and in its suppleness the ease and happiness of movement in the world of the future. Thus dressed, the bishop comes to anoint the candidate.[277] Immediately after the anointing the godfather, who has been standing behind the kneeling candidate, spreads an "*orarium*," or band of linen on his head, and then makes him stand erect:

> By your rising from your genuflection you show that you have cast away your ancient fall, that you have no more communion with earth and earthly things, that your adoration and prayer to God has been accepted, that you have received the stamp which is the sign of that ineffable military service, that you have been called to heaven, and that henceforth you ought to direct your course to its life and citizenship, while spurning all earthly things.[278]

The linen *orarium* which the godfather spreads on the candidate's head after he is anointed is, as Theodore explains, the emblem of freedom. Exiles and slaves stand bare-headed; free men spread linen on their hands as an adornment both at home and in the market-place.[279] The freedom symbolized by the *orarium*, is linked to the anointing:

> . . . it is through this signing that you are known to have been chosen for the service of heaven. This is the reason why immediately you rise up, you spread on your head linen, which is a mark of freedom, and this signifies that you have been chosen for the heavenly service, and been freed from communion with earthly things, while obtaining the freedom which is in heaven. If a slave is not allowed in this world to do military service to a king, how much

[277] *Bapt. Hom.* II.17 (*Ibid.*, 395; tr. *ibid.*, 45).

[278] *Ibid.*, II.19 (*Ibid.*, 398, 400; tr. *ibid.*, 47).

[279] On the *orarium* see J. Quasten, "A Pythagorean Idea in Jerome," *American Journal of Philology* 63 (1942) 207-215.

> more ought the person who has been detailed for the service of heaven to be remote from servitude. All of us, therefore, who have received communion with heavenly things are free men of that "free Jerusalem which is above. and which is mother of us all," as the blessed Paul said.[280]

Given this context of the ceremony, that is, the symbolism of the bishop's robe, rising and receiving the "orarium," both symbolizing aspects of the world to come and its freedom, it will be easier to appreciate Theodore's extraordinary and moving central interpretation of the anointing.

> . . . you, who have been chosen for the kingdom of heaven, . . . are first stamped on your forehead, that part of your head which is higher than the rest of your body, which is placed above all your body and above your face, and with which we usually draw near to one another and look at one another when we speak. You are stamped on that place so that you may be seen to possess great confidence (*παρρησια*). "Because now we see through a glass darkly, but then face to face, and with an open face we shall behold[281] as in a glass the glory of the Lord, and shall be changed into the same image from glory to glory, even as by the Spirit of the Lord,"[282] as the blessed Paul said, we are rightly stamped in a place that is higher than our face, so that from far we may frighten the demons, who will not then be able to come near us and injure us, and so that we may be known to possess so much confidence (*παρρησία*) with God that we look at Him with open face, and display before Him the stamp by which we are seen to be members of the household[283] and soldiers of Christ our Lord.[284]

280 *Ga.* 4:26. *Bapt. Hom.* III.1 (*Ibid.*, 404; tr. *ibid.*, 49).

281 Mingana translates here "we shall behold," *i.e.*, the future tense. But the Syriac text favors the present tense, as is also made clear by Theodore's own exposition of the first-fruits already present now in the following sentences. See W. Van Unnik, "*Parrhesia* in the 'Catechetical Homilies' of Theodore of Mopsuestia," in *Mélanges offertes à Chr. Mohrmann* (Utrecht, 1963), p. 18, n. 17.

282 *Cf.* 1 *Co.* 12:12; 2 *Co.* 3:18.

283 *Cf. Ep.* 3:19.

284 *Bapt. Hom.* II.17-18 (Tonneau-Devreesse, *SeT* 145, 396, 398; tr. Mingana, *WS* VI, 46-47).

By his act of renunciation and commitment, an interior transformation has taken place in the candidate as a result of which he receives "the first-fruits of the sacrament which we believe to be the earnest of the good and ineffable things found in heaven."[285] The sign on his forehead indicates that the candidate now possesses what for Theodore is a key notion, "confidence (παρρησία)." It is this confidence which comes to him as a result of his act of commitment, and the presence of which is indicated by the anointing on the forehead, a gift, the symbol of the first-fruits of the sacrament which gives the candidate free right of city in the heavenly world: "When the priest performs these things for you and signs you with a sign on your forehead, he separates you from the rest as a consequence of the aforesaid words, and decides that you are a soldier of the true King and a citizen of heaven.[286] The sign (with which you have been signed) demonstrates that you have communion with and participation in, all these things."[287]

The notion, so strong in Chrysostom, that the seal is a protection against the demons,[288] is present but receives minimal attention in the mystagogy of Theodore. It is, rather, the notion that the *sphragis* reveals the presence of *parrhesia* that is central. A parallel passage from Theodore's *Commentary on the Lord's Prayer* shows the profundity of this notion. In contrast to the children of the *Old Law* who worked under the servitude of the Law of Moses, Jesus says to His disciples:

> You have received through Me the grace of the Holy Spirit whereby you have obtained adoption of Sons,[289] and confidence (παρρησία) to call God, Father. "You have

[285] *Ibid.*, II.16 (*Ibid.*, 394; tr. *ibid.*, 45).

[286] *Cf. Ph.* 3:20. This is a favorite text of Theodore. For other occurrences see Tonneau-Devreesse, *SeT* 145, 608 (The Index of Scriptural Texts).

[287] *Bapt. Hom.* II.19 (Tonneau-Devreesse, *SeT* 145, 398; tr. Mingana, *WS* VI, 47).

[288] See above, p. 120-121. See also F. Dölger, *Sphragis*, p. 120; H. Green, *art. cit.*, p. 88 ff.

[289] *Cf. Ga.* 4:5.

> not received the Spirit in order to be again in servitude and fear, but to be worthy of the Spirit of adoption of sons, through which you call God, Father, with confidence."[290] From this you have obtained conversation[291] in Jerusalem, which is above,[292] and have been worthy of that life of freedom which will be the lot of those who, in the resurrection, will become immortal and immutable, and will live in heaven in such a nature.[293]

Thus, *parrhesia* is one of the specific elements of the new life of the Christian. In this connection Van Unnik notes:

> *Parrhesia* has not only the notion of "confidence" but also, and foremost that of "liberty" of "freedom of speech." In contrast with the Gentiles, the Christians know the only God; in contrast to the Jews they serve Him not as slaves but as Sons, and they have free intercourse with Almighty God. The depth of the great idea which is expressed here by Theodore is only righly understood if we realize on the one hand that *parrhesia* in secular Greek is the right of free citizens or the privilege of true friends, and on the other, that the service of God is awe-inspiring.[294]

The "awe-inspiring" aspect of the anointing had already been noted by Theodore when he remarked on the symbolism of the bishop's garments when he came to anoint the candidate: "He [the bishop] depicts these things [the next world] by means of the garments in which he is clad, and by the hidden symbol of the same garments he inspires you with fear, and with fear, he infuses love into you, so that you may, through the newness of his garments look into the power which it represents."[295]

[290] *Rm.* 8:15.
[291] *Cf. Ph.* 3:20.
[292] *Cf. Ga.* 4:26.
[293] *Commentary on the Lord's Prayer* (Tonneau-Devreesse, *SeT* 145, 297; Mingana, *WS* VI, 6-7).
[294] Van Unnik, *art cit.*, p. 14.
[295] *Bapt. Hom.*, II.17 (Tonneau-Devreesse, *SeT* 145, 396; tr. Mingana, *WS* VI, 46).

This whole usage of the fundamental Christian idea of *parrhesia* has been transformed by Theodore with his own particular mystagogical genius, and been applied to the theme of citizenship in heaven, a metaphor which he uses throughout his *Homilies.* The anointing on the forehead receives its interpretation in this way, as sign of this *parrhesia,* and all that it implies. In a previous *Homily* Theodore had said: "After we have, by our profession of faith, made our contracts and engagements with God our Lord, through the intermediary of the priest, we become worthy to enter His house and enjoy its sight, its knowledge and its habitation, and to be also enrolled in the city and its citizenship. We then become the owners of a great confidence."[296] On this passage Van Unnik remarks: "In view of the connection between *parrhesia* and the rights of a Greek *polites* the last part of this quotation is very striking: the political idea has been transferred to the city of God."[297]

But what exactly is this *parrhesia*, the presence of which is indicated by the *sphragis,* access to which has been obtained by the candidate's act of renunciation of Satan and his "promises" and "engagements" with Christ, a thing which Theodore calls the "first-fruits" of the sacrament, and which results in such a liberation of the candidate that he is able to stand up a free man and with the seal on his forehead as a sort of passport testifying to the presence of this *parrhesia,* gain confident access to the heavenly city as one of its citizens and even possess it to such a degree that he can look upon God with an uncovered face? The answer to this question lies in Theodore's christology. In his first homily on baptism with the express purpose of helping the candidate understand the mystagogy he is going to unfold ("We have spoken in this way so that our words might be better understood; and it is time to show you the reason for every act performed in the sacrament"),[298] Theodore pro-

[296]*Ibid.,* I.27 (*Ibid.,* 366; tr. *ibid.,* 34).

[297]*Art. cit.,* p.14.

[298]*Bapt. Hom.* I.10 (Tonneau-Devreeesse, *SeT* 145, 338; tr. Mingana, *WS* VI, 23).

vides a helpful summary of this christology. Summarizing the reason why God became man Theodore says: "From the fact that the man [Jesus] Who was assumed from us had such a confidence (with God), He became a messenger on behalf of all the human race, so that the rest of mankind might participate with Him in His great change."[299] Understanding this, the candidates will better grasp Theodore's presentation of the sacrament. Commenting on *Rm.* 6:3-4 he says: "Paul clearly taught here that we are baptized so that we might imitate in ourselves the death and resurrection of Our Lord, and that we might receive from our remembrance of the happenings that took place the confirmation of our hope in future things."[300] The full meaning of *parrhesia,* then, becomes clearer in this mystagogical explanation of the anointing when we see the christology and the sacramental theology of Theodore: "We draw nigh unto the sacrament because we perform in it the symbols of the freedom from calamities from which we were unexpectedly delivered, and of our participation in these new and great benefits which had their beginning in Christ our Lord."[301]

The *parrhesia* that we possess, shown by the anointing, is indeed confidence, but not merely my confidence, but a confidence which is a share in the confidence of Jesus Himself. Jesus Christ possessed *parrhesia* by which He was able to conquer death. This same *parrhesia* is given to the baptized, that we may share in Jesus' victory. And this *parrhesia* is not only Jesus' confidence that he would conquer death, but is the element which describes Jesus' perfect union with the Godhead. This free intercourse of men with God and with heavenly things which Theodore describes in his interpretation of the anointing is a result of *parrhesia,* a *parrhesia* which men share in, but which has its basis in Jesus' *parrhesia* with the Godhead.

[299] *Ibid.,* I.9 (*Ibid.,* 336; tr. *ibid.,* 22).
[300] *Ibid.,* I.7 (*Ibid.,* 332; tr. *ibid.,* 20).
[301] *Ibid.,* I.10 (*Ibid.,* 336, 338; tr. *ibid.,* 22).

Theodore's mystagogical explanation of this reality is what Van Unnik calls "proleptic eschatology." "This free intercourse of men with God will not only be a gift for the heavenly future, but it is already enjoyed here where the sacraments are 'proleptic eschatology,' and where the first-fruits of the Spirit are present."[302] As Theodore says: "We strive, therefore, to partake of the Sacrament, because we believe that through symbols, as through unspeakable signs, we possess sometime beforehand the realities themselves."[303]

In the central mystagogical text[304] Theodore's use of 1 *Co.* 13:12 and 2 *Co.* 3:18 to explain the *parrhesia,* the confidence which the stamping on the forehead with oil shows the baptizand as possessing, illustrates his idea of the sacraments as "proleptic eschatology." The Pauline texts, linked together by the words "face" and "mirror" indicate an already present share of the heavenly world which will one day be a complete reality. Furthermore, the stamp on the forehead reveals "so much confidence with God that we look at Him with uncovered face," as Theodore says,[305] repeating with some emphasis this Pauline phrase from the second text which he cites, 2 *Co.*

[302] *Art. cit.,* p. 15.

[303] *Homily on the Eucharist and the Liturgy* II.30 (Tonneau-Devreesse, *SeT* 145, 582; tr. Mingana, *WS* VI, 115). Van Unnik summarizes his analysis of Theodore's use of *parrhesia* thus: ". . . *parrhesia* is an expression of the new life of Christians; the 'freedom of the children of God' who, by the work of Jesus Christ, are no longer separated from the Almighty, Holy and Eternal God, and who, as citizens of God's world, converse with Him as citizens of God's world, converse with Him as their Father. It is a gift of the Holy Spirit which is enjoyed here in the sacraments and in prayer. It is remarkable that though this new life has its ethical implications, the word *parrhesia* is practically restricted to the sphere of the relation between God and man and is not applied to interhuman relationships, such as the preaching of the Gospel." *Art. cit.,* pp. 16-17.

[304] *Bapt. Hom.* II.18 (Tonneau-Devreesse, 396, 398; tr. Mingana, *WS* VI, 46-47).

[305] *Ibid., (Ibid.,* 398; tr. *ibid.,* 47).

3:18, as a link in his train of thought.[306] The notion of the "covered face" as a sign of awe is widespread in antiquity and occurs in a parallel text in Theodore's *Homily on the Eucharist and the Liturgy* where he describes the attitude of the seraphim in *Is.* 6:3: "The spiritual hosts appeared to look with great awe and reverence, since they were looking downwards and covering their faces completely with their wings."[307] An uncovered face is a sign that one feels no shame, as, for example, in the awesome presence of the Holy God.[308]

Thus, the sign on the forehead of the baptizand indicates that the baptizand possesses not a subjective feeling of confidence, but rather this ontological reality, this objective first-fruit of the Spirit, *parrhesia,* which enables him to have free access to God, and gives him the liberty to converse with the Holy God. This is the same objective sense of the word as used elsewhere in the *Homilies,* as we have seen. The anointing with the cross on the forehead, then, according to Theodore's mystagogy, is, so to speak, "the passport for free entrance into the presence of Almighty God."[309]

[306] There is close agreement with the use of these texts from 1 and 2 *Co.* in Cyril's mystagogy of the pre-baptismal anointing on the forehead, albeit seen as one anointing in a series of anointings on other parts of the body. See *Myst. Cat.* III.4 (Piédagnel, *SC* 126, 126; tr. Cross, *SPCK*, 65) and below, pp. 372-373. Chrysostom, without specifically applying it to an anointing, also has this mystagogy of seeing Christ in His glory, and he, too, like Theodore and Cyril, quotes 2 *Co.* 3:18: "But we all, with faces unveiled, reflect the glory of the Lord (Ἡμεῖς δὲ ἀνακεκαλυμμένῳ προσώπῳ τὴν δόξαν Κυρίου κατοπτριζόμεθα." *Stav.* 3.25 (Wenger, *SC* 50, 165; tr. Harkins, *ACW* 31, 64). In this same connection the passage of Ambrose should be mentioned, where he says that the candidate, after renouncing the devil to his face turns to the East and looks on the face of Christ. *Myst.* 7 (Botte, *SC* 25bis, 158; tr. Deferrari, *FC* 44, 7). See above, pp. 63.

[307] *Homily on the Eucharist and the Liturgy* II. 6 (Tonneau-Devreesse, *SeT* 145, 542, 544; tr. Mingana, *WS* VI, 100).

[308] See van Unnik, *Art. cit.,* pp. 20-21.

[309] *Ibid.,* p.21. Van Unnik puts forth "in a very tentative way" the hypothesis that Theodore's emphasis on the uncovered face might possibly indicate a practice in the baptismal ceremonies in which the candidates had their heads covered, and at this point they were uncovered. "This is a mere hypothesis for which no definite evidence has been found thus far, and it is superfluous to add how scanty our evidence for the baptismal practises in the 2nd and 3rd centuries is." *ibid.,* p. 22.

Comparative Summary

There are, in fact, two separate but related elements in this ceremony which form the point of departure for the mystagogical interpretation of Chrysostom and Theodore. The first is the fact of the signing of the candidate's forehead with the sign of the cross. This gesture may, in itself, but need not be performed by using oil to make the sign. The greater part of the mystagogy of Chrysostom and Theodore could conceivably be valid with some adjustments even if oil were not used in the ceremony, since their mystagogy, while utilizing the significance of the oil throughout, refers primarily to the signing with the cross. The second element of the ceremony is the fact that indeed, in these two liturgies in question, an oil is actually employed when the cross is traced on the candidate's forehead. This liturgical fact is taken into account in the interpretation of the ceremony. Here we have a pastoral example of how a liturgy, despite its possible historical changes, can, at a given point be given a plausible explanation using different materials. Here we see both a fundamental similarity in interpreting the ceremony from the standpoint ot the traditional *sphragis,* or seal of belonging. At the same time, in the variety of material which the two mystagogues bring to bear on this ceremony, we see their own particular attempt to utilize materials available to them to give a plausible and meaningful interpretation to the ceremony as it is in the framework of the whole initiation as it takes place at this particular juncture of liturgical history.

Both mystagogues find in the ceremony an apt conclusion to and symbolic expression of what has taken place in the all-important act of renunciation and commitment. Both are at pains to show that the sealing symbolizes *belonging and ownership* because the candidate has just made his contract of faith with Christ. It is this act which enables him to wear the cross as sign of belonging, because by his *syntaxis* he has gone over to the side of Christ. In choosing his Pauline text[310] Chrysostom takes advantage of the fact that the seal is made with oil in order to emphasize that Christ, as it were, takes direct possession of the candidate by Himself anointing Him with His cross. One sees in Chrysostom's use of such a text how a mystagogue is able to apply Scripture to a liturgical act of this sort effectively, even though there is no evidence that St. Paul was thinking of this particular liturgical ceremony when he said that it is "Christ, Who has anointed us."[311] The Pauline expression can quite well be figurative, and not a reference to a specific liturgical act, since anointing is a general biblical sign of election.

In a similar way, but using a different Pauline text and set of images Theodore explains the ceremony as a sign of ownership and belonging. By first drawing attention to the secular practice of tatooing soldiers or branding animals, he then uses *Ep.* 2:19 to link up this seal of the cross with the name-plate of ownership in a household. Through their engagements in the *apotaxis-syntaxis,* the candidates have qualified for membership in God's household, which membership is visibly symbolized by this sign of the cross on their forehead.

Thus, both mystagogues show the ceremony as sign of belonging and ownership, but through different approaches, Chrysostom utilizing the fact that the sealing is an anointing, and through St. Paul, showing Christ's direct action in performing it, and Theodore, not emphasizing the anointing, but rather the sign of the cross itself linked through a different Pauline text to the secular signs which represent membership in a household.

In interpreting the seal as a *sign of appointment for life task and protection,* it is the underlying theological emphasis on Christian Initiation which determines the difference of approach to the mystagogy of the essentially similar ceremony.

Chrysostom's pastoral emphasis on the Christian struggle

[310] See above, p. 118.
[311] 2 *Co.* 1:21.

which Christian Initiation imports leads him to link the seal with the combat arena. Joining the ranks or team of Christ in his *syntaxis* the candidate now wears His sign. Again, Chrysostom is able effectively to link *sphragis* and the liturgical fact that this sign of the cross is performed as an anointing. The olive oil which forms the substance for the anointing is a reminder for Chrysostom of the similar oil used to rub down athletes before combat. Thus, Chrysostom draws together the *sphragis* as sign of membership on Christ's team and the use of oil in making that sign through his theology of Christian combat against evil, thus again linking the ceremony mystagogically with the *apotaxis-syntaxis.* This same association of cross and anointing is carried yet further by Chrysostom in connection with his theology of struggle. Because the *sphragis* is the sign of the cross, it contains the power of the cross. It is apparently the glistening quality of the oil used in tracing this sign on the forehead which permits Chrysostom then to see the cross as the power of a brilliant lightning flash which blinds the eyes of the devil.

While also using this *sphragis* ceremony as an appointment for a life task, Theodore's theology is less on the combat metaphors of belonging to Christ's team and being His athlete. In this respect he concentrates not on the anointing but on the fact of the sign of the cross as sign of Christ's suffering, death and victory, using 2 *Tm.* 2:11-13 to interpret the sign of the cross made on the forehead as the call to follow Christ through suffering to glory.

It is Theodore's theology of the world to come, however, which leads him to choose quite remarkable materials to interpret this ceremony as sign of the *first-fruits of final victory,* materials not present in Chrysostom's mystagogy, and part of which, interestingly enough, are used by Cyril, but there in connection with the post-baptismal anointing! [312]

Theodore's mystagogy here rests on the central concept of freedom to which the candidate is tending, a freedom which will be complete in the heavenly city, but which through the

[312] See below, ch. 3, pp. 372-373.

sacrament is actually present in some way even now. Since, as we have seen, in the act of renunciation the candidate is liberated from a tyrant and by his act of commitment has come to the free service of Christ, this anointing becomes in Theodore's mystagogy one of several symbols of what this freedom means and it is in this sense that he selects the material for interpreting it, just as Chrysostom had concentrated on material such as the sign of membership on Christ's team or oil for the athlete which illustrates his message of Christian struggle. Here is an example of how two different emphases guide the selection of mystagogical materials. The combat aspect of the act of renunciation and commitment in Chrysostom determines his mystagogical emphasis of the *sphragis* ceremony; the freedom aspect of this act determines Theodore's mystagogy of the same ceremony.

The bishop's robe, sign of the freedom and joy of heaven, rising from the knees, the *orarium,* or linen head band of the free man, and then the remarkable application of 1 *Co.* 12:12 and 2 *Co.* to explain the fact that the candidate's forehead glistening with the sign of the cross is a sign of freedom, that is, of his ability to raise his head from shame and now look at God with open face because it reveals that he is now in possession of "*parrhesia*," or confidence, the very interior life with which the Son of God gazes eternally at His Father: this is the gift of the Spirit, the gift of adoption as Son of God as Christ is natural Son of God. All of this is presented by Theodore with the cultural reference to the concept of political freedom in the Greek city-state, where the candidate's *sphragis* becomes the sign of citizenship in the heavenly city.

Indeed, in this mystagogy it will not escape notice that Theodore, as mystagogue, is not only governed by "proleptic eschatology" in his sacramental theology, but also that he is employing in this interpretation a kind of liturgical prolepsis. The candidates, after all, are not even baptized at this point in the initiation rites, and yet Theodore is speaking of this ceremony as though the candidate had received all the prerogatives of baptism. This style of mystagogy becomes less surprising as a kind of unjustified anticipation, if we remember that in the Eastern mode of thought the process of initiation is seen not as a linear series of points on a straight line, but rather as a circle or ellipse, as a totality, the center of which can "unlogically" influence the other parts, even in an anticipatory way.[313] Theodore particularly disperses mystagogical material in application to different ceremonies which seems to overlap. The fact that Cyril uses certain material to interpret the post-baptismal anointing which Theodore uses here to interpret the *sphragis* anointing only serves to show how the mystagogues view Christian Initiation as a totality and feel free to use traditional materials to emphasize this or that particular point which concerned the Church at the time.[314] It is obvious that due to such progressive mystagogical development the actual historical origin of a ceremony can become blurred, and at a certain point the mystagogy no longer plausible as when the ceremony itself has nothing to do intrinsically with the explanation given to it, or when it degenerates into mere allegory.

In the case of Chrysostom and Theodore and their mystagogy of this *sphragis* anointing these errors are avoided and we see remarkable versatility in presenting an interpretation of the ceremony which takes into account the actual ceremony itself, the cross and the oil, its place in the whole unfolding of the initiation, the tradition of the *sphragis* as sign of belonging and ownership, the apt use of Pauline writings and the cultural awareness of the hearers.

If we compare, by way of conclusion, Chrysostom and Theodore in their christological approach to this concluding ceremony of the renunciation and commitment, we see that divergent though the two appear, they are actually facets of that unity of faith in Christ and participation in His life and sacrifice which is represented by the ceremonies of Christian Initiation. In Theodore's explanation, the interior gift which the candidate displays before God by virtue of the sign of his forehead, that confidence, *parrhesia,* is nothing other than the

[313]See also below, ch. 3, n. 144, p. 399.
[314]See below, ch. 3, n. 143, pp. 397-398.

participation in the *parrhesia* which the man Jesus possesses in His unity with the Godhead, and in which, as "first-fruits of the sacrament," the candidate participates. This is actually the same reality under a different mystagogical emphasis, of which Chrysostom, in his explanation of the sign has spoken, participation in the life of Christ. He expresses it, however, under the image of the cross, stamped by God Himself on the baptizand's forehead and shining forth like the rays of the sun, linking it, as we have seen,[315] through the image of this light to the sacrifice on Good Friday, when the culminating expression of *parrhesia* was uttered by Jesus in giving man access to the Holy God: "Father, into Thy hands I commend my Spirit." In both cases it is an interior apprehension of the life, sacrifice and eternal reality of Jesus Himself, whether seen as the cross, which shines forth from the candidate's forehead "like a lightning flash,"[316] or as the stamp which enables one to look at God confidently, "with uncovered face."[317]

This analysis of how two fathers, Chrysostom and Theodore approach the ceremony of anointing in their mystagogical explanations shows both their common unity in subsuming on the materials of tradition, such as the long history of the idea of the *sphragis,* and the underlying idea of union with Christ in His relationship to the Godhead, as well as their individual genius in interpreting what is essentially the same ceremony. Theodore has, in consistency with his notion of the "citizenship of heaven" taken the *NT* word *parrhesia* and blended it with the many personal and political overtones of the word as it is used in respect to the rights of a Greek citizen, and emphasizing the victory it represents. Chrysostom, in his profound meditation on the meaning of the cross of Jesus has concentrated on this sign of anointing, and with the same underlying reality of the life of Jesus, through the use of the athletic and combat metaphor, shown how the candidate through this ceremony is appointed to join in the struggle of Jesus, in

[315]See above, pp. 68-69.
[316]See above, pp. 121-122.
[317]See above, pp. 125, 130.

coming, under the protection of this sign, to the ultimate victory.[318]

[318]The mystagogical achievement of the fathers in combining the natural and cultural symbolism of their world with Christian revelation in the liturgical process is well summed up by G. Kretschmar, *op. cit.,* pp. 158-159: "In a society in which fundamental Christian principles were beginning to gain obvious recognition, these rites of the catechumenate and the requirement of the discipline of the secret – even though to a great extent by now a fiction – maintain the principle that being a Christian is not simply an obviosity. Union with the Holy God through Christ is not something that may be had cheaply. To confess Him and call Him Father is a gift and an authorization. In the Syrian liturgy explanations free access to God as characteristic of the Christian now begins to receive special emphasis. According to 2 *Co.* 3:18 the Christians may look upon the glory of God 'with uncovered face.' That is almost the language of the mysteries, however Paul originally understood this word. That being a Christian is a gift and not something earned – true, a gift that carries with it obligations – and that Christian faith lives not from the *loci communes* of a wordly metaphysic but from the Word of God in the writings of the *OT* and the *NT* in the fellowship of the Church – this could be expressed in the categories of the mystery theology better than with the intellectual apparatus of the philosophical enlightenment and theodicy, of which the Christian apologetes had so readily availed themselves. . . . On the threshold between pagan and Christian antiquity, in a world for which the ancient mysteries were no longer worthy of trust, but a world which still knew about them nonetheless, the new liturgy offered precisely new possibilities for understanding. The fact that at the time the dangers implicit in this did not yet appear is due to the achievement of the great theologians and pedagogues of the early imperial church. (In einer Gesellschaft, in der christliche Grundsätze begannen zur anerkannten Selbstverständlichkeit zu werden, halten diese Katechumenatsriten und die Forderung einer Arkandisziplin – auch wenn sie weithin Fiktion war – fest, dass Christsein das eben nicht Selbstverständliche ist. Gemeinschaft mit dem Heiligen Gott durch Christus ist nicht billig zu haben. Ihn zu bekennen und als Vater anzurufen ist Gabe und Ermächtigung. In den syrischen Liturgieerklärungen wird jetzt mit besonderer Betonung der freie Zugang zu Gott als Kennzeichnung des Christen genannt; sie dürfen nach 2. Kor 3,18 die Herrlichkeit des Herrn 'mit aufgedecktem Angesicht' schauen. Das ist schon fast die Sprache der Mysterien, wie auch immer dies Wort ursprünglich von Paulus gemeint war. Dass Christsein nicht Leistung sondern Gabe – allerdings verpflichtende Gabe – ist, und christlicher Glaube nicht von den Gemeinplätzen einer Allerweltsmetaphysik lebt, sondern vom Worte Gottes in der Schrift des Alten und Neuen Testaments in der Gemeinschaft der Kirche, das liess sich eben in den Kategorien einer Mysterientheologie besser ausdrücken als mit den Denkmitteln etwa der philosophischen Aufklärung und Götterkritik, die von den christlichen Apologeten so gern aufgegriffen worden waren. . . . An der Schwelle zwischen heidnischer und christlicher Antike, in einer Welt, der die alten Mysterien unglaubwürdig geworden waren, die aber noch um sie wusste, bot die neue Liturgik auch gerade neue Verstehensmöglichkeiten. Dass damals die Gefahren noch nicht so in Erscheinung traten, war eben auch das Werk der grossen Theologen und Pädagogen der frühen Reichskirche.)"

Summary and Conclusion

Viewed in the abstract, the preaching of the Good News calls the hearer to faith in Christ, an act which unavoidably implies a rejection of all that is disconsonant with this faith, a *metanoia.* It is the liturgy of initiation which in varied forms expresses in a body and soul concreteness this *metanoia.* Due to the very flesh and blood nature of a human being and his relationship to the world around him this expression must be dramatic: word and action. The function of mystagogy is to explain this liturgical drama, to reveal as deeply and as widely as possible the meaning of what is said and done.

In their mystagogy of this first major step in this liturgy of Christian Initiation the four fathers have chosen a variety of materials accessible to the understanding of their hearers in fulfilment of this purpose of interpretation.

By treating the fathers in detailed, individual analysis of the materials brought to bear on this rite we have attempted to reveal their individual style, their consistency, that which stamps each of the four mystagogies with the individual genius of its author. This task then carried out in detail, it has been possible to compare and contrast their several approaches, a comparison which, while methodologically admittedly difficult due to the wide scope of the material of the mystagogy, has still been rendered possible by the general basic unity of the initiation rites at this particular historical period. For the purpose of this analysis and comparison it has been necessary methodologically to group the rite under the headings: bodily movements, reciting the formula, and the concluding anointing.

Our study of the mystagogical interpretation of this rite has shown that natural symbol and contemporary cultural symbol have been related in an unforced way to the liturgical drama itself to reveal its meaning and that the use of the biblical framework of salvation history has been the guiding principle used to illumine the drama in its ultimate religious meaning, the presence in the liturgy of God's own activity. This last has been the means by which the fathers have attempted to bring the candidates to awareness of the unique and specifically Christian meaning of the liturgical events, the Christian "mystery" or "sacrament."

The cumulative effect of the mystagogy shows the vast effect which the act of faith, and its counterpole, rejection of non-faith, has on the individual, his relationship with himself, who he is, his position in time and history in relationship to God's salvific plan, his relationship to his cultural and social environment and its conflicting demands, the unique and absolute seriousness which characterizes his radical decision when the moment comes for him to accept the full responsibility of uttering the words, "I renounce you, Satan, and I commit myself to you, O Christ," words which then become a solemn public act and irrevocable "confession" both in heaven and on earth.

In the language of bodily gesture and in the solemnity of the human word, two worlds are shown to meet one another in a point of crisis, God's and man's, *kairos* and *chronos,* both, however, inextricably interwoven, yet distinct. And this interaction is the sacramental principle.

The adversary is named and confronted, in word and in bodily symbolic gesture, and this word and these gestures are shown in full scope of meaning by recourse to the varied meaning of such images as rising and falling, turning to Paradise, rejection and imploring and adoration, slavery and freedom, human unity, legal contract, light and darkness, the intimacy of bridal love, the longing for a new heaven and earth to come, yet appearing in the human struggle of the vision of the suffering Jesus already transfigured in glory, a curious rejection of the "world," yet in the very moment of rejection, a possession now deeper of the same world in Christ as Lord of all, present in faith, yet struggling to be born in the courageous and temporal rejection of all that is still disconsonant with the universal Lordship of Jesus Christ.

For example, the very choice of such a culturally meaningful symbol as slavery and freedom, which runs through so much of the mystagogy we have seen, shows how strongly the fathers saw the inextricable intertwinement between commitment to Christ and its social repercussions in one's context of life. The apparent simplicity of choosing such a symbol as that of slavery and freedom to interpret much of the liturgy ought not to appear, due to the dust of centuries, as a mere harmless obviosity. So much is made in this regard of the turning and kneeling and rising, and the personal confrontation with the adversary precisely because they carried with them implications for membership in the Christian Church which were based on an actual confrontation with the problems of the day. As a matter of fact, the dimensions of these human problems are made more acute precisely by revealing the deeper religious dimensions inherent in them. This the mystagogy does by combining cultural symbol with biblical material. Underlying this mystagogy are demands which would startle (and please) even the most enthusiastic and "radical" of the modern social apostles. As a matter of fact, the radical demand which such apostles today make on the church are, in the light of this patristic mystagogy of the rejection of Satan and the commitment to Christ anything but far-fetched. On the contrary, they just about come close to what the fathers consider the norm in rejecting Satan and being committed to Christ. The fathers are not presenting a detached, scholarly investigation into the liturgy, nor a mere esthetic exposition of liturgical ceremonies. They are dead serious, and their catecheses are for concrete candidates wrestling with concrete problems of the Christian life. One looks in vain through this mystagogy to find a single sentence that is not relentlessly uncompromising in its practical demands in the act of renunciation and commitment. People elsewhere may have other positions, but for these mystagogues, initiation into the Christian Church carries with it no "ifs" "ands" or "buts," and the unity of their mystagogical presentation reveals the inexorableness of their position, based on their understanding of the meaning of faith and its opposite. In their mystagogy they present really no alternative to an irrevocable life choice of universal dimension which infuses the entire life of the candidate.

The mystagogy of the anointing on the forehead with the sign of the cross continues and rounds off the deepening awareness of what happens in the rite of renunciation and commitment. The interpretation of the sign of the cross as a seal of belonging, a symbol imbedded in the culture of the times as was the anointing of the athlete for his struggle, the symbol of anointing the face as sign of the removal of shame and the intimacy of face-to-face gaze, a natural and cultural symbol of especial importance in the bible, this is the material which Chrysostom and Theodore use to interpret the concluding ceremony of the rite. The ceremony is seen as a kind of symbolic recapitulation of what has taken place in the act of renunciation and commitment itself. As Chrysostom's mystagogy had reached its high point when he considered the act of faith under the image of a dowry which the bride brings to the Bridegroom, so Theodore's presentation reaches its apex in his treatment of the anointing as sign of confidence, *parrhesia,* which permits the final face-to-face intimacy of man and God, present now through faith, and finally to be revealed in its completeness later.

Thus, by recourse to a rich variety of material, always allied plausibly to the given liturgical ceremony, Cyril, Chrysostom, Theodore and Ambrose have been able to present to their hearers an instruction on the meaning of the first of the initiation rites remarkable both in its depth and in its scope.

CHAPTER TWO

BAPTISM

The Mystagogical Catecheses of Cyril of Jerusalem, John Chrysostom, Theodore of Mopsuestia and Ambrose of Milan, whatever difference of detail they might reveal in describing this or that ceremony of Christian Initiation, or whatever presence or omission might be found in regard to certain ceremonies, all reveal a definite *caesura* in passing from their treatment of the rite of renunciation and profession to the rite of baptism itself. The interpretation of the ceremonies which they had undergone, given by the fathers to the newly baptized, demonstrate by the manner in which they are grouped in the catecheses, that the fathers considered the entire rite to be centered on two major poles, the first being the candidate's act of committing himself to Christ and renouncing Satan, and the second, the baptismal bath itself. The interpretation of the individual ceremonies derives from their implied relationship to these two centers of influence in the liturgical drama.[1]

This second chapter will deal with this second of the major poles, the baptismal act itself. It will take into consideration not only how the four fathers interpreted the baptismal bath itself, but will also include their interpretation of the ceremonies which precede this act, since the fathers themselves interpret these preceding ceremonies in relationship to the central ceremony of the baptismal bath. Whatever the historical origin of such ceremonies may have been, as, for example, customs from the world of secular antiquity, the mystagogical writings see them in the light of the baptismal act, with its central

[1] For a historical sketch of this development see A. Stenzel, *Die Taufe,* Forschungen zur Geschichte der Theologie und des innerkirchlichen Lebens, eds. H. Rahner, J. Jungmann, Heft VII/VIII (Innsbruck, 1957).

Christian meaning. Indeed, whatever the prior Christian liturgical history of the ceremonies might have been, the fathers apply their own particular "mystagogical" genius to them, and without doing violence to the Christian tradition, present to the newly baptized a comprehensive and unified interpretation of the rite. As in the preceding chapter, so here too, by comparing the main lines of mystagogical interpretation, by analyzing the materials the fathers use to construct their interpretations, by comparing and contrasting the several approaches, the individual genius of each father will be thrown into relief, and at the same time an attempt will always be made to point up the underlying unity which is at the heart of their diversified pastoral program of explaining the rite of initiation to their neophytes.

The method will be the same as in Chapter One. The synopsis of the ceremonies as found in each of the four fathers will be presented. Then, the mystagogical interpretations which the fathers give to these ceremonies will be analyzed and compared. As in the case of the rite of renunciation and commitment, so here too, the ceremonies are common enough to all four fathers to warrant such comparative analysis.

The mystagogical interpretation of the ceremonies of baptism is divided into two parts, *Part One* deals with the ceremonies which precede the baptismal bath itself, namely, (1) the removal of clothing and nakedness, and (2) the anointing before the baptismal bath. *Part Two* deals with the mystagogical interpretation of the baptismal bath proper.

Synopsis of the Ceremonies

Cyril

The rite of renunciation and commitment having been completed "in the outer chamber (*ἐν τῷ ἐξωτέρῳ . . . οἴκῳ*)"[2] of the baptistery, the candidates then proceed to the "inner chamber (*ἐσωτέρῳ οἴκῳ*)."[3]

[2] *Myst. Cat.* I.11 (Piédagnel, *SC* 126, 102; tr. Cross, *SPCK,* 58).
[3] *Ibid.,* II.1 (*Ibid.,* 104; tr. *ibid.,* 59).

Here they divest themselves of their garments, and stand there "naked in the sight of all (γυμνοὶ... ἐν ὄψεσι πάντων)."[4]

Once stripped of their clothing, the candidates were then anointed with "exorcised oil (ἐλαίῳ ἐπορκιστῷ)" "from the topmost hairs of their head, right down to their feet (ἀπ' ἄκρων κορυφῆς τριχῶν ἕως τῶν κατωτάτων)."[5]

After this anointing the candidates were led by the hand to the "holy pool (ἁγίαν κολυμβήθραν)"[6] of baptism.[7]

Arrived at the pool each candidate was asked separately whether he believed in the name of the Father and of the Son and of the Holy Spirit, and "you made this saving confession (ὡμολογεῖτε τὴν σωτήριον ὁμολογίαν)."[8]

[4] *Ibid.*, II.2 (*Ibid.*, 106; tr. *ibid.*, 60). Piédagnel, *SC* 126, 105, n. 1, remarks: "Il est probable que certaines précautions étaient prises pour respecter la pudeur," and notes how Cyril, in arranging the preparatory exorcisms takes pains to preclude any semblance of impropriety by having men and women sit in different groups. See *Procat.* 14 (Cross, *SPCK*, 9; tr. Cross, *SPCK*, 48-49). In imagining, however, what these precautions might be here and for the anointing of the body and descent into the pool, it must be born in mind that the symbolism of the return to the Garden of Eden is in play here, as we shall later see (below, p. 181). Therefore the unabashedness of the candidates in the fact of their mutual exposure is precisely the point which Cyril wishes to make in his idea of the return to primitive innocence. He says specifically: "O wondrous thing! You were naked in the sight of all, and were not ashamed; for truly you bore the likeness of the first-formed Adam, who was naked in the garden, and was not ashamed (ὢ θαυμασίου πράγματος· γύμνοι ἦτε ἐν ὄψεσι πάντων, καὶ οὐκ ῃσχύνεσθε. Ἀληθῶς γὰρ μίμημα ἐφέρετε τοῦ πρωτοπλάστου Ἀδάμ, ὃς ἐν τῷ παραδείσῳ γυμνὸς ἦν καὶ οὐκ ῃσχύνετο)." *Myst. Cat.* II.2 (Piédagnel, *SC* 126, 106; tr. Cross, *SPCK*, 60. Therefore, the precautions taken to protect modesty must not be imagined to be such as to destroy the symbolism of innocent nakedness. F. Dölger, *Der Exorzismus im altchristlichen Taufritual* (Paderborn, 1909), p. 107 ff, has shown that the term "γυμνός" need not necessarily mean of itself total nakedness, but can still apply even if one is wearing an undergarment.

[5] *Myst. Cat.* II.3 (Piédagnel, SC 126, 106; tr. Cross, *SPCK*, 60).

[6] *Ibid.*, II.4 (*Ibid.*, 110; tr. *ibid.*, 60).

[7] While Cyril makes no mention here of the blessing of the baptismal water, *Bapt. Cat.* III.3 (*MG* 33.428) alludes to it: "Ordinary water, having received the invocation of the Holy Spirit and of Christ and of the Father, receives sanctifying power (τὸ λιτὸν ὕδωρ Πνεύματος ἁγίου καὶ Χριστοῦ καὶ Πατρὸς τὴν ἐπίκλησιν λαβὸν δύναμιν ἁγιότητης ἐπικτᾶται)."
For further references see Piédagnel, *SC* 126, 110, n. 1.

[8] *Myst. Cat.* II.4 (Piédagnel, *SC* 126, 110; tr. Cross, *SPCK*, 60).

Then the candidate plunged three times into the water and similarly emerged from it three times.[9]

Chrysostom

The rite of renunciation and commitment having been completed by the first, or "sphragis" anointing, the candidate "in full darkness of night (*κατὰ τὸν τῆς νυκτὸς καιρὸν ὁλόκληρον*)"[10] has his robe stripped off him by the "priest (*ἱερεύς*)."[11]

Then, the priest (or bishop) causes the candidate's whole body to be anointed with the "olive oil of the spirit (*ἔλαιον πνευματικόν*)."[12]

[9] *Idem.*

[10] *Stav.* 2.24 (Wenger, *SC* 50, 147; tr. Harkins, *ACW* 31, 52). Since, according to *P.K.* 3.4 (*VGS,* 171; tr. Harkins, *ACW* 31, 166, no. 19) the rite of renunciation and commitment, along with its anointing took place on Good Friday afternoon at three o'clock, this note as to the time seems to indicate that this second anointing took place on Holy Saturday night, since baptism immediately follows it. See above, ch. 1, p. 28 and n. 29.

[11] *P.K.* 3.8 (*VGS,* 173; tr. Harkins, *ACW* 31, 170, no. 28). In the liturgies of Cyril and Theodore the candidates removed their clothes themselves. (See above, p. 144 and below, p. 147). The "Priest" here can also mean the bishop, given the interchangeability of terms as Chrysostom uses them. See above, ch. 1, p. 30 and n. 33.

[12] *Stav.* 2.24 (Wenger, *SC* 50, 147; tr. Harkins, *ACW* 31, 52). The way in which Chrysostom describes the liturgical action here, "he causes your whole body to be anointed (*ἅπαν τὸ σῶμα ἀλείφεσθαι παρασκευάζει*)," rather than stating directly that the priest or bishop anoints the body seems to indicate that not the priest or bishop , but others did the actual anointing. This is understandable, given a large number of candidates and an anointing of the entire body, rather than, *e.g.* merely of the forehead, as with the anointing after the act of renunciation and commitment. (See above, ch. 1, p. 31). Theodore mentions other ministers for this function, without specifying who they are. (See below, p. 148). The oil which was used in the first anointing was called "oil of the spirit (*ἔλαιον πνευματικόν*)," (see above, ch. 1. p. 31). It was a Chrism (*χρίσμα*)," which Chrysostom explained as being composed of "olive oil (*ἔλαιον ὁμου*)" and "unguent (*μύρον*)," (see above, ch. 1, p. 31 and n. 267). The oil in this second anointing seems, from this comparison of terms, to be only "olive oil (*ἔλαιον ὁμοῦ*)," since no mention of "unguent (*μύρον*)" is made. See also T. Finn, *op. cit.,* pp. 130-133.

The priest (or bishop) then leads the candidate down "into the flowing waters (*ἐπὶ τὰ νάματα*)".[13]

The priest (or bishop)[14] places his right hand on the candidate's head, pushes it down into the water and lifts it out three times saying, "So-and-so is baptized in the name of the Father and of the Son and of the Holy Spirit (*βαπτίζεται ὁ δεῖνα εἰς τὸ ὄνομα τοῦ πατρὸς καὶ τοῦ υἱοῦ καὶ τοῦ ἁγίου πνεύματος*)."[15]

Theodore

Upon completion of the "sphragis" anointing and the other ceremonies connected with the rite of renunciation and commitment, the candidates proceed to the "remaining part of the sacrament."[16]

Arrived at the place of baptism, the candidates take off all their garments.[17]

Then they are anointed on their whole body with the "oil of anointing."[18]

[13]*P.K.* 3.8 (*VGS,* 173; tr. Harkins, *ACW* 31, 170, no. 28). See also *Stav.* 2.25 (Wenger, *SC* 50, 147; tr. Harkins, *ACW* 31, 51) where the reading is: "He makes you go down into the flowing waters (*εἰς τὰ ἱερὰ νάματα καθίησιν*)."

Was there a blessing of the font? Drawing from a) parallels with Cyril (see above n. 7) and with Theodore (see below, n. 20); b) the fact that Chrysostom often calls the baptismal waters "sacred" and "divine;" c) *Stav.* 2.10 (Wenger *SC* 50, 138-139; tr. Harkins, *ACW* 31, 47), where Chrysostom says: It is the grace of the Spirit which sanctifies the nature of the water and touches your head together with the hand of the priest (*ἡ τοῦ Πνεύματος χάρις ἐστὶν ἡ καὶ τῶν ὑδάτων τὴν φύσιν ἁγιάζουσα καὶ μετὰ τῆς χειρὸς τοῦ ἱερέως ἐφαπτομένη σου τῆς κεφαλῆς*)," one may infer that the font was blessed. Apparently, however, Chrysostom. like Cyril and Theodore, does not bring an explanation of this ceremony into the *Baptismal Instructions* because it seems that this was not a rite in which the candidates actively participated. Theodore, for example, seems to be speaking of the rite as though describing to the candidates something which they themselves had not actually witnessed (see below, n. 20).

[14]See *Stav.* 2.10 (Wenger, *SC* 50, 138; tr. Harkins, *ACW* 31, 47.

[15]*Ibid.,* 2.26 (*Ibid.,* 147; tr. Harkins, *ACW* 31, 52). *Cf. P.K.* 3.3 (*VGS,* 169-170; tr. Harkins, *ACW* 31, 164, 165, nos. 12, 14).

[16]*Bapt. Hom.* II.20 (Tonneau-Devreesse, *SeT* 145, 400; tr. Mingana, *WS* VI, 47).

[17]*Ibid.,* III. text (*Ibid.,* 400; tr. *ibid.,* 48).

[18]*Idem.*

It is the bishop who begins this anointing saying, "So-and-so is anointed in the name of the Father and of the Son and of the Holy Spirit," and then, "others appointed for this service" continue the anointing on the entire body.[19]

The baptismal water has already been consecrated by the bishop by an invocation of the Holy Spirit.[20]

Clad in the same shining apparel that he had put on for the first of "sphragis" anointing,[21] the bishop conducts the baptism in the following way.

The candidate descends into the water.[22] The bishop, standing, extends his hand and places it on the candidate's head. Then he says, "So-and-so is baptized in the name of the Father," at the end of which phrase he exerts pressure on the candidate's head, who, hearing these words and following the leading pressure of the bishop's hand, bows down his head and immerses himself in the water. Then the candidate raises his head back up, out of the water. The bishop then says, "and of the Son," and in the same way, following the pressure of the bishop's hand as he says this phrase, the candidate bows down his head a second time and immerses himself in the water. After he raises his head back out of the water, the candidate hears the bishop say the third phrase, "and of the Holy Spirit," and for the third time, following the pressure of the bishop's hand, the candidate, bowing his head, submerges and raises his head back out of the water.

Then the candidate leaves the pool.[23]

[19]*Bapt. Hom.* III. text, 8 (Tonneau-Devreesse, *SeT* 145, 400, 402, 418; tr. Mingana, *WS* VI, 48, 54).

[20]*Ibid.,* text, 9, 14 (*Ibid.,* 402, 418, 430; tr. *ibid.,* 48, 54, 58). The only indication as to when this consecration of the baptismal water took place is the notation of Theodore that in undertaking it the bishop wore the same garment which he had changed into for the first or "*sphragis*" anointing concluding the ceremony of renunciation and commitment (see above, ch. 1, p. 33), and which he is still wearing for the baptism itself. *Bapt. Hom.* III.14 (Tonneau-Devreesse, *SeT* 145, 430; tr. Mingana, *WS* VI, 58).

[21]See above, ch. 1, p. 33.

[22]*Bapt. Hom.* III. text (Tonneau-Devreesse, *SeT* 145, 402; tr. Mingana, *WS* VI, 48).

[23]*Ibid.,* text, 14, 18-19 (*Ibid.,* 402, 430, 440, 442; tr. *ibid.,* 48, 58, 62-63).

Ambrose

The candidates, who had already entered the baptistery area for the first anointing and the subsequent act of renunciation,[24] now approach to within sight of the baptismal font.[25] The bishop consecrates the font[26] by exorcising the water

[24] See above, ch. 1, p. 27.

[25] See *Sacr.* I.9 (Botte, *SC* 25bis, 64; tr. Deferrari, *FC* 44, 272).

[26] See *Myst.* 8; *Sacr.* II.14 (*Ibid.,* 158, 80; tr. *ibid.,* 7, 283). Of the four fathers it is Ambrose alone who makes a specific mention of the ceremonies of the consecration of the font in this context of the chronological unfolding of the baptismal rite. It is the barest mention, depending on the word "consecrantem" of *Myst.* 8. This sparse picture of the action of the consecration of the font in the context of the baptismal ceremonies is not appreciably expanded by the other reference in *Sacr.* II.14, where essentially the same action is noted, namely, "the bishop comes and says a prayer at the font (venit sacerdos precem dicit ad fontem)." Indeed, the impression is conveyed particularly from the context of *Myst.* 8, where the arrival of the candidates at the font is described, that this ceremony was not one in which the candidates actively participated, but rather one which was already in progress from the side of the bishop when they arrived at the font. In this sense it seems to be a sacerdotal ceremony which does not have a direct liturgical significance or mystagogical importance, as do the other ceremonies in the Initiation.

As has already been noted (see above, n. 7, p. 145), *Cyril* alludes to a consecration of the font, but this allusion does not come in his *Mystagogical Catecheses,* but rather in his *Baptismal Catecheses.* It is not clear when this ceremony takes place. At any rate it is not treated in the ceremonies of the baptismal rite and their mystagogical interpretation. From evidence and supposition we have inferred a consecration of the font in *Chrysostom* (see above, n. 13, p. 147). But here, too, the ceremony plays no particular role in the general structure of the mystagogical explanation of the rite of Christian Initiation. *Theodore,* as has been pointed out (see above, p. 148 and n. 20), notes that the baptismal water has already been consecrated by the bishop, but he does not say when this took place, nor is it of particular importance in the ritual structure he is presenting. Further, it is uncertain whether the candidates took part in such a ritual of consecration. Theodore seems to be speaking of the ceremony as though describing to the candidates something which they themselves had not actually witnessed.

The ceremony of consecrating the font, then, even though evidence of it is present in the four fathers, is not one which they deal with with direct emphasis in the ritual structure they present for the mystagogical interpretation of the baptismal rite. The explanation of this is most probably due to the liturgical fact mentioned above, namely that this ceremony of consecrating the font is a sacerdotal ceremony concerned with the preparation of the font for baptism, and therefore not necessarily one in which the candidates were impressed by a primary form of active participation. For this reason it would not be central to "what was said and by an invocation plus a prayer for the sanctification of the font and for the presence of the Trinity.[27]

The candidate then descends into the font, where the bishop, a priest, and some deacons are standing.[28]

The candidate is asked, "Do you believe in God, the Father almighty (Credis in Deum, Patrem omnipotentem)?"

He replies, "I believe (Credo)." And he submerges in the water.

The candidate is asked, "Do you believe in our Lord Jesus Christ and in His cross (Credis in Dominum Nostrum Jesus Christum et in crucem ejus)?"

He replies, "I believe (Credo)." And he submerges a second time in the water.

The candidate is asked, "Do you believe also in the Holy Spirit (Credis et in Spiritum Sanctum)?"

He replies, "I believe (Credo)." And he submerges a third time in the water.[29]

Then the baptized climbs out of the font.[30]

and what was done" to the candidates on the night of their baptism (*cf. Myst. Cat.* I.1, Piédagnel, *SC* 126, 84; tr. Cross, *SPCK,* 53), and so is not directly emphasized by the fathers in presenting their mystagogy of Christian Initiation.

Allusion to the blessing of the font will occur, however, briefly in the mystagogy of baptism as new birth when Theodore presents the picture of the water womb (see below, p. 332). When Ambrose treats this same picture, and brings in the comparison of the miraculous birth of the baptized with the Virgin Birth, there is possibly also an echo of the ceremony of the blessing of the font (see below, pp. 309-311). Chrysostom, in presenting the mystagogy of baptism as new birth, presents the Church as mother womb, and, like Ambrose, uses the mystery of the Virgin Birth to elucidate the new birth of the baptized. It is possible, but by no means provable, that his mystagogy is also echoing the rite of the blessing of the font (see below, pp. 317-320).

On the blessing of the font see B. Neunheuser, "De benedictione aquae baptismalis," *Ephemerides Liturgicae* 44 (1930) 194-207, 258-281, 369-412, 455-492; H. Scheidt, *Die Taufwasserweihegebete* (Münster, 1935); E. Stommel, *Studien zur Epiclese der römischen Taufwasserweihe* (Bonn, 1950); J. Quasten, "The Blessing of the Baptismal Font in the Syrian Rite of the Fourth Century," *Theological Studies* 7 (1946) 309-313.

[27] See *Sacr.* I.18 (Botte, *SC* 25bis, 82; tr. Deferrari, *FC* 44, 275).

[28] See *ibid.,* II.16 (*Ibid.,* 82; tr. *ibid.,* 284).

[29] See *Sacr.* II.20; *Myst.* 28 (*Ibid.,* 84, 86, 170; tr. *ibid.,* 286, 15).

[30] See *Myst.* 29 (*Ibid.,* 172; tr. *ibid.,* 15).

Comparative Summary

This synopsis of the ceremonies comprising the rite of baptism is based on the indications of the mystagogical writings themselves. As has already been noted in discussing the synopsis of ceremonies connected with the rite of renunciation and commitment what is included for mention by each father and what is omitted is determined by his plan of mystagogical commentary. By his mention of this or that ceremony, for example, "after this you did such and such," or "and then you heard these words," he is presenting to the mind of the neophyte not the entire ritual structure in every detail, but such points as he intends to interpret in his mystagogical catechesis, and out of which he has tried to compose a certain unity of mystagogical commentary.

In bringing together the ceremonies mentioned in connection with the ritual of baptism in this synoptic form, one can see at a glance the remarkably similar ritual structure present in all four fathers. The very choice of such similar points of emphasis, which when drawn together in this synoptic way reveal such a similar ritual structure, is itself an indication of the unity of the mystagogical interpretation which these fathers attempt to provide for the given liturgy. These points of emphasis may be drawn together in the following summary way.

From the standpoint of ritual structure—and it must be borne in mind that this ritual structure as here presented in the mystagogical writings is not in the form of a handbook of ceremonies, but a structure the purpose of which is designed to provide a framework for a unified mystagogical interpretation of the ritual, and which thereby becomes itself in a sense part of the mystagogy—one notes *first* the *caesura* or transition emphasized between the previous rite of renunciation and commitment and this new phase of the initiation.

Cyril mentions the movement of the candidates in the framework of the physical structure of the baptistery, the change of position from the "outer chamber," where the ritual of renunciation and commitment had taken place to the "inner chamber," where the ritual of baptism will take place. *Chrysostom* brings out this transition by emphasizing the time difference between the rite of renunciation and commitment and that of baptism, the former having taken place on Good Friday at three in the afternoon, the latter "in the full darkness of night." *Theodore* divides the two parts of the initiation on the basis of inner structure, calling the baptismal rite, "the remaining part of the sacrament," as well as noting the physical movement of the candidates from one place to the other. *Ambrose* emphasizes the transition also by noting the change of position of the candidates, and in a way similar to Cyril reminds them that only after the renunciation and commitment do they come within sight of the baptismal font.

The *second* point which strikes one in this grouping of the ceremonies for mystagogical commentary is a frame of two ceremonies which preceed the baptismal act: the removal of garments and the anointing with oil. Ceremonies laden with both practical as well as pagan and Jewish-Christian background, the fathers manifest their intention to deal with them at length and to provide for them suitable mystagogical interpretation. These two ceremonies form the principal concern for the mystagogues prior to the baptismal act itself.

Further indications as seen in the synopsis of ceremonies make it obvious that a secondary transition then takes place between the treatment of these two pre-baptismal act ceremonies, the removal of garments and the anointing, and the actual baptism itself, which clearly becomes the climax and most important part of the initiation process as far as the mystagogical writings are concerned. This transition from the ceremonies at the edge of the baptismal pool and the baptismal bath itself is the *third* feature of the ritual structure which strikes one from the synopsis of ceremonies.

What is an obvious fact, namely that after everything else has been done, the candidate must finally enter the baptismal pool, is underscored, especially by Cyril and Chrysostom indicating by such dramatic emphasis that a central mystagogical interpretation will be applied to the entire complex of actions which make up the baptismal bath, starting with the very practical movement of going to the pool itself.

Finally, the *fourth* outstanding feature which emerges from this synoptic comparison of ceremonies is the presentation of the baptismal bath itself as the central action of the initiation process. Provided with a dramatic introduction which is forged out of an action of practical necessity, one sees the very detailed attention given to each particular of the baptismal act itself.

The following synoptic chart provides an overview of the ritual structure which has emerged as a result of collating the ceremonies in synoptic form from the indications provided in the mystagogical writing of the four fathers.

SYNOPTIC CHART

The Ceremonies of Baptism

Cyril	*Chrysostom*	*Theodore*	*Ambrose*
First: Caesura: Rite of Renunciation – Rite of Baptism:			
Outer Chamber-Inner Chamber	Day-Night	Remainder of Sacrament	Sight of Font
Second: Ceremonies preceding baptismal bath:			
Undressing	Undressing	Undressing	
Anointing with exorcised oil	Anointing with oil of spirit	Anointing with oil of anointing	
Third: Transition to baptismal bath proper:			
Led to pool	Led to pool		Approach pool
			Consecration

The Ceremonies of Baptism—continued

Cyril	*Chrysostom*	*Theodore*	*Ambrose*
Fourth: The baptismal bath:			
Confession of faith	Confession of faith (?)		
	Led into pool	Descent into pool	Descent into pool
Triple plunge	Triple immersion of head by priest (bishop)	Triple head bow & triple immersion, bishop directing with hand	Triple plunge
Triple emersion	Triple raising of head	Triple emersion & raising head	
	Formula by priest (bishop)	Formula (distributed) by bishop	Triple question-answer, formula distributed
		Leaves pool	Ascends from pool

The Mystagogical Interpretation of the Ceremonies

The newly-discovered *Stavronikita* series of the *Baptismal Instructions* of St. John Chrysostom contain two paragraphs which in remarkably condensed form reveal practically the entire mystagogical dynamic which is at work in these fourth century explanations of the rite of Christian Initiation:

> Next after this [i.e., the first, or "sphragis" anointing,] he [the priest or bishop] strips off your robe and, as if he were going to lead you into heaven itself by the ritual, he

> causes your whole body to be anointed with that olive oil of the spirit, so that all your limbs may be fortified and unconquered by the darts which the adversary aims at you.
>
> After this anointing the priest makes you go down into the sacred waters, burying the old man and at the same time raising up the new, who is renewed in the image of his Creator. It is at this moment that, through the words and the hand of the priest, the Holy Spirit descends upon you. Instead of the man who descended into the water, a different man comes forth, one who has wiped away all the filth of his sins, who has put off the old garment of sin, and put on the royal robe.[31]

Such a passage as this, highly compressed though it is and containing a number of themes which require separate development, reveals the central thought which the fathers will use to interpret the rite of baptism with all the attendant ceremonies. The central thought is the Pauline theology of Adam and Christ, the old man and the new man. In this light, the candidate who lays aside his clothes, is anointed, plunges into the pool where he is baptized, and the person who emerges, puts on new clothes and is anointed, are "two different men." A new birth, a new creation has taken place, which has many ramifications. The mystagogical writings show, step by step in their interpretation of these ceremonies, just how such a remarkable reality comes to be through this symbolic action, and they indicate some of its ramifications. This thought is the "magnetic pole" whose sphere of influence reaches out to the "satellite" ceremonies and provides their interpretation.

[31] *Stav.* 2.24-25 (Wenger, *SC* 50, 147; tr. Harkins, *ACW* 31, 52): *Εἶτα μετὰ τοῦτο κατὰ τὸν τῆς νυκτὸς καιρὸν ὁλόκληρον ἀποδύσας τὸ ἱματιον καὶ καθάπερ εἰς αὐτὸν τὸν οὐρανὸν εἰσάγειν μέλλων διὰ τῶν τελουμένων οὕτως ἅπαν τὸ σῶμα ἀλείφεοθαι παραοκευάζει τῷ ἐλαίῳ· ἐκείνῳ τῷ πνευματικῷ ὥστε τάντα τὰ μέλη διὰ τῆς ἀλοιφῆς τειχισθῆναι καὶ ἀχείρωτα γενέσθαι τοῖς παρὰ τοῦ ἐναντίου πεμπομένοις βέλεσι. Μετὰ τὴν ἀλοιφην τοίνυν ταύτην εἰς τὰ ἱερὰ νάματα καθίησιν, ὁμοῦ καὶ θάπτων τὸν παλαιὸν ἄνθρωπον καὶ ἀνιστὰς τὸν νέον τὸν ἀνακαινούμενον καὶ εἰκόνα τοῦ κτίσαντος αὐτόν. Τότε λοιπὸν διὰ τῶν ῥημάτων τοῦ ἱερέως καὶ τῆς τούτου χειρὸς ἡ ἐπιφοίτησις ἐφιπταται τοῦ Πνεύματος τοῦ ἁγίου καὶ ἄλλος ἀντ' ἄλλου ἄνεισι, πάντα τὸν ῥύπον τῶν ἁμαρτημάτων ἀποσμηξάμενος καὶ ἀποδυσάμενος τὸ παλαιὸν τῆς ἁμαρτίας ἱμάτιον καὶ ἐνδυσάμενος τὴν ἐσθητα τὴν βασιλικήν·*

I

THE CEREMONIES PRECEDING THE BAPTISMAL ACT

In his essay on the original structure of the baptismal rite, with its emphasis on the historical genesis and the forces which were at work gradually shaping this structure, A. Stenzel[32] shows that originally the two major poles of the initiation rite were not those which the four fathers imply in sketching their ritual structure for mystagogical interpretaion, namely the act of renunciation of Satan and commitment to Christ as a sort of self-enclosed rite on the one hand, and the rite of baptism on the other. The development of the initiation rite as the fathers encountered it in the fourth century led naturally to this division in their presentation, which reflects the actual liturgical state of development. The original center of the initiation, reflecting the scriptural admonition to believe and be baptized was the baptismal act itself, that is, the bath of water and just prior to it, or along with it, the baptismal confession of faith, the act of commitment to Jesus Christ. Because this positive confession of adherence to Christ, this *turning toward* Christ, intimately connected with the baptismal bath, implies a *turning away* from someone or something, a ritual of contrast was built up gradually, the negative side of the baptismal confession of faith in Christ, the "renunciation of Satan." Material for the development of this ritual lay in the elements which the candidate would renounce if he were really serious about his act of commitment to Christ. These would be spelled out in the practices of the pagan world which were to be rejected as a cultural entity opposed to God.

This ritual of renunciation, the "apotaxis," which grew up little by little and was actually the reverse side of the positive baptismal confession of faith, soon gained a ritual independence of its own as it gained in scope and importance. As it became more separated from the side of the baptismal pool,

[32] *Op. cit.*, p. 104.

so to speak, due, for example, to large numbers of candidates causing it to be held on another day than that of the baptism itself, it began to demand its own opposite piece for ritual balance, since its own original opposite, the baptismal confession of faith, had become so far removed from it. There developed, then, along with the original act of commitment joined with the baptismal bath, the original baptismal confession of faith, a second act of commitment, the "syntaxis" which formed the balanced opposite to the renunciation or "apotaxis." Particularly in the East was this development noticeable, and this is reflected in the treatment of the act of renunciation and commitment in Cyril, Chrysostom and Theodore, as has been treated in Chapter One.[33]

Since the "apotaxis," the original opposite piece to the baptismal confession of faith, and originally closer in time to the actual baptismal bath, was viewed as a turning away from a world which had fallen under the domination of Satan, it is not strange that numerous exorcistic motifs clustered around the rite of renunciation, and that exorcistic interpretations would be suggested for the ceremonies which were close to this act of renunciation. Even though the act of renunciation had removed itself ritually in time and space from the baptismal bath, ceremonies close to the baptismal bath, which, due to practical considerations, could not accompany the act of renunciation in its migration, remained under the influence of interpretation suggested by the act of renunciation, that

[33]See above, ch. 1, n. 17, pp. 25-26. Stenzel, (*op. cit.,* pp. 104-105), summarizes the development as follows: "A new word came into use: commitment. A rite which is verifiable with certainty only in the East and is determinant for many a characteristic of this area. In some way a surprising rite, when considered from the standpoint of the Western ritual, since structurally in the West there are two opposite pieces, baptismal-confession and renunciation. The decision as to which is the more original form is not difficult to make: the West remained more conservative. (Es war ein neuer Name gefallen: Zusage. Ein Ritus, der mit Sicherheit nur im Osten nachweisbar ist und für manche Eigentümlichkeit dieses Bereichs bestimmend ist. Ein irgendwie erstaunlicher Ritus, wenn man ihn vom westlichen Ritual her betrachtet. Da, im Westen, sind nämlich strukturmässig die Gegenstücke: Taufbekenntnis und Absage. Die Entscheidung darüber, was die ursprünglichere Form sei, fällt nicht schwer: der Westen ist konservativer geblieben)." See also Stenzel, p. 105, n. 99.

is, exorcistic interpretation. Such exorcistic interpretation of the ceremonies preceding the baptismal bath will be seen in this section of the fathers' mystagogy, where they treat the removal of clothing and nakedness and the anointing of the whole body.[34]

Such ceremonies, which lend themselves to an interpretation which underscores the renunciation of Satan, would seem to suggest classification by the fathers with the "pole" which has been treated in Chapter One, the act of renunciation. They belong to what Stenzel calls, "Gestures which underscore the active role of the candidate in the renunciation."[35] For practical reasons, however, the ceremonies are treated by the fathers in conjunction with the baptismal bath. Stripping and being anointed as preparation for the bath cannot practically be performed a day or more in advance, even though the ceremonies underscore the meaning of renunciation.[36] But also, for mystagogical reasons, as will become evident, the fathers treat these ceremonies in conjunction with the baptismal bath, because they wish to invest them

[34]"Since it is a question of dealing with the devil, it is not surprising that also exorcistic motifs occur in the accompanying ceremonial: the hair loosened (a significant meaning of this rite is contained in the fact that with the loosening of the hair, the ornaments have to be removed in which the demons could easily reside) – the nakedness (likewise to prevent the demons from entering the water along with the candidate . . .) and similar motifs. (Da es um die Auseinandersetzung mit dem Teufel geht, ist nicht verwunderlich, dass auch exorzistische Motive im Begleitzeremoniell auftauchen: die gelösten Haare (eine Sinnspitze dieses Ritus liegt darin, dass damit der Schmuck entfernt werden musste, in dem leicht die Dämonen sitzen konnten) – die Nacktheit (ebenfalls um zu verhindern, dass die Dämonen mit ins Wasser steigen . . .) u. a. mehr)." Stenzel, *op. cit.*, p. 102. The classical study on this subject is F. Dölger, *Der Exorzismus im altchristlichen Taufritual* (Paderborn, 1909).

[35]*Op. cit.*, p. 102; "Gestik, die die aktive Rolle des Täuflings in der Absage unterstreicht."

[36]"In a direct and 'practical' way, however, the loosening of the hair, undressing, etc., point to that ceremony which stands in closest relationship to the renunciation: to the anointing and the baptismal bath which follows it. Direkt und 'praktisch' aber weisen Lösen des Haares, Ausziehen usw. auf die Zeremonie hin, die mit der Absage in engstem Zusammenhang steht: auf die Salbung (und das nachfolgende Taufbad)." Stenzel, *op. cit.*, p. 102.

with a creative interpretation, which goes beyond the exorcistic, or better said, deepens and broadens the exorcistic motifs present in these ceremonies.

This brief historical portrayal is important to provide the proper perspective to appreciate how the fathers, confronted with "given" ceremonies, all of which had a secular and a Christian history behind them, were able to give a coherent and meaningful interpretation to these ceremonies.

A. Removal of Clothing and Nakedness

Apart from the practical considerations of removing one's clothing to facilitate either the anointing of the body or the baptismal bath, F. Dölger had already pointed out the exorcistic and cathartic considerations in the ancient world which made of this ceremony a symbolic act.[37] Moreover, both in pagan and in Jewish antiquity, the materials out of which clothing was made, putting on and taking off of clothing: all of this could have high symbolic value.[38]

It is most instructive, when considering such a point as this in the mystagogical writings to see how the fathers, given the various currents of tradition, pagan, Jewish and Christian, associated with clothing, managed to form for their neophytes an intelligible instruction in the meaning of the symbols, an instruction which is creative, that is, which receives a new focal point of unity through the application of Christian materials in the interpretation, chiefly Holy Scripture, and which at the same time includes in the interpretation an

[37] F. Dölger, *Der Exorzismus im altchristlichen Taufritual* (Paderborn, 1909), pp. 107-118.

[38] J. Quasten, "A Pythagorean Idea in Jerome," *American Journal of Philology*. 63 (1942) 207-215, deals with the significance of animal skins *vs.* linen. Shame, mortality, death is represented by such animal skins as wool. Joy, immortality, life, is represented by cloth made from plants, such as linen. Behind this idea of the mortality of the "tunics of skin" which Adam wore (*Cf. Gn.* 3:21) is the ancient conception that clothes are peculiarly liable to attract the influence of the spirits. See E. Peterson, *Pour une théologie du vêtement* (Lyons, 1943), p. 17. For clothing as symbol of passions and mortality in the ancient world, both pagan and Jewish, see P. Oppenheim, *Symbolik und religiöse Wertung des Mönchskleides im christlichen Altertum* (Münster, 1932), pp. 8-18.

awareness of the real environment from which the neophytes come.

This is precisely the creative nature and function of "mystagogy," and demonstrates why it must be done anew in each culture, using the same basic principles. One sees that the mystagogue must be aware of two worlds, the present culture around him along with some analysis of its historical and psychic presuppositions, and the world of revelation the underlying activity of which must be revealed through the words and actions of the liturgy, joined as they are in different ways and on different levels to secular symbols.

How, then, do the fathers interpret the action of the removal of clothing and the consequent nakedness so as to help the neophyte to that "deeper understanding" of the meaning of what was done to them?

The mystagogical interpretations which Cyril, Chrysostom and Theodore give to the laying aside of the garments and the ensuing nakedness may be grouped under three headings: *first,* the moralistic interpretation, *second,* the mortality-immortality theme, and *third,* the return to primeval innocence.

The following chart provides a synoptic view of the elements comprising the interpretation, the sources in the mystagogical writings, and the chief scriptural material used in the interpretation.

SYNOPTIC CHART

The Mystagogy of the Removal of Clothing and Nakedness

Cyril	*Chrysostom*	*Theodore*
The Moralistic Interpretation:		
Removal of old man & his deeds	Removal of old man & his deeds	
-Pauline Image *Myst.Cat.* II.2 *Col.* 3:9	-Pauline Image *Stav.* 2.25 *Col.* 3:9	
-Wedding Allegory *Procat.* 3-4	-Wedding Allegory *Montf.* 2.15-20	
Mt. 22:1-14	*Mt.* 22:1-14	
-Bridal Image *Bapt.Cat.* III.2 *Mt.* 22:9-10	-Bridal Image *Stav.* 1.3	
	-Old burden of Sin	
	Stav. 4.3,12 2 *Co.* 5:17	
	-Vain & Seductive Display *Stav.* 1.32-38 *Montf.* 2.39-47 *Ga.* 5:18-24 1 *Tm.* 2:9	
The Mortality-Immortality Dimension:		
Principalities & Powers *Myst.Cat.* II.2 *Col.* 2:15		Mortality of Adam *Bapt.Hom.* III.8 *Gn.* 3:21

The Mystagogy of the Removal of Clothing and Nakedness—continued

Cyril	*Chrysostom*	*Theodore*
Eschatological Symbolism *Myst.Cat.* I.10 *Is.* 25:8; 61:10 *Rv* 21:4 *Myst.Cat.* II.2 *Sg.* 5:3		
The Return to Primeval Innocence:		
Baptistery as Paradise *Procat.* 15 *Myst.Cat.* I.1 *Myst.Cat.* II.2 *Gn.* 2:25	Baptistery as Paradise *P.K.* 3.28-29 *Gn.* 2:25	Adam in Paradise *Bapt.Hom.* III.8 *Gn.* 2:25

1. The Moralistic Interpretation

a. *Cyril*

(1) *The Old Man and His Deeds*

(a) *The Pauline Image*

Cyril first employs a Pauline image to provide his first step in interpreting for the neophyte the meaning of stripping off his clothing before the baptismal act. The metaphor underlying St. Paul's statement, ". . . having stripped off the old man with his deeds (ἀπεκδυσάμενοι τὸν παλαιὸν ἄνθρωπον *σὺν ταῖς πράξεσιν αὐτοῦ*),"[39] is that of a person removing his clothing. With the removal of this clothing, then, symbolically the old self is peeled off as well, and the evil deeds which emanate from this old self. The counterpart of this will, of course, be the putting on a new self, and with it the corresponding Christian behavior which emanates from this new self.[40] Thus, St. Paul continues, ". . . having put on a new man, which will progress towards true knowledge the more it is renewed in the image of its Creator."[41]

Following this Pauline clothing metaphor, Cyril states explicitly the symbolism to be understood in the removal of garments at this point of the baptismal ceremonial: "As soon therefore as you entered in, you put off your garment; and this was an image of putting off the old man with his deeds (*εὐθὺς γ'οὖν εἰσελθόντες, ἀπεδύεσθε τὸν χιτῶνα· καὶ τοῦτο ἦν εἰκὼν τοῦ τὸν παλαιὸν ἄνθρωπον ἀπεκδύσασθαι σὺν ταῖς πράξεσιν*)."[42]

(b) *The Allegory of the Wedding*

Cyril also develops the idea of the garment as a sign of the vices of the old man in a rather long allegory based on the Gospel parable of the wedding feast.[43] In verses 11-13 of this parable the allegorical scene of the wedding shifts to the notion of the Last Judgement. With that background one of the guests at the banquet is condemned by the host for failing to dress for the occasion by wearing a proper wedding garment. The point in the Gospel is that good works (the proper garment) must go hand in hand with faith (the free invitation to the wedding banquet).

Cyril embellishes the story with a twist of his own suitable to his mystagogy of the old garment as a sign of the vices of the old self. In instructing those who are beginning their Lenten

[39] *Col.* 3:9.

[40] *Cf. Col.* 3:12-14.

[41] *Col.* 3:10.

[42] *Myst. Cat.* II.2 (Piédagnel, *SC* 126, 104, 106; tr. Cross, *SPCK,* 59).

[43] *Mt.* 22:1-14. See *Procat.* 3-4 (Cross, *SPCK,* 2-3; tr. Cross, *SPCK,* 41-43).

preparation for baptism[44] he has the bridegroom approach the guest (the baptismal candidate) and berate him for wearing "dirty clothes." Cyril applies dirty clothes then as a symbol of the guest's failure to get rid of his bad habits, his taking advantage of the host's generosity in slipping by the doorkeeper (his enrollment in the catechumenate, particulary in the intensive Lenten preparation for baptism) though improperly dressed: "You have been free to enter with a soul bemired with sins, and a defiled purpose."[45] Because he simply continued along with the many other guests, but never really made the conscientious effort to get rid of his "dirty clothes" and become like the others in fashion and purpose, he is thrown out of the wedding banquet.[46]

The garments which one has on represent the vices which one has and which cannot simply be cloaked over, but must be torn off, avarice, for example, fornication and uncleanness: "If avarice has been the fashion of your soul, put on another, and then come in: put off what you had, do not cloak over: put off, I pray you, fornication and uncleanness and put on the most bright robe of soberness."[47]

(c) *The Bridal Image*

Occuring outside of the *Mystagogical Catecheses* but closely allied to them, one finds Cyril using this same image of dirty clothing as morally unacceptable acts which must be changed before baptism. Again the Gospel image of the marriage banquet occurs[48] where the king's messengers go to the crossroads and invite everyone to the wedding banquet. The candidate is advised by Cyril "to set to work washing your garments

[44] See *Procat.* 4, where Cyril speaks of the forty days of penitential preparation.

[45] *Procat.* 4: *Ἐγχωρεῖ δὲ σε βεβορβορωμένην ἔχοντα τὴν ψυχὴν ἁμαρτίαις, καὶ τὴν προαίρεσιν ἐσπιλωμένην, εἰσελθειν.*

[46] See *Procat.* 3.

[47] *Procat.* 4: *Εἰ φιλάργυρον ἔχεις τὸ σχῆμα τῆς ψυχῆς, ἄλλο ἐνδυσάμενος εἴσελθε· ἐκδυσαί μοι πορνείαν καὶ ἀκαθαρσίαν, καὶ ἔνδυσαί μοι σωφροσύνης λαμπροτάτην στολήν.*

[48] *Cf. Mt.* 22:9-10.

through conversion so that the call of the nuptial chamber will find you ready."[49]

b. *Chrysostom*

(1) *The Old Man and His Deeds*

(a) *The Pauline Image*

Chrysostom uses the same metaphor from St. Paul[50] to interpret the removal of garments before the baptismal bath as does Cyril: "We put off the old garment, which has been made filthy with the abundance of our sins, we put on the new one, which is free from every stain."[51]

Later in the same *Instruction*, although referring to the cleansing of the baptismal bath, Chrysostom reverts back to the picture of the removal of garments at the side of the pool. He describes the man coming forth from the baptismal pool as the man "who has wiped away all the filth of his sins, who has put off the old garment of sin and put on the royal robe."[52]

Echoes of this Pauline image, the putting off of morally unacceptable actions as one puts off dirty clothes occur with great frequency throughout the *Baptismal Instructions* and this is a favorite pedagogical vehicle of Chrysostom.

(b) *The Allegory of the Wedding*

Like Cyril, Chrysostom also uses the Gospel image of the marriage banquet[53] to expand his mystagogy of the removal of garments before baptism. Cataloguing numerous aspects of conduct unworthy of the Christian[54] he urges the candi-

[49] *Bapt. Cat.* III. 2 (*MG* 33.425): Ἄρξασθε πλύνειν τὰς στολὰς ὑμῶν διὰ μετανοίας, ἵνα εἰς τὸν νυμφῶμα καθαροὶ κληθέντες εὑρεθῆτε.

[50] *Cf. Col.* 3:9-10.

[51] *Stav.* 2.11 (Wenger, *SC* 50, 130; tr. Harkins, *ACW* 31, 47): ἀποδυόμεθα μὲν τὸ παλαιὸν ἱμάτιον τὸ ὑπο τοῦ πλήθους τῶν ἡμαρτημένων καταρρυπωθέν, ἐνδυόμεθα δὲ τὸ καινὸν καὶ πάσης κηλῖδος ἀπηλλαγμένον.

[52] *Ibid.*, 2.25 (*Ibid.*, 147; tr. *ibid.*, 52): See above pp. 154-155 and n. 31.

[53] *Mt.* 22:1-14.

[54] *Montf.* 2.15-17 (*MG* 49.233-234; tr. Harkins, *ACW* 31, 177-178).

dates for baptism not to come to this feast wearing a garment covered with the filth of such works, but to take one suitable for the wedding feast.[55] The habit of evil deeds, the filthy garment, must be overcome, otherwise the new garment could become soiled as well.[56]

(c) *The Bridal Image*

Chrysostom also uses the image of the invitation of the bridegroom to the bride, as did Cyril. This bridal imagery is much more fully developed in Chrysostom's mystagogical writings than in those of Cyril, and is a frequently recurring image. The candidate for baptism is the bride, called to the nuptials. Called into the nuptial chamber, the bride must be stripped of her sordid garments, the sins of her past which have deformed her.[57]

(d) *The Old Burden of Sin*

Speaking to the neophytes of the benefits of baptism Chrysostom tells them of the confidence they can have since they are now God's sons. They have put on the royal robe. Before they put on this robe, however, they put off the burdens of their sins. The image here is that the weight of sins was symbolized by the weight of the old and soiled clothing which the candidates had put off before baptism: "They have put off their burdens of sins, and put on the royal robe."[58]

Further on in the same *Instruction* commenting on the Pauline idea of the old creation and the new creation,[59] Chrysostom contrasts this old and this new under the same image of putting off and taking on clothing. Those who believe in Christ have passed from the old creation to the new

[55] See *ibid.*, 2.18 (*MG* 49.234; tr. *ibid.*, 178).

[56] See *ibid.*, 2.20 (*MG* 49.234; tr. *ibid.*, 178-179).

[57] See *Stav.* 1.3 (Wenger, *SC* 50, 110; tr. *ACW* 31, 23-24).

[58] *Ibid.*, 4.3 (*Ibid.*, 183; tr. *ibid.*, 67): *τὰ τῶν ἁμαρτημάτων ἀποθεμένοι φορτία καὶ τὴν βασιλικὴν ἐνδυσάμενοι στολήν.*

[59] *Cf.* 2 *Co.* 5:17.

creation. A symbol of this is that they have "put off like an old cloak the burden of their sins."[60]

(e) *Vain and Seductive Display*

Up until this point Chrysostom reveals an almost identical parallel with Cyril in presenting his mystagogy of the removal of garments before the baptismal bath. Laying aside of garments as putting aside the old man and his deeds is treated in a general way by both. At this point, Chrysostom, the moral preacher, cannot leave the subject of the deeds of the old man without spelling out in some detail what these deeds might be, and warning and threatening against them. The mystagogical interpretation of the ceremony contained in these observations of Chrysostom is suggested by the very fact of clothing itself, and the sociological, moral and even esthetic considerations of clothing, and the ornaments such as jewelry which form an integral part of dress, form the materials of the mystagogy. If bad deeds in general should be stripped off, clothing itself, not only as symbol of the deeds of the old man, but actually as revelation of vain display and seduction, must be criticized and corrected in the candidate who wishes to adhere to Christ. This is the most literal of the moralistic interpretations of the ceremony, and is peculiar to Chrysostom.

Chrysostom's point of mystagogical departure is Pauline, the catalogue of virtues and vices which reflect the work of the flesh as opposed to the work of the Spirit.[61] Elaborate ramifications of the works of the flesh as a result of impropriety in the matter of clothing[62] show Chrysostom's concern for the moral probity and seriousness of purpose of the candidates.

Unnecessary luxury in the matter of dress and bodily adornments, expensive clothing and jewelry, is a sin against social justice: "That you may wear a single ruby, countless poor

[60] *Stav.* 4.12 (Wenger, *SC* 50, 189; tr. Harkins, *ACW* 31, 71): *καθάπερ ἱμάτιον παλαιὸν ἀποδυσάμενοι τῶν ἁμαρτημάτων τὸ φορτίον.*

[61] *Ga.* 5:18-24.

[62] See *Stav.* 1.34-38 (Wenger, *SC* 50, 125-128; tr. Harkins, *ACW* 31, 36-39); *Montf.* 2.39-47 (*MG* 49.237-238; tr. Harkins, *ACW* 31, 184-187).

are starved and crushed."[63] Moreover, such luxurious display signifies vanity, is an inducement to frivolous living and envy and even to thievery, in proportion to its luxury. This clothing and jewelry is to be stripped off, since it represents and leads to the deeds of the old man, and in its place should come good works, through which the soul will become attractive and shine.

It is particularly against luxury and seductiveness in the clothing of women that Chrysostom hurls his strongest rhetorical bolts. He advises them to adorn themselves with virtues rather than clothing and cosmetics. Since it is often the very clothing and adornment of women which prompt the vices disconsonant with the Christian life, suspicion, jealousy, quarrels,[64] best to be rid of this, and put on in its place such adornment as almsgiving and modesty.[65] In this way women will draw angels to themselves as their lovers, rather than men, and will have God's approval rather than man's admiration. God will win over their husbands to these women in every way, since their virtue, not their clothing and other adornments will shine forth. Using the classic passage from St. Paul, ". . . not with braided hair of gold or pearls or expensive clothing,"[66] Chrysostom advises the women candidates for baptism:

> Strip off your adornment and put it in Christ's hands through the hands of His poor. He will guard all your riches for you against the day when He will raise up your body with great glory. Then He will put on you a better wealth and a richer adornment, since your present wealth and adornment are really paltry and ridiculous.[67]

Attention to the frivolity of luxurious clothing rather than zeal in good deeds is, then, really a dangerous distraction for

[63] *Montf.* 2.41 (*MG* 49.237; tr. Harkins, *ACW* 31,185): Καὶ γὰρ ἵνα σὺ κόκκον ἕνα φορέσῃς, μυρίοι τῷ λιμῷ πένητες ἄγχονται.

[64] See *ibid.*, 2.42 (*MG* 49.237; tr. *ibid.*, 185).

[65] See *ibid.*, 2.42-43 (*MG* 49.237; tr. *ibid.*, 185-186).

[66] 1 *Tm.* 2:9.

[67] *Montf.* 2.46 (*MG* 49.238; tr. Harkins, *ACW* 31, 187): περιελομένη τὸν κόσμον ἅπαντα εἰς τὰς τοῦ Χριστοῦ χεῖρας ἀπόθου διὰ τῶν πενήτων. ἐκεῖνος σοι φυλάξει τὸν πλοῦτον ἅπαντα, ἐπειδὰν ἀναστήσῃ σου τὸ σῶμα μετὰ πολλῆς τῆς λαμπρότητος· τότε σοι βελτίονα περιθήσει πλοῦτον καὶ κόσμον μείζονα, ὡς ὅ γε παρὼν οὗτος εὐτελὴς καὶ καταγέλαστος.

those committed to Christ. The stripping away of such clothing, then, as exemplified in the ceremony in question, is a singularly apt and literal symbol of the true versus the false values that Christian Initiation will impart.

Not only luxury, and the vices which spring from that, but sheer seductiveness in the matter of women's clothing and what goes with it are also taken to task by Chrysostom. Cosmetics, such as rouge and eye-shadow, are an insult to the Creator, since such "painting of the face" implies that the Creator's workmanship was originally defective. Rather than adding to the beauty of the face, they actually destroy the soul:

> Especially are you heaping up abundant fire for yourself by exciting the looks of the young men, and attracting to yourself the eyes of the undisciplined; by making complete adulterers of them, you are bringing their downfall on your own head.[68]

Chrysostom concludes his diatribe by urging women to more good works, and directing that, at least when they come to Church, they are not to wear cosmetics and eye-shadow, which he calls an "outrageous practice," which St. Paul most certainly would have forbidden. Stripping off of such habits, like stripping off of clothing, will be a sign of return to good deeds, otherwise:

> But you have forsaken these virtues. You are trying to trip up many of the careless ones, even in church. By what thunderbolts do such actions deserve to be punished? You arrive in port and you cause your own shipwreck. You come to the physician to have your wounds cured, and you go away after making them worse.[69]

[68] *Stav.* 1.37 (Wenger, SC 50, 127-128; tr. Harkins, *ACW* 31, 38): Ἄλλως τε καὶ πολὺν ἐπισορεύεις διὰ τούτου σαυτῇ τὸ πῦρ, τὰς τῶν νέων ὄψεις ἀναπτε ροῦσα καὶ τοὺς τῶν ἀκολάστων ὀφθαλμους ἐπισπωμένη καὶ μοιχοὺς ἀπηρτισμένους ἐργαζομένη καὶ τὸν ἐκείνων ὄλισθον εἰς την σὴν ἕλκεις κεφαλήν.

[69] *Ibid.*, 1.38 (*Ibid.*, 128; tr. *ibid.*, 38): Συ δε ταῦτα καταλιποῦσα πολλους τῶν ῥαθύμων καὶ ἐν τῇ ἐκκλησία ὑποσκελιξείν ἐπιχειρεῖς. καὶ πόσων ταῦτα ἄξια σκηπτῶν; Εἰς τὸν λιμένα παραγίνῃ καὶ ναυάγιον σαυτῇ κατασκευάζῃ. πρὸς τὸν ἰατρὸν ἔρχῃ τὰ ἕλκη θεραπεῦσαι καὶ μείζονα αὖτα ἐργαζομένη ἀπέτχῃ.

Thus, from material connected with the cultural habits of everyday life as reflecting social and moral problems of the times, Chrysostom expands the mystagogical interpretation of a ceremony the very nature of which lends itself rather well to the suggestion of such literal interpretation. The Bishop or priest strips off the candidate's clothing before he can enter the pool of baptism says Chrysostom. Then in that stripping of garments, strip off luxury, vanity, seductiveness, and though naked, realize that what you have given to the poor through the hand of Christ, will be returned to you in a glory beyond that which fine clothing or jewelry of make-up could ever achieve. The material of this mystagogy, drawn though it is from the everyday life of the candidates whom Chrysostom is instructing, is never very far from the similar concern of St. Paul for the Christian community, a fact of which Chrysostom continually reminds his bearers by his constant reference to St. Paul.

Comparative Summary

On this level of the moralistic interpretation of the removal of clothing before baptism, Cyril and Chrysostom present a mystagogy which is quite parallel in imagery and in scriptural sources. Both proceed consciously from the Pauline metaphor of laying aside the deeds of the old man as one might lay aside old clothing. Both use the Gospel allegory of the wedding feast as an exhortation to increased moral effort, getting rid of the soiled clothes of bad inclinations and evil habits so as not to come improperly clothed to the feast. Cyril uses the image to make certain references to the stages of enrollment at the beginning of that Lent at the end of which the catechumen wished to be baptized. And so he compares the doorkeepers and the assembly where the instruction is held to the group assembling for the marriage feast, remarking how the candidate with soiled clothes can actually get by the doorkeepers by just following the crowd, but eventually must face the embarrassment of exposure. It is not too late, however, even now to change: "Depart in good time now, and enter in tomorrow better,"[70] and the reminder is given that the candidate has forty days to do penance. The ominous warning, however, is not omitted for those who show no serious intent to change: "for though the water shall receive you, the Spirit will not accept you."[71] Chrysostom applies the allegory in the same context, an instruction to those who are going to be baptized, and he likewise uses the urgency of the coming wedding feast to stress the necessity of serious moral purpose in the candidates.

Subjoined to the allegory of the wedding is then the image of the bridal call, also used in common by both Cyril and Chrysostom in their instructions to the candidates prior to baptism, and with a specific emphasis on the clothes of the bride. For both fathers, soiled clothing represents an unworthy condition for appearing for the marriage. For Cyril, the garments must be washed, representing conversion from evil deeds; for Chrysostom, the bridegroom himself will take care of this, and not reject the bride, even though these garments are soiled.

Chrysostom goes farther than Cyril in elaborating on the deeds of the old man. Aside from the small catalogue in the *Procatechesis*[72] Cyril does not go into detail on these deeds from the standpoint of a literal interpretation of the meaning of clothing for the Christian life. Chrysostom, on the other hand, adds a further mystagogical interpretation of the ceremony on this moralistic level. Since, as he points out, the acts of the old man are part of an old creation, which is passing away—here following Pauline instruction, sins, like old clothes are part of the old burden which can be laid aside and must be laid aside. In vivid and literal mystagogy, then, clothing becomes for Chrysostom not merely the Pauline symbol, but a reality of Christian conduct in its implications.

[70] *Procat.* 4 (Cross, *SPCK.* 3; tr. Cross, *SPCK,* 42): *ἔξελθε εὐκαίρως τὰ νῦν, καὶ εἴσελθε αὔριον εὐκαιρότατα.*

[71] *Idem (Idem;* tr. *ibid.,* 43): *τὸ μὲν γὰρ ὕδωρ σε δέξεται, τὸ δὲ πνεῦμά σε οὐ δέξεται.*

[72] *Idem (Idem;* tr. *ibid.,* 42).

Implications of the clothing which the candidates wear, and of which they are stripped before baptism, become the matter of this literal interpretation on the moralistic level of mystagogical interpretation. This includes economic considerations: the exploitation of the poor represented by jewelled clothing; social considerations: class envy, jealousy, represented by vain show in oversumptous dress; moral considerations: the question of seduction, represented particularly in dress and make-up of women.

This particular dimension based on pastoral realities in the environment of the baptismal candidates is added in particular detail and force by Chrysostom, while it is absent in such detail and literal interpretation of the ceremony in Cyril's approach. Apart from this development by Chrysostom, the two fathers are practically identical in the matter of their mystagogy, *NT,* that is, *Mt.* and St. Paul, identical texts, and in their application for the candidates for baptism.

2. The Mortality-Immortality Dimension

The stripping off of the candidates' garments as symbol of the stripping off of the old man and his deeds has been treated particularly from a moralistic viewpoint of interpretation. A second level of interpretation considers the nature of the "old man" and the repercussions of his deeds beyond the visibly measurable moral level. In other words, who is this old man viewed from the standpoint of salvation history? To what, or to whom are his deeds related, past, present and future? Is there a hidden relationship in what he is and does, a burden of the past, a call of the future, which should be revealed in order that he may understand more fully what his insertion into the Christian life means for him and for his conduct ?

In this ceremony of the stripping of garments before plunging into the baptismal pool, and the consequent state of nakedness, a second level of interpretation is emphasized particularly by Cyril and also by Theodore: the deeds of "mortal" man viewed against the framework of his actual divine call to immortality. In this dimension what does it actually mean that he put aside the old man and his deeds? What is this present moral striving when viewed in the perspective of the burden of the past and the call of the future? What forces surround the candidate as he removes his garment and is urged by virtue of that symbol to put off the old man and his deeds? Is he alone, or is there an invisible world surrounding him, a drama being played out? In their mystagogical interpretation of this ceremony Cyril particularly, and also Theodore, but to a lesser extent, attempt to present this dimension of mortality and immortality. The candidate is stripped of his clothing and stands naked. What does this mean?

a. *Cyril*

(1) *The Principalities and Powers*

In a most striking way Cyril, having presented the moralistic level of interpretation, then associates the candidate with Christ Himself, Who was also stripped of His garments and hung naked on the cross: "Having stripped yourselves, you were naked; in this also imitating Christ, Who hung naked on the Cross."[73] That this association of the naked candidate with the naked Christ on the cross is peculiar to Cyril alone of the four fathers is, no doubt, due in part to the unique dramatic advantage which Cyril had of presenting his mystagogical interpretation of the initiation ceremonies in the very place in Jerusalem where the *Anastasis* was, the small chapel containing the Holy Sepulchre. The physical proximity, both here and in other liturgical events, to the actual scene of Christ's crucifixion, death and resurrection, suggests automatically such vivid mystagogical interpretation.

Cyril then goes on to introduce the mystagogical meaning of the association of the candidate's nakedness with that of Christ, Who hung naked on the cross, "and by His nakedness

[73]*Myst. Cat.* II.2 (Piédagnel, *SC* 126, 106; tr. Cross, *SPCK,* 59): Ἀποδυθέντες γυμνοὶ ἦτε, μιμούμενοι καὶ ἐν τούτῳ τὸν ἐπὶ τοῦ σταυροῦ γυμνωθέντα Χριστόν.

spoiled principalities and powers, and openly triumphed over them on the tree."[74]

The candidate naked is the "old man," the man of sin, represented by Christ on the cross, humiliated by being stripped naked. To the invisible eye of faith, behind the scene of this outward humiliation, this nakedness, a battle with a triumphal outcome is in progress. Underlying Cyril's image of Christ's triumph on the cross is the image under which St. Paul presents this triumph of apparent humiliation turned to victory, the image of a military conqueror returning in triumphal procession through the streets of his city displaying the spoils of his victory.[75]

In the Pauline teaching, which Cyril is following, the discussion centers about the power of the Law, which ultimately can do nothing for the sinner, the "old man," but condemn him to death.[76] Since the "old man" stands under a curse of death, then his works cannot save him, and the Law only serves to point out the transgressions contained in his works, thus revealing the curse of death at work. It is this death sentence for man which God once and for all carries out on His own Son, Jesus, in order to abrogate it forever, to cancel the debt of humanity by "nailing it to the cross."[77] On the cross, Jesus is "made sin,"[78] "subject to the Law,"[79] and "cursed by the Law."[80] The death warrant, and the changes it made against humanity, are nailed up on the cross in the Person of God's Son. However, by carrying out this sentence of death against sinful humanity in His own body, Jesus overcomes those "powers" which in various ways, under the aegis of the curse of sin and death, work against the real destiny of man, insuring in one way or other that he will be corrupt and mortal, that

[74] *Idem: καὶ τῇ γυμνότητι ἀπεκδυσάμενοι τὰς ἀρχὰς καὶ τὰς ἐξουσίας, καὶ μετὰ παρρησίας ἐν τῷ ξύλῳ θριαμβεύσαντα.*

[75] *Cf. Col.* 2:15.

[76] *Cf. Rm.* 7:7.

[77] *Col.* 2:14.

[78] 2 *Co.* 5:21.

[79] *Ga.* 4:4.

[80] *Ga.* 3:13.

he will do those works leading to death, the works of the "old man" and finally die forever. The humiliation of Jesus on the cross, symbolized by His being stripped and naked, is, then transformed into a triumph of the Son of God. Man's enemies, the "sovereignties and the powers" are divested of their power of corrupting, and are forced to march in humiliation behind the conquering Son of God on the Cross, just as a military leader makes a public display of his captives, now stripped of their power. The stripping away of Christ's garments signified the stripping away of these evil powers, and the nakedness, meant to be a humiliation, becomes thereby the final sign of victory.

In the text in question[81] St. Paul seems to be thinking particularly of those "sovereignties and powers" who are in Jewish tradition the angels[82] who brought the Law down to Moses. By honoring them, and so making the Law a kind of idolatry[83] they and the Law gained a power over man. It is this power which Jesus conquers, "parading them in public, behind Him in His triumphal procession."

For Cyril, however, the "principalities and powers" in question are made broader than those which concern St. Paul in the particular passage to which Cyril alludes. They encompass, rather, the "sovereignties and powers"[84] that "spiritual army of evil in the heavens" who disobeyed God and who war against man in an attempt to enslave him to themselves in sin.[85] They are the spirits who induce men to live "sensual lives, ruled entirely by our own physical desires and our own ideas,"[86] with the result indicated by St. Paul, that the law of man's body "follows a different law that battles against the law which my reason dictates," with the result, "This is what makes me a prisoner of that law which lives inside my body."[87]

[81] *Col.* 2:15.
[82] *Ga.* 3:19.
[83] *Col.* 2:18.
[84] *Cf. Ep.* 6:12.
[85] *Cf. Ep.* 2:2
[86] *Ep.* 2:3.
[87] *Rm.* 7:23.

For in the same passage, after alluding to the image of Christ's "military triumph" on the cross over "the principalities and powers,"[88] Cyril goes on to interpret: "For since the powers of the enemy made their lair in your members, you may no longer wear that old tunic. I do not at all mean this visible one, but that old man, which is corrupt according to deceitful lusts."[89]

So, then, as the humiliation of Christ in being stripped and made naked is transformed into a triumph over the "principalities and powers" whose influence is represented by these clothes of mortality, and whose power is symbolically destroyed by their removal, so too in the candidate who imitates Christ in being himself stripped of his clothes before baptism, the old clothes, symbol of the mortal corruption and consequent vices of the "old man" are stripped away, and their symbolized evil effects are rendered powerless in and with Christ.

(2) *Eschatological Symbolism*

In addition to this vivid mystagogical interpretation of the stripping of the garments and nakedness, based both on the Pauline meditation on the crucifixion and the actual physical fact of the neophytes' presence at the actual site of the Holy Sepulcher, Cyril also draws from the *OT* to provide an eschatological framework to bring out the mortality-immortality dimension present in the ceremony. The image of the banquet, as we have already seen in Cyril's use of it, drawing from the Gospel parable of the allegory of the wedding, and there given a moralistic interpretation[90] recurs with Cyril in another context, in which he brings it beyond the moralistic interpretation: "In former times death was mighty and devoured; but

[88] *Cf. Col.* 2:15.

[89] *Myst. Cat.* II.2 (Piédagnel, *SC* 126, 106; tr. Cross, *SPCK*, 59): Ἐπειδὴ γὰρ τοῖς ἡμετέροις μέλεσιν ἐνεφώλευον αἱ ἀντικείμεναι δυνάμεις, οὐκ ἔτι φορεῖν ὑμῖν ἔξεστι τὸν παλαιὸν ἐκεῖνον χιτῶνα. οὐ τοῦτον πάντως λέγω τὸν αἰσθητόν, ἀλλα τὸν παλαιὸν ἄνθρωπον, τὸν φθειρόμενον ἐν ταῖς ἐπιθυμιαις τῆς ἀπάτης.

[90] See above, pp. 163-164.

at the holy bath of regeneration, God has wiped away every tear from every face.[91] For you will no longer weep, having put off the old man, but you will celebrate a feast day, having put on the garment of salvation,[92] Jesus Christ.[93]

Cyril presents here a mélange of scriptural echoes both from *OT* and *NT* with their primarily eschatological accent. The wiping away of tears by God is a scene of the last judgement, which is presented under the image of the Messianic banquet. As *Is.*[94] portrays it, God Himself is host, bidding the people to sit down at His feast. The scene anticipates the Gospel parable of the wedding feast[95] with its overtones of the last judgement. It recurs again in *Rv.* where the heavenly Jerusalem is described, which attends the disintegration of the "world of the past," and where the "water from the well of life" will be free.[96] In this framework Cyril sees the candidates putting off their garment, the old man, and putting on a new one in order to celebrate a feast day banquet. This clothing image also comes from *Is.*[97] where a "Magnificat" is presented, a song of rejoicing that God has clothed one. Here, too, the bridal image, which Cyril has already presented on the level of the moralistic interpretation, occurs, God clothing the bridegroom with a wreath or the bride with her jewels.

In this scriptural framework of eschatological dimensions, then, Cyril interprets the removal of the garment prior to baptism to be a sign of insertion into salvation history, not a matter-of-fact happening merely, but a symbol of the old and the new, the past, the present and the future, the dimension

[91] *Cf. Is.* 25:8.

[92] *Cf. Is.* 61:10.

[93] *Cf. Rm.* 13:14; *Ep.* 4:24; *Ga.* 3:27. *Myst. Cat.* I.10 (Piédagnel, *SC 126,* 100, 102; tr. Cross, *SPCK,* 58): *ἀλλ'ἐν μὲν τοῖς πρὸ τούτου χρόνοις κατέπιεν ὁ θάνατος ἰσχύσας· ἐπὶ δὲ τοῦ ἁγίου τῆς παλιγγενεσίας λουτροῦ, ἀφεῖλεν ὁ Θεος πᾶν δάκρυον ἀπο παντὸς προσώπου. οὐκ ἐτὶ γὰρ πενθεῖς, ἐκδεδυμένος τὸν παλαιὸν ἄνθρωπον. ἀλλὰ πανηγυρίζεις, ἐνδεδυμένος ἱμάτιον σωτηρίου, Ἰησοῦν Χριστόν.*

[94] *Cf. Is.* 25:8.

[95] *Cf. Mt.* 22:2-10.

[96] *Cf. Rv.* 21:4.

[97] *Is.* 61:10.

of mortality and immortality. The passage from this mortality, in which "death was mighty and devoured" into immortality, the cessation of tears, the banquet with God in the New Jerusalem, is signified by putting off these garments which are part of the "old man," the man subject to this power of death, the mortal man.

In this framework of the removal of clothing as sign of the passing from mortality to immortality, the bridal image, which Cyril had already used in the moralistic interpretation of the ceremony,[97a] recurs, this time as eschatological symbol. Putting off the old man with his corruption and deceits, like putting off a garment, signifies the entering of this new dimension of existence; it represents a turning from one way of life to another, infused by hope: "May no soul which has put him [the old man] off, again put him on, but say with the Spouse of Christ in the *Song of Songs,* 'I have put off my coat, how shall I put it on?' "[98]

b. *Theodore*

The Shame of Adam

The dimension of immortality-mortality, as symbolized by the removal of the garments before baptism is also presented in the mystagogy of Theodore. While not presenting the vivid christological association which Cyril had given, a remarkably similar thread of interpretation runs through the two fathers. Theodore reaches to *Gn.* for his interpretation, and the story of Adam and Eve.[99] Theodore explains why God made clothes out of skins for Adam and Eve after they had sinned. He relates these clothes to the clothes which the baptismal candidates wear and which they strip off. By breaking God's commandment Adam became mortal. This loss of trust in God,

[97a] See above, p. 164.
[98] *Sg.* 5:3. *Myst. Cat.* II.2 (Piédagnel, *SC* 126, 106; tr. Cross, *SPCK,* 59-60): *"Ὂν μὴ εἴη πάλιν, ἐνδύσασδαι τῇ ἅπαξ τοῦτον ἀποδυσαμένῃ ψυχῇ. ἀλλὰ λέγειν κατὰ τὴν ἐν τῷ "Αισματι τῶν ᾀσμάτων τοῦ Χριστοῦ νύμφην. "'Εξεδυσάμην τὸν χιτῶνά μου, πῶς ἐνδύσομαι αὐτον;"*
[99] *Cf. Gn.* 3:21.

and the consequent "self-consciousness" made him realize the need of a covering. This covering of animal skins which he received from God was a "sign of mortality and a reproving mark of that (divine) decree by which you were brought low to the necessity of a covering."[100] Since the candidate through baptism is about "to be born anew and become symbolically immortal," he duly removes his clothing, which is the symbol, since Adam, of his mortality.

Comparative Summary

Different though the mystagogy of Cyril and Theodore might appear at first glance, there is a similar underlying theme in Cyril's presentation of Christ stripped on the cross and so overcoming the power of corruption, and Theodore's reflection on the mortality of Adam, represented by the clothing God gave him to wear to cover this shame. The underlying point of unity is the notion of the old Adam and Christ as the new Adam. Indeed, Cyril presents his mystagogy with the vivid picture of the crucifixion, and the Pauline interpretation of the triumph it represents, a picture absent in Theodore. Yet, the point of the stripping of the garments, in Cyril, is from the body of Christ. In Theodore it is evident that these garments are none other than the clothing which Adam in his shame had to put on, a sign of his condemnation to mortality, to death. By stripping off these garments, the candidate shows, according to Theodore, his call to immortality, the reversal of the fall of Adam and its consequences. What Cyril has added, and that profoundly, is that it is through Christ, the new Adam, in actual historical fact, that this has taken place, and that these garments represent the history of sin and the power of sin and consequent mortality over man.

Thus, the mystagogy of the ceremony, even though it is approached from two different points of departure, actually

[100] *Bapt. Hom.* III.8 (Tonneau-Devreesse, *SeT* 145, 418; tr. Mingana, *WS* VI, 54).

converges in the ceremony itself and its interpretation: the symbolism of the clothing on Adam and on Christ, the new Adam. The matter of the mystagogy is salvation history, from Adam through Christ, and now in the candidate for baptism in whom both Adam and Christ are re-presented. The mystagogy is similar; Cyril adds the dimension of the actual fact of Christ being stripped of His garments.

3. *The Return to Primeval Innocence*

In addition to the moralistic interpretation and the dimension of immortality-mortality present in the mystagogical interpretation of the removal of clothing there is another interpretation common to Cyril, Chrysostom and Theodore. It looks particularly to the nakedness of the candidates as they make ready to plunge into the baptismal pool. This is the theme of the return to primeval innocence.

Gn. describes Adam and Eve in these terms: "Now both of them were naked, the man and his wife, but they felt no shame in front of each other."[101] After their disobedience, however, they hid from God, and when God finds Adam, and asks him why he hid, Adam answers, "I was afraid because I was naked." And God asks Adam, "Who told you that you were naked?"[102] After the sin is exposed, and the curse of mortality is visited on Adam and Eve, "Yahweh God made clothes out of skins for the man and for his wife, and they put them on."[103]

It is to this description of innocence and the trusting relationship with God lost, presented under the image of nakedness, first unashamed, then self-consciously in need of covering that Cyril, Chrysostom and Theodore all repair to present another level of interpretation for the nakedness of the candidates after they have been stripped of their garments.

[101] *Gn.* 2:25.
[102] *Gn.* 2:10-11.
[103] *Gn.* 2:21.

a. *Cyril*

Cyril had already stated that baptism was the "gate of paradise:" "At that time to each man and woman among you may the gate of paradise be opened."[104] This description of the event of baptism as the opening of the gate of paradise, occuring in the *Procatechesis,* recurs again in retrospect of the event, after the experience the neophytes have gone through on the night of their baptism. Cyril introduces his first *Mystagogical Catechesis* with an allusion to the fact that he wishes to lead the neophytes further into this paradise they have entered, "into the brighter and more fragrant meadow of this paradise."[105]

The scene thus set with such intimations as the baptistery as symbol of the garden of paradise, Cyril explains to the men and women who had stood naked before one another at the baptismal pool: "O wondrous thing! You were naked in the sight of all, and were not ashamed; for truly you bore the likeness of the first-formed Adam, who was naked in the garden and was not ashamed."[106]

The stripping of the garments, then, and the ensuing nakedness, far from an impoverishment or embarrassment, which it would naturally be, is symbol of a return to that innocence and intimate trust in God and openness with one another which characterized God's plan for man in the beginning.

b. *Chrysostom*

Of the three fathers who utilize this common material from *Gn.* to present this aspect of the mystagogical interpretation

[104] *Procat.* 15 (Cross, *SPCK,* 9; tr. Cross, *SPCK,* 49). (Text, see above, ch. 1, n. 125, p. 63).

[105] *Myst. Cat.* I.1 (Piédagnel, *SC* 126, 84; tr. Cross, *SPCK,* 53): "*εἰς τὸν ͵ωτεινότερον καὶ εὐωδέστερον λειμῶνα τοῦδε τοῦ παραδείσου.*"

[106] *Ibid.,* II.2 (*Ibid.,* 106; tr. *ibid.,* 60). (Text, see above, n. 4, p. 145).

of the ceremony, Chrysostom embellishes the scene the most:

> After stripping you of your robe, the priest himself leads you down into the flowing waters. But why naked? He reminds you of your former nakedness, when you were in Paradise and you were not ashamed. For Holy Writ says, "Adam and Eve were naked and were not ashamed," until they took up the garment of sin, a garment heavy with abundant shame.
> Do not, then, feel shame here, for the bath is much better than the garden of Paradise. There can be no serpent here, but Christ is here initiating you into the regeneration that comes from the water and the Spirit. You cannot see here beautiful trees and fruits, but you can see spiritual favors.[107]

For Chrysostom, as is obvious from the descriptive terms of the passage, the "flowing waters," the "beautiful trees and fruits," the baptistery is reminiscent of the garden of paradise, and nakedness of the candidates is a re-entering into that state of innocence and bliss that the first parents enjoyed before the fall.[108]

c. *Theodore*

Theodore similarly sees the nakedness of the candidates preparing to receive the gift of immortality back which Adam had lost, as a symbolic resemblance to Adam, who was formerly naked and not ashamed of himself.[109] He does not present the same mystagogy of the baptistery as symbol of paradies, however, as is present in both Cyril and Chrysostom.

[107] *P.K.* 3.8 (*VGS*, 173-174; tr. Harkins, *ACW* 31, 170, nos. 28-29): Τότε ἀποδύσας σε τὸ ἱμάτιον ὁ ἱερεύς, αὐτός σε κατάγει ἐπὶ τὰ νάματα. τίνος οὖν ἕνεκεν γυμνόν; ἀναμιμνήσκει σε τῆς προτέρας γυμνότητος ὅτε ἦς ἐν τῷ παραδείσῳ καὶ οὐκ ᾐσχύνου. "ἦσαν" γὰρ φησιν "'Αδὰμ καὶ Εὕα γυμνοὶ καὶ οὐκ ᾐσχύνοντο", ἕως ἔλαβον τὸ τῆς ἁμαρτίας ἱμάτιον, τὸ πολλῆς γέμον αισχύνης. μὴ τοίνυν μηδὲ ενταῦθα αἰσχύνου· πολὺ γὰρ τοῦ παραδείσου βελτίων ἡ κολυμβήθρα. οὔκ ἐστιν ἐνταῦθα ὄφις, ἀλλὰ Χριστός ἐστὶν ἐνταῦθα μυσταγωγῶν σε πρὸς τὴν ἐξ ὕδατος καὶ πνεύματος ἀναγέννησιν. οὐκ ἔστιν ἐνταυθα δένδρα καλὰ καὶ ὡραῖα ἰδεῖν. ἀλλ' ἔστιν ἐνταῦθα χαρίσματα πνευματικά.

[108] On the rivers of Paradise see J. Daniélou, *From Shadows to Reality: Studies in the Biblical Typology of the Fathers,* tr. W. Hibberd (London, 1960), pp. 23-26. On the Paradise symbolism of the baptistery in general see J. Daniélou, *The Bible and the Liturgy,* pp. 35-37.

[109] *Bapt. Hom.* III.8 (Tonneau-Devreesse, *SeT* 145, 416; tr. Mingana, *WS* VI, 54).

Comparative Summary

In dealing with the nakedness of the disrobed candidates, all three fathers, Cyril, Chrysostom, and Theodore converge in the single picture from *Gn.,* Adam and Eve naked and unashamed. It is the logical conclusion from the foregoing. Stripped of the garments which represent the old man and his deeds, a ceremony which further imports the placing of the candidate through Christ into a new dimension, a passing symbolically from mortality to immortality through the removal of those garments which symbolize in salvation history corruption and mortality, he finds himself then in a state of nakedness. This final dimension of the mystagogical interpretation of the ceremony shows the "result" of the ceremony: this nakedness is not the usual shame attendant on such a situation, but symbol of the restoration of the prerogatives lost by Adam, and his former enjoyment of which was represented by him and his wife naked and unashamed before one another. Both Cyril and Chrysostom simply make of the baptistery a garden of paradise by their allusions. While Theodore does not use the physical appointments, and the added innuendoes of imagery, his point is the same.

Conclusion

From this comparative analysis of the mystagogical interpretation of the ceremony of removing one's clothing prior to baptism, one can see how Cyril, Chrysostom and Theodore forged considerable pastoral meaning for a ceremony which was at once merely practical, the necessary disrobing before entering the baptismal pool, but that also had both a pagan and Christian-Jewish history behind it, and in which numerous echoes of different symbolism were present.

When one considers, for example, the magical notions which surrounded the idea of clothing, which to some degree or other perdured in the candidates for baptism, one can see the work of mystagogy in reforging such notions on a thoroughly

Christian basis. Primitive peoples had the idea that the clothing a person wore partook itself in the spiritual forces which the wearer encountered in his environment.[110] For this reason, so as not to defile sacred places, clothing had to be removed before entering these precincts. And conversely, one had to guard against bringing the influence of divinity from a sacred place into the profane world.[111] F. Dölger has shown how such notions perdured strongly into the second half of the second century[112] and cites a passage from the *Canons of Hippolytus,* explaining why women have to undo their hair and put aside their jewelry before entering the baptismal pool, so that evil spirits which may cluster about the hair or ornamentation will not accompany them into the water.[113] He notes that in the attitude of the time, complete divesting of one's garments prior to entering the water was strictly enjoined to prevent these evil spirits, which could lodge in the smallest ornament, from entering the baptismal water.

Comparing this attitude toward the removal of garments before baptism with the mystagogy of the fathers, one sees the advance of interpretation. Indeed there are evil spirits,

[110]"It was a common idea among primitive peoples that clothing is especially likely to become impregnated with the spiritual forces that have surrounded its wearer. There is danger, then, that the clothing would bring hostile emanations into the sacred places, or again, carry particles of divine fluid out into the profane world." A. Lods, *Israel des origines aux Prophètes,* p. 313, cited in Daniélou, *The Bible and the Liturgy,* p. 51.

[111]See F. Dölger, *Der Exorzismus im altchristlichen Taufritual,* pp. 107-118.

[112]*Idem.*

[113]"Mulieres deponant ornamenta et aurea et caetera. Solvant crinium nodos, ne cum illis descendat in aquam regenerationis quidquid peregrinum de spiritibus peregrinis." On this passage Dölger comments: "At that time the attitude was prevalent that in the smallest ornament a demon could reside which could make the blessing illusory. Therefore, the strict directive that the most complete removal of garments had to take place. The fear that the evil spirits could climb into the water with the baptismal candidate reaches certainly into the second half of the second century. (Es herrschte also damals die Auffassung, es könnte sich im kleinsten Schmuck ein Dämon verstecken, welcher die Weihe illusorisch machen könnte. Deshalb die strenge Bestimmung, dass die vollständigste Entkleidung stattfinden müsse. Die Furcht, dass böse Geister mit dem Täufling ins Wasser steigen könnten, reicht sicherlich bis in die zweite Hälfte des zweiten Jahrhunderts hinauf)." *Der Exorzismus,* pp. 112-113.

but not in the magical sense those who will defile the baptismal water and make the ceremony an illusion, but rather those evil spirits which will make of the ceremony a mockery if the candidate has not tried with sincere purpose to cooperate in his conversion process by the moral effort of uprooting his vices and bad habits. The connection of the evil spirits with the water of baptism, and the concomitant danger of "invalidating" the baptism is not magic but personal and moral. Using the Pauline image of the old man, the individual is exhorted to try to correct his bad habits, removing them as he removes his clothing. It is failure of this *sincerity,* and not "evil spirits" in the clothing, which jeopardize the baptism. As Cyril points out: "If you abide in your evil purpose . . . you must not look for grace: for though the water receive you, the Spirit will not accept you."[114] Not the emanations of any evil fluid into the water from the clothing of the wearer, but insincerity of purpose is the evil represented by the old clothing. For Chrysostom, too, if, indeed, clothing or jewelry are nests of demonic powers which the bishop must strip off the candidate before leading him into the baptismal pool, then he is at great pains to point out that the demonic force resides not in the folds of the garments or in the glint of the jewelry, but rather in the unexpurgated vices of the wearer, the unregenerate force of vain show, seductiveness and lack of concern for the poor.

A further step in the "re-personalization" of any such magic notions which still might be present in the candidates' attitude toward the removal of clothing is seen in the association of ceremony, through the use of the wedding allegory and the bridal image from *Mt.*, which places the whole ceremony in the context of response to a personal call toward an intimate and personal relationship on the part of God with the candidate. He is not merely symbolically divesting himself of a kind of uncleanness in getting rid of his old clothes, but preparing

[114]*Procat.* 4 (Cross, *SPCK,* 3; tr. Cross, *SPCK,* 43): Εἰ δὲ επιμένεις κακῇ προαιρέξει . . . σὺ δὲ μὴ προσδόπα λήψεσθαι τὴν χάριν· τὸ μὲν γὰρ ὕδωρ σε δέξεται, τὸ δὲ πνεῦμά σε οὐ δέξεται.

to answer a personal invitation to a banquet, to a wedding banquet, indeed, ultimately, to his own nuptials. Far removed from the magical fetishism which might still cling to the minds of the candidates in regard to the ceremony, this interpretation of Cyril and Chrysostom elevates them and their efforts to that of a joint partnership with God.

Cyril particularly, by his use of the Pauline interpretation of the crucifixion of Jesus, deals a final blow against the magical notions of the ceremony. The "principalities and powers," the evil spirits, are not simply a horde plaguing superstitious man, but rather a reflection of the sinfulness of the old man, the power of his evil deeds which have set up a net in himself and in his environment from which Christ alone can liberate him by emptying Himself on the cross and becoming naked. The magic spirits which might have resided in the candidate are then the power of the deeds of the old man. As Cyril says, quoting St. Paul: "For since the powers of the enemy made their lair in your members, you may no longer wear that old vestment; I do not at all mean this visible one, but that old man, which is corrupt according to deceitful lust."[115]

The spiritual horizon of the candidates is also taken beyond magic or the ritual uncleanness of natural religious ideas and placed through the mystagogy in the dimension of salvation history. The eschatological symbolism of dressing in new clothes, and removing the old is shown in *OT* and *NT,* through *Is.* and the *Sg.* over the Gospel call to the accomplishment envisioned in *Rv.* J. Quasten has already analyzed the notions of the material out of which garments were made as symbol of death or of life in pagan antiquity. Citing a letter of St. Jerome to Fabiola he brings out the cultural background which sees in the garments of wool, that is animal skin, a sign of death, and in the garments of linen, that is plant life, a sign of life.[116] Jerome remarks that the candidate upon emerging

[115] See above, p. 176 and n. 89.

[116] See J. Quasten, "A Pythagorean Idea in Jerome," *American Journal of Philology* 63 (1942) 207-215.

from the font is vested "in a garment of linen which has nothing of death in itself (veste linea nihil in se morte habente)."[117] Why the garment of linen has "nothing of death in itself" is understood when compared to the old clothing the candidates wore before baptism, which are called "tunicae pelliceae" in St. Jerome's letter, "woolen garments":

> We have here nothing else than the contrast between wool and linen. The old clothing which the candidates have taken off was made of wool, in other words, of material which comes from animals. Therefore it has something of death in itself, because it reminds us of creatures which are mortal, destined to die. That is the reason that these garments cannot be worn after baptism, the sacrament of regeneration. Death and life do not go together. On the other hand, the white garment is made of linen, the product of a plant, and has therefore nothing of death in itself. Nothing could be more fitting for the sacrament which was called "the garment of immortality." We are here in the middle of an interesting world of ideas, centering around "wool and linen," which goes back to the Pythagoreans and Egypt.[118]

Over against this notion of animal skin clothing as profane and a sign of death, the mystagogy of the fathers emphasizes the notion of immortality and mortality through their use of biblical materials, which both inherits this idea, but also lifts in into the dimension of salvation history. Both in the symbol of the banquet garment and the removal of the old garment which Cyril traces from *Is.* through *Rv.,* as well as Theodore's reference to the fact that the garments of animal skin which God gave Adam in his shame were a sign of mortality and corruption, one sees how the cultural notions of pagan antiquity are drawn into salvation history by mystagogical interpretation of this sort. They help the candidate to enlarge his horizon from natural religious symbolism to the Christian

[117] *Ibid.,* p. 207. *Ep.* 64, 19 (*CSEL* XIV, p. 610).
[118] Quasten, *art. cit.,* pp. 207-208.

horizon, here the dimension of mortality-immortality, life and death. By stripping his garment of death, the candidate is preparing for life.

The "result" of this ceremony, the nakedness of the candidate, also associates him with salvation history, the symbolic return of his lost past, in that he is Adam, standing unashamed in his first relationship of trust to God and to his fellow men, before his fall, corruption and mortality. Common to all three fathers is the idea that the nakedness of the candidates about to be baptized resembles the unashamed nakedness of the first parents in the garden of paradise, which for Cyril and Chrysostom is symbolically the baptistery itself. The covering, the "animal skins" which represented the loss of innocence have been removed, and the candidates stand ready to receive through the waters of baptism the gift of trust they had lost in the transgression of the protoparents. The shame that had led Adam and Eve to cover themselves before God and before one another would now disappear with the return of the filial trust, the "parrhesia" which had characterized Adam before the fall. And this state which baptism will bring about is symbolically anticipated by the nakedness of the candidates.

Personal moral effort as response to the divine call which is echoing in human life, the wedding allegory, the bridal image: this is the message of the first, or moralistic level of interpretation of the ceremony. The horizon of the divine plan, mortality and immortality, and the central role of Christ in achieving this plan: this is the message of the second level of mystagogical interpretation. And this future immortality: a restoration and return to the roots of man's history, the restoration of his lost innocence: this is the message which the mystagogy on the third level of interpretation presents.

Present, the Christian life now; future, the immortality to come; past, the restoration of man's original prerogatives: this is the unified picture of mystagogical interpretation which emerges. And the dynamic center: the candidate's resemblance to Christ, the symbolic "exinanitio" of the candidate stripping off his clothes and standing naked, brought into conjunction with Christ's "exinanitio" on the cross, also stripped and naked. The "having nothing," the humiliation of being found naked, the shame and degradation in the worldly sense of what it means when one's garments or jewelry are stripped from one, becomes, through the stripping and nakedness of Christ, the very path of overcoming the old man and his deeds, the very positive force of "exorcising" the principalities and powers. On the threshold of baptism, at the edge of the pool, the ceremony as interpreted by the fathers is one of singular force in underscoring the meaning of baptismal conversion, the paradox of belief.

B. The Anointing Before the Baptismal Bath

The Ceremony

In the synoptic presentation of the ceremonies in this chapter[119] we have seen that Cyril, Chrysostom and Theodore all speak of an anointing of the entire body just after the candidate removes this clothing and immediately prior to his entering the baptismal pool. As Cyril describes the rite of initiation in his *Mystagogical Catecheses* this is the first anointing which is mentioned. In the *Baptismal Instructions* of Chrysostom and in the *Baptismal Homilies* of Theodore, however, this anointing is the second anointing to be described. Because of its peculiar nature as "sphragis" anointing, this first anointing mentioned by Theodore and by Chrysostom, which concludes the rite of renunciation and commitment in these two fathers, has been given separate treatment in Chapter One.[120]

In addition to these anointings of the body before the baptismal bath as found in Cyril, Chrysostom and Theodore, we shall treat as well in this section the first anointing mentioned by Ambrose.[121] Although this anointing comes before the act of renunciation and commitment in the description given by Ambrose, both the interpretation which Ambrose gives to it,

[119]See above, pp. 144-148.
[120]See above, pp. 111-131. See also *Essay, The Anointings,* above, ch. 1, pp. 104-111.
[121]See above, ch. 1, p. 27.

and the fact that like the other anointing just prior to the baptismal bath in Cyril, Chrysostom and Theodore, it is apparently an anointing the entire body[122] indicate that it is similar in meaning, not to the "sphragis" anointings but rather to these body anointings before the baptismal bath in Cyril, Chrysostom and Theodore.

The *origin* of this ceremony of anointing the body with oil before the baptismal bath, which the fathers inherited in the rite upon which they were called to comment, is somewhat complex. Different indications of the ceremony in liturgical texts both prior to and contemporary with the fathers here in question, show a variety of symbolic interpretation, not to mention a variety of locations in the rite itself.[123]

In this connection A. Stenzel notes that this anointing did not belong to the central rite in antiquity, and since, as a general rule, local customs first proliferate when not tied down by traditional rites, and only later become unified, it will not be surprising that both the symbolic interpretation and the location of the ceremony in different initiation rites will vary. Since the anointing was not part of the ancient central rite, it was able to enter various local churches at different times and in different ways.[124]

The discovery that the fathers, in interpreting this anointing, use material from Holy Scripture rather sparingly, at least in comparison to the way in which they weave it into their explanations of the other ceremonies, will come as no surprise. One might contrast this lack of scriptural reference in explaining this pre-baptismal anointing to its frequent and well-

[122] *Idem.*

[123] See Stenzel, *op. cit.,* 102-104; Dölger, *Der Exorzismus,* 137-139.

[124] "Since the anointing from the standpoint of age does not belong to the fundamental ritual, because, according to a generally accepted law local plurality comes before unification, then the variations in the location alloted to the anointing and the variations in the symbolism as well, should not be very surprising. (Da die Salbung altersmässig nicht zum Kernritual gehört, da nach einem allgemein anerkannten Gesetz die örtliche Vielfalt vor der Vereinheitlichung ist, darf das Schwanken im angewiesenen Platz und manchmal in der Symbolik nicht viel wundernehmen)." Stenzel, *op. cit.,* p. 104.

integrated use, for example, in interpreting the post-baptismal anointing.[125] This singular reticence in applying biblical materials to the pre-baptismal anointing may well be explained by the fact that the ceremony penetrated the rite under strongly pagan influence, rather than belonging to original biblical, or Jewish-Christian influence, as is the case with the post-baptismal anointing.[126] Hence, the interpretative tradition was not as clear for this pre-baptismal anointing.

The Cultural Attitude toward Sickness

The pagan influence on this ceremony has been traced in general to two sources. The first of these is the cultural attitude toward sickness as the work of evil spirits, thus, the exorcistic element of this anointing, a source which will be seen reflected still to some degree in the mystagogical explanations of the ceremony.

Sickness, particularly such illnesses as epilepsy and lunacy, was viewed in antiquity as the work of evil spirits.[127] In this light, the transportation of the anointing with the oil of the sick[128] into the rite of Christian initiation is not difficult to understand. The catechumens are "ethically sick," and need release from those powers which are contributing to this condition. Anointing for sickness was quite common to the medicinal practice of the ancient world. Hence the intelligibility of this practice as an effective symbol of healing.[129]

[125] See above, ch. 3 pp. 359-363.

[126] See Stenzel, *op. cit.*, p. 103, n. 90.

[127] Even in the thirteenth century Durandus wrote: "Engergumeni sunt qui a daemonibus obsessi sunt, vel lunatici, sive morbum caducum patientes, sic dicti ab *ergon*, quod est labor, et *menoi*, quod est defectus, et *nous*, quod est mens, quia secundum defectum mentis in defectu lunae maxime patiuntur." *Rationale divinorum officiorum*, lib. II, c. VI, 5. See Dölger, *Der Exorzismus*, p. 153.

[128] *Cf. Jm.* 5:14; *Mt.* 6:12-13.

[129] Dölger, *Der Exorzismus*, p. 152 and Botte, *SC* 25bis, p. 62, n. 2, both bring liturgical texts attesting the similarity of formulas in the liturgy for this anointing of the catechumen and the anointing of the sick.

Bathing Customs

The second factor contributing to the presence of this pre-baptismal anointing was that of pagan bathing customs.[130] Since baptism, the "bath of rebirth (λουτρὸν παλιγγενεσίας)"[131] was executed as a real immersion, bathing customs such as anointing before a bath were taken over as a part of it. In addition, in the world of pagan Greek antiquity, anointing with oil and bathing were considered as cultic acts of reconciliation.[132]

In comparing the texts of the four fathers which interpret this pre-baptismal anointing, three motifs emerge in their handling of the ceremony, the exorcistic-healing motif, the motif of fortifying the candidate for a combat, and finally the motif of union with Christ.

[130] See Dölger, *Der Exorzismus,* pp. 156-158.

[131] *Tt.* 3:5.

[132] Dölger sums up the results of his investigations as follows: "The introduction of the exorcistic anointing prior to the baptism is not accidental, but is contingent on a number of reasons. The condition of the unbaptized was considered as sickness or possession. The idea suggested itself therefore, to cure the ethical sickness and possession as well as the physical by anointing with oil. Pagan bathing customs, which had an anointing prior to the bath, as well as the anointing of religious reconciliation which was practiced in the greco-roman culture, might well have contributed from their side toward facilitating the entrance of the Christian anointing ceremony into the ritual of exorcism. (Die Einführung der Exorzismussalbung vor der Taufe erscheint nicht zufällig, sondern ist durch eine Reihe von Gründen bedingt. Der Zustand des Ungetauften wurde gefasst als Krankheit und Besessenheit. Es lag daher nahe, die ethische Krankheit und Besessenheit wie die leibliche zu heilen: durch Ölsalbung. Die heidnische Badepraxis, welche eine Salbung vor dem Bade kannte, sowie die in der griechisch-römischen Kulturwelt geübte religiöse Sühnesalbung mögen ihrerseits dazu beigetragen haben, um der christlichen Salbungszeremonie leichteren Eingang in das Exorzismusritual zu ermöglichen)." p. 157.

SYNOPTIC CHART

The Mystagogy of the Anointing before the Baptismal Bath

Cyril	*Chrysostom*	*Theodore*	*Ambrose*
The Exorcistic-Healing Motif:			
From hairs of head to feet:			
Demonology *Myst.Cat.* II.3			
"Exorcised" oil:			
Ceremonies of catechumenate (*Procat.* 9)			
Purifying-healing agency *Myst.Cat.* II.3			
		Entire body:	
		Garment of immortality	
		Medicinal *Bapt.Hom.* III.8	
The Combat Motif:			
Oil as "charm" against evil:			
Preservative agency of oil *Myst.Cat.* II.3			
	Anointing as strengthening:		Anointing as strengthening:
	Soldier, armor, Athlete *Stav.* 2.24 *P.K.* 3.27		Athlete *Sacr.* I.4 1 *Co.* 9:24-25
			Baptismal Arena; Adversary *Myst.* 7

The Mystagogy of the Anointing before the Baptismal Bath—continued

Cyril	Chrysostom	Theodore	Ambrose
The Union with Christ Motif:			
"Olive" oil:			
Wild olive tree and good tree *Myst.Cat.* II.3 *Rm.* 11:17-24			
	Christ Himself anoints *P.K.* 3.27 *Stav.* 3-*P.K.* 4.9 2 *Co.* 1:21		
			Christ Himself gives crown *Sacr.* I.4 1 *Co.* 9:24-25

1. *Cyril*

Cyril, who provides the fullest explanation of this ceremony, touches upon all three of these motifs.

> Then, when you were stripped, you were anointed with exorcized oil, from the very hairs of your head to your feet, and were made partakers of the good olive-tree, Jesus Christ. For you were cut off from the wild olive-tree, and grafted into the good one, and were made to share in the fatness of the true olive-tree. The exorcized oil, therefore, was a symbol of the participation of the fatness of Christ, the charm to drive away every trace of hostile influence. For as the breathing of the saints and the invocation of the Name of God, like fiercest flame, scorch and drive out evil spirits, so also this exorcized oil receives such virtue by the invocation of God and by prayer, as not only to burn and cleanse away the traces

of sins, but also to chase away all the invisible powers of the evil one.[133]

a. *The Exorcistic-Healing Motif*

Although by this time it no longer comes to the fore as a consciously emphasized explanation of the ceremony, Cyril's pointed reference to the fact that the candidate is anointed "from the very hairs of your head," does seem to indicate some reminiscence of the prior exorcistic history of the ceremony, and the notions of pagan antiquity, which we have already seen in the ceremony of disrobing.[134] The hair had to be loosened, and any jewelry, which could be a nesting place for demons, had to be removed, lest the demons enter the baptismal water with the candidate.[135] In this reference, then, there is a faded echo of pagan purification rites, preventing the profane from entering the sacred precinct. This note indicates immediately the purificatory nature of the ceremony and so, like the stripping of the garments, underscores the whole idea of renunciation.

Cyril, however, does not for a minute remain in his mystagogy in any pagan or natural religious explanation of the ceremony, or magic superstition, but immediately weaves into his mystagogy the Christian meaning of the ceremony, even though he builds on the natural symbolism of the ceremony as purificatory and healing.

The anointing is done over the whole body with "exorcised oil (ἐλαίῳ ἐπορκιστῷ)." Using the matter of the oil itself for

[133] *Myst. Cat.* II.3 (Piédagnel, *SC* 126, 106, 108; tr. Cross, *SPCK*, 60): Εἶτα ἀποδυθέντες, ἐλαίῳ ἠλείφεσθε ἐπορκιστῷ ἀπ' ἄκρων κορυφῆς τριχῶν ἕως τῶν κατωτάτων. καὶ κοινωνοὶ ἐγίνεσθε τῆς καλλιελαίου Ἰησοῦ Χριστοῦ. Ἐκκοπέντες γὰρ ἐκ τῆς ἀγριελαίου, ἐνεκεντρίζεσθε εἰς τὴν καλλιέλαιον, καὶ κοινωνοὶ ἐγίνεσθε τῆς πιότητος τῆς ἀληθινῆς ἐλαίας. Τὸ οὖν ἐπορκιστον ἔλαιον σύμβολον ἦν τῆς κοινωνίας τῆς πιότητος τοῦ Χριστοῦ, φυλαδευτήριον τυλχάνον παντὸς ἴχνους ἀντικειμένης ἐνεργείας. Ὥσπερ γὰρ τὰ ἐμφυσήματα τῶν ἁγίων, καὶ ἡ τοῦ ὀνόματος τοῦ Θεοῦ ἐπίκλησις, ὥσπερ σφοδροτάτη φλόξ, καίει καὶ ἐκδιώκει δαίμονας, οὕτω τὸ ἐπορκιστὸν τοῦτο ἔλαιον ἐπικλήσει Θεοῦ καὶ εὐχῇ δυναμιν τηλικαύτην λαμβάνει ὡς οὐ μόνον καῖον τὰ ἴχνη τῶν ἁμαρτημάτων ἀποκαθαίρειν, ἀλλὰ καὶ τὰς ἀοράτους τοῦ πονηροῦ ἐκδιώκειν δυνάμεις.

[134] See above, pp. 183-189.

[135] See above, p. 184. See also W. Van Unnik, "Les cheveux défait des femmes baptisées," *Vigiliae Christianae* I (1947) 77-100.

his mystagogy, Cyril reaches back into the catechumenate to show how this oil has a purifying and healing effect. Not that it is some sort of magic element in itself, this oil, but it receives its efficacy because it is associated "with the invocation of God (ἐπικλήσει Θεοῦ)" and "with prayer (εὐχῇ)." Cyril puts the oil in dynamic relationship with the ceremonies of the catechumenate, with its purificatory and healing exorcisms.[136] There, the "insufflations of the saints (ἐμφυσήματα τῶν ἁγίων)"[137] and the "invocation of the Name of God (τοῦ ὀνόματος τοῦ Θεοῦ ἐπίκλησις)" drive out the "evil spirits (δαίμονας)."

Resting on the natural symbolism of oil which heals and purifies, the oil is brought into conjunction with Christian prayer, serving as a symbol of the purification and the healing from sin, viewed as a sickness of the soul, and the power of sin which reaches out into its environment. By bringing the oil into conjunction with the catechumenate, Cyril removes any temptation to a "magical" interpretation of the ceremony since the catechumenate was an integrated program of instruction, moral assistance and advice and prayer. The exorcisms contained in it, and to which Cyril makes reference, were imbedded in the symbolic view of sin as a power which reached interiorly into the candidate, the power of corruption, and which threw its net out into the environment in which the candidate lived, a thoroughly biblical view. Not in itself alone, but in conjunction with this view and Christian practice of prayer, does the oil have value as a symbol, resting as it does quite nicely on its widespread and common understanding as medicine.

The oil, then, receives a twofold power which is activated in the anointing ceremony, and which it has received as Cyril says, "by the invocation of God," and "by prayer." Resting on the worldview implied in the catechumenate, Cyril then indicates the twofold power of the oil: "not only to burn and cleanse away the traces of sins, but also to chase away all the invisibly powers of the evil one."

[136]See *Procat.* 9 (Cross, *SPCK*, 5-6; tr. Cross, *SPCK*, 45).

[137]The "saints" are probably the priest-exorcists who prepare the candidates. See Piédagnel, *SC* 126, 109, n. 1.

Just as in the earlier ceremony of exorcism, the "evil spirit (*ἐχθρὸς δαίμων*)" was driven out of the catechumen, those powers which contributed to his sickness of soul, so here, through anointing with this exorcised oil the final "traces of sins (*τὰ ἴχνη τῶν ἁμαρτημάτων*)," what remains from the ravages of evil in the soul, its marks and traces, are burned away in a final symbolic ceremony of purification and healing.

The material for Cyril's mystagogical interpretation of this ceremony of anointing before the baptismal bath is, then, the liturgy of the catechumenate plus the natural symbolism of oil as a purifying and healing agent. The natural healing and purifying power of oil is elevated through the liturgical prayers and in conjunction with the whole religious assistance and preparation program of the catechumenate into a symbol of supernatural healing and purification.

b. *The Combat Motif*

In addition to this exorcistic-healing motif, Cyril also attributes to the ceremony a power of fortifying and protecting the candidate against "the invisible powers of the evil one (*τὰς ἀοράτους τοῦ πονηροῦ δυνάμεις*)." Through the anointing, as it were by a "charm (*τυγχάνον*)" "every trace (*παντὸς ἴχνους*)" of "hostile influence (*ἀντικειμένης ἐνεργείας*)" is driven away.

In what sense is the anointing with oil a kind of charm which offers the candidate a kind of protection against every trace of hostile influence? Again the mystagogy is twofold. There is the natural symbolism of oil as a preservatice agent, which protects against corruption and decay, the forces which seek to erode or to dry up what would otherwise remain supple and alive. Cyril is not content, however, to remain on the level of this natural symbolism of oil, but elevates the symbol into the supernatural realm through his mystagogical interpretation of the anointing with oil as association with Christ.

c. *The Union with Christ Motif*

If, indeed, this anointing with oil produces a purifying and healing effect and protects the candidate from hostile influences, then this effect is explained in the mystagogy of Cyril by the fact that the anointing represents an incorporation into the life of Christ. It is from this incorporation, symbolized by the anointing with olive oil, that the ceremony produces such benefits.

To explain this symbolism of the olive oil Cyril once again repairs to the Pauline writings,[138] where the converted pagans are described as branches of a wild olive tree, growing in its natural state. Through the gift of faith they are grafted onto the cultivated olive tree, Israel, taking the place of those branches which were lopped off due to their refusal to believe. In this way the converted pagans are made participants of the "rich sap provided by the olive tree itself."[139]

As for Paul[140] so for Cyril, it is through the act of faith in Jesus Christ that one receives a share in His life. Cut off from the wild olive tree and grafted onto the good one, the candidates were made "partakers of the good olive-tree, Jesus Christ (*κοινωνοὶ . . . τῆς καλλιελαίου Ἰησοῦ Χριστοῦ*)."

In this context, then, the olive tree with which the candidates are anointed becomes a "symbol of the participation of the fatness of Christ (*σύμβολον . . . τῆς κοινωνίας τῆς πιότητος τοῦ Χριστοῦ*)." The life of Christ, represented by the symbolic richness of the sap of the true olive tree becomes manifest on the candidates, who are anointed with olive oil, manifesting symbolically their participation in this life of Christ.[141]

Relying on the natural symbolism of the well-known fruitfulness of the olive tree in its production of oil and in its symbol fertility, and adding material from St. Paul, Cyril gives a christological unity to his mystagogy of the anointing of the body before baptism.

Summary

By forging this mystagogical explanation of the ceremony through recourse to Pauline writings, Cyril has infused the

[138] *Cf. Rm.* 11:17-24.

[139] *Rm.* 11:18.

[140] *Cf. Rm.* 11:20.

[141] For a previous use of the same idea, see *Bapt. Cat.* I.4 (*MG* 33.373).

exorcistic-healing and the protective symbolism of this anointing with a profound christological character. In providing this explanation of the anointing ceremony, he has also carried the ceremony well beyond the pagan associations which might be familiar to the catechumens. Resting on the natural symbolism of oil as a purifying and healing agent, and as a preservative against decay, without destroying these legitimate cultural associations, Cyril elevates the ceremony in meaning by showing that the power from which the symbolic purifying, healing and the "charm" to drive away every hostile influence" derives is not some magical power inherent in the oil itself, which remains a symbol associated with the blessing in Christian prayer, but is rather the fruitful power of the life of Christ, symbolized by the richness of the olive-tree, and into which the candidate is symbolically grafted when he is anointed with the oil of this tree from head to foot. Without destroying the associations which were part of the thinking and the environment of the candidates, Cyril transforms them and anchors them in a "mystical" meditation on the life of Christ. This mystagogy, with its specific emphasis on the candidate's symbolic conformity to the life of Christ, through whose power the victory over the destructive forces from within and without, the sickness of soul and the hostile influences of the world, has been achieved, is similar to Cyril's mystagogy in interpreting the removal of clothing. There the symbolic power of corruption is overcome, the principalities and powers, also through the candidate's association with Christ stripped and naked on the cross. Just as in that section, so here too, Cyril contributes an interpretation unique among the four fathers to interpret the ceremony of the anointing with olive oil.

2. *Chrysostom*

a. *The Combat Motif*

The interpretative analysis which Chrysostom accords to this anointing of the entire body with the "olive-oil of the spirit (ἔλαιον πνευμετικόν)"[142] prior to the baptismal bath,

[142] See above, p. 146.

continues one of this favorite rhetorical figures, the image of the soldier-athlete entering into combat with Satan.[143] Derived from Christian antiquity[144] and already present, for example, in Cyril[145] and in Theodore,[146] though not as mystagogical explanations of the anointing, Chrysostom makes use of this image as the chief vehicle to explain the meaning of this anointing:

> Next after [the first anointing] in the full darkness of night, he [the priest] or [bishop] strips off your robe, and as if he were going to lead you into heaven itself by the ritual, he causes your whole body to be anointed with that olive-oil of the spirit, so that all your limbs may be fortified and unconquered by the darts which the adversary aims at you.[147]

> After He [Christ] anoints all your limbs with this ointment, you will be secure and able to hold the serpent in check; you will suffer no harm.[148]

These two texts of mystagogical interpretation must be read in conjunction with the interpretation of the first or "sphragis" anointing, which in the *Baptismal Instructions* though not in the actual time of the ceremonies, immediately precedes them. Although the two anointings, the "sphragis" anointing and this anointing of the whole body before the baptismal bath are separated in time[149] Chrysostom makes them interdependent in interpretation by virtue of his controlling rhetorical image. In the first, or "sphragis" anointing the candidate has been given the mark of Christ's ownership.[150] As a result of

[143] See P. Harkins, "Pre-Baptismal Rites in Chrysostom's Baptismal Catecheses," *SP,* ed. F. Cross, Vol. VIII, Part II, TU 93 (Berlin, 1966), pp. 236-238.

[144] See J. Daniélou, *The Bible and the Liturgy,* pp. 58-60; F. Dölger, "Sacramentum militiae," *AC* 2 (1930), 268-280.

[145] *Cf. Bapt. Cat.* I.3 (MG 33.372).

[146] See *Bapt. Hom.* II.17 (Tonneau Devreesse, *SeT* 145, 396; tr. Mingana, *WS* VI, 46).

[147] *Stav.* 2.24 (Wenger, *SC* 50, 147; tr. Harkins, *ACW* 31, 52). Text, see above n. 31, p. 155.

[148] *P.K.* 3.7 (*VGS,* 173; tr. Harkins, *ACW* 31, 169, no.27): *ἐπειδὰν δὲ τοῦτο τὸ ἄλειμμα ἀλείψῃ τὰντα τὰ μέλη, μετὰ ἀδείας τὸν δρὰκοντα κατέχειν δύνασαι καὶ οὐδ ἐν πείσῃ δεινόν.*

[149] See above, p. 146 and n. 10.

[150] See above, pp. 113-114,118.

this, a combat situation has been set up, since by the seal of the first anointing the candidate is recognized by Satan as one who has gone over to the side of Christ and thereby become an opponent to be challenged and attacked. Although, in Chrysostom's interpretation, the first anointing had already been viewed under its protective aspects, through the shining rays of which Satan would be confounded[151] this second anointing is viewed as a special form of protection for the soldier-athlete in the actual arena of combat.

Fundamental to the interpretation is the natural symbolism of oil as a preservative agent against corruption. To this the cultural symbolism is added, the practice of anointing the limbs of an athlete, particularly an athlete engaged in wrestling sports, to add strength and suppleness to his limbs for the combat with his adversary.[152] This image fits in completely with the program which Chrysostom has already laid down for the candidates in other parts of the *Baptismal Instructions*, where they were viewed as being trained for combat similar to the Olympic games, and finally made ready to enter the arena. Thus: "He [Christ] anointed us as we went into the combat, but He fettered the devil; He anointed us with the oil of gladness, but He bound the devil with fetters that cannot be broken to keep him shackled hand and foot for the combat. But if I happen to slip, He stretches out His hand, lifts me from my fall, and sets me on my feet again."[153]

Also present in Chrysostom's symbolic interpretation of this anointing is his view of the olive-oil as providing the candidate with a suit of armor which will render his limbs invulnerable to the darts which the adversary aims at him. This image of the anointing as a suit of armor is likewise a continuation

[151] See above, p. 121.

[152] See J. Sawhill, "*The Use of Athletic Metaphors in the Biblical Homilies of St. John Chrysostom*," (Princeton, New Jersey, 1928), pp. 10-27.

[153] *Stav. 3-P.K.* 4.9 (Wenger, *SC* 50, 156, tr. Harkins, *ACW* 31, 58): 'Ημᾶς εἰς τὸν ἀγῶνα εἰσιόντας ἤλειψεν, ἐκεῖνον ἔδησεν· ἡμᾶς ἤλειψεν ἔλαιον ἀγαλλιάσεως· ἐκεῖνον ἔδησε δεσμοῖς ἀλύτοις ἵνα συμποδίζηται πρὸς τὰ παλαίσματα.' Εμὸὶ κἂν ὑποσκελισθῆναι συμβῇ χεῖρα ὀρέγει καὶ πεσόντα ἀνίστησι καὶ πατεῖν αὐτὸν πάλιν ποιεῖ.

of Chrysostom's ideas of the training program of the catechumenate.[154]

Oil to give strength and suppleness to the athlete's limbs, oil which preserves and protects against destruction and decay, and so in symbolic form, a kind of covering, a soldier's armor, in view of the combat of the Christian life: these are the two pictures which Chrysostom uses to interpret the ceremony of the anointing before the baptismal bath from the standpoint of the combat motif.

b. *The Union with Christ Motif*

The motif of the candidates' union with Christ, the christological interpretation of the ceremony, such as was seen in Cyrils's use of the Pauline texts referring to the wild olive-tree and the cultivated olive-tree, occurs also in Chrysostom, but under a different modality. Characteristic of Chrysostom's view of the liturgical action is an interaction between the minister and Christ Himself: "And that you may again know that it is not a man but God Himself Who anoints you by the hand of the priest, listen to St. Paul when he says: 'It is God Who is warrant for us and for you in Christ, Who has anointed us.' " Then Chrysostom adds: "He [Christ] anoints all your limbs with this ointment."[155] It is Christ "Who anointed us as we went into the combat."[156]

Thus, by association with the life of Christ, a thread which has run consistently through Chrysostom's view of the combat, by the strength which the candidate shares with Christ Himself Whose athlete and soldier he is, he will become both strong for the battle and invulnerable against attack, symbolized by the oiling of the athlete and the anointing of the limbs as outfitting the candidate on his whole body with the necessary unfailing protective armor of the soldier.

[154] See *Ibid.*, 3.11 (*ibid.*, 157-158; tr. *ibid.*, 59-60).

[155] *P.K.* 3.7 (*VGS*, 173; tr. Harkins, *ACW* 31, 169, no. 27): *καὶ ὅτι πάλιν οὐκ ἄνθρωπος, ἀλλ' αὐτος σε χριει ὁ θεὸς διὰ τῆς τοῦ ἱερέως χειρός ἄκουσον τοῦ Πρύλου λέγοντος. "ὁ δε βεβαιῶν ἡμᾶς σὺν ἡμὶν εἰς Χριστον καὶ χρίσας ἡμας θεός." . . . τοῦτο τὸ ἄλλιμμα ἀλείψη πάντα τὰ μέλη.*

[156] *Stav.* 3-*P.K.* 4.9 (Wenger, *SC* 50, 156; tr. Harkins, *ACW* 31, 58) (Text, see above, n. 153, p. 201).

3. *Theodore*

Theodore's interpretation of the pre-baptismal anointing, which, as in Cyril, takes place immediately after the removal of the candidate's garments, seems at first inspection somewhat ingenious, given the symbolism which he uses:

> After you have taken off your garments, you are rightly anointed all over your body with the oil of anointing, a mark and sign that you will be receiving the covering of immortality, which through baptism you are about to put on. After you have taken off the covering which involves the sign of mortality, you receive through your anointing the sign of the covering of immortality, which you expect to receive through baptism. And you are anointed all over your body as a sign that unlike the covering used as a garment, which does not cover all the parts of the body, because although it may cover all the external limbs, it by no means covers the internal ones—all our nature will put on immortality at the time of the resurrection, and all that is seen in us, whether internal or external, will undoubtedly be changed into incorruptibility according to the working of the Holy Spirit which shall then be with us.[157]

The Exorcistic-Healing Motif

Despite this somewhat original approach of Theodore in seeing in the anointing of all the bodily limbs a sign which represents a bodily covering, the covering of immortality which the candidate is going to receive through his baptism, it should not be overlooked that this interpretation of the ceremony reduces itself fundamently to the exorcistic-healing motif, which was more explicitly present in Cyril's reference to the "oil of exorcism," to the blessing of this oil, and to the ceremonies of exorcism in the catechumenate.

[157] *Bapt. Hom.* III.8 (Tonneau-Devreesse, *SeT* 145, 418; tr. Mingana, *WS* VI, 54).

The term "oil of anointing" which Theodore uses is no different from the term he used to denote the oil used in the first anointing, after the act of renunciation and commitment.

Theodore's interpretation must be seen in conjunction with his interpretation of the removal of garments, and forms a unity with that ceremony. Echoing the various pagan cultural and biblical attitudes toward clothing, which we have already discussed, Theodore had seen in the garments which Adam put on when he had sinned and become shamefully aware of his nakedness, the sign of his fall, and his consequent mortality, "a reproving mark of that divine decree by which you were brought low to the necessity of a covering."[158]

The anointing, then, replaces as it does this garment of mortality, and the corruption and death which that involves, becomes the exorcistic-healing sign of the immortality to come. Underlying the interpretation is the natural-cultural use of oil as a medicinal agent, to heal. In this case, what is healed is the corruption of mortality, through the use of the oil. As it is spread on the entire body, it becomes a healing covering. It is even more effective in making the candidate immortal than were the garments in making him mortal—all in sign. The oil reaches and penetrates to where the garments could not, not only covering more of the external limbs than the garments would, but even penetrating into the interior of the candidate, presumably with an eye here in the symbolic elaboration to the penetrating quality of oil. Healing, penetrating, covering, Theodore's symbolism is fundamentally the exorcistic-healing one, albeit with a unique imaginative interpretation of the covering with oil as a garment, the garment of immortality.

The christological emphasis, found both in Cyril and in Chrysostom, is not present here. There is no explicit recourse to Holy Scripture to secure the material for interpretation. Theodore states his link to the divine action not in

[158] *Idem.*

christological terms, but rather "according to the working of the Holy Spirit, which shall then be with us."

If to the modern reader the description of an anointing with oil in terms of a garment seems a trifle contrived, allowance must be made for the mentality of Theodore's candidates, influenced by and able to relate more concretely to the various medicinal uses of oil in their environment. The two elements mentioned by F. Dölger[159] as possibly influencing the ceremony from the pagan environment, the healing uses of oil in medicine and the cultic reconciliation aspects of anointing as part of religious bathing customs have been Christianized by Theodore by a consistent imagery from the stripping of Adam of his garments to the promise of future immortality, and so, no less than in Cyril, it reveals the mystagogue at work.

4. *Ambrose*

The first anointing which Ambrose mentions takes place before the act of renunciation and commitment, rather than just prior to the baptismal bath as in Cyril, Chrysostom and Theodore. The reasons for this difference between East and West in the development of rites have already been discussed.[160] As has already been shown in the synopsis of the ceremonies in the place where this anointing occurs,[161] because this is most probably an anointing of the entire body, and because the interpretation which Ambrose attaches to it corresponds to that of the other fathers in treating the anointing which for them occurs after the act of renunciation and commitment, just prior to the baptismal bath, then this anointing in Ambrose is properly treated here in conjunction with Cyril, Chrysostom and Theodore.

Ambrose interprets this anointing as follows:

> We have come to the font; you have entered; you have been anointed. Consider what you have seen, what you have said; consider, repeat carefully. A levite meets you,

159 See above, pp. 191-192.
160 See above, pp. 135-136, 189-191; ch. 1, n. 17, p. 25.
161 See above, ch. 1, p. 27.

> a priest meets you; you are anointed as an athlete of Christ as if to contend in the contest of this world. You have professed the struggles of your contest. He who contends has what he hopes for; where there is struggle, there is crown. You contend in the world, but you are crowned by Christ. And for the struggles of the world you are crowned, for, although the reward is in heaven the merit for the reward is established here.[162]

a. *The Combat Motif*

Here the symbolism of the anointing is quite clear. As in Chrysostom, it is the oiling of the athlete, equipping him with increased agility and strength for the coming combat, which begins with the renunciation of Satan, a difficult and awesome step.

Although the fact of the anointing is not mentioned, this picture of the combat also emerges in another place, where the candidate's attitude is described prior to the renunciation: "Having entered, therefore, that you might recognize your adadversary, whom you think you should renounce to his face. ."[163]

The combat metaphor is further expanded by the fact of where the ceremony takes place. It is in the baptistery apparently, but a little bit removed from the font.[164] This could lend a somewhat dramatic emphasis to this anointing squaring off a sort of small arena where the face-to-face combat with the adversary takes place. The image is that of an athlete or gladiator in the arena.

b. *The Union with Christ Motif*

The motif of union with Christ also becomes present in this athletic metaphor. Without explicitly quoting him, Ambrose

---

[162] *Sacr.* I.4. (Botte, *SC* 25bis, 62; tr. Deferrari, *FC* 44, 270): "Venimus ad fontem, ingressus es, unctus es. Considera quos videris, quid locutus sis considera, repete diligenter. Occurrit tibi levita, occurrit presbyter. Unctus es quasi athleta Christi, quasi luctam hujus saeculi luctaturus, professus es luctaminis tui certamina. Qui luctatur habet quod speret; ubi certamen, ibi corona. Luctaris in saeculo, sed coronaris a Christo et pro certaminibus saeculi coronaris. Nam etsi in caelo praemium hic tamen meritum praemii conlocatur."

[163] *Myst.* 7 (*Ibid.*, 158; tr. *ibid.*, 7): "Ingressus igitur ut adversarium tuum cerneres cui renuntiandum in os putaris."

[164] See above, ch. 1, pp. 27, 49.

echoes St. Paul's usage of contemporary sporting terms of winning the crown as a result of one's efforts in the arena.[165] In Chrysostom it was Christ Himself Who anointed the athlete for the combat; here it is Christ Who gives the victorious combatant the crown in heaven, the title to which, the "meritum praemii" he has earned by his struggle in this world.

Comparative Summary

The three fundamental motifs which we have discovered in the mystagogical interpretation of the body anointing before the baptismal bath, the exorcistic-healing motif, the motif of fortifying and protecting, or the combat motif, and the motif of union with Christ, recur continually throughout the different interpretations which the four fathers give to this ceremony. Despite the nuances of approach, due to the mystagogical genius of each father, a remarkable unity of interpretation emerges, even there where the interpretations seem to diverge so much that they no longer seem tangential to one another.

The exorcistic-healing motif begins in both Cyril and Theodore with the natural symbolism of oil as a healing agent. Cyril then proceeds to explain and elucidate this image, and to "christianize" it by a consideration of the oil itself, the prayers used in its blessing, and the relationship to the "healing" program of the catechumenate, which brings his mystagogy beyond the merely natural symbolism into the symbolism of sin as corruption, as sickness of the soul, which, like a fever, leaves its traces and ravages in the patient which must be healed by this medicinal oil. Proceeding from the same fundamental natural symbolism of oil as healing agent, Theodore, on the other hand, does not devote any attention to the oil as such, or the prayers used in its blessing, but reverts to his previous image of clothing as sign of corruption. Then he elevates or "christianizes" the natural symbol of oil in its medicinal healing power by showing how it penetrates and covers the body,

165 1 *Co.* 9:24-25.

and in so doing removes sickness. This sickness for him, no less than for Cyril, is sin and its effects. But he sees the anointing, coming as it does immediately after the removing of garments, as replacing them, as a garment would, since it covers the entire body, and even as improving on the former garments, reaching further than they would. This picture, then, he sees under the light of immortality, healing power, over against mortality, the decaying power of corruption. Thus, both Cyril and Theodore, actually beginning from the same natural symbol, and with the same Christian concern to show sin as sickness, proceed in quite different ways, and yet remain united in what they do, namely, give a Christian interpretation to the ceremony reflecting common concerns.

Underlying the *combat motif* is the natural symbolism of oil as an agent that preserves from decay, that keeps alive and supple. Cyril goes no further than a mention of this symbolism, and builds no further in his imagery, although further pictures of the athlete and the soldier are not unknown to him in another context. Chrysostom and Ambrose both add the picture of the athlete, thus using the cultural symbol of the use of oil for athletes before entering the arena to increase the suppleness and agility of their muscles. And in addition, Chrysostom adds the picture of the soldier. If oil preserves and protects from corruption and decay, then the picture of the full body anointing suggest a protective covering similar to a soldier's armor. In this Chrysostom is not too removed from Theodore, who also saw in the anointing of the entire body a covering or garment. The glistening of the oil contains for Chrysostom a symbol of the power in which the athlete's body or the soldier's armor accompany him into the combat with the adversary.[166] Ambrose does not explicitly use the image of the sol-

[166] J. Daniélou, *The Bible and the Liturgy,* p. 41, says: "So the anointing with oil is meant to strengthen the initiate for his struggles with the demon. But it is important to notice that this does not refer only to the future struggles of the new Christian, but to the act of baptism itself." Daniélou then cites various texts showing that the waters were seen as the "dwelling places of diabolic powers and that Christ had conquered them by His baptism." (P. 42). Daniélou concludes

dier clad in armor, but in this context it is interesting to note a parallel text preserved by the Milanese liturgy for the anointing of the sick, which Botte thinks might perhaps be an ancient formula for the pre-baptismal anointing: "Ungo te oleo sanctificato ut more militis unctus et praeparatus ad luctam aerias possis superare catervas."[167] In addition to bringing out the military metaphor present in the interpretation of the anointing, this passage, referring as it does to the anointing of the sick, but perhaps previously belonging to the pre-baptismal anointing, points up the fundamentally exorcistic character at the root of all the interpretations of the pre-baptismal anointing we have seen.

In summary fashion one might state the interpretations in this way: by removing the traces of sin or "ethical sickness" by use of this medicinal oil, the candidate's weakness of "mortality" and "corruptibility" was removed and in its place comes an invulnerability or "cloak of immortality" which protects and strengthens him, as a soldier or an athlete is strengthened or protected.

---

from this that "it was for this victorious struggle against the powers of darkness that the candidates for baptism were prepared by receiving a symbolic anointing." (P. 42). Whatever merit this view of Daniélou has, and the texts are convincing, the problem of symbolism may be seen, (and the necessity of avoiding generalities, but rather of analyzing different approaches in their context before proceeding to general comparisons), in Chrysostom's contribution to this matter of the serpent dwelling in the water. In the text quoted from the *P.K. Instruction* (see above, p. 200 and n. 148), Chrysostom says that the anointing will so strengthen the limbs of the candidate that he will be able to hold the serpent in check and suffer no harm. But further on, continuing the comparison of the baptistery with the Garden of Paradise, which we have seen already, Chrysostom, in this same *Instruction* explicitly states: "Do not, then, feel shame here, for the bath is much better than the garden of Paradise. There can be no serpent here, but Christ is initiating you into the regeneration that comes from water and the Spirit." (See above, p. 182 and n. 107). Thus, for Chrysostom at least, in order to be consistent with his Paradise imagery, and the flowing waters of the garden, the serpent's presence in the waters is not tenable, and the symbolism of the anointing, therefore, applies more to the general Christian struggle, rather than to the encounter with the dragon in the waters of the baptismal font.

See also, F. Dölger, "Der Kampf mit dem Ägypter in der Perpetua-Vision. Das Martyrium als Kampf mit dem Teufel," *AC* 3 (1932) 177-188.

[167] Botte, *SC* 25bis, p. 62, n. 2. See also P. Borella, "Gli esorcismi nel battesimo e la estrema-unzione," *Ambrosius* 20 (1944), 40-45.

The final and perhaps most important step which the mystagogues take is, then, to relate these natural and cultural symbols, and their relationship to sin and healing of this sin to the power of Christ. This *union with Christ motif* is also brought out in different ways by different fathers. Cyril reaches to *Rm.* for the Pauline image of the wild olive-tree and the cultivated olive-tree and makes of this, in respect to the olive oil as symbol, a direct christological symbol, the oil being a sign of the richness of the life of Christ in the true olive-tree, and also shared then by the candidate as it is spread over him. Chrysostom, too, uses Pauline material, but different from Cyril. Consistent with his sacramental theology that it is Christ Who acts through the hand of the priest, then he visualizes Christ anointing the candidate, so that the candidate becomes an athlete and soldier of Christ, a member of His team, of His army. The essential point of departure is anchored in 2 *Co.*[168] The same motif of union with Christ as seen in the anointing occurs in Ambrose, but again in yet a different way. Using 1 *Co.*[169] Ambrose sets up the picture of the arena, and above this arena in heaven, it is Christ Who waits in heaven to crown the athlete who has received His anointing and entered the struggle for Him on earth. In Theodore, it is the action of the Holy Spirit Who in sign communicates the gift of heavenly immortality now.

Healing, which in its turn leads to increased strength, and ultimately to invulnerability, because it is God's healing power, all under the aspect of reconciling the candidate's life with the life of Christ Himself, His "becoming sin," His weakness and vulnerability unto death, His victory over these powers of corruption through His resurrection: these are the Christianized aspects which the mystagogues provide in a rich variety for a ceremony strongly anchored in the environment of the candidates, in natural and cultural as well as religious symbolism.

[168] 1:21.
[169] 9:24-25.

In his article on the pagan background of the "garment of immortality" as the name for baptism, J. Quasten remarks, "And here we have again an example which proves that ecclesiastical writers cannot be understood without a thorough knowledge of ancient culture."[170] By outlining the general cultural environment and its understanding of the healing and strengthening powers of oil as well as its cultic use as symbol of reconciliation attached to ancient bathing customs, and then giving an analysis and comparison of how the four fathers presented this symbolism in a Christian way, we have attempted to show how in this "given" historical ceremony of the anointing of the body before the baptismal bath, basic principles of creative mystagogy are contained and developed.

II

THE BAPTISMAL ACT

Historical Background

The triumph which the missionary preaching of the Church had achieved by the fourth century in rendering the pagan gods no longer trustworthy led to a curiously embarrassing development in the process of Christian initiation. As long as the Church remained in the ghetto vis-à-vis the powers of the secular city, her strong eschatological emphasis could retain the essential martyrdom witness of commitment to Christ in baptism. The "either-or" emphasis of membership in the community of the saved could be uniformly asserted without having to face the less radical but perhaps more subtle crisis of what the Christian commitment of baptism demanded when the Church was at peace with the empire, and when an ever increasing number of Christians were not merely members of a Church which was at war heretofore with the empire of the pagan city,

[170] J. Quasten, "A Pythagorean Idea in Jerome," *American Journal of Philology* 63(1942), p. 203.

but were also now officials in that very empire. The problem of how to live in both worlds had become the acute problem once Christians were no longer accustomed merely to withdraw from a condemned world with its pagan institutions, but rather to take up responsibility for the secular city. Conditions for entrance into the catechumenate in the pre-Nicene period[171] indicate how much of a sociological reality the separation of Church and State really was.

The problem of Christian initiation was reflected symbolically in the life of the emperor Constantine. He solved the conflict of being at once a Christian and yet *ex officio* the *Pontifex Maximus* of the religious cult of the empire by postponing baptism until his deathbed. Coming out of the ghetto, more and more Christians found themselves unable to answer the questions and the conflicts which peace with the empire posed, and for this reason, more, perhaps, than out of cynicism, growing numbers of catechumens followed Constantine's example.

[171] Kretschmar, *op. cit.*, p. 70, presents a section of the reconstructed *Apostolic Tradition* of Hippolytus which indicates the severity of the conditions for entry into the catechumenate in the pre-Nicene period: "Then there follows (ch. 16) an examination into the way in which the applicant earns his livelihood, with explicit directives. A keeper of a brothel, an actor, anyone appearing in the circus, a gladiator, a priest for idols, a high state official, a lewd person, a magician, an astrologer: all were required to give up their previous occupation otherwise they would be excluded. A sculptor or painter was not allowed to produce any more representations of idols. As far as possible, a school master must cease instructing the children in 'worldly wisdom.' 'If he has no other trade, let this be taken into consideration.' A soldier may kill no more and is not permitted to swear the military oath. Christians who become soldiers of their own free will are excluded. Further, for the difficult problem of concubinage rules are established. ("Dann folgt c. 16 eine Prufung, auf welche Weise sich der Bewerber seinen Lebensunterhalt verdient, mit klaren Weisungen: Ein Hurenwirt, Schauspieler, jemand der im Zirbus auftritt, ein Gladiator, Götzenpriester, hoher Staatsbeamter, Unzüchtiger, Magier oder Astrolog hat seine bisherige Beschäftigung aufzugeben, oder er wird abgewiesen. Ein Bildhauer oder Maler darf keine Götzenbilder mehr herstellen; ein Schullehrer soll möglichst den Kindern keine 'weltliche Weisheit' mehr beibringen, 'wenn er kein anderes Handwerk hat, so sei es ihm nachgesehen'; ein Soldat darf nicht mehr töten und keinen Militäreid schwören; Christen, die freiwillig Soldat werden wollen, werden ausgeschlossen. Weiter werden für die schwierige Frage des Konkubinate Regeln festgelegt)."

The necessity of leading a life of responsibility in the previously rejected world made of the original demand of radical obedience to the Gospel a seemingly impossible ideal, better not to be shouldered as long as one was involved in such a world.[172]

For such towering spirits as Basil, John Chrysostom, Theodore of Mopsuestia and Augustine, "conversion" was seen now as a decision for an ascetical life, one that would preclude an emerging lack of seriousness with Christian initiation, with baptism. This, however, did not solve the problem of the lack of what one might term today an ethic for the Christian layman. The growing practice of postponing baptism until the deathbed, because it was viewed as such a burden or even a danger given the task one was involved in in this world, and because it presented insoluble ethical problems, given the prior schism between church and world—and this atmosphere still dominated the thinking on baptism—this postponement of baptism was threatening to give this sacrament a purely eschatological orientation and make of it a highly individual rather than an ecclesial concern.

It was during this particular socio-religious crisis for the church, with its repercussions in the practice of Christian Initiation, that the theology of the ancient church reached a flowering. It was from this force that a deepened awareness of the meaning of baptism was to come. "Theology" meant preponderantly for the fathers of the church the exegesis of Holy Scripture. Of particular interest for the deepened reflection of the meaning of the baptismal act itself was the rediscovery of the writings of St. Paul as a means for making the theology of baptism more fruitful.[173]

In presenting the materials used in the mystagogical writings to interpret the ceremonies of initiation treated up to the

[172] For a summary of this tension between society and church see G. Kretschmar, *op. cit., pp.* 145-152. See also G. Kretschmar, "Die zwei Imperien und die zwei Reiche," in *Ecclesia und Res publica,* für K. D. Schmidt (Göttingen, 1961), pp. 89-112, esp. p. 102ff.

[173] See Kretschmar, *Der Taufgottesdienst,* p. 148.

baptismal act itself, we have already seen in numerous instances the influence of the Pauline writings on the four fathers. It will not be surprising, then, to discover that the chief source to which Cyril, Chrysostom, Theodore and Ambrose repair to explain the meaning of the baptismal bath itself is St. Paul. Both in their presentation of this ceremony as the central action of the initiation, as well as in the unified convergence of their mystagogy in emphasizing the Pauline view of its meaning, we see the attempt to lend deeper meaning to Christian Initiation in time of crisis, a crisis brought on not by the Church's "war" with the world, but embarrassingly, by its "peace."

Biblical background

As A. Stenzel has adequately outlined[174] the general mystagogical interpretation of the baptismal act is that of a purifying bath of water.[175] The word "baptize (βαπτίζειν)" itself is already a pre-Christian word meaning "to dip in water," in order to achieve, for example, purification from cultic uncleanness. In its basic *liturgical* understanding in the *NT*, the word "baptize" cannot be said to mean anything more than this: going into water and coming out of water as the indispensable movement in order to achieve a purificatory washing.[176]

This simple "*terminus technicus*," meaning a washing with water is, then, the fundamental liturgical term reflected in the *NT* when baptism is mentioned. The fact of the term's pre-Christian history connected with cultic purification brings with it to the *NT* the fundamental mystagogical interpretation of the liturgical action of entering the water and coming out

[174] See A. Stenzel, *Die Taufe,* pp. 15-42.

[175] *Cf. Col.* 2:11-13; 1 *Co.* 6:11; *Ep.* 5:26; *Heb.* 10:22.

[176] "In actual fact the earliest witnesses see in the entering and leaving the water nothing more than the unavoidable movement required for a purificatory washing (Tatsächlich sehen die frühesten Zeugnisse im Hinein – und Herausgehen aus dem Wasser nicht mehr als die nun einmal unvermeidliche Bewegung, um zur reinigenden Waschung zu kommen)." Stenzel, p. 23. See also A. Oepke, "βάπτω, βαπτίζω," *TWB* I.527-544.

of it as that of purification. The further interpretations of the meaning of baptism present in the *NT*, which go beyond this, cannot in themselves be always considered as a mystagogical interpretation of the *liturgical action,* but rather as a theologizing on the meaning of the baptismal event itself. For example, if a *NT* author describes baptism as a being buried with Christ, one may not immediately conclude thereby that this is a mystagogical interpretation of a liturgical action, which action would then necessarily be a complete immersion of the candidate in water in order to represent his death or entry into the grave etc. It can be, rather, a *theologizing on the meaning of baptism,* derived from other sources in the apostolic preaching, rather than a mystagogical interpretation of the liturgical ceremony as it actually was performed. True, such theologizing on the meaning of being baptized in Christ could then later affect the ritual itself so that it could be made to correspond to the theologizing, but this is a further step and represents a further development in the relationship of theology to the creation of liturgical symbols. Great caution is required before one can say that, over and above the simple *liturgical "terminus technicus"* of entering and leaving water, which baptism means, and the mystagogical interpretation of purification which is unavoidably attached to this action in the *NT*, given its pre-Christian origin, the other utterances in the *NT* about the meaning of baptism prove how the action was performed liturgically. Such utterances are a theologizing on the meaning of baptism, not a mystagogy on a given actual ceremony.[177]

[177]"Only the minimal meaning of the *terminus technicus* can serve as point of departure for conclusions about the general baptismal praxis. What the individual author provides as nuances and as complementary material must first be viewed as his own theologizing. (Nur der ärmere Gehalt des terminus technicus kann als Ausgangspunkt für Schlüsse auf allgemeinen Taufgebrauch dienen. Was der einzelne Autor darüber hinaus an Nuancen und Füllung bringt, muss zunächst als theologisierendes Eigengut angesehen werden)." Stenzel, p. 21.

"The images in their multiplicity neutralize one another. One is justified the more in seeing theology in them by the fact that they can only be partially drawn from the rite of the bath of water. At least caution is called for not to come to

Even when considering St. Paul's utterances on the meaning of being baptized in Christ, one sees that he is apparently not giving a mystagogical interpretation of the liturgical action of baptism as he saw it. His liturgical point of departure remains nothing more, apparently, than the basic purifying bath of water.[178] Thus, as Schnackenburg notes, St. Paul builds his baptismal interpretation from the basic christological scheme of the faith, that is, from a dogmatic conception rather than from a liturgical intuition.[179]

When St. Paul, in *Rm.* 6, goes beyond the fundamental tradition of the purifying bath in erecting his baptismal theology of being buried with Christ and rising again with Him, one would not be justified in saying that this is a mystagogical interpretation of a liturgical action the essence of which is the action of being plunged into water as into a grave, and which action therefore requires or suggests the interpretation of burial and resurrection. Neither *Rm.* 6 nor descriptions of baptism in the earliest Christian literature support the assumption that the decisive meaning of the "bath of water" consists in providing the medium under the surface of which one could be "buried" by immersing in it.[180] The basic liturgical action remains, rather, a movement in and out of the water as a purificatory washing, at least as far as the earliest testimonies are concerned. For them baptism is the purifying bath of water. As St. Paul describes it: "cleansed by the bath of water (*καθαρίσας τῷ λουτρῷ τοῦ ὕδατος*)."[181]

---

overhasty conclusions about the sacramental rite ("efficiunt quod significant") on the basis of one of these many images. (Die Bilder in ihrer Vielzahl neutralisieren einander; in ihnen Theologie zu sehen ist man um so mehr berechtigt, als sie nur zum Teil aus dem Ritus des Wasserbades ableitbar sind. Zu einer Vorsicht wird man mindestens gedrängt: nicht voreilig aus einem dieser vielen Bilder auf den sakramentalen Ritus ("efficiunt quod significant") zu schliessen)." Stenzel, p. 21, n. 12.

[178] *Cf. Rm.* 6; *Col.* 2:11; 1 *Co.* 6:11; *Ep.* 5:26; *Heb.* 10:22.

[179] ". . . aus dem Christusschema des Glaubens argumentiert . . . aus dogmatischer Konzeption, nicht liturgischer Intuition." R. Schnackenburg, *Das Heilsgeschehen bei der Taufe nach dem Apostel Paulus* (Munich, 1950), p. 64.

[180] See Stenzel, p. 23.

[181] *Ep.* 5:26.

Stenzel summarizes the *NT* situation. In the time for which the *NT* writings are witness, the Church had no unified and binding baptismal order other than that which comprised entering the water and the act of faith. And this is not surprising in a time of missionary expansion. The extent of our knowledge is small and can be summarily described. The mission sermon reaches someone whose heart is ready. Perhaps there follows a personal dialogue with the missionary. The individual is prepared to confess the faith which was proclaimed, and when the missionary feels that he is ready—a matter of hours or perhaps days—then he baptized him upon his confession of faith.[182]

Theological Background

In addition to the historical currents and the *NT* background which are necessary for understanding the approach of the four fathers to the mystagogical interpretation of the baptismal act, there are, of course, also numerous theological meanings which in the course of previous Christian history had been attached to the baptismal act. These theological approaches are many and varied, and the fathers obviously do not develop all of them by incorporation into their mystagogy in the same degree. They are aware of these several meanings, however, and list them in general or "catalogue" fashion. Since they form a background out of which the central mystagogical interpretation arises, it will be useful to list them as part of the general background material to which the fathers reach for their mystagogy.

Cyril

Cyril summarizes the effects of baptism in the following passage: "It is a ransom to captives; the remission of offenses; the death of sin; the regeneration of the soul; the garment of light; the holy seal indissoluble; the chariot to heaven; the lux-

[182]See Stenzel, pp. 41-42.

ury of paradise; a procuring of the kingdom; the gift of adoption."[183]

Chrysostom

Chrysostom brings together a survey of Pauline quotations to show the candidates the variety of names which may be given to baptism. Describing it as a mystic cleansing he says: "This cleansing is called the bath of regeneration.[184] . . . It is also called baptism.[186] It is called a burial.[187] . . . It is called a circumcision.[188] . . . It is called a cross."[189]

The unusual rhetorical flight present in another summary of what baptism means in its effects might prompt one to overlook how totally Chrysostom's analysis is based, not on arbitrary symbols, but completely in the *NT.* Although he does not list the pertinent *NT* references in his text, an analysis shows that of the ten fruits of baptism which Chrysostom enumerates, nine of them come from either the Gospels or from the Pauline Epistles.[190]

> Before yesterday you were captives, but now you are *free*[191] and citizens of the Church; lately you lived in the shame of your sins, but now you live in freedom and justice. You are not only free, but also *holy,*[192] not only holy but also *just,*[193] not only just, but also *sons,*[194] not only sons, but also *heirs,*[195] not only heirs, but also *brothers* of

[183] *Procat.* 16 (Cross, *SPCK,* 10; tr. Cross, *SPCK,* 50): *αἰχμαλώτοις λύτρον· ἁμαρτημάτων ἄφεσις· θάνατος ἁμαρτίας· παλιγγενεσία ψυχῆς· ἔνδυμα φωτεινόν· σφραγὶς ἁγία ἀκατάλυτος· ὄχημα πρὸς οὐρανόν· παραδείσου τρυφή· βασιλείας πρόξενον· υἱοθεσίας χάρισμα.*

[184] *Cf. Tt.* 3:5.

[185] *Cf. Heb.* 10:32; 6:4-6.

[186] *Cf. Ga.* 3:27.

[187] *Cf. Rm.* 6:4.

[188] *Cf. Col.* 2:11.

[189] *Cf. Rm.* 6:6 *Montf.* 1-*P.K.* 1.12 (*MG* 49.225; tr. Harkins, *ACW* 31, 135): *τὸ καθάρσιον τοῦτο καλεῖται λουτρὸν παλιγγενεσίας· . . . καλεῖται φωτίσμα, . . . καλεῖται και βαπτίσμα· . . . καλεῖται ταφή· . . . καλεῖται περιτομή· . . . καλειται σταυρός.*

[190] See Harkins, *ACW* 31, 232, n. 9.

[191] *Cf. Jn.* 8:36.

[192] *Cf. Rm.* 1:7.

[193] *Cf. Rm.* 2:13.

[194] *Cf. Rm.* 8:14.

[195] *Cf. Rm.* 8:17.

Christ,[196] not only brothers of Christ, but also *joint heirs,*[197] not only joint heirs, but also *members,*[198] not only members, but also the *temple,*[199] not only the temple, but also *instruments* of the Spirit.[200]

Theodore

Less directly leaning on Holy Scripture than Chrysostom and somewhat less concrete than Cyril's presentation, Theodore also lists a summary of the effects of baptism.

> In the same way the sentence: "In the name of the Father and of the Son and of the Holy Spirit" reveals the giver of the benefits of baptism which are: second birth, renewal, immortality, incorruptibility, impassibility, immutability, deliverance from death and servitude to all evils, happiness of freedom, and participation in the ineffable good things which we are expecting. The person who is baptized is baptized for these things.[201]

Ambrose

While not providing a similar summary of the effects of baptism they may be gleaned from various places in the Paschal catechesis of Ambrose. They are: salvation, healing, purification, new creation, new birth, transformation, illumination.[202]

[196] *Cf. Mt.* 12:50.

[197] *Cf. Rm.* 8:17.

[198] *Cf.* 1 *Co.* 6:15.

[199] *Cf.* 1 *Co.* 3:16.

[200] The italics in the text are ours. As Harkins notes, only this last term, "instruments of the Spirit,"is not found in Scripture as such. *Stav.* 3-*P.K.* 4.5 (Wenger, *SC* 50, 153; tr. Harkins, *ACW* 31, 57): *Οἱ πρὸ τῆς χθὲς αἰχμάλωτοι, νῦν ἐλεύθεροι καὶ πολῖται τῆς ἐκκλησίας· οἱ πρώην ἐν αἰσχύνῃ ἁμαρτιῶν, νῦν ἐν παρρησίᾳ καὶ σύνῃ. Οὐ γὰρ ἐλεύθεροι μόνον ἀλλὰ καὶ ἅγιοι, οὐχ ἅγιοι μόνον ἀλλὰ καὶ δίκαιοι, οὐ δίκαιοι μόνον ἀλλὰ καὶ υἱοί, οὐχ υἱοὶ μόνον ἀλλὰ καὶ κληρονόμοι, βὐ κληρονόμοι μόνον ἀλλὰ καὶ ἀδελφοὶ τοῦ Χριστοῦ, οὐκ ἀδελφοὶ τοῦ Χριστοῦ μόνον ἀλλὰ καὶ συγκληρονόμοι, οὐ συγκληρονόμοι μόνον ἀλλὰ καὶ μέλη, οὐ μέλη μόνον ἀλλὰ καὶ ναός, οὐ ναὸς μόνον ἀλλὰ καὶ ὄργανα τοῦ Πνεύματος.*

[201] *Bapt. Hom.* III.17 (Tonneau-Devreesse, *SeT* 145, 438; tr. Mingana, *WS* VI, 62).

[202] See Botte, *SC* 25bis, 35.

The Mystagogical Problem

Such listings as the above of the meaning or effects of baptism are grounded in scripture and tradition. They show the scriptural, theological and traditional overview which the fathers had of the meaning of the baptismal act. They are, obviously, not in themselves, nor do they intend to be, the *actual mystagogical interpretation of the act of baptism* as the fathers found in the respective liturgies in which their neophytes had participated on the night of their baptism. They do, however, form the traditional matter of interpretation of the meaning of baptism, even though they are not arrived at through the specific mystagogical interpretation of the liturgical action itself. What interests us, especially, is this: given the traditional development of the meaning expressed, as we have seen in the above listings, in a variety of ways, how did the fathers relate this material to the given ceremony of baptism upon which they commented?

Since the purpose of a mystagogical catechesis is to bring the neophytes to a deeper meaning of what was said and what was done, then the materials used to explain this meaning cannot be a mere theologizing, or application of past theologizings to the liturgical ceremony, without reference to how the ceremony itself indicates what is asserted. Otherwise, the relationship of the theological meaning to the ceremony itself would be unauthentic, forced or nil. This would not be mystagogy, but mere catechism. At worst, one would be tempted to read into the ceremony things which really are not present, in order to make it correspond in meaning with the theology, or even more disturbing, alter the ceremonies themselves so that they would conform, howbeit artificially, to the theology. This not entirely unknown phenomenon would be a perversion of the order of liturgy.[203]

[203] See A. Kavanagh, "Liturgical Needs for Today and Tomorrow," *Worship* 43 (1969), pp. 488-495, esp. 490-491.

From this it follows that one unavoidable factor of mystagogy is its uniqueness in a given situation. Since the liturgical event is in a sense "unique" even though "repeatable," so too a mystagogical explanation of this unique event, given to these individuals who have participated, has perforce an element of creative uniqueness about it which, for example, a catalogue listing of abstract "truths" would not have to possess. A list of abstract truths is one thing. When such a list is presented to a candidate to learn perhaps even by heart, one does not have the same kind of situation which faces the mystagogue who has not to present a series of truths catechetical style to his hearers, but rather to help them to understand the meaning of what they have actually done. This, then, is the reason for the uniqueness of a mystagogical catechesis. The *actual liturgical ceremony* must be taken into account, with its traditional givens, and some historical explanation of these givens, at least implied. But that is still not sufficient. The candidates themselves, their environment, the church's needs of the present moment against its sociological backdrop, these factors must be calculated by the mystagogue. Both of these elements, the ceremony itself and the *Sitz im Leben* of the candidates must be combined in order to present not a forced or far-fetched, but a coherent explanation of the significance of the ceremonies. One cannot ignore the real ceremony in an excessive zeal to present theological meaning, else the ceremony is reduced to inauthenticity. Then the ceremony really would not matter at all, but would be reduced to a quasi-magic backdrop against which the really "important" thing, the theology, would be presented without concern for its link to the liturgy itself. At the same time, one cannot ignore the candidate's awareness and background, how he relates to the liturgy anthropologically, otherwise the mystagogical explanation of the ceremony—no matter how valid it might have been in a previous set of circumstances—could appear to the candidate to be ludicrous.

Faced then with the uniqueness of the problem of helping *these neophytes* discover the meaning of *these rites* of Christian initiation, let us examine what principles were adopted, what materials were used by Cyril, Theodore, Chrysostom and Ambrose to present to their neophytes the meaning of the central action of the initiation rite, the bath of water itself.

A. *Conformity to Christ in Death and Resurrection*

The Convergence on Pauline Theology

Three main factors might be isolated to explain the remarkable convergence of emphasis in all four fathers in employing the Pauline theology of baptism as a sharing in the crucifixion, death and resurrection of Jesus Christ in order to provide the central "material" to construct the mystagogical explanation of the baptismal act.

The Hearers: Eschatological Versus Incarnational Spirituality

As we have seen in the historical sketch, it was imperative that baptism be rescued from the fate of becoming a merely eschatological sacrament, an individualistic act often postponed until the deathbed, which would wash away all one's sins, and at the most convenient moment, when the struggle and doubt as to what it meant to be a Christian in the world was well-nigh over, would throw open the gates of heaven to the fortunate recipient. In this connection Chrysostom somewhat caustically describes three kinds of Christians: those who receive baptism as babies, those who have no particular inclination to make the final commitment which baptism requires, but immediately seek it in event of a serious illness, from which they later recover and finally those who receive baptism as healthy, adult human beings.[204]

By emphasizing baptism not only as the saving bath which purified from all sin and threw open the gates of heaven, but showing the relationship of this salvation to the salvific action of the life, death and resurrection of Christ, and the candidates' conformity to this through faith, and the expression of this faith in the act of baptism, then a major step had been

[204]See *In act. apost.* 23 (*MG* 60.182). See Kretschmar, *op. cit.*, p. 147.

taken toward providing the candidate with a spirituality for a Christian life in this world, central focus of which is his dynamic union with the humanity of Christ.

The Material: The Renascence of Pauline Studies

The second factor which led the fathers to utilize in their mystagogical explanation of the baptismal act the material found in the Pauline theology of baptism was the renascence of Pauline studies at the time.[205] In dealing with the other ceremonies we have already seen how the fathers prefer material from Holy Scripture as far as possible for use in providing their mystagogical explanations, wherever this is possible. Precisely in the Pauline theology of baptism with its constant referral to the relationship between Christ and the Christian, and to the Adam-Christ, old man-new man comparison, the fathers could find the suitable vehicle to emphasize the baptismal act, not merely as the final act of remission of sins and passage through the portals of heaven, but as the beginning of the candidate's life in Christ now, in this world, his transfiguration.

The Ceremony: State of Development

A third factor which made the Pauline view of baptism as conformity to the death and resurrection of Christ suitable from a mystagogical viewpoint was the state of development of the liturgical action of baptism at the time. From the synopsis of the ceremonies in which the act of baptism is reconstructed from the indications of it given in the mystagogical writings of the four fathers,[206] it is clear that immersion of the candidate in the baptismal water, or at least something closely approximating immersion and seen as the equivalent thereof, was the liturgical practice.[207]

[205] See Kretschmar, *op. cit.*, p. 148.

[206] See above, pp. 144-150.

[207] The "equivalent" of immersion could be, *e.g.*, having the candidate stand in the pool, with the water reaching only a certain point on his body, as would be the case of many pools which were hardly deep enough to make complete immersion feasible. The person baptizing then pours water over his head, so that in a sense

The practice of baptism by immersion lent itself readily, of course, to the application of the Pauline theology of *Rm.* 6:3-4 and *Col.* 2:12 as a suitable vehicle and remarkably apposite mystagogical explanation of the way the baptismal act was performed, immersion into the water being immersion into death, even though, as we have already pointed out in the treatment of the *NT* background this Pauline theology was apparently not originally meant to be a mystagogical explanation of a liturgical action, but rather a theological reflection on the meaning of baptism in Christ in general, regardless of whether or not the actual ceremony provided a corroborative symbolism. Be that as it may, the baptismal act of immersion described by the fathers did actually provide this symbolism, and given the other factors at work, the needs of the hearers and the Pauline exegesis, they seized upon it as an excellent and graphic way to describe to the neophytes what had actually taken place when they descended into the baptismal pool.

---

the candidate is for a few moments covered with a mantle of water, or "immersed." Such is often found in pictorial representations of the baptism of Jesus by John in the Jordan. In such a case one might still speak of baptism by *immersion,* and not by mere pouring, or *infusion.* In the latter case the candidate would not be standing in any kind of pool at all. For a historical summary of these practices see Stenzel, pp. 108-110.

SYNOPTIC CHART

Baptism as Conformity to Christ in Death and Resurrection

Cyril	*Ambrose*	*Chrysostom*	*Theodore*
GENERAL:			
ENTERING AND LEAVING POOL:	IMMERSION AND LEAVING POOL:	ENTERING AND LEAVING POOL:	IMMERSION AND LEAVING POOL:
DEATH AND RESUR-RECTION WITH CHRIST.	DEATH AND RESUR-RECTION WITH CHRIST: FORGIVENESS OF SINS.	DEATH AND RESUR-RECTION WITH CHRIST.	DEATH AND RESUR-RECTION WITH CHRIST.
Myst.Cat. II.8 *Rm.* 6:4,13 (*Procat.* 2 *Bapt.Cat.* III.12)	*Sacr.* II.16,20; III.1 *Rm.* 6:4	*Stav.* 2.25,29 *P.K.* 2.11 *Col.* 3:10 *Rm.* 6:4,8	*Bapt.Hom.* I.6-7 III. 5,25 *Rm.* 6:3
-Anastasis: *Myst.Cat.* II.4 -Reading: *Rm.* 6:3-14: *Myst.Cat.* II.6			
SIN AND DEATH:			
Movement to Pool: Christ to Sepulcher *Myst.Cat.* II.4	*1st Immersion: Sin and Death* -Biblical Theology: *Sacr.* II.17-18 *Gn.* 3:17-23 *Rm.* 6:7	*Entering Pool: Death* *Stav.* 2.25	*Immersion: Death* *Bapt.Hom.* III. 5,25

Baptism as Conformity to Christ in Death and Resurrection—continued

Cyril	*Ambrose*	*Chrysostom*	*Theodore*
	-Baptistery Tomb: *Sacr.* III.1; II.19	-Baptistery Paradise: *P.K.* 3.28 *Col.* 3:10	-Baptistery Furnace, Potter's Vessel: *Bapt.Hom.* III. 10-11 *Jr.* 18:1-6 *Jb.* 33:6; 4:19
	-Earth-Water: *Sacr.* II.17,19 *Gn.* 3:19		-Earth-Water; *Bapt.Hom.* I.10
		-Death as Detachment: *Stav.* 7.21-23 *Col.* 3:1-4 *Rm.* 6:6	
Triple Immersion-Emersion: 3 Days: *Myst.Cat.* II.4 *Mt.* 12:46 *Jon.* 2:1			
THE CROSS:			
Fellowship in Christ's Sufferings *Myst.Cat.* II.5-7 *Rm.* 6:5 *Jn.* 15:1-8 *Mt.* 27:59	*2nd Immersion: the Cross* *Myst.* 28 *Sacr.* II.23 *Rm.* 6:3	*Baptism and the Cross*	
		-Sons of Zebedee: *P.K.* 2.9-10 *Mt.* 20:20; 26:39 *Mk.* 10:38 *Lk.* 12:50	
		-Blood-Water: *Stav.* 3- *P.K.* 4.16 *Jn.* 19:33-34	

Baptism as Conformity to Christ in Death and Resurrection—continued

Cyril	*Ambrose*	*Chrysostom*	*Theodore*
FORGIVENESS:			
	Triple Immersion: Sin and Forgiveness *Sacr.* II.21-22		*Power of Forgiveness* *Bapt.Hom.* III 15-16
	-Peter: *Jn.* 21:17		
	-Trinity		-Trinity
	-Name of Jesus *Ac.* 4:12		-Name of Jesus *Ac.* 3:6
RESURRECTION:			
Leaving Pool: Resurrection *Myst.Cat.* II.8 *Rm.* 6:4,13 (*Procat.* 2) (*Bapt.Cat.* III.12)	*Leaving Pool: Resurrection* *Sacr.* III.1-2	*Leaving Pool: Resurrection* *Stav.* 2.29 *P.K.* 2.11	*Leaving Pool: Resurrection* *Bapt.Hom.* III. 5,25
			Future Resurrection of Body *Bapt.Hom.* III.6 *Rm.* 6:5
			-Body of Christ *Bapt.Hom.* III. 21-22 1 *Co.* 2:3 *Ph.* 3:20-21 *Col.* 2:19

1. Cyril

Presuppositions

The Place

Cyril enjoyed the most advantageous position to capitalize on this mystagogical explanation of the act of baptism as meaning a participation in the sufferings, death and resurrection of Jesus. His mystagogical discourses, delivered in Easter week, were held, it will be remembered, in the *Anastasis,* the rotunda of the resurrection. Listening to Cyril's catecheses, the neophytes had, as he himself points out to them, the holy sepulcher itself before their very eyes.[208] This "on-the-scene" advantage is the first material from which Cyril draws the interpretation of the baptismal act as a being buried with Christ.

The Scripture Reading

Assembled in the *Anastasis,* and with this point about to be emphasized by the mystagogue, the neophytes who had come to hear a discourse revealing to them the meaning of the baptismal act which they had done on Holy Saturday night, the neophytes heard the reader deliver *Rm.* 6:3-14, a kind of *Magna Charta* for the mystagogical interpretation of baptism by immersion as burial with Christ, and also for the spirituality of Christian life in the world as conformity to Christ. In the course of the catechesis, Cyril has occasion to quote several verses of this scripture reading which the neophytes had just heard. His use of them forms the key to his mystagogical interpretation of the baptismal act, that is, the sinner, being "baptized" or "immersed" in water, is thus symbolically "buried" with Christ: "Do you not know that as many of us as were baptized into Christ Jesus, were baptized into His death? Therefore we are buried with Him by baptism."[209]

[208] See *Myst. Cat.* II.4 (Piédagnel, *SC* 126, 119; tr. Cross, *SPCK,* 60). *Cf. Bapt. Cat.* XVIII.33 (*MG* 33, 1056); *Peregrinatio Aetheriae* 47, *SC* 21, 260.

[209] *Cf. Rm.* 6:3-4. *Myst. Cat.* II.6 (Piédagnel, *SC* 126, 114; tr. Cross, *SPCK,* 62): "'Η ἀγνοεῖτε ὅτι ὅσοι ἐβαπτίσθημεν εἰς Χριστὸν Ἰησοῦν, εἰς τὸν θάνατον αὐτοῦ ἐβαπτίσθημεν; Συνετάφημεν οὖν αὐτῷ διὰ τοῦ βαπτίσματος."

Even though Cyril touches on other aspects of the meaning of baptism from traditional sources, such as rebirth, remission of sins, adoption into sonship, it is obvious that his chief concern as mystagogue is to link the liturgical ceremony of the baptismal act as the neophytes had undergone it with the real historical event of the burial of Christ. Through the act of baptism the baptized is intimately associated with the salvific event of Christ's death and burial, and by consequence, of course, with His passion and resurrection. This is the Pauline message, proceeding, as we have pointed out before[210] not from a mystagogical interpretation from the liturgical action of immersion necessarily, but from the basic christological scheme of faith, that is, from a dogmatic conception rather than from a liturgical intuition. Cyril takes this Pauline dogmatic message, the reality of baptism as association with Christ from which the act contains its transforming force, and applies it to the actual ceremony as a central building block in his mystagogical interpretation of this ceremony. How does Cyril show his hearers that this is the meaning of what was actually done in the ceremony which they underwent, the immersion in the baptismal pool?

a. *The Movement to the Font: From Cross to Tomb*

Cyril's introductory sentence to his mystagogical interpretation of the baptismal act contains a strikingly concrete image which indicates from the very outset the direction his mystagogical interpretation of the baptismal act will take: "After these things [that is, the removal of garments and the prebaptismal anointing], you were led by the hand to the holy pool of divine baptism, as Christ was carried from the cross to the sepulcher, which is before you."[211]

[210] See above pp. 214-217.

[211] *Myst. Cat.* II.4 (Piédagnel, *SC* 126, 110; tr. Cross, *SPCK,* 60): *Μετὰ ταῦτα ἐπὶ τὴν ἁγίαν τοῦ θείου βαστίσματος ἐχειραγωγεῖσθε κολυμβήθραν, ὡς ὁ Χριστὸς ἀπὸ τοῦ σταυροῦ ἐπὶ τὸ προκείμενον μνῆμα.*

Thus the stage is set for a kind of one-to-one comparison of the actions of the candidate with the burial of the body of Christ. The candidate's transit from the room where he had removed his clothing and the place where he had been anointed to the baptismal pool itself becomes equated symbolically with the carrying of the body of Jesus from the cross to the tomb.[212]

This image continues the idea of mystical association of the candidate with Christ through the symbolism which Cyril attaches to the ritual action and which he had used previously, when the stripping off of the candidate's clothing was compared to the stripping of Christ on the cross.[213]

b. *The Triple Immersion-Emersion: 3 Days and 3 Nights*

In the next stage of the liturgical action, the immersion in the water, Cyril proceeds along the same mystagogical line, the interpretation of the details of the liturgical action as symbolizing the events of the burial of Jesus. Thus he interprets the triple immersion and the triple emersion in the baptismal water: ". . . and you were immersed three times in the water and came up again, here too in a symbolic way signifying the three-day burial of Christ."[214]

[212]According to the "topography" of Cyril's baptistery this movement was between the room designated for the removal of clothing and anointing and the place where the baptismal pool itself was located, in the same building. The renunciation had taken place in the "vestibule of the baptistery," that is, "in the exterior edifice." (See above, ch. 1, p. 24). The rest of the ritual takes place "in the interior edifice (*ἐν τῷ ἐσωτέρῳ . . . οἴκῳ*)." *Myst. Cat.* II.1 (Piédagnel, *SC* 126, 104; tr. Cross, *SPCK*, 59). Possibly the "holy of holies (*ἅγια τῶν ἁγίων*)" referred to earlier by Cyril, *Myst. Cat.* I.11 (Piédagnel, *SC* 126, 102; tr. Cross, *SPCK*, the entire interior edifice. Ambrose uses the same term, "sancta sanctorum." *Myst.* 5 (Botte, *SC* 25bis, 158; tr. Deferrari, *FC* 44, 6), but in a more general symbolic sense, rather than in a strict local allusion from which a mystagogical interpretation is derived, since his candidates had already entered the baptistery before he makes the statement.

[213]See above, pp. 173-176.

[214]*Myst. Cat.* II.4 (Piédagnel, *SC* 126, 110; tr. Cross, *SPCK*, 60): *καὶ κατεδύετε τρίτον εἰς τὸ ὕδωρ καὶ πάλιν ἀνεδύετε, καὶ ἐνταῦθα διὰ συμβόλου τὴν τριήμερον τοῦ Χριστοῦ αἰνιττόμενοι ταφήν.*

Thus, the baptismal pool becomes the mystagogical equivalent of the tomb of Jesus. The triple immersion, and emersion, which was a part of the baptismal ritual in Jerusalem at the time, is then construed by Cyril in a somewhat complex symbolic explanation:

> Just as our Savior passed three days and three nights in the heart of the earth, so you also in your first emersion out of the water represented the first day of Christ in the earth, and by your [first] immersion into the water the [first] night; for, just as a person in the night does not see any more, whereas a person during the daytime remains in the light, so you, too, in your immersion saw nothing, just as in the night, but in your emersion again, you found yourself as in the daytime.[215]

The triple emersion should not be confused here with the candidate's coming out of the baptismal pool itself. He remains in the pool itself, but ducks and comes up three times. And wandering in the daytime must not be confused with the resurrection. Rather Cyril has taken the given rite, where the candidate's head is immersed into the water three times, and, of course, comes back up three times, and interpreted it as a symbol of three days and three nights, the nights being when the head is under water, the days being when the head is above water. To further this interpretation of the ceremony, which, of course, at this point borrows from the natural symbol of light and darkness to symbolize day and night, he borrows the expression from the bible, "three days and three nights in the heart of the earth (*ἐν τῇ καρδίᾳ τῆς γῆς τρεῖς ἡμέρας καὶ τρεῖς νύκτας*)"[216] where the St. Matthew Gospel treats the sign of Jonah, "who remained in the belly of the fish for three

[215] *Ibid.*, II.4 (*Ibid.*, 112; tr. *ibid.*, 60-61): Καθάπερ γὰρ ὁ Σωτὴρ ἡμῶν τρεῖς ἡμέρας καὶ τρεῖς νύκτας ἐν τῇ καρδίᾳ τῆς γῆς πεποίηκεν, οὕτω καὶ ὑμεῖς ἐν τῇ πρώτῃ ἀναδύσει τὴν πρώτην ἐμιμεῖσθε τοῦ Χριστοῦ ἐν τῇ γῇ ἡμέραν καὶ τῇ καταδύσει τὴν νύκτα· ὥσπερ γὰρ ὁ ἐν νυκτὶ οὐκέτι βλέπει, ὁ δὲ ἐν ἡμέρᾳ φωτὶ διάγει, οὕτως ἐν τῇ καταδύσει ὡς ἐν νυκτὶ οὐδεν ἑωρᾶτε, ἐν δὲ τῇ ἀναδύσει πάλιν ὡς ἐν ἡμέρᾳ ἐτυγχάνετε ὄντες.

[216] *Mt.* 12:40.

days and three nights."[217] Both the immersion, where the candidate's head is submerged in the darkness of the water, as in the night, and the emersion, where his head comes out of the water, and he can see as in the day—both of these gestures represent time spent in the heart of the earth, three nights and three days according to the biblical reckoning.

Cyril's interpretation of the triple immersion and the triple emersion as symbolizing the three days and three nights of Christ in the "heart of the earth" will stand in marked difference with that of Ambrose, Theodore and Chrysostom, as we shall later see.[218] Cyril's main concern is not in the Trinitarian symbolism of the three immersions, but rather in continuing to make graphic the christological symbolism of the act of baptism.[219]

c. *Coming out of the Pool: Resurrection*

Does Cyril employ the symbolism which would normally suggest itself at this point, namely, that since the baptismal pool represents the tomb, and the baptized's entering the pool and triple immersion and emersion represents Christ's entering the tomb and remaining there three days and three nights, so the newly baptized in climbing up out of the pool would be an apt symbol of Jesus rising from the tomb? Strangely enough, Cyril, at this point in his mystagogy, does not mention this seemingly obvious mystagogical interpretation. His concern turns almost immediately to the theology of how the neophyte is actually conformed sacramentally to the passion, death and resurrection of Christ, and this is what occupies him next.[220]

[217] *Idem. Cf. Jon.* 2:1.

[218] See below, pp. 244-252, 255-259, 261-266, 271-278.

[219] That such traditional Trinitarian interpretation of the triple immersion could be readily used by Cyril is obvious from the confession of faith which the candidates make: "And each one of you was asked if he believed in the name of the Father and of the Son and of the Holy Spirit. And you made that saving confession. (*Καὶ ἠρωτᾶτω ἕκαστος εἰ πιστεύει εἰς τὸ ὄνομα τοῦ Πατρός, καὶ τοῦ Υἱοῦ καὶ τοῦ αγίου Πνεύματος. Καὶ ὡμολογεῖτε τὴν σωτηρίον ὁμολογίαν*)." *Myst. Cat.* II.4 (Piédagnel, *SC* 126, 110; tr. Cross, *SPCK,* 60). See Stenzel, pp. 110-111.

[220] For parallels in other authors where such an interpretation is explicitly used see Piédagnel, *SC* 126, 113, n. 1.

That Cyril was, however, aware of such an interpretation for the coming out of the pool is clear from several other passages in his writings. A direct parallel, that is, entering the water as being buried with Christ in the tomb, and coming up out of the pool as being raised with Him, is used by Cyril in the *Procatechesis.* Speaking of Simon Magus[221] as an example for anyone who might come to baptism with improper dispositions, Cyril says: "Even Simon Magus once came to the bath of baptism . . . he dipped his body in the water . . . his body went down and came up, but his soul was not buried with Christ, nor was it raised with Him."[222] And in another place Cyril says: "You in the same way [as Jesus] having descended into the water, and, in a certain manner, having been buried in the waters as He was buried in the rock, you are raised up, 'walking in newness of life.' "[223] The Pauline quotation is the same one with which Cyril concludes his *Mystagogical Catechesis* on the baptismal act: "God is powerful, He Who having established you as it were living from the dead[224] and will grant you to walk in newness of life."[225]

Still, an examination of these passages shows that a specific reference to coming out of the baptismal pool in concrete mystagogical terms as a symbol of rising from the tomb with Christ, is not unequivocally present, and the passages might be said to hover between theological explanation of a salvific event and mystagogical interpretation of an concrete liturgical action, the coming out of the pool associated with the resurrection of Jesus from the tomb.

[221] *Cf. Ac.* 8:13.

[222] *Procat.* 2 (Cross, *SPCK,* 1; tr. Cross, *SPCK,* 40-41): Προσῆλθέ ποτὲ καὶ Σίμων τῷ λουτρῷ ὁ μάγος· . . . τὸ μὲν σῶμα ἔβαψεν ὕδατι, . . . κατέβη μέν τὸ σῶμα, καὶ ἀνέβη· ἡ δὲ ψυχὴ οὐ συνετάφη Χριστῷ, οὐδε συνηγέρθη.

[223] *Cf. Rm.* 6:4, *Bapt. Cat.* III.12 (*MG* 33.444): οὕτω καὶ σὺ καταβὰς εἰς τὸ ὕδωρ, καὶ τρόπον τινὰ ἐν τοῖς ὕδασι ταφείς, ὥσπερ ἐκεινος ἐν τῇ πέτρᾳ ἐγείρῃ πάλιν "ἐν καινότητι ζωῆς περιπατῶν."

[224] *Cf. Rm.* 6:13.

[225] *Cf. Rm.* 6:4. *Myst. Cat.* II.8 (Piédagnel, *SC* 126, 118; tr. Cross, *SPCK,* 63): Δυνατὸς δὲ ἐστὶν ὁ Θεός, ὁ παραστήσας ὑμᾶς ὡς ἐκ νεκρῶν ζῶντας, δοῦναι ὑμῖν ἐν καινότητι ζωῆς περιπατεῖν.

Essay: "Fellowship in Christ's Sufferings"

Perhaps the reason why Cyril does not draw the obvious mystagogical conclusion for the neophytes of the coming out of the pool in the same way that he presents entering the pool as entering the tomb, just as Christ's body was placed in the tomb, is due to his preeminent concern at this point with the neophyte's relationship to the sufferings of Christ, and just *how* the efficacy of the cross is present in the baptismal rite, To this particular point Cyril addresses himself with an earnestness which practically pushes the other meaning of baptism, which he does mention, into the background. A polemical note resounds here:

> Let no one, then, suppose that baptism is merely the grace of the remission of sins, or further, that of adoption; as John's baptism bestowed only the remission of sins. No, we know full well, that as it purges sins, and conveys to us the gift of the Holy Spirit, so also it is the counterpart (*ἀντιτυπον*) of Christ's sufferings. For this reason Paul, just now read, cried aloud and says, "Do you know that as many of us as were baptized into Christ Jesus were baptized into His death? Therefore we are buried with Him by baptism." These words he spoke to them who had settled with themselves that baptism ministers the remission of sins, and adoption, but not that further it has communion (*κοινωνίαν*) also in representation (*ἐν μιμήσει*) with Christ's true sufferings.[226]

[226]*Myst. Cat.* II.6 (Piédagnel, *SC* 126, 114, 116; tr. Cross, *SPCK,* 61-62): Μηδεὶς οὖν νομιζέτω τὸ βάπτισμα ἀφέσεως ἁμαρτιῶν μόνον καὶ υἱοθεσίας χάριν τυγχάνειν, ὡς τὸ Ἰωάννου ἐτύγχανε βάπτισμα μόνης ἀφέσεως ἁμαρτημάτων παρεκτικόν. ἀλλ 'ἀκριβῶς εἰδότων ἡμῶν, ὅτι ὡς ἔστιν ἁμαρτημάτων καθαρτήριον καὶ Πνεύματος ἁγίου δωρεᾶς πρόξενον, οὕτω καὶ τῶν τοῦ Χριστοῦ παθημάτων ἀντίτυπον. Διὰ τοῦτο γὰρ καὶ Παῦλος ἀρτίως βοῶν ἔλεγεν· "Ἢ ἀγνοεῖτε ὅτι ὅσοι ἐβαπτισθημεν εἰς Χριστον Ἰησοῦν, εἰς τὸν θάνατον αὐτοῦ ἐβαπτίσθημεν; Συνετάφημεν οὐν αὐτῷ διὰ τοῦ βαπτίσματος." Ἴσως γὰρ πρὸς τινὰς ταῦτα ἔλεγε διατεθέντας, ὡς ἀφέσεως ἁμαρτημάτων καὶ βίοθεσίας προξενητικὸν τὸ βάπτισμα, οὐκ ἔτι δὲ καὶ τῶν ἀληθινῶν τοῦ Χριστοῦ παθημάτων ἐν μιμήσει ἔχον τὴν κοινωνίαν.

While mentioning here that baptism is a remission of sins and adoption into sonship, Cyril elects to concentrate attention on a third effect, baptism as a "participation (*κοινωνία*)" "in imitation (*ἐν μιμήσει*)" in the sufferings of Christ. In a beautiful and moving passage just preceding this, Cyril exclaims:

> O strange and inconceivable thing! We did not really die, we were not really buried, we were not really crucified and raised again, but our imitation (*μίμησις*) was but in a figure (*ἐν εἰκόνι*), while our salvation is in reality (*ἐν ἀληθείᾳ*). Christ was actually crucified, and actually buried and truly rose again; and all these things have been vouchsafed to us, that we, by imitation (*μιμήσει*) communicating (*κοινωνήσαντες*) in His sufferings, might gain salvation in reality (*ἀληθείᾳ*). O surpassing loving kindness! Christ received the nails in His undefiled hands and feet, and endured anguish; while to me without suffering or toil, by the fellowship (*κοινωνίας*) of His pain, He vouchsafes salvation.[227]

From the key words in these given texts, one might summarize Cyril's thought as follows:

(1.) Christ suffered once "in reality (*ἐν ἀληθείᾳ*)," not just in appearance.

(2.) I have a "share (*κοινωνία*)" in these true sufferings of Christ.

(3.) The means whereby I am enabled to share in these true sufferings of Christ is the sacramental action, in which there is an "imitation" or "representation (*μίμησις*)" of these true sufferings.

[227] *Ibid.*, II.5 (*Ibid.*, 112-114; tr. *ibid.*, 61): *Ὢ ξένου καὶ παραδόξου πράγματος· οὐκ ἀληθῶς ἀπεθάνομεν, οὐδ 'ἀληθῶς ἐτάφημεν, οὐδ 'ἀληθῶς σταυρωθέντες ἀνέστημεν, ἀλλ' ἐν εἰκόνι ἡ μίμησις, ἐν ἀληθείᾳ δὲ ἡ σωτηρία· Χριστὸς ὄντως ἐσταυρωθη καὶ ὄντως ἐτάφη καὶ ἀληθῶς ἀνέστη· καὶ πάντα ἡμῖν ταῦτα κεχάρισται, ἵνα μιμήσει τῶν παθῶν αυτοῦ κοινωνήσαντες, ἀληθείᾳ τήν σωτηρίαν κερδήσωμεν· Ὢ φιλανθρωπίας ὑπερβαλλούσης· Χριστὸς ἐδέξατο ἐπὶ τῶν ἀχράντων χειρῶν ἥλους καὶ ἤλγησε, κἀμοὶ ἀναλγητὶ καὶ ἀπονητὶ χαρίζεται διὰ τῆς κοινωνίας τὴν σωτηρίαν.*

(4.) This "imitation (*μίμησις*)" does not consist obviously in actual suffering on my part. Rather, my participation in the sufferings of Christ is achieved through the medium of an "image (*ἐν εἰκόνι*)" in the sacramental act.

(5.) Even though my participation in the sufferings of Christ is "imitation through the medium of an image (*μίμησις ἐν εἰκόνι*)," the salvation is not "imitation (*μίμησις*)" but rather "in reality (*ἐν ἀληθείᾳ*)."

(6.) Baptism may thus be called the "antitype (*ἀντίτυπον*)" of Christ's sufferings.

In point of historical fact, Christ really suffered, and in this suffering achieved salvation for me. The content of saving grace thus gained is present in the sacrament of baptism, and I participate really in this grace. But my participation in this content of saving grace brings with it a relationship to the sufferings of Christ. But how is this relationship achieved, since Christ's sufferings were historically a past act, and in baptism I do not suffer, as Christ suffered? To this question, Cyril would answer that the sacrament of baptism is a "counterpart (*ἀντίτυπον*)" of Christ's sufferings, that is, the sacramental action "represents in an image (*μίμησις ἐν εἰκόνι*)" this suffering. It is through the medium of this "image (*ἐν εἰκόνι*)" that I, even though I do not suffer, can participate in the sufferings of Christ.

Cyril is offering, through a mystagogical explanation of the rite of baptism itself, an explanation of how I, without actually reliving Christ's sufferings, can actually relate to them in "imitation by means of an image (*μίμησις ἐν εἰκόνι*)." The content of saving grace is, of course, not merely "imitation by means of an image," but something that comes "in reality (*ἐν ἀληθείᾳ*)." Cyril is going beyond what one would call "sacramental theology" in an attempt to show not only *that* the sacrament contains the saving grace, but also through his mystagogical explanation to show *how* it contains it.

It must be observed at this point that Cyril manifests a subtle, but real shift from mystagogy strictly speaking to theological interpretation of the sacrament based more on the christological scheme of the faith than on the actual sacramental rite as it was performed, such a scheme of interpretation as is found, for example, in *Rm.* 6, where St. Paul explains the meaning of baptism not necessarily from the rite, but from christological catechesis and preaching. It is a question of the Adam-Christ parallel, and the theme of spiritual transfiguration through divine grace as mediated through the life, death and resurrection of Jesus.

As we have already seen, just as St. Paul is not presenting a mystagogical interpretation of the baptismal rite, but a theological consideration of what is means to be baptized, so, too, Cyril's mystagogical line, the one-for-one parallel between the events of Christ's crucifixion and death and their "imitation" in the baptismal rite, as, for example, the walk from the place of the anointing to the pool being compared to the carrying of the body of Jesus to the tomb, begins to blur somewhat, and so mystagogy passes over into theology, and this of necessity.

This question, then, suggests itself: In what part of the baptismal ritual are, for example, the sufferings of Christ "represented in image (*μίμησις ἐν εἰκόνι*)?" True, the burial of Christ can be interpreted mystagogically as a "*μίμησις ἐν εἰκόνι*" in the rite upon which Cyril is commenting, in that the baptizand enters the water as the body of Christ entered the tomb. This ritual action is the "image (*εἰκών*)" through the medium of which the baptizand can "imitate (*μίμησις*)" the burial of Christ. Cyril uses this mystagogical interpretation clearly in explaining the baptismal rite as he found it. But when he passes on further to the "theology" of imitating the sufferings of Christ. His hands being pierced with the nails, His anguish, one fails to see just where in the rite of baptism such things are "represented in an image (*μίμησις ἐν εἰκόνι*)" through the medium of which image one can relate to the real events in Christ's suffering. Perhaps one must assume that the whole idea of death, symbolized by the immersion of the candidate, brings with it more or less the notion of anguish, suffering, and dread, and all of this is contained in the "image (εἰκών)" of going into the water-tomb. But such an assumption does not really suffice, since Cyril goes into explicit details of Christ's crucifixion, and says that the baptizand communicates in His actual sufferings by "imitation through the medium of an image (μίμησις ἐν εἰκόνι)," by which he seems to indicate his understanding of the sacramental rite as nothing less than an efficacious symbol of the Passion and Resurrection.

In this one sees the weakness of such a mystagogy. It could (and later actually did) lead to an attempt to create symbols which would signify the historical reality which one wished to portray in order to bring out graphically its relationship to the sacramental event. This can easily become forced or excessive, or it can lead to a distorted mystagogical interpretation of the real liturgical action which really goes beyond the "givens" and becomes far-fetched and unconvincing. It can also lead to "creating" symbols and eventually inserting them into the rite itself in order to suit the theological concern. We have already seen that the basic form of the baptismal bath does not of itself require immersion in the sense in which it was performed in Cyril's time. Cyril's use of *Rm.* 6 to provide a mystagogical interpretation of the rite as he had it, the immersion, happens to be quite apt, particularly given the circumstances of his presence at the historical sites of the passion and resurrection. That such favorable circumstances will not always be the case is obvious, and for this reason one must be aware of the transistory nature of different approaches to the mystagogical interpretation. Thus, when Cyril says that the Passion of Christ is imitated in an image, "μίμησις ἐν εἰκόνι", one must ask, where is this image in the baptismal rite? Entering the water-tomb is an image of death, but not of crucifixion as such. Here, then, a line must be traced between theologizing and mystagogical interpretation of a given liturgy.

Theologically, the baptized share in the reality of the passion, death and resurrection of Christ according to Pauline teaching. If, however—and this is what Cyril seems to lean toward—one tries to find in a given liturgical rite the image through which this imitation takes place, and then make of this image the efficacious sign of the reality, one has gone too far in the attempt to show *how* the passion, death and resurrection of Christ are actually present in baptism. The liturgical rite will simply not admit this sort of one-for-one parity of historical actuality and liturgical image, despite occasional appositeness, which the mystagogue will, of course, seize upon as a way of presenting the theological reality, which he is trying to emphasize.

The problem becomes clearer, perhaps, in summary, through Cyril's final exposition of the relationship:

> In order therefore that we may learn that whatever things Christ endured, He suffered them for us and our salvation, and that in reality (*ἐν ἀληθείᾳ*) and not in appearance we also are made partakers of His sufferings, Paul cried with all exactness of truth, "For if we have planted (*σύμφυτοι*) together with Christ in the likeness (*ὁμοιώματι*) of His death, we shall also be in the likeness of His resurrection."[228] Well has he said "planted together." For since the true vine was planted in this place, we also by partaking in the baptism of death "have been planted together with Him." And fix your mind with much attention on the words of the Apostle. He has not said, "For if we have been planted together in His death," but "in the likeness of His death." For upon Christ death came in reality, for His soul was truly separated from His body, and His burial was true, for His holy body was wrapt in pure linen[229] and everything happened to Him truly; but in your case only the likeness (*ὁμοίωμα*) of death and sufferings, and of salvation, not the likeness but the reality (*ἀλήθεια*).[230]

[228] *Rm.* 6:5.

[229] *Cf. Mt.* 27:59.

[230] *Myst. Cat.* II.7 (Piédagnel, *SC* 126, 116, 118; tr. Cross, *SPCK,* 62-63): Ἵνα οὖν μάθωμεν, ὅτι ὅσα ὁ Χριστὸς ὑπέμεινε, δι 'ἡμας καὶ τὴν ἡμετέραν σωτηρίαν ἐν ἀληθείᾳ καὶ οὐκ ἐν δοκήσει ταῦτα πέπονθε, καὶ ἡμεῖς κοινωνοὶ αὐτοῦ τῶν παθημάτων γινόμεθα· μετὰ πάσης ἐβόα Παῦλος τῆς ἀκριβείας· "Εἰ γὰρ σύμφυτοι γεγόναμεν τῷ ομοιώματι τοῦ θανάτου αὐτοῦ, ἀλλὰ καὶ τῆς ἀναστα-

As one can see, as far as mystagogical interpretation goes, the "likeness (ὁμοίωμα) of *death* has been indicated because the baptismal rite was well-suited to it, as well as the two factors of the needs of the hearers and the renascence of Pauline exegesis at the time. But does not Cyril go beyond this in attempting to see in the ceremony a likeness, for example, of the sufferings of Christ? How? Where? Again, the influence of the locale has been the factor chiefly at work in Cyril's development of this line of mystagogy. This is clear from the paragraph where Cyril interprets the Pauline expression "σύμφυτοι" which means to be united intimately in the sense of coalescing with someone, in terms of the historical image of the cross. When he says, ". . . here the true vine has been planted (ἐνταῦθα πεφύτευται ἡ ἄμπελος ἡ ἀληθινή)," he is referring to the cross of Jesus, planted, as it were, in Jerusalem, where he is delivering the catechesis. The image is further artfully carried through in that the phrase "the true vine (ἡ ἄμπελος ἡ ἀληθινή)," is drawn from John's discourse on the vine and the branches.[231] The vine, the cross, is that into which the Christians have been grafted by baptism, and so a further "likeness (ὁμοίωμα)" by virtue of *locale*. Still, this remains a symbol, and not an exclusive efficacious sign which actually shows how the Christian is united to the cross of Jesus.

Cyril has emphasized the reality of Christ's suffering, and the fact that in Christian baptism the suffering, death and resurrection of Christ is somehow actually present, though not *in the same way* as in the unique historical event. However, his mystagogical presentation of *how* this mystery of Christ is present is not entirely consequent, and is also open to some objection, particularly since we have seen that the rite of bap-

σεως ἐσόμεθα." Καλῶς δὲ καὶ τὸ "σύμφυτοι." Ἐπειδὴ γὰρ ἐνταῦθα πεφύτευται ἡ ἄμπελος ἡ ἀληθινή, καὶ ἡμεῖς κοινωνίᾳ τοῦ βαπτίσματος τοῦ θανάτου "σύμφυτοι" αὐτοῦ γεγόναμεν· Ἐπίστησον δὲ μετὰ πολλῆς προσοχῆς τὸν νοῦν τοῖς τοῦ ἀποστόλου λόγοις· Οὐκ εἶπεν, εἰ γὰρ σύμφυτοι γεγόναμεν τῷ θανάτῳ, ἀλλά, τῷ ὁμοιώματι τοῦ θανάτου· Ἀληθῶς γὰρ ἐπὶ Χριστοῦ θάνατος ἀληθής, ἐχωρίζετο γὰρ τοῦ σώματος ἡ ψυχὴ καὶ ἀληθινη ταφή· ἐν σινδόνι γὰρ καθαρᾷ τὸ ἅγιον αὐτοῦ σῶμα ειλεῖτο, καὶ πάντα ἀληθῶς ἐν αὐτῷ συνέβαινεν. Ἐπὶ δὲ ἡμῶν θανάτου μὲν καὶ παθημάτων ὁμοίωμα-σωτηρίας δὲ οὐχ ὁμοίωμα, ἀλλὰ ἀλήθεια.

[231] *Cf. Jn.* 15:1-8.

tism, which Cyril interprets with the help of *Rm.* 6 was not always the same, and previously in history, as well as subsequently, could hardly bear such a mystagogical interpretation without a great leap of the imagination. Cyril's attempts, and inadequacies, in this area, are explainable in great part to the unusual position he held in being actually on scene where the historical events of Christ's life took place.[232]

Summary

Cyril's principal mystagogical point has been an interpretation of the baptismal act as an imitation of the burial of Christ. He has applied the theology of baptism from *Rm.* 6 to the liturgical ceremony at Jerusalem. His material has been the actual *locale*, that is, the place where Christ's tomb is located, to reinforce his mystagogy, and then the action of the baptismal ritual itself, the movement to the font compared to the carrying of Christ's body to the sepulcher, the triple immersion-emersion with its natural symbol of seeing as by day and not seeing as by night for the three days and three nights of Christ

[232]Commenting on this passage (see above, p. 239), J. Daniélou, *The Bible and the Liturgy,* p. 45, says: "This text is admirable in every way. Baptism is an 'antitype' of the Passion and Resurrection, that is to say, it is at the same time like and unlike the original. And the text explains in what the likeness consists and in what the unlikeness. In the death and Passion of Christ, there are two aspects which must be distinguished: the historical fact and the content of saving grace. The his torical fact is only imitated; the sacramental rite symbolizes it. But the content of saving grace allows us a true participation (*κοινωνία*): The two aspects of the sacrament are thus defined perfectly: it is an efficacious symbol of the Passion and resurrection, representing them corporeally and actualizing them spiritually."

In view of our analysis it is difficult to agree with Daniélou that "the two aspects of the sacrament are thus defined perfectly." On the contrary, there is an apposite mystagogical interpretation of a liturgical rite which lends itself to the interpretation of burial, but not much more. To say, "The historical fact is only imitated; the sacramental rite symbolizes it, represents it," really seems to go beyond the facts into an unsubstantiated generality. So, too, to call this "an efficacious symbol of the Passion and Resurrection, representing them corporeally" seems quite untenable, since this symbolism is so limited. Daniélou seems here to have failed to distinguish mystagogy and sacramental theology, and to have asserted more than is warranted by careful analysis of this catechesis.

in the tomb, reinforced by the scriptural image of the sign of Jonah. He has implied that the coming out of the pool is a sign of the resurrection, again using *Rm.* 6 to subsume on the natural symbolism of walking and daylight, "walking as in the day," but this has been done in places other than the second of the *Mystagogical Catecheses,* although it is also indicated there.

He has gone beyond the mystagogy of the actual ceremony and presented the theological meaning of how baptism is a sharing in Christ's sufferings. The strictly mystagogical interpretation of the *actual ceremony* as opposed to the theological interpretation of the *meaning* of the ceremony has, in this consideration of the cross, been at least anchored in the notion of the "planting" of the true cross in the ground at Jerusalem, symbolizing the planting or grafting of the baptizand onto the death of Christ when he enters the water-tomb, which implies not only burial but the cross. And for this image he has employed the Johannine meditation on the vine and the branches, as well as *Rm.* 6:5. At this point, however, he reaches the outer limits of mystagogy.

2. Ambrose

The theme of conformity to Christ in death and resurrection as a mystagogical explanation of the meaning of the act of baptism is worked out in the catecheses of Ambrose in a way that bears a remarkable similarity to the thought of Cyril.[233]

It will be remembered that except for the "Effetha" ceremony, apparently all the ceremonies were conducted in the bap-

[233] In respect to Ambrose's use of Greek sources, Kretschmar, *op. cit.,* p. 233, warns that sometimes a discrepancy is found in Ambrose's explanations between the actual liturgy and the theology of this liturgy, the reason being that Ambrose's liturgy is not always the same as that presupposed by the Greek sources which he uses. ". . . gelegentlich tritt aber auch heraus, dass Liturgie and Theologie der Taufe sich bei Ambrosius nicht mehr so decken wie bei den von ihm als Vorlagen benutzten griechischen Quellen." This will not be the case here, however, where the basic lines of the liturgy and its explanation are similar, but will be noted later in considering the explanation of the triple formula and its relationship to the Arian struggle.

tismal room.[234] After explaining the meaning of the consecration of the font, Ambrose reminds the neophytes: "Now let us examine what is it that is called baptism. You came to the font; you went down into it; you gave heed to the highest priest; you saw the Levites and the priest at the font. What is baptism?"[235] Then, in lapidary form, Ambrose gives a summary statement of his mystagogy of the baptismal act:

> You were asked: "Do you believe in God, the Father almighty? " You said: "I do believe," and you submerged, that is, you were buried. Again you were asked: "Do you believe in Our Lord Jesus Christ and in His Cross? " You said: "I do believe," and you submerged. So you were also buried together with Christ.[236] For he who is buried with Christ rises again with Christ. A third time you were asked: "Do you believe in the Holy Spirit? " You said: "I do believe," you submerged a third time, so that the threefold confession absolved the multiple lapse of the previous life.[237]

The mystagogy contained in this passage is then considerably amplified by Ambrose's different explanations for the significance he attaches to the triple immersion.

[234]See above, ch. 1, p. 27, and n. 20.

[235]*Sacr.* II.16 (Botte, *SC* 25bis, 82; tr. Deferrari, *FC* 44, 284): "Nunc disputemus quid sit quod dicitur baptisma. Venisti ad fontem, descendisti in eum, adtendisti summum sacerdotem, levitas, presbyterum in fonte vidisti. Quid est baptismum?"

[236]*Cf. Rm.* 6:4.

[237]*Sacr.* II.20 (Botte, *SC* 25bis, 84,86; tr. Deferrari, *FC* 44, 286): "Interrogatus es: *Credis in Deum Patrem omnipotentem?* Dixisti: *Credo,* et mersisti, hoc est, sepultus es. Iterum interrogatus es: *Credis in Dominum nostrum Jesum Christum et in crucem ejus*? Dixisti: *Credo,* et mersisti. Ideo et Christo es consepultus. Qui enim Christo consepelitur cum Christo resurgit. Tertio interrogatus es: *Credis et in Spiritum Sanctum?* Dixisti: *Credo,* tertio mersisti ut multiplicem lapsum superioris aetatis absolveret trina confessio."

a. *The First Immersion: Burial*

The candidate is asked the first question, "Do you believe in God the Father almighty? " After saying, "I do believe," he then submerges in the water, and this immersion is called by Ambrose the candidate's burial. In what sense is this symbol to be understood?

(1) *Biblical Theology of Death*

As will be seen, Ambrose, like Cyril, makes use of *Rm.* 6 to explain the significance of the baptismal act as a representation of death, linking it to the liturgical act of immersion into the water. To explain this meaning in his mystagogy, however, Ambrose lays a much larger foundation from biblical sources and natural symbolic exposition. In his biblical exposition Ambrose fills in the large picture from the Adam-Christ parallel, that is, why we should die a physical death at all, in other words, the meaning of death as a penalty for sin. This teaching on the symbolic meaning of death, and its necessity, is summed up in the following passage, which exegetically links *Gn.* and *Rm.*

> In the beginning our Lord God made man so that, if he has not tasted sin, he would not have died the death. He contracted sin; he was made subject to death; he was ejected from paradise.[238] But the Lord, Who wished His benefits to endure and to abolish all the snares of the serpent, also to abolish everything that caused harm, first, however, passed sentence on man: "Dust thou art and unto dust thou shalt return,"[239] and He made man subject to death. It was a divine sentence; it could not be resolved by human condition. A remedy was given: that man should die and rise again. Why? That that also, which before had ceded to a place of damnation, might cede to a place of benefit. What

[238] *Cf. Gn.* 3:17-23.
[239] *Gn.* 3:19.

> is this except death? Do you ask how? Because death, intervening, makes an end of sin. For when we die, surely we have ceased to sin.[240] The satisfaction of the sentence seemed to be that man, who had been made to live, if he had not sinned, began to die. But that the perpetual grace of God might perservere, man died, but Christ found resurrection, that is, to restore the heavenly benefit which had been lost by the deceit of the serpent. Both, then, are for our good, for death is an end of sins and resurrection is the reformation of nature.[241]

Here Ambrose's argument, which is based on *Rm*. 6:7, runs as follows: Man would have been immortal had he not sinned. Man did sin, however, thereby failing to fulfil the condition which would have given him immortality. At this point a merciful design of God begins, "Sed dominus qui sua vellet beneficia permanere . . ." Ejected from paradise, destined for immortality but no longer able to reach it because of his sin, man begins to encounter death, he becomes subject to death as the obvious alternative to immortality. The sentence which God utters against man, then, "Terra es et in terram ibis," is not only a specification of the penalty which naturally comes from man's lost chance for immortality, but rather, a merciful utterance of God manifesting the divine plan to bring man to

[240] *Rm*. 6:7.

[241] *Sacr*. II.17 (Botte, *SC* 25bis, 82,84; tr. Deferrari, *FC* 44, 284-285): "In principio dominus deus noster hominem fecit ut, si peccatum non gustaret, morte non moreretur. Peccatum contraxit, factus est obnoxius morti, ejectus est de paradiso. Sed dominus qui sua vellet beneficia permanere et insidias omnes abolere serpentis, rescindere quoque omne quod nocuit, primo quidem sententiam tulit in hominem: 'Terra es et in terram ibis,' et morti hominem fecit obnoxium. Erat divina sententia, solvi humana conditione non poterat. Remedium datum est ut homo moreretur et resurgeret. Quare? Ut et illud quod ante damnationis loco cesserat loco cederet beneficii. Quid illud est nisi mors? Quaeris quomodo? Quia mors interveniens finem facit peccati. Quando enim morimus, utique peccare desistimus. Satisfactum ergo sententiae videbatur quia homo qui factus fuerat ut viveret, si tamen non peccaret, incipiebat mori. Sed ut dei perpetua gratia perseveraret, mortuus est homo, sed Christus invenit resurrectionem, id est: ut redintegraret caeleste beneficium quod fraude fuerat serpentis amissum. Utrumque ergo pro nobis, quia et mors finis est peccatorum et resurrectio naturae est reformatio."

his destined immortality despite his sin. God's sentence of death becomes a benefit for man, showing that it is God Who will save man, since man cannot of himself reverse this sentence. Why should this sentence of death be a benefit? "Ut et illud quod ante damnationis loco cesserat loco cederet beneficii." By sentencing man to death, God makes of this normal consequence of his lost immortality a positive means of recovery. By dying, namely, as fulfilment of a positive divine sentence, man stops sinning. Death puts an end to sin, and thereby removes the unfulfilled condition to immortality, that man not sin. When a man is dead, he can no longer commit sin, no longer continue to violate the condition of this receiving immortality. Death, then, is God's gift, the remedy which stops man from sinning, and so clears the way for the gift of immortality, which man could not otherwise have, since he had at the outset failed to fulfil the condition for immortality, that is, not to sin. Death, then, is God's benefit to man, "quia mors interveniens finem facit peccati. Quando enim morimur, utique peccare desistimus."

The condition of not sinning now guaranteed through this gift of death, man now awaits the restoration of the lost promise of life. Man has indeed stopped sinning because dead, and so the impediment to his immortaly is removed. But now the reintegration must take place to put man back on his course to immortality. This is done through the resurrection of Christ: "Sed ut dei perpetua gratia perseveraret, mortuus est homo, sed Christus invenit resurrectionem, id est: ut redistegraret caeleste beneficuim quod fraude fuerat serpentis amissum."

This entire explanation, leaning on the Pauline teaching in *Rm.* 6, is then applied by Ambrose to the action of baptism. This is his mystagogical explanation of what is actually happening in the act of baptism, and is actually "mystagogy" and not only "theology" because in the subsequent paragraphs, beginning with the sentence, "truly then, in order that the fraud or the tricks of the devil might not prevail in this world, baptism was invented." (Verumtamen ne in hoc saeculo diaboli fraus vel insidiae praevalerent, inventum est baptisma),"[242] Ambrose takes pains to explain how his scriptural presentation is corroborated in the liturgical action of baptism, which he calls the "design of God," a great grace: "Ergo baptismum consilium dei est. Quanta est gratia ubi est consilium dei." [243]

This material from *Gn.* and *Rm.*, as explained by Ambrose, forms the scriptural material by which he explains the deeper meaning of the symbolism of immersion in water as entering one's own tomb, one's own death with Christ.

(2) *The Baptistery-Tomb*

In presenting the mystagogical interpretation of the act of baptism, Ambrose does not possess the special advantage of Cyril in being able to refer to the presence of the sites of the passion and death of Christ and His resurrection as being physically present to the hearers. There is, for example, no mention of the movement to the font as the transit of the body of Christ from the cross to the sepulcher. However, Ambrose is not without reference to the physical appointment of the place of baptism to reinforce his mystagogical explanation of baptism as signifying death. He reminds the baptized: "Yesterday we treated the font, which in appearance looks something like a tomb."[244]

In this connection it might be noted that the baptistery recently discovered adjacent to Ambrose's cathedral in Milan manifests in its style a similarity to the way sepulchers were constructed.[245] Kretschmar also suggest that an inscription, which is now preserved only in literary form might indeed well have stood in this baptistery: "[Christus,] qui claustra resolvit mortis et e tumulis suscitat exanimes.[246] This would

[242] *Ibid.*, II.18 (*Ibid.*, 84; tr. *ibid.*, 285).

[243] *Idem.*

[244] *Ibid.*, III.1 (*Ibid.*, 90; tr. *ibid.*, 289): "Hesterno de fonte disputavimus, cujus species veluti quaedam sepulcri forma est."

[245] See above, ch. 1, n. 20.

[246] See Kretschmar, *op. cit.*, p. 234, n. 307.

summarize the entire mystagogy of Ambrose, and if, indeed, such an inscription stood in the "baptistery-tomb" would summarize well the symbolism of the place in contributing to the exposition of the meaning of immersion in water as immersion in death.

(3) *Water-Earth Symbolism*

In addition to presenting the scriptural theology of death in the framework of the Adam-Christ parallel, which shows the meaning of "spiritual death," as a result of sin, and also drawing attention to the symbolism of the baptistery as tomb, Ambrose takes pains to develop the mystagogy even more fully by recourse to a natural symbol drawn from the general notion of the natural physics of his time. Having shown the "benefit" of death and its necessity, and having announced that the first immersion means burial, Ambrose shows then in detail how the immersion in water without causing physical death, is actually the symbolism of the death to sin which God's curse requires to save man:

> For, that in this world also, the grip of the devil might be loosened, there was discovered how man alive might die and alive might rise again. What is "alive?" That is, the living life of the body, when it comes to the font, and is immersed into the font. What is water but of the earth? So it satisfied the heavenly sentence without the stupor of death. Because you immerse, that sentence is resolved: "Thou are dust and into dust thou shalt return." When the sentence has been fulfilled, there is opportunity for heavenly benefit and remedy. So water is of the earth, but the potentials of our life did not permit that we be covered with earth and rise again from earth. Then, earth does not wash, but water washes. Therefore, the font is like a sepulcher.[247]

[247] *Sacr.* II.19 (Botte, *SC* 25bis, 84; tr. Deferrari, *FC* 44, 285-286): "Audi, ergo, nam ut in hoc quoque saeculo nexus diaboli solveretur, inventum est quomodo homo vivus moreretur et vivus resurgeret. Quid est vivus? Hoc est, vita corporis vivens, cum veniret ad fontem et mergeretur in fontem. Quis est aqua nisi de terra? Satisfit ergo sententiae caelesti sine mortis stupore. Quod mergis solvitur sen-

In this passage Ambrose is explaining how immersion in water can truly be called a "burial," and how, therefore, man can fulfil the sentence of death given against him in the book of *Gn.*, that he return to the earth from which he came, without at the same time actually experiencing physical death. It must be possible for man to return to the earth from which he came, without actually dying physically, otherwise he cannot fulfil the heavenly sentence, the condition of his rising to new life. For man actually to enter the earth, to be covered over with earth, would, as Ambrose points out, destroy our physical life, and quite preclude that we expect to rise again after such an experience. God, however, in His mercy, as Ambrose has shown, has provided a way of fulfilling the sentence. without the irreversible fact of physically dying. And here Ambrose explains how this provision of God, immersion in water, manifests this act of death.

The element in ancient physics which was closely related to earth was water. Although man could not be covered over with earth, and so fulfil the divine sentence, he could be covered over with its sister element, water. "What is water, but of the earth?" Man thus returns to dust, according to God's command, the dust in this case being the element most closely allied to dust, namely water, and so man by his imersion in the water could fulfil the sentence in *Gn.* to return to earth as a penalty of sin.

When the candidate immerses, then, it is as though he were being buried in his own grace, and thereby, without destruction to his physical life, he is able to anticipate his death handed on as penalty of sin, and fulfil this penalty through the expedient of baptism.

Thus, through recourse to the presentation of the biblical theology of death, the physical resemblance of the tomb as a sepulcher, and the natural symbolism of earth and water, Ambrose presents a consequent mystagogy of baptism in the sense

---

tentia illa: 'Terra es et in terram ibis.' Inpleta sententia locus est beneficio remedioque caelesti. Ergo aqua de terra, possibilitas autem vitae nostrae non admittebat ut terra operiremur et de terra resurgeremus. Deinde non terra lavat, sed aqua lavat. Ideo fons quasi sepultura est.

of burial. He attaches this mystagogy particularly to the first line of the baptismal formula which he cites along with its attendant action of submerging: "You were asked: 'Do you believe in God the Father almighty?' You said: 'I do believe, and you submerged, that is: you were buried."[248]

b. *The Second Immersion: The Cross*

The candidate is asked the second question: "Do you believe in our Lord Jesus Christ and in His cross?" After saying, "I do believe," he submerges a second time in the water, and this second immersion is explained by Ambrose as a "being buried together with Christ."[249]

In this formula as given by Ambrose, there is a remarkable and unique insertion, the words, "and in His cross," which already indicates the direction of his mystagogy. The way in which Ambrose himself emphasizes the importance of this insertion is reminiscent of the concern, polemical in tone, which Cyril revealed when he dealt with the same matter:[250] "You descended, then, into the water; remember what you replied to the questions . . . with this only exception, that you confessed you must believe in the cross of the only Lord Jesus."[251]

The unusual addition to the formula, the notion of believing in the cross of Jesus, reveals the similarity of Ambrose's concern to relate the passion and death of Christ to the baptismal act. The very fact of the form's singularity[252] indicates the measure of emphasis which Ambrose wishes to accord to it.

Having explained how sin and the sentence of death are related to the candidate's burial in the waters of baptism, as explanation of the first immersion, Ambrose now goes a step further, and in his mystagogical explanation of the second

[248]See above, p. 243.
[249]See above, p. 243.
[250]See above, p. 234 ff.
[251]*Myst.* 28 (Botte, *SC* 25bis, 170; tr. Deferrari, *FC* 44, 15): "Descendisti igitur. Recordare quid responderis, . . . hoc solo excepto quod in crucem solius domini Jesu fateris tibi esse credendum."
[252]See Kretschmar, *op. cit.,* p. 233.

immersion wishes to show how the passion, death and burial of Christ are related to the candidate's burial in the waters of baptism. By submerging the first time, after I had proclaimed faith in God, the Father almighty, who in his mercy had instituted this means of recovering from the penalty of my death, I was buried. Then, after the second question, proclaiming my faith in Christ and in His cross, I submerge again, and this time, says Ambrose, I was not only buried, but I was "buried together with Christ."

How does Ambrose explain this mystagogical assertion of the meaning of the second immersion? In what sense can I be said, by this immersion, to be buried with Christ from the standpoint of the liturgical action?

Ambrose avails himself of the explanation of the meaning of baptism in respect to the death of Jesus as found in *Rm.* 6: "So the Apostle exclaims, as you just heard read, that whoever is baptized, is baptized in the death of Jesus."[253] But the candidate's "death" in baptismal "burial" and the death of Jesus are not just any death, but a death with a particular meaning:

"What does 'in the death' means? That, just as Christ died, so you also taste death;[254] just as Christ died to sin and lives to God, so you, too, died to the former allurements of sins through the sacrament of baptism and rose again through the grace of Christ."[255]

The candidate's baptismal death, Ambrose is saying, is contained in the death of Christ. As Christ died to sin for all of mankind on calvary, the atoning death on the cross, so the candidate's baptismal death is an association with this death to sin on the part of Christ. Christ dies to sin for mankind; the candidate dies to the allurements of sin in his baptismal death.

[253] *Cf. Rm.* 6:3. *Sacr.* II.23 (Botte, *SC* 25bis, 86; tr. Deferrari, *FC* 44, 287) : "Clamat ergo apostolus, sicut audistis in lectione praesenti quoniam quicumque baptizatur, in morte Jesu baptizatur."

[254] *Cf. Mt.* 16:28; *Mk.* 8:39; *Lk.* 9:27; *Jn.* 8:52.

[255] *Sacr.* II.23 (Botte, *SC* 25bis, 86; tr. Deferrari, *FC* 44, 287): "Quid est in morte? Ut quomodo Christus mortuus est, sic et tu mortem degustes, quomodo Christus mortuus est peccato et deo vivit, ita et tu superioribus inlecebris peccatorum mortuus sis per baptismatis sacramentum et resurrexeris per gratiam Christi."

Christ's death, however, was a physical death; the candidate's baptismal death is not physical. Christ's death was brought about by a crucifixion. Can the candidate's baptismal death be said to be an association in the crucifixion, the cause of Christ's death externally, just as his baptismal death can be said to be an association in the death of Christ, because in baptismal death the candidate dies to sin's allurements as Christ died to sin? Yes, because not only the death of Christ was caused by sin, but also the suffering He underwent. So just as the candidate shares in Christ's death to sin, by dying to the allurements of sin in his baptism, so he also has a share by this death in that struggle against sin which the crucifixion of Jesus represents: "So [baptism] is a death, but not in the reality of corporal death but in likeness. For when you immerse, you take on the likeness of death and burial, you receive the sacrament of that cross, because Christ hung on that cross, and His body was transfixed with nails. You, then, are crucified with Him; you cling to Christ, you cling to the nails of our Lord Jesus Christ, lest the devil be able to take you away. Let the nails of Christ hold you, whom the weakness of human nature recalls."[256]

If baptism is association in the death of Christ as death to sin, so by extenuation baptism is association in the sufferings of Christ, a suffering brought about by sin. This teaching, then, relying on *Rm.* 6, is Ambrose's explanation for the addition of the phrase ". . . and in His cross," to show how burial with Christ in baptism is also a sign of sharing in His crucifixion.

Essay: Ambrose and Cyril: The Mystagogical Problem

In examining Ambrose's attempt in the above passage to show *how* the passion of Christ is represented in the baptismal act,

[256] *Ibid. (Ibid.,* 86,88; tr. *ibid.,* 287): "Mors ergo est, sed non in mortis corporalis veritate, sed in similitudine. Cum enim mergis, mortis suscipis et sepulturae similitudinem, crucis illius accipis sacramentum, quod in cruce Christus pependit et clavis confixum est corpus. Tu ergo concrucifigeris, Christo adhaeres, clavis domini nostri Jesu Christi adhaeres, ne te diabolus inde possit abstrahere. Teneat te clavus Christi, quem revocat humanae conditionis infirmitas."

one encounters the same mystagogical problem as in Cyril.[257] Death is symbolized by entering the water. Since this is a likeness of Christ's death, the two points of comparison are clear, the meaning and the symbolizing of the meaning in the actual ceremony. But in the question of the passion of Christ, while the meaning is clear in the baptismal act from *Rm.* 6, and also from the logical connection of the death of Christ with His sufferings (that is, if baptism is a share in the death of Christ, it must also logically be a share in the way He died, a share in the crucifixion) the second point of the comparison is not clear, namely, how is this meaning, this passion, symbolized in the actual ceremony. Death is symbolized by entering the water-tomb. Where in the ceremony is the symbol of the passion?

The mystagogy which Ambrose offers at this point is strongly reminiscent of Cyril's attempt to show "representation through image (*μίμησις ἐν εἰκόνι*)." Most striking in this connection is Ambrose's phrase. ". . . non in mortis corporalis *veritate,* sed in *similitudine.*" Here is the same basic theological attempt which is found in Cyril's mystagogy. The concepts: "reality (veritas) (*ἀλήθεια*)," and "likeness (similitudo) (*ὁμοίωμα*)," are the same. Ambrose does not make the same elaborate attempt to show how the sacramental action is actually "*μίμησις ἐν εἰκόνι*" as Cyril has done. After showing how the descent into the font is like death, without further attempt at "sacramental theology" he returns to what preceded the death of Christ, namely His crucifixion, and simply states an equation of association, ". . . crucis illius accipis sacramentum."

The justification for such a mystagogical explanation which, just as in Cyril, goes actually beyond the mystagogical interpretation, which has its limits in the liturgical symbolism of death and burial, is derived not from the liturgical action of baptism as such, but from *Rm.* 6:3 which, just as in Jerusalem,

[257] See above, pp. 234-241.

so here in Milan[258] was the text which the baptized had just heard read to them. If it is the death of Christ, symbolized by certain features of the liturgical action, into which one has been baptized, then it follows that one is associated with the crucifixion of the same Christ. As in Cyril, so here in Ambrose, it is difficult to see precisely this association with the cross in symbolic terms as one could show association with the burial in the font-tomb in symbolic terms.

Through the use of *Rm.* 6, then, Ambrose, like Cyril, in some sense passes over from "mystagogy" to "theology." The inner link to facilitate this passage is the Pauline teaching of the union between Adam and Christ and the baptized. Christ dies; you die. Christ dies "in veritate"; you die "in similitudine". The content of grace, however, is real: Christ's death was a death to sin, that is, the death of the old Adam, the fulfilment of the sentence of death, that man might sin no more. But this death was a crucifixion. You, then, dying with Christ to sin, who has associated Himself totally with mankind by taking on the image of the old Adam, are associated with Him in the manner of His death, a crucifixion, which thereby makes legitimate from a theological standpoint Ambrose's statement: "Tu ergo concrucifigeris Christo adhaeres, clavis domini nostri Jesu Christ adhaeres."

In summary form the argument might be stated:

> Christ dies *really* (in veritate); you die in *likeness* (in similitudine); this likeness is represented in the liturgical action of immersion into the water-tomb.
>
> Christ is *really* crucified; you are crucified in *likeness*; this likeness is "crucis illius . . . sacramentum."
> (Ambrose, however, like Cyril, is unable to provide a mystagogical explanation strictly speaking for the likeness of the crucifixion in the liturgical ceremony).

[258] See *Sacr.* II.23 (Botte, *SC* 25bis, 86; tr. Deferrari, *FC* 44, 287), and above, p. 251 and n. 253.

The content of grace, gained, according to the Pauline teaching, by the crucifixion and death of Christ as Head of the human race and the new Adam, is really conveyed to the baptized through this sacrament. Therefore, in some way, they share in the actual event of Christ's crucifixion and death, since they share in the sin of Adam. Christ's death being a death to sin, and taking the form of a crucifixion, manifests itself also, then, in the act of baptism. Thus, on the basis of this Pauline theology Ambrose can conclude, theologically if not mystagogically, with St. Paul, that in baptism the baptized not only dies with Christ, but is also crucified with Him, not only dies to sin, but adheres to this position over against the allurements of the old life, the life of the old Adam, in the same way that Christ went in dying to sin, the way of the cross: "Teneat te clavus Christi quem revocat humanae conditionis infirmitas."

From such a graphic statement on the part of Ambrose and a similar statement of the part of Cyril, we can see how the concern of the fathers in this part of the fourth century for a baptismal understanding which would provide a spirituality for life in the world, and not just a gate to heaven, was worked out using the sacramental rites available, plus natural symbolism and Pauline theology. The similarity of the message and approach of both Ambrose and Cyril is clear in their attempt to unfold in the baptismal action the presence of the cross of Christ, and the baptized's mystical union with Him in His cross and in His death.

c. *The Triple Immersion and Confession*

(1)*Sin and Forgiveness*

The third line of the baptismal formula, "Credis in Spiritum Sanctum," received no particular explanation from Ambrose. As in the first line, the expression of belief in the Father, what concerns Ambrose as mystagogue is the attendant action, the third immersion. According to Ambrose's plan of interpretation, the first and second immersion had each received a particular interpretation, the first being the exposition of death which had a relationship to the mention of God the Father in the formula in the sense of *Gn.,* and in God's creative plan, His attendant sentence of death and His plan for man's redemption, and the second being the interpretation of the sacrament of the cross, which had a relationship to the unique words "in crucem ejus" contained in the formula. The first immersion meant *death,* the second immersion meant crucifixion and death *with Christ.*

In dealing with the third immersion, no particualr relationship to the third Person of the Trinity is expressly stated, nor is the third immersion as a single immersion interpreted. Rather, with the accomplishment of the third immersion, Ambrose links it with the other two, in order to present his interpretation.[259]

Ambrose shifts, in his mystagogical exposition of the third immersion, to a rather unexpected christological interpretation, which is very concretely based on the situation of the person being baptized. Perhaps because of its sudden contrast in conjunction with the rather lengthy interpretation of the first immersion, with its notions of death and burial, water and earth, sin and God's merciful plan, and with the moving interpretation of the second line of the formula, with its graphic presentation of Christ on the cross, and the picture of the baptizand crucified with Him, based on Pauline mysticism, the simple biblical picture which Ambrose uses to interpret the third immersion, not as an individual immersion, but as the completion of three, is strikinglly effective.

[259]It might be argued that there is a relationship implied in Ambrose's Trinitarian pattern in respect to the third immersion and the Holy Spirit. The first immersion and burial – God the Father and Creator, the destruction of His divine plan and His mercy. The second immersion – God the Son, Redeemer, through His cross and death and man's configuration to Him in this cross and death. Both of these are present in Ambrose's interpretation of these liturgical words and actions. By the same token one might perhaps say, the third immersion – God the Holy Spirit, the Sanctifier, Who, as it were, presents to the Church the fruits of the redemption. This third, however, receives very little, or rather, no development, while the first two, as we have seen in the analysis, are justifiably illated.

First, situating the picture in the general framework of sin and forgiveness, which has been the general presupposition of this entire mystagogical section, ". . . you submerged a third time, so that the threefold confession absolved the multiple lapse of the previous life," Ambrose says:

> Finally to furnish you an example, the holy Apostle Peter, after he seemed to have lapsed during the Passion of the Lord due to the weakness of his human condition, he who previously had denied, afterwards, that he might wipe out and repair that lapse, is asked a third time by Christ if he loves Christ. Then he says, "You know, Lord, that I love you."[260] He answered a third time, that he might be absolved a third time.[261]

Thus, in the dramatic structure of the baptismal questions and immersions, three in number, the triple question evokes a reminiscence of the triple question of Christ to the fallen Peter, in this case the fallen Peter being the baptizand, who is in sin, manifest by the falls of his previous life as was Peter's fall manifest by his triple denial. The triple "Credo" of the baptizand becomes the triple assurance of Peter to the question posed three times by Christ. The triple immersion becomes the symbol of the triple fall of Peter, or applied to the baptizand, the multiple falls of his previous life, the "infirmitas conditionis humanae."

By using the scene from the life of St. Peter, Ambrose has evoked an elaborate parallel for the liturgy of baptism. If the answers to the baptismal questions, "Do you believe in the Father, etc," are the answers of Peter-the baptizand to Christ's

[260] *Jn.* 21:17.

[261] *Sacr.* II.21 (Botte, *SC* 25bis, 86; tr. Deferrari, *FC* 44, 286): "Denique, ut uobis adferamus exemplum, sanctus apostolus Petrus, posteaquam in passione domini lapsus videretur infirmitate conditionis humanae, qui ante negaverat, postea ut illum lapsum aboleret et solveret tertio interrogatur a Christo si Christum amaret. Tum ille dicit: 'Tu nosti, Domine, quia amo te.' Tertio dixit ut tertio absolveretur."

questions, "Do you love me," then in the baptismal action the person who is posing the questions to the candidate is Christ Himself. This helps to explain Ambrose's subsequent observation on the trinitarian formula, where he says:

> But do not marvel that we are baptized in one name, that is in the name of the Father and of the Son and of the Holy Spirit, because He said one name, in which is one substance, one divinity, one majesty. This is the name of which it is said, "In this [name] all must be saved."[262] In this name you have all been saved; you have returned to the grace of life.[263]

Unusual here is that the word "name" from the baptismal formula is identified by Ambrose with the name of Jesus, which is the meaning of "name" in *Ac.* 4:12 to which he alludes. Such a mode of thought confirms the christological emphasis in respect to the baptismal liturgy.[264]

(2) *Trinitarian Symbolism*

Trinitarian symbolism, not used by Cyril, is conveyed here briefly by Ambrose, but in conjunction with the general theme which governs this whole section, sin and redemption. The triple immersion symbolizing the triple fall of Peter, the threefold question and answer representing Christ and Peter after the fall, suggest to Ambrose that the three Persons named in the questions forgive the baptized's sins: "It is thus that the Father forgives sins, thus that the Son forgives them, and so, too, the Holy Spirit. In one name, however, we are baptized, that

[262] *Ac.* 4:12.

[263] *Sacr.* II.22 (Botte, *SC* 25bis, 86; tr. Deferrari, *FC* 44, 287): "In uno autem nomine baptizari nos, hoc est, *in nomine patris et filii et spiritus sancti,* noli mirari, quia dixit unum nomen ubi est una substantia, una divinitas, una majestas. Hoc est nomen de quo dictum est: *In quo oportet omnes salvos fieri.* In hoc nomine omnes salvati estis, redditi estis ad gratiam vitae."

[264] Such a way of thinking permitted Ambrose to accept baptism in the name of Jesus, provided that therewith a denial of another Person of the Trinity was not implied. See Kretschmar, *op. cit.,* p. 235.

is, 'in the name of the Father and of the Son and of the Holy Spirit,' "[265]

Thus, the triple naming of the Persons of the Trinity signify for Ambrose in this mystagogical interpretation, the triple action of each person in forgiving the sins of the candidate, while at the same time, however, he upholds the unity of the divine action.

d. *Coming out of the Pool: Resurrection*

Ambrose, indicates his understanding that just as being immersed into the baptismal water represented death, so coming out of the font is a symbol of resurrection: "Yesterday we discussed the font, whose likeness is as a kind of sepulcher into which, believing in the Father and the Son and the Holy Spirit, we are received, and immerse, and come up out of it again, that is, we are resuscitated."[266] And he reinforces this idea further: "Because baptism is a likeness of death, without doubt, when you immerse and when you come back out again there is a likeness of the resurrection."[267]

Summary

Basing his presentation of the mystagogy of the baptismal act on the fact of the triple immersion, Ambrose has presented a varied mystagogy from different sources to show how

[265] *Sacr.* II.22 (Botte, *SC* 25bis, 86; tr. Deferrari, *FC* 44, 286-287): "Sic ergo peccatum dimittit pater, sic dimittit filius, sic et spiritus sanctus. In uno autem nomine baptizari nos, hoc est, *in nomine patris et filii et spiritus sancti.*"

[266] *Ibid.*, III.1 (*Ibid.*, 90; tr. *ibid.*, 289): "Hesterno de fonte disputavimus, cujus species veluti quaedam sepulcri forma est, in quem credentes in patrem et filium et spiritum sanctum recipimur et demergimur ut resurgimus, hoc est, resuscitamur."

[267] *Ibid.*, III.2 (*Ibid.*, 90; tr. *ibid.*, 290): ". . . quoniam [baptisma] similitudo mortis est, sine dubio dum mergis et resurgis similitudo fit resurrectionis." Further mystagogical exposition of this action of rising from the font as resurrection will be treated in the section on baptism as rebirth, below, pp. 305-311 which is the standpoint from which Ambrose interprets it.

this act is a sign of conformity to Christ in death and resurrection. In the *first immersion* sin and death have been treated from the standpoint of the biblical theology in *Genesis* and *Romans,* and then the appearance of the baptistery as a tomb, and the possible inscription interpreting its meaning, plus the exposition of how immersion in water is similar to immersion in earth from the view of the natural physics of the time have formed the mystagogical exposition to show the meaning of this immersion as death and burial in its deeper aspects. In the *second immersion* Ambrose has again used *Rm.* 6 to relate the candidate's death to the death of Jesus, and then he has developed the association further by extending it to an association not only in the fact of the death of Jesus, but also to an association in His cross and passion. In this area, he has left the strictly mystagogical interpretation of the ceremony itself, and moved into a theological explanation of the meaning of baptism, following Pauline teaching. For the *triple immersion* Ambrose has used the scene from *Jn.* 21 where Christ asks Peter if he loves Him, the triple question reflecting Peter's triple denial. The candidate is thus associated in the scene by the triple question and answer of the baptismal formula, and by the triple immersion, which represents the triple fall of Peter or the multiple lapse in the previous life of the baptismal candidate. The christological emphasis in this interpretation of the baptismal act is also reinforced by the use of *Ac.* 4:12, noting that the "Name" in the formula of baptism contains the power of Jesus, the Name by which men are saved. The conclusion has been clearly stated by Ambrose that *coming out of the pool* symbolizes the resurrection of the candidate, just as entering it symbolized his death and burial, all with the background of the Pauline Adam-Christ parallel, old-man, new-man. Further, Ambrose has added a reference to the *Trinity* in that he sees the three Persons as mentioned in the baptismal formula as each involved in the forgiveness of sins.

While the materials of the mystagogy are varied, and their application dispersed according to the framework of the triple question-answer and the triple immersion-emersion, the central *leitmotiv* of the candidate's conformity to the passion, death, burial and resurrection of Jesus remains the predominant factor in the mystagogical exposition.

3. *Chrysostom*

The Pauline teaching of *Rm.* 6 that baptism is a participation in the mystery of the death and resurrection of Christ is taken over as well by Chrysostom, and he uses this material throughout the *Baptismal Instructions* to provide one of his principal interpretations of the meaning of the baptismal act.[268]

As with Cyril, Ambrose and Theodore, the liturgy of the baptismal act upon which Chrysostom was commenting, with its action of immersion and emersion[269] was particulary well-suited to support the application of the Pauline teaching in a symbolic way.

In using this material and developing his mystagogical exposition of the baptismal act, Chrysostom's work will be seen to be less "finished" than that of the other fathers. It bears the impress more of the *ad hoc* preacher than of the developing literary genus of mystagogical catecheses, and hence his intuitions must be collated from remarks here and there throughout the series of the *Instructions.*

a. *Entering and Leaving the Pool: Death and Resurrection*

Chrysostom does not go into detailed commentary on the action of the baptism itself, as do Cyril and Ambrose. For him, the essential action which forms the framework of his mystagogical exposition is simply the fact that the candidate enters and leaves the baptismal pool. Using this liturgical action as a point of departure, Chrysostom applies then his other material to elaborate the meaning of this entering and leaving the baptismal pool as a sign of conformity to Christ in death and resurrection: "For in baptism there are both burial and resurrection at the same time."[270] This burial is signified by enter-

[268] According to Finn, Chrysostom cites the pertinent Pauline texts, *Rm.* 6:1-13; *Col.* 2:12-15; *Col.* 3:1-4, at least thirteen times, Finn, *op. cit.*, p. 158.

[269] See above, p. 147.

[270] *P.K.* 2.4 (*VGS*, 159; tr. Harkins, *ACW* 31, 152, no. 11): ὁμοῦ γὰρ καὶ ταφὴ καὶ ἀναστασίς ἐστὶν ἐν τῷ βαπτίσματι κατὰ τὸν αὐτὸν καιρόν.

ing the baptismal waters, and the resurrection is signified by coming up out of the waters: "After this anointing the priest makes you go down into the sacred waters, burying the old man and at the same time raising up the new, who is renewed in the image of his Creator."[271] And even more explicitly for the movement up out of the pool as sign of the resurrection Chrysostom says later in the same *Instruction:* "As you come forth from the waters, symbolizing your resurrection by rising up from them . . ."[272]

In these quotations the familiar Adam-Christ parallel is found as well as the parallel of baptism and the creation of man. Going-down, water, burial, rising up, these are the actions upon which Chrysostom focuses the Pauline teaching of the anamnesis of the death and resurrection of Christ to show the candidate how his baptism is a configuration in the death and resurrection of Christ.

(1) The Baptistery-Paradise

Chrysostom speaks of "going down into the sacred waters."[273] It will be remembered that the scene in the baptistery was a dramatic suggestion of the garden of Paradise. The word which Chrysostom frequently uses for the baptismal waters, "*νάματα*"[274] means the flowing waters of a spring or a stream. This evocative word may be considered part of Chrysostom's own mystagogical application to the baptismal act. In one place[275] where he describes the baptismal scene step by step, its recurrence indicates, along with the other features mentioned there, a deliberate recreation of the Paradise scene. By

[271] *Cf. Col.* 3:10. *Stav.* 2.25 (Wenger, *SC* 50, 147; tr. Harkins, *ACW* 31, 52) (Text, see above, n. 31 p. 155).

[272] *Stav.* 2.29 (*Ibid.*, 149-150; tr. *ibid.*, 54): Ἐπιβαίνοντες τοίνυν τῶν θείων ἐκείνων ναμάτων καὶ τὸ σύμβολον τῆς ἀναστάσεως διὰ τῆς ἐκεῖθεν ἀνόδου ἐπιδεικνύμενοι.

[273] *Stav.* 2.25. See above, n. 271.

[274] See *e.g.* *P.K.* 3.8 (*VGS,* 173; tr. Harkins, *ACW* 31, 170, no. 28). This word occurs again in *Stav.* 2.25, 27, 29; 3.26; 7.10 (Wenger, *SC* 50, 147, 148, 149; 167; 234; tr. Harkins, *ACW* 31, 52, 54; 65; 107).

[275] *P.K.* 3.8 (*VGS,* 173-174; tr. Harkins, *ACW* 31, 170, no. 28).

bringing the candidate symbolically into the garden of Paradise, he automatically evokes in an imaginative way the history of creation and of the fall. By his skillful use of suggestive words and pictures, Chrysostom provides a kind of imaginative composition of place, evoking scenes from *Gn.*, supported to some degree, no doubt, by the actual physical features of the baptistery. This rhetorical provision serves the mystagogical interpretation of the baptismal act by its general evoking of the mysteries of salvation history, creation, sin, redemption.[276]

(2) Death as Detachment

A good example of the mystagogical method peculiar to Chrysostom is contained in one of the *Instructions* given to the neophytes shortly after their baptism. If going into the baptismal waters meant dying, here Chrysostom explains in what sense the neophytes can be said to have died.

The neophytes are gathered at the tombs of the martyrs,[277] an apt location from the standpoint of symbolic place, for

[276]This does not necessarily prove that the actual baptismal font in which baptism took place for Chrysostom's candidates was outfitted with a baptismal font of flowing waters, although in the early Church such was preferred. See J. Jungmann, *The Early Liturgy to the Time of Gregory the Great,* tr. F. Brunner (Notre Dame, Indiana, 1959), pp. 81-82. Th. Klauser, "Taufet in lebendigem Wasser," in *Pisciculi, Studien zur Religion und Kultur des Altertums* (Münster, 1939), pp. 157-164. Quite obviously, flowing water could not at all times and everywhere be had for baptism in all Christian communities. What is important is Chrysostom's use of the word, which may be considered part of his own mystagogical application.

[277]The *Instruction* is a Paschal homily addressed to the neophytes in particular although others are present: (". . . both you who have just now been judged worthy of the gift of baptism, and all of us who shared in this grace in the past"). They have gathered at one of Antioch's many *martyria* or shrines dedicated to the martyrs. Harkins suggests that the homily may have been held on the Friday of Easter week, since in the Syrian church from the fourth century this day was dedicated to the memory of Christian martyrs who died under Sapor II on Good Friday of the year 341. "Since their feast could not be celebrated on Good Friday, it was transferred to the following Friday, and very soon it became a kind of commemoration of all the martyrs." Harkins, *ACW* 31, 268, n. 1. See also A. Baumstark, *Festbrevier und Kirchenjahr der syrischen Jakobiten* (Paderborn, 1910), pp. 251-252.

Chrysostom to elaborate the symbolic meaning of death in the baptismal act. Using one of the central Pauline anamnesis texts Chrysostom explains:

> [Paul] did not want those who hear these words of his to think that his counsel goes beyond their strength, nor that what he enjoins is impossible, nor that to adopt a purpose so lofty transcends the powers of human nature. So after he said: "Mind the things that are above, not the things that are of the earth," he went on to add: "For you have died."[278] What a burning soul he has, and filled with what great yearning for God! "For you have died," he says; but this is practically saying: What do you have in common with the present life? Why do you gape after the things of earth? You have died, that is, you are corpses as far as sin is concerned. Once and for all you have renounced the present life. Nor did he want them to be upset when they heard him say: "You have died," so he quickly added: "and your life is hidden with Christ in God."[279] Your life is no longer seen, for it is hidden. Therefore, do not be active in the things of this life as if you were living, but be as if you had died and were corpses. For tell me this. Is it possible for one who has died as far as this life is concerned to be active thereafter in the affairs of this life? Of course not. So, too, with you, he says. After you have died and become dead to sin once and for all by your baptism, accordingly have nothing to do with the passions of the flesh and the affairs of the world. "For our old self," he says, "has been crucified and buried through baptism,"[280] Therefore get for yourself none of the things that are one earth, and be not active in the affairs of the present life. For your life is hidden now and unseen by those who do not believe, but the time will come when it will be seen. But now is not your time. Since you have died once and for all, refuse to mind the things that are on earth. The greatness of your virtue is plainly seen especially when you have prevailed over the arrogance of the flesh and act toward the good things of the world just as if you were dead to this life. Let us listen to these truths, both you who have just now been judged

[278] *Col.* 3:3.
[279] *Idem.*
[280] *Rm.* 6:6.

worthy of the gift of baptism and all of us who shared in this grace in the past. Let us accept the counsel of Paul, the teacher of the whole world. Let us consider what disposition he desires in those who have once and for all shared in the ineffable mysteries; let us consider how, he wishes them to be strangers to the present life. His purpose is not to have them emigrate somewhere far from this world, but while they go about in the midst of it, he would have them act like strangers to it. He would have them shine like stars and by their actions prove to the infidels that they have changed their citizenship to another country; he would have them prove that they have nothing in common with the earth nor with the things which are one earth.[281]

[281] *Stav.* 7.21-23 (Wenger, *SC* 50, 239 - 241; tr. Harkins, *ACW* 31, 112-113): Καὶ ἵνα μὴ νομίσωσι πάλιν οἱ ταῦτα ἀκούοντες ὑπερβαίνειν αὐτοὺς τὴν συμβουλὴν καὶ ἀδύνατα εἰναι τὰ ἐπιτάγματα καὶ ὑπερ τὴν ἀνθρωπίνην δύναμιν εἶναι τὸ τοιοῦτον φρόνημα ἀναλαβεῖν, εἰπών· "Τὰ ἄνω φρονεῖτε μὴ τὰ ἐπι τῆς γῆς", ἐπηγαγεν· "'Απεθάνετε γάρ." Ὢ ψυχῆς πεπυρωμένης καὶ πολὺν ἐχούσης τὸν πόθον περὶ τὸν Θεόν. "'Απεθάνετε γάρ, φησί", μονονουχὶ λέγων· Τὶ κοινὸν ἔχετε πρὸς τὸν παρόντα βίον λοιπόν; Τὶ κεχήνατε πρὸς τὰ τῆς γῆς πρὰγματα; 'Απεθὰνετε, τουτέστι νεκροὶ γεγόνατε τῇ ἁμαρτία, καθάπαξ ἀπετάξεσθε τῇ παρούσῃ ζωῇ·

Εἶτα ἵνα μὴ θορυβηθῶσιν ἀκούοντες ἀπεθάνετε, ταχέως ἐπήγαγε· "καὶ ἡ ζωὴ ὑμῶν κέκρυπται σὺν τῷ Χριστῷ ἐν τῷ Θεῷ." Ἡ ζωή, φησίν, ἡ ὑμετέρα νῦν οὐ φαίνεται, κέκρυπται γάρ· μὴ τοίνυν ὡς ζῶντες οὕτως ἐνεργεῖτε πρὸς τὰ τοῦ παρόντος βίου πράγματα, ἀλλ 'ὡσανει ἀποθανόντες καὶ νεκροὶ ὄντες οὕτω διάκεισθε· Εἰπὲ γάρ μοι, μὴ ἔστι τὸν ἀποθὰνοντα κατὰ τὸν βίον τοῦτον ἐνεργεῖν τὶ λοιπὸν ἐις τὰ παρόντα πράγματα; Οὐδαμῶς. Οὕτω, φησί, καὶ ὑμᾶς ἀποθανόντας καθάπαξ καὶ νεκρωθέντας τῇ ἁμαρτία διὰ τοῦ βαπτίσματος, ἀκόλουθον μηδὲν κοινὸν ἔχειν πρὸς τὰ τῆς σαρκὸς πάθη καὶ τὰ ἐπι τῆς γῆς πράγματα. "'Ο παλαιὸς γὰρ ἡμῶν ἄνθρωπος, φησί, συνεσταυρώθη καὶ ἐτάφη διὰ τοῦ βαπτίσματος." Μηδὲν τοίνυν τῶν ἐπι τῆς γῆς διαπράττεσθε μηδὲ ὡς ζῶντες ἐν τοῖς παροῦσι πρὰγμασιν ἐνεργεῖτε. Ἡ γὰρ ζωὴ ἡ ὑμετερα νῦν μὲν κέκρυπται καὶ ἄδηλος ἐστὶ τοῖς ἀπίστοις, ἔσται δὲ καιρὸς ὅτε φανερὰ γενήσεται. Νῦν οὐκ ἔστιν ὑμέτερος ὁ καιρός. ἀποθανόντες τοίνυν καθάπαξ μὴ θελήσητε τὰ ἐπὶ τῆς γῆς φρονεῖν. Τὸ γὰρ τῆς ἀρετῆς ὑμῶν μέγεθος οὕτω μάλισα διαδείκνυται ὅταν τὸ φρόνημα τῆς σαρκὸς καταγωνισαμενοι ὡσανεὶ νεκροὶ τῷ βίῳ γεγενημένοι οὕτω διάκεισθε πρὸς ἅπαντα τὰ βιωτικά.

'Ακουέτωσαν ταῦτα καὶ οἱ πρόσφατον τῆς τοῦ βαπτίσματος δωρεᾶς ἀξιωθέντες καὶ ἡμεῖς ἅπαντες οἱ πάλαι ταύτης μετασχόντες τῆς χάριτος καὶ δεχώμεθα τὴν συμβουλὴν τοῦ τῆς οἰκουμένης διδασκάλου καὶ εννοήσωμεν οἵους εἶναι βούλεται τούς ἅπαξ τῶν ἀπορρήτων μυστηρίων μετόχους γεγενημένους, πῶς ἀλλοτρίους αὐτους τοῦ παρόντος βίου, οὐχ ἵνα ἔξω τοῦ κόσμου τούτου καὶ μακράν που ἀποικισθῶσιν, ἀλλ 'ἵνα ἐν τῷ μέσῳ στρεφόμενοι τῶν μακραν ὄντων μηδὲν διαφέρωσιν ἀλλὰ φωστήρων δίκην διαλάμπωσι καὶ διὰ πραγμάτων δεικνύωσι τοῖς ἀπίστοις ὅτι ἐις ἑτέρνα πολιτείαν ἑαυτους μετέστησαν καὶ οὐδὲν κοινὸν ἔχουσι πρὸς τὴν γῆν καὶ τὰ ἐπὶ τῆς γῆς πράγματα.

This text reveals well the particular style and main features of Chrysostom's mystagogical interpretation of baptism as death. For the sake of his hearers, drawing from the setting at the shrine of the martyrs, and remarking on the brilliance and symbolism of the white robes of the neophytes[282] Chrysostom, presupposing the liturgical action of the past week, immersion into the font, used the Pauline material to explain in what sense this immersion meant "death", what this "death" means.

The martyrs died, but the neophytes should not fear when they hear that they "die" in baptism, for, as Paul teaches, they died to live a new life. For the neophytes their baptismal death, if not martyrdom, will mean death to sin and to the life of the "flesh" just as Christ's death was a death to sin and a living to God. Since their "death" in baptism is joined to Christ's death, Who rose again, they need not fear it.

Essay: Chrysostom's Mystagogical Approach

Chrysostom, more the preacher than the theologian, or perhaps more correctly put, Chrysostom, whose theology is distributed throughout his instructions more according to the homiletic of the immediate needs of his hearers, rather than being placed in any compact scheme, reveals his view of baptism as related to the Pauline anamnesis of the death and resurrection of Christ not so much in terms of any attempted sacramental theology of *how* this can be so, but rather in the awesome announcement *that* it is so. In the above passage, which it has been necessary to quote at length in order to show the style of Chrysostom, he announces the Pauline words, "You have died!" The solemn announcement of what happened at the baptismal immersion is repeated again and again with rhetorical skill, and each time developed further to show the meaning of this baptismal death to the neophytes and others gathered for the sermon at the shrine of the martyrs.

[282] *Ibid.*, 7.24 (*Ibid.*, 241; tr. *ibid.*, 114).

Cyril, Ambrose, Theodore: all clearly reveal their attempt at the sacramental theology which will show *how* in the ceremony the Christian can be said to die, or to rise again, proceeding from the same Pauline theology. From the texts in Chrysostom it is clear that he is at one with these other three fathers in his mystagogical interpretation of the liturgical action of baptism, the immersion and emersion as symbolizing death and resurrection, and the candidate's conformity to Christ in this death and resurrection. What distinguishes Chrysostom's mystagogical approach from that of the other fathers is precisely his homiletic style, the style of the preacher filled with reverence before the mystery, and communicating with no less skill, but in a different way, the message to those coming to belief.

The ceremony is the same, the material, *Rm.* 6 is the same, yet his presentation is governed by his concern not so much to explain intellectually the meaning of the ceremony, *how* from the standpoint of sacramental theology the ceremony of immersion can be said to be death, as to present in a multifaceted way the actuality of the mystery as it applies to the hearers in front of him.

Reverence calls to reverence, and in this approach one sees the devoted preacher eagerly accepting the ceremony and the traditional materials of interpretation, and skillfully handing it on in a way tailored to the needs of those before him, without digressing into a theological speculation on details of the ceremony, which, apparently, would not particularly serve the needs of those who have come to the point of taking a major step in the Christian life, and need a mystagogical explanation of baptism which will, in the good sense of the word, be more edifying than speculative. He speaks directly to his hearers, weaving in the Pauline texts in a very plastic way to make his point. Chrysostom speaks rather than *writes* a theology which will satisfy an intellectual curiosity, which curiosity would hardly be paramount in the minds of those who have struggled through the difficult preparation and renunciation required, and come now to the firm desire to be baptized, a step which will mean for them something eminently practical and realistic as far as their lives are concerned. He takes them by the hand, supporting them by his own faith, anchored in solid tradition.

In Chrysostom, more than in the other three fathers, one becomes aware of the actual hearers of the *Instructions,* because one sees how the mystagogical interpretation is geared to them, and their needs at the occasion of their baptism.

This passage quoted at length above, explaining the meaning of death in the framework of the ceremony of immersion in the baptismal pool, is a good example of Chrysostom's mystagogical approach. Since, as we have already seen, St. Paul's comments on the meaning of baptism were not necessarily a mystagogy of the liturgy of baptism as he himself experienced its performance, but rather a reflection on the meaning of baptism as such, arguing from the scheme of christological preaching rather than from liturgical action, and attempting to show what baptism meant for the style of Christian life in this world, one might say that the way in which Chrysostom follows St. Paul here is closer to Paul's original intention. Chrysostom does not "pass over" the ceremonies in order to explain the meaning of the Pauline anamnesis. He gives the ceremonies their due, using them as a point of departure, but his main emphasis, and this is his particular mystagogical approach, is to let these ceremonies echo and refract in the life of the neophytes, so that their liturgy on Holy Saturday night will influence their life style and conduct, in accordance with the meaning which the ceremonies of baptism have for the Christian life.

In this sense Chrysostom fulfils in an eminent degree one of the concerns of the Church in the fourth century in seizing upon the Pauline exegesis at all, namely of showing how the sacrament of initiation is not merely the gate to heaven, but a program for the Christian life here and now. One can see in the very situation and in the words of this instruction this precise kind of mystagogical concern in explaining the sacrament, to make of baptism a serious commitment in life here and now, something which will immediately after its reception manifest itself in the life style of the neophytes, and not a death-bed experience to which the sacrament had, to some degree, degenerated.[283] The passage speaks of the meaning of baptismal death, and shows the line between this world and the next world. But this death reveals itself now in the conduct of the Christian in this world, not only as preparation for the next.

The *Instruction* is held at a "martyrium", and thus the link with baptism and martyrdom, the strong point of emphasis in the persecution conditions of the Church of the martyrs, but now transformed in time of peace to the "martyrdom" or "witness" of a Christian life reflecting the "death" of baptism, in detachment from sin. Chrysostom uses the phrases of strict ascetical life, the way of life which many earnest Christians had been led to take up now that the Church was "at peace" with the Empire. At the same time he addresses not only the ascetics, who had gathered from the region to hear the discourse,[284] but all Christians in whatever walk of life. He avows that these Christians must live and give example in this world, and, as he says, not "emigrate somewhere far from this world," but "go about in the midst of it."

The very paradoxes inherent in Chrysostom's mystagogical interpretation of baptism, martyrdom, or its continuation in time of peace through monastic-ascetical life, having, as he says, "nothing to do with the affairs of this world" until one's life hidden with Christ through baptism is revealed in the eschaton, and yet still present, still giving example, still leading

[283] See above, pp. 211-214.

[284] Later in this discourse Chrysostom uses the example of Cornelius the centurion (*cf. Ac.* 10:1-4) saying: "He will be a trustworthy teacher not only for the military but also for all of us, as well as those who have chosen the monastic life and those dedicated to the service of the Church (*Τάχα δὲ οὐκ ἐκεινοίς μόνοις ἀξιόπιστος οὗτος γενήσεται διδάσκαλος· ἀλλὰ καὶ πᾶσιν ἡμῖν καὶ αυτοῖς τοῖς τὸν τῶν μοναχῶν βίον ἐκανηρημένοις καὶ τὴν ἐκκλησιαστικὴν λειτουργίαν ἀναδεδειγμένοις*)."
Stav. 7.31 (Wenger, *SC* 50, 245; tr. Harkins, *ACW* 31, 117). In Chrysostom's audience were, no doubt, monks who were quite numerous in the mountains of the Antioch area. Chrysostom had himself once been a monk, a state for which he never lost his longing. (*Cf. In Mt.* 55, *MG* 58.545-550). See C. Baur, *John Chrysostom and His Time,* tr. M. Gonzaga, Vol. I, Antioch (Westminster, Maryland, 1959), pp. 104-114.

human life, and a nimbus from this hidden life begun in the baptismal font reflecting on one's conduct in this life—these very paradoxes reflect the Church's grappling with an ethic of the Christian life in changed conditions. They also show the preacher—mystagogue at work in something of a model passage, taking into account in a very skillful and creative way the actual liturgical ceremony itself as it was experienced by the baptized, the newest Pauline exegesis, and the application to the real needs of his neophytes. It might from the standpoint of the principles underlying it serve as a model of mystagogy.[285]

[285] A particularly apt passage, not from the mystagogical writings, however, shows very well how Chrysostom has actually assimilated the different themes we have already seen in Cyril, Ambrose and Theodore, and then applies them with rhetorical skill: "Let us not grieve when we fail to enjoy honor. If this life is not life, but is hidden, we should live this life as though we were dead. 'Then you too will appear with Him in glory'. (*Col.* 3:4) Nor did Paul say 'in glory' to no purpose for the pearl is hidden as long as it is in the oyster. If, therefore, we are insulted or suffer some hurt, let us not be grieved, for this life of ours is not life; we are strangers and sojourners, for 'you have died,' as Paul says. Who is so foolish that he buys slaves for one who is dead and buried, or builds houses, or has rich garments made for a corpse? No one. Let us not do so, then, but just as we seek one thing, namely, that we be not naked, so also let us seek one thing here. The man we were is buried; he is buried not in the earth but in water. Death did not destroy him, but He who destroyed death has buried him. This is not done by nature's law, but by a command that is stronger than nature and its power. For anyone could destroy what is sprung from nature; what issues from this command no one can ever destroy. There is nothing more blessed than this burial, at which all rejoice—angels, men and the Master of the angels. For this burial there is no need of a garment or a tomb or any other thing like that. Do you wish to see the symbol? I shall show you the baptismal pool, in which the man we were is buried and from which the new man arises. In the Red Sea the Egyptians were drowned, but the Israelites arose. The same thing buries the one and begets the other." *In Col.* 7 (*MG* 62.346 A-B; tr. Harkins, *ACW* 31, 276, n. 37):

Μὴ ἀλγῶμεν, ὅταν τιμῆς μὴ ἀπολαύωμεν· εἰ μὴ ἐστὶν αὔτη ἡ ζωὴ ζωή, ἀλλὰ κέκρυπται, ὡς νεκροὶ ζῆν ὀφείλομεν ταύτην τὴν ζωήν. Τότε καὶ ὑμεις, φησί, συὺ αὐτῷ φανερωθήσεσθε ἐν δόξῃ. — Ἐν δόξῃ εἶπεν, οὐχ ἁπλῶς· ἐπεὶ καὶ ὁ μαργαρίτης κέκρυπται, ἕως ἂν ᾖ ἐν τῷ ὀστρέῳ. Ἀν τὲ οὖν ὑβριζώμεθα, μὴ ἀλγῶμεν' ἔν τὰ ὁτιοῦν πάσχωμεν· οὐ γὰρ ἐστὶν ἡμῶν ζωὴ αὔτη ἡ ζωή· ξένοι

Chrysostom's mystagogy, more than that of the other fathers, is clothed in the dynamics of the preacher. Because Chrysostom does not become involved in the speculations of "sacramental theology" one should not conclude thereupon that this mystagogy is the less profound. It is entirely Pauline, not merely in the sense of deriving from St. Paul the ideas for his mystagogical interpretation, but absorbing St. Paul as preacher, and giving him forth to a given group as well.

(3) *Death and Resurrection with Christ*

In Chrysostom's constant reference to the Pauline texts one can see the dynamic process at work of providing for these candidates a mystagogical exposition of the sacrament, in its action and in the inseparable relationship of that liturgical action to the Christian life. Thus, in an *Instruction* given to

---

γὰρ καὶ παρεπίδημοί ἐσμέν. Ἀπέθανετε γὰρ, φησί. Τίς ἐστὶν οὕτως ἀνόητος, ὡς τῷ νεκρῷ σώματι τῷ ταφέντι ἢ οἰκέτας ἀγοράζειν, ἢ οἰκίας οἰκοδομεῖν, ἢ ἱμάτια κατασκευάζειν πολυτελῆ; Οὐδείς. Μὴ τοίνυν μηδὲ ἡμεῖς· ἀλλ' ὥσπερ ἓν μόνον ζητοῦμεν, ὥστε μὴ γεγυμνῶσθαι, οὕτω καὶ ἐνταῦθα ἓν μόνον ζητῶμεν. Ἐτάφη ἡμῶν ὁ πρῶτος ἄνθρωπος· ἐτάφη οὐκ ἐν γῇ, ἀλλ' ἐν ὕδατι, οὐ τοῦ θανάτου αὐτὸν καταλύοντος, ἀλλὰ τοῦ τὸν θάνατον καταλύσαντος θάψαντος αὐτὸν οὐ φύσεως νόμῳ, ἀλλὰ τῷ τῆς φύσεως ἰσχυροτέρῳ προστάγματι τῆς δεσποτείας. Τὰ μὲν γὰρ ὑπὸ φύσεως γενόμενα κἂν ἀναλύσειέ τις, τὰ δὲ ὑπὸ τοῦ προστάγματος αὐτοῦ, οὐκέτι. Οὐδὲν ταύτης μακαριώτερον τῆς ταφῆς, ἐφ' ᾗ πάντες χαίρουσι, καὶ ἄγγελοι καὶ ἄνθρωποι καὶ ὁ τῶν ἀγγέλων Δεσπότης. ταύτῃ τῇ ταφῇ οὐχ ἱματίων, οὐ λάρνακος, οὐκ ἄλλου τῶν τοιούτων οὐδενος χρεία. Βούλει τὸ σύμβολον ἰδεῖν; Δείξω σοι κολυμβήθραν ἐν ᾗ ὁ μὲν ἐτάφη, ὁ δὲ ἀνέστη· ἐν τῇ Ἐρυθρᾷ θαλάσσῃ κατεποντίσθησαν Αἰγύπτιοι, ἀνῆλθον δὲ Ἰσραηλῖται· καὶ τὸ αὐτὸ πρᾶγμα τὸν μὲν θάπτει, τὸν δὲ γεννᾷ.

In this passage one sees Chrysostom's awareness of the traditional mystagogical interpretation in explaining dying and rising in the baptismal act. The metaphor of the hidden life as a pearl in the oyster, which in a rhetorical way says much the same thing as Theodore in his theology of participation in the coming eschaton, which is really already present; the distinction between earth burial and burial in water, which we saw emphasized in Ambrose; the fact that his baptismal burial traces back to a merciful command of God to help man reverse the sentence "in terram ibis," which Ambrose had likewise spent much time explaining, and hence the same conclusion, that this death is a gift of God.

the candidates shortly before baptism[286] Chrysostom says: "Baptism is a burial and a resurrection. For the old man is buried with his sin, and the new man is resurrected, "being renewed according to the image of his Creator".[287]

An enlargement of this statement, with its Pauline Adam-Christ parallel of baptism as death and resurrection, is found in another pre-baptismal *Instruction:*

> Listen, then, to what St. Paul says and how he speaks of baptism as both the death of sin and the cross. "Do you not know that all you who have been baptized into Christ, have been baptized into His death? "[288] And again: "Our old self has been crucified with Him, in order that the body of sin may be destroyed."[289] That you may not be frightened when you hear the words "death" and "cross", St. Paul added that the cross is the death of sin.[290]
> Hence, St. Paul also says: "For if we have been united with Him in the likeness of His death through baptism."[291]

[286] See Harkins, *ACW* 31, 213, n. 1.

[287] *Col.* 3:10. *Stav.* 2.11 (Wenger, *SC* 50, 139; tr. Harkins, *ACW* 1, 47): *Καὶ γὰρ τάφος ἐστὶ καὶ ἀνάστασις τὸ βάπτισμα· "Συνθάπτεται γὰρ ὁ παλαιος ἄνθρωπος τῇ ἁμαρτία καὶ ἀνίσταται ὁ νέος ὁ ἀνακαινούμενος κατ' εἰκόνα τοῦ κτίσαντος."*

[288] *Rm.* 6:3.

[289] *Rm.* 6:6.

[290] *P.K.* 2.4 (*VGS,* 158; tr. Harkins, *ACW* 31, 151, no. 8): *Ἄκουσον γοῦν, τί φησιν ὁ Παῦλος, πῶς ἀμφότερα λέγει περὶ τοῦ βαπτίσματος ὅτι θάνατός ἐστὶν ἁμαρτίας καὶ ὁ σταυρός· "ἤ ἀγνοεῖτε ὅτι ὅσοι εἰς Χριστὸν ἐβαπτίσθητε, εἰς τὸν θάνατον αὐτοῦ ἐβαπτίσθητε"; καὶ πάλιν· "ὁ παλαιὸς ἡμῶν ἄνθρωπος συνεσταυρώθη, ἵνα καταργηθῇ τὸ σῶμα τῆς ἁμαρτίας". ἵνα οὖν μὴ ακούσας θάνατον καὶ ἀκούσας σταυρὸν φοβηθῇς, ἐπήγαγεν ὅτι ἁμαρτίας θάνατός ἐστὶν ὁ σταυρός.*

[291] *Cf. Rm.* 6:5. The words, "through baptism" have been added to the verse from the preceding verse. There is a parallel commentary on the same Pauline text: "Nor did Paul say: if we become sharers in the likeness of His death. What did he say? 'If we have been united with Him,' hinting by the word 'unite' at the fruit that comes to us from it. His body was buried in the earth and brought forth salvation as its fruit for the world, so also our body was buried in baptism, and produced as its fruit justice, holiness, adoption and countless blessings. And it will bring the final gift of resurrection. Since we were buried in water. He in the earth, we in the nature of our sin. He in the nature of His flesh, Paul did not say 'in death'

> He did not say "in death" but "in the likeness of His death". For both the first and the second are death, but not the death of the same thing; the first is the death of the body, the second is the death of sin. Hence, it is the "likeness of death."[292]

Through these "fontal" Pauline texts, and his explanation of them, Chrysostom presents the mystagogy of how the death of the Christian is not only a death to sin, and a sign of radical detachment, but also how his death is associated with the death of Christ and His resurrection. It is immediately evident that his explanation is at one with that of the other fathers. Christ died physically on the cross, and His death was a death to sin undertaken for humanity. The candidate does not die a physical death when he immerses in the font, but he shares nonetheless not only in the sign of radical detachment through the sign of death, but he does this in association with the death of Christ Himself, a death to sin. So he does not die physically, but in the "likeness (ὁμοίωμα)" of death, not the death of the body, but one like it, the death to sin. Christ died really; His death was a death to sin. The candidate does not die really in physical fact, yet he does die to sin, and through the baptismal act is really associated in Christ's death, really, but not physically. The act of baptism permits the candidate to die

but 'in the likeness of death.' Both the one and the other are death, but not of the same thing." *In Rm.* 11 (*MG* 60.484; tr. Harkins, *ACW* 31, 307, n. 35): Καὶ οὐκ εἶπεν, Εἰ γὰρ ἐκοινωνήσαμεν τῷ ὁμοιώματι τοῦ θανάτου· ἀλλὰ τί; Εἰ γὰρ σύμφυτοι γεγόναμεν, τῷ τῆς φυτείας ὀνόματι τὸν ἐκ ταύτης καρπὸν ἡμῖν αἰνιξαμένος· Καθάπερ γὰρ τὸ σῶμα ἀυτοῦ ταφὲν ἐν τῇ γῇ καρπὸν τῆς οἰκουμένης τὴν σωτηρίαν ἤνεγκεν· οὕτω καὶ τὸ ἡμέτερον ταφὲν ἐν τῷ βαπτίσματι, καρπὸν ἤνεγκε τὴν δικαιοσύνην, τὸν ἁγιασμόν, τὴν υἱοθεσιαν. τὰ μυρία ἀγαθά· οἴσει δὲ καὶ τὸ τῆς ἀναστάσεως ὕστερον δῶρον. Ἐπεὶ οὖν ἡμεῖς μὲν ἐν ὕδατι, αὐτος δὲ ἐν γῆ, καὶ ἡμεῖς μὲν κατὰ τὸν τῆς ἁμαρτίας λόγον, ἐκεῖνος δὲ κατα τὸν τοῦ σώματος ἐταφη, διὰ τοῦτο οὐκ εἶπε, Σύμφυτοι τῷ θανάτῳ, ἀλλά, "Τῷ ὁμοιώματι τοῦ θανάτου." θάνατος μὲν γὰρ καὶ τοῦτο καὶ ἐκεῖνο, ἀλλ 'οὐ τοῦ αὐτοῦ ὑποκειμένου.

[292] *P.K.* 2. 4 (*VGS*, 159; tr. Harkins, *ACW* 31, 151-152, no. 10): Διὰ τοῦτο καὶ ὁ Παῦλος φησί. "εἰ σύμφυτοι γεγόναμεν τῷ ὁμοιώματι τοῦ θανάτου αὐτου διὰ τοῦ βαπτίσματος". οὐκ εἶπε "τῷ θανάτῳ", ἀλλὰ "τῷ ὁμοιώματι τοῦ θανάτου αὐτοῦ". θάνατος μὲν γὰρ κακεῖνο καὶ τοῦτο, ἀλλ 'οὐ τοῦ αὐτοῦ πράγματος· ἐκεῖνο μὲν γὰρ σωματος, τοῦτο δὲ ἁμαρτίας· δια τοῦτο ὁμοίωμα θανάτου.

with Christ without really dying physically. But it also unites the candidate in a *real* way, and not merely in "likeness" with Christ's death to sin. In "likeness" he is united to Christ's physical death; in reality to His death for sin. The "likeness" to Christ's death comes from the fact that the candidate does not die a physical death, as did Christ. He *really* shares, however, in Christ's death to sin. In other words the real grace of Christ's death is contained in the sacrament. The manner of death, however, is not the same, Christ's being physical, the candidate's through the symbolism of baptism, and particularly through his Christian life, being in the "likeness". That this is Chrysostom's thought is clear from what he says in his commentary on *Rm.*[293]

Not only is the baptismal act a dying with Christ, not only does it contain the grace of the cross, but in its emersion-resurrection aspects it also associates the Christian with the new, risen life of Christ. Both death and resurrection derive their significance from the historical death and resurrection of Christ, and what that means in terms of overcoming sin and living a new life.

> What about this, then? Are we only dying with the Master and are we only sharing in His sadness? Most of all let me say that sharing the Master's death is no sadness. Only wait a little and you shall see yourself sharing in His benefits. "For if we have died with Him," says St. Paul, "we believe that we shall also live together with Him."[294] For in baptism there are both burial and resurrection at the same time. He who is baptized puts off the old man, takes the new, and rises up, "just as Christ has arisen through the glory of the Father."[295] Do you see how, again, St. Paul calls baptism a resurrection?[296]

[293] See above, n. 291, p. 272.

[294] *Rm.* 6:8.

[295] *Rm.* 6:4.

[296] *P.K.* 2.4 (*VGS,* 159; tr. Harkins, *ACW* 31, 152, no. 11):

Τί οὖν; ἀποθνῄσκομεν μόνον μετὰ τοῦ δεσπότου καὶ ἐν τοῖς σκυθρωποῖς κοινωνοῦμεν μόνον; μάλιστα μὲν οὐδὲ τοῦτο σκυθρωπόν, τὸ κοινωνῆσαι θανάτῳ

In this way Chrysostom explains in what sense the death and resurrection of Jesus is re-presented in the Christian's baptism. It will be a death to sin in this world, sharing through baptism in the crucifixion of Jesus by living a life in this world crucified to sin, and invisibly, but really, risen to God. This latter is the meaning of the emersion in the baptismal act, in which the new life is associated with the resurrection of Christ, in the Pauline sense, a life dead to sin, hidden, but real awaiting full revelation later, but nevertheless, because real, and like Christ, now alive to God, manifesting itself in some way in the Christian life of the baptized in this world.

These passages, then, with their emphasis on Pauline teaching from *Rm.* and *Col.* form the heart of Chrysostom's mystagogical instruction on the meaning of baptism in as far as it is seen as a configuration to Christ in death and resurrection.[297]

b. *Baptism and the Cross*

Since the other fathers emphasized the presence of the cross in baptism, particularly Cyril and Ambrose,[298] one would expect to find this aspect of the mystagogical explanation in Chrysostom. And this especially because two of the strongest dramatically rhetorical passages in both Cyril and Ambrose are concerned with the relation of the cross to baptism.[299] This aspect of the mystagogical explanation would seem, then, to be a most apt subject for Chrysostom, the rhetorician *par ex-*

δεσποτικῷ. πλὴν μικρὸν ἀνάμεινον καὶ ὄψει καὶ ἐν τοῖς χρηστοῖς κοινωνοῦτά σε. "εἰ γὰρ ἀπεθάνομεν σὺν αὐτω", φησί, "πιστεύομεν ὅτι καὶ συζήσομεν αὐτῷ". ὁμοῦ γὰρ καὶ ταφὴ καὶ ἀνάστασις ἐστὶν ἐν τῷ βαπτίσματι κατὰ τὸν αὐτον καιρόν. αφίησι κάτω τὸν παλαιὸν ἄνθρωπὸν καὶ λαμβανει τὸν καινὸν καὶ ἀνίσταται, "ὥσπερ ἠγέρθη ὁ Χριστὸς διὰ τῆς δόξης τοῦ πατρός". ορᾷς. πῶς πάλιν τὴν ἀνάστασιν λέγει.

[297] For further corroboration see also *In Rm.* 11. 1-3 (*MG* 60.483-488); *In Col.* 6 (*MG* 62.339-340); *In 1 Co.* 7.2 (*MG* 61.56-57); *In 1 Co.* 40.1-3 (*MG* 61.347-350).

[298] See above, pp. 234-241, 250-252.

[299] See above, pp. 235-236, 252.

cellence. We have already seen how he had brought to bear the idea of the crucifixion and the good thief in connection with the hour of the ceremony on Good Friday.[300] Surprisingly, however, Chrysostom does not deal as vividly with the crucifixion and its presence in the baptismal act as do Cyril and Ambrose, who emphasize as far as possible the reality of the physical aspects of the crucifixion. Indeed, as we have just seen, Chrysostom elaborates on baptismal death as sharing in the death of Jesus to sin, but his emphasis here is on the meaning of dying to sin in the Christian life, and not a focus on the actual role of the cross itself in the liturgy of baptism

Chrysostom treats the cross in baptism in the following:

> Do you see how baptism is a cross? Learn that even Christ called baptism a cross when He used the name interchangeably (with that of the cross). He calls your baptism a cross. "I call my baptism a cross," He says. Where does He say this? "I have a baptism to be baptized with, of which you do not know."[301] And how is it clear that He is speaking of the cross? The sons of Zebedee came up to Him—rather "the mother of the sons of Zebedee,"[302] saying: "Command that these my two sons may sit, one at thy right hand and one at thy left hand in the kingdom."[303] A mother's request, even if it was an inconsiderate one! How, then, did Christ answer? "Can you drink of the cup of which I am about to drink, and be baptized with the baptism with which I am baptized? "[304] You see that He called the cross a baptism. How is this clear? "Can you drink." He says, "of the cup of which I am about to drink? "[305] He calls His passion a cup and on this account He says: "Father, if it is possible, let this cup pass away

[300]See above, ch. 1, p. 68.
[301]*Cf. Lk.* 12:50.
[302]*Mt.* 20:20.
[303]*Mt.* 20:21.
[304]A conflation from *Mt.* 20:22 and *Mk.* 10:38.
[305]*Mt.* 20:22.

> from me,"[306] Do you see how He called the cross a baptism and the passion a cup? He did not speak of them in this way because He Himself was washed clean—How could "He Who did no sin, neither was deceit in His mouth?"[307] but because the blood which flowed from the passion and the cross washed the whole world clean.[308]

This choice of the scene from the request of the mother of the sons of Zebedee as a text used to relate the cross to baptism is unusual in that the other fathers do not use such an approach. It is rather the quasi-apologetical approach of the preacher seeking *topoi,* rather than that of the sacramental theologian. To show that the cross and baptism are related Chrysostom reverts to a scene from the earthly life of Jesus, in which Jesus Himself calls the cross a baptism, thus, showing from the mouth of our Lord Himself that His consequent death by crucifixion is that in which His followers will be bap-

[306] *Mt.* 26:39.

[307] 1 *P.* 2:22.

[308] *P.K.* 2.4 (*VGS,* 158-159; tr. Harkins, *ACW* 31, 151, nos. 9-10): Εἶδες, πῶς σταυρὸς τὸ βάπτισμα; μάθε, ὅτι καὶ τὸν σταυρὸν βάπτισμα ἐκάλεσεν ὁ Χριστός, ἀντιδιδούς σοι καὶ ἀντιλαμβάνων τὸ ὄνομα τοῦ βαπτίσματος. τὸ βάπτισμα τὸ σὸν ἐκάλεσε σταυρόν. τὸν σταυρὸν τὸν ἐμόν. φησί, καλω βάπτισμα. καὶ ποῦ τοῦτο φησί; "βάπτισμα ἔχω βαπτισθῆναι. ὃ ὑμεῖς οὐκ οἴδατε". καὶ πόθεν δῆλον. ὅτι περὶ τοῦ σταυροῦ λέγει; προσῆλθον αὐτῷ υἱοὶ Ζεβεδαίου, μᾶλλον δέ "ἡ μήτηρ τῶν υἱῶν Ζεβεδαίου" λέγουσα· "Εἰπέ, ἵνα οὗτοι οἱ δύο υἱοί μου καθίσωσιν, εἷς ἐκ δεξιῶν καὶ εἷς ἐξ εὐωνύμων ἐν τῇ βασιλείᾳ σου". μητρος ἡ αἴτησις, εἰ καὶ ἀπερίσκεπτος. τί οὖν Χριστός; "δύνασθε πιεῖν τὸ ποτήριον, ὃ ἐγω μέλλω πίνειν, καὶ τὸ βάπτισμα ὃ ἐγω βαπτίζομαι βαπτισθῆναι"; ὁρᾶς, ὅτι βάπτισμα τὸν σταυρὸν ἐκάλεσε. πόθεν τοῦτο δῆλον; "δύνασθε", φησί, "πιεῖν τὸ ποτήριον, ὃ ἐγω μέλλω πίνειν"; ποτήριον τὸ πάθος λέγει καὶ διὰ τοῦτο φησί· "πάτερ, εἰ δυνατόν, παρελθέτω τὸ ποτήριον τοῦτο ἀπ 'ἐμου". ειδες, πῶς βέπτισμα τὸν σταυρὸν ἐκάλεσε καὶ τὸ πάθος ποτήριον;

ἐκάλεσε δὲ οὕτως, οὐκ ἐπειδὴ αὐτος ἐκαθαίρετο (πῶς γάρ, "ὅς γε ἁμαρτίαν οὐκ ἐποίησεν οὐδε δόλος ἦν ἐν τῷ στόματι αὐτοῦ";), ἀλλ 'ἐπειδη τὸ αἷμα τὸ ῥεῦσαν ἐκεῖθεν ἅπασαν τὴν οἰκουμένην ἐκάθηρε.

[309] In discussing baptism as contract in ch. one (see above, pp. 98-99), we saw how Chrysostom quoted St. Paul, "The decree of our sins which was against us, He has taken it completely away, nailing it to the cross." (*Col.* 2:14). Chrysostom concluded: "The nails of the cross tore up the decree and destroyed it utterly (*οἱ γὰρ ἧλοι τοῦ σταυροῦ διέρρηξαν αὐτὸ καὶ διεύθειραν ἵνα ἄχρηστον γένηται τοῦ λοιποῦ*)." *Stav. 3-P.K.* 4.21 (Wenger, *SC* 50, 163; tr. Harkins, *ACW* 31, 63).

tized. What gives Christian baptism its effect, then, is the fact that it is related to the passion of Christ, which is His baptism, even though He needed no cleansing. And Chrysostom shows this relationship by citing Christ Himself to prove it. Because, as Chrysostom points out, the blood which flowed from the cross provided the unique historical act of wiping out sin, those who are baptized in this death of Christ will also be involved in this act; according to Christ's own words. In this sense the cross is present in baptism, because Christ's baptism, in which His followers share, was the baptism of the cross.

Chrysostom also pursues a more mystical explanation, once cross and baptism are associated, using a Johannine text:

> Do you wish to learn from another source as well the strength of this blood? Look from where it first flowed and where it had its source! It flowed down from the cross, from the Master's side. St. John says that when Christ was dead, but still on the cross, the soldier came and pierced His side with a lance and straightway there came out water and blood.[310] The one was a symbol of baptism the other of the mysteries.[311]

The water of baptism is seen, then, as symbolized by the water which came forth from the side of Christ, giving the baptized access to the temple: "It was the soldier, then, who opened Christ's side and dug through the rampart of the holy temple, but I am the one who has found the treasure and gotten the wealth."[312]

Thus, in an apologetical and then mystical way, Chrysostom takes his own approach to show the presence of the cross in the baptismal act.

[310] *Cf. Jn.* 19:33-34.

[311] *Stav. 3-P.K.* 4.16 (Wenger, *SC* 50, 160; tr. Harkins, *ACW* 31, 61): Βούλει *μαθεῖν καὶ ἑτέρωθεν τοῦ αἵματος τούτου τὴν ἰσχύν;* Βλέπε *πόθεν ἔρρευσε τὴν ἀρχὴν καὶ πόθεν τὴν πηγὴν ἔσχεν, ἄνωθεν ἀπο τοῦ σταυροῦ, ἀπὸ τῆς πλευρᾶς τῆς δεσποτικῆς.* Τ*εθνηκότος γάρ, φησί, τοῦ* Χ*ριστοῦ καὶ ἐν τῷ σταυρῷ ὄντος ἔτι, προσελθων ὁ στρατιώτης ἔνυξε τὴν πλευρὰν τῇ λόγχῃ, εἶτα ἐξῆλθεν ὕδωρ καὶ αἷμα.* Καὶ *τὸ μὲν τοῦ βεπτίσματος σύμβολον ἦν, τὸ δὲ τῶν μυστηρίων.*

[312] *Ibid.:* Ἔνυξε *τοίνυν τὴν πλευρὰν ὁ στρατιώτης ἐκεῖνος, διώρυξε τὸν τοῖχον τοῦ ἁγίου ναοῦ καὶ ἐγω τὸν θησαυρὸν εὗρον καὶ τὸν πλοῦτον ἔλαβον.*

Summary

Proceeding from the assumption that entering and leaving the baptismal pool symbolize death and resurrection Chrysostom uses *Rm.* 6:4,8 and *Col.* 3:10 as material to construct a mystagogy which will explain the meaning of this liturgical action. He evokes the mysteries of salvation history by portraying the baptistery in terms which evoke the garden of Paradise. His concern in explaining the death symbolized by the baptismal act centers around the message of Christian detachment in *Col.* 3:1-4 and *Rm.* 6:6, that the Christian, having "died" to this world, lives *in* the world, but is not *of* the world.

This death to sin and detachment from this world, however, is not an action of the Christian alone in his baptism, but one in which he is joined to the death and resurrection of Christ. Using *Col.* 3:10 and *Rm.* 6:3-6 Chrysostom demonstrates how baptism may be seen as the "likeness" of Christ's death. Chrysostom explains the meaning of the Pauline term "likeness" in showing the difference between Christ's physical death as a result of sin, and the candidate's symbolic death, one, however, in which he really shares, though not physically, in Christ's death to sin. If the immersion symbolizes death with Christ, the emersion signifies resurrection with Christ. Using *Rm.* 6:8 and 4 Chrysostom shows how dying to the old life of sin with Christ brings one to a participation in the new life which the risen Christ is already living for God, although the final revelation of that life will only come later.

Chrysostom accords special treatment to the question of how the cross is present in baptism. He reminds the hearers of Christ's own description to the mother of the sons of Zebedee of His coming cross as a baptism, one in which His followers would also share. The "cup" is the passion; the "baptism" is the cross. Pursuing then a more mystical line Chrysostom also shows the association of cross with baptism through the picture of the water flowing from the pierced side of Christ in *Jn.* 19:33-34.

4. Theodore

Essay: Baptism, Sign of the Future

Like Cyril, Ambrose and Chrysostom, Theodore's principal mystagogical explanations of the baptismal liturgy converge on the act of baptism itself. Even though Theodore develops a rather elaborate mystagogy for all the ceremonies connected with baptism, from the first enrollment to the final anointing, discussing with those to be baptized what he calls the "reason for all the mysteries and signs."[313] still it is the baptismal bath itself which is central to "the events we sacramentally perform which took place in connection with Christ our Lord, in order that, by means of these signs, our communion with Him might strengthen our hope."[314]

Like the other mystagogues, Theodore chooses the Pauline *anmnesis* of the death and resurrection of Christ as his principal means for explaining what happens in the baptismal act: "It is indeed evident to us, according to the words of the Apostle, that when we perform either baptism or the Eucharist, we perform them in remembrance of the death and resurrection of Christ, in order that the hope of the latter may be strengthened in us."[315] Like them, he quotes *Rm.* 6:3-4, and explains: "He [Paul] clearly taught here that we are baptized so that we might imitate in ourselves the death and resurrection of our Lord, and that we might receive from our remembrance of the happenings which took place the confirmation of our hope in future things."[316]

This is Theodore's principal statement, as it were, in respect to baptism. Furthermore, and this is an emphasis which is not underscored by Cyril, Ambrose or Chrysostom, but it is given an exceptional emphasis in the thinking of Theodore, the baptismal act is also a sign of future realities: "As we have a firm

[313] *Bapt. Hom.* I.7 (Tonneau-Devreesse, *SeT* 145, 332; tr. Mingana, *WS* VI, 21).
[314] *Idem.*
[315] *Ibid.*, I.6 (*Ibid.*, 330-332; tr. *ibid.*, 20).
[316] *Ibid.*, I.7 (*Ibid.*, 332; tr. *ibid.*, 20).

belief that things that have already happened will happen to us, so [the things that happened at the resurrection of our Lord] we believe that they will happen to us. We perform, therefore, this ineffable sacrament, which contains the incomprehensible signs of the Economy of Christ our Lord, as we believe that the things implied in it will happen to us."[317]

As we have already discovered in dealing with the other fathers, however, such a theological statement of the meaning of baptism is not a mystagogical interpretation of the ceremony itself. It states that the act of baptism is associated in some way with the death and resurrection of Christ. While Cyril, Ambrose and Chrysostom attempted to relate the liturgical action especially to the passion and death of Christ, and to develop a mystagogy of the ceremonies under this *leitmotiv,* and beyond that, to make some attempt at a sacramental theology which would explain and justify this mystagogical interpretation of these ceremonies, Theodore's program will call for an emphasis on the ceremonies as sign of future realities, as well as a representation of the passion and death.

After these introductory statements outlining the program of analysis which Theodore will undertake in order to show how the sacrament makes present in some way the past historical event of Christ's death and resurrection, and also represents in some way the baptizand's participation in the future world, he prepares the ground for his mystagogical interpretation of the sacrament as sign of these realities. Similar to Ambrose's portrayal[318] he repairs to *Gn.* for the history of man's creation and fall, and the consequent power of death and of Satan over man, and he outlines the saving work of Christ, concluding: "We draw nigh unto the sacrament because we perform in it the symbols of the freedom from calamities from which we were unexpectedly delivered, and of our participation in these new and great benefits which had their beginning in our Christ Lord."[319]

[317] *Ibid.,* I.6 (*Ibid.,* 330; tr. *ibid.,* 20).

[318] See above, pp. 244-247.

[319] *Bapt. Hom.* I.10 (Tonneau-Devreesse, *SeT* 145, 336,338; tr. Mingana, *WS* VI, 22).

In this sense, the sacramental action which Theodore calls by various names, such as symbol, type, emblem, mystery, not only represents the past historical event of Christ's salvific act, but somehow looks toward and represents the full realization of this salvation at the neophyte's final resurrection from the dead. The sacramental action will contain, then, not only symbols of the passion, death, and resurrection of Christ and our participation in this, but also be a symbol of our participation in the fulfilment to come, which this resurrection of Christ implies. In this program of Theodore, the future will somehow be made present symbolically.[320]

In a *Catechetical Homily* on the mass Theodore states his position as follows:

> We walk by faith and not by sight because we are not yet in the reality, as yet we are not yet in the heavenly benefits. We wait here in faith until we ascend into heaven and set out on our journey to our Lord, where we shall not see through a glass and in a riddle, but shall look face to face.[321] These things, however, we expect to receive in reality through the resurrection at the time decreed by God, and it is not only by faith we draw nigh unto the first fruits of these good things: to Christ our Lord and the high

[320] According to R. Greer, *Theodore of Mopsuestia: Exegete and Theologian* (London, 1961), pp. 66-85, esp. 73-80, Theodore's sacramental theology is based on his doctrine of the Two Ages. T. Finn, "Baptismal Death and Resurrection: A Study in Fourth Century Eastern Baptismal Terminology," *Worship* 43 (1969), 184-185, sums this up as follows; "The First Age is the visible and ever-changing world of time, space and human life and choice, in short, 'the world.' The Second Age is the invisible and immutable future, the world of paradise regained, in short, the *eschaton.* But the Two Ages are not discontinuous. The Second is hidden in the First, the invisible behind the visible, the immutable beneath the mutable, the eternal and heavenly within the temporal and terrestrial. For in His incarnation, Christ entered the First Age and fully established the Second through His death and resurrection. The risen Lord is the real but invisible link between the Two Ages, for in virtue of the "risen-ness" of Christ's humanity, the Second is ontologically linked to the First, as its consummation. Further, Christ, precisely as *homo assumptus,* has established within human nature itself the pattern by which all men progress from the First to the Second Age, namely death and resurrection."

[321] 1 *Co.* 13:12.

> priest of things that belong to us. We are ordered to perform in this world the symbols and signs of the future things, so that, through the service of the Sacrament we may be like men who enjoy symbolically the happiness of the heavenly benefits, and thus acquire a sense of possession and a strong hope of the things for which we look.[322]

From such statements one can see that in Theodore's view the "types" or "signs" performed in the sacrament reflect future salvation, but this not only as reflection: they also contain this future salvation, because they participate in it, and mediate such participation to the receiver.[323] The sacramental "signs" are able to do this because they are related to the death and resurrection of Christ. Precisely "how" they are so related is not explained by Theodore. It is not by "participation" since he reserves this word for future goods, already exemplified by the resurrection of Christ.

a. *Immersion-Leaving Pool: Death and Resurrection with Christ*

Here the sacramental analysis gives way to the mystagogical statement. As in the other three fathers, the liturgical action of baptism in Theodore is seen as a sign of the death and resurrection of Christ, and the candidate's configuration to this:

> Because Christ our Lord abolished the power of death by His own resurrection [the Apostle] said: "As many of us as were baptized into Jesus Christ, were baptized into His death."[324] As if one were saying: "We know that death has been abolished a long time ago by Christ our Lord, and

[322] *Homily on the Eucharist and the Liturgy* I. 18 (Tonneau-Devreesse, *SeT* 145, 492; tr. Mingana, *WS* VI, 82).

[323] For the centrality of the concept of participation see L. Abramowski, "Zur Theologie Theodors von Mopsuestia," *Zeitschrift für Kirchengeschichte* 72 (1961), 263-293, esp. 274ff; J. Quasten, "The Liturgical Mysticism of Theodore of Mopsuestia," *Theological Studies* 15 (1954), 431-439; Kretschmar, *op. cit.*, p. 176.

[324] *Rm.* 6:3.

> we draw nigh unto Him, and are baptized with such a faith because we desire to participate in His death, in the hope of participating also in the future resurrection from the dead, in the way in which He Himself arose.[325]

Presenting, then, this summary of the historical event of Christ's salvific acts, Theodore goes on in a central mystagogical statement to explain to the candidates how this reality is exemplified by what they do in the liturgical action of the baptismal act: "This is the reason why, when at my baptism I plunge my head I receive the death of Christ our Lord, and desire to have his burial, and because of this I firmly believe in the resurrection of our Lord; and when I rise from this water, I think I have symbolically risen a long time ago."[326]

Thus, in rather brief and summary form, Theodore asserts the same fundamental mystagogical interpretation of the baptismal act as did Cyril, Ambrose and Chrysostom. The water is the tomb of Christ into which I enter, being buried with Him, and my rising from this water is a sign of my resurrection, just as He rose from the tomb. This is Theodore's central mystagogical interpretation of the action of immersing in the water and coming out of it. In comparison to Cyril and Ambrose in particular, the statement is quite brief. Like Chrysostom, Theodore takes it for granted that this is the meaning of the liturgical action.

(1) Earth-Water; Baptistery-Furnace Symbolism

Theodore does analyze the notion of entering the water as sign of corruption and death, which has reminiscences of the biblical notion of creation and the chaos of the flood, sin and the sentence of death, which he had already outlined, in a later passage in connection with a symbol of the baptismal pool as a forge, where mortal nature will be changed into immortal:

[325] *Bapt. Hom.* III.5 (Tonneau-Devreesse, *SeT* 145, 412; tr. Mingana, *WS* VI, 52).
[326] *Idem.*

> It behooves you, therefore, to think that you are going into the water as into a furnace, where you will be renewed and refashioned in order that you may move to a higher nature, after having cast away your old mortality and fully assumed an immortal and incorruptible nature. These things dealing with birth happen to you in the water, because you were fashioned at the beginning from earth and water, and having fallen later into sin you assumed a thorough corruption through the sentence of death.[327]

Here, through the use of natural symbolism of earth and water, and its biblical counterpart, together with the artificial symbol of the furnace, Theodore explains how plunging into the water exemplifies the corruption of death. Man, who was originally fashioned by God out of earth and water, because of the sentence of death, now returns to these elements. Entering the pool, then, is the sign of dissolution and death. Made in water, we return to the water and are dissolved in it, in order to be re-made.

(2) The Symbol of the Potter's Vessel

Theodore adds a further symbol based on *Jr.* 18:1-6 to explain the meaning of entering the water as dissolution, a dissolution made necessary by the fact that the artefact was marred, and had like a clay vessel to be immersed into the water in order to be refashioned:

> The potters are also in the habit, when the vessels which they fashion are damaged, to refashion them again with water so that they may be remade and reconstructed and given the wanted form. This is the reason why God ordered also the prophet Jeremiah to repair to a potter; and he went and saw him working on a vessel which, because it was marred, he cast in the water, remade, and brought to its former state; and then God said to him: "O house of Israel, cannot I do with you as this potter? said the Lord." Because we also were made of earth and clay—as

[327] *Ibid.*, III.11 (*Ibid.*, 424; tr. *ibid.*, 56-57).

> it is said: "For thou are also made of clay like me,"[328] and "forgive them that dwell in a house of clay because we are also made of the same clay."[329] when we fell and sin corrupted us, we received a complete dissolution from the [Divine] sentence of death, but afterwards our Maker and our Lord refashioned us and remade us by His ineffable power, because He abolished death by resurrection and granted to all of us the hope of resurrection from the dead, and a world higher than the present, where we shall not only dwell but also become immortal and incorruptible.[330]

Thus, through biblical and natural symbol Theodore explains the meaning of immersion in the baptismal pool. They are related to creation-redemption, Adam-Christ parallels.

b. *Coming out of the Pool: Sign of Future Resurrection*

Unlike Cyril and Ambrose, Theodore does not concentrate special attention on the baptismal action in its relationship to the crucifixion of Christ. Having shown cursorily the meaning of baptism as a death, and its relationship theologically to the death of Christ and the penalty of sin, he passes on quickly to his main point, baptism as a sign of resurrection. His emphasis is not on how the crucifixion and death are symbolized in the baptismal act, but rather how this act is a symbol of the resurrection, related indeed in a backward glance to Christ's actual resurrection, but more especially as symbol of the baptized's participation now in the eschatological reality which is to come.

A good indication of this shift of emphasis, in which Theodore sees the sacramental action as a sign of participation in the future principally rather than an "imitation" of the past historical events of Christ's death and resurrection – is his use of a text in this connection which Cyril had used in graphic

[328] *Jb.* 33:6 *LXX.*
[329] *Jb.* 4:19 *LXX.*
[330] *Bapt. Hom.* III.11 (Tonneau-Devreesse, *SeT* 145, 424, 426; tr. Mingana, *WS* VI, 57).

reference to his notion of the sacrament as imitation of the crucifixion of Christ.

> Since, however, all this is done in symbols and signs in order to show that we do not make use of vain signs only, but of realities in which we believe and ardently desire, [Paul] said: "For if we have been planted together in the likeness of His death, we shall be also [in the likeness] of His resurrection."[331] In using the future tense he confirms the present event by the future reality, and from the greatness of the coming reality, he demonstrates the credibility of the greatness of its symbols, and the symbol of the coming reality is baptism. The working of the Holy Spirit is that it is in hope of the future things that you receive the grace of baptism, and that you draw nigh unto the gift of baptism in order to die and to rise with Christ so that you may be born again to the new life, and thus, after having been led by these symbols to the participation in the realities you will perform the symbol of that true second birth.[332]

While Cyril had used this text of *Rm.* to emphasize the baptized's being planted in union with the crucifixion of Christ, as the true cross was planted in Jerusalem[333] to show his union in baptism with the Crucified, Theodore, on the other hand, concentrates on the second part of the text, the notion of baptism as sign of future resurrection. Cyril had concentrated on the term "likeness (ὁμοίωμα)," in reference to the death of Christ; Theodore is interested in the word as it refers to the resurrection of Christ, and points grammatically to Paul's use of the future tense, "we shall be (ἐσόμεθα)" to show that, while the historical resurrection of Christ is present in the baptismal act, the act also looks forward to the future accomplishment of this resurrection for the baptized in the eschaton.

[331] *Rm.* 6:5.

[332] *Bapt. Hom.* III.6 (Tonneau-Devreesse, *SeT* 145,412, 414; tr. Mingana, *WS* VI, 52).

[333] See above. p. 239.

Thus, in his use of *Rm.* 6, Theodore interprets the baptismal act, mystagogically, the emerging from the water, as not only an imitation of the historical resurrection of Christ emerging from the tomb, but as a participation, mediated by the symbols of the sacramental action, in future salvation. These future goods are exemplified by the salvation events in the historical life Jesus, and this presence of these events in the baptismal act is what makes the participation in future goods possible now, through the action of the sacrament.

The Body of Christ

This underscoring of the resurrection leads Theodore to other Pauline texts not used by the other fathers, to provide the mystagogical interpretation of the coming out of the water in relationship to Christ's resurrection in the past and the neophites resurrection in the future.

> We believe in one Godhead and are baptized and through it we become one body, according to the working on us of the Holy Spirit, in baptism, which makes us children of God and one Body of Christ our Lord, Whom we consider our Head[334] as He is from our nature and was the first to rise from the dead, and as it is through Him that we received participation in benefits . . . . And we become one body of Christ, because we consider Christ our Lord in the flesh as our Head, since He was assumed from us and was the first to rise from the dead, and thus He confirmed for us our participation in the resurrection from which we expect our body to be similar to His body. Indeed, "our conversation is in heaven from whence also we look for our Savior, our Lord Jesus Christ, Who shall change our vile body that it may be fashioned alike unto His glorious body . . . .[335] This will take place in reality in heaven, but we perform its symbols and its signs in baptism.[336]

[334] *Cf.* 1 *Co.* 11:3.

[335] *Ph.* 3:20-21.

[336] *Bapt. Hom.* III.21-22 (Tonneau-Devreesse, *SeT* 145, 446,448; tr. Mingana, *WS* VI, 64-65.

As Cyril had considered the baptized's body to be similar to the crucified body of Christ that was taken down from the cross and buried, so here Theodore considers the body of the baptized, coming up out of the pool, to be similar to the risen body of Christ, using the Pauline theology of the headship of Christ to ground his mystagogy. And so Theodore goes on to say: "We are also called the Body of Christ our Lord, Christ our Lord being our Head, as the blessed Paul said: 'Christ is the head from which all the body is joined together and increases with the increase of God.' "[337]

Here we have, then, the same Pauline theology of Adam-Christ, death to sin, resurrection to a new life for God, as is found in Cyril and Ambrose. In his mystagogy, however, Theodore has concentrated more on the resurrection, and that as sign of participation in the coming eschaton, more than had either Cyril or Ambrose.

Theodore summarizes this aspect of his mystagogy, baptism as configuration to the death and resurrection of Christ, insofar as entering and emerging from the baptismal pool signify this:

> You have fulfilled by your baptism in water the rite of burial, and you have received the sign of the resurrection by your rising out of the water; . . . you are no more part of Adam who was mutable and burdened and made wretched by sin, but of Christ, who was completely freed from sin through the resurrection, while even before it He never drew nigh to it. It was congrous that [this sinless state] should have had its beginning in Him before [His resurrection] and that at His resurrection He should fully receive an immutable nature. In this way He confirmed to us the resurrection from the dead and our participation in incorruptibility.[338]

[337] *Col.* 2:19. *Bapt. Hom.* III.22 (Tonneau-Devreesse, *SeT* 145, 448; tr. Mingana, *WS* VI, 65).

[338] *Bapt. Hom.* III.25 (*Ibid.,* 454; tr. *ibid.,* 67).

Theodore develops his mystagogy of how baptism signifies the life to come more fully under the aspect of baptism as second birth, and this part of Theodore's presentation will be treated in that section.[339]

c. *Trinitarian Symbolism*

Other aspects of the baptismal ceremony, such as the triple immersion or the invocation of the Trinity do not receive from Theodore the mystagogical interpretation under this aspect of death and resurrection as they did in Cyril or in Ambrose. These features of the ceremony have been interpreted in the light of Trinitarian concerns, rather than the christological development. How completely this change has taken place may be seen in one passage which Theodore uses from *Ac.* 3:6 where Peter orders a lame man to get up and walk in the name of Jesus of Nazareth. Just as Ambrose had used the example of the triple denial and the triple question of Christ to Peter after His resurrection to give a mystagogical interpretation to the triple immersion, so in this passage Theodore could have conceivably used such material as this in relationship to the theme of baptism as configuration to the passion and resurrection of Christ. The man, lame, a symbol of sin, raised up and renewed, an eschatalogical symbol of the resurrection, by the power of Christ. In actual fact Theodore uses the passage to justify baptism in the name of the Trinity, emphasizing that in that name the saving power is given, just as in *Ac.* it was the name of Christ.

> When, therefore [the priest] utters these words: "In the name of the Father and of the Son and of the Holy Spirit," he reveals to you the cause of the things that take place. In as much as the one who said: "In the name of Jesus of Nazareth rise up and walk,"[340] alluded to Christ as the cause of what would take place, and to the fact that it

[339]See below, pp. 325ff.
[340]*Ac.* 3:6.

> would be He who would give [to the lame man] the power of rising and walking, so also the [priest] who says, "In the name of the Father and of the Son and of the Holy Spirit," refers to them as the cause of the benefits conferred upon us in baptism . . . . The priest does not say "In the name of the Father and in the Name of the Son, and in the Name of the Holy Spirit," because every one of them has a separate name that does not fit that of the other.[341]

From this example one can see that further mystagogical interpretation of the actions accompanying the rite of the baptismal act, the triple immersion, the triple formula, which in Cyril and in Ambrose had received interpretation relating to the paschal mystery of death and resurrection, here in Theodore are subsumed into Trinitarian concerns.[342]

Summary

Like the other mystagogue, Theodore applies the Pauline *anamnesis* to the liturgy of the baptismal act. Immersion in the water and leaving the pool symbolize death and resurrection with Christ. The element of the baptismal water is presented in the light of the biblical account of man's creation from earth and water, his death as a return to these elements as a penalty for sin. The baptismal pool becomes the "furnace" where this symbolic dissolution of man and his "reforging" take place: water of creation, water of death, water of re-creation. The candidate is also seen in the pool as a potter's vessel, made of clay. It is dunked in the water to the point of dissolving its former imperfect shape, and re-fashioned by God, the potter.

[341] *Bapt. Hom.* III.15-16 (Tonneau-Devreesse, *SeT* 145, 434, 436; tr. Mingana, *WS* VI, 60).

[342] *Cf. ibid.,* III.18-20 (*Ibid.,* 440, 442, 444; tr. *ibid.,* 62-64).

Special attention is devoted to the action of coming out of the pool. Re-enacting in symbol Christ's resurrection from the tomb, the neophyte, planted in the likeness of Christ's death in the water, emerges also from the water in the likeness of Christ's resurrection, now in symbol, awaiting future revelation. The real presence of the resurrection of Christ in the baptismal act ensures the reality of this resurrection, thus making the sacrament more than a mere symbol.

Theodore reinforces this part of the mystagogy, showing how the baptized, coming out of the tomb, is really united to the risen Body of Christ, by appeal to Pauline texts representing the mystical Body of Christ, the Head, Christ as Firstborn from the dead, Who will change our "vile Body" into His "glorious Body", the old Adam becoming the new Adam.

Aspects of the ceremony like the triple immersion which might have been treated under the aspect of baptism as conformity to Christ in death and resurrection, are treated by Theodore under the aspect of Trinitarian symbolism.

Comparative Summary

The central piece in the catecheses, the mystagogy of the baptismal act as a conformity to Christ in death and resurrection, reveals, upon analysis, the fundamental unity of view among the four fathers despite their individuality of style. The message contained in the biblical material, the view of salvation history with creation, destruction and new creation, sin and death, forgiveness and resurrection, converges upon the cross and death, burial and resurrection of the new Adam, Jesus Christ. The fathers rely on this material, particularly as it is fixed in the Pauline lens, to explain what happens in the baptismal act itself. In this Pauline view adopted by the fathers as their principal material for providing a mystagogy of the liturgical action, Christian baptism bespeaks nothing less than a mystical transubstantiation of the candidate into Christ. The various elements of the liturgy, the locale where baptism takes place, entering the pool, the immersions into and the emersions from the water, the coming out of the pool, the element of water itself: these are the elements of the given liturgy in the framework of which the fathers must show how this mystagogical transubstantiation is taking place, how, in other words, the elements of the given liturgy in some way reveal what faith and tradition say is actually happening.

In *general* mystagogical terms, the association with the death and resurrection of Christ which Christian baptism bespeaks is seen by all four fathers as signified by entering or immersing in the water and leaving the pool. This is the basic framework in which their interpretation takes place. The rest of what they do is to show how, by this or that liturgical indication, the view of the baptismal ceremony as a sign of association in the death and resurrection of Christ is revealed. The four fathers quote from *Rm.* 6. Cyril possesses a particular advantage of being at the very scene of the events of Christ's death and resurrection, and presses this advantage to make his mystagogy more graphic in relating the liturgical action to the actions of Christ's crucifixion, death, burial and resurrection.

From the standpoint of the elements of *sin and death,* as represented by the ceremony, Cyril presents the stark comparison between the body of Christ brought from the cross and buried in the sepulcher, and the movement of the candidate to the pool. This literal presentation of the "imitation" of the surrounding events of Christ's death, then, extends its influence to the interpretation of the triple immersion-emersion as a sign of the three days of Christ in the tomb, a symbolic interpretation unique to Cyril among the four fathers.

In using *Rm.* 6 to explain the baptismal act as representation of death, Ambrose lays a much larger foundation from biblical theology of death as penalty for sin, exegetically linking *Gn.* and *Rm.* Cyril concerned himself with Paul's idea of our death as "likeness" to the death of Christ, trying to show how this takes place in the baptismal act by "imitation". Ambrose, on the other hand, fills in the larger picture from the Adam-Christ parallel, that is, why man should die at all, in other words, the meaning of death as penalty of sin. The symbolism of the baptismal pool as a tomb is the same, however, although Ambrose does not have the privilege of being at the *Anastasis* as does Cyril, but he reminds his hearers of the tomblike aspects of the baptistery. Ambrose also takes pains, through his explanation based on the reigning physics, to make plausible the immersion in water as sign of death and burial, linking this symbolic burial to the curse of *Gn., "Ibis in terram,"* death as penalty for sin. Cyril had contented himself with the allusion to the burial of Christ, comparing it to the immersion of the baptized, and then moved into his theology of baptism being an imitation in image of the death of Jesus. In the passages preceeding and subsequent to the one describing the baptismal questioning, Ambrose, on the other hand, has elaborated the whole biblical story of man's fall from grace and consequent death as penalty for sin, beginning immediately after this question, "What is baptism (Quid est baptismum)?" with the introduction: "In the beginning the Lord our God made man so that he would not die, provided that he would not taste sin."[343] Ambrose does not interpret the therefold immersion as Cyril, but uses it rather as a somewhat arbitrary framework on which to spread out his mystagogy of death, the cross and forgiveness.

Chrysostom's approach to the sin and death aspects of the baptismal act is in agreement that entering the pool represents burial with Christ, and he puts the candidate into touch with salvation history through his reminiscence of the baptistery as the garden of Eden. Thus, from the standpoint of locale as serving an interpretative function of the baptismal rite one might say that what Cyril had available by virtue of his position at the actual scene of the salvific events of Christ's life in Jerusalem, and which he used so obviously in presenting his mystagogical interpretation of the sacrament, Chrysostom, for his part, failing the geographic advantage, has created a rhetorical advantage through his skillful use of suggestive words Chrysostom does not draw the large picture of creation, death and sin like Ambrose, but rather presents the meaning of

[343]See above, pp. 244-245.

Christ's death to sin and the Christian's detachment. His concern is more pastoral than theological, nor does he give much detailed liturgical commentary. While Ambrose had used such liturgical elements as the tomblike aspects of the baptistery and the water in inter-action with his theology of creation and redemption, Chrysostom explains in a more pastoral way how Christ's death to sin must be revealed in the Christian's detachment to sin.

Theodore recreates the salvation history of sin and death also by allusion to water and earth as the elements of creation. Then, in an imaginative allusion, the pool is not only the tomb, but also a furnace for refashioning the corrupted vessel. Death or dissolution is also seen in the allusion to the baptistery as a potter's tank into which the Maker casts the clay pot to be remade.

Each father, then, while in common mystagogical agreement he sees entering the pool as entering one's own death symbolically with Christ buried, brings out different aspects of the locale or the liturgical elements, or the interpretation of biblical history which the elements suggest.

From a mystagogical viewpoint, the truth that baptism is an *association in the cross of Christ* is much more difficult to portray than baptism as association in the death and burial of Christ, a matter already discussed.[344] Cyril, Chrysostom and Ambrose are all at pains to insist on the traditional truth that baptism forgives sins. But it not only does this; it has this power because it is related to the crucifixion of Christ, an act which contains the power which forgive sins. It is the relationship of the power of baptism to forgive sins to the crucifixion of Christ which the fathers also attempt to bring out in their mystagogical interpretation of the baptismal act. From a mystagogical standpoint they are not entirely successful.

Cyril's approach to the problem of how the crucifixion of Christ may be indicated in the liturgical ceremony passes of

[344]See above, pp. 234-241, 252-255.

necessity from mystagogical interpretation to theological statement. The mystagogical "convenience" of the death-resurrection-water tomb symbolism is simply absent when one goes to seek in the ceremony a similar representation of the crucifixion. This, of course, shows the limitation of mystagogical interpretation of any sacramental action, just as it also shows the dependence of mystagogy on the given liturgical ceremonies at any given time of their history. Ambrose in his distribution of the three immersions attempts a certain connection of the cross with the liturgy of the baptismal act when he uses the second immersion to emphasize the presence of the cross in baptism, no doubt because the second immersion is done in the name of the second Person of the Trinity—the redemption therefore—and because it contains the unusual addition to the Trinitarian baptismal formula of the words, "Do you believe . . . in His Cross?" Ambrose had used the first immersion, referring to God the Father, for his mystagogy, logically, of creation, the fall, the curse of death from the Creator. Ambrose's solution to the mystagogical problem here, in addition to the relationship to the second immersion, is to show that since the candidate's death is a share in Christ's death to sin (based on the Christ-Adam theology), so the candidate, sharing not in the corporal death of Christ, but in its "likeness," similary shares, by virtue of this "likeness" in the reason for Christ's death, a death caused by sin in the new Adam, taking the form of a crucifixion. The similarity to Cyril's solution, the "imitation" theology, is manifest. The Pauline message, "With Christ I am nailed to the cross,"[345] emerges clearly in the utterances of both Cyril and Ambrose who see the candidate mystically nailed to the cross with Christ in the process of Christian Initiation.

While Cyril and Ambrose emphasize the cross, but direct their attention more to the sacramental theology of *how* the cross is present in the baptismal act, Chrysostom also occupies himself explicitly with the question of how baptism is the cross. His line, however, proceeds to show not so much *how* the cross is contained in the baptismal act from the standpoint

[345] *Ga.* 2:19. See above, pp. 235-236, 252.

of sacramental theology, but rather he answers the question by presenting as "proof" the word of Jesus to the mother of the sons of Zebedee that the baptism of His followers in an association in His cross, and as further proof Chrysostom adds the mystical symbolism of the blood and water from the side of Christ which links the baptismal bath of water with the crucifixion, here touching, like the other fathers, on the "likeness" theology which has its roots in St. Paul, "If we have been united with Him in the likeness of His death through baptism . . ."[346]

Unlike Cyril, Ambrose and Chrysostom, Theodore does not occupy himself particularly with the question of how baptism is related to the crucifixion of Christ.

It is Ambrose who develops the mystagogy of baptism as *forgiveness of sins* by relating the triple fall of Peter to the triple immersion of the baptismal act, and the triple question-answer confession of faith to the triple question-answer dialogue of Christ and Peter after the resurrection, "Simon Peter, do you love me?" "You know, Lord, that I love you." This mystagogy, as is seen in Ambrose's subsequent observation that the name in which one is baptized is the name of Jesus, also reflects the theological problem of the Trinitarian formula of baptism and the other traditional formula of baptism in the name of Jesus.

In all four fathers the coming out of the pool is mystagogically interpreted as a sign of the *resurrection.* Cyril does not develop the point in the *Mystagogical Catecheses.* The chief point of his mystagogy of the baptismal act had been conformity to Christ's crucifixion and death. While mentioning this interpretation specifically, Ambrose also attempts no further development. He, too, had been concerned particularly with the mystagogical explanation of the baptismal act and the problem of death. Chrysostom links the mystagogy of the resurrection to that of death, placing it under his pastoral emphasis of death to and detachment from sin. Crucified to sin the baptized emerges from the pool possessing the new, resurrected,

[346] *Rm.* 6:5.

but hidden life of Christ which will manifest itself to the world in his Christian conduct.

It is Theodore who takes the emerging from the pool as sign of resurrection and develops it more fully than the others, in conformity with his whole emphasis on the sacrament as participation in the future reality rather than "imitation" of past historical events of salvation. The text, *Rm.* 6:5, the first part of which Cyril had emphasized to bring out baptism as an association in Christ's sufferings ("For if we have been planted together in the likeness of His death"), the being planted in the earth like a vine as the true cross was planted in Jerusalem, is used by Theodore in its latter part ("We shall be also in the likeness of His resurrection") to emphasize the baptized's conformity to the risen Christ in the eschaton. Because of this emphasis on emerging from the font as future resurrection, Theodore chooses texts referring to the glorious body of Christ to which the baptized will be ultimately conformed. While Cyril had emphasized the body of Christ taken down from the cross and wrapped in linen, in mystagogical comparison to the baptized's body going as it were from cross to tomb, Theodore emphasizes the association of the baptized's body coming out of the font as sign of his future conformity to the risen body of Christ. He continues this development particularly in his mystagogy of baptism as new birth.

B. New Birth

Biblical Background

Baptism as a configuration to the death and the resurrection of Christ is a particularly Pauline symbol. It is this Pauline material which plays the most prominent role in the mystagogical writings of Cyril, Ambrose, Chrysostom and Theodore in their attempt to explain to their neophytes the meaning of the baptismal act. There is a second symbol, closely affiliated with that of death and resurrection, and likewise rooted in the *NT* teaching on baptism, which the fathers employ in their mystagogy of the baptismal act. This symbol describes baptism as a "new birth".

Central passages in the *NT* where this descriptive designation of baptism occurs are the following. In *Tt.* 3:5 God's compassionate salvation is described as affecting its purpose "by means of the bath of rebirth (*διὰ λουτροῦ παλιγγενεσιάς*)." And in the dialogue between Jesus and Nicodemus we read: "I tell you most solemnly, unless a man is born from above [or, again] (*γεννηθῇ ἄνωθεν*), he cannot see the kingdom of God. Nicodemus said, "How can a grown man be born (*γεννηθῆναι*)? Can he go back into his mother's womb and be born again (*γεννηθῆναι*)? " Jesus answered: "I tell you most solemnly, unless a man is born (*γεννηθῇ*) through water and the Spirit, he cannot enter the kingdom of God."[347]

St. Paul had made the connection between the resurrection of Christ and the new life of the baptized in *Rm.* 6:4: ". . . as Christ was raised from the dead by the Father's glory, we too might live a new life." And this same juxtaposition of new life, or, in this case, new birth together with the raising up of Jesus from the dead, is also found in 1 *P.* 1:3: "Blessed be God the Father of our Lord Jesus Christ, who in his great mercy has given us a new birth (*ἀναγεννήσας*) into a living hope through the resurrection of Jesus Christ from the dead." And in the same letter the condition of the baptized is further described as "newborn:" "You are new-born (*ἀναγεγεννημένοι*), not from any mortal seed, but from the everlasting word of the living and the eternal God."[348] And the description of the baptized as new-born continues with the exhortation that they seek after spiritual milk, "like newborn babes (*ἀρτιγέννητα βρέφη*)."[349]

From such scripture texts the picture emerges of baptismal conversion as a being born into a new life, and this new life is related to the risen life of Christ Himself. It must be remembered, however, that such scripture texts are not mystagogical interpretations of baptismal ceremonies necessarily, such as

[347] *Jn.* 3:3-5.
[348] 1 *P.* 1:23.
[349] 1 *P.* 2:2.

they were performed at the time of the *NT* witness, but rather they argue from the general scheme of Christian belief in attempting to show the meaning of baptismal conversion in general, and the relationship of Christian conversion to the salvific events of the death and resurrection of Christ. From such texts, of course, it is clear that the Christian conversion being spoken of involves baptism specifically.

The Petrine text and the text from *Rm.* show the relationship between the new life of Christ risen from the dead, and the new life of the Christian. Since the Christian has "died" with Christ, he also rises with Him to a new life. If this is so, then an obviously apt symbol from the natural realm to describe such a phenomenon as a new beginning, or a new life, is that symbol derived from human birth. The *NT* has developed the idea of "new birth" (παλιγγενεσία) thus far in its reflection on the meaning of baptism.

How do the fathers apply this scriptural image of baptism as new birth to the baptismal act in order to provide a plausible mystagogy of the liturgy of baptism as they found it in their respective churches?

SYNOPTIC CHART

Baptism as New Birth

Cyril	*Ambrose*	*Chrysostom*	*Theodore*
	RISING FROM FONT: REGENERATION	BATH OF REBIRTH	REBIRTH: IMAGE OF FUTURE
	Sacr. III.2 *Ac.* 13:33 *Ps.* 2:7 *Col.* 1:18	*Stav.* 1.17 *Stav.* 3-*P.K.* 4.23 *Mont.*1-*P.K.* 1.12 *Tt.* 3:5	*Bapt.Hom.* III. 2,3,5-7,21-23 *Ph.* 3:20-21 *Rm.* 6:5 *Jn.* 3:3-5
		Bridal Bath: *Ep.* 5:25-27 -Blood-Water *Stav.* 1.17	

Baptism as New Birth—continued

Cyril	*Ambrose*	*Chrysostom*	*Theodore*
		Stav. 3-*P.K.* 4.17 *Jn.* 19:34	
		-Adam-Eve; Church-Christ *Stav.* 3-*P.K.* 4.18 *Gn.* 2:21-23	
		-Christ as Mother with New Born *Stav.* 3-*P.K.* 4.19	
Water Womb: *Myst.Cat.* II.4 *Qo.* 3:2	*Water Womb:*	*Church as* *Mother Womb:* *Stav.* 4.1	*Water Womb:* (Blessing of Font) *Bapt.Hom.* III 9-10 *Jn.* 3:4-5 1 *Co.* 15:42-44
		-No Labor Pains *Mont.* 1-*P.K.* 1.19 1 *Co.* 6:11	
	-Natural-Super- natural; Water *Sacr.* III.3 *Gn.* 1:20-21	-Natural-Super- natural; Earth-Water *Mont* 1-*P.K.* 1.20	
	-Virgin Birth (Blessing of Font) *Myst.* 59 *Mt.* 1:18 *Jn.* 3:4	-Virgin Birth *P.K.* 3.16-17 *Mt.* 1:18 *Lk.* 1:35	
		Potter's Vessel *Mont.* 1-*P.K.* 1. 20-26 *Jr.* 18:6; 19:11 *Ps.* 2:7-9	*Potter's Vessel* *Bapt.Hom.* III. 11-13 *Jr.* 18:1-6 *Jb.* 4:9; 33:6, *LXX*

1. *Cyril*

Water Tomb as Mother Womb

Cyril's use of the symbol of new-birth in his mystagogical explanation of the baptismal act provides one of the best examples to show how this symbol of new birth is affiliated with that of baptism as dying and rising with Christ in the context of the concrete liturgy of baptism: "At the self-same time you died and were born; and that water of salvation was at once your grave and your mother. And what Solomon spoke of others will suit you also for, he said, 'There is a time to bear and a time to die',[350] but to you, on the contrary, the time to die is also a time to be born; and one and the same season brings about both of these things, and your birth went hand in hand with your death."[351]

The descent into the font had been a parallel for the burial of Christ's body, carried from cross to sepulcher. The image now shifts from the water-grave symbol, or water as symbol of death and destruction, to the natural symbolism of water as a creative force from which life springs, the death bearing water-tomb to the life bearing water-womb. The use of the scriptural quotation from *Qo.*, with its foundation in the natural rhythms of nature and the natural phenomena of birth and death, is especially apt at this point. By reversing the natural idea as he has done, showing how the natural rhythm of nature, first birth then death, is reversed in baptism, where there is first death, and at the very same moment, out of this death a birth, Cyril shows ingeniously the paradox of the act of baptism over against the rules of natural life, and thereby he underscores the astounding fact of new life, new birth, coming out of death, a reversal of the usual order of things, where one does not die in order to be born.

[350] *Qo.* 3:2.

[351] *Myst. Cat.* II.4 (Piédagnel, *SC* 126, 112; tr. Cross, *SPCK,* 61): "Καιρὸς *τοῦ τεκεῖν, καὶ καιρὸς τοῦ ἀποθανεῖν.*" Ἐφ *ὑμῖν δὲ τὸ ἀνάπαλιν· καιρὸς τοῦ ἀποθανεῖν.*" *καὶ καιρὸς τοῦ γεννηθῆναι.* Καὶ *εἷς καιρὸς ἀμφοτέρων τούτων ποιητικός, καὶ σύνδρομος ἐγίνετο τῷ θανάτῳ ἡ γέννησις ἡ ὑμετέρα.*

The connection of the two symbols is clear. The death and resurrection of Christ are somehow present in baptism. The symbol of the candidate's sharing in the death of Christ was his immersion in the water-tomb. The symbol of the candidate's sharing in the resurrection of Christ is his emersion from the water-tomb. First the candidate's death is symbolized, in relationship to Christ's death: he is buried as Christ was buried. Then the candidate's resurrection is symbolized: he arises from his death as Christ rose. But to this second place of the symbolism, rising from the font as symbol of rising with Christ, something additional enters in order to explain symbolically what this rising means, and this something additional is precisely the *symbol of new birth, new life,* which is necessary to describe the mysterious phenomenon of baptism as new life, a phenomenon accessible only to the eyes of faith. This mystagogical symbol of new birth helps the eyes of faith to understand the meaning "of what was said and done on that evening of your baptism." Faith believes that baptism gives a share in the resurrection of Christ. Somehow baptism brings the candidate into relationship to the resurrection of Christ. This truth of the faith is concretized mystagogically two ways by Cyril, first by likening the baptized's rising from the font to the rising of Jesus from the tomb, a matter already discussed in the section on configuration to Christ in death and resurrection,[352] and then he goes a step further in the symbolism in order to explain more fully in what this resurrection with Jesus consists, namely the beginning of a new life. Symbol to explain this is, then, symbol of birth and new life. So the water-tomb, into which one had immersed in death with Christ and from which one had emersed in resurrection with Christ receives now a second symbolism, and becomes the water-womb. Of course, with the addition of this new symbolism for the font, the parallel line of the action of immersion, which corresponds to Christ's burial and emersion, which corresponds to His resurrection, must come to a halt, and the development of the new symbol must be on an inde-

[352]See above, pp. 232-233.

pendent track. Since the emersion is interpreted to symbolize the resurrection of Christ from the tomb, one could not here, without jarring the images, begin to speak of a parallel between the candidate's new birth and the birth of Christ, since the emersion symbolizes not Christ's birth, but His resurrection. Such a development, at least by suggestion, is not entirely absent however, as we shall see later.[353]

The problem, then, of how to show the neophytes what the new life of baptism means, was met by this new-birth symbolism. Already present in Holy Scripture, and archetypally imbedded in human nature in the idea of water as a creative force from which life teems forth, an idea on which the biblical account of creation relies, the symbol lay ready to hand for the fathers' application to the baptismal act.[354]

Because of his concern to show how the passion of Christ is present in the baptismal act, Cyril does not expend any more time developing the symbolism of baptism as new birth, but contents himself with the statement which has been quoted, and then passes on to his more paramount concern, baptism as conformity to Christ in death and resurrection.[355]

[353] See below, pp. 309-311, 318-320, 341.

[354] The notion of tomb and mother is found among other authors besides these four mystagogues, *e.g.*, Tertullian, Cyprian, Didymus the Blind, Zeno of Verona. For texts, see J. Daniélou, *The Bible and the Liturgy*, pp. 47-48.

[355] In connection with the maternal or procreative power of the water in the font attention should be drawn to several other statements of Cyril, which probably are connected with the idea of the blessing of the font, and so the power invested in the water through that blessing. In *Procat.* 15 (Cross, *SPCK*, 9; tr. Cross *SPCK*, 49): ". . . may you then enjoy the fragrant waters which contain Christ (. . . Τότε ὑδάτων ἀπολαύσητε Χριστοφόρων, ἐχόντων εὐωδίαν)." In *Bapt. Cat.* III.5 (*MG* 33.432) Cyril gives an analysis of the power of the water as opposed to the other elements resting on an analysis of Holy Scripture. In the same *Catechesis*, III.3 (*MG* 33.428) he warns the candidates not to approach the baptismal water as though it were ordinary water. Just as the offerings brought to idols become impure through the invocation of the idols, so ordinary water, through the invocation of the Holy Spirit, Christ and the Father, acquires a sanctifying power. (See n. 7, p. 145).

2. *Ambrose*

Coming out of Font: Regeneration

Jesus as Cyril, Ambrose demonstrates his mystagogical concern to expand the symbol of rising from the font as rising with Christ by the addition of the symbol of rebirth. He does this in a somewhat more elaborate way than Cyril's flat statement that the font is both tomb and womb. In order to develop this mystagogy, Ambrose reaches for material to the great inaugural discourse of St. Paul, which Luke offers in *Ac.* 13: 17-31 as a typical model of the apostle's preaching to the Jews:

> What is regeneration? You have it in the *Acts of the Apostles*, for that line, which is mentioned in the second psalm, "You are my Son; this day have I begotten You."[356] seems to refer to the resurrection. For the Holy Apostle Peter[357] in the Acts of the Apostles thus interpreted that at that time when the Son rose from the dead, the voice of the Father resounded, "You are my Son; this day have I begotten You."[358] Therefore he is also called "the firstborn from the dead."[359] So, what is the resurrection other than we rise from death to life? Thus, even in baptism, since it is a likeness of death, undoubtedly, when you dip and rise again, it becomes a likeness of the resurrection. Thus, according to the interpretation of the apostle, just as that resurrection was a regeneration, so that resurrection from the font is a regeneration.[360]

[356] *Ps.* 2:7.

[357] Possibly a *lapsus memoriae* because of the similarity of Paul's prayer (*Ac.* 13:15-41) and Peter's prayer (*Ac.* 2:14-36).

[358] *Ac.* 13:33.

[359] *Col.* 1:18.

[360] *Sacr.* III.2 (Botte, *SC* 25bis, 90; tr. Deferrari, *FC* 44, 289-290): "Quid est regeneratio? Habes in actibus apostolorum quod ille versiculus qui dictus est in psalmo secundo: 'Filius meus es tu, ego hodie genui te,' ad resurrectionem spectare videatur. Namque sanctus apostolus Petrus in actibus apostolorum sic interpretatus est quod tunc, quando resurrexit filius a morte, patria vox resultaverit: 'Filius meus es tu, ego hodie genui te.' Unde et 'promogenitus a mortuis' dicitur. Ergo resurrectio quid est nisi quando de morte ad vitam resurgimus? Sic ergo et in baptismate, quoniam similitudo mortis est, sine dubio dum mergis et resurgis similitudo fit resurrectionis. Itaque secundum interpretationem apostoli sicut illa resurrectio regeneratio fuit, ita et ista resurrectio de fonte regeneratio est."

According to the Pauline teaching, as represented in Paul's use of *Ps.* 2:7 here in the passage of *Ac.* to which Ambrose refers, Christ is enthroned as Messiah by his resurrection, and from then on His human nature enjoyed all the privileges of the Son of God.[361] It is, then, in His resurrection where Christ's Sonship is affirmed, and this, then, is His "birth" as Son of God, Christ being, as Ambrose says, following St. Paul, "the first-born from the dead (πρωτότοκος ἐκ τῶν νεκρῶν)."[362] Such biblical phrases, then, as "first-born (πρωτότοκος)," or "begotten (γεγέννηκα)" form the foundation of Ambrose's application to the baptismal liturgy.

Ambrose argues thus: Having already pointed out that rising from the font is a symbol of the baptized rising with Christ, Ambrose now shows that Christ's actual resurrection was, as it were, not only a resurrection, but also a new-birth. And this regeneration is valid not only for Christ (here, of course, following the Pauline theology that Christ the man received full prerogatives of divine Sonship through the power of His Father in His resurrection) but for the whole human race, Christ being the first-born. Here, again, we find the Christ-Adam parallel. If Christ's resurrection was a new-birth, a regeneration, then the baptized, who participates in this resurrection, symbolically manifest in his rising from the font, which had been his and Christ's tomb, also participates in this regeneration. As Christ is His resurrection is "regenerated" into full Sonship, so baptism is regeneration for the baptized.

This is the basic statement of Ambrose to ground his mystagogy of the baptismal act as new birth. However, this is a theological argument, and as mystagogy, it is rather thin. Mystagogy must show how the given ceremony in a plastic way demonstrates the meaning of what is done. Rising from the font signifies rising from the tomb. This is a concrete picture. This rising is also a regeneration. This is a theological argument,

[361] *Cf. Rm.* 1:4: "This news is about Jesus Christ our Lord, Who in the order of the spirit, the spirit of holiness that was in Him, was proclaimed Son of God in all His power through His resurrection from the dead."

[362] *Col.* 1:18.

an analysis of meaning, but not yet a mystagogy. The next step is to show how the ceremony represents this regeneration, which has been theologically asserted. That the ceremony of rising from the font represents in some way Christ rising from the tomb is clear. How can the ceremony be shown to represent in some way a new birth?

a. *Water: Natural and Supernatural Generation*

In order to provide this mystagogy for his argument that resurrection is also regeneration, Ambrose reaches to the concrete element of the water, just as he had done to make graphic the symbolism of death: "But why do you say that you dip in water? . . . You have read about water: 'Let the waters bring forth creatures having life,'[363] and creatures having life were born. They indeed were in the beginning of creation, but for you it was reserved for water to regenerate you unto grace, just as waters generated other creatures unto life."[364]

By drawing this parallel between natural and supernatural life, Ambrose begins to apply to the ceremony, using the concrete element of the water, the mystagogy of regeneration. In both the case of natural creation and supernatural generation, the creatures were born in water, the waters of creation described in *Gn.*, and the waters of the baptismal font. In the former case, through God's Word, creatures were born into natural life, the beginning of creation. In the case of those emerging from the font, they have been re-born in these waters through God's Word to the life of grace, creation and re-creation; birth and re-birth, and the common symbol in the natural order and in the supernatural is the element of water.[365]

[363] *Gn.* 1:20-21.

[364] *Sacr.* III.3 (Botte, *SC* 25bis, 90,92; tr. Deferrari, *FC* 44, 290): "Sed quid dicis quia in aqua mergis? . . . De aquis legisti: 'Producant aquae animantia, et nata sunt animantia.' Illa quidem in principio creaturae, sed tibi reservatum est ut aqua te regeneraret ad gratiam sicut alia generavit ad vitam."

[365] In this connection J. Daniélou, "Die Symbolik des Taufritus," *Liturgie und Mönchtum* 5 (1949), 64 draws attention to the fish as Christian symbol. That the fish, "ἰχθύς" is symbol of Christ is a well-known fact. What is less well-known is what F. Dölger, *Das Fischsymbol* (Münster, 1928), pp. 3-7, has established: that this symbol has its origin in this mystagogy of baptism. The paintings on the

Ambrose then draws out this mystagogical explanation with a charming and often-quoted bit of advice for the neophytes, in fine rhetorical style:

> Imitate the fish, which indeed has obtained less grace, yet should be an object of wonder to you. It is in the sea and is upon the waters; it is in the sea and it swims upon the floods. A tempest rages in the sea, storms shriek, but the fish swims; it is not submerged, because it is accustomed to swim. So even for you this world is a sea. It has diverse floods, heavy waters, severe storms. And do you be a fish that the water of the world may not submerge you.[366]

Such a passage is rooted in Ambrose's guiding idea in his whole treatment of baptism, that it is a transformation which reaches out to the whole of creation.[367] We have seen already how he considered death to be a gift of God, in view of His whole salvific plan, a chance for man to work out the sentence against him, achieved in the act of baptism as death.[368] Here, in this section, the waters of the world, biblically symbolized as chaos, death, destruction, begin to lose their destructive force, and begin to take on regenerative force. Instead of destroying the candidate by swallowing him up, they are sufficiently transformed by God's redeeming Word to regenerate him to new life. As the chaos of the waters of creation brought forth natural life, so the waters of recreation, symbolizing death, paradoxically are able to bring forth supernatural life.

---

catacombs show small fish, "pisciculi" swimming in the water. As we see in the text of Ambrose, the water of baptism brings forth these fish, the baptized, who are "regenerated" as Christ is "reborn" through His resurrection, just as the waters of creation brought forth fish on the natural level. Thus Cyril says: "Baptized in Christ, . . . you have become christs (Εἰς Χριστὸν βεβαπτισμένοι ··· χριστοὶ δὲ γεγόνατε)." *Myst. Cat.* III.1 (Piédagnel, *SC* 126, 120; tr. Cross, *SPCK,* 63).

[366] *Sacr.* III.3 (Botte, *SC* 25bis, 92; tr. Deferrari, *FC 44,* 290): "Imitare illum piscem qui minorem quidem adeptus est gratiam, tamen debet tibi esse miraculo. In mari est et super undas est, in mari est et super fluctus natat. In mari tempestas furit, stridunt procellae, sed piscis natat, non demergitur quia natare consuevit. Ergo et tibi saeculum hoc mare est. Habet diversos fluctus, undas graves, saevas tempestates. Et tu esto piscis ut saeculi te unda non mergat."

[367] See Kretschmar, *op. cit.,* pp. 232-233.

[368] See above, p. 302.

The neophyte is not taken out of the world in his baptismal rebirth, any more than the fish is taken out of water. Rather, the world loses its destructive force, because the neophyte is now like the fish who can swim. The unbenign waters of death have become regenerative waters. What is evil becomes for the baptized a force for good, for creativity, through the re-birth of baptism.

While Cyril had not used this symbolism, his central thought is the same: "Your death went hand in hand with your birth."[369] The positive acceptance of death through faith in Christ brings the good out of the evil through the power of God, as is seen in the resurrection of Jesus.

In dispensing this moral advice for the neophytes on the basis of this mystagogy of regeneration in the waters of baptism, not merely as the static reality of resurrection rebirth with Christ as a theological statement, but through the development of the regeneration symbolism, he moves to the explanation of how this new life, which is given birth in the waters of baptism is so manifest itself in the world. This is one of the principal concerns of the fourth century mystagogy. Such symbolism is a rich font for Christian asceticism and the development of a Christian baptismal spirituality.

b. *Water-Womb: The Virgin Birth*

Given his emphasis on the baptismal font as a tomb, and his obvious familiarity with the idea-world of the Jerusalem catecheses, it would be surprising if Ambrose failed to use the tomb-womb symbolism in trying to make graphic how the baptismal ceremony represents new birth. Ambrose concludes *De Mysteriis* with the following paragraph:

> Thus, having obtained everything, let us know that we have been regenerated. Let us not say: "How were we regenerated? We have not entered into the womb of our mother and been born again.[370] I do not recognize the course of

[370] *Cf. Jn.* 3:4.

> nature." But no order of nature is here, where there is an excellence of grace. Finally the course of nature does not always produce generation; we confess that Christ our Lord was conceived of a Virgin, and we deny the order of nature. For Mary did not conceive of man, but received the Holy Spirit in her womb, as Matthew says: "She was found with child of the Holy Spirit."[371] If, then, the Holy Spirit coming upon the Virgin effected conception and effected the work of generation, surely there must be no doubt that the Spirit coming upon the font, or upon those who obtain baptism, effects the truth of regeneration.[372]

As has already been noted[373] that mystagogical explanation which emphasizes baptism as regeneration will naturally seek as model for its explanation elements connected with the birth of Christ. We have seen how Ambrose, following St. Paul, sees in the resurrection of Christ the birth of the new Adam. It is but a short step from the mystagogical parallel of rising from the pool—resurrection of Christ and the candidate, to further reflection on how this regeneration, which the resurrection implies, may be shown.

While not explicitly stated, as in Cyril, the womb-tomb parallel is present here. If the rising from the font is resurrection, and resurrection is regeneration, how is this seen in the ceremony? To this Ambrose answers: How was Christ generated in the womb of His mother? The Holy Spirit came over Mary and effected generation in her womb in a supernatural way:

[371] *Mt.* 1:18.

[372] *Myst.* 59 (Botte, *SC* 25bis, 190-192; tr. Deferrari, *FC* 44,28): "Unde adepti omnia sciamus regeneratos nos esse, nec dicamus: Quomodo regenerati sumus? Numquid in ventrem matris nostrae introivimus et renati sumus? Non agnosco usum naturae. Sed nullus hic naturae ordo ubi excellentia gratiae. Denique non semper usus naturae generationem facit: generatum ex virgine Christum dominum confitemur et naturae ordinem denegamus. Non enim ex viro Maria concepit, sed de spiritu sancto, ut dicit Matthaeus quia 'inventa est in utero habens de spiritu sancto.' Si ergo superveniens spiritus sanctus in virginem conceptionem operatus est et generationis munus implevit, non est utique dubitandum quod superveniens in fontem spiritus vel super eos qui baptismum consequuntur veritatem regenerationis operatur."

[373] See above, p. 304.

the Holy Spirit comes over—and then Ambrose offers a choice —the font, *or* the baptized. In the former case, the symbol is then the font as mother womb, and so mystagogy. In the latter case, there is more of a theological attempt to explain, than a mystagogical picture. We are dealing with symbolism here, and not mere logic, and Ambrose is attempting to illuminate from different standpoints, using Scripture in a way that the neophytes might be helped to understand the mystery. The blessing of the font, at any rate, with the invocation of the Holy Spirit, has been used to make the parallel: as the Holy Spirit can bring forth a miraculous birth in the womb of the Virgin Mary, so too, in the womb which is the baptismal font, he can bring forth a new creature in a miraculous way.[374]

[374] As in Cyril (see above, n. 355, p. 304), such references to the power of water are not without reference to the blessing of the font. (See above, n. 7, p. 145; n. 26, pp. 149-150; Kretschmar, pp. 231-232). Ambrose's particular mode of thinking here, which leads to what seem like contradictions, is the problem of the static and the dynamic, or, in contemporary terms, the essential and the existential, object or action. If the *leitmotiv* of Ambrose's entire sacramental theology is transformation, then this transformation is also supposition and content of his baptismal teaching. As Kretschmar shows (*op. cit.*, pp. 231-232) when one compares the texts of Ambrose which refer to the consecration of the baptismal water, one might almost think that he is teaching a "transsubstantiation" of the water similar to that of the bread and wine of the Eucharist. In using scriptural examples, and the creation-recreation parallel with the image of water, he naturally reaches to the symbolism of the water receiving power from God's Word, just as the waters of creation brought forth a creation at the Word of God. At the same time he realizes that it is the Spirit and not the water itself which conveys the regeneration at baptism. That it is not the water which becomes a "new creature," but the baptized, is seen from a text referring to the Mass liturgy:

"What is the expression of Christ? Surely that by which all things were made. . . . The heaven was not, the earth was not, the sea was not, but hear David when he says: 'He spoke and they were made; he commanded, and they were created.' (*Ps.* 32:9; 148:5). Therefore, to reply to you, there was no body of Christ before the consecration, but after the consecration I say to you there is the body of Christ. He Himself spoke, and it was made; He himself commanded and it was created. You yourself were, but you were an old creature; after you were consecrated, you began to be a new creature. Do you wish to know how a new creature? It says: 'every creature is new in Christ.' (2 *Co.* 5:17) (Quis est sermo Christi? Nempe is quo facta sunt omnia. . . . Caelum non erat, mare non erat, terra non erat, sed audi dicentem David: 'Ipse dixit et facta sunt, ipse mandavit et creata sunt.' Ergo, tibi ut respondeam, non erat corpus Christi ante consecrationem, sed post consecrationem dico tibi qiua jam corpus est Christi. Ipse dixit et factum est, ipse mandavit et creatum est. Tu ipse eras, sed eras vetus creatura; posteaquam consecratus es, nova creatura esse coepisti. Vis scire quam nova creatura? 'Omnis,' inquit, 'in Christo nova creatura.' " *Sacr.* IV. 15-16 (Botte, *SC* 25bis, 110; tr. Deferrari, *FC* 44, 302-303. (On this problem see also the discussion, ch. 3, n. 64, pp. 370-371.

Summary

Ambrose has taken the Pauline theology that Christ receives His full prerogatives as Son of God at His resurrection, that this, therefore, is Christ's "birth" as Son of God, and he uses it as point of departure for the mystagogy of baptism as second birth. Since, as Ambrose has already shown in the mystagogy of the emersion from the pool, the Christian shares in Christ's resurrection, he also shares in Christ's "birth" as Son of God, since this is what the resurrection is. And he hears God say also to him, as He said to Jesus: "You are my Son, this day have I begotten you".

To apply this idea mystagogically, Ambrose reminds his hearers that the water of the ceremony is that *Ur*-element of creation which brought forth all creation at God's Word. So, too, this water of baptism is a fitting element for the new, supernatural, re-creation, also effected through God's Word. His charming metaphor of the fish continues along the same line of theology of transformation: the paradox that the waters, which can be destructive, can also be rendered benign, and at God's power bring forth a creature which is capable of negotiating in them: here, the fish, which can swim and does not drown, in baptism the Christian, he to whom God gives this regenerative power of becoming the kind of new creature that will never again drown, but can swim in the waters of this world.

A second application of the idea of regeneration to the baptismal act is the implication that the baptismal font is womb, which is capable of producing a supernatural birth. Ambrose combines the fact of the blessing of the font upon which the Holy Spirit comes, with the coming of the Holy Spirit on the womb of the Virgin Mary. In both cases a miraculous generation takes place.

3. *Chrysostom*

The Bath of Rebirth

St. John Chrysostom intersperses his mystagogical interpretation of the baptismal act under the image of interpretation of the baptismal act under the image of second birth throughout his *Baptismal Instructions*. As a result, his use of the regeneration imagery is dependent on the context, mostly scriptural meditations, in which it occurs. The common point of departure for the application of this image of baptism as a rebirth is Chrysostom's preference for the Pauline term "bath of rebirth (λουτρὸν παλιγγενεσίας)."[375] This term occurs frequently as the central focus point in those passages which develop the idea of regeneration.[376]

Chrysostom's reason for developing the regeneration image from the Pauline "bath of rebirth" as a point of departure is not difficult to discern. The regeneration is seen over against the remission of sins, and it is precisely this twofold aspect of baptism which Chrysostom the preacher and Christian educator throughout his *Instruction* is constantly emphasizing. The "regeneration" demonstrates God's gift, but the "bath" idea emphasizes the fact that the candidate was sinful, was filthy, and so was in need of washing, of forgiveness. The consciousness of sin, and the need of educating the baptized for the Christian life and its difficulties, is something never lost sight of in Chrysostom's *Instructions*. As has been noted before, Chrysostom, more than Cyril, Theodore or Ambrose, is the preacher, and paramount in the thinking which governs his choice and use of his imagery, are the needs of his hearers.

[375] *Tt.* 3:5.

[376] See *e.g.*, *Stav.* 1.17; *Stav.* 3-*P.K.* 4.17,23 (Wenger, *SC* 50, 117, 161, 164; tr. Harkins, *ACW* 31, 29, 62, 63).

a. *The Bridal Bath*

If baptism is a "bath of regeneration" in what sense can this fact be portrayed in the ceremony? A favorite image of Chrysostom is the bridal metaphor, where Christ is the bridegroom and the baptizand or the Church is the bride. This image, which is, of course, Pauline[377] is taken by Chrysostom and applied in his mystagogy to the baptismal act itself, which then becomes the bridal bath. The reason why this bridal bath has such power to cleanse the bride and make her beautiful for the Bridegroom comes from the fact that it has been invested with the love of Christ, symbolized by His Blood, which has the power to cleanse from sins and to regenerate. It is in this context, the love of Christ for His Church, symbolized by the outpouring of His Blood, and conveyed by the spiritual marriage metaphor that the term "bath of rebirth" occurs in the first of the *Stavronikita* series of *Baptismal Instructions.* In the framework of *Ep.* 5:25-27, where St. Paul advises husbands to love their wives as Christ loved the Church, Chrysostom says:

> No man would ever have allowed himself to do this, namely, to pour out his blood for the woman who was going to be his bride. But the kindly Master, imitating His own goodness, has accepted this great and marvellous sacrifice because of His solicitude for her, that by His own Blood He might sanctify her, that, having cleansed her by the bath of baptism, He might present her to Himself a Church in all her glory. To this end He poured forth His Blood and endured the cross, that through this He might freely give sanctification to us too, and might cleanse us through the bath of regeneration, and might present to Himself those who before were in dishonor, and unable to speak with

[377] *Cf. Ep.* 5:21-33; *Ezk.* 16.

[378] On the image of the bridal bath see Kretschmar, *op. cit.*, pp. 31-32; O. Casel, "Die Taufe als Brautbad der Kirche," *Jahrbuch für Liturgiewissenschaft* 5 (1925), 144-147; T. Finn, *op. cit.*, p. 165.

> confidence, but now are glorious, without spot or wrinkle, or any such thing.[379]

The power of "regeneration" contained in the baptismal bath is seen as a result of the Blood of Christ, sign of His self-giving love, which is powerful enough to cleanse, erase the sordidness of the past, and bring about a regeneration. The baptismal act, then, becomes the symbolic bridal bath, which prepares the bride for the Bridegroom by a process of regeneration.

A further reason why the baptismal act as bridal bath contains the power of regeneration is found by Chrysostom in his meditation on the Johannine scene of the piercing of the side of Jesus, where blood and water issued forth as symbols of baptism and the Eucharist:

> "There came out of His side water and blood."[380] Beloved, do not pass this mystery by without a thought. For I have still another mystical explanation to give. I said that there was a symbol of baptism and the mysteries in that blood and water. It is from both of these that the Church is sprung, "through the bath of regeneration and renewal by the Holy Spirit,"[381] through baptism and the mysteries.[382]

[379] *Cf. Ep.* 5:27. *Stav.* 1.17 (Wenger, *SC* 50, 117-118; tr. Harkins, *ACW* 31, 29-30):

Τοῦτο οὐκ ἄν τίς ποτε ποιῆσαι κατεδέξατο, τὸ αἷμα ἐκχεῖν ὑπὲρ τῆς μελλούσης αὐτῷ συνάπτεσθαι. Ἀλλ ὁ φιλάνθρωπος δεσπότης τὴν οἰκείαν μιμούμενος ἀγαθότητα, τοῦτο τὸ μέγα καὶ πατάδοξον διὰ τὴν περὶ αὐτην κηδεμονίαν κατεδέξατο, ἵνα διὰ τοῦ αἵματος τοῦ ἰδίου ταύτην ἁγιάσῃ, ἵνα καθαρίσας τῷ λουτρῷ του βαπτίσματος παραστήσῃ ἑαυτῷ ἔνδοξον τὴν ἐκκλησίαν. Διὰ τοῦτο τὸ αἷμα, ἐξέχεε καὶ σταυρὸν ὑπέμεινεν ἵνα καὶ ἡμῖν διὰ τούτου τὸν ἁγιασμὸν χαρίσητε καὶ καθαρίσῃ ἡμᾶς διὰ τῆς τοῦ λουτροῦ ἀναγεννήσεως καὶ τούς πρότερον ἠτιμωμένους καὶ μηδεμίαν παρρησίαν δυναμένους ἔχειν παραστήσῃ ἑαυτῷ ἐνδόξους μὴ ἔχοντας σπίλον ἤ ῥυτίδα ἤ τι τῶν τοιούτων.

[380] *Cf. Jn.* 19:34.

[381] *Tt.* 3:5.

[382] *Stav. 3-P.K.* 4.17 (Wenger, *SC* 50, 161; tr. Harkins, *ACW* 31, 62): "*'Εξῆλθεν ἀπὸ τῆς πλευρᾶς ὕδωρ καὶ αἷμα.*" *Μὴ παραδράμῃς ἁπλῶς, ἀγαπητέ, τὸ μυστήριον. Ἔχω γὰρ καὶ ἕτερον λόγον εἰπει μυστικόν. εἶπον ὅτι τοῦ βαπτίσματος σύμβολον καὶ τῶν μυστηρίων ἐστι τὸ αἷμα ἐκεῖνο καὶ τὸ ὕδωρ. Ἐξ ἑκατέρων τούτων ἡ ἐκκλησία γεγένηται, "διὰ λουτροῦ παλιγγενεσίας καὶ ἀνακαινώσεως Πνεύματος ἁγίου", διὰ βαπτίσματος καὶ διὰ μυστηρίων.*

Here it is the water of baptism particularly which is associated with the water flowing from the side of Christ, as sign of the cleansing power of the baptismal bath. Through the power of the Holy Spirit, says Chrysostom, associated with the water of baptism, a cleansing and regeneration from the sordid past is effected.

It is Christ, then, Who, in the power of His Blood, symbol of His love, cleanses the Church, the baptized, and this cleansing is seen under the image of spiritual marriage, a Pauline notion from *Ep.*, who has borrowed from the customs of antiquity, the bridal bath, showing how the baptized, cleansed in the "bath of rebirth" comes, as it were, reborn by this cleansing bath to her husband.[383]

In a not unexpected way, Chrysostom goes on in this same *Instruction*[384] to develop the consequences of this spiritual marriage, in terms of rebirth and the image of the Blood of Christ which has brought this rebirth about. As Eve was formed by God from the side of Adam while he slept[385] so in the Blood and water from the side of the second Adam, while he "slept" on the cross, the Church is formed.

The metaphor of bride and bridegroom is then blended by Chrysostom with the metaphor of the mother feeding her child, a picture he will develop elsewhere at greater length in this mystagogy. Adam-Christ and Eve-the baptized now becomes Christ the mother and the baptized as the child whom he nurtures: "Have you seen how Christ unites us to Himself His bride? Have you seen with what food He nurtures us all? It is by the same food that we have been formed and are fed. Just as a woman nurtures her offspring with her own blood and milk, so also Christ continuosly nurtures with His own blood those whom He has begotten."[386] Here Chrysostom, like

[383] *Cf. Ezk.* 16. The reference in Chrysostom and in *Ep.* 5:27 is to the ancient custom of the bridal bath. *Cf.* above, n. 378, p. 314.

[384] *Stav. 3-P.K.* 4.18 (Wenger, *SC* 50, 161-162; tr. Harkins, *ACW* 31, 62).

[385] *Cf. Gn.* 2:21-22.

[386] *Stav. 3-P.K.* 4.19 (Wenger, *SC* 50, 162; tr. Harkins, *ACW* 31, 62):
Εἴδετε πῶς συνῆψεν ἑαυτῷ τὴν νύμφην ὁ Χριστός; Εἴδετε ποίᾳ πάντας ἡμᾶς τρέφει τροφῇ; Ἐκ τῆς αὐτῆς τροφῆς καὶ συνεστήκαμεν καὶ τρεφόμεθα. Καθάπερ γὰρ γυνὴ τὸ τεχθεν οἰκείῳ τρέφει αἵματι καὶ γάλακτι, οὕτω καὶ ὁ Χριστὸς οὓς ἐγέννησεν αὐτὸς οἰκείῳ τρέφει διηνεκῶς αἵματι.

Theodore has taken advantage of the image of rebirth in baptism to develop and allusion to the Eucharist in the sense that it will be the nutriment for those who are new born in baptism.[387]

Instead of the rather lengthy and detailed biological metaphor of conception and birth which we shall see in Theodore, as explanation of the scriptural reference to baptism as new birth, Chrysostom has chosen to employ a mystical meditation of primarily christological overtones as his main emphasis, resting on the spiritual marriage metaphor, with its image of the bridal bath.

b. *Church as Mother Womb*

While not applying the word "womb" explicitly to the baptismal font, preferring instead to use the Pauline phrase "bath or rebirth" throughout the *Instructions,* Chrysostom nevertheless echoes his familiarity with this patristic image.[388] While the baptismal font may not explicitly be called the womb, the Church is, however, the mother which brings to birth the baptized on the night of their baptism. The baptismal act, then, is seen in this mystagogy under the metaphor of child-bearing. If, then, in the words of the apostle, baptism is a rebirth, the baptismal act demonstrates by its similarity to childbirth, the baptized coming out of the baptismal pool like a child from the womb of his mother, that this regeneration is taking place: "See how many children this spiritual mother has brought forth suddenly and in a single night. But we must not be surprised. Spiritual child-bearing is such that it needs neither time nor a period of months."[389]

[387]The comparison between Christ and a mother based on the fact that both nurture their offspring is found again in *In Mt.* 82 (*MG* 58.744). See Harkins, *ACW* 31, 238, n. 38.

[388]On the Eastern tradition, which sees the font itself as the virginal mother, and the Western tradition, which sees the font as the virginal womb of the Mother Church see W. Bedard, *The Symbolism of the Baptismal Font in Early Christian Thought* (Washington, D.C., 1951), p. 18. Chrysostom here is more in line with the Western tradition.

[389]*Stav.* 4.1 (Wenger, *SC* 50, 182-183; tr. Harkins, *ACW* 1, 66): 'Ιδοὺ γὰρ *ἐν μιᾶ νυκτὶ πόσους ἀθρόον ἀπέτεκεν ἡ πνευματικη αὔτη μήτηρ.* Καὶ *μὴ θαυμάσῃς· Τοιαῦται γὰρ αἱ ὠδῖνες αἱ πνευματικαί· οὐ δέονται χρόνου καὶ περιόδου μηνῶν.*

Further, commenting on 1 *Co.* 6:11, Chrysostom, wishing to make the point that baptism is not only a washing from sin, but also, positively, justification and sanctification, uses an image from the labor pains of childbirth: "What could be more unexpected than that justification come to forth without labor or sweat or good works?"[390]

Pursuing the same thought further in this *Instruction* Chrysostom applies the birth image to describe the baptismal bath. Even though he does not use the word "womb" the notion is implied:

> And why, someone will say, if the bath takes away all our sins, is it not called the bath of the remission of sins, or the bath of cleansing, rather than the bath of regeneration ? The reason is that it does not simply cleanse us of our faults, but it does this just as if we were born anew. For it does create us anew and it fashions us again, not molding us from earth, but creating us from a different element, the nature of water.[391]

The Virgin Birth

In an indirect way Chrysostom uses the mystery of the Virgin Birth as did Ambrose, but in a larger context. To the question, "How are we regenerated in baptism, since we cannot reenter our mother's womb?" a question echoing the Nicodemus-Jesus discourse, Ambrose had answered with the text of *Mt.* 1:18, showing that if Mary could conceive in a way exceeding the order of nature, so the Holy Spirit, coming upon the font or upon the baptized could also bring about regeneration in a supernatural way.[392] Chrysostom, speaking in the

[390] *Montf.* 1-*P.K.* 1.19 (*MG* 49.226; tr. Harkins, *ACW* 31, 137): *Τί τούτου γένοιτ 'ἄν παραδοξότερον, ὅταν πόνων καὶ ἱδρώτων χωρὶς καὶ κατορθωμάτων δικαιοσύνη τικτομένη ᾖ;*

[391] *Ibid.*, 20 (*MG* 49.227; tr. *ibid.*, 138): "*Καὶ τίνος ἕνεκεν, φησίν, εἰ τά ἁμαρτήματα ἡμῖν ἅπαντα ἀφίησι τὸ λουτρόν, οὐχὶ λουτρὸν ἀφέσεως ἁμαρτημάτων καλεῖται, οὔτε λουτρὸν καθάρσεως, ἀλλὰ λουτρον παλιγγενεσίας; Ὅτι οὐχ ἁπλῶς ἡμῖν ἀφίησι τὰ ἁμαρτήματα, οὐδὲ ἁπλῶς ἡμᾶς καθαίρει τῶν πλημμελημάτων, ἀλλ 'οὕτως ὡς ἂν εἰ ἄνωθεν ἐγεννηθήμεν. Καὶ γὰρ ἄνωθεν ἡμᾶς δημιουργεῖ καὶ κατασκευάζει, οὐκ ἀπὸ γῆς διαπλάττον πάλιν, ἀλλ' ἐξ ἑτέρου στοιχείου τῆς τῶν ὑδάτων φύσεως δημιουργοῦν.*"

[392] See above, pp. 309-310.

context of the gift of faith, alludes to the baptismal act, noting its mysterious and incomprehensible nature as a rebirth, since the rebirth cannot be actually seen by natural eyes. As a help to the general problem of the act of faith, and with it, the mysterious act of rebirth in baptism, he quotes the same text of *Mt.*

> Let me pass over that mysterious birth which has no human witnesses.[393] Let me bring before you that birth which took place here below and was witnessed by many.[394] Through this very explanation I shall secure your faith in things, because without faith you would never be able to accept it. He who cannot be contained, He who contains all and rules all, came into a virgin's womb. How, tell me, and in what way? You cannot explain it. But if you come to believe, your faith will be able to satisfy you to the full. In matters that surpass the weakness of our reasoning, we must turn to the teaching of faith. Matthew, who wrote of it, did not understand the manner of that begetting, for he said: "She was found to be with child by the Holy Spirit,"[395] but he did not teach us how this came to pass. Nor did Gabriel understand, for he had only this to say, "The Holy Spirit shall come upon thee, and the power of the Most High shall overshadow thee."[396] But he did not understand how and in what way.[397]

[393] *I.e.,* the regeneration which takes place in the act of baptism. Although others are present, the actual rebirth is itself a mystery, accessible only to the eyes of faith. In this sense, despite the bystanders at the font, the re-birth has no witnesses.

[394] *I.e.,* the shepherds, the Magi.

[395] *Mt.* 1:18.

[396] *Lk.* 1:35.

[397] *P.K.* 3.3 (*VGS,* 170; tr. Harkins, *ACW* 31, 165-166, nos. 16-17): *Καὶ ἵνα τὴν ἄρρητον ἐκείνην καὶ ἀμάρτυρον παραλείπω γέννησιν, ταύτην τὴν κάτω γενομένην, ἧς πολλοὶ μάρτυρες ἐγένοντο, παραγαγὼν εἰς μέσον δι' αὐτῆς σε τῶν, πραγμάτων τῆς ἀποδείξεως πιστώσομαι, ὅτι πίστεως ἄνευ οὐ δυνατὸν οὐδὲ ταύτην καταδέξασθαί ποτε. ὁ ἀχώρητος, ὁ πάντα συνέχων καὶ διακρατῶν, εἰς μήτραν ἦλθε παρθενικήν. πῶς, εἰπέ μοι, καὶ τίνι τρόπῳ; αποδειξαι μεν ουκ ἔστιν. ἂν δὲ ἐπὶ τὴν πίστιν ἔλθῃς, ἐκείνη σε πληροφορῆσαι δυνήσεται· τὰ γὰρ ὑπερβαίνοντα τῶν ἡμετέρων λογισμῶν τὴν ἀσθένειαν τῇ τῆς πίστεως ἐπιτρέπειν διδασκαλίᾳ χρή. τοῦτον τὸν τρόπον τῆς γεννήσεως οὔτε Ματθαῖος οἶδεν αὐτὸς ὁ γράψας. ὅτι μὲν γὰρ "εὑρέθη ἐν γαστρὶ ἔχουσα ἐκ πνεύματος ἁγίου" εἶπεν, τὸν δὲ τρόπον οὐκ ἐδίδαξεν. οὔτε Γαβριὴλ ἐπίσταται, καὶ γὰρ καὶ ἐκεῖνος τοῦτό φησι μόνον· "πνεῦμα ἅγιον ἐπελεύσεται ἐπὶ σε καὶ δύναμις ὑψίστου ἐπισκιάσει σοι". τὸ δὲ πῶς καὶ τίνι τρόπῳ οὐδὲ αὐτὸς ἐπίσταται.*

In this sense, the baptismal font is the womb for the supernatural rebirth. A true generation takes place there, though it is invisible, much as the miraculous generation of Christ took place in the womb of His mother.

c. *The Image of the Potter's Vessel*

Proceeding from the basic elements of earth and water as the elements of creation, just as Theodore does,[398] Chrysostom uses the same image of the potter and the vessels, quoting the same text, *Jr.* 18:6 as is found in Theodore. Here, as in Theodore, the image serves to elaborate somewhat further what the regeneration in baptism means:

> For baptism does create us anew and it fashions us again, not molding us from earth, but creating us from a different element, the nature of water.
>
> This bath does not merely cleanse the vessel, but melts the whole thing down again. Even if a vessel has been wiped off and carefully cleaned, it still has the marks of what it is and still bears the traces of the stain. But when it is thrown into the smelting furnace and is renewed by the flame, it puts aside all dross and, when it comes from the furnace, it gives forth the same sheen as newly-molded vessels. When a man takes and melts down a gold statue which has become filthy with the filth of years and smoke and dirt and rust, he returns it to us all clean and shining. So, too, God takes this nature of ours when it is rusted with the rust of sin, when our faults have covered it with abundant soot, and when it has destroyed the beauty He put into it in the beginning and He smelts it anew. He plunges it into the waters as into a smelting furnace and lets the grace of the Spirit fall on it instead of the flames.[399] Then he brings us forth from the furnace, renewed like newly-molded vessels, to rival the rays of the sun with our bright-

[398] See below, pp. 336-337.
[399] *Cf. In Jn.* 11 (*MG* 59.75-76).

> ness. He has broken the old man to pieces but has produced a new man who shines brighter than the old.[400]

To support this image of destruction and cleansing, Chrysostom then applies the Messianic *Ps.* 2, showing how it refers to the act of baptism:

> The Psalmist of old hinted at this destruction and this mystic cleansing when he said: "Thou shalt break them in pieces like a potter's vessel."[401] And that he is speaking of the faithful is made clear by what precedes, when he says: "Thou art my son, this day have I begotten thee. Ask of me, and I will give thee the nations of the earth for thy inheritance, and the utmost parts of the earth for thy possession."[402] Did you see how he called to mind the Church of the Gentiles and spoke of the Church of Christ as reaching the whole world? Then he says again: "Thou shalt rule them with a rod of iron," not burdensome, but strong, as if "thou shalt break them in pieces like a potter's vessel."[403]

[400] *Montf.* 1-*P.K.* 1.20-22 (*MG* 49.227; tr. Harkins, *ACW* 31, 138-139): Καὶ γὰρ ἄνωθεν ἡμᾶς δημιουργεῖ καὶ κατασκευάζει, οὐκ ἀπὸ γῆς διαπλάττον πάλιν, ἀλλ 'ἐξ ἑτέρου στοιχείου τῆς τῶν ὑδάτων φύσεως δημιουργοῦν. Οὐ γὰρ ἁπλῶς ἀποσμήχει τὸ σκευὸς, ἀλλ 'ὁλόκληρον αὐτὸ ἀναχωνεύει πάλιν. Τὰ μὲν γὰρ ἀποσμηχόμενα, κἂν μετὰ ἀκριβείας ἐκκαθαίρηται, ἔχει τῆς ποιότητος ἴχνη καὶ τῆς κηλῖδος φέρει τὰ λείψανα· τὰ δὲ εἰς χωνευτήριον ἐμπεσόντα καὶ διὰ τῆς φλογὸς ἀνανεωθέντα, πᾶσαν ἀποθέμενα ῥυπαρίαν, τὴν αὐτην τοῖς νεοπαγέσιν ἀπὸ τῆς καμίνου προελθόντα τὴν λαμπηδόνα ἀφίησιν. "Ωσπερ οὖν ανδριάντα χρυσοῦν πολλῷ τῷ χρόνῳ καὶ τῷ καπνῷ καὶ τῇ κόνει καὶ ἰῷ ῥυπωθέντα λαβὼν τις καὶ χωνεύσας, καθαρώτατον ἡμῖν καὶ αστράπτοντα ἀποδίδωσιν, οὕτω καὶ τὴν φύσιν τὴν ἡμετέραν ὁ Θεὸς ἰωθεῖσαν τῷ τῆς ἁμαρτίας ἰῷ καὶ πολὺν δεξαμένην τὸν καπνὸν τὸν ἀπο τῶν πλημμελημάτων, καὶ τὸ κάλλος ἀπολέσασαν, ὅπερ παρ' αὐτοῦ παρὰ τὴν ἀρχὴν ἐγκατέθηκε, λαβὼν ἄνωθεν ἐχώνευσε, καὶ καθάπερ εἰς χωνευτήριον ἐμβαλὼν τὰ ὕδατα, καὶ τὴν τοῦ Πνεύματος ἐπαφεις χάριν ἀντι φλογός, εἶτα νεοπαγεῖς ἐκεῖθεν καὶ καινοὺς γενομένους, ἀντιβλέψαι λοιπὸν ταῖς ἡλιακαῖς ἀκτῖσι μετὰ πολλῆς ἀνάγει τῆς λαμπρότητος, τὸν μὲν παλαιὸν συντρίψας ἄνθρωπον, νέον δὲ κατασκευάσας τοῦ προτέρου λαμπρότερον.

[401] *Ps.* 2:9.

[402] *Ps.* 2:7-8.

[403] *Montf. 1-P.K.* 1.23 (*MG* 49.227; tr. Harkins, *ACW* 31, 139): Καὶ ταύτην ἡμῖν τὴν συντριβὴν καὶ τὸν μυστικὸν τοῦτον καθαρμὸν αἰνιττόμενος ὁ προφήτης ἄνωθεν ἔλεγεν· Ὡς σκεῦος κεραμέως συντρίψεις ἀυτούς. Ὅτι γὰρ περὶ τῶν πιστῶν ὁ λόγος, ἡμῖν τὰ ἀνωτέρω δείκουσι σαφῶς· Υἱὸς γὰρ μου εἰ συ, φησίν. ἐγω σήμερον γεγέννηκα σε. Αἴτησαι πὰρ 'ἐμοῦ, καὶ δώσω σοι τὰ ἔθνη τὴν κληρονομίαν σου, καὶ τὴν κατάσχεσίν σου τὰ πέρατα τῆς γῆς. Εἶδες πῶς τῆς ἐκ τῶν ἐθνῶν 'Εκκλησίας ἐμνημόνευσε, καὶ τὴν πανταχοῦ τοῦ Χριστοῦ τεταμένην βεσιλείαν εἶπεν; Εἶτά φησι πάλιν· Ποιμανεῖς αὐτους ἐν ῥάβδῳ σιδηρᾷ. οὐ φορτικῇ, ἀλλ 'ἰσχυρᾷ. ὡς σκεῦος κεραμέως συντρίψεις αὐτούς.

For the sake of his application of this image to the baptismal act, Chrysostom, then goes on to explain the difference between vessel of baked clay, or *terra-cotta,* which once it is smashed to pieces, cannot be put together again, and a potter's vessel, which is made of muddy clay, which muddy clay can be given another shape by the craftsman's skill:

> When Holy Writ speaks of an irremediable disaster, it does not speak of the potter's vessel but of a *terra-cotta* one. For when God wished to teach his prophet and the Jews that he had given over the city to irremediable destruction, he bade Jeremias to take a *terra-cotta* jar, to break it to pieces before all the people, and to say: "Even so will the city be destroyed and broken to pieces."[404] But when God wished to extend hope to them he led his prophet into a potter's workshop and showed him not a vessel of baked clay but one of muddy clay which had fallen from the potter's hands, saying: "If this potter took up the vessel which had fallen and brought it back into proportion again, will I not all the more be able to set you up aright again after you have fallen."[405]

Chrysostom then concludes his application of this imagery to explain the bath or regeneration on a rather unique note: "It is possible for God not only to correct us through the bath of regeneration, since we are clay, but also after we have received the working of the Spirit and then have slipped, He can lead us back through sincere repentance to our former state."[406]

[404] *Jr.* 19:11.

[405] *Jr.* 18:6. *Montf. 1-P.K.* 1.25-26 (*MG* 49.227-228; tr. Harkins, *ACW* 31, 139-140): *Ὅταν μὲν οὖν συμφορὰν ἀνίατον λέγῃ, οὐ σκεύη κεραμέως φησίν, ἀλλὰ σκεῦος ὀστράκινον. Ὅτε γοῦν ἐβούλετο διδάξαι τὸν προφητήν καὶ τοὺς Ἰουδαίους, ὅτι συμφορᾷ ἀνιάτῳ παρέδωκε τὴν πόλιν, ἐκέλευσε λαβεῖν βίκον ὀστράκινον, καὶ συντρίψαι ἔμπροσθεν παντὸς τοῦ δήμου, καὶ εἰπεῖν. Οὕτως ἀπολεῖται καὶ ἡ πόλις, καὶ συντριβήσεται. Ἐπειδὰν δὲ βούληται χρηστὰς αὐτοῖς ὑποτείνειν ἐλπιδας, εἰς περαμεῖον κατάγει τὸν προφήτην, καὶ οὐ δείκνυσιν αὐτῷ σκεῦος ὀσταάκινον, ἀλλὰ δείκνυσιν αὐτῷ σκεῦος πήλινον ἐν ταῖς χερσὶ τοῦ κεραμέως γινόμενον, διαπίπτὸν, καὶ ἐπάγει λέγων· Εἰ ὁ κεραμεὺς οὗτος τὸ σκεῦος τὸ διαπεσὸν ἀναλαβὼν ἐρρύθμισε πάλιν, οὐ πολλῷ μᾶλλον ἐγὼ δυνήσομαι διαπεσόντας ὑμας ἐπανορθῶσαι;*

[406] *Montf. 1 P.K.* 1.26 (*MG* 49.228; tr. Harkins, *ACW* 31, 140): *Δυνατὸν μὲν οὖν τῷ Θεῷ οὐχι πηλίνους ὄντας μόνον διορθῶσαι διὰ λουτροῦ παλιγγενεσίας, ἀλλὰ καὶ τὴν τοῦ Πνεύματος δεξαυένους ἐνέργειαν, καὶ διολισθήσαντας διὰ μετανοίας ἠκριβωμένης πρὸς τὸ αρχαῖον ἐπαναγαγεῖν.*

The note here is somewhat unique, because the connection between falling into sin and repenting of it after baptism is not brought up by the other three fathers, nor by Chrysostom, except here, in passages which concern themselves with the mystagogical explanation of the act of baptism. Perhaps, again, it is the realism of the preacher, as well as his own life experience.[407] After presenting the mystagogy of baptism as rebirth, Chrysostom the pastor wishes to temper its absoluteness by realistic appraisal of the struggle to come. There is no question here of a second baptism[408] but rather of the works of penance to expiate the sins committed after baptism. In Chrysostom's use of this idea in conjunction with his presentation of the mystagogy of the baptismal act as second birth, the observation suggests itself as to how important the life experience of the mystagogue himself can be in the selection and arrangement of his material and his emphasis, his awareness of the needs of his hearers, and his own personal affinity to the liturgical ceremony itself.

[407] *P.K.* 3.5 (*VGS*, 172; tr. Harkins, *ACW* 31, 167, no. 23) records that Chrysostom had to interrupt his discourse because he started to cry at the thought of his own falls after baptism while he was explaining to the candidates the words, "I renounce you, Satan."

"Just now tears welled up in my eyes; my mind was confounded and bitterly did I groan. Why did I mention that holy night on which I was brought to the dreadful and holy initiation. I remember my purity at that time and the sins which I have piled up from that day to this (*Δακρῦσαί μοι νῦν ἐπῆλθε καὶ συνεχύθην τὴν διάνοιαν καὶ πικρὸν ἐστέναξα. τίνος ἕνεκεν ἀνεμνήσθην τῆς ἱερᾶς ἑσπέρας ἐκείνης, καθ' ἥν τὴν μακαρίαν ταύτην κατηξιώθην ἀφεῖναι φωνήν, καθ' ἥν ἐπὶ τὴν φρικώδη καὶ ἁγίαν μυσταγωγίαν ἠγόμην; ἀνεμνήσθην τῆς τότε καθαρότητος καὶ τῶν ἁμαρτημάτων, ὅσα μετ' ἐκείνην εἰς τὴν παροῦσαν ἡμέραν συνέλεξα*)."

After drawing a brief lesson from his own experience Chrysostom then apologizes to the hearers for drawing their attention to the gloomy theme of his own troubles. *Stav.* 2.19 (Wenger, *SC* 50, 144; tr. Harkins, *ACW* 31, 50) records a similar digression, also occasioned by the words, "I renounce you, Satan." Considering his own sins after baptism Chrysostom uses the occasion to request intercession with God for him on the part of those who are baptized.

[408] *Stav.* 3.23 (Wenger, *SC* 50, 164; tr. Harkins, *ACW* 31, 164): "There is no second cross, nor a second remission by the bath of regeneration. There is remission, but not a second remission by baptism (*δεύτερος γὰρ σταυρὸς οὐκ ἔστιν, οὐ δευτέρα ἄφεσις διὰ λουτροῦ παλιγγενεσίας. Ἄφεσις μὲν γὰρ ἔστι, διὰ λουτροῦ δὲ παλιγγενεσίας. Ἄφεσις μὲν γὰρ ἔστι, διὰ λουτροῦ δὲ οὐκ ἔστι δευτέρα ἄφεσις*)."

Summary

Proceeding from the description of baptism in *Tt.* 3:5 as the "bath of rebirth" Chrysostom links a series of images together to provide a mystagogy of the baptismal act, showing how it reveals itself as a regeneration or new birth. The Pauline metaphor of *Ep.* 5, Christ as Bridegroom and the Church as bride, centers here on baptism as the bridal bath, the cleansing and regeneration power of which is derived from the love of the Bridegroom under the mystical signs of the blood and water which flow into it from the Savior's open side. Similarly, from this open side of the new Adam "asleep" on the cross the Church is born in this blood and water, just as in the story of natural creation Eve was generated from the side of Adam as he lay asleep. This mystical description of generation and supernatural rebirth suggests the image of Christ as mother nourishing her new born with her own blood, an image which moves into the mystagogy of the Eucharist.

The mystagogy continues further seeing the baptismal act as the mother church who brings forth from the font as from a womb new offspring, yet without the natural time lapse or pains of childbirth. As God brought forth man from earth, the second birth comes out of water. The miracle of the virgin birth is cited as parallel to help in the understanding of how this mystery of rebirth in the womb of the baptismal font can be possible for the eyes of faith.

The idea of creation and recreation as part of God's plan at work is illustrated from *Jr.* in the image of the baptismal act as the action of the potter's furnace into which the dirty vessel is plunged to be refurbished and remoulded. The vessel is not one of *terra-cotta,* which, when broken, cannot be put together again, but rather one of muddy clay, put out of shape by an accidental fall from the potter's hands, but which can be remoulded by immersion in the water (the baptismal font) and the skill of the potter's hands (God).

4. *Theodore*

Essay: The Second Birth Image in the Perspective of Theodore's Sacramental Theology

The basic symbols of creation and re-creation, natural birth and supernatural birth, which we have seen in Cyril, Ambrose and Chrysostom also form the foundation of Theodore's mystagogical explanation of the baptismal act as regeneration, or second birth. He elaborates then much more extensively and eloquently, however, than the other fathers, and the perspective of his sacramental theology is somewhat different, one might also say, more elaborate, even more subtle and refined. They reflect more imaginative development.

Accepting the basic mystagogy of the rising of Christ from the tomb compared with the rising of the Christian from the font, Theodore's principal mystagogical symbolism to explain what this resurrection of the Christian in baptism actually imports is the symbolism of second birth. This is also true of Ambrose and Chrysostom, and the beginnings of the same outline are found in Cyril. The perspective which Theodore adds, however, and which therefore distinguishes his handling of the mystagogical symbolism of second birth from that of Ambrose and Chrysostom in his emphasis on the *future* resurrection of the baptized, at the arrival of the eschaton. The other fathers emphasized the presence in baptism of the past salvific event of Christ's actual resurrection, and showed the Christian's participation in this through imitation. Baptism contained the resurrection by "imitation (*μίμησις*) (similitudo)." Christ rises from the tomb; the Christian rises from the font. Theodore also sees this "re-enactment" of the resurrection of Christ in the relationship of the sacrament to past event. But, unlike the others, he then draws the line further: indeed, the Christian is risen with Christ. Christ dies physically, the Christian dies spiritually in baptismal death; Christ rises physically, the Christian rises spiritually in baptismal resurrection. Thus far the relationship to the past made present in the baptismal act. But what, then, of the Christian's physical resurrection from the dead? This obviously has not yet taken place (nor has his physical death). What is the relationship of the baptismal action to the future resurrection of the Christian after he has actually died and been buried, not in water but in earth? Such a relationship to future resurrection is, of course, *implied* in every backward look to the event of Christ's resurrection, since this historical event is also trans-historical in its full implications. But Theodore spells out this relationship to the risen Christ not merely by reference to "imitation" of the past event, but by his mystagogy of baptism as sign of hope in the future: "And we become one body of Christ, because we consider Christ our Lord in the flesh as our Head, and thus He confirmed for us our participation in the resurrection from which we expect our body to be similar to His body. Indeed, our conversation is in heaven, from which we look for our Lord Jesus Christ, Who will change our vile body that it may be fashioned like unto His glorious body."[409]

We do share by imitation in baptism in the resurrection of Christ, but we also really participate in the heavenly life to come, and this real participation in this coming risen life is mediated by the sacrament. Thus, Theodore immediately adds: "This will take place in reality in heaven, but we perform its symbol and signs in baptism."[410] The reality will, indeed, take place in the eschaton. This does not mean, however, that the sacrament is an empty symbol. It is, rather, a *real participation* in this reality, not physical incorruptibility, but a relationship to the future in a hope which contains the whole potency of this future.

Thus, although the "true" second birth will take place in the eschaton, baptism is also a second birth, because by virtue of the "symbols" a real participation in this future second birth has actually been established: "You should now proceed towards baptism in which the symbols of this second birth are

[409] *Cf. Phil.* 3:20-21. *Bapt. Hom.* III.21 (Tonneau-Devreesse, *SeT* 145, 446; tr. Mingana, *WS* VI, 64-65).

[410] *Bapt. Hom.* III.22 (*Ibid.*, 448; tr. *ibid.*, 65).

performed, because you will in reality receive the true second birth only after you have risen from the dead and obtained the favor to be in the state of which you were deprived by death." Thus, Theodore instructs the candidates before their approach to the font on the meaning of baptism as second birth in terms of the eschaton. Then he adds: "All these things will happen to you in reality at the time appointed for your birth at the resurrection; as to now you have for them the word of Christ our Lord, and in the expectation of them taking place you rightly receive their symbols and signs through this awe-inspiring sacrament, so that you may not question your participation in future things."[411]

This perspective of Theodore, the relationship of baptism to the future flowering of the potencies which are contained in it must be borne in mind in order to appreciate his employment of the image of "second birth" as a mystagogical explanation of the baptismal act. The perspective might be aptly labelled one of "dynamic tension." Second birth will indeed be accomplished in the eschaton. The act of baptism, however, because it looks back to the actual resurrection of Christ with Whom the candidate is associated, and because it contains a real relationship in hope that its recipient will one day achieve this glorious resurrection, may itself be interpreted in the terms of the image of second birth, even though, as Theodore points out, the true second birth will take place in the resurrection itself. Because, as has already been pointed out, the act of baptism is more than a mere symbol, but a reality in hope, Theodore's use of the image of second birth—and he unfolds it rather elaborately, as we are about to see—will constantly hover between second birth, in which is understood the event which will transpire at the baptizand's resurrection from the dead, and second birth, in which is understood the symbolic explanation of the potentialities which the act of baptism here and now, related to the actual past resurrection of Christ and really related to the future second birth in hope, actually contains.

[411] *Ibid.,* III.2 (*Ibid.,* 404, 406; tr. *ibid.,* 49-50).

In the case of all four fathers, baptism is related to resurrection. The other three, however, view the resurrection in so far as it is related to the baptismal act in its perspective as a past salvific act, that is, the resurrection of Jesus. When they then apply the image of new birth, it is to show how the Christian is related to the inner meaning of Christ's resurrection. As Jesus becomes "Son of God" in the resurrection, so too the Christian, participating through the baptismal act in this resurrection receives a new birth into sonship. Theodore, while acknowledging this backward look, emphasizes with his second birth symbolism the perspective of futurity: the resurrection of Jesus is not only a past salvific act, represented mystagogically in the emersion of the baptized from the pool, but an eschatological act as well, which meets history in its future as well as in its past and present.

The act of baptism, corresponding to this emphasis, is interpreted in this perspective of looking to that future resurrection of the baptized, of which the past resurrection of Jesus is the model.

Cast in the language of typology, Theodore's frame of reference would read as follows. The actual resurrection of Jesus of Nazareth is the *type.* To this extent Theodore parallels the other fathers. Baptism is the *antitype.* Then,—and this is where Theodore's emphasis differs—from the perspective of futurity, baptism itself is the *type.* The eschaton, the coming resurrection of the candidate from the dead, his true new birth, is the *antitype.*

When Theodore says that baptism "contains the symbol of the birth which we expect"[412] he does not understand symbol primarily as Cyril and Ambrose, who could speak of baptism containing the salvific events of the earthly crucifixion, death and resurrection of Jesus "*εν μιμήσει*" or "in similitudine", which is also Chrysostom's understanding. He means, rather, a symbol which denotes and contains actually in hope the future resurrection. This being the case, it is not difficult to see why Theodore makes greater use of the image of second birth

[412] *Ibid.,* III.3 (*Ibid.,* 406; tr. *ibid.,* 50).

than do the other fathers. One can, indeed, explain the baptismal act mystagogically by comparing the burial of Christ to immersion in the font, and the resurrection of Christ to emersing from the font. But when emphasis is shifted from the reference primarily to the past salvific act of Jesus of Nazareth, His death and resurrection onto the future eschaton, one has no longer a tangible historical reality which one can imitate "in similitudine". The eschaton, being unimaginable future, can hardly be represented in image in the act of baptism. The best one can do is to represent in image the rising of Jesus from the tomb, and then add the images of second birth in so far as they fit into some kind of plausible relationship to the liturgical ceremony, *e.g.* water-creation-womb. So, Theodore, wishing to emphasize the reality contained in the baptismal act in its reference to the future, is confronted with a mystagogical problem: how represent the future in a way related to the liturgical ceremonies? To solve this problem what he does is to develop an imaginative metaphor, that of second birth, with some elaborateness. In so doing he has to sever himself to some extent from the liturgy itself, which really does not provide such material, and pursue the route of metaphorical imagination, based on an elaboration of the image of second birth. This is the nature of Theodore's sacramental eschatology, or eschatological mystagogy, a process not without certain dangers of severing onesself from the liturgy itself, and moving ever further even into allegory, rather than mystagogy.

This "dynamic tension" and "sacramental eschatology" of Theodore, in which he provides in his mystagogy for past salvific act, present sacrament and future reality, and in which, in his mystagogical explanations, he hovers between these realities, is exemplified in the following passage:

> This is the reason why, at my baptism I plunge my head, I receive the death of Christ our Lord, and desire to have His burial, and because of this I firmly believe in the resurrection of our Lord; and when I rise from the water I think I have symbolically risen a long time ago.
>
> Since, however, all this is done in symbols and signs, in order to show that we do not make use of vain signs only,

> but of realities in which we believe, and which we ardently desire, Paul said: "For if we have been planted together in the likeness of his death we shall be also [in the likeness] of his resurrection."[413] In using the future tense, he confirms the present event by the future reality, and from the greatness of the coming reality he demonstrates the credibility of the greatness of its symbols, and the symbol of the coming realities is baptism. The working of the Holy Spirit is that it is in the hope of the future things that you receive the grace of baptism, and that you draw nigh unto the gift of baptism in order to die and to rise with Christ so that you may be born again to the new life, and thus, after having been led by these symbols to the participation in the realities, you will perform the symbol of that true second birth.[414]

Theodore's interest in baptism as symbol of the life to come in the resurrection leads him to an emphasis in the application of the Jesus-Nicodemus dialogue somewhat different from Ambrose, who had used the same scriptural passage,[415] at least by allusion:

> You draw nigh, therefore, unto the holy baptism which contains the symbol of the birth which we expect. This is the reason why our Lord called it second birth when He said to Nicodemus: "Except a man be born again, he cannot see the kingdom of God."[416]
> In this He showed that those who will enter the kingdom of God must have a second birth. Nicodemus, however, thought that they will be born according to a carnal birth from a woman, and said: "How can a man be born when he is old? Can he enter the second time into his mother's womb and be born?"[417] He said this because he believed we shall be born in a way similar to our first birth. As to our Lord, He did not disclose to him then that there are

[413] *Rm.* 6:5.
[414] *Bapt. Hom.* III.5-6 (Tonneau-Devreesse, *SeT* 145, 412, 414; tr. Mingana, *WS* VI, 52).
[415] *Jn.* 3:1-8.
[416] *Jn.* 3:3.
[417] *Jn.* 3:4.

> two ways in which we shall in reality receive this, one of which is at the resurrection, because He knew that the subject was too much for his hearing. He, therefore, only disclosed to him the symbolic birth which is accomplished through baptism, unto which all those who believe must draw nigh so that by means of its symbols they may move to the happiness of the reality itself, and answered: "Unless a man be born of water and of the Spirit, He cannot enter the Kingdom of God."[418]

Ambrose had used the Nicodemus passage to emphasize the power of the Holy Spirit in bringing about a new birth, comparing it to the work of the Spirit in bringing about the conception of Jesus in the womb of Mary.[419]

While not mentioning the virgin birth as a point of comparison, Theodore also emphasizes the role of the Holy Spirit, "because this birth is accomplished by his action,"[420] in his continuation of his explanation of the Nicodemus passage. The striking addition in Theodore, however, is his interpretation that there was here a question of *two ways* to receive the second birth, one in baptism, which Jesus described to Nicodemus, from water and the Spirit, but also another, "at the resurrection," and that Jesus withheld description of this second way since the mystery would have at the moment exceeded Nicodemus' capacity to understand. Theodore explains that this second way of receiving a new birth is directly related to the first way, "so that by means of its symbols [baptism] they may move to the happiness of the reality itself [the resurrection]." Thus, Theodore can conclude: "[Jesus] called baptism a second birth because it contains the symbol of this second birth."[421]

Theodore concludes this introductory section, in which he expounds the connection between the symbols of baptism and

[418] *Jn.* 3:5. *Bapt. Hom.* III.3 (Tonneau-Devreesse, *SeT* 145, 406, 408; tr. Mingana *WS* VI, 50).

[419] See above, pp. 309-310.

[420] *Bapt. Hom.* III.3 (Tonneau-Devreesse, *SeT* 145, 408; tr. Mingana, *WS* VI, 50).

[421] *Ibid.*, III.4 (*Ibid.*, 410; tr. *ibid.*, 51).

the resurrection under the image of second birth with the words:

> The power of holy baptism consists in this: it implants in you the hope of future benefits, enables you to participate in the things which we expect, and by means of the symbols and signs of the future good things it informs you with the gift of the Holy Spirit, the first-fruits of whom you receive when you are baptized.[422]

a. *The Water Womb*

Like the other fathers, Theodore sees the font as becoming a womb for the sacramental birth. In his allusion to the fact that the baptized descend into water which has received a priestly blessing, he notes that the power thereby imparted to the water was a power of conception and of becoming a womb to shelter the child conceived:

> You descend into the water, which has been consecrated by the benediction of the priest, as you are not baptised with ordinary water only, but with the water of the second birth, which cannot become so except through the coming of the Holy Spirit [on it]. For this it is necessary that the priest should have beforehand made use of clear words, according to the rite of the priestly service, and asked God that the grace of the Holy Spirit might come on the water and impart to it the power both of conceiving that awe-inspiring child and becoming a womb to the sacramental birth.[423]

In a similar reference to the blessing of the water, Theodore indicates the purpose of the blessing in terms of empowering it to serve as a womb for the second birth:

> [The priest] prays that the grace of the Holy Spirit come upon the water and prepare it with His holy and awe-inspiring presence for the task of performing all these things, so that it may become a reverential womb for the

[422] *Ibid.*, III.7 (*Ibid.*, 416; tr. *ibid.*, 53-54).
[423] *Ibid.*, III.9 (*Ibid.*, 418, 420; tr. *ibid.*, 54-55).

> second birth, and so that those who descend into it may be fashioned afresh by the grace of the Holy Spirit and born again into a new and virtuous human nature.[424]

Material for elaboration of this womb-image Theodore finds by returning a second time to the Nicodemus passage of *Jn.* 3. Although rather lengthy, the passage deserves citation because it is a key example of the manner in which Theodore proceeds as mystagogue, showing how he blends Scripture and his own theological orientation, along with the natural image, that of human conception, birth and growth, and uses these to explain the act of baptism.

> Our Lord also, when Nicodemus asked Him whether a man "can enter the second time into his mother's womb, and be born," answered: "Except a man be born of water and of the Spirit, he cannot enter into the kingdom of God."[425] He shows in this that as in a carnal birth the womb of the mother receives the human seed, and the Divine hand fashions it according to an ancient decree, so also in baptism, the water of which becomes a womb to the one who is being born, and the grace of the Spirit fashions in it, into the second birth, the one who is being baptized, and changes him completely into a new man. And inasmuch as the seed that falls into the womb of the mother has neither life, nor soul nor feeling, but after it has been fashioned by the Divine hand, it results in a living man, endowed with soul and feeling, and in a human nature capable of all human acts, so also here the one who is baptized falls into the water as into a womb, like a seed which bears no resemblance of any kind to the mark of an immortal nature, but after he has been baptized and has received the Divine and spiritual grace, he will undoubtedly undergo a complete change: he will be fashioned from a mortal into an immortal, from a corruptible into a incorruptible, and from a mutable into an immutable, nature;

[424] *Ibid.*, III.10 (*Ibid.*, 424; tr. *Ibid.*, 56).

[425] *Jn.* 3:4-5.

> he will be changed completely into a new man according to the power of the one who fashions him.
> And inasmuch as the one who is born of a woman has potentially in him the faculty of speaking, hearing, walking and working with his hands, but is very weak to perform all these acts in reality till the time in which God has decreed for him to perform them, so also is the case in connection with the one who is born of baptism. This one has indeed in him and possesses potentially all the faculties of an immortal and incorruptible nature, but is not now in a position to make use of them and put them into a complete and perfect act of incorruptibility, immortality, inpassibility and immutability He who receives through baptism the potential faculty of performing all these acts, will receive the power of performing them in reality at the time when he is no more a natural but a spiritual man, and when the working of the (Holy) Spirit renders the body incorruptible and the soul immutable, while sustaining and keeping the both of them by His power, as the blessed Paul said: "It is sown in corruption, it is raised in incorruption; it is sown in weakness, it is raised in power; it is sown in dishonor, it is raised in glory; it is sown a natural body, it is raised a spiritual body."[426] He shows here that incorruption, glory and power will come then to man throught the working of the Holy Spirit, which affects both his soul and body, the former with immortality and the latter with immutability; and that the body which will rise from the dead and which (man) will put on will be a spiritual and not a natural body.[427]

In this central passage of Theodore's mystagogical explanation of what happens when the candidate plunges into the baptismal pool, he subsumes on the Nicodemus passage, which he had used before to bring out a parallel between new birth in baptism and new birth in the resurrection and from the resurrection.[428] This time he uses the passage, not to emphasize what

[426] 1 *Co.* 15:42-44.

[427] *Bapt. Hom.* III.9-10 (Tonneau-Devreesse, *SeT* 145, 420, 422, 424; tr. Mingana, *WS* VI, 55-56).

[428] See above, p. 333.

is not said in it, that is the second birth in the resurrection, which Theodore had argued was too difficult for Nicodemus to understand, but to draw the parallel between carnal birth and what happens in the act of baptism, proceeding from the womb and rebirth imagery contained in the Nicodemus passage.

The womb of a mother parallels the water of the baptismal font. The male seed enters the mother's womb, the seed containing in itself no human feeling or life. The candidate enters the baptismal font devoid of immortal life and all that it implies. In the mother's womb the process of conception takes place, and a living human being is the result, following the divinely ordained process. In the baptismal font a process likewise takes place, in which the mortal man is transformed and an immortal being is the result, brought about by the power of the Holy Spirit.

The child conceived in the mother's womb receives all the potential faculties of human activity, but cannot yet use them. The immortal being, conceived in the womb of the baptismal font, also possesses the faculties of immortal and incorruptible activity, but cannot yet use them. The child will be able to use his human faculties at the time when God decrees him to be born. The baptised likewise has the faculties of an immortal and incorruptible nature, but is not yet in a position to exercise these potential powers until God decrees it. When is that time? Theodore explains: "At the time when he is no more a natural but a spiritual man, and when the working of the (Holy) Spirit renders the body incorruptible and the soul immutable," that is, at the resurrection. Theodore then confirms this by drawing in the Pauline passage on the resurrection.[429]

One notes here the "dynamic tension" which characterizes Theodore's mystagogy. Baptism itself is a second birth, yet the second birth really does not take place until the resurrection. Baptism is a second birth, but in hope, and containing really the potentialities which will be actualized at the resurrection,

[429] *I.e.*, 1 *Co.* 15:42-44.

when the "real" second birth takes place. Thus Theodore's particular pains to explain the meaning of the Nicodemus discourse, and to relate the second birth to the resurrection, and his efforts, through the use of natural imagery and comparison from human life, to make graphic for his baptismal candidates the meaning of baptism in terms of the life of the resurrection. The future resurrection is the focus of attention which determines his mystagogy.

b. *The Image of the Potter's Vessel*

Using the idea of earth and water as the natural elements from which the creation of man took place, and echoes of which we have already seen in the other fathers, Theodore draws on the *OT* image of the potter to draw out the image of regeneration, using here the idea of recreation or reconstruction of the vessel of clay:[430]

> It behooves you therefore, to think that you are going into the water as into a furnace, where you will be renewed and refashioned in order that you may move to a higher nature, after having cast away your old mortality and fully assumed an immortal and incorruptible nature. These things dealing with birth happen to you in the water, because you were fashioned at the beginning from earth and water, and having fallen later into sin you assumed a thorough corruption through the sentence of death. The potters are also in the habit, when the vessels which they fashion are damaged, to refashion them again with water so that they may be remade and reconstructed and given the wanted form. . . . when we fell and sin corrupted us, we received a complete dissolution from the (Divine) sentence of death, but afterwards our Maker and our Lord refashioned us and remade us by his ineffable power, because He abolished death by resurrection and granted to all of us the hope of resurrection from the dead, and a world higher than the present, where we shall not only dwell but also become immortal and incorruptible.[431]

[430] *Cf. Jr.* 18:1-6; *Jb.* 33:6; 4:19 *LXX.*

[431] *Bapt. Hom.* III.11 (Tonneau-Devreesse, *SeT* 145, 424, 426; Mingana, *WS* VI, 56-57).

Theodore passes here from the image of the womb, and human conception and birth, to the image of the artefact, the earthern vessel, reconstructed in the potter's furnace. The same parallel is here present as in the previous image. God is the potter who does the refashioning, and it takes place in the water, now a potter's furnace instead of a womb. The clay vessel is particularly apt in the imagery because of its connection with the earth and water from which man was made according to the *Gn.* account. Likewise, in the emphasis on the resurrection, the "dynamic tension" is present in the image. God remade man through the resurrection of Christ. But this resurrection, as a salvific event of past history, looks to the future resurrection, "because He abolished death by resurrection and granted to all of us the hope of resurrection from the dead." Theodore enunciates this perspective of baptism in his conclusion to this section once again:

> We perform the symbols and signs of these things in water and are renewed and reconstructed according to the working of the Spirit on it. We who draw nigh unto baptism receive therefore, these benefits from the Sacrament in symbol, while in the next world we shall all of us receive renewal of our nature in reality. As an earthen vessel, which is being remade and refashioned in water, will remain in its soft nature and be clay as long as it has not come in contact with fire, but when it has been thrown on fire and baked on it, it will undoubtedly be remade and refashion—so also we, who are in a mortal nature, rightly receive the grace of the Holy Spirit, which hardens us more than any fire can do.[432]

We see, once again, how Theodore, in his view of the baptismal act, and his mystagogy in explaining it, hovers between the actuality of the second birth, here seen in the image of the reconstructed clay vessel, in the act of baptism, yet at the same time, its inescapable reference to the revelation of this second birth at the resurrection. Here, Theodore emphasizes that the reconstruction has actually taken place—through the baptismal act, the power of the Holy Spirit has hardened the baptized,

[432] *Ibid.,* III.12-13 (*Ibid.,* 428; tr. *ibid.,* 57-58).

that is, reconstructed him, just as the potter's fire eventually bakes the soft clay vessel to hardness. The refashioning took place in the water, the hardening fire was the fire of the Holy Spirit. Baptism is the actual rebirth. In the previous passage, however,[433] Theodore is careful to point out that this refashioning, however real in baptism, is a reality always in hope. It is this reality in hope which permits this mystagogical interpretation using the image of womb and human birth, and the construction and reconstruction of artefacts.[434]

Summary

Theodore himself summarizes his image and reviews the theological perspective by which he has provided a mystagogical interpretation of the baptismal act as a second birth:

> As such is the second birth that comes to us through baptism, unto which you are about to draw nigh, and from which we expect to move into that real and awe-inspiring second birth of the resurrection. It confirms in us that which comes to us in symbols and signs through faith, and strengthens us in relation to it. It is not to be wondered when we receive two births, and that we shall move from the present birth to the future one, as even in our carnal birth we receive a two-fold birth, one of which comes from the male, the other, which comes later, from the female. We are first born of the male in the form of human semen, which has not a single vestige of human form. It is indeed clear to everyone that the semen has no human form of any kind and that it receives the form of the human nature according to the laws formulated by God for our nature after it has been conceived, fashioned, formed and born of

[433]See above, pp. 330-331.

[434]The guiding image of rebirth and its relationship to the resurrection occurs in a brief allusion as well to the garments which the priest wears, the same apparel which he wore for the first, or *sphragis* anointing (see above, ch. 1, p. 33): "It is in this apparel that he performs the gift of baptism, because it behooves him to perform all the sacraments while wearing it, as it denotes the renovation found in the next world, to which you will be transferred through this same sacrament." *Bapt. Hom.* III.14 (Tonneau-Devreesse, *SeT* 145, 430; tr. Mingana, *WS* VI, 58).

> a woman. It is in this same way that we are also born, first in the form of semen through baptism, before we are born of the resurrection and have taken shape in the immortal nature into which we expect to be changed, but when by faith and hope in the future things we have been formed and fashioned into the life of Christ and remained till the time of the resurrection, then we shall receive according to the decree of God, a second birth from dust, and assume an immortal and incorruptible nature, and "our vile body will be changed by Christ, our Lord, that it may be fashioned into His glorious body," as blessed Paul said.[435]

In this conclusion and summary of his mystagogical interpretation of the baptismal act under the aspect of second birth, Theodore has actually added a refinement. The new birth, or re-birth, or second birth (as opposed to our first, natural human birth), is actually not one birth, but two. When Theodore says, "It is not to be wondered that we receive two births," he is not speaking about natural birth and baptismal birth, but about baptismal birth alone, which he then shows to be two births, the birth of baptism and the birth of the resurrection. These are the two births which constitute spiritual re-birth. This is the dynamic tension between spiritual re-birth in hope through baptism, and the fulfilment of this hope through spiritual re-birth in the resurrection. In his urgency to stress this point in his mystagogical exposition for the candidates who are about to enter the pool, Theodore attempts to show the relationship of the two supernatural births, the baptismal and the resurrectional, by comparing the process with carnal birth, in which he also sees two separate though interrelated moments, which he calls a "two-fold" birth. The first phase in the carnal process he calls "being born of the male," that is, the conception and gestation process in the mother's womb. In this prenatal period, as Theodore has pointed out earlier, the fetus has all the human potentialities, but they become activated at birth, which is the second phase of the process. Baptism, in the order

[435] *Ph.* 3:21. *Bapt. Hom.* III. 28 (Tonneau-Devreesse, *SeT* 145, 458, 460; tr. Mingana, *WS* VI, 69).

of supernatural birth, is then, the first new birth, that is, the first phase, comparable in the carnal process to the conception, and gestation process. "It is in this same way that we are also born, first in the form of semen through baptism." The second phase in the natural process is the "birth" itself. In the supernatural process this phase occurs in the resurrection, where, "we have taken shape in the immortal nature into which we expect to be changed."

A somewhat new element enters Theodore's use of the new-birth symbolism when he indicates that the first phase of the supernatural birth, the baptism, is not merely an act, containing germinally the entire potentiality of the second phase, the resurrection, but, similar to the gestation period in the natural birth explanation, where the fetus is "fashioned and formed" before being born of a woman, there is also, in this first phase of the supernatural birth, a kind of formation or gestation period. What is this period? A period, after our "birth" in the form of semen through baptism, (that is, the first phase of our supernatural birth) "when by faith and hope in the future things we have been formed and fashioned into the life of Christ and remained till the time of the resurrection." Here would be the point of departure for the baptismal spirituality which takes into account the life of the baptized in this world. Though already born anew through baptism, his period of waiting for the second phase of this supernatural rebirth, its revelation in the resurrection, is to be filled by being fashioned into the life of Christ, with "faith and hope in the future things."

Like Ambrose, Theodore's mystagogy has concentrated on using scripture and natural imagery relating to the idea of new birth in order to explain the meaning of the baptismal act itself. Ambrose, in his advice to the baptized to "imitate the fish,"[436] who, once begotten in the water, swims through the

[436] See above, p. 308.

breakers and storms of life without drowning, and Theodore, who in the passage just quoted draws his new birth image at least far enough to indicate that between the time of the "first" rebirth of baptism and the "second" rebirth of resurrection a period of "being formed and fashioned into the life of Christ" must take place; both only touch upon this aspect of the life of the baptized in their mystagogy without developing the theme any further.

Several further very brief touches along this line are indicated by Theodore before he closes this instruction and passes on to consideration of First Communion:

> After you have received in this way a sacramental birth through baptism, you draw nigh unto an immortal food, consonant with your birth, with which you will be nourished . . . For the present, however, because you have received through (our) teaching the birth of baptism, and have drawn nigh, through this second birth, unto communion with that ineffable light, and because we have, by what we have said, wrapped you tightly in swaddling clothes, so that you may grasp firmly and unshakeably the birth that takes place, we shall soothe you by silence . . ."[437]

As is clear from the passage, Theodore has carried his image of new birth further by the notion of nourishment for the new born child, suggested by the coming discourse on the Eucharist, and by the allusion to the swaddling clothes for the new born baby. Here, too, is further indication of the Christian life of the newly baptized, when the new birth, which he has received, a reality in hope, will have to be nourished until the day when he is finally born, not only in hope, but in full reality in the resurrection.

Comparative Summary

Analysis of the mystagogy of the baptismal act as new birth shows that while all of the fathers employ this image, each one

[437]*Bapt. Hom.* III.29 (Tonneau-Devreesse, *SeT* 145, 460; tr. Mingana, *WS* VI, 69-70).

uses it according to an individual teleology in his presentation. The image of baptism as a new birth is rooted in the *NT* as we have seen, and it is from the *NT* principally that the fathers derive their principal material for this mystagogy. However, the theological statement of the *NT* that baptism is a regeneration is not necessarily a mystagogical interpretation of the liturgy of baptism. Each of the fathers takes the *NT* image of new birth and attempts to apply it to his baptismal liturgy in order to show how the liturgical ceremony itself can suggest in some way the *NT* truth that in Christian baptism one is reborn. And this application of the *NT* image must fit plausibly not only into the given liturgy, but into the complex of each father's entire mystagogy. It is for this reason that the use of the image, while retaining many common features among the four fathers, will reveal different emphasis and nuances. After having analyzed how each father employs the image, we are now in a position to make a comparative inspection to reveal these different nuances and emphases, and to understand some of the reasons for them, and so to see how mystagogy is created from the given materials and demands. Particularly with such a difficult image to represent mystagogically, which, because it looks to a future fulfilment in eternity, reaches the outer rim of possibilities for use in mystagogy, a comparative analysis will be rewarding, since it will reveal how each father dealt with this particular problem in the framework of his particular liturgy.

Common to all four fathers is the fact that the image of baptism as new birth is offered by way of supplementary mystagogy to the principal mystagogy of the baptismal act as conformity to Christ in death and resurrection. The image itself is not parallel to, but rather unfolds out of the notion – difficult to portray at all – of resurrection. The baptismal resurrection of the "new man" following the baptismal death of the "old man" is, in its newness, seen as a recreation or regeneration. The image, then, is related particularly to resurrection. If going into the font meant death, then coming out of the font meant resurrection. What is resurrection, however, if not a recreation, since it comes out of death, and here begins the point where the image of new birth begins to explain this resurrection – but to explain it mystagogically, that is, with reference to the liturgical ceremonies, and not merely as a suitable metaphor to describe an interior spiritual change which, according to *NT* teaching, is effected by baptism. As we have already seen, the coming out of the pool means for all four fathers resurrection with Christ. How can this resurrection with Christ be explained further, *mystagogically,* using the *NT* image of new birth?

Ambrose reaches to the Pauline idea that Christ's Sonship is ratified, comes to full revelation, in His actual resurrection from the dead. "You are my Son; this day have I begotten You,"[438] is viewed by Ambrose as referring to the resurrection. Hence, the resurrection is a "generation" into Sonship, a "birth" of God's Son. Ambrose continues his logical parallel. Since emerging from the font signifies resurrection, it, too, is a regeneration for the baptized, just as Christ's resurrection was His "rebirth" as Son of God.

Chrysostom's point of departure is different. He concentrates on the scriptural description of baptism as the "bath of rebirth" and builds his mystagogy on just this image, without making Ambrose's attempt to show *how* resurrection of the candidate is rebirth in the sense of Christ's rebirth to Sonship. In this sense Chrysostom is less apologetic than Ambrose, who seems to wish to show *how* this can be so. Chrysostom accepts the scriptural statement of rebirth and presents more of a mystical and pastoral meditation than an explanation. We have already seen how this approach to mystagogy is more characteristic of Chrysostom.[439] This mystical approach is particularly evident in Chrysostom through his application of the bridal metaphor, seeing the baptismal bath as a bridal bath. The element of "regeneration" here is seen in terms of the power of the love of the Bridegroom for His bride. This mystagogy is presented in terms of the blood and water flowing from Christ's open side into the baptismal font, giving the bath

[438] *Ps.* 2:7.
[439] See above, pp. 266-271.

its power of cleansing and regenerating, in terms of the baptized "begotten" from the side of Christ "asleep" on the cross, as Eve was begotten from the side of the sleeping Adam, and even in terms of Christ as a mother feeding her new born child with her own blood. The elaboration of this mystical imagery in connection with baptism as regeneration belongs to Chrysostom alone of the four fathers. The imagery is related to the liturgical action because baptism is a bath of water.

Theodore's approach differs from either the apologetic tone of Ambrose or the more mystical tone of Chrysostom. Theodore seizes upon the image of new birth as the most apt, from the standpoint of the imagination, to get across the theological point which most preoccupies him: the future. His method is to combine scriptural references about the coming resurrection with a detailed imagery of the whole process of conception and birth in order to show how baptism is a new birth, and that it is a "symbol" of the "real" new birth which will take place in the eschatological resurrection of the body. For Theodore, then, as he interprets the Jesus-Nicodemus dialogue, there are not one, but two "new births," one in baptism and one in future resurrection. To support this mystagogy in showing baptism as *type* and future resurrection as *antitype*, Theodore has to go much further than the other fathers in unfolding in imaginative detail the picture of new birth. The other fathers, since their perspective is not so future-oriented, do not go quite so far in developing the image of new birth, but content themselves with limiting the image to the baptismal act, rather than trying to extend it to future resurrection, which the baptismal act germinally contains. Theodore, it must be said, provides the most fullsome development of the image as such.

Ambrose, Chrysostom and Theodore, then, each has a different style in presenting the common scriptural image of rebirth as mystagogical interpretation of the baptismal act.

Despite these differences of approach and in handling the scriptural material concerned with baptism as a regeneration, the four fathers converge in their mystagogy relating the new birth image to the actual liturgy *via* the consideration of the baptismal pool as a *womb* from which the new born child emerges. With this image *Cyril* is able to state the paradox of death and resurrection very graphically, that the candidate died and was born at the same time, and that the baptismal pool became both grave and mother womb. He indicates the paradox, natural-supernatural, death-birth, further in his quotation from *Qo.* that the water pool which had been construed as grave paradoxically becomes mother womb, since the baptized on coming out of it is new born. This image is also the occasion for Ambrose and Chrysostom to contrast natural and supernatural generation which the new birth implies. Ambrose sees the element of water common to both the first creation of the universe, and finds it fitting that God's Word should also bring the new creation out of the water. This is part of his transformation theology in which God touches the fallen material universe at the root of all interconnected elements so that they work to good according to His plan of resurrection. In a somewhat different way Chrysostom, too, considers the element of water itself in treating the natural-supernatural paradox. Different from Ambrose, however, he sees not creation and recreation from water, but rather creation of man from earth, and recreation of man from water. Chrysostom does not have throughout his *Instructions* the elaborate universal transformation theology of creation and recreation which characterizes Ambrose, and so his statement limits itself to the paradox nature-supernature and its symbol, earth-water, for the creation and recreation of man himself. The difference in development in dealing with such elements is seen further in Ambrose's charming picture of the baptized as little fishes swimming in the storms of this world. Chrysostom, on the other hand, in order to stress God's sovereign power, does not deal here like Ambrose with the creation of the world from water, but continues the image of the mother womb, stating that the baptized are brought forth without the customary pains or time of birth labor.

However, both Ambrose and Chrysostom reach to the Virgin Birth parallel to explain what takes place in the baptismal font in its supernatural character, and this is a continuation of the water womb image of the font. In this connection Ambrose makes a comparison as well to the blessing of the font. Just as Christ was conceived in the womb of His mother by the power of the Holy Spirit, so the font receives the power to beget new birth through the invocation of the Holy Spirit. While not referring specifically to the mystery of the Virgin Birth as do Ambrose and Chrysostom, Theodore also makes the allusion to the blessing of the font in connection with the image of the font as water womb. It is the invocation of the Holy Spirit which makes the font into a womb capable of giving birth to the awe-inspiring child.[440] Like Ambrose, Theodore uses here the Jesus-Nicodemus dialogue to emphasize the power of the Holy Spirit in bringing about a new birth. However, Theodore then goes on to use this text as a point of departure for his very elaborate development of the idea of the two births, that of baptism and that at the final resurrection, showing by means of this development how the two are interrelated. He asserts that Jesus withheld the secret of the second new birth from Nicodemus because of the latter's incapacity to understand it. In this exegesis of the Jesus-Nicodemus dialogue Theodore explains why Jesus called baptism a second birth. He bases his explanation on the distinction between the child in the womb, who in a sense is "born" there in his conception, i.e., who has all the potential faculties of living man but cannot yet use them, and the actual coming out of the womb and being born, when the child begins to be able to walk and speak and use his faculties. This latter is the second birth of the resurrection in the future eschaton; the former is the second birth of the baptismal act, where the child "born" in the womb has all the potential faculties, but cannot yet use them.

[440] It is, no doubt, due to Chrysostom's christological or *Logos* orientation that direct allusions to the role of the Holy Spirit empowering the water to produce the new born are not obvious in this connection, as they are in Theodore (see above, p. 332), and in Ambrose as well (see above, p. 309). The maternal images of conception, birth, nourishment are governed in Chrysostom by the christological or *Logos* principle, rather than the theology of the Holy Spirit. For further discussion see ch. 3, n. 143, pp. 397-398; n. 159; pp. 404-406.

It is quite possible that the explanation for Theodore's omission of any reference to the Virgin Birth here, such as is found in Ambrose and Chrysostom, lies in the confusion of imagery it could engender in Theodore's somewhat ingenious explanation of the "two" new births, the first in the symbol of hope (baptism) and the second in "reality" (the resurrection). Instead of looking back to the birth of Christ in *Mt.* and *Lk.*, as do Ambrose and Chrysostom, he quotes 1 *Co.* 15:42-44 in his text, a passage from St. Paul which looks ahead to the supernatural act of the resurrection of the body rather than backward to the supernatural birth of Christ. Given the obvious similarities to Ambrose—the reference to the power of the Holy Spirit in the blessing of the font and the use of the Jesus-Nicodemus dialogue, one would expect that Theodore, since like Ambrose and Chrysostom he is working in the water womb image framework, would also like these other two fathers allude to the Virgin Birth. Given his unusual exegesis of the Jesus-Nicodemus dialogue, however, and his consistent concern with the future resurrection, this startling omission makes pedagogical sense. After Theodore has finally made his point about the second birth as the reality of future resurrection, he does make what seems to be a deftly imaginative allusion to the birth of Christ, not explicit indeed, but at least by the innuendo of his choice of words, it is strongly reminiscent of the Bethlehem scene. He tells his hearers: ". . . because we have, by what we have said, wrapped you tightly in swaddling clothes, so that you may grasp firmly and unshakeably the birth that takes place, we shall soothe you by silence . . ."[441]

Obvious interdependence between Chrysostom and Theodore is seen in the treatment of the image of the baptismal act as the process of a potter at work remaking in his creative power the imperfect clay vessel in his furnace. Earth and water are the elements of creation, God is the craftsman, the font is His furnace, the baptized is His clay vessel. As expected, Theodore nuances the picture slightly to show that the artefact will reach

[441] See above, p. 341.

its final restoration only in the eschaton. Chrysostom the pastor draws the distinction between the *terra-cotta* vessel, which, once shattered, can never be restored, and a clay vessel which can be remade, to encourage his hearers in respect to God's power of forgiveness, and he alone of the four fathers adds the realistic pastoral note that God's forgiveness which brings about the regeneration in baptism can extend to post-baptismal falls as well. It should be noted that Chrysostom in this section also quotes the line, "Thou art my Son; this day have I begotten you,"[442] in reference to the baptismal act as a regeneration, the same text Ambrose had used as a point of departure for his mystagogy of baptism as a new birth.

In this comparative summary of the mystagogy of the baptismal act as new birth one sees how a traditional scriptural image, that of regeneration, finds its application in the hands of these four mystagogues both according to their individual style and the theology of their respective catecheses with reference to the possibilities which the given liturgy and its various elements suggest. While the role of the creative imagination is in the case of the new birth image particularly strong, it cannot be said that the fathers – not even Theodore who goes the farthest along the line of imaginative development – depart from the objective requirements of the given liturgical elements themselves and move into *mere* allegory. While exercising the imagination vigorously to explain the meaning of the ceremony, the connection with the liturgical elements themselves always remains intact.

[442]See above, p. 321.

CHAPTER THREE

THE POST-BAPTISMAL CEREMONIES

Synopsis of the Ceremonies

Cyril

After the newly-baptized come up out of the baptismal pool, a "chrismation" takes place.[1] That is, the newly-baptized are anointed with a kind of perfumed oil, which is called "*μύρον*." "You were christened with perfume (*ὑμεῖς δὲ μύρῳ ἐχρίσθητε*)."[2] This "*μύρον*" is applied to the forehead, the ears, the nostrils, and the breast of the neophytes.[3]

Although not mentioned in this third *Mystagogical Catechesis* it is quite clear that the garment which the neophyte would have put on after emerging from the baptismal font would be the ceremonial white garment, indicated in the writings of Chrysostom, Theodore and Ambrose, and which seems to have been a universal usage in both Orient and Occident in the fourth century.[4] Not only is there the obvious symbolic contrast with the stripping of the garments before the baptismal

[1] *Myst. Cat.* III.1 (Piédagnel, *SC* 126, 120-122; tr. Cross, *SPCK*, 63-64). In describing this ceremony Cyril prefers to use derivatives of the verb "*χρίειν*," which means "to anoint with chrism," rather than the simpler word "to anoint (*ἀλείφειν*)" which he had used for the pre-baptismal anointing. (See above, ch. 2, p. 145). Because of this word's association with "Christ," "to christen," "chrismation," "Christian," it is already in itself interpretative of the action of this particular anointing.

[2] *Myst. Cat.* III.2 (Piédagnel, *SC* 126, 124; tr. Cross, *SPCK*, 65). For the pre-baptismal anointing Cyril had said: "You were anointed with exorcized oil (ἐλαίῳ ἠλείφεσθε ἐπορκιστῷ)." *Myst. Cat.* II.3 (Piédagnel, *SC* 126, 106; tr. Cross, *SPCK*, 60).

[3] *Myst. Cat.* III.4 (Piédagnel, *SC* 126, 126; tr. Cross, *SPCK*, 65-66).

[4] In addition to the presence of the baptismal garment in the four fathers treated here, it is also mentioned in the following; Palladius, *Dialogue* 9 (*MG* 47.34); *Peregrinatio Aetheriae* 38 (*SC* 21, ed. H. Pétré, p. 240); Augustine, *Sermo* 172 (*De Tempore* 157, *ML* 39.2075); Proclus of Constantinople, *Catechesis de baptismo mystagogica, Codex Sinaïticus graecus* 491, foll. 138 v.-139. (*SC* 50, ed. A. Wenger, p. 100 and p. 101, n. 1). For text (and tr.) see also below, n. 180, p. 417.

act,[5] but also Cyril makes positive allusion to the white garments in two other places. In giving a summary description of the whole baptismal service he describes the neophyte entering the church for the Eucharist as though they were stars, "bright in the outward man (φαιδροὶ τῷ σώματι)" as well as radiant in their souls.[6] Cyril also alludes to the fact that although the white garments need not be continually worn, their spiritual significance must be lived.[7]

[5] See above, ch. 2, p. 145.

[6] *Procat.* 15 (Cross, *SPCK*, 10; tr. *ibid.*, 50).

[7] *Myst. Cat.* IV.8 (Piédagnel, *SC* 126, 142; tr. Cross, *SPCK*, 70). Whether the ceremonial white garment was donned before the anointing or after it is not clear. Theodore (see below, p. 352) states that this garment was received before the anointing, that is; immediately on emerging from the pool, after which the bishop anoints the forehead. In Ambrose (see below, p. 353) the bishop anoints the head first, then begins the foot-washing, after which the white garment is received and then there follows the consignation. Though there is no conclusive evidence, small indices suggest that the white garment is put on after the anointing has taken place, and not before it. *First,* since the breast had to be anointed, there is the matter of convenience. *Second,* there is Cyril's mystagogy of the anointing which emphasizes the River Jordan - Baptismal pool comparison (see below, pp. 364-367). A concrete ceremonial reproduction of such a scene as Christ's baptism in the Jordan, which, as we have already seen, is a favorite mystagogical method of the Jerusalem catecheses, could well reflect the fact that in the liturgy itself the anointing was as near as possible to the leaving of the pool. *Third,* there is Cyril's mystagogy based on the etymology of the word "Christian," (see below, p. 376). According to this the neophyte cannot be rightly called a Christian until he has received this anointing. The white garment, however, as Cyril's mystagogy shows, symbolizes a completion of this process of "christification," or "anointing," and would, therefore, come naturally after this anointing. The theme of the white garment as symbol for purity of life which Cyril treats in his mystagogy (see below, pp. 418-419) would also seem to presuppose the mystagogy of the anointing where Cyril sees it as providing the Christian with the first-fruits of the Spirit now already in his life on earth (see below, pp. 367-369), as well as emphasizing the transforming effects of the *myron* (see below, pp. 370-371). The white garment symbolizes the end result of what Cyril sees as taking place in the anointing. While this reasoning is inconclusive since the guiding ideas of the mystagogical presentation cannot be used absolutely to argue to the precise facts of the actual liturgical ceremonies, they do suggest that we place the ceremony of donning the white garment in the Jerusalem liturgy reflected in Cyril's *Catecheses after* the ceremony of the anointing, and not before it.

Chrysostom

Emerging from the baptismal font, the neophytes are embraced, greeted and kissed by all present.[8]

Other than this kiss, Chrysostom does not make any further specific mention of post-baptismal ceremonies. Internal and external evidence, however, indicates the following. The neophytes probably received a lamp or candle. Proclus, Patriarch of Antioch in A.D. 434 and rehabilitator of Chrysostom in the see of Constantinople[9] attests to the custom of the neophytes holding "lamps (λαμπάδες)" in their hands.[10] Furthermore, there are in the *Baptismal Instructions* numerous indications of an imagery suggested by light and fire applied to the newly baptized,[11] for whom Chrysostom's favorite name is "the newly-illuminated (οἱ νεοφώτιστοι)," a term which occurs in all the titles of the *Stavronitika* series except the second.

Even more certainly attested is the reception of the ritual white garment. Also mentioned in the text of Proclus, "the shining garment (λάμπρον τὸ ἔσθημα),"[12] Chrysostom refers to this more than thirty times in the *Instructions.*[13]

[8]*Stav.* 2.27. (Wenger, *SC* 50, 148; tr. Harkins, *ACW* 31, 53). This ceremonial kiss immediately after the baptism itself is apparently a different one from the kiss mentioned in *P.K.* 3.10 (*VGS,* 175; tr. Harkins, *ACW* 31, 171-172, nos. 32-34). This latter kiss, as emerges from the context of the *Instruction,* is the Eucharistic *pax.* Further, the interpretation given to this second kiss is different from the interpretation given to the kiss which follows on the coming out of the font. A similar context and interpretation for the first kiss which corroborates its distinction from the Eucharistic *pax* is found in *In prin. act.* 3 (*MG* 51.98). See J. Quasten, "Der Kuss des Neugetauften in altchristlicher Taufliturgie," in *Liturgie: Gestalt und Vollzug,* Festschrift J. Pascher, ed., W. Dürig (Munich, 1953) 269-270; Finn, *op. cit.,* pp. 197-199.

[9]See J. Quasten, *Patrology,* 3 (Westminster, Maryland, 1960) 521-525.

[10]Proclus, *loc. cit.* For text (and tr.), see below n. 180, p. 417.

[11]See esp. *Stav.* 4.3 (Wenger, *SC* 50, 184; tr. Harkins, *ACW* 31, 66-67) and our discussion of this below, p. 431. See also Finn. *op. cit.,* 190-191.

[12]*Loc. cit.* For text (and tr.), see below, n. 180, p. 417.

[13]See esp. *Stav.* 4.18; 7.24 (Wenger, *SC* 50, 192, 241; tr. Harkins, *ACW* 31, 73, 114). See also Finn, *op. cit.,* p. 194.

Chrysostom makes no mention of any post-baptismal anointing.[14]

Theodore

Upon emerging from the water, the neophyte puts on a shining, white garment.[15] The bishop then approaches and

[14]In the liturgy reflected in the *Baptismal Instructions* no anointing is mentioned after the baptismal bath. The fact that Chrysostom's fourth century contemporaries, Cyril (see above, p. 349), Theodore (see below, p. 353), the compilers of the *Apostolic Constitutions (Constitutiones Apostolorum* 7, 22. F. Funk, ed., *Didascalia et Constitutiones apostolorum* (Paderborn, 1911) 406), and the *Testament of Our Lord (Testamentum Domini Nostri Jesu Christi* 2, 8-9. FP 7, ed. J. Quasten, pp. 270-271) all mention an anointing after baptism raises a question concerning the apparent absence of this anointing in the *Baptismal Instructions.* One may rule out the unlikely explanation that Chrysostom simply did not choose to mention the anointing in his mystagogy, although it was actually present in the liturgy. In all probability, if such an anointing were present, Chrysostom, the mystagogue and preacher, would be acting quite out of character in the *Baptismal Instructions* were he to miss the opportunity for commenting on its meaning. The fact is, other sources show that the baptismal liturgy upon which Chrysostom comments did, indeed, have no post-baptismal anointing. The mystagogical instruction of Proclus (d. 446) upon the baptismal liturgy of Constantinople does not reflect the presence of a post-baptismal anointing. (*Op. cit.,* for text and tr. see *SC* 50, ed. A. Wenger p. 100 and p. 101, n. 1, and below, n. 180, p. 417. This only serves to corroborate what R. Connolly confirmed in his study of the *Didascalia apostolorum* (Oxford, 1929), Introduction, pp. XLVIII-L) and of Narsai (R. Connolly, ed., *Liturgical Homilies of Narsai.* Texts and Studies VIII.1 (Cambridge, 1909), Introduction, pp. XLII-L), namely that third, fourth and fifth century Syrian documents pertaining to baptismal practices reflect no post-baptismal anointing. Speaking in the jubilee year of Connolly's edition of the *Liturgical Homilies of Narsai,* H. Benedict Green sums up the research in respect to the Syrian baptismal tradition apropos of Connolly's Work:

> The apocryphal *Acts of Judas Thomas* and of *John,* the *Didascalia Apostolorum,* Ephraim, Aphraates and two Syriac narratives of the 5th-6th centuries were all laid under contribution to establish to the general satisfaction of scholars that the Syrian initiation rite from the 3rd century onwards consisted of a sealing (*rushmā*) of the candidate in oil, followed by an anointing of the whole body, followed by baptism in water, with no further ceremony intervening between this last and the Eucharist. A post-baptismal anointing did not establish itself among the Nestorians, the true heirs of the Syrian liturgical tradition, until the patriarchate of the westerniser Ishoyābh III in the mid-7th century. (H. Benedict Green, "The Significance of the Pre-Baptismal Seal in St. John Chrysostom," in *SP,* Vol. VI, Part IV, *TU* 81 (Berlin, 1962), p. 84).

On the question of why Theodore, then, should mention a post-baptismal anointing, when Chrysostom and the Syrian baptismal tradition has none, see below, n. 143, p. 397.

[15]*Bapt. Hom.* III. text and 26 (Tonneau-Devreesse, *SeT* 145, 402, 454; tr. Mingana, *WS* VI, 48, 68).

signs him on the forehead saying, "So-and-so is signed in the name of the Father and of the Son and of the Holy Spirit."[16] Although nothing specific is indicated as to the kind of oil used for this consignation, it is clear from the context and the interpretative remarks concerning anointing that the consignation actually did take place with the use of oil.

Ambrose

The neophytes come out of the font and approach the bishop.[17] The bishop spreads chrism, ("myrum,") ("unguentum,") on their heads,[18] and recites this formula: "God the Father almighty, Who regenerated you by water and the Holy Spirit and forgave you your sins, will Himself anoint you unto life everlasting."[19]

Jn. 13 is then read[20] whereupon the bishop begins to wash the feet of the neophytes, and after he has begun this act, the priest continues it.[21]

After the foot-washing the neophytes receive the white garment.[22]

"There follows a spiritual seal (sequitur spiritale signaculum)"[23] is what describes the ceremony which follows the washing of the feet. Little is said which would indicate how the ceremony is performed. It is accompanied by an invocation of the bishop: "at the invocation of the bishop the Holy Spirit is poured forth (ad invocationem sacerdotis spiritus in-

[16] *Ibid.*, III. text and 27 (*Ibid.*, 400, 402, 456; tr. *idem).*

[17] *Myst.* 29 (Botte, *SC* 25bis, 172; tr. Deferrari, *FC* 44, 15-16).

[18] *Sacr.* III.1 (*Ibid.*, 90; tr. *ibid.*, 289).

[19] *Sacr.* II. 24 (*Ibid.*, 88. tr. *ibid.*, 287): "Deus, pater omnipotens, qui te regeneravit ex aqua et spiritu concessitque tibi peccata tua, ipse te unguet in vitam aeternam."

[20] *Sacr.* II. 24 (*Ibid.*, 92, 94; tr. *ibid.*, 291); *Myst.* 31 (*Ibid.*, 172; tr. *ibid.*, 16).

[21] *Sacr.* III.4 (*Ibid.*, 92; tr. *ibid.*, 291).

[22] *Myst.* 34 (*Ibid.*, 174; tr. *ibid.*, 17). While not indicating it explicitly, the reception of the white garment is implied also in *Sacr.* V.14 (*Ibid.*, 126; tr. *ibid.*, 313). Here the communicants, that is, the neophytes who have come to the altar to receive their first Communion, are described as a "household dressed in white (familia candidata)."

[23] *Sacr.* III.8 (*Ibid.*, 96; tr. *ibid.*, 293).

funditur.)"[24] It is also called a "consignation," ("quando consignaris").[25] In the same way the ceremony is described in *De Mysteriis* simply as a spiritual seal, "you have received the spiritual seal (accepisti signaculum spiritale)."[26] One may safely assume that what is meant ceremonially by the consignation is the sign of the cross, probably on the forehead. In conjunction with this ceremony *De Sacramentis* says specifically: "Therefore God anointed you, Christ sealed you. How? You were marked with the sign of His cross, of His passion."[27]

A reading from Scripture accompanies this ceremony. The Scripture text is not indicated in *De Sacramentis* but in *De Mysteriis* we learn that the reading was 2 *Co.* 1:21-22, which makes reference to being anointed with the seal of the Spirit.[28]

Was this ceremony of the spiritual seal performed as an anointing? Neither in *De Sacramentis* nor in *De Mysteriis* is certain information given in the matter.

Such a consignation, "σφραγίζειν," separate from the anointing just after baptism, and performed by the bishop by placing his hand on the neophyte's head and signing him with oil on the forehead with an invocation of the Holy Spirit, is described in the *Apostolic Tradition* of Hippolytus.[29] Botte notes that the rite is specifically Roman, but nevertheless it is absent from other primitive Western liturgies, and concludes that the term "consignatio" in Ambrose probably implies an anointing.[30]

[24] *Idem.*

[25] *Ibid.*, III.10 (*Idem*).

[26] *Myst.* 42 (*Ibid.*, 178; tr. *ibid.*, 20).

[27] *Sacr.* VI.7 (*Ibid.*, 140; tr. *ibid.*, 320-321): "Ergo unxit te deus, signavit te Christus. Quomodo? Quia ad crucis ipsius signatus es formam, ad illius passionem."

[28] *Myst.* 42 (*Ibid.*, 178; tr. *ibid.*, 20).

[29] Hippolytus, *Traditio Apostolica* 21, ed. B. Botte, *LQF*, 39 (Münster, 1963), pp. 52-54.

[30] Botte, *SC* 25bis, p. 97, n. 5. Botte's assumption that the consignation implies an anointing rests on the similarity of the rite described by Ambrose to that described by Hippolytus. In the *Traditio Apostolica* after the neophyte comes out of the water, the priest ("presbyter") anoints him with the oil of thanksgiving ("oleo gratiarum actionis," "εὐχαριστία"), with the formula, "Ungo te oleo sancto, in

Both *De Sacramentis* and *De Mysteriis* give what appears to be a liturgical formula connected with this ceremony of consignation, mentioning the invocation of the bishop for the impouring of the Holy Spirit in these terms: "the spirit of wisdom

---

nomine Jesu Christi," and then the neophyte proceeds into the church. (Botte, ed., *Traditio Apostolica*, p. 50). There the bishop ("episcopus") imposes his hand on him saying. "Domine Deus, sicut fecisti illos dignos accipere remissionem peccatorum in saeculum venturum, fac eos dignos ut repleantur spiritu sancto et mitte super eos gratiam tuam ut ("ἵνα") tibi serviant secundum voluntatem tuam; quoniam tibi gloria patri et filio cum spiritu sancto, in sancta ecclesia, nunc et semper et in saecula saeculorum." The bishop then pours the oil of thanksgiving ("oleum gratiarum actionis," "εὐχαριστία,") on his own hand, and places his hand on the head of the neophyte saying, "Ungo te oleo sancto in deo patre omnipotenti et Jesu Christo et spiritu sancto." Then he signs him on the forehead ("Et consignabit ('σφραγίζειν') in fronte ejus.") (Botte, ed., *Traditio Apostolica*, pp. 52-54.) In Ambrose the neophyte upon coming out of the water is anointed with *myron* by having it spread on his head, with the formula quoted by Ambrose. His feet are then washed, and he is brought back to the bishop who signs him on the forehead, making the sign of the cross and using the formula containing the enumeration of the sevenfold gifts of the Spirit. Due to this similarity of rites, Botte supposes that since the consignation in Hippolytus is made by the bishop immediately after he places his anointed hand on the neophyte's head, and so presumably making the sign of the cross on the neophyte's forehead with his hand still moist with the oil, so too this is what happens in the consignation described by Ambrose, even though this second anointing on the head after the foot-washing is not mentioned, and Ambrose makes no mention of oil at this point.

Kretschmar, on the other hand, is of the opinion that the consignation described by Ambrose is performed without an anointing, it being a descendant of the old episcopal laying on of hands after the baptismal bath, as, for example, in Tertullian. (See Kretschmar, *op. cit.*, p. 235). In Tertullian there are three distinct rites, an anointing, a signing on the forehead, and finally a laying on of hands. (See *De bapt.* 8, *CCL* I, 283; *De carn. res.* 8, *CCL* II, 931). Since the West knows no anointing in connection with confirmation until the time of Innocent I (d. 417) (see H. Elfers, *Die Kirchenordnung Hippolyts von Rom* (Paderborn, 1938), pp. 101-160), it seems that as far as the Western tradition is concerned, Hippolytus is something of an exception with his anointing as part of the consignation, an exception which was not imitated in the West for almost two centuries. Jungmann's thesis that the anointing as part of the consignation in Hippolytus is a question of the adoption of Eastern ceremonial and so for the Western tradition where this anointing is absent, an exception, corroborates this. (See J. Jungmann, *Zeitschrift für katholische Theologie* 63 (1939), p. 235). (For an analysis of this intricate problem, see Stenzel, *op. cit.*, pp. 127-129, 170. Also P. Galtier, "La consignation dans les églises d'Occident," *Revue d'Histoire ecclésiastique* 13 (1912) 257-301; L. Mitchell, "Ambrosian Baptismal Rites," *Studia Liturgica* I (1961) 248-252.

and of understanding, the spirit of counsel and of fortitude, the spirit of knowledge and of piety, the spirit of holy fear."[31] As Mitchell points out,[32] the principal argument against this being a liturgical formula is the fact that it is contained in *De Mysteriis* as well as *De Sacramentis.* However, due to the *disciplina arcani*, *De Mysteriis* intended for the general reader, never quotes liturgical texts. However, the similarity to the biblical text, *Is.* 11:2, might make it possible to include it in the general disquisition of *De Mysteriis*, without the risk of revealing it to be a liturgical formula as such.

In fact, *De Mysteriis* does omit the words, "when at the invocation of the bishop (quando ad invocationem sacerdotis)," which occur in *De Sacramentis.* Hence, it is thinkable that these words actually formed the liturgical invocation mentioned in this ceremony of consignation.

While the question remains unsolved as to whether the consignation described by Ambrose was performed with or without an anointing, it seems to this author at least worthy of note in the discussion to observe that Ambrose's mystagogy of the consignation nowhere indicates that oil was used. Given the ready-made mystagogy which the use of such oil would provide, as it provided for Theodore, and especially for Cyril, it would seem that if oil were actually used in the consignation this fact would certainly be reflected in the mystagogy. (See below, pp. 390ff). The absence of such mystagogy reflecting the use of oil in the consignation lends weight to the supposition that the consignation with oil had not yet become part of the Milanese liturgy, but that rather, similar to other Western liturgies, it was performed without an anointing.

[31] *Sacr.* III.8 (Botte, *SC* 25bis, 96; tr. Deferrari, *FC* 44, 293); *Myst.* 42 (*Ibid.*, 178; tr. *ibid.*, 20): ". . . spiritum sapientiae et intellectus, spiritum consilii atque virtutis, spiritum cognitionis atque pietatis, spiritum sancti timoris. . . ."

[32] *Art. Cit.*, p. 250.

SYNOPTIC CHART

The Post-Baptismal Ceremonies

Cyril	*Chrysostom*	*Theodore*	*Ambrose*
			Anointing with "*myrum*", by bishop, on head, with formula
			Reading: *Jn.* 13
			Foot-washing, begun by bishop, continued by priests
	White garment	White garment	White garment
			Reading: 2 *Co.* 1:21-22
Anointing with "μύρον," on forehead, ears, nostrils, breast		Anointing with oil ("μύρον?") by bishop, on forehead, with formula	Signing (anointing?), of cross (?), by bishop, on forehead (?), with invocation by bishop
White garment			
	Lamp (?)		

THE MYSTAGOGICAL INTERPRETATION OF THE CEREMONIES

I

THE ANOINTING

It goes beyond the scope of this dissertation to enter the problematic area of the difference between the sacraments of "baptism" and "confirmation," as they are designated according to modern usage. This much discussed and controversial area pertains to the field of sacramental theology.[33] In ancient terminology, that is, before the third century, the word "σφραγίς," "signum," "signaculum," is not so limited in its usage as to designate only what is known in current theological terminology as "confirmation," but is a more general word for Christian Initiation in a broader sense.[34]

In treating the fathers' mystagogy of the anointing after the baptismal bath, then, our question will not be, where does "baptism" end and "confirmation" begin, since such a question would do violence to the structure of Christian Initiation both in the mystagogical writings which are under consideration and to the complex ritual traditions upon which they comment. It is sufficient to note for our purpose here that from the beginning there were two steps required for full Christian

[33] For a resumé of the *status quaestionis* in this area, see Stenzel, *op. cit.,* pp. 125-132. Standard works are J. Coppens, *L'imposition des mains et les rites connexes dans le Nouveau Testament et dans l'église ancienne* (Paris, 1925); B. Welte, *Die postbaptismale Salbung,* Freiburger Theologische Studien 51 (Freiburg, 1939); G. Lampe, *The Seal of the Spirit,* 2nd ed., (London, 1967). For recent and valuable surveys of the confirmation controversy see; M. Bohen, *The Mystery of Confirmation* (New York, 1963) 15-46; T. Marsh, "Confirmation and its Relation to Baptism," *The Irish Theological Quarterly* 27 (1960) 284-293; T. Marsh, "The History and Significance of the Post-Baptismal Rites," *The Irish Theological Quarterly* 29 (1962) 175-206.

[34] See Stenzel, *op. cit.,* p. 125; F. Dölger, *Sphragis. Eine altchristliche Taufbezeichnung in ihren Beziehungen zur profanen und religiösen Kultur des Altertums* (Paderborn, 1911); J. Ysebaert, *Greek Baptismal Terminology: Its Origins and Early Development, GCP* 1 (Nijmegen, 1962).

Initiation, and that the second step had to do with a particular communication of the Holy Spirit.[35] Or to state the matter even more circumspectly, of the two steps which may be discerned in Christian Initiation, one of them involves a particular communication of the Holy Spirit.

Our purpose here is not to solve this problem of "baptism", "confirmation" in sacramental theology, but rather, having determined what was said and done after the baptized came out of the pool, to analyze and compare the meaning which the fathers saw in these ceremonies. By performing this task in conscientious detail, it is possible that the picture which emerges from such a treatment of the mystagogical interpretation of the ceremonies might serve some useful purpose for those who continue the as yet uncompleted task of analyzing the realtionship between "baptism" and "confirmation" as a problem of sacramental theology and the history of the development of liturgical rites.[36]

[35] See Stenzel, *op. cit.*, p. 126.
[36] For further discussion, see below, pp. 396-407.

SYNOPTIC CHART

The Mystagogy of the Post-Baptismal Anointing

Cyril	*Theodore*	*Ambrose*
		(The anointing directly after baptism) *ETERNAL VS. TEMPORAL LIFE* -Anointing *Formula*: Oil of Paradise Tree *Sacr.* II.24 -Anointing on *head*: Regeneration *Sacr.* III.1 *Myst.* 30 *Qo.* 2.14

The Mystagogy of the Post-Baptismal Anointing—continued

Cyril	*Theodore*	*Ambrose*
		-*Odor* of chrism: Attraction of risen Jesus *Sacr.* IV:3 *Myst.* 30 *Sg.* 1:2-3
		PRIESTLY AND REGAL People of God *Sacr.* IV:3 *Myst.* 30 1 *P.* 2:9
THE COMMUNICATION OF THE HOLY SPIRIT:		
		(Consignation anointing? after washing of feet)
Anointing from Holy One *Myst. Cat.* III 1 *Jn.* 2:20-28	Descent of Spirit *Bapt. Hom.* III.27 In Name of Trinity	Spirit as Pledge/Seal *Myst.* 42; *Sacr.* III.8 2 *Co.* 1:21-22 7 Gifts of Spirit *Myst.* 42; *Sacr.* III.8 *Is.* 11:2 *Ep.* 3:10 A Special Gift *Sacr.* VI.8 1 *Co.* 12:4-6
CHRIST AND THE CHRISTIAN:		
Christ "anointed" with Spirit *Myst. Cat.* III.2 *Ac.* 10:38 *Ps.* 44:7	Christ "anointed" with Spirit *Bapt.Hom.* III.27 *Lk.* 4:18 *Ac.* 10:38	

The Mystagogy of the Post-Baptismal Anointing—continued

Cyril	*Theodore*	*Ambrose*
Christian anointed with Spirit (chrism) *Myst. Cat.* III.1 *Heb.* 3:14 *Ps.* 104:15	Christian anointed with Spirit (chrism) *Bapt.Hom.* III.27	
Christ emerges from Jordan Spirit-dove: *type* Christian emerges from pool Spirit-chrism: *antitype* *Myst.Cat.* III.1,2 *Is.*61:1 - *Lk.*4:18	Christ emerges from Jordan Spirit-dove Christian emerges from pool Spirit-chrism: *type* *Bapt. Hom.* III.27 *Is.*61:1 - *Lk.*4:18 *Ac.* 10:38	
OT Prefiguration *Myst.Cat.* III.6 Aaron, priest *Lv.* 8:6 Solomon, king 1 *K.* 1:38-39, 45 *NT* Fulfilment *Myst.Cat.* III.6 Christ/Christian as first-fruits *Rm.* 11:16	Anointing: first-fruits of resurrection: *antitype* *Bapt.Hom.* III.27 *Rm.* 11.16	
		Christ Himself seals with His Spirit *Sacr.* VI:6 2 *Co.* 1:21-22 *Sg.* 8:6 Sealed to form of Cross *Sacr.* VI:7 *Rm.* 6:4,6,10

The Mystagogy of the Post-Baptismal Anointing—continued

Cyril	*Theodore*	*Ambrose*
PARTICULAR EFFECTS *Myst.Cat.* III.3 -Myron: Transformation Epiclesis theology	*PARTICULAR EFFECTS*	
-Forehead Shame and glory *Gn.* 3:7-10 2 *Co.* 3:18 -Ears: Messianic message *Is.* 50:5 *Mt.* 11:15 -Nostrils: Good odor of Christ for believers 2 *Co.* 2:15 -Breast: Armor of Messiah and of Christian *Ep.* 6:14,11 (*Is.* 11) Spirit strengthens Jesus is desert before messianic work *Mt.* 4:1-11 Christian strengthened for evangelization *Ph.* 4:13		
-The Name "Christian" *Myst.Cat.* III.5 Actualized now Etymology		

The Mystagogy of the Post-Baptismal Anointing—continued

Cyril	*Theodore*	*Ambrose*
-Teacher and Protector *Myst.Cat.* III.7 Body and Soul 1 *Jn.* 2:20-28	-Durable and insepa-rable, as with Jesus *Bapt. Hom.* III.27 *Lk.* 4.18 *Ac.* 10:38	
ESCHATOLOGY *Myst.Cat.* III.7 Anointing at Messianic Banquet *Is.* 2:2-3; 15:7; 25:6		

A. Cyril

Cyril provides the fullest mystagogical exposition of the anointing which takes place after the baptismal bath, devoting his entire third *Mystagogical Catechesis* to this ceremony. What does it mean when the baptized is anointed with chrism directly upon emerging from the baptismal pool?

1. *The Communication of the Holy Spirit*

It is clear that Cyril sees in this ceremony of anointing after the baptismal bath a very particular form of communication of the Holy Spirit. This is indicated at the outset of his mystagogy by the Scripture reading which opens the catechesis and to which Cyril alludes in the closing paragraph.[37] The reading is 1 *Jn.* 2:20-28, in which the faithful are reminded that

[37]*Myst. Cat.* III.7 (Piédagnel, *SC* 126, 130; tr. Cross *SPCK*, 66).

they have an "anointing by the Holy One (*χρῖσμα ἀπὸ τοῦ ἁγίου*)."[38] His further comments interpreting this christening with *myron* as Cyril calls it[39] imports the special coming of the Holy Spirit on the neophytes.

2. *Christ and the Christian*

Since, as we have often seen, it is the concern of the Jerusalem Catecheses to relate the ceremonies of Christian Initiation to the actual salvific events which took place in the earthly life of Christ, so here too, the mystagogical explanation of the gift of the Spirit, which is communicated by the anointing, is worked out from the central christological viewpoint: the Christian is transformed into the full image of Christ through the liturgical ceremonies, which are an "imitation in image (*μίμησις ἐν εἰκόνι*)." What particular aspect of the Christian's full growth into the image of Christ is contributed by this ceremony of anointing which was not present before?

Cyril introduces his answer to this question at the beginning of the catechesis. Reminding his listeners that they have been "conformed (*σύμμορφοι*)" to the Son of God and to the glorious Body of Christ through the act of the baptismal immersion by which God has predestined them to "sonship (*υἱοθεσίαν*)," he proceeds to show how the anointing with the *myron* continues this process of mystical transformation and brings it an essential step further: "Being therefore made 'partakers of Christ,'[40] you are properly called Christs, and of you God said 'Touch not my Christ.' "[41] Here, and throughout this Catechesis, Cyril is, of course, playing on the word for Christ, "Χριστός," which means the "anointed." The neophyte may be called a "Christ," because he, too, is an "anointed," a

[38] *Vs.* 20.

[39] *Myst. Cat.* III.2 (Piédagnel, *SC* 126, 124; tr. Cross, *SPCK*, 65).

[40] *Cf. Heb.* 3:14.

[41] *Ps.* 104:15. *Myst. Cat.* III.1 (Piédagnel, *SC* 126, 120; tr. Cross, *SPCK*, 63): Μέτοχοι οὖν τοῦ Χριστοῦ γενόμενοι, χριστοὶ εἰκότως καλεῖσθε, καὶ περὶ ὑμῶν ἔλεγεν ὁ Θεός· Μὴ ἅπτεσθε τῶν χριστῶν μου.

"christened" one. How this came about is explained by Cyril: "Now you were made Christs by receiving the mark (*ἀντίτυπον*) of the Holy Spirit."[42]

Then, in a manner consistent with his previous mystagogical explanation of the baptismal act, Cyril proceeds to show how this ceremony of anointing, refers back "in imitation" to a specific event in the life of Christ, reproducing, as it were, in a figure this event: "And all of this was accomplished in you in a figure (*εἰκονικῶς*), because you are figures (*εἰκόνες*) of Christ."[43] In his mimesis theology of associating the saving events of Christ's life with the ceremonies of baptism, Cyril now shifts his image from the body of Christ taken down from the cross, buried in the earth and rising as type of the Christian, dead to sin, "buried" in water and "rising" from the font-tomb. He now uses the image of Christ being baptized in the waters of the Jordan by John, and then coming up out of the waters whereupon the Holy Spirit descended upon Him in the form of a dove.[44] This was Christ's "anointing," that is, his designation as the "Messiah," the "Christ," the "Anointed," Who is now equipped for His Messianic mission by this "anointing" of the Spirit, although material oil is not used, but rather the voice of the Father and the dove: "For Christ was not christened by men with oil of material ointment, but the Father, having appointed Him to be the Savior of the whole world, christened Him with the Holy Spirit."[45] And as corroboration of the link between Christ's designation as the Messiah and its symbol in material anointing, which will be for

[42]*Myst. Cat.* III.1 (*Idem;* tr. *ibid.*, 63-64): *Χριστοὶ δὲ γεγόνατε, τοῦ ἁγίου Πνεύματος τὸ ἀντίτυπον δεξάμενοι.*

[43]*Idem.* (*Idem.*, tr. *ibid.*, 64): *καὶ πάντα εἰκονικῶς ἐφ' ὑμῶν γεγένηται, ἐπειδὴ εἰκόνες ἐστὲ Χριστοῦ.*

[44]*Cf. Mt.* 3:16-17; *Jn.* 1:32-34.

[45]*Myst. Cat.* III.2 (Piédagnel, *SC* 126, 122; tr. Cross, *SPCK*, 64): *Ἐλαίῳ γὰρ ἢ μύρῳ σωματικῷ Χριστὸς ὑπ' ἀνθρώπου οὐκ ἐχρίσθη, ἀλλ' ὁ Πατὴρ αὐτὸν Σωτῆρα προχειρισάμενος τοῦ παντὸς κόσμου Πνεύματι ἔχρισεν ἁγίῳ.*

Cyril the antitype, he adds two scriptural texts which already contain the word linking the outpouring of the Holy Spirit with the symbol of material anointing with oil: "As Peter says: 'Jesus of Nazareth, Whom God anointed (ἔχρισεν) with the Holy Spirit,'"[46] and Cyril concludes with the text of royal Messianic anointing: "therefore God your God has anointed (ἔχρισε) you with the oil of gladness above your fellows."[47]

This scene in the Jordan, where Jesus of Nazareth became the "Messiah," the "Christ," the Anointed One through the designation and descent upon Him of the Holy Spirit, "like resting upon like"[48] as Cyril is careful to add, though without material anointing with oil, but with the "anointing" of the Holy Spirit, is now repeated in the anointing of the neophyte with *myron* as he comes out of the baptismal pool: "In the same manner for you also, after you had come up from the pool of sacred streams (ναμάτων) there was the chrismation (χρῖσμα), the exact figure (ἀντίτυπον) of that with which Christ was christened; and this was the Holy Spirit."[49]

Cyril further elucidates the meaning of this event in which Christ and the neophyte are associated, Christ by the appearance of the Holy Spirit in the form of a dove after He emerges from the waters of the Jordan, and the neophyte by the anointing with chrism after he emerges from the baptismal pool, by adding another text associated with the inauguration of Christ's Messianic ministry after receiving the designation of the Spirit: "The Spirit of the Lord is upon Me, that is why He has anointed (ἔχρισέ) me, to preach the good news to the poor He has sent me."[50]

46 *Ac.* 10:38. *Myst. Cat.* III.2 *(Idem):* ὡς Πέτρος φησίν· "Ἰησοῦν τὸν Ναζωραῖον, ὃν ἔχρισεν ὁ Θεὸς Πνεύματι ἁγίῳ."

47 *Ps.* 44:7. *Myst. Cat.* III.2 (*Ibid.,* 124; tr. *idem):* διὰ τοῦτο ἔχρισέ σε ὁ Θεός, ὁ Θεός σου, ἔλαιον ἀγαλλιάσεως παρὰ τοὺς μετόχους σου.

48 *Myst. Cat.* III.1 (*Ibid.,* 122; tr. *idem):* τῷ ὁμοίῳ ἐπαναπαυομένου τοῦ ὁμοίου.

49 *Idem:* Καὶ ὑμῖν ὁμοίως ἀναβεβηκόσιν ἀπὸ τῆς κολυμβήθρας τῶν ἱερῶν ναμάτων χρῖσμα, τὸ ἀντίτυπον ὃ ἐχρίσθη Χριστός. Τοῦτο δὲ ἐστὶ τὸ ἅλιον Πνεῦμα.

50 *Is.* 61:1; *Lk.* 4:18. *Idem:* Πνεῦμα Κυρίου ἐπ' ἐμέ, οὗ εἵνεκεν ἔχρισέ με. εὐαγγελίσασθαι πτωχοῖς ἀπέσταλκέ με.

In this mystagogical interpretation of the anointing ceremony then, the baptismal pool is not merely the "pool (*κολυμβήθρας*)," as before,[51] but the pool "of sacred streams (*ναμάτων*)," the reference being to the baptismal pool not now as tomb, but as symbol of the waters of the River Jordan.[52] The "type (*τύπος*)" is the coming of the Holy Spirit upon Jesus and what it implies Messianically; the "antitype (*ἀντίτυπος*)" to this salvific event is the "chrismation (*χρῖσμα*)" of the neophyte, as Cyril says: "the chrismation, the exact figure (*ἀντίτυπον*) of that with which Christ was christened."

Cyril confirms his mimesis theology applied to this ceremony in the following passage:

> And as Christ was in truth crucified, and buried, and raised, and you in likeness (*ἐν ὁμοιώματι*) are in Baptism accounted worthy of being crucified, buried and raised together with Him, so it is with the chrismation also. As He was christened with the spiritual oil of gladness, the Holy Spirit, Who is so-called, because He is the author of spiritual gladness, so you were christened with ointment (*μύρῳ*) having been made partakers (*κοινωνοὶ*) and companions of Christ.[53]

Pre-figuration and Fulfilment

Cyril structures his mystagogy of the anointing of the neophyte as antitype of the anointing of Jesus even more fully by drawing attention to two figures from the *OT*, Aaron, the priest and Solomon, the king, who bathed and were anointed

[51]See *Myst. Cat.* II.4 (*Ibid.*, 110; tr. *ibid.*, 60).

[52]See *Myst. Cat.* III.1 (*Ibid.*, 122; tr. *ibid.*, 64). We have seen previously how Chrysostom applies this word for flowing waters to the baptismal pool in order to evoke the image of the waters of the rivers of Paradise. (See above, ch. 2,pp. 262-263).

[53]*Myst. Cat.* III.2 (Piédagnel, *SC* 126, 124; tr. Cross, *SPCK*, 64-65): *Καὶ ὥσπερ Χριστὸς ἀληθῶς ἐσταυροῦτο καὶ ἐθάπτετο καὶ ἠγείρετο, ὑμεῖς δὲ κατὰ τὸ βάπτισμα ἐν ὁμοιώματι καὶ συσταυρωθῆναι καὶ συνταφῆναι καὶ συναναστῆναι αὐτῷ καταξιοῦσθε, οὕτω καὶ ἐπι τοῦ χρίσματος. Ἐκεῖνος ἐλαίῳ νοητῷ ἀγαλλιάσεως ἐχρίετο, τοῦτ ᾽ἔστι Πνεύματι ἁγίῳ, ἀγαλλιάσεως καλουμένῳ ἐλαίῳ. διὰ τὸ αἴτιον, αὐτο τῆς πνευματικῆς ἀγαλλιάσεως τυγχανέιν· ὑμεις δὲ μύρῳ ἐχρίσθητε, κοινωνοὶ· καὶ μέτοχοι τοῦ Χριστοῦ γενόμενοι.*

with oil into their respective functions. In bringing in these two parallels, his purpose, as he states, is to show that the chrismation has its "symbol (*σύμβολον*)" in the *OT.*[54] The symbolism is ready-made. Moses washes Aaron and his sons with water.[55] Moses pours chrism on Aaron's head, by this anointing consecrating him for his priestly task.[56] "He anointed [him,] and he was called Christ [or the Anointed,] (*ἔχρισε, καὶ ἐκαλεῖτο Χριστός*)."[57] David fulfils his oath to Bathsheba by designating Solomon, their son, to be king.[58] Zadok, the priest, and Nathan, the prophet, bring Solomon to the river Gihon and there anoint him with a horn of oil.[59]

Cyril's point, however, in mentioning these *OT* anointings is not for purpose of comparison, but rather of contrast. The chrismation into the priestly and royal function in the *OT* are similar in rite, that is, anointing with chrism,[60] to the anointing of the neophyte after the baptismal bath. "To them, however, these things happened in a figure (*τυπικῶς*); but to you not in a figure, but in truth (*ἀληθῶς*)."[61] The difference between "*τυπικῶς*" and "*ἀληθῶς*" in the two ritual events of anointing is explained by Cyril to be the fact that Christian anointing is done by the power of Christ, Who was christened by the Holy Spirit, and that here no longer a prefiguration but the actual beginning of salvation is established. The ritual of the *OT* was no such reality vested with the power of the Holy Spirit which had been sent through the salvific grace attained through the life, death, and resurrection of Jesus. Cyril, then, is not interested in showing how the Christian by his anointing

[54] *Ibid.,* III.6 (*Ibid.,* 128; tr. *ibid.,* 66).

[55] *Lv.* 8:6.

[56] *Lv.* 8:12.

[57] *Myst. Cat.* III.6 (Piédagnel, *SC* 126, 128, tr. Cross *SPCK,* 66). *Cf. Lv.* 4:5.

[58] 1 *K.* 1:30.

[59] 1 *K.* 1:38-39, 45.

[60] The chrism of the *OT* was composed in the same way as that used in the Christian liturgy, a compound of olive oil and fragrant herbs. See *Ex.* 30:22-26.

[61] *Myst. Cat.* III.6 (Piédagnel, *SC* 126, 128; tr. Cross, *SPCK,* 66): Ἀλλὰ ταῦτα μὲν ἐκείνοις συνέβαινε τυπικῶς, ὑμῖν δὲ οὐ τυπικῶς, ἀλλ᾽ ἀληθῶς.

received "priestly" and "royal" prerogatives. His purpose, rather, in drawing on the material of the royal and priestly anointing in the *OT* is to contrast such anointing into priesthood and kingship with the new reality of sharing through chrismation the unique communication of the Holy Spirit which comes through Christ, and in the consequent mission which this communication implies, a mission adumbrated in the roles of the priest and king in the *OT*.

The perfection of transformation into Christ, Who Himself is the Anointed One of the Father, is what occurs in this post-baptismal anointing, a point which Cyril brings out in concluding his *OT* considerations by echoing the Pauline notion of Christ as the "first-fruits" of the new cosmic order, and those who have fellowship with Him as the whole batch of dough, the entire bread, which is thus by association sanctified: "He is the first-fruit, and you are the mass; but if the first-fruit be holy, it is manifest that its holiness will pass to the mass also."[62]

3. *Particular Effects of the Anointing*

According to Cyril the anointing bespeaks a particular communication of the Holy Spirit, and by his typology of Christ's baptism in the Jordan he shows that this communication of the Holy Spirit transforms the Christian according to a particular modality of the life of Christ, namely the modality of Christ's Messianic mission. This mystagogical explanation

[62] *Idem. (Ibid.,* 130; tr. *Idem): ἐκεῖνος γὰρ ἀληθῶς ἀπαρχή, καὶ υμεῖς τὸ φύραμα· εἰ δὲ ἡ ἀπαρχη ἁγία, δηλονότι μεταβήσεται ἐπὶ τὸ φύραμα ἡ ἁγιότης.* By "first-fruits (*ἀπραχή*)" is meant this first handful of dough which is offered as "first-fruits" in order to make the whole offering sacred. (See *Nb.* 15:19-21). The "*φύραμα*" is the entire mass of dough. This Pauline image is found in *Rm.* 11:16, and recurs again in 1 *Co.* 5:6-7; 15:23. That Cyril intends this contrast between the old and the new dispensation may be gathered from a passage in *Bapt. Cat.* X.14 (*MG* 33.680) where he speaks at greater length on the priesthood of Christ. Christ's priesthood is changeless, it did not begin in time, there is no successor to Him as High Priest. It is not a priesthood of corporal succession, as, for example, Moses appointing his brother Aaron, nor was Christ anointed with material oil, as were the priests of the *OT* (*cf. Myst. Cat.* III.2, tr. above, p. 365, text above, n. 45, p.365, but He received His priesthood from the Father before all ages.

of the ceremony, resting on scriptural texts referring to the relationship of anointing to the communication of the Spirit for a certain mission and the actuality of the baptismal pool-Jordan River symbol, is then further supported by Cyril in his exposition of certain detailed features of the ceremony. This part of the mystagogy considers the ointment itself, the "*μύρον*," which is used in the ceremony, the meaning of the anointing of different parts of the body, the etymology of the word "chrismation," and a consideration of the relationship of the anointing to a certain *NT* description of the effect of the Holy Spirit on body and soul.

a. *The Myron Theology*

Cyril adds a striking consideration to the theology of the *myron,* that is, the perfumed oil, a combination of olive oil base to which balsam and other aromatic herbs are added to produce a perfumed fragrance.[63] What Cyril does is to draw a kind of parallel between the epiclesis over the bread, after which it is no longer bread, but the Body of Christ, and the epiclesis over the *myron.* He warns the neophytes to beware of thinking that this chrism is mere ordinary ointment once this epiclesis over it has taken place. It is rather the gift of Christ, the Holy Spirit giving it divine efficacy.[64] Cyril concludes this exposition with a somewhat classic statement of its kind in sacramental theology: "While your body is christened with visible

[63] For details concerning the composition of *myron,* see Ph. Hofmeister, *Die heiligen Öle in der morgen und abendländischen Kirche. Eine kirchenrechtliche liturgische Abhandlung,* Das östliche Christentum, Neue Folge, Heft 6/7 (Würzburg, 1948) 29ff. For a general survey, uncritical however, since it is used in support of his thesis on the meaning of "confirmation," and so open in some aspects to debate, see Daniélou, *op. cit.,* pp. 121-126.

[64] *Myst. Cat.* III.3 (Piédagnel, *SC* 126; 124; tr Cross, *SPCK,* 65).One must, of course, avoid applying the framework of later "transubstantiation" theology in this context. Cyril's primary interest is not in explaining the oil as object, but rather its dynamic use in conjunction with the operation of the Holy Spirit. One must compare Cyril's thinking in this passage with other examples where mention of the epiclesis occur. In *Myst. Cat.* I. 7 (Piédagnel, *SC* 126, 94; tr. Cross, *SPCK,* 56), for example, Cyril compares bread and wine which has through the epiclesis become the body and blood of Christ with the transformation which takes place in other foods such as bread or meat when idolatrous invocations are made over them. They become then part of the impure "pomps of Satan." That Cyril is thinking in

ointment, your soul is sanctified by the Holy and life-giving Spirit."[65]

In this contribution to the mystagogy of the ceremony, then, Cyril uses material from the *myron* theology, placing particular emphasis on the fact that the anointing brings about a transformation because of the inner working of the Holy Spirit associated with the *myron.* This *myron* is made holy by the work of the Holy Spirit, not independent of, but rather in a dynamic relationship to its use in the liturgical ceremony. With the use of the sanctified *myron,* the neophyte himself is sanctified. This takes place through the Holy Spirit, but the Holy Spirit working through the "sacrament" of the anointing. And this inner change which is wrought in the neophyte, far beyond any mere symbol, as in the *OT,* is nothing less than the effecting of a "participation" in the Anointed One Himself, in the Messiah Christ.

---

the theology of dynamic transformation rather than in the static terms of a transsubstantiated object may also be seen in his remarks in *Myst. Cat.* V.7,19 (Piédagnel, *SC* 126, 154, 168; tr. Cross, *SPCK,* 74, 78). Speaking of the epiclesis over the bread and wine he says: "Whatever the Holy Spirit touches is sanctified and changed (*παντὸς γὰρ οὗ ἂν ἐφάψηται τὸ ἅγιον Πνεῦμα, τοῦτο ἡγίασται καὶ μεταβέβληται*)." *Myst. Cat.* V. 7 (Piédagnel, *SC* 126,154; tr. Cross, *SPCK*, 74). (For further analysis of this passage, see Piédagnel, *SC* 126, 155, n. 1). Even more revealing of the transformation theology which lies at the heart of Cyril's mystagogy are his remarks in the same catechesis prior to receiving Holy Communion, apropos of the liturgical admonition which he cites, "Holy things to the holy (*τὰ ἅγια τοῖς ἁγίοις*)." *Myst. Cat.* V. 19 (Piédagnel, *SC* 126, 168; tr. Cross, *SPCK,* 78). The gifts are holy through the epiclesis of the Holy Spirit. The communicants are holy because they have received the Holy Spirit. Holy things and holy people. To the objection that One alone is holy, the One Lord Jesus Christ, Cyril answers that this is true, but the people also may be called holy, not by "nature (*φύσει*)" as is Jesus Christ, but by "participation (*μετοχῇ*)" as well as by effort and prayer. This word "*μετοχῇ*" is the same word which Cyril uses to describe what takes place in the post-baptismal anointing, where the neophytes become "companions and participants of Christ (*κοινωνοὶ καὶ μέτοχοι τοῦ Χριστοῦ*)." (*Myst. Cat.* III.2) (Tr. and text, see above, p. 367 and n. 53). (For indications of the epiclesis apart from the Eucharist among other authors, see Piédagnel, *SC* 126, 125, n. 1).

65 *Myst. Cat.* III.3 (Piédagnel, *SC* 126, 124; tr. Cross, *SPCK,* 65): *καὶ τῷ μὲν φαινομένῳ μύρῳ τὸ σῶμα χρίεται, τῷ δὲ ἁγίῳ και ζωοποιῷ Πνεύματι ἡ ψυχὴ ἁγιάζεται.*

Cf. in Ambrose a similar statement of the relationship between sensible sign and invisible mystery: "For although we are apparently sealed on the body, yet truly we are sealed on the heart, that the Holy Spirit may express in us the likeness of the heavenly image. (Nam etsi specie signemur in corpore, veritate tamen in corde signamur, ut Spiritus Sanctus exprimat in nobis imaginis caelestis effigiem)." *De Spiritu,* Lib. I, 6, 79 (*ML* 16.725; tr. Deferrari *FC* 44, 63).

b. *The Anointings of the Different Parts of the Body*

Consequent to the *myron* theology, which reveals the transforming power of the anointment, Cyril then proceeds to explain in detail particular aspects of this transformation as it is connected with the application of the *myron* to different parts of the neophyte's body, namely the forehead, the ears, the nostrils and the breast.[66] His mystagogical method here is to draw on a scriptural quotation for each anointing and to add a brief word of explanation. The form is quite condensed and requires some elucidation in order to understand just how the Scripture text which Cyril draws on as his material relates to his entire picture of the anointing ceremony.

(1) The Anointing of the Forehead

Man's loss of the "glory of God (*δόξα τοῦ Θεοῦ*)" as a result of his fall in Paradise brought with it a sense of shame, a darkening of man's countenance, which no longer reflected his intimate gaze of union with God. He hid from God in his shame, and even before his partner found a heretofore unknown sense of shame in his own nakedness.[67] God had communicated His Spirit to man, but through man's sin there was an alienation from this Spirit. The anointing precisely on the forehead, man's countenance, represents the restoration of this gift of God's Spirit. Its effect is to remove this shame, restoring in principle the paradisal condition, so that—and here Cyril uses St. Paul—"with uncovered face you might reflect as in a mirror the glory of the Lord"[68] In this same verse Paul explains that this is the work of the Spirit of Jesus, the Holy Spirit. By the anointing of the Spirit the neophyte is restored to God's image, and growing in this inner contemplation of the divine Essence, the

[66]*Myst. Cat.* III.4 (Piédagnel, *SC* 126, 126; tr. Cross, *SPCK*, 65).
[67]See *Gn.* 3:7-10.

[68]*Cf.* 2 *Co.* 3:18. *Myst. Cat.* III.4 (Piédagnel, *SC* 126, 126; tr. Cross, *SPCK*, 65): ἀνακεκαλυμμένῳ προσώπῳ τὴν δόξαν Κυρίου κατοπτρίζησθε.

restored "*δόξα τοῦ Θεοῦ*," the neophyte's own countenance, with the veil of separation from this divine Essence now removed, and the shame on his countenance as a result now gone, mirrors forth in even brighter form the glory of God, which is found in Christ, to Whom he has been joined by the communication of the Spirit.

From the context of the Pauline passage which Cyril has chosen as illustration of this anointing of the forehead, one may conclude that he understands this effect of the Spirit to be not one single act, but a process, an ever brighter reflecting of Christ's glory on the part of the neophyte, a transformation, as Paul describes it, into the very image which one is reflecting, a progress "from glory to glory (*ἀπὸ δόξης εἰς δόξαν*),"[69] that is, to a reflection which grows brighter and brighter as one becomes in time more closely associated with Christ through the work of the Spirit communicated to him. Cyril's emphasis in explaining this effect of the anointing is on its power in bringing about in the neophyte an active mirroring forth of the glory of God, through the presence of the Spirit linking him with Christ, Who is the image of God.[70]

(2) The Anointing of the Ears

The effect that this anointing has is explained by Cyril with two scriptural references. In the third song of the Servant of Yahweh, the servant announces that God has opened his ear,[71] that is, God has communicated to him a divine message which, like a disciple, he will listen to and learn, becoming versed in this divine communication. The purpose of the anointing of the ears is just this, symbolically through the sense of hearing, to awaken one to the communication of a spiritual reality, a spiritual world transcending what is verifiable only by the

[69] 2 *Co.* 3:18.

[70] This notion of "process" is confirmed by Cyril's idea of holiness in *Myst. Cat.* V.19 (Piédagnel, *SC* 126, 168; tr. Cross, *SPCK* 78) where he says that holiness is a result of "participation and spiritual exercises and prayer (*μετοχῇ καὶ ἀσκήσει καὶ εὐχῇ*)." *Cf.* above, n. 64, p. 370.

[71] *Is.* 50:5.

senses. That the communication of the Spirit to this end involves process and task is confirmed further by the second scriptural quotation used here by Cyril, "He that has ears to hear, let him hear."[72] Not chosen at random, the context relates to the preaching of the kingdom. Jesus explains the prophets, particularly John the Baptist, as messengers of the kingdom and of his own Messiahship. The coming of the Spirit, symbolized by the anointing of the ears then, brings with it the spiritual awareness which makes one learn and transmit the message of the kingdom, in other words, association in Christ's Messianic work.

(3) The Anointing of the Nostrils

The sweet-smelling *myron*, the communication of the Spirit of Christ, this symbolic fragance makes the neophytes aware that he is participating in Christ Himself. Just as for the explanation of the anointing of the ears, so, too, here, Cyril chooses a Pauline quotation delivered in a context of apostolic concern: "We are the good odor of Christ for God among those who are saved."[73]

(4) The Anointing of the Breast

To elucidate the meaning of this anointing Cyril also choses Pauline verses. Joining two texts[74] he instructs the neophytes that they were anointed on the breast in order that having put on the breastplate of righteousness, they might resist the manoeuvres of the devil. This image itself of the breastplate of righteousness derives from the *OT* notion of Yahweh arming Himself and going forth to meet His enemies. The phrase occurs in *Is.* 11[75] which describes in some detail the characteristics of the coming Messiah. The Spirit of Yahweh rests upon the Messianic king, and here are enumerated the familiar char-

[72] *Mt.* 11:15. *Myst. Cat.* III.4 (Piédagnel, *SC* 126, 126; tr. Cross, *SPCK,* 65): ὁ ἔκων ὦτα ἀκούειν, ἀκουέτω.

[73] 2 *Co.* 2:15. *Idem:* Χριστοῦ εὐωδία ἐσμὲν τῷ Θεῷ ἐν τοῖς σωζομένοις. For a comparative development of the notion of divine perfume among other fathers, see Daniélou, *op. cit.*, pp. 122-126.

[74] *Ep.* 6:14,11.

[75] *Vs.* 4.

acteristics, the spirit of wisdom and insight, the spirit of counsel and power, the spirit of knowledge and of the fear of Yahweh. In the *LXX* these qualities as listed there have become the traditional Christian seven gifts of the Holy Spirit. (Piety has been added, a repetition of the "fear of Yahweh.") Cyril immediately ties in this echo of the Messianic king, fortified by the spirit of Yahweh, with the picture of Jesus, after His baptism and the coming of the Holy Spirit on Him, going to struggle with Satan, prelude to His Messianic work.[76] So, too, the Christian after his baptism and his "mystical chrismation (*τὸ μυστικὸν χρῖσμα*)," invested with God's armor, like the Messiah fortified by the Spirit of Yahweh, the armor of the Holy Spirit, must go into the combat like Jesus, with the words of St. Paul on his lips: "I can do all things in Him Who strengthens me, the Christ."[77] Like the other texts, this one too from *Ph.* comes in the context of the apostolic mission, and Paul is expressing his confidence that in Christ he will be able to endure all in the service of evangelization.[78]

Summary

This detailed mystagogy of the anointing of the senses leaves no doubt as to Cyril's main emphasis. His mystagogical interpretation of each of the anointings converges on the view that the coming of the Spirit in the post-baptismal anointing seizes the neophyte and transforms him into an apostolic instrument, just as Christ, the anointed One, the Messiah, was also the

[76]See *Mt.* 4:1-11; *Mk.* 1:12-13; *Lk.* 4:1-3.

[77]*Ph.* 4:13. *Myst. Cat.* III.4. (Piédagnel, *SC* 126, 126; tr. Cross, *SPCK*, 66): Πάντα ἰσχύω ἐν τῷ ἐνδυναμοῦντί με Χριστῷ.

[78]*Bapt. Cat.* III.13 (*MG* 33.444) contains a similar passage referring to Jesus' struggle with Satan after His baptism, and drawing the parallel with the Christian who, before his chrismation, did not dare such a combat. This, too, comes in the context of evangelization, and Cyril offers there an invitation to do evangelical work. The same image of scriptural warfare occurs in *Bapt. Cat.* XVII.36 (*MG* 33.1009). What fortifies the Christian, as is clear from this catechesis on the Holy Spirit, is his chrismation. Here it is called the baptismal "seal (σφραγῖδα)." *Cf.* also *Bapt. Cat.* XVII.35 (*MG* 33.1009).

"Apostle," the One sent from God. After showing the effects of the anointing on the forehead to import a restoration in principle of the paradisal condition, man once again reflecting the glory of God, the texts of Scripture which Cyril chooses to elucidate the meaning of the other anointings all come from contexts of kingdom of God, apostleship, discipleship, evangelization, mission. God's kingdom, restored in Christ and communicated to the neophyte through the anointing of the Spirit of Christ, must now manifest itself in a dynamic way, interacting with the forces in the world opposed to it, until it reaches its full growth and maturity. A new presence of Christ's Spirit will manifest itself in the Christian himself, both providing the Christian with his task in this world, and giving him the strength to perform it. Cyril's presentation of the mystagogy of these anointings is a model of the mystagogy of Christian spirituality.

c. *The Name "Christian"*

A sort of substantiation of the end effect of the transformation which the anointing brings is seen by Cyril in his consideration of the etymology of the word "Christian." Only after receiving this anointing can the neophyte properly be called "Christian." "When you are counted worthy of this Holy Chrism (χρίσματος), you are called Christians (χριστιανοί)."[79] In this particular mystagogical explanation Cyril is, of course, playing on the similarity between the words "chrism (χρῖσμα)," "Christ (χριστός)," and "Christian (χριστιανός)." Prior to this "christianization" through the chrism, the catechumen, according to Cyril's interpretation here, was not yet a Christian, but on the way to becoming one.[80] While as a catechumen he might have been termed loosely a "Christian," the verification

[79] *Myst. Cat.* III.5 (Piédagnel, *SC* 126, 128; tr. Cross, *SPCK,* 66): Τούτου τοῦ ἁγίου Χρίσματος καταξιωθέντες καλεῖσθε Χριστιανοί.

[80] The distinction which Cyril uses here for the sake of his mystagogy is, of course, not always so strictly verified in tradition. The word "Χριστιανός" is sometimes also applied to the catechumens. (For examples of this see Piédagnel, *SC* 126, 128, n. 1). (For a history of the word "Christian" from its apparent first use in 1 *P.* 4:16, see E. Peterson, *Christianos,* Miscellanea Mercati I (Vatican City, 1946).

of this new name, its "actuation," occurs only after this final step in initiation.

d. "*Teacher and Protector*"

At the end of this Catechesis Cyril returns to the Scripture text which had been read at the outset,[81] repeating the notion found there that the "anointing" which the neophytes have received will be their teacher, and then adding that this anointing is a "preservative of the body and a safeguard for the soul (*σώματος φυλακτήριον καὶ ψυχῆς σωτήριον*)."[82] Although he does not further explain the meaning of this latter part of the statement, it reflects the mystagogical explanation already seen in Cyril's treatment of the *myron* theology, the relationship between the external sign performed on the body, and the interior action which takes place in the soul. The use of oil to preserve, make supple, protect is perhaps echoed here and so becomes the symbol of protection.

4. *The Eschatological Dimension*

As in the first *Mystagogical Catechesis* where he explained the renunciation of Satan and the act of profession for Christ,[83] Cyril also here draws his mystagogical explanation of the anointing into eschatological dimensions.[84] He uses the image of the temple of Yahweh lifted above the mountains with the nations streaming into it to learn God's ways and to walk in His paths,[85] applying it to the Church. He uses the image of the Messianic banquet on Mount Sion, that the banqueters shall be anointed with ointment,[86] and that the gifts of the banquet, including the anointing, would be given to the nations.[87]

[81] See above, p. 363.

[82] *Myst. Cat.* III.7 (Piédagnel, *SC* 126, 130; tr. Cross, *SPCK,* 66-67): *σώματος φυλακτήρτον καὶ ψυχῆς σωτήριον.*

[83] See above, ch. 1, p. 61.

[84] *Myst. Cat.* III.7 (Piédagnel, *SC* 126, 130, 132; tr. Cross, *SPCK*; 66-67).

[85] *Is.* 2:2-3.

[86] *Is.* 25:6 *LXX*, Cyril had quoted from this same chapter of *Is.* at the conclusion of the first *Myst. Cat.* See above, ch. 2, p. 177.

[87] *Is.* 25:7 *LXX.*

Cyril's consistent mystagogy of the anointing up to this conclusion in the eschatological scenes is continued right to the end. The anointing is already the first-fruits of a gift which, through given on earth in sacrament, must be exercised in a mission, a Messianic mission, by the Christian, in the Church, and through this Church to the final restoration in all men of the gift of the Spirit lost in Paradise, and now sent in this sacrament to the faithful to be the first-fruit of and the strength for the mission in this world leading up to the consummation. The earthly anointing, in this final imagery of Cyril, is reflection of the completion of the work, seen in the image of the anointing of all men with joy at the heavenly banquet. The anointing is more than a mere symbol, but, because of its relationship to Messianic fulfilment, something which Cyril calls "mystical." It is already part of this future fulfilment, the gift already received, and for that reason he admonishes the neophytes to keep this anointing unspotted and unblemished in them. At the same time it is functional, even as the Spirit which is communicated through it is in function of mission, helping the neophytes to cooperate with the spread of the Messianic work completed by Christ and now poured out in the Holy Spirit, working to final fulfilment, universal salvation.

Summary

From this analysis of Cyril's mystagogical interpretation of the anointing which takes place after the baptismal bath, it becomes very clear that whatever the pagan or Christian history of the anointing might have been, Cyril clearly links it with that particular communication of the Holy Spirit which comprises traditionally one of the steps of Christian Initiation. His mystagogy is consequent, unified and carefully worked out.

Central to this mystagogy of the ceremony as a special communication of the Holy Spirit are two things: first, the fact that there is an anointing of the neophyte with oil, and second, the fact that this anointing comes just at this point of the ceremony. As a result of this liturgical structure Cyril can readily and plausibly make great use of biblical material to explain the ceremony. The symbol of anointing itself is already present in both *OT* examples and *NT* vocabulary (e.g. "Jesus of Nazareth, Whom God *anointed* with the Holy Spirit,")[88] as sign of consecrating and outfitting certain individuals for a particular mission.

Together with this biblical "given" in regard to anointing, the fact of the ceremony's place immediately after the neophyte comes out of the baptismal pool, where he has been made conformed to Christ, lends itself readily to the imagery of the scene on the Jordan. The fact that Christ receives here a particular Messianic mandate fits perfectly the notion of why the Spirit is given anyway as well as the preceding mystagogy of baptism as conformity to Christ. A key insight into the working of mystagogy itself, and its manner of dealing with given ceremonies can be seen here in the fact that the mystagogue allows himself quite readily to shift from the baptismal font as tomb, which formed the high point of the mystagogy of the baptismal act using the ideas of *Rm.* 6,[89] to the baptismal water as the waters of the River Jordan, in order to make use of another aspect of the mystery of Christ, his inauguration into Messianic mission. While such mystagogical shifts remain plausible in Cyril's writings, one can readily surmise that further development in less responsible hands could lead to far-fetched interpretation, which would even effect the liturgy itself in turn.

From the fact of the anointing and its biblical echoes, and from the fact that it is *this* anointing, after the baptismal bath interpreted as it had been, Cyril's further elaborations as to the particular effects of this anointing follow obviously. The anointing with oil which has undergone an epiclesis, and its use on different parts of the body, will logically be interpreted according to the mission purpose inherent in the coming of the Holy Spirit, with constant comparison between Christ's mission and that of the Christian.

[88] *Ac.* 10:38.
[89] See above, ch. 2, pp. 229-232.

Even the final consummation of the mission, the universal salvation of all mankind intended in the coming of the Holy Spirit, finds a ready image in the oil of the Messianic banquet, where the participants are anointed as sign of joy and welcome, the oil of gladness, first-fruits of which are already present in the anointing of the candidate for his mission on earth. The centrality of the symbol of oil to the entire mystagogy might best be realized if one were to ask: how would Cyril present his mystagogy if no oil were used (but rather, for example, a laying on of hand only as sign of the particular communication of the Spirit)? In studying Ambrose we shall see a good example of how such a mystagogy would be presented, where the particular communication of the Spirit is recognized, but where the consideration of oil is not present in the mystagogical interpretation.

B. Theodore

The post-baptismal anointing is treated in much less detail by Theodore than by Cyril. Nevertheless the same theological presuppositions are at work here as in the Jerusalem *Catecheses*, and similar material is used to provide the mystagogical interpretation of this anointing. In comparison to Cyril's entire catechesis on the subject, Theodore's mystagogy is condensed into the following passage. For purpose of comparison, now that Cyril's mystagogy has been so minutely analyzed, it will be valuable to quote Theodore in entirety:

> After you have received the grace of baptism and worn a white garment that shines, the priest draws nigh unto you on your forehead and says: "So-and-so is signed in the Name of the Father and of the Son and of the Holy Spirit." When Jesus came out of the water He received the grace of the Holy Spirit who descended like a dove and lighted on Him, and this is the reason why He is said to have been anointed: "The Spirit of the Lord is upon me, because of which the Lord has anointed me,"[90] and: "Jesus

[90] *Lk.* 4:18.

of Nazareth whom God has anointed with the Holy Spirit and with power,"[91] texts which show that the Holy Spirit is never separated from Him, like the anointment with oil which has a durable effect on the men who are anointed, and is not separated from them. It is right, therefore, that you should receive the signing on your forehead.

When (the priest) signs you he says: "So-and-so is signed in the name of the Father and of the Son and of the Holy Spirit," so that it may be an indication to you that it is in the name of the Father and of the Son and of the Holy Spirit that the Holy Spirit descended on you also, and you were anointed and received grace; and He will be and remain with you, as it is through Him that you possess the first-fruits. Indeed, at present you only receive symbolically the happiness of the future benefits, but at the time of the resurrection you will receive all the grace from which you will become immortal, incorruptible, impassible and immutable; even your body will then remain for ever and will not perish, while your soul will be exempt from all inclination, however slight, towards evil.[92]

1. *The Communication of the Holy Spirit*

As in Cyril's cathechesis, so here in Theodore's work this post-baptismal anointing is associated in a particular way with that step in Christian Initiation which has to do with a particular communication of the Holy Spirit. Of the anointing with its formula Theodore tells the neophytes that this is an indication "that the Holy Spirit descended on you also."

2. *Christ and the Christian*

That it is Theodore's intention in this remark not merely to explain the baptismal act as the act in which the Holy Spirit is communicated in a particular way, then "symbolized" afterward in a kind of explanatory rite, that of the anointing, is

[91] *Ac.* 10:38.

[92] *Bapt. Hom.* III.27 (Tonneau-Devreese, *SeT* 145, 456, 458; tr. Mingana, *WS* VI, 68-69.

clear from his use of the kind of mimesis theology as is found in Cyril's explanation of the ceremony. The anointing of the neophyte is linked with the event in Christ's life where He emerges from his baptism in the Jordan, and the Holy Spirit descends on Him in the form of a dove.[93] Explanatory texts from *Lk.* and *Ac.* indicate the Messianic understanding of the anointing of Jesus, and so thereby underscore the missionary interpretation of this anointing for the Christian after his emerging from the font. They are the same texts Cyril had used in the Jordan scene.[94]

As might be expected from our analysis of Theodore's typological emphasis in relationship to the baptismal bath,[95] even though the use of the Jordan scene and the scriptural texts interpreting it are identical with Cyril's use, the typological explanation shifts somewhat as a result of Theodore's constant emphasis on future resurrection. The relationship of the past event in the life of Jesus to the liturgical act of anointing is for Cyril a relationship of type (the anointing of Jesus by the Holy Spirit) and antitype (the anointing of the Christian after emerging from the font). Theodore's framework of the coming resurrection, on the other hand, causes him to emphasize the post-baptismal anointing as looking to the future, while, at the same time, not neglecting the reference to the past salvific event in the Jordan. In this emphasis, the liturgical anointing would be the type, related in retrospect to the anointing of Jesus with the Spirit, and the future benefits of the resurrected body would be the antitype.

3. *Particular Effects of the Anointing*

The liturgical anointing itself, then, communicates a possession of the Holy Spirit, looking to future revelation but already begun now: "He will be with you and remain with you, as it is through Him that you possess now the first-fruits."[96]

[93] See *Mt.* 3:16-17; *Jn.* 1:32-34.
[94] See above, pp. 365-366.
[95] See above, ch. 2, pp. 325-332, esp. 328.
[96] See above, p. 381.

Without going into Cyril's more elaborate explanation of the *myron* theology, or the analysis of the anointing on the different parts of the body, which apparently did not take place save for the forehead, and without using Cyril's classic formulation that the soul is being sanctified while the body is being anointed, Theodore's explanation of the particular effects of the anointing comes to the same conclusion as that of Cyril, that the anointing is a reality of durable effect, because it contains in re-presentation the mystery of the conferring of the Spirit looking toward the Messianic task of the Christian, just as Jesus was anointed for this task. Commenting on the texts which both he and Cyril had used to explain the meaning of Christ's anointing,[97] Theodore says: "[These texts] show that the Holy Spirit is never separated from [Jesus], like the anointing with oil which has a durable effect on the men who are anointed and is not separated from them."[98]

Essay: The Anointing on the Forehead: Theodore and Cyril

In the baptismal liturgy which finds its reflection in the *Baptismal Homilies* of Theodore and in the *Mystagogical Catecheses* of Cyril the anointing after the baptismal act is performed as an anointing on the forehead. Cyril also describes further anointing on other bodily parts; Theodore does not. Cyril offers a mystagogical interpretation of this anointing on the forehead, and this mystagogical interpretation forms his point of departure for the mystagogy of the anointing on the ears, the nostrils and the breast, and this mystagogy, as we have seen, is the theme of participation in the Messianic mission of Christ. Theodore, on the other hand, does not offer any mystagogical interpretation of the anointing on the forehead, save the most general and not entirely intelligible statement: "It is right, therefore, that you should receive the anointing on your forehead."[99] In context this statement seems

[97] *Lk.* 4:18; *Ac.* 10:38.
[98] See above, p. 381.
[99] See above, p. 381.

to be nothing more than a general summary of the equation between Christ's anointing and that of the candidate, and a conclusion about the durable effects of the anointing. It is a statement about the *anointing,* not particularly about the anointing *on the forehead.*

The reason for Theodore's silence on the mystagogy of the anointing on the forehead might be twofold. First, since there is no further room for development of a mystagogy for the anointing of any other bodily parts, there being no such anointings, a specific mystagogy of the forehead anointing could not go very far. It sufficed to draw attention to the fact of the anointing, disregarding the specific question as to *why the forehead,* and relate it to the mystagogy of the anointing which has already been given, namely that it is a special communication of the Holy Spirit, its relationship to the Jordan scene, and its particular effect of durability in and inseparability from those who are anointed.

The second, and more important reason that might explain Theodore's silence on the mystagogy of the forehead anointing, is the fact that Theodore has already provided a very lengthy commentary on an anointing of the forehead when he dealt with his first, or *sphragis* anointing, which concludes the rite of renunciation and profession in his liturgy.[100] This *sphragis* anointing in the rite of renunciation and profession, it will be remembered, is absent in the Jerusalem liturgy.

What is most striking, however, is the remarkable similarity between Theodore's mystagogy of this forehead anointing at the conclusion of the rite of renunciation and profession, and Cyril's mystagogy of the forehead anointing after the baptismal bath.[101] Theodore's development of the mystagogical interpretation of the forehead anointing as a sign of confidence, "*parrhesia*," in this place[102] is quite similar to Cyril's development of the mystagogy of the forehead anointing after baptism. In both interpretations the forehead anointing signifies

[100]See above, ch. 1, pp. 123-131.
[101]See above, pp. 372-373.
[102]See above, ch. 1, pp. 125-126.

the removal of shame, and the ability to view the glory of God with unveiled face. Both fathers employ the same Pauline text[103] in their mystagogy of this ceremony.

We have already noted the possibility that both fathers may well be drawing on the same traditional matter of exposition in order to explain the meaning of the anointing of the forehead.[104] That Cyril uses such an explanation for the post-baptismal forehead anointing, while Theodore develops the material in conjunction with the *sphragis* anointing concluding the rite of renunciation and profession, is apparently due to the mystagogical emphasis into which this somewhat fluid and adaptable material is incorporated. This mystagogical emphasis and distribution of material will also be determined by the differences of the given liturgies among the different fathers.

Cyril is able to bring the material meaningfully into the interpretation of an anointing which bespeaks in a particular way the communication of the Holy Spirit. He links the *Gn.* notion of the Spirit of God active in creation, and the loss of this Spirit through man's sin, with the coming of the Holy Spirit as sign of the new creation, hence of the removal of man's shame and his new ability to look at God with unveiled face, and reflect His image with increasing clarity. This same material, the anointing of the forehead as sign of removal of shame, can be used by Theodore to explain the *sphragis* anointing, where, among the other meanings attached to this anointing, the sign of the first-fruits of heavenly victory and the final possession of heavenly life is implied.[105] (This same thought occurs in Theodore's explanation of the post-baptismal anointing as well, but as a bare statement without specific explanation of how it is connected with the placing of oil on the forehead.)

It is in this context that the idea of the removal of the shame of unfreedom, and the restoration of *parrhesia,* of confidence, of being able to look at God with open face as full citizen of

[103] 2 *Co.* 3:18.

[104] See above, ch. 1, pp. 136-137 and n. 306, p. 131.

[105] See above, ch. 1, pp. 123-131.

the heavenly city is developed by Theodore. He unfolds the idea in the context of the sign of belonging, *sphragis,* and what that ultimately means in the total picture of redemption and its fruits, eternal, heavenly life.

A second, interesting contextual difference for using this Pauline material from 2 *Co.* to explain the forehead anointing by Theodore and Cyril lies in the christological emphasis which each author employs in a different way. For Theodore the *sphragis* anointing, sealing the act of renunciation and profession, is a sign of belonging to Christ. Belonging to Christ, however, means an inward, mystical transformation by which the Christian lives with the very inner life which Christ Himself possesses. This contemplative explanation is actually developed in detail by Theodore[106] and is a chief piece in the mystagogical explanation using the "face-to-face" material of 2 *Co.* The main point of emphasis in which this explanation is located is a contemplation of the heavenly life, already begun. Cyril, on the other hand, whose liturgy has no anointing to conclude the rite of renunciation and commitment, brings this material into another christological aspect. Cyril's whole framework, as we have seen, proceeds from Christ's anointing after baptism in the Jordan, the "mission" aspect of Christ's life. His explanation of the anointing of the other senses was entirely qualified by this mission thought. His explanation of the anointing of the forehead is made, then, the source or point of departure for an expository unity which comprises the explanation of the anointings of the other body parts. The material from 2 *Co.,* the contemplative idea also present in Cyril is the same. But he does not use his mystagogy primarily in consideration of this aspect of the life of heaven already begun, but rather in consideration of the loss and return of the Holy Spirit to man. He notes the loss by his reference to *Gn.,* but then emphasiizes the task and mission of the Christian with Christ to cooperate in the restoration of the Spirit. His explanation of the anointing of the forehead, then, becomes, as it were, the source, or the point of departure from which the

[106]See above, ch. 1, pp. 126ff.

Christian is able to participate in the mission-anointing of Christ. The Spirit is both "*Gabe und Aufgabe*," gift and task. The Spirit, Who anoints Christ with this mission, and Who anoints the Christian and provides him with the "equipment" for the mission, is the Spirit Who is inwardly communicated, enabling the Christian to gaze interiorly at God with uncovered face, and grow "from glory to glory."[107] This inner dynamic of growth, provided by the communication of the Spirit, then exercises itself outwardly in the mission task of the Christian, hence the "missionary" explanation of the other parts of the body in Cyril. The communication of the Spirit for "now", the association of the Christian with Christ in His missionary task, is Cyril's main emphasis at this point, and so this is where he places the Pauline matter for explaining the anointing of the forehead. The belonging to Christ through renunciation and commitment, and the concomitant mystical association with the inner life of Christ as a sign of the heavenly life of confidence, of full right in the heavenly city, of seeing God face-to-face, is Theodore's main emphasis, and so it is with the *sphragis* anointing and not the post-baptismal anointing that he puts the same Pauline material.

Despite these differences of typological emphasis, and the differences dictated by christological emphasis, as this comparison between Theodore's mystagogy of the *sphragis* anointing and Cyril's mystagogy of the post-baptismal anointing show, the mystagogy of Theodore in the post-baptismal anointing is fundamentally similar to that of Cyril, as the texts of Theodore show. It is just that for the reasons just given Theodore does not develop the mystagogy of the forehead anointing as does Cyril. This, however, does not alter the other similarities. That is, the anointing is associated with a particular gift of the Holy Spirit, it implies Messianic mission in association with Christ (though this aspect is emphasized in much greater detail in Cyril than in Theodore), it is a present help, and so "functional" for the Christian life now, but because it

[107]See above, p. 125.

is "first-fruits" it is already anchored in its final fulfilment in the world to come, the eschaton.

C. Ambrose

As has been indicated in the Synopsis of Ceremonies,[108] in the liturgy upon which Ambrose comments there is an anointing on the head with *myron* immediately after the baptismal bath. Then the washing of feet intervenes, and this is followed, after the reception of the white garment, by the ceremony of "consignation," which may or may not have involved an anointing. Each of these ceremonies represents a different mystagogical complex and so each must be considered separately.

1. *The Post-baptismal Anointing*

Ambrose's mystagogical interpretation of the ceremony in which the bishop spreads *myron* on the head of the newly baptized, reciting the liturgical formula[109] is two-fold.

a. *Eternal Life versus Temporal Life*

The Anointing Formula

As the formula itself indicates with the words, "He Himself [God] will anoint you unto everlasting life (ipse te unguet in vitam aeternam),"[110] there is contained in this anointing the ancient tradition of associating anointing with resurrection. In Jewish apocalyptic literature the symbol of the life-giving oil of the tree of Paradise, which will again be given to mankind at the end of time, lends itself to an interpretation of the anointing as a participation in this future resurrection, and this symbolism has been used in interpreting the baptismal anointing.[111] This tradition, which is reflected in the accompanying formula for the anointing, is followed by Ambrose in his mystagogical interpretation of the ceremony. He tells the baptized that they are anointed for eternal life, contrasting

[108] See above, pp. 353-359.
[109] See above, p.353.
[110] *Idem.*
[111] See Kretschmar, *op. cit.,* p. 27 and n. 35, 35a.

eternal life with temporal life, instructing them that even temporal death is to be preferred to the loss of this eternal life, should some enemy perchance wish to destroy their faith: "See where you have been anointed. Into eternal life, he [the bishop] says . . . Do not choose that in which you have not been anointed, but choose that in which you have been anointed in such a way that you prefer eternal life to temporal life."[112]

Anointing on the Head

The fact that the myron is *spread* on the head of the baptized is a sign indicating regeneration. Ambrose grounds this interpretation, which he treats in the context of a discussion of regeneration, where immersion in the font symbolized death, and emersion symbolized resurrection, with a sentence adapted from *Qo.* 2:14: "The sense of the wise man is in his head (sensus sapientis in capite ejus?)"[113] The anointing of the head indicates the grace which comes to the seat of natural wisdom. This natural wisdom will atrophy without the help of grace, but given the grace, then a more perfect form of life is begun, or a "regeneration:" "for wisdom without grace grows cold. But when wisdom has received grace, then its work begins to be perfect. This is called regeneration."[114]

The Odor of the Chrism

Ambrose also makes the association between this anointing and the resurrection by using a picture drawn from *Sg.*, where he compares the fragrant smell of the ointment with the odor of the Resurrection: "This is the ointment of which Solomon also says: 'Thy name is as ointment poured out; therefore young maidens have loved thee and drawn thee.'[115] How many souls renewed today have loved Thee, Lord Jesus, saying,

[112] *Sacr.* II.24 (Botte, *SC* 25bis, 88; tr. Deferrari, *FC* 44, 287-288): "Vide ubi unctus es: in vitam, inquit, aeternam . . . Noli eligere illud in quo non es unctus, sed illud elige in quo unctus es, ut vitam aeternam vitae praeferas temporali."

[113] *Sacr.* III.1 (Botte, *SC* 25bis, 90; tr. Deferrari, *FC* 44, 289). The quotation in its original biblical form occurs also in *Myst.* 30 (*ibid.*, 172; tr. *ibid.*, 16). Here "oculi" is used instead of "sensus."

[114] *Sacr.* III.1 (Botte, *SC* 25 bis, 90; tr. Deferrari, *FC* 44, 289): "Friget enim sapientia sine gratia, sed ubi gratiam acceperit sapientia, tunc opus ejus incipit esse perfectum. Heac regeneratio dicitur."

[115] *Sg.* 1:2.

'Draw us after Thee; let us run after the odor of Thy garments,'[116] that they may drink in the odor of the resurrection."[117] In this sense, the ointment itself, in its fragrance, is a symbol of the resurrected Christ. In His association with the baptized, symbolized by the anointing with the perfumed ointment, He is drawing them from temporal life into eternal life.

b. *Priestly and Regal People*

A second, and no less ancient line of tradition is followed by Ambrose in his interpretation of this anointing after baptism, the interpretation of the anointing as a sacerdotal and regal anointing.[118] Coupling the idea of the anointing of Aaron and the priestly character of the people of Israel with 1 *P.* 2:9, Ambrose reminds his hearers that this anointing was an anointing symbolizing participation in the kingdom of God and in the priesthood: "What is the people itself, if not a priestly people? To these it was said, 'But you are a chosen generation, a royal priesthood, a holy nation,' as the apostle Peter says.[119] Everyone is anointed into the priesthood, into the kingdom, but the spiritual kingdom is also the spiritual priesthood."[120] This same thought, together with specific mention of Aaron occurs in *De Mysteriis*, 30.

Summary

Although certain echoes appear in Ambrose's interpretation of this anointing which remind one of Cyril's material in inter-

[116] *Sg.* 1:3.

[117] *Myst.* 29 (Botte, *SC* 25bis, 172; tr. Deferrari, *FC* 44, 16): "Hoc est unguentum de quo et Salomon ait: 'Unguentum exinanitum est nomen tuum, propterea adulescentulae dilexerunt te et adtraxerunt te.' Quantae hodie renovatae animae dilexerunt te, domine Jesu, dicentes: 'Adtrahe nos post te, in odorem vestimentorum tuorum curremus,' ut odorem resurrectionis haurirent."

[118] See Kretschmar, *op. cit.,* pp. 27-30.

[119] 1 *P.* 2:9.

[120] *Sacr.* IV.3 (Botte, *SC* 25bis, 102; tr. Deferrari, *FC* 44, 298): "Populus ipse qui est nisi sacerdotalis? Quibis dictum est: 'Vos autem genus electum, regale sacerdotium, gens sancta,' ut ait apostolus Petrus? Unusquisque unguitur in sacerdotium, unguitur in regnum, sed spiritale regnum est et sacerdotium spiritale."

preting the post-baptismal anointing, it is quite clear that Ambrose is using ancient traditional material *without* working it into the framework of an anointing as a particular communication of the Holy Spirit, as Cyril and Theodore actually do. Using traditional material, Ambrose attaches symbolic interpretation to a ceremony which was probably originally connected with ancient bathing customs of anointing after the bath.[121] This anointing is a symbol of what has taken place in the baptismal bath. It brings out the fact of the association of the neophite through that bath with the resurrected Christ. The material of the mystagogy, the formula reflecting the Paradise tree tradition, the fact of the anointing on the head indicating regeneration, and the fact of the odor of the chrism representing the attraction of the risen Jesus: the entire mystagogical material shows that this anointing is seen as a symbolic unfolding of what took place in the act of baptism, and it is not material brought into conjunction with the Holy Spirit.

The very fact that both Ambrose and Cyril use the image of *OT* anointing, as in the mention of Aaron, in different ways, shows the different directions of their purpose.[122] For Cyril, this *OT* image comes to fulfilment precisely because the anointing is more than symbolic anointing, but, as he says, a true anointing of the Holy Spirit. While Ambrose shows through his Petrine text that the *OT* anointing finds a fulfilment in the *NT* people of God, the holy nation, the royal priesthood, still the fulfilment is not seen precisely as the operation of the Holy Spirit communicated through the anointing, but rather as a symbol of the result of baptism in general, or the baptismal act specifically. The mystagogy of each father serves a different purpose.

Therefore, what Ambrose sees in this ceremony of anointing after baptism is not what Cyril and Theodore see, what would *now* be called an interpretation of the anointing as "confirmation," but rather the presentation of a mystagogical interpretation of this anointing which more fully unfolds the meaning of the baptismal bath.

[121]See Stenzel, *op. cit.,* p. 128.
[122]See above, pp. 367-369, 390.

2. *The Consignation*

This is not the case, however, when Ambrose comes to interpret the "consignation," that ceremony which takes place (with or without an anointing is uncertain) after the foot-washing and the reception of the white garment.[123] Ambrose's mystagogical interpretation of this ceremony brings it into the same frame of reference which is found in both Cyril and Theodore, that is, into conjunction with a particular communication of the Holy Spirit. Ambrose signals his mystagogy of this ceremony by introducing it as a "spiritual seal (spiritale signaculum)," which is first described in general terms as a perfecting of what was done in the font, "quia post fontem superest ut perfectio fiat."[124]

a. *The Communication of the Holy Spirit*

There is no doubt that this ceremony of the consignation is interpreted to be a particular outpouring of the Holy Spirit. In the Scripture reading which accompanies the ceremony[125] St. Paul reminds the faithful that God has anointed them and marked them with His seal and given them a pledge, the Spirit in their hearts. The text of *Is.* which also occurs,[126] probably as part of the liturgical formula,[127] mentions the sevenfold

[123] See above, pp. 353-354.

[124] *Sacr.* III.8 (Botte, *SC* 25bis, 96; tr. Deferrari, *FC* 44, 293). For Tertullian, the word "*signaculum*" means baptism. See *De pudic.* 9 (*CCL* 2, 1298); *De spect.* 4, 24 (*CCL* 1, 231, 248). For Cyprian, on the other hand, it means the gift of the Spirit. See *Epist.* 73.9 (*CSEL* 3.2, 785): "per nostram orationem ac manus impositionem spiritum sanctum consequantur et signaculo dominico consummentur." See also Dölger, *Sphragis,* pp. 173, 189.

[125] 2 *Co.* 1:21-22. *Sacr.* III.8 (Botte, *SC* 25bis, 96; tr. Deferrari, *FC* 44, 293) mentions the fact of a scripture reading; *Myst.* 42 (Botte, *SC* 25bis, 178; tr. Deferrari, *FC* 44, 20) specifies what the reading is. This reading contains essentially the same thought as 1 *Jn.* 2:20,27, two of the verses which form part of the reading which accompanies Cyril's catechesis. See above, p. 353.

[126] *Is.* 11:2.

[127] See above, p. 353.

gift of the Holy Spirit.[128] In his mystagogy Ambrose presents a discourse on these gifts[129] concluding with an allusion to *Ep.* 3:10 and a comment on the richness of God's wisdom, and the fact that it possesses a variety of gifts, as may be seen through the sevenfold gift of the Holy Spirit. Ambrose also says that there is "something special when you receive the spiritual seal,"[130] He also notes specifically that "at the invocation of the bishop the Holy Spirit is poured forth."[131]

b. *Christ and the Christian*

Christ Himself Seals

Ambrose is also concerned to link the communication of the Holy Spirit to the Christian with the idea of a conformity to Christ in greater degree than before. This christological concern, in the framework of an obvious concern for Trinitarian theology, emerges, for example, in the following passage. The context is a question of sacramental participation. Baptized in the name of the Trinity, although three Persons, there is one operation, one sanctifying action. At the same time, however, there are particular traits, which may be attributed to the different persons:

> How? It is God, Who anointed you and the Lord Who sealed you, and put the Spirit in your heart. Therefore you have received the Holy Spirit in your heart.[132] Take another example. As the Holy Spirit is in the heart, so also is Christ in the heart. How? You have this in the *Canticle of Canticles,* Christ saying to the Church: "Put me as a

[128]Cyril has used the same text of *Is.* in conjunction with his mystagogy of the anointing of the breast, and he worked it into his mystagogy much more elaborately. See above, pp. 374-375.

[129]*Sacr.* III.9-10 (Botte, *SC* 25bis, 96, 98; tr. Deferrari, *FC* 44, 293).

[130]*Sacr.* VI:8 (*Ibid.,* 140; tr. *ibid.,* 321): "deinde quasi speciale quando accipis spiritale signaculum."

[131]*Sacr.* III.8 (*Ibid.,* 96; tr. *ibid.,* 293): "ad invocationem sacerdotis, Spiritus Sanctus infunditur."

[132]*Cf.* 2 *Co.* 1:21-22.

> seal (signaculum) upon thy heart, as a seal (signaculum) upon thy arm."[133]

Ambrose is here attempting to show the relationship of Christ and the Christian *apropos* of the consignation, the coming of the Holy Spirit. He says, actually, that the liturgical action of the consignation is actually an action of Christ Himself. "The Lord sealed you (signavit te Dominus)." And in this action of sealing you, He put the Holy Spirit in the hearts of the baptized. This Spirit, however, is the Spirit of Christ Himself. "As the Holy Spirit is in the heart, so also is Christ in the heart." And then follows the Ambrosian explanation of how this is so, the reference to the *Canticle of Canticles,* that in the sacramental action a mystical union occurs between Christ and the Christian.

Ambrose's remarks occur under a somewhat apologetic influence, because he is obviously concerned with the doctrine of the Trinity, and the relationship of the activity of the Three Persons in the sacramental action.[134]

The Sign of the Cross

Ambrose further explains the relationship of Christ and the Christian by proceeding from the liturgical action of the sign of the cross, which apparently was the way the consignation was performed. His mystagogy refers the action of the sealing back not to the Jordan and anointing, but to the crucifixion and resurrection, hence to the baptismal act:

> Therefore God anointed you, Christ sealed you. How? Because you were sealed unto the form of the cross itself,

[133] *Sg.* 8:6. *Sacr.* VI.6 (Botte, *SC* 25bis, 140; tr. Deferrari, *FC* 44, 320): "Quomodo? Deus, qui te unxit et signavit te Dominus, et posuit spiritum sanctum in corde tuo. Accepisti ergo spiritum sanctum in corde tuo. Accipe aliud, quia quemadmodum sanctus spiritus in corde, ita etiam Christus in corde. Quomodo? Habes hoc in Canticis canticorum, Christum dicentem ad ecclesiam: 'Pone me sicut signaculum in corde tuo, sicut signaculum in bracchiis tuis.' "

[134] Several paragraphs later, Ambrose specifically mentions the Arians, showing his preoccupation with this problem in this section of the mystagogy: "The Arians think that they detract from the Holy Spirit, if they call the Spirit Paraclete." *Sacr.* VI.10 (Botte, *SC* 25bis, 142; tr. Deferrari, *FC* 44, 321): "Arriani putant se derogare sancto spiritui si dicant illum spiritum paraclitum."

> unto His passion. You have received the seal unto His likeness, that you may rise again unto His form, may live unto His figure, who was crucified to sin and liveth to God. And your old man is dipped in the font, was crucified to sin, but arose again to God.[135]

By referring in his mystagogy of the consignation as a conformity to Christ in greater degree than before back to the baptismal action, and its association with the crucifixion and the resurrection, by means of reference to the fact that the "sealing" is a sealing with a sign of the cross, Ambrose, while emphasizing the action as a conformity to Christ in a special way, is also able to take care of his concern to show the unity of Trinitarian activity in the whole of the Initiation, and to show that the community of the Holy Spirit is not something totally separate from the act of baptism. The very baptismal formula indicates a communication of the Holy Spirit in the water bath. Further, if Ambrose were to divide the bath of water as the forgiveness of sins, and the "sealing" as the communication of the Spirit – such a division would contravene completely his argumentation about the unity of Trinitarian activity in the *whole* of baptism. With this particular mystagogy, of Christ's special relationship in the consignation, yet through the idea of the sign of the cross related back to the baptismal act, Ambrose is able to manage his anti-Arian concern for the unity of Trinitarian action, while at the same time showing the particularity of the consignation.

It is, then, Christ who "seals" the newly baptized, and the Spirit which is communicated is the Spirit, but seen as the fruit of the salvific work of Jesus on the cross, because the sign of this sealing is the sign of the cross. It is a sealing into the new life of the Spirit, revealed through the crucifixion and

[135] *Sacr.* VI.7 (Botte, *SC* 25bis, 140; tr. Deferrari, *FC* 44, 320-321): "Ergo unxit te deus, signavit te Christus. Quomodo? Quia ad crucis ipsius signatus es formam, ad illius passionem. Accepisti signaculum ad illius similitudinem, ut ad ipsius formam resurgas, ad ipsius vivas figuram qui peccato crucifixus est et deo vivit. Et tuus homo vetus in fonte demersus peccato crucifixus est, sed deo resurrexit."

resurrection of Jesus, and now living in the baptized, who is thereby conformed to this new life of Christ Who lives for God, "that you may live unto His figure, Who was crucified to sin and liveth to God."[136]

Despite this necessary emphasis on the unity in the initiation rite, based on the actual salvific events of Christ's life, and required by Ambrose's defense of the unity of Trinitarian activity, he concludes by emphasizing as well that the sealing is something particular and distinct:

> You find, then, elsewhere, something particular: it is God, Who has called you[137] then in respect to baptism, it is with Christ that you have been crucified in a special way;[138] then also there is something special when you receive the spiritual seal. You see that there is a distinction of persons, but that the whole mystery of the Trinity is connected.[139]

Reminding his hearers of a recent liturgical reading, on the diversity of graces, but the one Spirit[140] Ambrose admonishes his hearers to bear in mind particularly: ". . . that the spirit of God is the Spirit of Christ. And hold to this: He is the Holy Spirit; He is the Spirit of God; He is the Spirit of Christ; He is the Paraclete Spirit."[141]

Essay: "Confirmation"

At the start of this section which treats of the mystagogical interpretation of the post-baptismal anointing, it has been stated that it goes beyond the scope of this work to enter the

[136] *Idem. Cf. Rm.* 6:4,6,10.

[137] *Cf. Ga.* 1:6.

[138] *Cf. Rm.* 6:6.

[139] *Sacr.* VI.8 (Botte, *SC* 25bis, 140; tr. Deferrari, *FC* 44, 321): "Deinde habes alibi speciale quod te vocaverit deus, in baptismate autem quasi specialiter concrucifigeris Christo, deinde quasi speciale, quando accipis spiritale signaculum, vides distinctionem personarum esse, sed conexum omne mysterium trinitatis."

[140] 1 *Co.* 12:4-6.

[141] *Sacr.* VI.9 (Botte, *SC* 25bis, 142; tr. Deferrari, *FC* 44, 321): ". . . quia spiritus dei spiritus Christi est. Et illud tenete ipsum esse spiritum sanctum, ipsum spiritum dei, ipsum spiritum Christi, ipsum spiritum paraclitum."

problematic area of the difference between the sacraments of "baptism" and "confirmation."[142] However, it will be of value to draw together the main points of the mystagogical study just made of the post-baptismal anointing, and to place its results over against the problematic of "confirmation." In this way, the mystagogical interpretation which we have analyzed of Cyril, Theodore and Ambrose (and indirectly of Chrysostom), can shed some light on the understanding of this problem, and underscore an approach to the question which is a dimension sometimes insufficiently regarded in sacramental theology.

In the mystagogical interpretation of the post-baptismal anointing in Cyril, Theodore and Ambrose (the consignation), we find an awareness that this ceremony of anointing (Cyril and Theodore) or consignation, with or without anointing (Ambrose) is associated with a very particular step in the process of Christian Initiation. In the case of *Ambrose,* this step, at least in the particular stage of liturgical development in his church, corresponds to the traditional Christian communication of the Holy Spirit known in current terminology as "confirmation." In the case of *Cyril,* despite his highly developed mystagogy of the communication of the Holy Spirit in the anointing, a mystagogical development due strongly to the development of the theology of the Holy Spirit at the time,[143]

[142] See above, pp. 358-359.

[143] The fact that Chrysostom and the Syrian baptismal tradition at this time has no post-baptismal anointing, while Theodore mentions one, as do the *Apostolic Constitutions* though without clearly indicating its significance (see above, n. 14, p.352), reflects the development in Syrian baptismal liturgy and theology in the last part of the fourth century, in the time, indeed, between Chrysostom and Theodore in their mystagogy. The greater emphasis on clarifying the explicit role of the Holy Spirit in the liturgy of Christian Initiation reflected the controversies of the First Council of Constantinople (381) about His divinity and personality. (Fourth century development on the theology of the Holy Spirit and its effect on the liturgy in both East and West is treated by J. Quasten in "The Blessing of the Baptismal Font in the Syrian Rite of the Fourth Century," *Theological Studies* 7 (1946) 309-313). Quasten concludes in his study of the consecration of the waters of the baptismal font: "Here as elsewhere the third Person of the Trinity becomes more and more prominent. The theology of the *Logos,* which attributed the incarnation, the inspiration of the prophets, and the consecration of the eucharistic bread,

one cannot absolutely say that Cyril is maintaining that this ceremony of anointing is the "sacramental sign" exclusively in his liturgy of what is now called "confirmation." Because of Cyril's almost ingenious use of traditional materials associated with the communication of the Holy Spirit, one is tempted to say this anointing is "confirmation." But this would be an unjustifiable application of later thought categories to more undifferentiated beliefs of earlier times, and can only result finally in an indiscriminate polemic or theological dead-end. That Cyril uses the ceremony of the anointing as an apt vehicle for a mystagogical interpretation of the fact that the Holy Spirit is communicated in Christian Initiation is clear, and his motive is clear: greater emphasis on the role of the Holy Spirit, and its meaning in Christian Initiation. Despite Cyril's "mystagogical" success here, however, one cannot say this anointing which Cyril the mystagogue treats so effectively, is the "sacramental sign" of "confirmation." The careful analysis of the texts of Cyril which we have tried to present lead more and more to the conclusion that Cyril was not writing with such later theological thought patterns in mind, and that he was not really treating the question in a way in which later theology puts it. Therefore, one must not come to Cyril's mystagogy to find an answer to the question of where was the *locus,* the "sacramental sign" of "confirmation". The communication of the Holy Spirit takes place in Christian Initiation.

---

as well as the sanctification of the baptismal font to Christ, now gives way to the theology of the Holy Spirit." (*Ibid.,* p. 312).

From our comparative study of the mystagogy of the post-baptismal anointing in Cyril and the consignation in Ambrose, we see how strongly Ambrose reflects the *Logos* theology in his explanation of how it is Christ Who seals the candidate with the seal of the cross, yet at the same time with an obvious concern to do justice to the particular action of the Holy Spirit. (See above, pp. 434-436). Cyril's emphasis, on the other hand, on the epiclesis of the *myron,* the symbolism of the anointing, the placing of the christological aspects of the ceremony totally under the picutre of the "anointing with the Holy Spirit" of Christ in the Jordan, and the concern for the apostolic mission of the anointed: all of this manifests an almost complete preocupation with the theology and the role of the Holy Spirit.

The precise question of later sacramental theology of "where specifically as visible sign" does not really emerge as a concern in Cyril, and cannot be pursued further without misunderstanding the modality of his instructions. When Cyril says that the neophyte received the Holy Spirit in the anointing after baptism, he is thinking "inclusively" and not "exclusively," for in the Eastern fathers, the communication of the Holy Spirit is seen in the totality of Christian Initiation. Hence, their thinking does not admit of too much application of a more linear Western mode of thought.[144]

Now the statements of *Theodore,* that the Holy Spirit is communicated in the anointing after baptism, clear though they seem at first glance, cannot be totally convincing as proof that he considered this anointing the *locus* for what is now

[144] Speaking of the relationship of baptism to the consignation in Ambrose, Kretschmar sums up this phenomenon well: "Already by the fourth century we encounter a peculiarity of the Latin baptismal theology as opposed to the Easterners, a peculiarity which will determine the way of baptism in the West in the following centuries. Among the Greeks the capacity grew ever stronger to view the various rites of baptism looking out from a central point as it were, the baptismal bath, as the unfolding of the one baptism according to the laws of the divine economy of salvation. Ambrose is able to understand the individual partial actions of the baptism only as divinely established rites which follow one another in consecutive order and whose respective function must be kept separate from one another. The circle, or even the ellipse, corresponds to the structure of the Greek thinking; the straight line corresponds to the structure of the Latin thinking. For this reason among the Greeks baptism in the fullness of its rites remained a unity; among the Latins it could come back to a unity only when the consignation had finally separated itself from the baptism and become a "sacrament" of its own. (Wir stossen hier im vierten Jahrhundert auf eine Besonderheit der lateinischen Tauftheologie gegenüber den Orientalien, die den Weg der Taufe in Westen in den folgenden Jahrhunderten bestimmen wird. Die Griechen lernten es immer stärker, die mancherlei Riten der Taufe gleichsam von einer Mitte aus zu sehen, dem Taufbad, als Entfaltung der einen Taufe nach den Gesetzen der göttlichen Heilsökonomie. Ambrosius kann die einzelnen Teilhandlungen der Taufe nur als aufeinander folgende gottgesetzte Riten verstehen, deren Funktion voneinander abgehoben werden muss. Der Struktur des griechischen Denkens entspricht der Kreis oder auch die Ellipse, dem des lateinischen die Gerade. Die Taufe ist bei den Griechen deshalb in der Fülle ihrer Riten eine Einheit geblieben; bei den Lateinern konnte sie erst wieder zur Einheit werden, als die Konsignation schliesslich sich als eigenes 'Sakrament' von der Taufe gelöst hatte)." Kretschmar, *op. cit.,* p. 236.

known as "confirmation" either. Hesitation in regard to Theodore's actual intention is based on the fact that the Syrian liturgical tradition at this time knows no post-baptismal anointing.[145] Given this salient fact, it is possible that the anointing which Theodore calls a communication of the Holy Spirit could be rather a *symbol* coupled with a mystagogical explanation, of the gift of the Spirit which is included in the baptismal act itself, a mystagogical emphasis and symbolism which would reflect the growth in emphasis on the theology of the Holy Spirit at this time.[146]

There is, *first,* the fact of the unusual brevity in Theodore's mystagogy of the post-baptismal anointing. His single condensed paragraph,[147] as opposed, for example, to Cyril's full development, almost gives the impression of a hasty digest inserted at this point, designed, perhaps, to support a changing tradition which previously had no anointing at this point in the ceremony, but which now had one in view of the changed emphasis on the explicit action of the Holy Spirit in Initiation. Thus, certain traditional materials in regard to the communication of the Spirit in Christian Initiation are brought to bear *via* mystagogy on this ceremony in condensed form. When one compares, as we have done, Cyril's mystagogy of the anointing of the forehead in the post-baptismal anointing with that of Theodore in the prebaptismal *sphragis* anointing,[148] seeing how identical material was taken by Cyril and worked into a mystagogy of the communication of the Spirit and by Theodore where it remained in a much different framework, one becomes aware of the changes taking place in the liturgical tradition at this juncture.

Second, there is the pronounced emphasis in the directives of Theodore's liturgy on the laying on of the bishop's hand in the baptismal act itself.[149] coupled with the fact that he de-

[145] See above, n. 14, p. 352.
[146] See above, n. 143, p. 397.
[147] See above, pp. 380-381.
[148] See above, pp. 382-388.
[149] See above, ch. 2, pp. 147-148.

votes much more time and traditional material to describing the action of the Holy Spirit in the baptismal act itself than in his few brief remarks on the anointing after baptism. A case in point is the following passage which comes in the context of Theodore's explanation of what the baptismal bath means, and not specifically the anointing after the baptismal bath:

> If you say that the greatness of the symbols and of the signs is in the visible water, it would be an unimportant affair, as this has already happened before, but because this second birth, which you now receive sacramentally as the symbol of an earnest, is accomplished by the action of the Holy Spirit, great is the Sacrament which is performed and awe-inspiring and worthy of credence is the virtue of the symbols, which will also without doubt grant us to participate in the future benefits. We expect to delight in these benefits, because as an earnest of them we have received the grace of the Holy Spirit, from which we have now obtained also the gift of performing this Sacrament. This is the reason why blessed Paul said: "In whom we believed and were sealed with the Holy Spirit of promise which is the earnest of our inheritance to the praise of His glory."[150] He calls here the "Spirit of promise" the grace which is vouchsafed unto us by the Holy Spirit, as we receive it in the promise of future benefits, and he calls it "the earnest of our inheritance" because it is from it that we become partakers of those future benefits. He said therefore in another passage: "God has established us with you in Christ and anointed us and sealed us and given the earnest of His Spirit in our hearts."[151] And again he said in another passage: "And not only they but ourselves also which have the firstfruits of the Spirit, even we ourselves groan within ourselves waiting for the adoption of children unto the redemption of our bodies."[152] He uses the words "first-fruits of the Spirit which we have here" to imply that, when we shall dwell in the joy of the realities, we

[150] *Ep.* 1:13-14.
[151] 2 *Co.* 1:21-22.
[152] *Rm.* 8:23.

> shall receive *all* the grace, and by the words "we wait for the adoption of children, unto the redemption of our bodies" he shows that here we only receive the symbol of the adoption of children, but that hereafter, having been born afresh, risen from the dead, become also immortal and incorruptible, and received complete abolition of pains from our bodies, we shall receive the real adoption. He clearly calls "redemption of our bodies" the assumption of incorruptibility and immortality, because it is through these things that a complete abolition of calamities from our bodies is affected. The power of holy baptism consists in this: it implants in you the hope of future benefits, enables you to participate in the things which we expect, and by means of the symbols and signs of the future good things, it informs you with the gift of the Holy Spirit,[153] the first-fruits of whom you receive when you are baptized.[154]

After this introduction , Theodore then begins his exposition of the steps of baptism, beginning with the removal of the garments. It is clear from this passage, with its use of such traditional Pauline material concerned with the effect of the Holy Spirit, such as *Ep.* 1:13-14, 2 *Co.* 1:21-22; *Rm.* 8:23, that Theodore, despite the development which makes him devote particular attention to the post-baptismal anointing as communication of the Holy Spirit in another passage, sees the communication of the Holy Spirit in the baptismal liturgy taken as a whole. The passage 2 *Co.* 1:21-22, which Theodore uses here, is one used by Ambrose as part of the specific mystagogy of the consignation.[155] It is clear, then, that Theodore's mode of thinking is not "linear" but "circular." That is, he views the baptismal rite not so much as separated events on a linear plane, *e.g.*, baptismal bath and then anointing, with the corresponding and clearly divided mystagogical material, but rather as a totality, baptismal bath *and* anointing together. His

[153] *Cf. Idem.*

[154] *Bapt. Hom.* III.6-7 (Tonneau-Devreesse, *SeT* 145, 414, 416; tr. Mingana, *WS* VI, 52-54).

[155] See above, p. 392.

distribution of mystagogical material, then, is not as clearly delineated as is the case with Ambrose, for example, who represents not this Eastern "circular" mode of thinking, but the Western, "linear" mode.[156] In Ambrose there is the baptismal bath and its corresponding mystagogy of burial and rising with Christ and second birth, then, consignation, a "special" gift of the Spirit, with its corresponding mystagogy. While Theodore does manifest this same division, and devotes a special small section to the post-baptismal anointing as communication of the Spirit[157] still, just as much and more traditional material on the communication of the Holy Spirit is treated in such a way as to refer not exclusively to the anointing, but to the totality of the baptismal bath *and* anointing taken together. Thus, if no post-baptismal anointing were present in Theodore's liturgy, his mystagogy on the coming of the Holy Spirit could without contradiction apply equally to the baptismal bath, or rather, even to the entire complex of initiation rites taken as a whole. The fact of this doubling of materials, that is, the mystagogy of the baptismal act as the communication of the Holy Spirit, and then, in condensed form, a particular section in which this mystagogy is applied specifically to the post-baptismal anointing, confirms this feeling that the presence of a post-baptismal anointing in Theodore reflects a change in the normal Syrian tradition, which had no post-baptismal anointing, as we see, for example, in Chrysostom's *Baptismal Instructions.* In this case, Theodore is providing a mystagogy for this anointing. Yet, this mystagogy has not yet become so developed that it is separated entirely from the previous supposition under which there was no post-baptismal anointing at all, and where the mystagogy of the communication of the Spirit was included in the consideration of the baptismal bath itself, as it actually still is in Theodore, and, as a matter of fact, in Chrysostom.

[156]See above, n. 144, p. 399.
[157]See above, pp. 380-381.

Cyril and Ambrose have a clearly delineated mystagogy of the communication of the Holy Spirit applied to the post-baptismal anointing (or, in Ambrose, consignation), but for different reasons. Ambrose reflects the Western "linear" tradition (and probably, as far as the reflection of the two separate steps of Initiation is concerned, the more ancient tradition. In other words, Ambrose has found the right "ceremony" for his mystagogy of the special communication of the Holy Spirit.)[158] Cyril's clear separation of baptismal bath and post-baptismal anointing in his *Mystagogical Catecheses* on the liturgy is a reflection of his concern with the growing emphasis on the theology and working in the liturgy of the Holy Spirit. He, of the four fathers, develops this mystagogy in the most detailed and unified form, and proceeds to attach it to the post-baptismal anointing, for the reasons of the obvious suitability of this ceremony for developing a mystagogy of the communication of the Holy Spirit under the emphasis of Christian apostleship in the Initiation.

Third, the very fact that Chrysostom has apparently no post-baptismal anointing at all, reflecting the Syrian tradition, shows that the *locus* of the traditional communication of the Holy Spirit seen as "sacrament of confirmation" could well be elsewhere than in the post-baptismal anointing, apt though this anointing is *mystagogically,* as Cyril amply demonstrates, for teaching the doctrine of the Holy Spirit in regard to Christian Initiation. Chrysostom himself says that the Holy Spirit is communicated in the baptismal act itself: "through the words and hands of the priest (bishop) the Holy Spirit descends upon you."[159]

[158] The fact that Ambrose must constantly refer the consignation back to the baptismal act does not detract from this linear presentation of baptism in the death and burial of Christ and then consignation with the Spirit. The emphasis is due rather to the pressure of combatting Arianism.

[159] *Stav.* 2.25 (See above, ch. 2, p. 155). By this observation we do not mean to assert that the prominence which Chrysostom gives to the imposition of hand should lead one too hastily to the conclusion that here is the rite of "confirmation." J. Lécuyer ("San Juan Crisóstomo y la Confirmación" in *Orbis Catholicus* (Herder, Barcelona), November, 1958, pp. 385-387) seems to fall into this error when he

For these three reasons, then one must also hesitate to say that the post-baptismal anointing in Theodore is the *locus* of the "sacrament of confirmation."

---

tentatively infers that Chrysostom is thinking of two distinct sacramental actions going on simultaneously, baptism and confirmation. This is a perspective of sacramental theology representing a Western mentality which fails to take into account what we have already described, namely the circular mode of Greek thinking which sees the Initiation as a totality, not as individually separated ceremonies on a linear plane. (See above, n. 144, p. 399). Of course, Chrysostom does see the communication of the Holy Spirit associated with the imposition of hand. See as well as *Stav.* 2.25 also *Stav.* 2.10 (Wenger, *SC* 50, 138; tr. Harkins, *ACW* 31, 47): "It is the grace of the Spirit which . . . touches your head together with the hand of the priest." (Text, see above, ch. 2, n. 13, p. 147). But it is also clear the he, like Theodore, sees the Holy Spirit operative in all the phases of Christian Initiation, and not exclusively in the imposition of hand. Moreover, another of Chrysostom's reasons for associating the imposition of hand with the work of the Holy Spirit was the growing acuteness in his time of the controversy about the validity of baptism by sinful ministers, (See Finn, *op. cit.*, pp. 176-177). Presumably what H. Benedict Green must mean in his article, when he concludes that Chrysostom's liturgy lacked the rite of confirmation altogether ("The Significance of the Pre-Baptismal Seal in St. John Chrysostom," *SP*, Vol. VI, Part IV, TU 81 (Berlin, (1962), p. 90), is not that something essential was lacking in Christian Initiation according to the Syrian liturgy, but rather that Chrysostom's liturgy lacks what in some other liturgies (like that of Ambrose, or the development which seems to be taking place in Theodore) is a clearly delineated post-baptismal gift of the Holy Spirit. Even without this clearly delineated post-baptismal gift, one need not have recourse, as Lécuyer does, to the laying on of hand in Chrysostom's liturgy as the welcome missing link of "confirmation." The communication of the Spirit is seen by Chrysostom in the initiation as a whole. A good example of how the profile of the special action of the Holy Spirit, in conjunction with the post-baptismal anointing, which is beginning to emerge in Theodore, and has gained clear profile in Cyril, both of whom use the Jordan scene in their mystagogy, and has in Chrysostom not yet severed itself from the baptismal act viewed as a whole, is seen in *P.K.* 3.3 (*VGS*, 169-170; tr. Harkins, *ACW* 31, 164-165, no. 13): "And what happened in the case of our Master's body also happens in the case of your own. Although John appeared to be holding His body by the head, it was the divine Word which led His body down into the streams of Jordan and baptized Him. The Master's body was baptized by the Word, and by the voice of His Father from heaven which said: 'This is my beloved Son,' (*Mt.* 3:17) and by manifestation of the Holy Spirit which descended upon Him. This also happens in the case of your body. The baptism is given in the name of the Father and of the Son and of the Holy Spirit. There, John the Baptist told us, for our instruction, that man does not baptize us, but God; 'There comes after me one who is mightier than I, and I am not worthy to loose the strap of His sandal. He will baptize you with the Holy Spirit and with fire.'" (Καὶ ὅπερ ἐπὶ τῆς δεσποτικῆς *ἐγένετο σαρκός, τοῦτο καὶ ἐπὶ τῆς ἡμετέρας γί-νεται· καθάπερ γὰρ ἐκείνην τῷ μὲν δοκεῖν Ἰωάννης ἀπὸ τῆς κεφαλῆς κατεῖχεν,*

When Cyril quotes 1 *Jn.* 2:20-28 to the effect that Christians have an anointing from the Holy One and then proceeds to link this picture to the post-baptismal anointing as he finds it in his liturgy, it does not prove that 1 *Jn.* was referring to just this ceremony as being the liturgical *locus* where that "anointing" took place at all times and in all liturgies. 1 *Jn.* is merely stating that Christians received the Holy Spirit in their Initiation, and using the biblical image of an anointing to explain this. From this one could not even conclude that an *anointing* is indispensable to the sacramental communication of the Holy Spirit, since the image in 1 *Jn.* is not necessarily the description of a liturgical action, but rather a biblical image which aptly and traditionally describes the coming of the Holy Spirit. What Cyril the mystagogue is doing is using 1 *Jn.* for his purposes, and the text is most apposite for the liturgical ceremony as he finds it, which is an anointing in physical fact, and it fits in with his entire mystagogy of oil, with the epiclesis theology and the growing emphasis on the theology of the Holy Spirit as opposed to *Logos* theology, and with the entire biblical imagery of anointing, which then becomes for Cyril enormously suitable for building a coherent mystagogy. The very fact that Ambrose can construct a mystagogy of the consignation, making do entirely without any reference whatever to the use of oil, and this mystagogy serves the same liturgical

---

ὁ δὲ θεὸς λόγος εἰς τὰ Ἰορδάνεια ῥεῖθρα κατῆγε καὶ ἐβάπτιζε καὶ ἄνωθεν ἡ πατρικὴ φωνὴ λέγουσα, "οὗτός ἐστὶν ὁ υἱός μου ὁ ἀγαπητός", οὕτω καὶ τὸ πνεῦμα τὸ ἅγιον διὰ τῆς ἐπιφοιτήσεως· τοῦτο καὶ ἐπὶ τῆς σῆς γίνεται σαρκός· εἰς γὰρ ὄνομα πατρὸς καὶ υἱοῦ καὶ ἁγίου πνεύματος τὸ βάπτισμα γίνεται· διὰ τοῦτο καὶ Ἰωάννης ἔλεγε παιδεύων ἡμᾶς, ὅτι οὐκ ἄνθρωπος ἡμᾶς βαπτίζει, ἀλλ ̓ὁ θεός· "ὀπίσω μου ἔρχεται ὁ ἰσχυρότερός μου, οὗ οὐκ εἰμὶ ἱκανος λῦσαι τὸν ἱμάντα τοῦ ὑποδήματος αὐτοῦ. αὐτὸς ὑμᾶς βαπτισει ἐν πνεύματι ἁγίῳ καὶ πυρί).
Where Cyril particularly, and Theodore at least in inceptive form used the Jordan scene particularly in relation to the anointing, showing how the gift of the Spirit outfitted the Christian particularly for the mission similar to Christ's Messiahship, here the scene is less differentiated in its profile. The idea of the coming of the Holy Spirit is not reserved particularly to the anointing (which is not present in Chrysostom) but applies to the baptismal act. Notice also the emphasis on the *Logos* Theology, which in Theodore and Cyril particularly yields to the epiclesis theology of the Holy Spirit.

event as in Cyril, reveals the danger of coming to overhasty conclusions in sacramental theology without a more profound understanding of the function of mystagogy.

Our study of mystagogical materials, then, leads to an awareness of development and change in liturgical tradition, based frequently on theological emphasis, an emphasis which leads to different distribution of materials among the three fathers. This very study shows the danger of picking out single statements of the fathers, separated from the entire mystagogical development, a development which a comparative study as we are making here throws into clearer relief. If one uses isolated statements of different fathers, or fails to compare mystagogical development among several fathers, in order to confirm sacramental theology theories which belong to a more logical and schematic school tradition, one is in danger of misreading the fathers entirely. Precisely in this point of the post-baptismal anointing one sees such danger clearly. If one were to take the statement of Theodore in regard to the post-baptismal anointing as "proof" of the "sacrament of confirmation," without comparing within his work as a whole his mystagogy of the baptismal act, and externally with other fathers on the same ceremony, one might then be forced to the conclusion that Chrysostom either has no "confirmation" at all, since he has no post-baptismal anointing, or that there really must be an anointing which Chrysostom does not mention. Such a conclusion is quite unnecessary, however, when we see how different mystagogical materials are employed by different fathers to suit the historical exigencies, and how both Chrysostom and Theodore speak of the communication of the Spirit in the baptismal act itself.

Comparative Summary

The mystagogical interpretation of the post-baptismal anointing in Cyril and Theodore, and the consignation in Ambrose, in what concerns the theme of the *communication of the Holy*

Spirit may be thus compared. Both Cyril and Ambrose use *NT* material, Cyril a reading from 1 *Jn.*[160] and Ambrose a reading from 2 *Co.*[161] both of which speak specifically of the communication of the Holy Spirit. Cyril immediately takes up the emphasis on the idea of this communication as an *anointing* from the Holy One, and this will form the central focus of this entire mystagogy, the actual anointing of the candidate as well, the anointing of Jesus, the epiclesis theology of the *myron*, the specific effects of the several anointings, and final the eschatological symbolism of the anointing. Ambrose, on the other hand, does not place oil in the foreground at all as his mystagogical point of departure. One could not even prove from his mystagogy that oil was used in the ceremony of consignation. After connecting the *NT* reading with the consignation, he immediately adds a specification of what this communication of the Spirit means by using the text of *Is.*[162] describing the gifts of the Holy Spirit, and concludes with a reference to *Ep.*[163] to the effect that the sevenfold gift is a sign of the manifold variety of God's wisdom. This same text of *Is.* is taken by Cyril and used in connection with the anointing of the breast, mediated through the imagery of *Ep.*,[164] where the messianic armor is described. Cyril, then, distributes this text to suit the specific graphic framework of his anointing mystagogy, while Ambrose leaves it in the general framework of communication of the Spirit, without an application to the specific anointing. Ambrose also uses 1 *Co.*[165] to emphasize that this is a special gift, since his mystagogy will take him, far more than Cyril, back to the baptismal act to explain the relationship of the Holy Spirit to Christ in view of Arian difficulties. Cyril need not bother about this, and so he is able to use his materials in a freer way to work out the mystagogy of the communication of the Spirit, unencumbered by the necessity

[160] 2:20-28.
[161] 1:21-22.
[162] 11:2.
[163] 3:10.
[164] 6:14,11.
[165] 12:4-6.

of relating it to the baptismal act. Cyril obviously has a freer hand as mystagogue than Ambrose, a fact that reveals itself in his ability to use his materials in a more unified and even picturesque way.

Theodore does not use a *NT* text to provide a framework for this ceremony of anointing as a communication of the Spirit. As in so many other places in his mystagogical writing, he sees the action as a work of the entire Trinity.

The theme of how the communication of the Holy Spirit bring *Christ and the Christian* into closer union is worked out mystagogically in a different way by Cyril and by Ambrose. In presenting the communication of the Spirit in relationship to Christ, and to the Christian's conformity to Christ, Cyril particularly, Theodore to a lesser degree, emphasizes the anointing itself, and with his mimesis theology develops the whole from the picture of Christ in the Jordan, anointed after His baptism. This picture leads to the entire mystagogical interpretation of the anointing of the different senses under the aspect of the Christian's conformity to Christ in respect to his mission in the world. For this purpose Cyril has chosen scriptural texts all of which pertains to this mission. Theodore, faithful to his *leitmotiv* of seeing in the liturgical action the "symbol" of the world to come, places the emphasis not to much on the Spirit given to struggle with Christ in His Messianic mission, as on the anointing as sign of the coming resurrection, the Spirit being present as the "first-fruit" Who will protect the Christian on his way to incorruptibility. While adopting the texts and the mystagogy of the Jordan scene, and the mimesis theology as in Cyril, he does not go into the detailed anointing of the senses under the mission idea. Both Cyril and Theodore converge in the idea of the Spirit as "first-fruits." The mystagogy of the Christian's own union with Christ, in a mystical way, and also under the aspect of the world to come, had already been treated by Theodore in the *sphragis* anointing after the act of renunciation and commitment, where, as we have already noted, he used materials which Cyril uses to interpret the post-baptismal anointing.[166]

[166]See above, pp. 384-385.

The mimesis theology of Cyril, and his association of the baptized with Christ in the Jordan, coupled with his lengthy elaboration of the play on the words "Christ" and "Christian" and "chrism" had enabled him to present the communication of the Spirit as a closer association with Christ Himself in this way, showing how the Holy Spirit is the Spirit of Christ. The Christian becomes another Christ, and Cyril's particular mimesis mystagogy attempts to show how this takes place. The most striking difference between Ambrose and Cyril is the absence in the former of this mystagogy which uses the Jordan scene. Nor does Ambrose attempt the *sphragis* theology which Theodore had so richly developed, showing how the Christian, sealed, belongs to Christ, and so is associated with Christ's own "*parrhesia*," "confidence," and already lives with His heavenly life. He presents, rather, a mystical allusion the simplicity of which, in comparison to Cyril and Theodore, might at first glance be mistaken for superficiality. Ambrose says that the liturgical action of the consignation is an action of Christ Himself. "The Lord sealed you."[167] And in so doing He put the Holy Spirit in the hearts of the baptized. This Spirit, however, is the Spirit of Christ Himself. "As the Spirit is in your heart, so Christ is in your heart.[168] And then the Ambrosian explanation of how this is so, the reference to *Sg.*[169] that in the sacramental action a mystical union occurs between Christ and the Christian. This is somewhat differently expressed than by Cyril, who in showing the effects of the anointing had developed the traditional theology of the "*myron*."[170] Ambrose, in fact, comes to no different conclusion than the classic formulation of Cyril, that while the body is anointed, the soul is sanctified.

[167]See above, p. 393.

[168]*Idem.*

[169]8:6.

[170]See above, pp. 370-371. In this difference of approach between Cyril and Ambrose, one sees the different emphasis exerted on the mystagogy of the increasingly important epiclesis theology with the role of the Holy Spirit in the East and the more ancient Logos theology in the West. See above, n. 143, p. 397.

In further explaining the relationship to Christ and the Christian as a result of this spiritual sealing, Ambrose does not make the distinction which Cyril is able to make on the basis of his mimesis theology, that the baptismal act is a being buried with Christ and rising, while the anointing is a coming out of the Jordan with Christ, and receiving His anointing.[171] Ambrose's mystagogy at this point proceeds rather from the liturgical action of the sign of the cross, which apparently was the way the consignation was performed, rather than from the meaning of the anointing with oil. His mystagogy refers the action of the consignation back not to the Jordan and anointing, but to the crucifixion and resurrection, hence to the baptismal act, and so shows that the communication of the Holy Spirit is not something totally separate from the act of baptism. For Cyril's mystagogy, the mediating point to link the Christian with Christ in the communication of the Holy Spirit is the *anointing with oil*; for Ambrose's mystagogy it is the *sign of the cross.* The Spirit is the Spirit of Christ in Cyril *via* the oil and the Jordan scene and the mimesis theology of the baptismal ceremony of coming out of the font. The Spirit is the Spirit of Christ in Ambrose *via* the mystical notion it is Christ who seals, and seals with the cross. This difference between Ambrose and Cyril reflects the different development of the *Logos* theology and the theology of the Spirit.

In his particular emphasis Ambrose is close to Chrysostom, whose mystagogy of the *sphragis* anointing after the act of renunciation and commitment is characterized by the theology of the cross, although Chrysostom develops this *sphragis* theology much more extensively than does Ambrose.[172] For both Chrysostom[173] and Ambrose, it is Christ Himself who signs the candidate with His cross. Anointing and the theology of the Spirit characterize Cyril, and at least the beginnings of the same are found in Theodore. The sign of the cross and the *Logos*

[171] See above, pp. 363-367.
[172] See above, ch. 1, pp. 118ff.
[173] *Ibid.*, p. 118.

theology remain the traditional material from which Ambrose attempts to explain the cosignation.

While Cyril is able to develop a spirituality of the Christian life from his mystagogy of the anointing, Ambrose's mystagogy seems hobbled by the necessity of his Trinitarian concern, to show how the communication of the Spirit is the communication of the Spirit of Jesus Himself in a way that is related to the baptismal act. His point of mediation is the sign of the cross in the ceremony. He continues to emphasize that the consignation is something "special," yet is obliged to constantly relate it to the baptismal act itself, to show the unity of Trinitarian action.

The *particular effects* of this communication of the Spirit pertain to the *myron* theology of Cyril, and neither Theodore nor Ambrose develop them.

In all three fathers, the *eschatological dimension* of the ceremony receives different treatment. With the help of *Is.*[174] and the image of the banquet with its anointing of the guests, Cyril is able to give a fitting conclusion to his entire mystagogical piece, thoroughly biblical in tone: the Spirit as the eschatological gift already anticipated in the Initiation ceremonies, in which Christ and the Christian are united in the Messianic work which leads the world to this final goal. Theodore does not use this image of the banquet and the anointing of the guests. He reiterates a frequent theme, showing that the first-fruits of the Spirit will flower in incorruptibility and immortality, impassibility and immutability. Ambrose does not bring this eschatological dimension into the sealing at all. To some extent the eschatological dimension had been anticipated by Ambrose in his mystagogy of the anointing directly after the baptismal bath.[175] But here the emphasis was more on personal immortality rather than the Messianic function in contributing to the final consummation, and this was really an unfolding of the mystagogy of the baptismal act, rather than the mystagogy of the communication of the Spirit.

[174] *Is.* 2:2-3; 15:7; 25:6.
[175] See above, pp. 388-390.

II

THE BAPTISMAL GARMENT

The putting on of a garment after the baptized comes out of the pool is, of course, a matter of practical necessity. This necessity, however, is converted by all four fathers, in line with tradition, into the occasion for a mystagogical interpretation of the meaning of the garment which the newly baptized assumes. This interpretation corresponds with the interpretation given to the stripping off of the garments just prior to the baptismal bath, a mystagogy which we have already dealt with in detail.[176] One should not, however, expect a programmatic comparison in the mystagogical writings where the interpretation of the removal of garments is covered point by point by the interpretation of the putting on of the baptismal robe. This would be too schematic a presentation to suit the nature of the baptismal instructions. In presenting the interpretation of this ceremony, and the materials used in providing a mystagogy for it, such a schematization will, of course, be indispensable. It must be remembered, however, that the comments of the fathers on this ceremony are not systematic, and are scattered throughout different sections of their writings.

SYNOPTIC CHART

The Mystagogy of the Baptismal Garment

Cyril	*Chrysostom*	*Theodore*	*Ambrose*
A Symbol of Union with the Risen Christ:			
Robe: Putting on the Risen Christ:	Robe: Putting on the Risen Christ:	Robe:	Robe: Robe of Christ risen and ascended:
Myst.Cat. III.1 *Ga.* 3:27	*Stav.* 2.27 *Ga.* 3:27		*Myst.* 36 *Ps.* 23:7-8 *Is.* 63:1

[176]See above, ch. 2, pp. 159ff.

The Mystagogy of the Baptismal Garment—continued

Cyril	*Chrysostom*	*Theodore*	*Ambrose*
-Conformity to risen body: *Ph.* 3:21			
	-New Robe-New Man: *Stav.* 2.11;4.12 *Col.* 3:10 2 *Co.* 5:17		
	-Bridal Garment: *P.K.* 3.6-7 *Ps.* 44:10		-Bridal Garment: *Myst.* 37 *Zc.* 3:3; *Sg.*4:1
	-Radiance as Indwelling of Trinity: *Stav.* 4.3-4 *Mt.* 13:43 *Jn.* 14:23	-Radiance as happiness of eschaton: *Bapt.Hom.* III.26	-Whiteness as blossoming of grace: *Sacr.* V.14 *Myst.* 37-41 *Sg.* 5:1
A Symbol for Purity of Life:			
Whiteness of Robe:	Radiance of Robe: Christ's indwelling shines in works: *Stav.* 5.18 *Ga.* 3.27 Spotless Robe: *Stav.* 8.25;5.24-26 Luster increased by works: *Stav.* 7:24-25 Apostolic instrument to attract: *Stav.* 4.17-19 *Mt.* 5:16	Radiance of Robe:	Radiance of Robe: Christ's indwelling shines in works: *Myst.* 41 *Sg.* 8.6

The Mystagogy of the Baptismal Garment—continued

Cyril	*Chrysostom*	*Theodore*	*Ambrose*
Good deeds now under sign of eschatological joy: *Myst.Cat.*IV. 3, 8 (2 *P.* 1:4) *Qo.* 9:7;1:2 *Is.* 61:10	Preserved for eschatological wedding banquet: *Stav.* 6:24-25	Reflects joy now of eschaton: *Bapt.Hom.* III.26	
A Symbol of the Forgiveness of Sins:			
Radiance of Robe: *Procat.* 15 *Ps.* 32:1	Radiance of Robe: *Stav.* 7.24 Royal Robe: *Stav.* 2.25 Bridal robe for nakedness: *P.K.* 3:6-7 *Ga.* 3:27		Whiteness of Robe: -Washed snow-white: *Myst.* 34 *Ps.* 50:9 *Ex.* 12:22 *Mt.* 17:2 -Scarlet to snow-white: *Myst.* 34 *Is.* 1:18 -Black to white: *Myst.* 35 *Sg.* 1:4;8:5 (*Tt.* 3:5)

A. Cyril

Unlike Chrysostom, Theodore and Ambrose, Cyril presents no concrete mystagogy of the baptismal robe, at least in place in the unfolding of the ceremonies. The second *Mystagogical Catechesis* concludes with the interpretation of the baptismal bath as death and resurrection. Then the third concerns itself immediately with the chrismation. As has been indicated, however, in the synopsis of ceremonies,[177] Cyril is aware of the symbolism of the white robe, since he alludes to it in other places, and so provides a mystagogy.

1. *A Symbol of Union with the Risen Christ*

Although Cyril does not specifically refer the passage to the putting on of the baptismal robe, it seems highly probable that his description of the baptized after they have emerged from the font in the opening sentence of the third *Mystagogical Catechesis* as "having put on Christ (χριστὸν ἐνδυσάμενοι),"[178] could well be an allusion to the baptismal garment and its significance. The phrase itself is taken from *Ga.* 3:27, where the metaphor is one of being clothed, and it is one of the most common texts used in association with the baptismal garment.

Using this Pauline metaphor, Cyril goes on to explain what "putting on Christ" as one would put on a garment means. Through the act of baptism, the neophyte has been made "conformable to the glorious body of Christ."[179] One puts on Christ as one puts on a garment. Participating in the death and resurrection of Christ through the baptismal act, one's own mortal body is joined to the resurrected body of Christ. The putting on of the baptismal robe, then, would be an expressive symbol of the event of rising with Christ which Cyril had just described in his mystagogy of the baptismal bath.

This brief, and compact sentence seems, indeed, to be actually alluding to the white robe donned after baptism.

[177]See above, pp. 349-350.

[178]*Myst. Cat.* III.1 (Piédagnel, *SC* 126, 120; tr. Cross, *SPCK*, 63).

[179]*Idem.* συμμόρφους · · · τοῦ σώματος τῆς δόξης τοῦ Χριστοῦ. *Cf. Ph.* 3:21.

2. *A Symbol of the Forgiveness of Sins*

Cyril also sees in the putting on of the white robe a symbol that the sins of the baptized have been forgiven or covered over. In a general *visio* of what the whole liturgy of baptism will mean, he mentions a psalm being sung, presumably as the newly-baptized enter the Church for the Eucharist. He advises the candidates to long to hear the words of this psalm sung over them after they will have been baptized: " 'Blessed are they whose iniquities are forgiven, and whose sins have been covered;'[180] when, like stars of the Church, you shall enter in it, bright in the outward man and radiant in your souls."[181]

[180] *Ps.* 32:1 The liturgy of baptism at Constantinople in the time of Proclus, patriarch in 434, also mentions that *Ps.* 32:1 is sung. See Proclus of Constantinople, *Catechesis de baptismo mystagogica, Codex Sinaïticus graecus* 491, folios 138 v.-139. Text cited in Wenger, *SC* 50, 101, n. 1; tr. Finn, *op. cit.*, p. 189. Tr. and text as follows:

You have in yourself the meaning of the actions which have been performed on you. You appear naked, as one coming from the foe stripped of your garment by your enemies. Your bare feet give testimony of your poverty. As one in grief, you walk on sack cloth. As one in need you lift up your hands to heaven. In this you may know how poor you are whom the Master receives, how He enriches your nakedness with His grace, how with the chrism He puts on you the odor of good deeds, how with the oil, He makes you shine brilliantly, how you lay aside your corruption in the grave of the bath, how the Spirit raises you up to a new life, how he clothes your body with shining garments, how the lamps you hold in your hands symbolize the illumination of the soul, now David lifts his voice for you in the victory song: "blessed are those whose iniquities have been forgiven and whose sins have been covered over."

"Ἐχεις ἐν σοι τῶν περὶ σε πραγμάτων τὸ σύμβολον· γυμνὸς ὡς ἐκ πολεμίου προσφαίνῃ· ὡς ἐξ ἐχθρῶν ἡ στολὴ σου διήρπασται, ὁ πους τὴν πτωχείαν προσμαρτυρεῖ τῇ γυμνότητι· ὡς ἐν πένθει καθεστὼς τοῖς τριχίνοις ἐπιβαίνεις ὑφάσμασιν· ὡς ἐπιδεὴς πρὸς οὐρανὸν ἀνατείνεις τὰς χεῖρας ἵνα γνῷς πῶς ἔρημόν σε τῶν κακῶν ὁ δεσπότης προσδέχεται, πῶς σε γυμνὸν ὄντα πλουτίζει τῇ χάριτι πῶς μύρῳ σοι τῶν καλῶν τὴν εὐωδίαν ἐντίθησιν, πῶς ἐλαίῳ φαιδρύνει πρὸς ἔκλαμψιν, πῶς ἐν τάφῳ τῇ κολυμβήθρᾳ τὴν φθορὰν ἀποτίθης, πῶς νέος πρὸς ζωὴν ἀνεγείρῃ τῷ πνεύματι, πῶς λαμπροῖς ἐσθήμασιν μεταμφιάζει τὸ σῶμα, πῶς τὸν τῆς ψυχῆς φωτισμὸν αἱ κρατούμεναι ταῖς χερσὶν λαμπάδες γνωρίζουσιν, πῶς Δαβιδ ὡς πρὸς νίκην σοι τῆς μελωδίας ἐξάρχει. Μακάρισι ὧν ἀφέθησαν αἱ ἀνομίαι καὶ ὧν ἐπεκαλύφθησαν αἱ ἁμαρτίαι).

[181] *Procat.* 15 (Cross, *SPCK,* 10; tr. *ibid.,* 50): Χακάριοι ὧν ἀφέθησαν αἱ ἀνομίαι, ὅτε, ὥσπερ ἀστέρες τῆς ἐκκλησίας, εἰσέλθητε φαιδροι τῷ σώματι καὶ φωτεινοὶ τῇ ψυχῇ.

It may be assumed that the reference to the brightness of the outward man pertains to the wearing of the white garments in which the newly-baptized are clothed. The transformation which has taken place in baptism, the forgiveness of sins, specified by the interpretative word of the psalm which Cyril attaches here, causes a radiance in the soul, which is symbolized by the "brightness of the outward man," symbolized, that is, by the white baptismal robe.

3. *A Symbol for Purity of Life*

A further development of the white garment as symbol of the baptized's conformity to the resurrected life of Christ may be found in the fourth *Mystagogical Catechesis* which is devoted to the Eucharist. Cyril is explaining a theme from 2 *P.* 1:4, showing how through the Eucharist the Christian becomes a partaker of the divine nature.[182] Among such symbols as the bread and wine, the table and the anointing, he makes specific allusion to the baptismal garment:

> "Let thy garments always be white, for God now accepts thy works."[183] For before you came to baptism, your works were "vanity of vanities,"[184] but now, having put off your old garments, and put on those which are spiritually white, you must be continually robed in white; we mean not this, that you must always wear white raiment; but with truly white and glistening attire you be clothed whithal that you may say with blessed Isaiah, "My soul shall be joyful in my God; for He has clothed me in the garments of salvation; He has covered me with the robe of gladness."[185]

[182] *Myst. Cat.* IV.3 (Piédagnel, *SC* 126, 136; tr. Cross, *SPCK*, 68).

[183] *Cf. Qo.* 9:7-8.

[184] *Ibid.*, 1:2.

[185] *Is.* 61:10. *Myst. Cat.* IV.8 (Piédagnel, *SC* 126, 142, 144; tr. Cross, *SPCK*, 70):

"Διαπαντὸς ἔστω σου τὰ ἱμάτια λευκά, ὅτι ηὐδόκησε Κύριος τὰ ποιήματά σου·" νῦν ηὐδόκησε Κύριος τὰ ποιήματά σου. Πρὶν γὰρ προσελθεῖν τῇ χάριτι, "ματαιότης ματαιοτήτων" ἦν τὰ ποιήματά σου.

Νῦν δὲ ἀποδυσάμενος τὰ παλαιὰ ἱμάτια καὶ ἐνδυσάμενος τὰ πνευματικῶς λευκά,

The passages chosen to interpret the meaning of the white garment are eschatological in tone, and refer to action performed under the aspect and sign of future consummation. Here, in this mystagogy, the white garment has been brought into association with the eschatological symbolism, the robe of gladness, sign of the consummation of life. The white baptismal robe is to be worn, says Cyril, as sign of the presence of this eschatological clothing. And this white robe is worn, not always physically, but spiritually in that the good deeds one performs are actual emanations resulting from the baptized's association with the final eschatological fulfilment of his works. "Let thy garments always be white, for God accepts thy works."[186]

This, then, is a further extension of the idea of the baptized being conformed to the resurrected Christ. The life of the Christian, even before the consummation of the world, associated as it is with the resurrection of Jesus, in which this consummation has already begun, will reflect the purity and joy of the coming kingdom. This mystagogy of the white garment, particularly of its eschatological significance, goes beyond the "moralistic" interpretation to which Cyril has devoted some attention in the *Procatechesis*.[187] It sees, rather, the life of Christian action as emanating from mystical union with the risen Christ, and performed under the sign of the eschaton, to which this risen life tends in the Christian.

χρὴ λευχειμονεῖν διαπαντός. Οὐ πάντως τοῦτο λέγομεν, ὅτι σε δεῖ λευκὰ περιβεβλῆσθαι ἱμάτια ἀεί, ἀλλὰ τὰ ὄντως λευκὰ καὶ λαμπρὰ καὶ πνευματικὰ ἀναγκαῖον ἐστὶ περιβεβλῆσθαι, ἵνα λέγῃς κατὰ τὸν μακάριον Ἡσαίαν· "Ἀγαλλιάσθω ἡ ψυχή μου ἐπὶ τῷ Κυρίῳ· ἐνέδυσε γάρ με ἱμάτιον σωτηρίου καὶ χιτῶνα εὐφροσύνης περιέθηκέ μοι."

[186] Both this interpretation of the white garment as a sign of the immortality of the resurrection, and its consequent significance as symbol of purity of life, correspond to Cyril's analysis of the meaning of the stripping of garments before baptism under the aspect of mortality and immortality. The same texts used here, the references to putting on the garment of salvation from *Is.* 61:10 and putting on Jesus Christ from *Ga.* 3:27 to explain the symbolism, are also used there. See above, ch. 2, pp. 176-178.

[187] See above, ch. 2, pp. 163-164.

Summary

As is customary with Cyril, his mystagogy makes a wide arc, encompassing past, present and future. By using the Pauline metaphor of "putting on Christ" and further explaining it in terms of the baptismal act, that "putting on Christ" means being conformed to the risen body of Christ, a reality that transpired in the baptismal act, he shows the *robe* itself to be a symbol of the union of the risen Christ and the candidate. He carries this mystagogy further by interpreting the *radiance* of the white garment as a sign of the interior *radiance* which shines in the baptized as a result of the forgiveness of sins which baptism implies, that is, the overcoming of the sting of death in union with the resurrection of Christ. The material for thus interpreting this radiance of the baptismal robe is provided by the liturgical psalm itself which is sung over the candidates as they march from the baptistery into the church radiant in their white garments. It explains that the radiance comes from the sins being "covered over and forgiven." And this interpretation is offered (in *visio*) for the movement of the candidates from baptistery to church, the development of the mystagogy thus dovetailing nicely with the actual progression of the liturgical ceremonies. Once baptized, having "put on Christ," the baptized then move into the church like "stars," reflecting in this radiance of the robe what has taken place interiorly. Finally, the *whiteness* of the robe itself is used as the biblical symbol for man's actions performed under the eschatological sign of God's pleasure. The neophyte, in union with the risen Christ, has the guarantee that his works are accepted by God, as long as he remains unsevered from this union. And so his white garment is a sign of his "continually being robed in white," that is, of his future works being performed under this sign of eschatological fulfilment, pointing to this future.

The *robe* as sign of union with the risen Christ, the *radiance* of the robe as sign of the interior transformation wrought by the forgiveness of sins, the *whiteness* of the robe as sign of a life lived acceptable to God under the sign of eschatological fulfilment: through this mystagogy of the baptismal garment Cyril links neophyte with the past event of Christ's actual resurrection, its apprehension now in sacrament manifesting itself in the candidate's transformation, and to the future consummation of this risen life, under sign of which and through the power of which he now leads his life "continually robed in white."

B. Chrysostom

Like Cyril, Chrysostom does not deal specifically with the baptismal robe in the context of the ceremonies as they unfold. As we have already seen in the synopsis of ceremonies,[188] however, there is enough internal evidence from other parts of the *Baptismal Instructions* to indicate that Chrysostom takes its presence to be a fact, and he alludes to it with great frequency in a variety of figurative language.[189] Although more frequent and more widely dispersed throughout the *Instructions* than are Cyril's few allusions to the baptismal robe, Chrysostom's mystagogy bears close resemblance to that of Cyril, and groups itself under the same three headings: union with Christ, forgiveness of sins, purity of life. This strong similarity testifies, no doubt, to the antiquity of the tradition associated with the white robe, a tradition dating quite beyond Christian times.[190]

1. *A Symbol of Union with the Risen Christ*

In a context similar to that of Cyril, that is, in an explanation which is following in general the chronological unfolding of the initiation ceremonies, Chrysostom describes the neophytes as they come up from the waters of the baptismal pool and before they go into the Eucharistic celebration in the fol-

[188] See above, pp. 351-352.

[189] Finn reports more than thirty allusions of one kind or another to the "white robe." *Op. cit.*, p. 194.

[190] See J. Quasten, "A Pythagorean Idea in Jerome," in *American Journal of Philology* 63 (1942) 207-215. For further literature on this subject, see above, ch. 2, n. 38, p. 159.

lowing terms: "Since they have put on Christ Himself (Χριστὸν ἐνδεδυμένοι), wherever they go they are like angels on earth, rivalling the brilliance of the rays of the sun."[191]

Both in the context, and in the occurrence of the Pauline metaphor of *Ga.* 3:27, to "put on Christ," or "to clothe oneself in Christ," the mystagogy is the same as that of Cyril: the baptismal robe symbolizes the union of the baptized with the risen Christ which has been effected through the baptismal act. The color and tone of the description with its notion of angels and the brilliance of the sun, its context where the neophytes are described as being greeted when they come out of the pool, having passed from slavery to freedom: the scene is borrowed from Easter Sunday morning. Even though Chrysostom in this place does not present this specifically as a mystagogy of the baptismal garment, just as Cyril had not, it would seem that the white garment of the neophyte actually suggests the picture, and that it in its turn is determined by the thought of the resurrection, as far as its symbolic meaning goes. Both from the context in the ceremonies, where the neophyte, having just emerged from the font puts on the white garment, and from the use both of the Pauline clothing metaphor and the resurrection imagery of angels and the brilliance of the sun, it is clear that a mystagogy of the baptismal garment is being constructed by Chrysostom.

Proceeding from the Pauline metaphor of putting on Christ, Chrysostom has, in various other places in the *Instructions* brought other materials to bear to show how this baptismal robe symbolizes the union with the risen Christ which the neophyte has acquires through the baptismal act. If putting on the robe itself symbolizes the putting on of the risen Christ which baptism effects, then certain features of this robe will suggest more fully what this union with Christ imports. These features are the newness of the robe, its resemblance to a bridal garment, and its radiance.

[191] *Stav.* 2.27 (Wenger, *SC* 50, 148; tr. Harkins, *ACW* 31, 53): *καθάπερ αὐτὸν τὸν Χριστὸν ἐνδεδυμένοι οὕτω περιΐασιν, ὥσπερ ἄγγελοί τινες ἐπίγειοι πανταχοῦ φαινόμενοι καὶ ταῖς ἀκτῖσι τοὺ ἡλίου ἀντιλάμποντες.*

a. *New Robe – New Man*

The Pauline notion of man's renewal according to the image of his Creator is the scriptural foundation which Chrysostom uses to support the mystagogy of the *newness* of the robe being a sign of the renewal in God's image which has taken place in baptism:

> Baptism is a burial and resurrection. For the old man is buried with his sin, and the new man is resurrected, "being renewed according to the image of his Creator."[192] We put off the old garment which has been made filthy with the abundance of our sins; we put on the new one which is free from every stain. What am I saying? We put on Christ Himself. "For all of you," says St. Paul, "who have been baptized in Christ, have put on Christ."[193]

This newness of the creature, which will, of course, form the root of Christian conduct, is also explained in a further *Instruction* explaining the relationship between the renewal which takes place in Christian baptism and consequent conduct, and again St. Paul is used:

> . . . [Paul] showed . . . that those who by their faith in Christ had put off like an old cloak the burden of their sins, those who had been set free from their error and been illumined by the light of justification, had put on this new and shining cloak, this royal robe. This is why he said: "If any man is in Christ, he is a new creature: the former things have passed away; behold they are all made new."[194]

[192] *Cf. Col.* 3:10.

[193] *Ga.* 3:27. *Stav.* 2.11 (Wenger, *SC* 50, 139; tr. Harkins, *ACW* 31, 47): *Τάφος ἐστὶ καὶ ἀνάστασις τὸ βάπτισμα. "Συνθάπτεται γὰρ ὁ παλαιὸς ἄνθρωπος τῇ ἁμαρτίᾳ καὶ ἀνίσταται ὁ νέος ὁ ἀνακαινούμενος καὶ 'εἰκόνα τοῦ κτίσαντος." Ἀποδυόμεθα καὶ ἐνδυόμεθα· ἀποδυόμεθα μὲν τὸ παλαιὸν ἱμάτιον τὸ ὑπο τοῦ πλήθους τῶν ἡμαρτημένων καταρρυπωθέν, ἐνδυόμεθα δὲ τὸ καινὸν καὶ πάσης κηλῖδος ἀπηλλαγμένον. Τί δὲ λέγω; Αὐτὸν τὸν Χριστὸν ἐνδυόμεθα." Ὅσοι γάρ, φησίν εἰς Χριστὸν ἐβαπτίσθητε, Χριστὸν ἐνεδύσασθε."*

[194] 2 *Co.* 5:17. *Stav.* 4.12 (Wenger, *SC* 50, 189; tr. Harkins, *ACW* 31, 71): *Δεικνὺς ὅτι καθάπερ ἱμάτιον παλαιὸν ἀποδυσάμενοι τῶν ἁμαρτημάτων τὸ φορτίον διὰ τῆς εἰς τὸν Χριστὸν πίστεως, τὸ καινὸν τοῦτο καὶ φαιδρὸν ἱνάτιον καὶ τὴν στολὴν τὴν βασιλικὴν περιέθεντο οἱ τῆς πλάνης ἐλευθερωθέντες καὶ τῷ φωτὶ τῆς δικαιοσύνης καταυγασθέντες. διὰ τοῦτο ἔλεγεν· "εἰ τις ἐν Χριστῷ, καινὴ κτίσις· τὰ ἀρχαῖα παρῆλθεν, ἰδοὺ γέγονε τὰ πάντα καινά."*

The newness of the robe, then, is expressive of the transformation which the baptismal act has achieved. By putting on the robe, that is, putting on Christ, Chrysostom shows by the use of these two Pauline texts that its very newness indicates and reveals a particular aspect of the baptismal act; that the baptized is a new creature, renewed in the image of his Creator.

b. *A Bridal Garment*

The resemblance of the baptismal robe to a bridal garment is also an apt point for Chrysostom to teach the meaning of baptism. In a final instruction to candidates before baptism, he uses this, one of his favorite images. Christ as bridegroom and the Church, or the baptized, as bride, to provide a mystagogy for the baptismal robe:

> He came to her who was about to become His bride, and found her naked and disgracing herself. He threw around her a clean robe, whose brightness and glory no mind or word will be able to describe. How shall I say it ? He has thrown Himself around us as a garment: "For all of you who have been baptized into Christ have put on Christ."[195] When David saw this garment from afar with his prophetic eyes, he cried aloud and said: "The queen stood on thy right hand."[196] Suddenly the beggar and outcast has become a queen, and stands beside the King. And the prophet shows Christ and the Church and Bridegroom and bride standing in the holy bridal chamber "in gilded clothing surrounded with variety."[197] Behold, even the garment has told you.[198]

[195] *Ga.* 3:27.

[196] *Ps.* 44:10.

[197] *Idem.*

[198] *P.K.* 3.2 (*VGS,* 168, tr. Harkins, *ACW* 31, 162-163, nos. 6 and 7): *Καὶ ἐλθων καὶ εὑρων τὴν μέλλουσαν αὐτῷ νυμφαγωγεῖσθαι γυμνὴν καὶ ἀσχημονοῦσαν ἱμάτιον αὐτὴν περιέβαλε καθαρὸν καὶ οὗ τὴν λαμπρότητα καὶ τὴν δόξαν οὐδεὶς οὐ λόγος οὐ νοῦς παραστῆσαι δυνήσεται. ὥς εἴπω; ὡς ἱμάτιον ἑαυτὸν ἡμῖν περιέβαλεν. "ὅσοι γὰρ εἰς Χριστὸν ἐβαπτίσθητε, Χριστὸν ἐνεδύσασθε". τοῦτο τὸ ἱμάτιον ἄνωθεν ἰδὼν προφητικοῖς ὀφθαλμοις ὁ Δαυὶδ ἐβόα καὶ ἔλεγε. "παρέστη ἡ βασίλισσα ἐκ δεξιῶν σου". βασίλισσα ᾽αθρόον γέγονεν ἡ πτωχὴ καὶ ἀπερριμένη καὶ πλησίον ἕστηκε τοῦ βασιλέως, καὶ καθάπερ νυμφίον καὶ νύμφην ἐν ἱερᾷ παστάδι ἑστῶτας οὕτω δείκνυσι τὴν ᾽Εκκλησίαν καὶ τὸν Χριστὸν ὁ προφήτης. "ἐν ἱματισμῷ διαχρύσῳ περιβεβλημένη, πεποικιλμένη". ἰδοὺ καὶ τὸ ἱματίον εἶπέ σοι.*

Here, "putting on Christ" becomes more than merely putting on a robe, or a new robe. Through the interweaving of *OT* thought, and the notion of the outcast woman become queen by being wrapped about with the garment, Chrysostom suggests that the beauty of the robe as bridal robe reflects the union of greatest intimacy with Christ as the Bridegroom.[199]

c. *The Radiance of the Robe*

The fact of the radiance of the baptismal garment is also seized upon by Chrysostom to illustrate the background of baptism as effecting an interior transformation of justification by grace and the indwelling of the Holy Trinity. He combines the idea of the natural light of the sun and stars, and with the help of two Gospel quotations shows that the radiance of the neophytes in their transformed state surpasses this light: "They have put off their burdens of sins and put on the royal robe; they almost vie in brilliance with heaven itself. We see them shine more brilliantly than the stars, as they light up the faces of those who look at them."[200] Chrysostom carries out this comparison with the stars by explaining that the stars shine only at night, whereas the neophytes shine day and night, because they are spiritual stars, which rival and even surpass the light of the sun. He then quotes *Mt.* 13:43, "Then the just will shine forth like the light of the sun," and explains that the interior grace of baptism is more brilliant than any material thing, even than the sun, than which nothing is brighter. And he continues in the same passage: "Let me exhort them [the neophytes] to ponder on the excess of the Master's generosity and

[199]Chrysostom goes into further detail on the exterior garment and the interior reality when he deals with *Ga.* 3:27 in *Exp. in Ps. 44 (MG* 55.199) and he also explains further the meaning of the passages in *Ps.* 44. (For tr. of the passage, see Harkins, *ACW* 31, p. 317, n. 20).

[200]*Stav.* 4.3 (Wenger, *SC* 50, 183-184; tr. Harkins, *ACW* 31, 67): *τὰ τῶν ἁμαρτημάτων ἀποθέμενοι φορτία καὶ τὴν βασιλικὴν ἐνδυσάμενοι στολήν, αὐτῷ σχεδὸν· ἀντιλάμπουσι τῷ οὐρανῷ καὶ φαιδρότερον τῶν ἀστέρων τούτων ὀφθέντες τὸ φῶς καταυγάζουσι τῶν εἰς αὐτοὺς ὁρώντων τὰς ὄψεις.*

Cyril had used the same comparison, stressing the brilliance of the assembly and calling the neophytes the stars of the Church. See above, p. 417.

the luster of the garment which they have been judged worthy to wear. St. Paul says: 'For all of you who have been baptized into Christ have put on Christ.'[201] . . . And when I say Christ, I mean also the Father and the Holy Spirit. For this is what Christ Himself promised us when He said: 'If anyone love me and will keep my commandments, the Father and I will come to Him and make our abode with him'."[202]

2. *A Symbol of the Forgiveness of Sins*

Like Cyril, Chrysostom sees also in the *radiance* of the robe the symbol of the forgiveness of sins. His application is specific to the baptismal robe, since he points out during the homily, delivered during Easter week at one of the martyrs' shrines, that the other bystanders in the congregation are in admiration at the splendor of the neophytes' robes, which they wore for the occasion: "Your shining robe now arouses admiration in the eyes of all who behold you, and the radiance of your garments proves that your souls are free from every blemish."[203] Further mystagogical interpretation of the robe as symbol of the forgiveness of sin occurs when Chrysostom sees the robe as a "*royal robe*:" "Instead of the man who descended into the water, a different man comes forth, one who has wiped

[201] *Ga.* 3:27.

[202] *Cf. Jn.* 14:23. *Stav.* 4.4 (Wenger, *SC* 50, 184; tr. Harkins, *ACW.* 31, 67): *Παρακαλέσωμεν, ἐννοήσαντας τῆς φιλοτιμίας τοῦ δεσπότου τὴν ὑπερβολην καὶ τοῦ ἱματίου τὴν φαιδρότητα ὅπερ ἐνδύσασθαι κατηξιώθησαν· "Ὅσοι γάρ φησίν εἰς Χριστὸν ἐβαπτίσθητε, Χριστὸν ἐνεδύσασθε" . . . Ὅταν δὲ εἴπω τὸν Χριστόν, καὶ τὸν· Πατέρα λέγω καὶ τὸ Πνεῦμα τὸ ἅγιον. Καὶ γὰρ αὐτὸς ὑπέσχετο λέγων. "'Εάν τις ἀγαπᾷ με καὶ τὰς ἐντολάς μου τηρήσῃ, ἐγῷ καὶ ὁ Πατὴρ ἐλευσόμεθα καὶ μονὴν παρ' αὐτῷ ποιήσομεν."*
The same idea of Cyril, that the Christian is "conformed" to Christ (see above, p. 416) is handled quite directly, that is, without the intermediary symbolism of the white robe, in Chrysostom's commentary *In Gal.* 3 (*MG* 61.656), where Chrysostom tells the Christians that they have the same "form (*μορφήν*)" and "image (*ἀτύπον*)" as Christ, and that they "show forth Christ (*δεικνὺς τὸν Χριστόν*)." (For tr. of this passage see Harkins, *ACW* 31, p. 316, n. 16).

[203] *Stav.* 7. 24 (Wenger, *SC* 50, 241; tr. Harkins, *ACW* 31, 114): *Καὶ καθάπερ νῦν διὰ τῆς φαιδρᾶς ἐσθῆτος πᾶσι περίβλεποι τυγχάνετε καὶ δείκνυσιν ὑμῶν τῆς ἐν τῇ ψυχῇ καθαρότητος τὴν ὑπερβολὴν καὶ ἡ τῶν ἱματίων φαιδρότης.*

away all the filth of his sins, who has put off the old garment of sin and has put on the royal robe."[204] Although it cannot be said that this passage is a specific mystagogy of the actual baptismal garment, it may be safely assumed from the context (the instruction follows much of the chronological sequence of the ceremonies, and in this point particularly describes what happens right after the baptismal act), and from other texts, that the "royal robe" is not merely a figurative expression, but is a mystagogical interpretation of the baptismal robe, just as the old garments of sin were not merely figurative, but were part of the mystagogy based on the actual stripping of the candidates in preparation for entering the pool.

The passage already quoted[205] also contains in its imagery of the bridal robe covering over the nakedness of the sinful bride the mystagogy of the robe as sign of the forgiveness of sins.

3. *A Symbol for Purity of Life*

Like Cyril, Chrysostom's mystagogy of the white robe as a sign of the purity of life to which the Christian is called through his baptism, is not merely a moralistic presentation of Christian obligations, based for example, on the whiteness or the spotlessness of the robe as sign of sinlessness. In his strictures on excessive luxury and seductiveness in the matter of clothing, we have already seen how Chrysostom, as moral preacher, was able to deliver his fair share of that kind of mystagogical interpretation based on the literal contemplation of luxurious clothing and jewelry when he saw the need of it.[206] Here, however, in interpreting the meaning of the baptismal robe, Chrysostom sees the Christian life not as a series of moral obligations only, but rather a reflection of the Christian's union with the risen Christ within him. Two passages in the *Baptismal*

[204] *Stav.* 2.25 (Wenger, *SC* 50, 147; tr. Harkins, *ACW* 31, 52). (Text, see above, ch. 2, n. 31, p. 155).

[205] See above, n. 198, p. 424.

[206] See above, ch. 2, pp. 167-170.

Instructions particularly demonstrate how Chrysostom's mystagogy of the white robe makes the transition from the robe as symbol of union with the risen Christ to a symbol for the kind of life to which the Christian is called. In an exhortation strongly moralistic in tone, urging abstention from various vices like softness, extravagance and drunkenness, Chrysostom, toward the end of his catalogue of vices, resorts to the symbolism of the baptismal robe to relate Christian moral life to the indwelling of the risen Christ: "Especially you who have recently been judged worthy of divine initiation, who have put off the burden of your sins, and put on the shining robe – and what do I mean by the shining robe? – do you, who have put on Christ Himself and have received the Master of all things to dwell within you, show forth a conduct worthy of Him who dwells within you."[207] Under the image of the radiance of the robe Chrysostom relates the abstention from vices and the profession of virtue in the Christian life to the Christian's partnership with the risen Christ, which the white robe expresses symbolically. The conduct of the Christian must be worthy of the radiance of the robe, that is, worthy of Him Who dwells within him. Again, the central image is from *Ga.* 3:27; putting on Christ.

The same image also occurs in the second of these transitional passages, Chrysostom concludes an Easter week address at one of the countryside shrines or "martyria" in the vicinity of Antioch with a final exhortation to the neophytes:

> And especially do I exhort you who have recently put on Christ and received the descent of the Holy Spirit. Each day look to the luster of your garment, that it may never receive any spot or wrinkle, either by untimely words, or idle listening, or by evil thoughts, or by eyes which rush foolishly to see whatever goes on. Let us build a rampart about ourselves on every side and keep constantly before

[207] *Stav* 5.18 (Wenger, *SC* 50, 209; tr. Harkins, *ACW* 31, 87-88): *Καὶ μάλιστα ὑμεις οἱ πρόσφατον τῆς θείας καταξιωθέντες μυσταγωγίας καὶ τὰ τῶν ἁμαρτημάτων ἀποθέμενοι φορτία καὶ λαμπρὰν τὴν στολὴν περιβαλόμενοι· καὶ τί λέγω λαμπρὰν στολήν, οἱ τὸν Χριστὸν αὐτον ἐνδεδυμένοι καὶ τὸν τῶν ὅλων δεσπότην ἔνοικον δεξάμενοι, ἀξίαν τοῦ ἐνοικοῦντος τὴν πολιτείαν ἐπιδείξασθε.*

> our minds that dread day, so that we may abide in our shining brightness, keep our garment of immortality unspotted and unstained, and deserve those ineffable gifts.[208]

In these two passages Chrysostom uses the natural quality of the garment, its clean whiteness and its lack of spot and wrinkle, its shining quality, both as sign of Christ's indwelling, and as symbol of a blameless life according to this indwelling. In addition a further note of mystagogical interpretation begins to sound in the passages, the fact that the effort required to keep the garment white, spotless, without wrinkle not only corresponds to the indwelling of Christ through participation in His resurrection in baptism, but also it puts the neophyte in line with the eschatological fulfilment to which his moral life tends in partnership with Christ. Expressions like "that dread day," and the "garment of immortality" signal this symbolic interpretation of the white garment.

In numerous other passages as well Chrysostom shows his particular attention to the mystagogical interpretation of the baptismal robe as a symbol for purity of life, related to the risen Christ in one, and looking to the life to come. He urges the neophytes to keep their new garment clean, that is, their souls unsullied, comparing the shining garment to the soul in grace.[209] He adds a further aspect of the robe as symbol of purity of life, based on the image of the robe's brightness and cleanness.[210] If one, he explains, guards the present brightness of the new baptismal robe by purity of life, in the course of time the luster of the robe will actually increase. He advises

[208] *Stav.* 8.25 (*Ibid.*, 260; tr. *ibid.*, 130): *Καὶ μάλιστα ὑμείς οἱ νεωστὶ τὸν Χριστὸν ἐνδυσάμενοι καὶ τοῦ Πνεύματος τὴν ἐπιφοίτησιν ὑποδεξάμενοι, καθ᾽ἑκάστην ἡμέραν, παρακαλῶ, ὑμῶν περισκοπεῖτε τοῦ ἐνδύματος τὴν φαιδρότητα ὥστε μηδαμου σπιλον ἤ ῥυτίδα δέξασθαι, μὴ διὰ λόγων ἀκαίρων, μὴ δι᾽ἀκοῆς ματαίας μὴ διὰ λογισμῶν πονηρῶν, μὴ δι᾽ὀφθαλμῶν ἁπλῶς καὶ εἰκῇ τοῖς προστυγχανουσιν ἐπιπηδώντων. Πανταχόθεν τοίνυν ἑαυτους ἅπαντας τειχίζωμεν τῇ διηνεκεῖ μνήμῃ τῆς φοβερᾶς ἐκείνης ἡμέρας ἵνα ἐν φαιδρότητι διαμείναντες καὶ τὸ τῆς ἀφθαρσίας ἔνδυμα ἄσπιλον καὶ ἀκηλίδωτον διαφυλάξαντες τῶν ἀπορρήτων ἐκείνων ἀξιωθῶμεν δωρεῶν.*

[209] *Stav.* 5.24-26 (*Ibid.*, 212-213; tr. *ibid.*, 90-91).

[210] *Stav.* 7.24-25 (*Ibid.*, 241-242; tr. *ibid.*, 114).

prayer and almsgiving as practices which can maintain and even increase the luster of the robe. He makes the contrast between ordinary clothing, which due to wear and tear, aging or attacks of moths finally becomes dull, and spiritual clothing, which will actually increase in brilliance with age due to the practice of virtue.

The image of the robe as bridal garment, used previously to express the intimacy of union with Christ in baptism, and forgiveness of sins,[211] is also taken by Chrysostom, this time as a way of explaining the eschatological significance of the robe.[212] The more good works we do, he explains, the more grace increases, causing the spiritual garment to shine forth with greater luster. This will draw the Bridegroom to a greater love of the bride. This will culminate in the heavenly marriage banquet. Here on earth the white robe is worn for seven days, but when it is worn in the wedding banquet in heaven, it goes beyond the seven days, into the eighth or the eternal day. Thus, the white garment as wedding garment signifies the heavenly wedding banquet, which one can enter, if one has been faithful to the white garment on earth, keeping it unspotted.

Chrysostom's mystagogy also sees the white garment as an apostolic instrument, a means of drawing others to Christ, symbolically speaking. Basis of the mystagogy here are the insignia and robes of imperial officials. Because they bear this insignia, they are careful to do nothing that would compromise their reputation. So, too, Christians, having put on Christ, signified by the insignia of the white garment, must be careful in the conduct of their lives, and in so doing will attract others to praise Christ: "Now the robe you wear and your gleaming garments attract the eyes of all; if you should will to do so, by keeping your royal robe shining even more brightly than it does now, by your godly conduct and your strict discipline,

[211] See above, pp. 421-427.
[212] *Stav.* 6.24-25 (*Ibid.,* 227-228; tr. *ibid.,* 102-103).

you will always be able to draw all who behold you to show the same zeal and praise for the Master."[213]

Material for this mystagogy of the robe as apostolic instrument is found in *Mt.* 5:16, which urges the Christian to let his light shine before men, the note on which Chrysostom begins his explanation of the relationship of the symbol of the garment to the conduct of Christian life: "Did you see how [Christ] urges us to let the light within us shine forth not by garments but by deeds?"[214]

Summary

As with Cyril, the point of departure for Chrysostom's mystagogical interpretation of the white robe which the neophyte puts on after his baptism is the Pauline metaphor of "putting on Christ," often quoted by Chrysostom in the numerous passages he devotes to the baptismal garment and its meaning. As a symbol of the union with the risen Christ which the baptismal act has effected, Chrysostom sees the *newness* of the garment as reflecting the new creation which the very resurrection of Christ implies, and he uses Pauline material relating to the new creation and the restoration of God's image in the baptized as a new creature to support this mystagogical interpretation. The resemblance of the white robe to a *bridal garment* suggests the biblical imagery of union with God achieved by baptism. And the very *radiance* of the white robe suggests the interior illumination which the indwelling of Christ and indeed of the entire Trinity provide. To Gospel texts attesting

[213] *Stav.* 4.18 (*ibid.*, 192; tr. *ibid.*, 73): *Καὶ ὃν τρόπον νῦν ἡ τῆς ἐσθῆτος ὑμων περιβολη καὶ τὸ φαιδρὸν τῶν ἱματίων πάντων ἐπισπᾶται τὰς ὄψεις, οὕτω καὶ εἰς τὸ διηνεκες, εἰ βουληθείητε, δυνήσεσθε τὴν φαιρότητα τοῦ ἐνδυματος τοῦ βασιλικοῦ διατηροῦντες, ἀκριβέστερον ἢ νῦν διὰ τῆς κατὰ Θεὸν πολιτείας καὶ τῆς πολλῆς ἀκριβείας τοὺς ὁρῶντας ἅπαντας εἰς τὸν ὅμοιον ἐπισπάσεσθαι ζῆλον εἰς τὴν τοῦ δεσπότου δοξολογίαν.*

[214] *Stav.* 4.19 (*Ibid.*, 192; tr. *ibid.*, 73): *Εἶδες πῶς παραινεῖ λάμπειν τὸ φῶς τὸ ἐν ἡμῖν οὐ δια τῶν ἱματίων ἀλλὰ διὰ τῶν ἔργων;"*

to this illumination and indwelling, he adds his suggestion of the stars and the sun. These features are perhaps suggested by the fact of the night vigil and the coming of dawn itself, in which time the initiation was held. He contrasts here starlight with the greater light of the sun, and moves from the natural image to resurrection imagery itself, which the Gospels use to surround the description of the resurrection of Christ from the tomb. His remark that the brilliance of the neophytes' garments "light up the faces of those who look at them"[215] might very probably refer as well to the light of the candle, which, it seems, the neophytes also carried.[216]

Overlapping this mystagogy of the garment as symbol of union with Christ, Chrysostom also sees in the *radiance* of the robe the symbol of the forgiveness of sins effected interiorly by baptism. He emphasizes this mystagogy by pointing to the fact that the old clothes are exchanged for what resembles a "royal robe", the beggarly garments of humiliation and sin for kingly prerogatives. His most forceful and moving imagery in this section comes again in considering the robe as a bridal robe which the Bridegroom has not hesitated to place on the bride, despite the fact that He found her naked and debauched by sin.

Corresponding to Chrysostom's detailed pastoral attention to the significance of the removal of garments before baptism as a removal of vices, he devotes considerable time to a mystagogy of the white garment as symbol of purity of life. More than merely using the obvious qualities of spotlessness and whiteness, or the garment without wrinkle for moralistic lessons, Chrysostom relates these images to the indwelling of Christ, showing how these qualities in the garment are maintained and even increased by good deeds performed in union with the risen Christ. He draws on the natural qualities of earthly clothing which can so easily become soiled and decay to show the lesson of the garment as sign of supernatural clothing which becomes more attractive through good works, as no

[215] See above, p. 425.
[216] See above, p. 351.

earthly clothing can. With the help of the image of the heavenly wedding banquet, and the wedding garment which the worthy guests are privileged to wear, he moves into the eschatological significance of the garment, comparing the seven day earthly wedding feast, custom of his time, with the never ending wedding feast to which the garment will admit one, provided it is kept clean by a faithful life in partnership with Christ. In this image, which he uses in a homily toward the end of the Easter week celebration, he finds the liturgical octave a suitable parallel to the week's wedding celebration in earthly festivity which enables him to show the significance of the garment which will not then be put off to return to daily life, but more into the eighth day or everlasting wedding feast in heaven. A further point of mystagogy is provided by seeing the garment, symbol of purity of life, as an apostolic instrument to attract others by a good life. Material for this mystagogy Chrysostom finds both in the comparison to the garments of imperial officials, which bespeak their integrity and impress others, as well as the Gospel injunction to let one's light shine before men.

Chrysostom's mystagogy of the baptismal garment, given the amount of space he devotes to it throughout his *Baptismal Instructions* directly and indirectly, seems really to be for him the most important of his pastoral tools in explaining the meaning of baptism for the Christian life. His ingenious manner of combining natural symbolism of clothing and its meaning in the ordinary lives of his hearers, *OT* and *NT* materials which subsume on this natural symbolism, plus his capitalizing on the very real aspects of the liturgical ceremonies in which his people are involved, both in the baptismal night and in the time preceeding and the week following (as, for example, his use of the light and darkness themes of the night vigil, or the seven day aspects of the liturgical and natural celebrations) mark him as a pastoral mediator of foremost rank in providing a meaningful mystagogy for his people, characterized by acute awareness of Christian revelation, presented never bookishly, but with compassionate human awareness of the intellectual and emotional and imaginative patterns of his hearers, in the actual framework of liturgical event.

C. Theodore

In its proper place in the normal unfolding of the baptismal ritual, Theodore treats the symbolism of the baptismal garment, and attaches to it an explicit mystagogical interpretation.

1. *A Symbol of Union with the Risen Christ*

Like Cyril, Theodore interprets the white garment, which the baptized don when they emerge from the pool, from the christological viewpoint, with, however, nuances and emphases peculiar to Theodore. His interpretation of the garment comes in the same context as does that of Cyril.[217] That is, in both Cyril's *Catecheses* and those of Theodore, the treatment of the baptismal garment is surrounded by a general summary of the mystagogical meaning of the baptismal bath, with the particular stress on the mystagogical meaning of the bath in relationship to the death and resurrection of Jesus.[218] These summaries round off the interpretation of the baptismal bath, and what follows, the interpretation of the garment, has its natural place in the course of the ceremonies, since it is in coming out of the pool that the garment is a necessity for the neophytes. As in Cyril, so in Theodore, as would be expected, the interpretation of the white garment comes in the context of the resurrection. Theodore, however, consistent with his constant emphasis on the typology of the resurrection as the looking forward to the eschaton more than looking back to the actual resurrection of Jesus (though this latter, as we have seen, is an ever-present acknowledged reality) relates his interpretation of the garment to the resurrection of Jesus as sign of eschatological fulfilment. His mystagogical point is to draw attention to the *radiance* of the garment as he had already

[217]See above, p. 416

[218]See *Bapt. Hom.* III.25, above, ch. 2, p. 289.

done when describing the awe with which the bishop's garment inspires the candidates as sign of the world to come.[219] It is, in fact, peculiar to Theodore, that the very symbolic basis of his mystagogical interpretation of the garment is its very iridescence: "When you go out [of the water] you wear a garment that is wholly radiant. This denotes the next world which is shining and radiant, and the life into which you had a long time before moved through symbols."[220]

In Theodore's context, it is clear that the garment is a sign of the resurrection, of conformity to the new life of Christ. But Theodore's immediate mystagogical concern is to take the fact of the iridescence of this garment, to show how this union with the risen Christ looks to the eschatological fulfilment which the resurrection implies.[221]

2. *A Symbol for Purity of Life*

Like Cyril, Theodore sees in the white garment the sign of the happiness of eschatological fulfilment. Quite unlike Cyril and Chrysostom, however, he does not spell out the conclusion that the white garment, being a sign of the heavenly life already begun, should symbolize the conduct of Christian life now, lived under this sign of the eschaton, and reflecting this grace-filled condition, symbol of which are the white garments of joy. Rather, Theodore remains in the eschatological realm in his remarks, seeing in the garments a sign of the hap-

[219] See above, ch. 1, pp. 123-124.

[220] *Bapt. Hom.* III.26 (Tonneau-Devreesse, *SeT* 145, 454; tr. Mingana, *WS* VI, 68.

[221] It will be remembered that Theodore had already treated the pre-baptismal anointing under the image of a "garment of immortality." (See above, pp. 203-205). Perhaps for this reason he does not develop the idea of the white robe as a covering of immortality, since the point, so to speak, has already been made by the image of the anointing as garment. Nakedness and mortality *vs.* covering and immortality had already been treated in the removal of garments — anointing as garment of immortality picture, in line with Theodore's special concern for the idea of the liturgy of baptism as symbol of immortality.

piness of the world to come, based on the symbolism of white garments denoting joy:

> When you have received the resurrection in reality and put on immortality and incorruptibility, such a garment will be wholly unnecessary, but since you do not possess such things in reality, and have only received them sacramentally and symbolically, you are in need of garments. Of these you wear those which denote happiness, which you have now received symbolically, but which you will one day possess in reality.[222]

In a sense, this interpretation is a warranted counterpart to Theodore's interpretation of the stripping of the candidates' garments before baptism.[223] The clothing of Adam and Eve the garments of skins, were symbol of mortality and shame. The candidates had to remove these garments before baptism, through which they would be born anew and become, in symbol, immortal. Following this line of interpretation to its logical conclusion, then, after baptism no clothing should be worn. Theodore admits this, seeing in the present clothing a temporary necessity only. Indeed, this will be the case in the future, where clothing will no longer be necessary, since man will have regained his paradisal condition. The baptismal garment, then, Theodore must be at pains to explain, cannot be the resumption of the garments of mortality, but must be transformed into a forward looking symbol, a very special article of clothing. It is precisely in emphasizing the iridescence of the garment that Theodore lets the light of the coming world, as it were, shine through the garments, and make of them this peculiar symbol. The real sign of the new life is nakedness.[224] The baptismal garment, then, is not a denial of this, but a necessary intermediate step, one which in its iridescence already begins to manifest the life to come.

[222] *Bapt. Hom.* III.26 (Tonneau-Devreesse, *SeT* 145, 454-456; tr. Mingana, *WS* VI, 68).

[223] See above, ch. 2, pp. 178-179.

[224] See above, ch. 2, p. 182.

One might expect, then, that in this sense the garment, since it is a necessary covering in this world, would also be a symbol of the purity of Christian action in the Christian who wears it. In a certain sense, this mystagogy is implied by Theodore, when he says that the garment is a sign of happiness, the happiness of the coming fulfilment, and that it must be worn as an intermediate step before the resurrection is actualized in the eschaton. In this sense, the garment symbolizes in action this reality. Theodore, however, takes no pains whatever, to spell out this message in a concrete way, as did Cyril, and particularly Chrysostom in his elaborate mystagogy.

Such emphasis on the world to come, to the exclusion of emphasis on other factors, such as the living of the Christian life now, has been noted before in Theodore.[225] In this context particularly it will be recalled that Theodore's interpretation of the pre-baptismal anointing[226] as a kind of garment also emphasized the notion of immortality to the exclusion of other features of this exorcistic anointing which naturally presented themselves, as, for example, the idea of preparation for the Christian combat as an athlete.

Summary

The baptismal garment as symbol of union with the risen Christ is based on the *iridescence* of the garment, seen in the context of baptism as conformity to the resurrection of Christ. The point emphasized, however, is not primarily the relationship to the resurrection of Christ as historical event in the past, but rather to the significance of the resurrection in as much as it is already a hidden sign of the life of immortality which is to be revealed later.

As a symbol for the purity of life, the white garment being a sign of joy reflects the Christian's temporary sojourn. Reflecting the joy of the heavenly life to come, where no garment

[225] See above, ch. 2, pp. 280-283.
[226] See above, ch. 2, pp. 203-205.

will be necessary, because the body will have come to the promised glory, it is a present symbol of this coming happiness. As such it may be seen as symbol of the purity of Christian life now, which is lived in this interim condition of sacramental reality, looking to the life to come. Theodore, however, goes into no further detail mystagogically of how the garment represents purity of life.

D. Ambrose

A specific mystagogical interpretation of the baptismal robe is provided by Ambrose, and occurs in its proper place in the chronological sequence of the ceremonies.[227] The manner in which Ambrose handles the mystagogical interpretation of the white robe seems at first glance somewhat different in manner from that of the other fathers. However, the basic elements noted in them also occur in Ambrose's mystagogy of the white robe. The material of the mystagogy is almost entirely a concatenation of quotations from both the *OT* and the *NT*, executed on a rather poetic plane.

1. *A Symbol of Union with the Risen Christ*

To put on the white baptismal robe is to symbolize the union with the risen Christ which the baptismal act has sacramentally effected. The Pauline metaphor of "putting on Christ"[228] quoted by Cyril and so frequently by Chrysostom is not used specifically by Ambrose. He comes to essentially the same idea, however, of mystagogical interpretation of the robe by using two other scriptural quotations. He evokes the mystery of the resurrection of Christ, and its corrollary mystery, the ascension, by quoting the *Psalm* dialogue[229] of the entrance of the King of Glory into heaven, with the question of the angels,

[227] See above, p. 353.
[228] *Ga.* 3:27.
[229] *Ps.* 23:7-8.

"Who is this King of Glory?" and combining it with another *OT* reference to the fact that the King of Glory came dressed in a white robe: "Who is this that comes from Edom, the redness of his garments from Bosra, beautiful in his white robe?"[230] Here the powers of heaven are in "consternation" that mortal flesh should ascend.[231] Christ has brought mortal flesh to resurrection and ascension into heaven, as described in this *OT* image of the King entering in his white robe. Ambrose means to show the neophytes that the white robe which they are wearing signifies their participation in the resurrection and ascension of Christ, the King of.Glory, depicted also in a white robe. The white robe of Christ, resurrected and ascended, and the baptismal robe of the candidate are one. Using these texts from the *OT* which refer pictorially specifically to the white robe, Ambrose shows in this mystagogy how the white robe signifies incorporation of the neophytes into the mystery of the resurrection and ascension of Christ.

A corrollary of this mystical association of the neophyte with the mystery of the resurrection-ascension of Christ is the personal union of living intimacy which this implies. His mystagogy to underscore this point is the view of the baptismal robe as a *bridal garment,* along with the reminiscenses of the cultural preparations for wedding which this bridal garment imply, namely the bridal bath and the use of perfumes. Such a mystagogy fits admirably, of course, the fact that baptism was a bath, and the fact of the perfumed anointing after the baptismal bath, to which Ambrose, as we have seen, had already alluded in treating of the symbolism of the perfumed *myron*: "Christ, moreover, on seeing His Church in white vestments – for which He Himself, as you have it in the book of Zacharias the prophet, had put on 'filthy garments,'[232] – that is, a soul pure and washed by the bath of regeneration, says:

[230] *Is.* 63:1.
[231] *Myst.* 36 (Botte, *SC* 25bis, 174; tr. Deferrari, *FC* 44,18).
[232] *Cf. Zc.* 3:3.

'Behold, you are fair, my love, you are fair, your eyes are as a dove's'."[233]

Such mystagogy of the baptismal robe as a bridal garment, and all that that implies, which we have encountered in part already in Chrysostom[234] is then continued in some detail by Ambrose, following *Sg.* It shows the baptized as being attractive to Christ, and so moving to closer union with Him. The point of departure for this mystagogy had been the picture of the baptized dressed in their white robes, sign of their beauty to Christ because of the grace of baptism.

The use of *Sg.* with its bridal imagery, to express the union of the baptized with the risen Christ also occurs as a mystagogical explanation of the white robes in *Sacr.* V.14. Ambrose describes the neophytes after their baptism having come to the altar for the Eucharistic celebration saying: "The Church rejoices in the redemption of many, and is glad with spiritual exultation that the members of her household are at hand dressed in white."[235] The Church prepares a banquet and invokes Christ. Using *Sg.* 5:1 "Let my beloved come into his garden and eat the fruit of his apple trees," Ambrose says: "What are these apple trees? You were made dry wood in Adam, but now through the grace of Christ you flower as apple trees."[236] The suggestion of the apple trees in bloom with their white blossoms is related imaginatively to Ambrose's picture of the neophytes standing at the altar "dressed in white," a sign of the flowering of grace which baptism has brought about, a flowering from the dry wood in Adam, which could not have been expected to produce such attractive fruit.

[233] *Sg.* 4:1. *Myst.* 37 (Botte, *SC* 25bis, 176; tr. Deferrari, *FC* 44, 18): "Christus autem videns ecclesiam suam in vestimentis candidis – pro qua ipse, ut habes in Zachariae libro prophetae, 'sordida vestimenta' susceperat – vel animam regenerationis lavacro mundam atque ablutam, dicit: 'Ecce formosa es, proxima mea, ecce es formosa, oculi tui sicut columbae.' . . ."

[234] See above, pp. 424-425.

[235] *Sacr.* V.14 (Botte, *SC* 25bis, 126; tr. Deferrari, *FC* 44, 313): "Gaudet ecclesia redemptione multorum et adstare sibi familiam candidatam spiritali exultatione laetatur."

[236] *Idem:* "Quae sunt istae pomiferae? Lignum aridum factus eras in Adam, sed nunc per gratiam Christi pomiferae arbores pullulatis."

None of the other fathers uses *Sg.* in quite such a flamboyant and detailed way in his mystagogy of the white garments.

The mystagogy here employed by Ambrose, with its lyrical enchancement based on *Sg.* is based on the actual picture of the liturgy as it unfolds, where the candidates all dressed in white come into the Church and gather for the Eucharist. Ambrose's mystagogy is a meditation on this scene.

2. *A Symbol of the Forgiveness of Sins*

A fundamental statement of the mystagogy of the baptismal robe is for Ambrose the symbolic interpretation of the robe as a sign of the forgiveness of sins: "After this [the foot-washing] you received white garments as a sign you had put off the covering of sins, and had put on the chaste robes of innocence, of which the prophet said: 'sprinkle me with hyssop and I shall be cleansed; wash me and I shall be whiter than snow.' "[237]

Here the common theme of the contrast between removing the garments before baptism, the "covering of sins (involucrum peccatorum)," and putting on the shining white garment after baptism as sign of the return to primitive innocence is once again sounded. In what sense are the white garments a sign of the return to innocence? The symbol is their shining whiteness, representing the cleansing of the soul from sordid defilement. This is contained in the interpretative word of *Ps.* 50, which contains the both notions of washing and of whiteness similar to snow. This idea of cleansing from the stain of sin to a shining whiteness is further corroborated by Ambrose immediately after when he says that the baptized have been cleansed according to the law, the symbol here being Moses' sprinkling of the blood of the lamb,[238] and according to the Gospel. In mentioning the example of this latter, namely the whiteness of Christ's garments, "when in the Gospel he showed the

[237] *Ps.* 50:9. *Myst.* 34 (Botte, *SC* 25bis, 174; tr. Deferrari, *FC* 44, 17): "Accepisti post haec vestimenta candida ut esset indicio quod exueris involucrum peccatorum, indueris innocentiae casta velamina de quibus dixit proheta: 'Adsperges me hysopo et mundabor, lavabis me et super nivem dealbabor.' "

[238] *Ex.* 12:22.

glory of His resurrection,"[239] Ambrose associates the resurrection of Christ with the forgiveness of sins, and thereby, in a somewhat ingenious way, ties in the symbolism with both, forgiveness and resurrection: "He whose sin is forgiven is made whiter than snow (super nivem dealbatur, cui culpa dimittitur)."[240] The whiteness of Christ's garments in this context refers to the transfiguration scene, in which the glory of the resurrection is anticipated.

Yet another scriptural reference in connection with the forgiveness of sins and the symbolism of color – scarlet versus the whiteness of snow – is drawn in by Ambrose: "And so the Lord said through Isaiah: 'If you sins be as scarlet, I shall make them white as snow.' "[241]

Then Ambrose adds the black-white contrast to show the white robe as symbol of the forgiveness of sins. The image here is not that of the individual neophyte alone, but of the entire Church, clothed in white vestments. The interpretative material comes from *Sg.:*

> The Church, having assumed these vestments through the bath of regeneration,[242] says in the Canticles: "I am black but beautiful, O ye daughters of Jerusalem,"[243] black through the frailty of human condition, beautiful through grace; black, because I am made up of sinners, beautiful by the sacrament of grace. Perceiving these vestments, the daughters of Jerusalem in amazement say: "Who is this that comes up made white?"[244] She was black; how was she suddenly made white?[245]

[239] *Cf. Mt.* 17:2. *Myst.* 34 (Botte, *SC* 25bis, 174; tr. Deferrari, *FC* 44, 17): ... cum resurrectionis suae gloriam in evangelio demostraret."

[240] *Myst.* 34 (*Idem*).

[241] *Is.* 1:18. *Myst.* 34 (*Idem*): "Unde et per Esaiam dominus ait: 'Si fuerint peccata vestra sicut phoenicium, ut nivem dealbabo.' "

[242] *Cf. Tt.* 3:5.

[243] *Sg.* 1:4.

[244] *Sg.* 8:5.

[245] *Myst.* 35 (Botte, *SC* 25bis, 174; tr. Deferrari, *FC* 44, 17-18): "Haec vestimenta habens ecclesia per lavacrum regenerationis adsumpta dicit in Cànticis: 'Nigra sum et decora, filiae Hierusalem.' Nigra per fragilitatem conditionis humanae, decora per gratiam, nigra quia ex peccatoribus, decora fidei sacramento. Haec vestimenta cernentes filiae Hierusalem stupefactae dicunt: 'Quae est haec quae adscendit dealbata?' Haec erat nigra, unde nunc subito dealbata?"

Here the idea of baptism as a washing, the "bath of regeneration,"[246] from sins, seen as "blackness" to the "whiteness" which represents the forgiveness of sins, is represented by the white garment.

Through use of *Ps., Ex., Mt., Is.,* and *Sg.* Ambrose selects passages having to do with this imagery of washing and whiteness, and makes of them a rather rich mystagogy to demonstrate to the neophytes the meaning of his original mystagogical assertion, namely that the white garment was a "sign that you had put off the covering of sins, and had put on the chaste robe of innocence."[247]

3. *A Symbol for Purity of Life*

A transition in Ambrose's thought, from the presentation of the mystagogy of the white robe as sign of personal union with the risen Christ, to the meaning of this relationship for Christian life occurs when he describes Christ drawn by the beauty of the baptized, and telling the Chruch in the words of the Canticle[248] to put Him as a seal on her heart and a sign on her arm. "Let your works also shine," Christ says to the Church, "and bring forth the image of God, according to whose image you were made."[249] This section, begun by the mystagogical consideration of the white robe, then leads in to the seal of the Spirit which the candidates have on their hearts.

Summary

Ambrose's means of showing that the baptismal garment is a *symbol of union with the risen Christ* is to depict the mystery of the King of Glory using *OT* terms describing his dramatic entrance into heaven, where it is explicitly stated that

[246] *Tt.* 3:5.
[247] *Myst.* 34. See above, p. 441.
[248] *Sg.* 8:6.
[249] *Myst.* 41 (Botte, *SC* 25bis, 178; tr. Deferrari, *FC* 44, 20): "Opera quoque tua luceant et imaginem dei praeferant ad cujus imaginem facta es."

He comes "beautiful in his white robe."[250] Thus associated with the risen and ascended Christ by the symbol of the robe, Ambrose also shows the neophyte that this union with the risen Christ is one of close intimacy. His mystagogy here is to view the robe as a bridal garment, along with deft allusion to bridal customs, such as the bridal bath and the anointing with perfume after this bath. The allusion to *Zc.* where the Bridegroom has sought the bride, to *Sg.*, where the bride after her bath has become beautiful to the Bridegroom, and also from *Sg.*, the picture of the apple trees white with their perfumed blossoms: this is a lyrical imagery, but by no means arbitrary, since each image is based on the liturgical action and its inner meaning. There is the exchange of the "dirty clothes" before the baptism, the "bath of regeneration" itself, the anointing with the perfumed *myron* after the bath, and then the fragrant assembly of the neophytes all dressed in their resplendent white robes before the altar to celebrate the marriage banquet itself. A real touch of genius is manifest here in the extraordinary synthetic capacity which Ambrose's mystagogy of the white garment reveals. By combining the actual liturgical ceremonies themselves, removal of clothing, baptism, anointing, clothing, and the assembly for the Eucharist, along with biblical imagery to support its meaning from this imaginative record of salvation history, Ambrose shows the neophytes in an unforgettably beautiful way the profound inner meaning of union with the risen Christ which baptism has effected. And his central piece in this picture is the baptismal robe itself and all that it implies as symbol of union with the risen Christ. The unfolding of the liturgical events themselves, the interpretative imagery from the bible with which he has provided these events, the natural symbolism at the base of all of this: all combine in a most effective mystagogy of the baptismal robe.

The baptismal robe as *symbol of the forgiveness of sins* receives particular emphasis by Ambrose. The mystagogical point here is the shining whiteness of the garment, symbol of re-

[250]See above, p. 439.

gained innocence, over against the dirty clothing, the "covering of sins." This mystagogical point is supported by biblical references to washing which makes whiter than snow, to cleansing with the blood of the lamb. That this cleansing takes place in baptism is shown by relationship to the Gospel scene of the Transfiguration of Christ, a prefiguring of the Resurrection, where Christ's garments were white as snow. Further *OT* reference is provided in this mystagogy by the allusion to sins which were once scarlet, but now are white as snow. The black-white imagery for sin and forgiveness is also provided by the picture of the Church, the "*familia candidata*" standing in white robes before the altar, formerly black with sin, now white by the grace of forgiveness, again with reference to *Sg.*

Finally, the baptismal garment as symbol for *purity* of Christian conduct is seen in the shining radiance of the robe, a reflection of the life to be lived in partnership with Christ, who dwells within the neophyte as a seal on his heart, moving him to live a life which will reflect the image of God, in Whose image he was made, and which image is now restored through baptism and which will shine forth in Christian conduct, just as the garments themselves shine.

Comparative Summary

The most important aspect in the mystagogy of the white baptismal robe is the *symbolism of union with the Risen Christ.* As a practical necessity some clothing is necessary after the neophyte emerges from the baptismal pool. The very closeness of this action of clothing with the act of baptism, and its mystagogy of union with the resurrection with Christ, suggest, if at all possible, a symbolic interpretation of the clothing which will manifest more fully the meaning of the baptismal act, particularly the emersion from the pool in connection with the symbolism of the resurrection. The act of clothing also forms a counterpart to the act of removing the garments before entering the pool, which has been interpreted in close association with the baptismal act, particularly the entering the pool as association with the crucifixion, death and burial of Jesus as a result of sin. Whatever the previous development of this ceremony of putting on and wearing the white garment from practical necessity of some article of clothing to ritual white robe, it is clear that by the time of the fathers here in question the article of clothing was a ritual garment. We have already seen how the notion of linen *versus* animal skins formed a cultural background for the natural religious symbolism of mortality *versus* immortality.[251]

If putting off the old man and his deeds, putting off the old Adam and that mortality which sin had wrought, had been a controlling image for the removal of clothing, then putting on the new man and his deeds, the new Adam, and the immortality which the forgiveness of Christ's resurrection restores becomes the controlling image for the putting on of the white garment.

Since the new Adam, the new man, is Christ Himself, and since the deeds of this new man are the deeds of Christ Himself, then to "put on" Christ will be to associate onesself in the new Adam, the new man, and the deeds of this new man. To exemplify this reality which takes place in baptism, the baptismal robe as sign of union with the risen Christ becomes a most apt symbol, because its various qualities on the natural symbolic level lend themselves so well to the exemplification of what has happened in the baptismal act. The fathers take these natural symbolic qualities of the robe, couple them with different biblical images which correspond to the message, and form a mystagogy suggested by the liturgical tableaux themselves at various points in the entire initiation where the white robe is particularly impressive.

To exemplify union with Christ, Cyril and Chrysostom both reach to the ready-made imagery of *Ga.* 3:27. putting on the garment is like putting on Christ, just as they had used Pauline imagery to show that removing the garments was like removing the old man and his deeds. After the initial mention of this Pauline image of putting on Christ, Cyril is content to spell

[251]See above, ch. 2, pp. 186-188.

this out literally by stating that this means conformity to the risen body of Christ, using *Ph.* 3:21. Chrysostom, on the other hand, avails himself of such features of the robe as its newness, its resemblance to a bridal garment and its radiance to spell out in detail, backed up by *OT* and *NT* references, what conformity to this risen body of Christ means. He does this not in a single passage, but as the pastoral occasion suggests itself throughout his *Baptismal Instructions*. The robe thus becomes for Chrysostom a central symbol to call to mind the different aspects of the mystery of baptism. While Ambrose does not take the obvious cue of *Ga.* 3:27, he uses the biblical imagery of the robe of the King of Glory risen and ascended linking it, and so that association in the mystery itself, to the robe which the neophyte wears. Like Chrysostom he develops the imagery of the robe as a bridal garment in order to show the intimacy of union with the baptized and Christ. While Chrysostom sees in the radiance of the robe the manifestation in the individual of the indwelling of the Trinity, Ambrose sees in the total picture of the group of newly baptized gathered before the altar the vision of an apple orchard in white bloom, and with the help of imagery from *Sg.* applies this to the flowering of grace of baptism in the Church. He reaches back to his emphasis on the cross[252] in baptism to carry the image to artful completion by noting that before baptism the candidates were dead wood in Adam, but now this dead wood has bloomed. Irrigated by the waters of baptism, the tree of the cross, place of death, has bloomed into life.

These different approaches are clearly suggested in no small measure by the actual unfolding of the liturgical action. The very scene which the neophytes present to the eye indicates a direction for the mystagogy. Thus, when Chrysostom mentions that the white-robed neophyte illuminates the face of the onlooker, the glow very possibly enhanced by the candle he carries, this radiance suggests the power of the interior dwelling of the Trinity. When Ambrose sees the picture of the apple orchard in bloom, he is thinking apparently of the white-robed neophytes standing before the altar, and the

[252] See above, ch. 2, pp. 250-252.

perfumed fragance of the *myron* with which they had all been anointed.

Theodore is sparse in his mystagogy, mentioning only a single thought in connection with the radiance of the robe: his ever-present concern with the liturgy as symbol of the world to come. He seems to assume as obvious that the robe is sign of union with the risen Christ without spelling out the mystagogy here as did the other three fathers, and he simply associates this resurrection image with its final fulfilment in the hereafter. The radiant white robe is a sign of this coming joy.

Since the resurrection of Christ is sign of forgiving love, those associated with it in baptism will reflect that transformation of the forgiveness of their sins, those deeds of the old man emanating from their alienation from the life of God. So, obvious as *symbol of the forgiveness of sins* as having taken place by association in the resurrection of Christ through the baptismal act is the white garment. Features of the liturgical procession into the church for the Eucharist are combined by Cyril to produce this mystagogy of the white garment as symbol of the forgiveness of sins. The church choir becomes the choir of angels singing the psalm of forgiveness which rings in the ears of the neophytes. Their radiant white garment reflects their inner transformation, the forgiveness which has made of them "stars of the Church." A liturgical assembly later in the week is the occasion for Chrysostom to note that the radiance of the white garment, so impressive to the others, indicates that the inner transformation of forgiveness has taken place in the neophytes. Chrysostom also adds two further aspects of the robe to reinforce this mystagogy of the symbol of forgiveness: it is a royal robe for the former beggar and it is a bridal robe thrown over the shame of nakedness.

For Ambrose, it is the scene of the "familia candidata" gathered before the altar which leads him to a rather elaborate meditation on the symbol of whiteness as renewed innocence. Again, his point of departure is the baptismal act as a bath which cleanses to a whiteness. And through the use of *OT* texts this whiteness which the cleansing bath has brought about is contrasted with scarlet or black as sign of sin. The whole is unified in the picture of the transfiguration of Jesus, prelude to the resurrection, whose garments are as white as snow. Of the three fathers who treat the robe as symbol of forgiveness, Ambrose has the most detailed mystagogy. Chrysostom and Cyril contented themselves with the fairly obvious symbolism of the robe's radiance as sign of the inner transformation of forgiveness. Ambrose has gone to work to produce something quite more elaborate by this interweaving of color symbolism, *OT* imagery, the picture of the transfigured Christ in his snow-white robe, all proceeding from the traditional Pauline view of baptism as a "bath," and the cultural symbolism of the bridal bath.

The natural symbolism of a clean, white robe as *symbol of purity of life* is utilized by all four fathers. As might be expected, particularly in view of his development of the mystagogy of the removal of garments before baptism, it is Chrysostom who develops this aspect of the symbolism most thoroughly. He views the robe from all possible sides, basing his mystagogy on the natural awareness of clothing and its purposes in his hearers, running the gamut of symbolism from the radiance as sign of Christ acting in the works of the neophytes, through the effort required to keep it spotless, to increase its luster by good works, to attract others by a good life, that is, the robe's beauty, right up to the transformation from the robe reflecting good works, to the robe worn at the fulfilment of these good works in heaven, the eschatological banquet robe. Cyril's mystagogy is really the same, but only in kernel form in a single passage concerned actually with the Eucharist, of more precisely, how one partakes in the Divine Nature through the Eucharist. There we find the reference to the white robe as symbol of good deeds performed under the sign of eschatological joy by those whom God has justified in baptism. Theodore, too, sees in the works represented by the wearing of the robe the reflection of the joy of eschatological fulfilment already present in Christian action.

Neither Cyril nor Theodore provide the wealth of day-to-day style applications which characterize Chrysostom's unfolding of the mystagogy of the baptismal robe under this aspect of symbolism for purity of life. The essence of the mystagogy is the same, but the statements of Theodore and Cyril are summary in tone; Chrysostom's go into pastoral detail.[253] Ambrose, who has presented the chief burden of his mystagogy in the robe as sign of forgiveness and of union with Christ notes only that Christ's indwelling, symbolized by the robe, shines in the neophytes's works, using *Sg.* to indicate the mystical partnership existing between Christ and the neophyte.

Common to all fathers in their treatment of the robe as symbol of purity of life is the clear notion that the Christian performs his works not alone, but in union with Christ dwelling within him. Whether it be in the specific reference to the robe's radiance as sign of Christ's indwelling or the references to the robe as sign of the heavenly banquet robe, when life's deeds find their completion, one becomes conscious of their view of

[253]In a certain sense, Chrysostom provides a mystagogy for the conduct of the Christian life in his mystagogy of the white garment, while Cyril provides this mystagogy for Christian life in association with the meaning of the baptismal anointing. This distribution of emphasis is not surprising, since, as we have seen, Cyril has built up a full-fledged mystagogy of the Holy Spirit and Christian mission around the post-baptismal anointing, while Chrysostom's liturgy, lacking such an anointing, would naturally provide other ceremonies as the point of departure for such mission emphasis. The mystagogy for these ceremonies would be more oriented to the *Logos* theology, proceeding from the baptismal act as union with Christ, rather than to the theology of the Holy Spirit equipping the Christian for his mission as He equipped Christ in the Jordan scene. As a matter of fact, this is precisely the emphasis which Chrysostom accords the white garment as symbol of union with the risen Christ (see above, pp. 421-425), while Cyril hardly develops this symbol at all (see above, p. 416), reserving all for the post-baptismal anointing. Whether "one with Christ" (symbol: white garment) and so obligated to the Christian life (Chrysostom), or "anointed with the Holy Spirit" (symbol: post-baptismal unction) and so commited to the Christian life (Cyril), the meaning is the same. The different mystagogical emphasis reflects the difference in theological development and also the different points of departure provided for the mystagogues by the actual liturgies themselves with their different ceremonies, as well as the reference to the different cultural climates of the hearers. While it is obvious that the mystagogues did not take a free hand in altering traditional liturgies on a grand scale, it is however obvious that their mystagogical emphasis as a result of the currents they had to take into account, theological and cultural, will work back, causing alteration and reform of the liturgical ceremonies themselves, an ongoing and never-finished process guided by the principle "sacramenta propter homines."

the resurrection of Christ both as past event, as well as hidden sign of the consummation to which all earthly effort tends. The robe is for them the mystical symbol of this view of reality. The mystagogy is never left at the mere moralistic level, which the spotlessness or the whiteness might suggest, but always placed in the larger scope of resurrection of Christ, apprehension of this through baptism of the candidate and continued union with it throughout life, and already shining through the robe, in one's works, the shimmer of final fulfilment in the symbolic joy of the heavenly wedding banquet. Their success in preserving the fullness of this symbolism is due in no small measure to their use of biblical imagery in supplementing the natural symbolism which the robe suggests.

CONCLUSION

The work of the four fathers that we have subjected to investigation is manifestly a work of pastoral theology in the fullest sense of this term. They have taken seriously the fundamental principle of any existing Christian community that God actually addresses Himself to man here and now, and that man, in view of this address of God, can answer this call in the individual circumstances of his actual life. As mystagogues, those whose office it is to guide men in this encounter with God, they have availed themselves with singular awareness of the means available to give man the possibility of hearing this call of God and responding to it, thus fulfilling the central role of the Christian guide, that of service to the mystery of God's encounter with man.

They have accepted the fact of salvation history that God has chosen to reveal Himself and address man through the medium of certain signs which He has given to His Church, signs which derive their meaning and efficacy from the life, death and resurrection of His Son Jesus, Who is Himself the primary mystery and sign of man's encounter with God. These are the signs, the words and actions which comprise the sacred liturgy itself. Because they see these liturgical signs as God-given means of address and response they accept them as the means *par excellence* through which the encounter of God and man takes place. They view this liturgy not as something arbitrary, but as filled with the mystery which is the life of Christ Himself. Their basic attitude, then, can be nothing other than one of responsible and imaginative conservatism. The liturgical signs are seriously accepted as the vehicle through which the meeting of God and man takes place, and each word and gesture of this liturgy, as an expression of the Christian community of the time, is one of indisputable seriousness because it is viewed as the tradition of the Church, and so ultimately a revelation containing in symbol the reality of Christ.

At the same time this traditional faithfulness to the Church's expression of itself and of Christ at work in it at any given time in history and through the liturgical signs does not preclude creative and imaginative attention to the fact that these signs of the given liturgy must be made meaningful to the individuals who participate in it. As seriously as they take the tradition of the liturgical signs, just as seriously do they take the actual awareness and needs of their hearers. It is this aspect of the mystagogy especially which reveals the creative possibilities of which they avail themselves in their individual approaches and genius, which, while not doing violence to the given liturgy or distracting their hearers with extraneous theological disputes, still allows for unique and sensitive creativity in revealing to their hearers, on the basis of their own capacity for understanding, the wide flow of meaning which the liturgical signs possess.

Thus, *Cyril,* given his particular position at the very scene where the death and resurrection of Jesus took place, gives particular emphasis for his hearers at the *Anastasis* to the liturgical signs in their relationship to the actual past events of Christ's life, revealing graphically in his mystagogical interpretation how the liturgical signs are related to the mystery of the salvific events of the life, death and resurrection of Jesus, an emphasis of the liturgical exposition very strong in the Church since the beginnings of the Jerusalem pilgrimage.

Chrysostom, in the melée of the secular empire and the Church's struggle to maintain her unique identity vis-à-vis the "embarrassing" peace with this empire, shows his candidates how the life, cross and death of Jesus, which once took place in the past, reveal themselves again in the encounter of the Christian with the radical challenges which the secular city provides. And he shows this precisely by recourse to the meaning of the words and symbolic actions of the liturgy as a revelation and identity-producing re-presentation of the life, death and resurrection of Jesus now taking place in the Christian's new life with which he approaches the challenges of this world. By his exposition of the sign value of the liturgy in its constant reference to the daily lives of the neophytes he provides them with the possibility of carrying into their lives in the world the mystery of the past-made-present, the re-living of the mystery of Christ, showing how the initiation liturgy's central images are a call and a constant help in the interior meaning of dying to sin and living for God.

Where Cyril showed the vividness of Christ's offering present in the liturgical signs, and Chrysostom the reality of the past-made-present in the struggle of re-living Christ's life in the day-to-day struggle in the world through these signs, *Theodore's* genius is to take the same liturgical signs and move them in an arc pointing to the future. The past salvific events of Christ's life, death and resurrection, present in the liturgical "symbols" become for the Christian now, through the medium of the liturgical signs the already present, yet hidden actuality of the trans-temporal reality which the actual past resurrection of Christ guarantees. As such, his interpretation of the liturgy is the message of hope, and he reveals the liturgical signs as symbols of hope, repositories of a reality already begun and yet to be revealed, the baptismal birth and resurrection as a symbol and real beginning of the final birth and resurrection of the new man in the world to come.

Ambrose brings to this same liturgy of initiation a unique element which can only be called the redemption of the imagination. Due to his theology of the transformation of all the elements of creation, the intersection of the original creation with the redemptive plan of God in the mystery of Christ's historical death and resurrection, Ambrose is able to see in such liturgical signs as the creative source of water, the tomb and re-birth, the "familia candidata", the fragrance of the assembly of neophytes anointed with *myron*, in a uniquely imaginative and even sensual way the very beginnings of the new creation achieved in the mystery of Christ and already visible and tangible—in the "visibility" and "tangibility" of faith—revealed in the concrete signs of the liturgy.

All four fathers deal with fundamentally the same liturgy of initiation, yet in view of the needs of their hearers and their world, they are able to provide a mystagogy of the initiation rites of widely varied genius and scope, which makes salvation history a real presence in the lives of their hearers. Their mediation between the realities of this world and their symbolic expression of it was understood by their hearers, and their familiarity with the symbolic expression of Holy Scripture as the basis of their mystagogy assured an approach to the mystagogy of the rite of Christian Initiation which was at once thoroughly orthodox in its adherence to the historical reality of God's revelation to man, and at the same time thoroughly cognizant and in tune with the real needs of their hearers. As such this classical mystagogy of Christian Initiation of St. Cyril of Jerusalem, St. John Chrysostom, Theodore of Mopsuestia and St. Ambrose of Milan offers a valuable model to the Christian mystagogue of today.

INDEXES

1. OLD AND NEW TESTAMENT

OLD TESTAMENT

NEW TESTAMENT

2. ANCIENT CHRISTIAN WRITERS

(Text citations, paraphrases, references—See also General Index).

Principal Authors

Other Authors

3. MODERN AUTHORS

4. GENERAL INDEX